2x 6/11 2/12

Britain

Perfect places to stay, eat & explore

Contents

Rural Idylls

Cities

Coast & Country

Britain

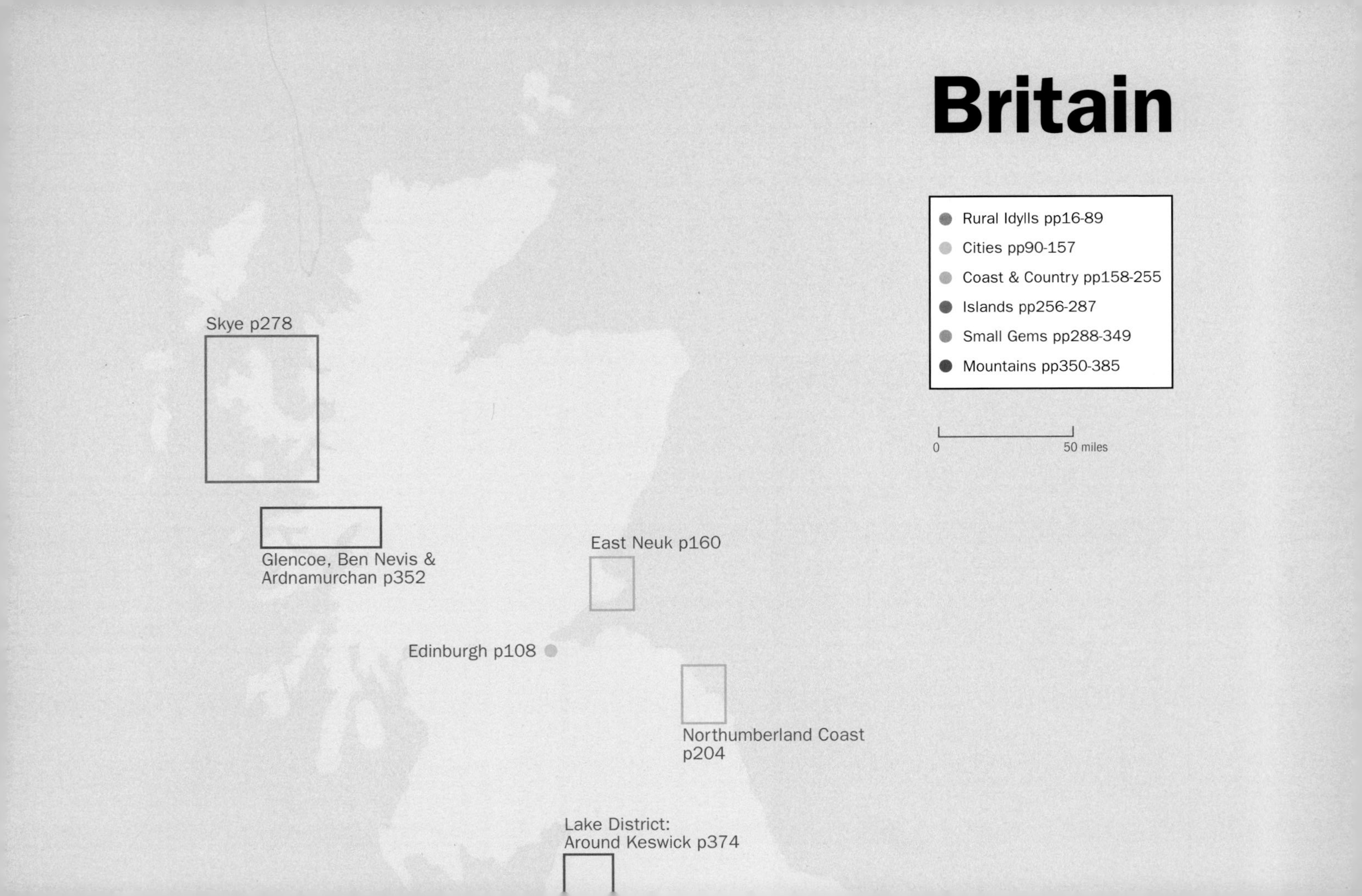

Rural Idylls pp16-89
Cities pp90-157
Coast & Country pp158-255
Islands pp256-287
Small Gems pp288-349
Mountains pp350-385
0
50 miles
Skye p278
Glencoe, Ben Nevis & Ardnamurchan p352
East Neuk p160
Edinburgh p108
Northumberland Coast p204
Lake District: Around Keswick p374

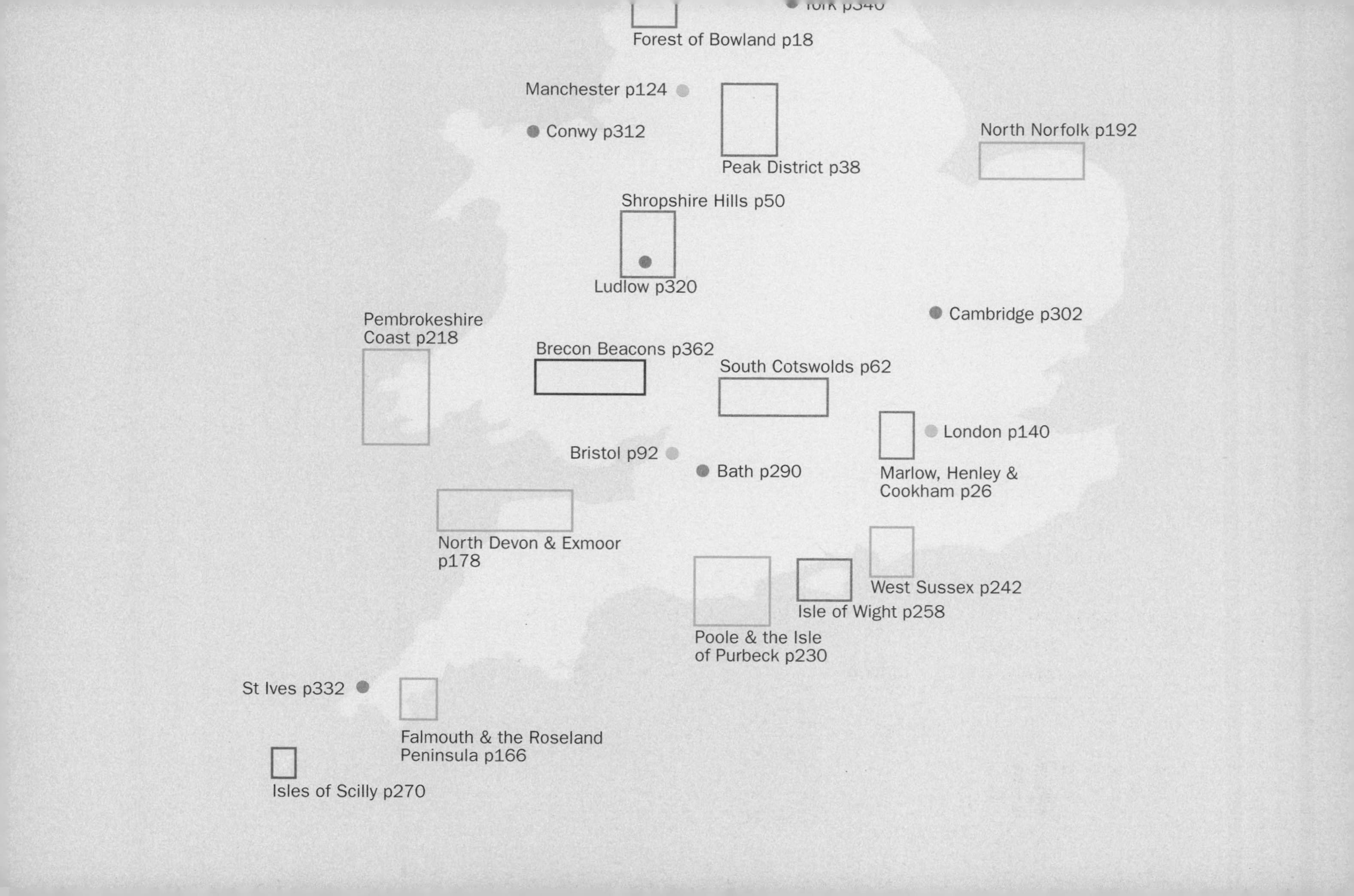

North Norfolk p192

Cambridge p302

London p140

Marlow, Henley &
Cookham p26

West Sussex p242

Isle of Wight p258

Poole & the Isle
of Purbeck p230

Forest of Bowland p18

Peak District p38

Shropshire Hills p50

South Cotswolds p62

Bath p290

Manchester p124

Conwy p312

Ludlow p320

Brecon Beacons p362

Bristol p92

North Devon & Exmoor
p178

Pembrokeshire
Coast p218

Falmouth & the Roseland
Peninsula p166

St Ives p332

Isles of Scilly p270

Published by Time Out Guides Ltd, a wholly owned subsidiary of Time Out Group Ltd.
Time Out and the Time Out logo are trademarks of Time Out Group Ltd.

© **Time Out Group Ltd 2009**

10 9 8 7 6 5 4 3 2 1

This edition first published in Great Britain in 2009 by Ebury Publishing
A Random House Group Company
20 Vauxhall Bridge Road, London SW1V 2SA

Random House Australia Pty Limited 20 Alfred Street, Milsons Point, Sydney, New South Wales 2061, Australia
Random House New Zealand Limited 18 Poland Road, Glenfield, Auckland 10, New Zealand
Random House South Africa (Pty) Limited Isle of Houghton, Corner Boundary, Road & Carse O'Gowrie,
Houghton 2198, South Africa

Random House UK Limited Reg. No. 954009

Distributed in USA by Publishers Group West
1700 Fourth Street, Berkeley, California 94710

Distributed in Canada by Publishers Group Canada
250A Carlton Street, Toronto, Ontario M5A 2L1

For further distribution details, see www.timeout.com

ISBN: 978-1-84670-157-3

A CIP catalogue record for this book is available from the British Library

Printed and bound by Firmengruppe APPL, aprinta druck, Wemding, Germany

The Random House Group Limited supports The Forest Stewardship Council (FSC), the leading international forest
certification organisation. All our titles that are printed on Greenpeace approved FSC certified paper carry the FSC
logo. Our paper procurement policy can be found at http://www.rbooks.co.uk/environment.

Time Out carbon-offsets all its flights with Trees for Cities (www.treesforcities.org).

While every effort has been made to ensure the accuracy of the information contained within this guide, the publishers
cannot accept responsibility for any errors it may contain.

Introduction

Welcome to *Time Out Britain: Perfect places to stay, eat & explore*, one in a new series of guidebooks that picks the very best of a country. We've chosen 30 of Britain's most inspiring destinations and for each of them singled out the most appealing hotels, shops and places to eat and drink. Some are in the luxury price bracket, but we also highlight the best good-value accommodation and restaurants.

It wasn't so long ago that, for the British, a 'proper' holiday or short break meant abroad. A few years ago that started to change. Aviation guilt and recession have played their part, but there is more to the story. First, the British have begun to rediscover what visitors have always known: that the country has miles of wonderfully diverse coast and countryside, historic interest aplenty and culturally vibrant towns and cities. Second, as far as accommodation and – especially – food is concerned, Britain has simply got better. All over the country, restaurants are connecting with their local roots, while chefs have absorbed influences from around the world. The once-familiar glass of tinned orange juice as starter is long gone, more often than not replaced with fine local ingredients, rigorously sourced and skillfully assembled.

Our team of writers – mostly locals, others with local knowledge – focused on areas with the most compelling sights and landscapes, exploring the wild, windy and remote Shropshire Hills, and the wide swathes of sand and mystical castles of the Northumberland coast; dramatic Scottish mountains and the gently green and bucolic topographies of West Sussex and the Cotswolds. We picked distinctive cities, packed with cultural interest as well as fascinating architecture; and small towns that are big draws, like Ludlow, now a centre of good food as well as Tudor buildings, and jewel-like St Ives on the Cornish coast, where the beauty of the setting and special quality of light turned a fishing village into an artists' colony. We hope you find some inspiration amid the diversity.

A word about the listings. The £ symbols indicate the price bracket of a venue: £=budget, ££=moderate, £££=expensive and ££££=luxury. Unless otherwise stated, all venues accept Visa and MasterCard credit cards. Some restaurants and hotels are hidden away deep in the countryside. In these cases we've indicated a location relative to a nearby town or village, but do check venues' websites for detailed directions.

All our listings are double-checked, but businesses do sometimes close or change their hours and prices, so we recommend that you check particulars by phone or online before visiting.

Burford House Hotel

BURFORD - THE COTSWOLDS

The pretty town of Burford is often described as the 'Gateway to the Cotswolds', situated just 20 miles west of the historical city of Oxford and within a short journey to many pretty golden Cotswold villages. Situated at the heart of Burford is the impressive five-star 17th Century Burford House Hotel offering bed and breakfast accommodation for families, groups of friends or couples wishing to truly 'escape to the country.' Described by visitors as 'a wonderful, friendly and charming hotel' it's no wonder guests continue to return year after year...

Built from original Cotswold stone the hotel stands on the main high street giving easy access to shops, public houses and restaurants. The accommodation consists of eight tastefully decorated en-suite double bedrooms all with their own individual style and a touch of elegance. King and Queen sized four-poster beds draped with Egyptian cotton linen, antique furniture, roll-top bathtubs and fine porcelain combine with the flat screen televisions, DVD/CD players, complimentary toiletries, bathrobes and a hospitality tray to make your stay truly luxurious.

Award winning Breakfast, light Lunches and Dinner, which is available on a Thursday, Friday or Saturday evening is served in the theatrically themed restaurant, Centre Stage, where diners can tuck into freshly prepared meals, cooked from locally sourced organic produce where possible, to the sound of musicals. Two comfortable lounge areas, one of which features a log-burning stove, provide guests with somewhere pleasant to relax after a busy day exploring, or before and after dinner.

Many walks lead from Burford and meander through the glorious Cotswold countryside surrounding the town. An excellent base for sightseers there are plenty of gardens, Stately homes and activities to be enjoyed within a short walk or drive.

The Burford House Hotel is also available to hire for larger parties wanting exclusive access to the entire home – ideal for special occasions and family get-togethers. For further information or to make a booking please telephone 01993 823151. Additional details regarding the accommodation and things to see and do in the surrounding area can be found on their website www.burfordhouse.co.uk. All email enquiries are welcomed at stay@burfordhouse.co.uk.

JANE AUSTEN'S HOUSE MUSEUM

Chawton, Alton, Hampshire
Tel: 01420 83262
Web: www.jane-austens-house-museum.org.uk

17th century house where Jane Austen lived from 1809 to 1817. She wrote and revised her six novels, including Pride and Prejudice and Emma.

Newly improved services for visitors include: new shop, learning centre with hands-on exhibits, the Austens' kitchen, and audio-visual.

Supported by Heritage Lottery Fund to celebrate the 200th anniversary of Jane Austen's arrival in Chawton in July 2009.

Full programme of events.

Admission fee charged
Book & Souvenir shop
Pleasant garden ideal for picnics
Refreshments opposite

Open
Jan - Feb weekends only   10.30am – 4.30pm
March - April daily   10.30am – 4.30pm
June - July - Aug daily   10am – 5pm
Sept - Oct - Nov - Dec daily   10.30am – 4.30pm
Closed Christmas Day and Boxing Day

Contributors

Edoardo Albert has written and edited guides for Time Out to places as diverse as Barcelona and Beijing, but Bamburgh in Northumberland remains his favourite place on the planet.

Ismay Atkins is a writer and editor living in West Cornwall. She has edited and contributed to a variety of Time Out publications; for this book she reported on St Ives, one of Britain's loveliest corners.

Jessica Cargill Thompson is a freelance writer and editor, and a former deputy editor of *Time Out London* magazine. She is the author of *40 Architects Under 40*, and editor of both *Time Out Cities* and *London Calling: high art and low life in the capital since 1968* and. She lived in Pittenweem, East Neuk, for four years.

Simon Coppock is a freelance writer and editor based in London. He has been the editor of Time Out's London travel guides since 2007, as well as contributing travel pieces on his favourite city to the *Sunday Times*, *Sunday Telegraph* and other publications.

Keith Davidson is the editor of Time Out's Edinburgh guides and is a resident of the city. He has also contributed Scottish chapters to Time Out's *Flight Free Europe* and *Seaside* books. As a freelance, he works for AA Publishing and other media.

Dominic Earle is a freelance travel journalist. In addition to editing Time Out City Guides to Paris, Copenhagen and Stockholm, he has also contributed to publications including the *Guardian* and *Independent*.

Charlie Godfrey-Faussett is a feature writer, author and editor who has contributed to many Time Out guides and was a theatre reviewer for six years for *Time Out London*. He has written travel guides to London, Edinburgh and England, and after a couple of years in central Europe has returned re-invigorated to explore his homeland.

Hugh Graham is the editor of Time Out's *Seaside* book and the Time Out Guides to Miami and gay London. His writing has appeared in *The Week*, the *Observer* and *Gay Times*.

Gayle Hetherington made the move to Bristol at the start of 2008, after working as a travel writer for over eight years. She now writes about sensible shoes – and Bristol – for a living.

Ruth Jarvis, one of Time Out's editorial directors, is from the Manchester area and a frequent explorer of the northern countryside, but was was relatively unfamiliar with the little-known Forest of Bowland, having last visited for Brownie Guide camp. She was happy to discover that Ribble Valley cuisine has moved on immeasurably from bangers and beans.

Natalia Marshall is a writer specialising in green issues, who has written four books and edited several travel guides. She lives in London but likes to escape whenever she can.

Daniel Neilson is a freelance journalist and editor, and an outdoors enthusiast. He has contributed words and pictures to *CNN Traveller*, *Four Four Two*, the *Observer* and the *Wire*, and has edited several guides for Time Out. After several years in South America, Daniel is enjoying exploring Britain's great outdoors.

Anna Norman is a staff editor at Time Out, and has written for and edited guidebooks for destinations in the UK, Europe and Latin America. Always stimulated and nourished by the cultural and architectural offerings of cities, she relished the opportunity to explore and write about one of England's most genteel urban centres: Bath.

Charlotte Packer is a freelance journalist based in Bristol. She writes about travel, design and interiors for a number of publications including the *Guardian*, *Telegraph* and *BBC Homes & Antiques*; she has also written several books on lifestyle and interiors.

Cyrus Shahrad currently writes and produces music in London. He first travelled to the Lake District as a teenage rock-climbing enthusiast, and still retreats there for a spiritual pitstop whenever the slings and arrows of city life become too much to bear.

Daniel Smith is a freelance journalist, researcher and musician. He edited Time Out's guide to Florence and Tuscany and contributed to *1000 Books to Change Your Life*.

Jill Turton has lived all her life on both sides of the Pennines. A former TV producer, she now writes about food and travel from her base in York.

Susie Stubbs is a freelance writer who lives in Manchester. She has written for the *Guardian*, *Independent* and *Time Out*, and recently published a book on abstract and figurative art for Tate Liverpool. Although not a Mancunian by birth, Susie reckons Manchester is the only place she's ever felt at home.

Yolanda Zappaterra is a travel and design writer and editor who writes regularly for *Time Out* magazine and guides, Virgin Media, and *Design Week* magazine. She has also written a number of books on art and design. As a child born in south Wales she was often dragged kicking and screaming to the Brecon Beacons, but has grown to love it dearly over the years. For this guide she happily went back to this beautiful part of Wales, and explored Norfolk and the Isle of Wight.

Contributors by chapter

Forest of Bowland Ruth Jarvis. **Marlow, Henley & Cookham** Charlie Godfrey-Faussett. **Peak District** Daniel Neilson. **Shropshire Hills** Edoardo Albert. **South Cotswolds** Natalia Marshall. **Yorkshire Dales** Jill Turton. **Bristol** Gayle Hetherington, Charlotte Packer; *Wall art* Gayle Hetherington. **Edinburgh** Keith Davidson. **Manchester** Susie Stubbs; *Manchester International Festival* Will Fulford-Jones. **London** Simon Coppock; *Nightlife confidential* Simone Baird. **East Neuk** Jessica Cargill-Thompson. **Falmouth & the Roseland Peninsula** Ismay Atkins. **North Devon & Exmoor** Charlie Godfrey-Faussett; *Board room* Alex Wade. **North Norfolk** Yolanda Zappaterra. **Northumberland Coast** Edoardo Albert. **Pembrokeshire Coast** Hugh Graham. **Poole & the Isle of Purbeck** Charlie Godfrey-Faussett. **West Sussex** Daniel Neilson. **Isle of Wight** Yolanda Zappaterra. **Scilly Isles** Simon Coppock. **Skye** Keith Davidson. **Bath** Anna Norman. **Cambridge** Simon Coppock. **Conwy** Daniel Smith. **Ludlow** Edoardo Albert; *Ludlow Food Festival* Charmaine Mok. **St Ives** Ismay Atkins. **York** Jill Turton. **Glencoe, Ben Nevis & Ardnamurchan** Dominic Earle. **Brecon Beacons** Yolanda Zappaterra. **Lake District: Keswick & Around** Cyrus Shahrad.

Editor's Picks

FIVE-STAR DESTINATIONS

Each destination in the book is rated by a series of catergories . Here are the top performers in each:

ART & ARCHITECTURE

Bath p290
Cambridge p302
Edinburgh p108
London p140
Manchester p124
Poole & the Isle of Purbeck p230
West Sussex p242
York p340

EATING & DRINKING

Edinburgh p108
Forest of Bowland p18
London p140
Ludlow p320
Marlow, Henley & Cookham p26

HISTORIC SITES

Bath p290
Cambridge p302
Northumberland Coast p204
Shropshire Hills p50
York p340

HOTELS

Falmouth & Roseland Peninsula p166
London p140

NIGHTLIFE

London p140
Manchester p124

OUTDOOR ACTIVITIES

Brecon Beacons p362
Glencoe, Ben Nevis & Ardnamurchan p352
Isle of Wight p258
Lake District: Around Keswick p374
Skye p278
Yorkshire Dales p74

SCENERY

Brecon Beacons p362
Falmouth & Roseland p166
Glencoe, Ben Nevis & Ardnamurchan p352
Isle of Wight p258
Isles of Scilly p270
Lake District: Around Keswick p374
North Devon & Exmoor p178
North Norfolk p192

Northumberland Coast p204
Peak District p38
Pembrokeshire Coast p218
Poole & the Isle of Purbeck p230
Shropshire Hills p50
Skye p278
South Cotswolds p62
Yorkshire Dales p74

SHOPPING

London p140
Manchester p124

ACCOMMODATION

LAP OF LUXURY

Amberley Castle; West Sussex p252
Balmoral; Edinburgh p120
Cliveden; Marlow, Henley & Cookham p36
Cowley Manor; South Cotswolds p72
Devonshire Arms Country House Hotel;
    Yorkshire Dales p86
Hotel Tresanton; Falmouth & Roseland
    Peninsula p176
Kinloch Lodge Hotel; Skye p287
Malmaison; Manchester p137

BUDGET BEDS

Alexander House; York p347
Ben Nevis Inn; Glencoe, Ben Nevis
    & Ardnamurchan p361
Bridges Long Mynd Youth Hostel; Shropshire
    Hills p60
Clachaig Inn; Glencoe, Ben Nevis &
    Ardnamurchan p361
Grinton Youth Hostel; Yorkshire Dales p88
Joiners Shop Bunkhouse; Northumberland
    Coast p215
Kings House Hotel; Glencoe, Ben Nevis
    & Ardnamurchan p361
Pot-a-Doodle-Do; Northumberland Coast p215
Longthorn Farm Campsite (tipis); Poole &
    Isle of Purbeck p239
Old Smithy; Pembrokeshire Coast p228
Wilderhope Manor; Shropshire Hills p60
Windmill Inn; Isle of Wight p267

RESTAURANTS

L'Autre Pied; London p150
La Bécasse; Ludlow p325
Burlington Restaurant; Yorkshire Dales p85
Fat Duck; Marlow, Henley & Cookham p35

**2 Kemplay Road
London
NW3 1SY**

www.hampsteadguesthouse.com

020 7435 8679

HAMPSTEAD VILLAGE GUESTHOUSE

We never planned to start a hotel in our family home but, when life changed, it was a natural development for the house, which had always welcomed a steady stream of visitors, to become a Guesthouse.

Whilst preserving the Victorian character of the house, all rooms have good writing tables, free wi-fi access and guests can use a laptop and mobile phone at no extra charge. Most important for families is the fridge and kettle in each room and, for general use, there are baby monitors, cots, high chairs, changing mat and a selection of toys which most children make a beeline for.

We have a beautiful garden which is a haven in summer. Hampstead Heath, which is very nearby, is an ideal place for children, with a playground just at the bottom of the road and paddling pool within walking distance. Kentish Town City Farm, also a wonderful place for children, is nearby.

Peaceful setting, close to Hampstead Heath, yet in the heart of lively Hampstead Village

~

Close to underground and bus. Centre of London in 15 minutes.

~

Large rooms full of character, plus modern amenities: TV, fridge, kettle and direct-dial telephone.

~

Breakfast in the garden, weather permitting

~

Accommodation from £55

~

No smoking

Felin Fach Griffin Inn; Brecon Beacons p367
Hakkasan, London p151
Hambrough, Isle of Wight p267
Kinloch Lodge Hotel; Skye p284
The Kitchin; Edinburgh p119
Mr Underhill's; Ludlow p326
Morston Hall, North Norfolk p200
Neptune, North Norfolk p200
Northcote; Forest of Bowland p24
Restaurant Martin Wishart; Edinburgh p119
St John; London p151
Walnut Tree; Brecon Beacons p370
Waterside Inn; Marlow, Henley & Cookham p35
Yorke Arms; Yorkshire Dales p88

ART

Barbara Hepworth Museum & Sculpture Garden;
   St Ives p334
Blenheim Palace; South Cotswolds p64
Kettle's Yard; Cambridge p306
Manchester Art Gallery; Manchester p124
National Gallery; London p145
Pallant House Gallery; West Sussex p249
Stanley Spencer Gallery; Marlow, Henley &
   Cookham p29
Tate St Ives St Ives p334
Royal Cambrian Academy; Conwy p315
Royal Scottish Academy, Edinburgh p114
Urbis; Manchester p125

BUILDINGS

CASTLES

Alnwick Castle; Northumberland Coast p213
Bamburgh Castle; Northumberland Coast p209
Corfe Castle; Poole & the Isle of Purbeck p233
Lindisfarne Castle; Northumberland Coast p206
Stokesay Castle; Shropshire Hills p56
St Mawes Castle, Falmouth & the Roseland
   Peninsula p168

CHURCHES & CATHEDRALS

All Saints, Bisham; Marlow, Henley, Cookham p31
Arundel Cathedral; West Sussex p249
Bath Abbey; Bath p292
High Kirk of St Giles; Edinburgh p110
King's College Chapel; Cambridge p306
Westminster Abbey; London p145
York Minster; York p345

HOUSES

Arlington Court; North Devon & Exmoor p185
Blenheim Palace; South Cotswolds p64
Cliveden; Marlow, Henley & Cookham
Goodwood House; West Sussex p247
Haddon Hall; Peak District p45
Lulworth Castle; Poole & the Isle of Purbeck, p234
Palace of Holyrood House; Edinburgh p113
Petworth House & Park p249

GARDENS

Abbey Gardens; Isles of Scilly p273
Alnwick Gardens; Northumberland Coast p213
Armadale Castle Gardens & Museum of the Isles;
   Skye p280
Austwick Hall; Yorkshire Dales p88
Barbara Hepworth Museum & Sculpture Garden;
   St Ives p334
Chatsworth House; Peak District p45
Forbidden Corner; Yorkshire Dales p79
Kew Gardens; London p150
Rousham House; South Cotswolds p64
Trewyn Subtropical Gardens; St Ives p334

OUTDOOR ACTIVITIES

WALKING

Borrowdale; Lake District: Around Keswick p377
Brecon Beacons p364-367
Forest of Bowland pp20-22
Isle of Purbeck; Poole & the Isle of Purbeck p233
Peak District pp38-49
Pembrokeshire Coast Path; Pembrokeshire
   Coast p220
Shropshire Hills pp50-61
South Downs; West Sussex p244
Yorkshire Dales pp76-82

ROCK-CLIMBING, MOUNTAINEERING

Glencoe, Ben Nevis & Ardnamurchan 354-258
Lake District: Around Keswick p376-379
St Govan's Head; Pembrokeshire Coast p220
Skye pp280-284

SAILING

Around Falmouth; Isle of Wight p172
West Wittering & Around; West Sussex p250

SKIING

Glencoe p356

SURFING & WINDSURFING

Freshwater West; Pembrokeshire Coast p223
Saunton Sands; North Devon & Exmoor p184
West Wittering; West Sussex p250

WILDLIFE

Arundel Wildfowl & Wetlands Trust;
   West Sussex p249
Cotswold Wildlife Park South Cotswolds p67
Farne Islands bird breeding ground;
   Northumberland Coast p210
The Islands; Pembrokeshire Coast p223
Lundy Island, North Devon & Exmoor p183
Titchwell Marsh p194, p197
Whalespotting; Skye p282

Time Out Guides Limited
Universal House
251 Tottenham Court Road
London W1T 7AB
Tel + 44 (0)20 7813 3000
Fax + 44 (0)20 7813 6001
Email guides@timeout.com
www.timeout.com

Editorial
Editor Ros Sales
Copy editors Jan Fuscoe, Phil Harriss
Listings checkers Alex Brown, William Crow
Proofreader Marion Moisy
Indexer Jackie Brind

Managing Director Peter Fiennes
Editorial Directors Sarah Guy, Ruth Jarvis
Financial Director Dan Allen
Editorial Manager Holly Pick
Assistant Management Accountant Ija Krasnikova

Design
Art Director Scott Moore
Art Editor Pinelope Kourmouzoglou
Senior Designer Henry Elphick
Graphic Designers Kei Ishimaru, Nicola Wilson
Advertising Designer Jodi Sher

Picture Desk
Picture Editor Jael Marschner
Deputy Picture Editor Lynn Chambers
Picture Researcher Gemma Walters
Picture Desk Assistant Marzena Zoladz

Advertising
Commercial Director Mark Phillips
Sales Manager Alison Wallen
Advertising Sales Ben Holt, Matt Peel, Jason Trotman
Copy Controller Alison Bourke

Marketing
Marketing Manager Yvonne Poon
Sales & Marketing Director, North America Lisa Levinson
Senior Publishing Brand Manager Luthfa Begum
Marketing Designer Anthony Huggins

Production
Group Production Director Mark Lamond
Production Manager Brendan McKeown
Production Controller Damian Bennett
Production Coordinator Kelly Fenlon

Time Out Group
Chairman Tony Elliott
Chief Executive Officer David King
Group General Manager/Director Nichola Coulthard
Time Out Communications Ltd MD David Pepper
Time Out International Ltd MD Cathy Runciman
Time Out Magazine Ltd Publisher/Managing Director Mark Elliott
Group IT Director Simon Chappell
Marketing Circulation Director Catherine Demajo

Maps Kei Ishimaru. Street maps by JS Graphics (john@jsgraphics.co.uk).

Cover photography Durdle Door, Dorset by Ruth Tomlinson/photolibrary.com; back cover courtesy of Great John Street Hotel, Armathwaite Hall and photographer Emma Beddard.

Photography by page 2 (right) Andrew Kneath; pages 3 (left), 21, 23, 38, 41, 47 (top), 48, 312, 316 Charlie Pinder; pages 2 (middle), 125 (top left) Joel Fildes; pages 3 (right), 146, 160, 162, 242, 245 (bottom), 248, 253, 278, 281, 285, 287, 352, 355, 356, 359 Jonathan Perugia; pages 3 (left), 270, 302 Simon Coppock; pages 16, 17, 50 (bottom right), 50 (bottom left), 53, 54 (top), 59, 60, 62, 65, 71, 218, 222, 226, 245, 256, 257, 288, 289, 320, 323, 326, 330, 332 (top right), 335, 362, 365, 368, 371 Britta Jaschinski; page 18 (middle right), 18 (bottom left) Chris Pierre; page 18 (top), 18 (middle right) Ruth Jarvis; pages 38 (bottom right), 44, 47 (bottom) Daniel Nielson; page 54 (bottom) Shropshire Tourism; pages 57 English Heritage; page 68 courtesy of Barnsley House; pages 75 (top), 77 (top), 80 (top right) www.yorkshire.com; pages 75 (bottom right), 75 (bottom left), 77 (bottom), 350, 351, 374, 380, 383 Michael Sayles; page 80 The Devonshire Fell; pages 80 (bottom right), 83 courtesy of The Red Lion hotel; page 84 courtesy the Shepherd's Purse Creamery; page 90, 91 Visit London Images/Britain On View; pages 92, 95 (top), 95 (left) Destination Bristol; page 98 courtesy of 45 RPM; page 108, 111, 112, 115, 116, 118 (bottom left), 143 (top) Olivia Rutherford; page 125 (bottom) Simon Buckley; page 131 Jill Jennings; page 131 (bottom right) Nathan Cox; page 140 (top left) Lee Mawdsley; page 140 (top right) Anthony Webb; page 140 (middle right) Damir Fabijanic; page 140 (bottom right) Heloise Berman; page 140 (left) Tim Motion; page 143 (bottom) Simon Leigh; page 153 Heike Bohnstengel; pages 158, 159, 166 (left), 166 (top right), 169 (bottom right), 172 Michelle Grant; pages 166, 169 (left), 172 (top left), 172 (top right), Emma Beddard; page 169 (top) courtesy of Jeff Meadows; page 169 (middle right) English Heritage; pages 178, 187 Walter Weber; pages 178 (top), 181, 188 Peter Hendrie; page 184 Lydia Evans; pages 192, 195, 199, 200 (bottom) Chris Herring; page 196 Sam Robbins; pages 205 (right), 205 (bottom right), 207, 208 (middle left), 212, 215, 216 Brian Young; pages 205 (top left), 205 (bottom left), 208 (bottom) Northumberland Tourism; page 221 Andrew Kneath; pages 230 (top), 230 (bottom right), 230 (bottom left), 230 (middle left), 236, 238 Ann-Marie Peña; page 230 (bottom) www.visitswanageandpurbeck.co.uk; page 235 (top) Lynn Chambers; page 251 (top) Daniel Neilson; page 258 (bottom), 266 Tove Breitstein; pages 258, 261, 262, 263 Steve Thearle; page 266 (top left) courtesy the Priory Hotel; page 290 www.visitbath.co.uk; page 293 (top) Colin Hawkes; page 292 Bath & North East Somerset Council; page 302 (top right) John Dalkin; page 309 Cambridge Folk Festival; page 335 www.stives-cornwall-co.uk; page 340 © visityork.org; page 340 (middle left) Sam Atkins.

The following images were provided by the featured establishments/artists: page 26, 30, 33, 34, 87, 92 (bottom right), 95 (middle right), 95 (bottom right), 101, 102, 118, 125, 132, 135, 149, 152, 174, 188 (bottom), 201, 209 (top), 209 (middle right), 211, 223, 242 (bottom), 251 (bottom), 256, 275, 282, 288 (middle), 290 (middle), 299, 310, 326 (top), 329, 332, 335 (top right), 336, 344, 347, 384.

The editor would like to thank Christine Cort, Ann-Marie Peña, Paul Shorrock, Jane Thurley, John Thurley.

Rural Idylls

Top & bottom right:
Whitewell; left & top right:
Forest of Bowland.

The Forest of Bowland

Remote fells, stern stone villages and the food-forward Ribble Valley.

Even within northern England the Forest of Bowland is little known. Thousands drive by this officially designated Area of Outstanding Natural Beauty every day on the M6 motorway that marks its western edge, noticing, if anything, only its most distinctive landmark, the barrow-like Pendle Hill, as they zoom past to the Lake District to the north or the Yorkshire Dales to the east. With no famous mountains or romanticised lakes, nor any tourist attractions as such, Bowland is overshadowed by its more cherished neighbours. Yet visitors who are interested in more than ticking off sights and summits find rich pleasures here, all the more satisfying for their lack of tourist traffic.

The Forest of Bowland is not a forest: the name arises from Bowland's medieval role as a royal hunting ground (the Queen is still said to be fond). It's dominated by its wild uplandsm huge hump-backed fells covered with heather and grouse moor. The rivers that rise in their boggy tops cut valleys, steep and tree-lined at first and then meandering into generous flood plains. The drystone walls of hill farms reach geometrically towards the summits. There are probably more sheep here than people.

To the south, the Forest is bisected by the pretty Ribble Valley, home of picturesque Clitheroe with its Norman keep. With an affluent population and the livestock, game and other produce of Bowland on its doorstep, the area has been a pioneer in local food sourcing and is home to a happily disproportionate number of excellent restaurants and pubs.

Explore

Forest of Bowland hotels have no bristling stacks of attractions leaflets. The main activities are outdoor ones: walking, cycling, birdwatching, hunting, fishing are all notably good here; the area is also known for gliding, paragliding, paramotoring and other air sports. The small towns and villages, cut out of the local grey stone, tend to be functional rather than chocolate box, handsome rather than twee. They are worth a wander for their pretty churches (particularly Ribchester, Dunsop Bridge and Wray), village pubs and variety of bridges. Some have a pleasing uniformity thanks to estate ownership – Downham is owned by Lord Clitheroe, who doesn't allow overhead electricity cables or excessive signage, a fact appreciated by the makers of period dramas.

RIBBLE VALLEY

From its source near Ingleton in the Yorkshire Dales, the River Ribble swoops down to its estuary near Preston in lazy meanders. Walkers can follow the Ribble the 70 miles of its length along the waymarked **Ribble Way**.

The Lancashire section that this chapter covers cuts a valley between the northern Bowland uplands and Pendle Hill to the south-east, running through **Gisburn**, **Sawley** and the handsome town of **Ribchester**, with its Roman remains and museum (Riverside, 01254 878261, www.ribchestermuseum.org). This is verdantly pretty countryside peppered with villages and small towns, with frequent views to the hills. Tolkein stayed here when he was writing *The Lord of the Rings*, and echoes of the landscapes have supposedly found their way into Middle Earth.

The Ribble brushes the edges of **Clitheroe**, a vital local market town worth a morning's explorations. There are some very browsable independent shops and a rather bijou Norman keep, with a newly remodelled museum (Clitheroe Castle Museum, 01200 424568, www.lancashire.gov.uk/museums).

PENDLE HILL

The unmistakable silhouette of Pendle Hill dominates the skyline for miles around. Its looming presence is a fitting monument to the 11 local women, the 'Pendle witches', who were tried and executed for witchcraft in 1612. There are various witch trails (see www.pendle.gov.uk) and witch paraphernalia abounds. For an informed take on the affair, along with a broader perspective on the area, visit the creditable **Pendle Heritage Centre** (01282 661704, www.htnw.co.uk) in **Barrowford**.

The village of **Barley**, criss-crossed by footpaths, is the best place to tackle an ascent of Pendle, possible in an afternoon. It's worth a visit in its own right, with a pretty stream-bordered picnic area in summer and a good pub, the Pendle Inn, for a pint to celebrate summitting.

Forest of Bowland

Historic sites
● ● ● ● ●

Art & architecture
● ● ● ● ●

Hotels
● ● ● ● ●

Eating & drinking
● ● ● ● ●

Scenery
● ● ● ● ●

Outdoor activities
● ● ● ● ●

INTO THE FELLS

The Forest of Bowland uplands are wildernesses of bog and heather, cut by characteristic cloughs of ash and oak and remote river valleys. Wildlife flourishes, from the unusually prolific birdlife (the hen harrier is the symbol of the Forest of Bowland AONB) to game to grazing animals.

In the south, notable villages are **Dunsop Bridge**, the official centre of Great Britain, with a slightly forlorn 1990s telephone box on its village green to mark its status; the hamlet of **Whitewell** comprising just a church and inn; picturesque **Chipping**; and remote, grey stone **Slaidburn**.

In the north, the **Lune Valley** is a picturesque way in from Lancaster. **Wray** is the nicest village, with access to walks along Roeburndale.

If you're exploring the fells on foot – and you should, to fully appreciate them – be sure to equip yourself wisely, with a map, waterproof boots and, if you plan to take advantage of the copious open access, a compass. There are good walks on www.fellscape.co.uk.

The less active will enjoy the gardens and livestock at working hill farm **Cobble Hey** (Garstang, 01995 602643, www.cobblehey. co.uk), and **Bowland Wild Boar Park** (Chipping, 01995 61554, www.wildboarpark.co.uk).

Eat

With a wealth of good local ingredients and a passionate, informed and affluent population, the **Ribble Valley** in particular has developed a unique gastronomic microclimate, sustaining a high number of excellent pubs, restaurants and food producers. Local sourcing has become something of an obsession, with some places posting detailed lists of all their suppliers.

Many hotels listed in the Stay section also serve excellent food.

Bay Horse Inn

Bay Horse, 5 miles S of Lancaster *Bay Horse Lane (01524 791204/www.bayhorseinn.com). Open noon-2pm, 7-9.15pm Tue-Sat; noon-3pm Sun. £££. Modern British.*
The Bay Horse is small and pretty, and its modern British dishes are rigorously sourced and prepared with a nose for flavour and an eye for detail by chef Craig Wilkinson. We've had intensely tasty soups (parsnip and roast garlic) and proper sandwiches (poached salmon) but more evolved dishes might include loin of venison with walnut mash, marinated raisins and port sauce. Decor and atmosphere are quite genteel: evidence of fell-walking is better left outside the door.

Bridge House Farm

Wray, 1 mile SW of Hornby *(01524 222496/ www.bridgehousefarm.co.uk). Open Café Summer 10am-5pm Tue-Sun. Winter 10am-4pm Tue-Sun. Bistro 6-9.30pm Thur-Sat. ££. Café/bistro.*
On the edge of Wray in the northern secton of Bowland, this one-time farmhouse is now home to a café, evening bistro, garden centre and gift shop, all on a small and personal scale. Café food always includes a generous number of cakes and tray bakes, plus filling, tasty versions of café standards, such as bacon, brie and cranberry ciabatta with fruity couscous and chutney, or individual cottage pies with red cabbage. Everything is made on site.

Duke of York

Grindleton, 2 miles NE of Clitheroe *Brow Top (01200 441266/www.dukeofyorkgrindleton.com). Open noon-2pm, 6-9pm Tue-Sat; noon-2pm, 5-8pm Sun. ££. Gastropub.*
There are some great deals at this village pub – a two-course menu for £7.50 when we visited. Our goat's cheese and beetroot salad, followed by herb-crusted haddock, were far better than they deserved to be at that price; though the à la carte dishes of Pendleton lamb and steak and ale pudding were probably worth the extra (and we loved the big chips). Presentation and detail were good, too; we reckon the little-fêted proprietor and chef, Michael Heathcote, deserves more attention. Surroundings are pleasant rather than cosy, with lots of light and modern prints on the wall.

Food by Breda Murphy

Whalley, 4 miles S of Clitheroe *Abbots Court, 41 Station Road (01254 823446/www.foodbybreda murphy.com). Open 10am-6pm Tue-Sat. £££. Global.*
Proprietor Breda Murphy was previously head chef at the Inn at Whitewell (*see p25*), where she built a reputation that has followed her to this catering business and deli, with a pretty, informal dining room painted duck-egg blue, where food is served during shop opening hours. At press time, it was opening for dinner only occasionally: shame, for head chef Gareth Bevan's menu is certainly interesting enough to merit a bigger audience. It draws from Asia and the Mediterranean, Britain and Ireland, in dishes such as salmon with beetroot and coconut sauce with fennel bhajis and pea risotto with artichokes and parsley oil. More casual food is available, too.

Highwayman

Burrow, 2 miles S of Kirkby Lonsdale *(01524 273 338/www.highwaymaninn.co.uk). Open noon-2pm, 6-9pm Mon-Fri; noon-2pm, 5.30-9pm Sat; noon-8.30pm Sun. ££. Gastropub/British.*
The Highwayman started life as an 18th-century coaching inn, but, with its high-capacity kitchen, dining rooms, car park and garden, and enormous horse logo, feels like a very contemporary rendering of your wayside hostelry. A Ribble Valley Inns property, it's perhaps a little impersonal, but the spruce surroundings (a handsome modern version of traditional pub decor, real fires and all), smart service and not too beery atmosphere draw hundreds of customers. The appetising and well-turned out menu bears the Ribble Valley hallmarks of unfussy, reasonably priced food sourced with impeccable detail – the lamb grazes on heather, the mutton is a local breed, and the regional dishes reflect the location on the Cumbria/Lancashire border. Cartmel sticky toffee pudding, anyone?

The Inn at Whitewell.

Northcote

Langho, 6.5 miles S of Clitheroe *Northcote Road (01254 240555/www.northcote.com). Open 7-9.45am, noon-1.30pm, 7-9.30pm Mon-Fri; 7.45-9.45am, noon-1.30pm, 6-9.30pm Sat; 7.45-9.45am, noon-2pm, 7-9pm Sun. ££££. British.*

Nigel Haworth, Northcote's long-time chef and proprietor, has been a key figure in the renaissance of British food, advocating local sourcing and a sense of *terroir* long before they were fashionable, and earning a Michelin star in the process. His menu starts long before the kitchen, with discussions with farmers over breeds of sheep (Lonk is the house choice, reared about ten miles away) and plans for planting in Northcote's own vegetable garden. On the plate food can be hearty or full of finesse, as the dish demands. We've enjoyed lobster ravioli, beetroot salad with goat's curd and even a simple salad (of 'tiny garden leaves'). The hotel operation is gradually gaining parity: attractive rooms are decorated in a mix of classic and current country-house styles and come with robes and iPod connectors alongside other mod cons. Some have pretty private gardens.

Parkers Arms

Newton-in-Bowland, 4 miles NW of Clitheroe *(01200 446236/www.parkersarms.co.uk). Open Summer noon-3pm, 6-8.30pm Mon-Fri; noon-8.30pm Sat, Sun. Winter noon-3pm, 6-8pm Tue-Sun. ££. Gastropub.*

This unreconstructed village pub/restaurant looks as if it's barely changed in 30 years, offering little in the way of decor but lots in the way of atmosphere, with a sympatico proprietor, small knots of locals, fireplaces and candlelight. A revamp is on the cards, but we are assured 'no chrome, spotlights or laid tables'. Tasty, good-value food comes from a short menu, which might include Goosnargh duck liver pâté, whitebait, Lancashire rarebit, pork and dumpling ragout and chestnut tart. Provenance is, as de rigeur, thoroughly local – even the slaughterhouse is namechecked – and everything down to the delicious Eccles cakes is made on the premises. A dartboard and brandied hot chocolate are two enjoyable idiosyncracies.

Spread Eagle

Sawley, 3 miles NE of Clitheroe *(01200 441202/ www.spreadeaglesawley.co.uk). Open noon-2pm, 6-9.30pm Mon-Sat; noon-7.30pm Sun. £££. British/Mediterranean.*

This capacious pub-restaurant was regularly full within weeks of opening in late 2008. That's partly down to the location, just across the road from the river and next to ruined Sawley Abbey, and partly down to its well-rendered smart-comfortable update of trad pub decor. But it's a lot to do with the food too – snacks, platters, nibbles and proper mains, with crowd pleasers from the comfort foody to the classic. There's plenty of local stuff but an Italian slant is noticeable: this might be the only place to offer black pudding fritters next to bruschetta. We've enjoyed the fishcakes, roast chicken and pork chop and, outstandingly, the English pudding plate. There's a good selection of wines and an on-site wine shop.

Taste@Backridge

Waddington, 2 miles N of Clitheroe *Backridge Farm, Twitter Lane (01200 427304/www.backridge.co.uk). Open 8am-6pm Mon-Sat; 10am-5pm Sun. ££. Café.*

This handsome wood-furnished café in the Backridge retail complex is a classy modern venture, with most of its fare premises-made, bread included. As well as the usual soups and quiches there are what you could call gastro-caff dishes: casual international classics fancied up just a tad: bruschetta with local air-dried ham, for example, or minute steak with sticky onions on a teacake with hand-cut chips. There are also cakes of all descriptions.

Three Fishes

Mitton, 3.5 miles SW of Clitheroe *Mitton Road (01254 826888/www.thethreefishes.com). Open noon-2pm, 6-9pm Mon-Fri; noon-2pm, 5.30-9pm Sat; noon-8.30pm Sun. ££. Gastropub/British.*

The successful Ribble Valley Inns company re-invented the dining pub when it refurbed and reopened this 400-year-old inn in 2004. Surroundings are attractive and comfortable, and retain an open-fire cosiness; there's generous outdoor seating and friendly staff. This commercial awareness is matched by a formidable kitchen nous: food is sourced and made with a palpable passion and is affordable. The commitment to local suppliers sings from a menu of crowd-pleasers. Warm Morecambe Bay shrimps are a sensory pleasure; fish pie is crusted with Mrs Kirham's Lancashire cheese and the excellent battered haddock comes with dripping-fried chips. Beer-wise, some nicely kept Hen Harrier from the Bowland Brewery and Hawkshead's Brodie's Prime were on offer when we visited. Bookings aren't accepted, so turn up early.

White Bull Hotel

Ribchester *Water Street (01254 878303/www.white bullrib.co.uk). Open noon-2.30pm, 6-9.30pm Tue-Sat; noon-3pm, 5-8pm Sun. £££. Gastropub.*

This large, comfortable pub buys into the culinary standards of gastropubbery but not its restaurant mores. Its capacious rooms, furnished with big tables and padded benches, are 100% pub, right down to the domino-playing drinkers and local real ales on tap. It's a handsome old building, unselfconscious and agreeably unmodernised. As chef-patron Chris Bell, alumnus of Paul Heathcote and Gordon Ramsay kitchens, says, all the money's gone into the kitchen: food is unshowy but excellent, precisely and painstakingly rendered. Local notes are here in produce like pheasant and mallard and Lancashire staples including hotpot and battered black pudding; there both simple grills and more complex dishes such as duck leg confit and pig cheeks with sage mash. Three bedrooms are decorated in beige-y contemporary style.

Stay

The **Bay Horse** (*see p22*), **Northcote** (*see above*) and **White Bull** (*see above*), also offer rooms.

Backfold Cottage

Waddington, 2 miles N of Clitheroe *The Square (01200 422367). ££. No credit cards.*

This B&B bills itself, with typical eccentric humour, as 'a mini country hotel'. Mini indeed: it's a tiny 17th-century cottage on a narrow cobbled street whose front door opens directly into the living room/diner. Here you'll likely find the proprietor, retired catering scientist Daphne Forbes, along with her home-made cakes: non-guests are welcome for afternoon tea, and guests are offered all-day refreshments, plus candlelit silver-service dinner. The three rooms are small, pretty, a tad old-fashioned and excellent value.

Hipping Hall
Cowan Bridge, 8 miles NW of Wray *(01524 271187/www.hippinghall.com). ££££.*
This impeccably kept restaurant with rooms is ten or so miles north of Bowland; it wins its place here despite the slightly far-flung location for its lovely romantic style and renowned kitchen. Six rooms in the main house and three in the cottage employ luxurious fabrics and materials to create a pampered feel. The restaurant is housed in a 15th-century hall, with minstrels' gallery. Chef Michael Wilson's menu displays contemporary aspirations and classic abilities, in dishes like scallops with cauliflower, apple and cumin foam and artichoke tart with parsnip purée, chestnut and celery velouté.

Inn at Whitewell
Whitewell, 5 miles N of Clitheroe *(01400 448222/www.innatwhitewell.com). £££.*
Fabulously set on the River Hodder with views across to the fells, this rambling country inn seduces with its effortlessly hospitable attitude. Children, dogs and muddy boots are all welcome. The ground floor is a flagstoned warren of cosy, rug-strewn rooms, with an abundance of real fires, capacious tables and window seats and a slightly more formal dining room. The whole place is furnished with a comfortable mix of antiques discovered by proprietor Charles Bowman, along with hunting, fishing and cricketing paraphernalia. Rooms are all different but all have their charms, both in the main building and in the annexe; several have peat-burning fires and while all have notably sybaritic bathrooms, some are home to the antique baths and showers that Charles collects.

Due attention is given to food here: Whitewell is a dining destination in its own right. The only dish that has never left the menu is the fish pie; otherwise it's a mix of fairly straightforward palate pleasers, plus some more developed dishes in the restaurant. Wines are knowledgeably chosen and available in small glasses (and also in the on-site shop).

Mitton Hall
Mitton, 3.5 miles SW of Clitheroe *near Whalley (01254 826544/www.mittonhall.co.uk). £££.*
Impressive not just for its age (500 and some years), Mitton Hall is also extremely beautiful. Its graceful honey-coloured frontage doesn't prepare you for the drama of the galleried hall within, now effectively put to use as a foyer and bar, with giant chandelier, grand piano and baronial fireplace. The bedrooms can't really compete, nor do they try to, with a not wholly successful stab at comfortable contemporary styling. Upgrades are in progress, though, and meanwhile prices are moderate. Food is international in scope, safe in the bar and more ambitious and expensive in the elegant dining rooms of the brasserie. The bar, where cocktails are poured, is a player on the local scene, attracting a dressy young crowd.

Park House
Gisburn, 6 miles NE of Clitheroe *Church View (01200 445269/www.parkhousegisburn.co.uk). ££.*
Park House is a bit of a find: it has all the charms of a small, personal hotel and none of the institutional tics of the B&B that it really is, with concomitantly reasonable prices. It's a handsome Georgian house opposite Gisburn church, with five rooms and a beautifully furnished guest lounge. Proprietor Glenis Jollys has a passion for antiquing and an eye for style: the rooms are furnished with pretty and individual one-off pieces, and the details are thoughtful. Beds are comfortable, glasses are cut glass, the flowers fresh and the fires real. Park House doesn't serve dinner, but there's a decent pub nearby, the White Bull, along with a smart and friendly Italian restaurant, La Locanda.

Stanley House
Mellor, 5 miles S of Ribchester *(01254 769200/www.stanleyhouse.co.uk). £££.*
This extravagant country house hotel is a substantial enterprise with a rated restaurant, landscaped grounds and a thriving corporate trade; locals are a bit suspicious of its showy aesthetic, but it's well done with a good eye for detail and some interesting artwork. The 12 rooms are well-specced and lavishly furnished: features might include a carved bed, slipper bath, wood-burning stove or Oriental theming.

Factfile

When to go
You're here to enjoy the outdoors, so weather is part of the package. The fells have their own microclimate: it can be sunny here when raining in Clitheroe. Pubs and restaurants are reliably cosy in winter, with real fires.

Getting there & around
A car is useful – and the area is convenient for the M6 and M65 – but not essential. Train travellers are best arriving at Clitheroe, to which there is a regular train service from Manchester via Blackburn and from where there are good local bus services. The B10 and B11 ply a circuit that takes in Whitewell and Slaidburn. You can also get the train to Preston, Lancaster or Blackburn to access the Forest of Bowland, but the connections aren't as good.

Tourist information
Bowland Visitor Centre Beacon Fell Country Park (01995 640557/www.forestofbowland.com). Open 10.30am-4.30pm daily.
Clitheroe 12-14 Market Place (01200 442226/ www.forestofbowland.com). Open 10am-5pm Mon-Sat; 11am-4pm Sun.

Marlow.

Marlow, Henley & Cookham

Quiet Thames-side towns and villages, with artistic and literary links.

'Hooray for Henley' goes up the cry. Surely one of the last places in England where boaters can still be worn with pride, Henley not only has the hat, but it still has the boats.

The middle reaches of the Thames to the west of London, for many centuries the most important thoroughfare in southern England, have long had royal associations. Henley is close to Windsor, where William the Conqueror established a castle, and Eton, where Henry IV founded a school, so it comes as no surprise that its regatta is a royal affair. 'Sweet Thames, run softly' could well be the motto of these three charming bridge towns, because for at least the last 150 years they've been dedicated to seriously affluent riverside leisure. Cliveden House represents the apotheosis of that fashion, with its pleasure gardens overlooking the adorable old village of Cookham, immortalised in the paintings of Sir Stanley Spencer. And Marlow remains a handsome old riverside town with strong literary associations, one of the most splendid bridges above London, and a brace of interesting churches. These river banks also boast the finest dining outside the capital, with a clutch of Michelin-starred establishments, old and new, in the pretty village of Bray, and various others within easy reach around the countryside.

As well as the sense of bucolic affluence, the fine food and Thames-side walks, visitors also come to enjoy the nearby countryside. The chalky Chiltern hills, with their hanging beech woods, red kites and profusion of wildflowers, provide some of the most inspiring rambles within an hour of London.

Explore

COOKHAM

On a kind of island formed by the river, Maidenhead and the roaring A404, Cookham is in fact a trinity of villages, and remains almost as described by its most celebrated son, the visionary figurative artist Sir Stanley Spencer (1891–1959) – a 'village in heaven'. Cookham itself, with its quaint old High Street, where Spencer was born at the Victorian semi called Fernlea (he spent much of his life painting the village and its people), runs down to the river bridge. It is separated by the quarter mile of wide common called Cookham Moor from **Cookham Rise**, on the railway line. **Cookham Dean** lies scattered about on Mount Hill a mile west, with famous views of Marlow and the river below from **Winter Hill**, and wonderful walks through beech hangers in the Woodland Trust's **Bisham Woods**. No visit to Cookham is complete without a look into the **Stanley Spencer Gallery** (*see p29*), which also publishes an excellent booklet mapping out a guided walk round the scenes that the artist painted both in the centre of the village and further afield. The walk begins at the gallery, and takes visitors past the Tarry Stone, believed by some locals to be a meteorite, then down to the river and into the churchyard of **Holy Trinity**, founded in 1140, where Spencer is buried and the setting for his extraordinary *The Resurrection, Cookham*. Also unmissable is a look around **Cliveden** (*see p29*), perched high above the village and river on the east bank. As well as walking through the National Trust woodlands along one of the most beautiful stretches of the river to the south of the house, it's also worth taking time to drop in on **Taplow** to find the lonely and atmospheric **Old Churchyard of St Nicolas**, next door to Taplow Court. It's the site of a prominent Anglo-Saxon burial mound and has been in continuous use since the seventh century. Treasure found in the mound in 1833 is preserved in the British Museum.

Taplow overlooks Maidenhead, on the west bank of the river, one part of an unholy trinity with Slough and Windsor, the 'gateway towns' of the pulsating M4 corridor west of London. Downriver from Cookham, just beyond Maidenhead, is **Bray**, celebrated in a satirical 18th-century song 'The Vicar of Bray', about a cleric who boasts that he has three times changed his creed to keep his living. Today it is most famous for its improbably priced cluster of gourmet restaurants and riverside housing stock. Well worth a look from the outside, on the main road to Bray Wick, is the **Jesus Hospital**, red-brick almshouses founded in 1609 by William Goddard of the Worshipful Company of Fishmongers, their entrance surmounted by a full-size effigy of the man.

Hidden away just north of Slough is **Stoke Poges churchyard**, known for its connection with Thomas Gray (1716-71) and for the churchyard where his

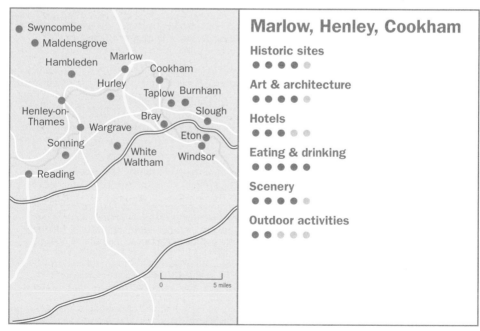

Marlow, Henley, Cookham

Historic sites
● ● ● ● ◐

Art & architecture
● ● ● ● ○

Hotels
● ● ● ◐ ◐

Eating & drinking
● ● ● ● ●

Scenery
● ● ● ● ◐

Outdoor activities
● ● ◐ ◐ ◐

Swyncombe · Maldensgrove · Hambleden · Marlow · Hurley · Cookham · Taplow · Burnham · Henley-on-Thames · Bray · Slough · Wargrave · Eton · Sonning · White Waltham · Windsor · Reading

0 — 5 miles

'Elegy in a Country Churchyard' (1751) was probably written. There is a monument to him by James Wyatt (1799) east of the churchyard, and he is buried with his mother near the east wall of the church. Stoke Pogres church is also famous for its 'Bicycle Window' (1643), showing a man on a hobby-horse with a horn and very little besides. Next door are the **Stoke Poges Memorial Gardens** (open dawn to dusk), laid out in 1934 for the 'repose of the ashes of cremated persons' and probably unique in Britain for their stipulation that here 'there will be no buildings, structures or monuments of any kind likely to remind one of a cemetery'. A small, old-fashioned museum is dedicated to the history of the gardens, the church, and Stoke Park, which is now a pretty swanky golf and tennis hotel.

"The current house is an Italianate villa designed by Charles 'Houses of Parliament' Barry in 1851, with an amazing Italian garden laid out by the Astors."

Cliveden

Taplow, nr Cookham *(01494 755562/www.national trust.org.uk). Open Grounds Mar-Oct 11am-6pm daily. Nov, Dec 11am-4pm daily. House Apr-Oct 3-5.30pm Thur, Sun. Admission £8; £4 reductions (house £1 extra; 50p reductions).*

On a phenomenal site above the Thames, Cliveden was the pleasure palace of the decadent Duke of Buckingham in the 17th century. The current house (now a five-star hotel, *see p36*) is an Italianate villa designed by Charles 'Houses of Parliament' Barry in 1851, with an amazing Italian garden laid out by the Astors, the super-rich American owners of the place from 1893 until 1967. All that remains of Buckingham's house is a red-brick arcade and terrace, complete with an 18th-century hi-fi 'sounding room'. It's fenced off from the astonishing spread of lawn and flowerbed that is the parterre, with its unmatchable views downstream, by the Borghese Balustrade, imported here from the Villa Borghese in Rome by William Waldorf Astor, the first of three generations of Astors to hold court here. They are buried in the remarkable chapel, overlooking the river and designed by Giacomo Leoni in 1735. The interior is resplendent throughout with glass mosaics by those Victorian masters of the arts and crafts, Clayton and Bell. Behind the altar is a golden triptych depicting the Adoration of the Magi. Also unmissable nearby is the Canadian War Memorial Garden, presided over by a distinctive statue of Peace with outstretched arms, apparently modelled on Nancy Astor, the most beautiful and celebrated of Cliveden chatelaines.

Stanley Spencer Gallery

Cookham *High Street (01628 471885/www.stanley spencer.org.uk). Open Apr-Oct 10.30am-5.30pm daily. Nov-Mar 11am-4.30pm Thur-Sun. Admission £3; £2 reductions.*

Occupying the small Wesleyan chapel where the artist worshipped as a child, the gallery is a unique repository of the works of this frankly tortured local genius who dedicated his life to finding and portraying devotional, non-denominational delight in the everyday scenes and sex of the village of his birth. Highlights include his *View from Cookham Bridge, the Resurrection* – set in Holy Trinity churchyard – and *Cows on Odney Common*, as well as the unfinished *Cookham Regatta*. Many of the local places that he painted are still perfectly recognisable today. Something of a child prodigy – witness the drawing here done aged 14 – Stanley Spencer was the home-schooled second youngest of a musical family of 11. A very poor businessman, forced to churn out his masterful landscapes as lucrative 'pot-boilers', his personal life was a shambles and he died a pauper, of cancer, in 1959. The gallery holds 120 of his works and shows about 50 in rotation, in summer and winter hangings.

MARLOW & AROUND

Marlow is a charming riverside town with attractive houses and a wobbly old suspension bridge across the Thames. The bridge was designed in 1831–36 by William Tierney Clark, also responsible for Hammersmith Bridge in London, and it's a miniature version of his famous Chain Bridge across the Danube linking Buda and Pest in Hungary. The parish church beside the bridge contains a curious monument to Sir Miles Hobart (died 1632), paid for by Parliament, depicting the accident that killed him, and also a painting of George Alexander the 'spotted negro boy', a St Vincent slave child suffering from piebaldism who was exhibited as a freak in John Richardson's travelling theatre from 1810, when he was baptised, until 1813, when he died. A path leads to the riverside through the churchyard, via a stone memorial inscribed with lines about time past and time future from *Burnt Norton* by TS Eliot, one of Marlow's many famous literary residents (others include Jerome K Jerome, Thomas Love Peacock and the Shelleys, Percy Bysshe and Mary). The path emerges opposite the Two Brewers (see *p32*), with fabulous views of the river and bridge, at the bottom of St Peter's Street, which is well worth a stroll along to see the outside of the medieval 'Old Priory', and the Roman Catholic church of **St Peter's** (1845-48) designed by AWN Pugin. The church contains an unusual relic of uncertain age, a shrivelled hand in a glass casket, viewable on request, which was apparently rescued from the ruins of Reading Abbey during the construction of Reading Gaol in the 1780s.

Marlow;
Stanley Spencer Gallery.

It has been venerated by some as the left hand of St James the Apostle. Back on West Street, at the top of the High Street, is **Remnantz**, a grand old Georgian house that was the first home, in the 18th century, of the Royal Military Academy, the officer training school now at Sandhurst.

On the south bank, minor roads lead from Marlow bridge up to Cookham Dean and along the river to **Bisham**, where the very picturesque, riverside **All Saints** church was founded in the 12th century. The western tower is built of clunch (chalk). Apart from its position on the river, the church is chiefly remarkable for the monuments erected by Lady Hoby for her husband Sir Thomas, Elizabeth I's guardian and ambassador to the French court, who died in Paris at the age of 36. As well as commissioning her own tomb, on which she is depicted with all her children, she is also responsible for the monument to 'two knights' (her husband and brother), lying side by side in their armour. Beyond Bisham is **Hurley**, another handsome old riverside settlement, with the remains of a priory, a large campsite, a couple of above-average pubs including the **Olde Bell Inn** (High Street, 01628 825881, www.theoldebell.co.uk), recently refurbished and with a distinctly above-average menu and rooms.

On the north bank of the river, after four miles the main road from Marlow to Henley passes the turning on the right up to the idyllic village of **Hambleden** and the Chiltern hills beyond. In Hambleden church, the muniment chest belonging to James Brudenell, the seventh Earl of Cardigan, who led the Charge of the Light Brigade, can be found next to the impressive D'Oyley Monument. It's well worth pressing on up into the rolling hills to find the Chiltern Valley Winery (*see below*). Also worth the detour up into the hills is **Fawley**, with its spooky churchyard containing the stumpy 18th-century mausoleum of John Freeman, massive 13th-century west tower, and John Piper window.

Chiltern Valley Winery & Brewery

Hambleden *Old Luxters Vineyard (01491 638330/ www.chilternvalley.co.uk). Open Apr-Sept 9.30am-6pm Mon-Fri; 11am-6pm Sat, Sun. Oct-Mar 9.30am-5pm Mon-Fri; 11am-5pm Sat, Sun.*
Deep in the beech woods, Old Luxter's Vineyard, home to the Chiltern Valley Winery, specialises in slow food, real ketchup, interesting liqueurs, mead, and some exceptional champagne. Since 1984, the winery has been producing award-winning vintages, and the brewery, by appointment to HM The Queen, does full mash real ales by the cask or bottle. The gift shop furnishes a treasure trove of delicious handmade treats.

HENLEY-ON-THAMES

Henley is a very jolly, proper old market town, with a good selection of independent shops, congenial atmosphere and an expansive riverside to boot. With plenty of timber-framed and 18th-century

houses, it stands on the west bank of the river, in Oxfordshire. At the town's east end is the bridge, built in 1786 and adorned with masks of the Thames and Isis over its central arches. Hart Street leads uphill west of the bridge and into the wide Market Place, dominated by the grand Victorian town hall. Bell Street, a good shopping street, leads off to the right, with a right turn again down New Street leading back towards the river past the adorable old Kenton Theatre, still on the top of its game after two centuries of raising the curtain, and the former Brakspear Brewery, now converted into the Hotel du Vin & Bistro (*see p36*).

> ## 'The church, burned down by suffragettes in 1914, was rebuilt in 1916, when Norman masonry was discovered beneath the 17th-century casing of the tower.'

The town is best known for the **Henley Royal Regatta**, held here in the first week of July over a course of about a mile between Temple Island and Poplar Point, just north of the bridge. Founded in 1839, this peculiar combination of social one-upmanship, strenuous oarsmanship and generally amiable riverside drunkenness has become the most important amateur regatta in the world. If you can't make it – or face it – there are several other less prestigious regattas of various types held here on various dates in July and August, all just as much fun – or not, depending on your attitude.

The **Oxfordshire Way** long-distance footpath winds its way north from the town. It begins at the foot of No Man's Hill, on Fair Mile, the wide, tree-lined boulevard of the Nettlebed and Wallingford road. After a couple of miles, it passes through **Middle Assendon**, where the Rainbow Inn (01491 574879) does better food than many pubs, before heading up to **Maidensgrove** through a hidden valley concealing the overgrown ruins of St James's church. At the top of the valley, after another couple of miles, it skirts the **Warburg Nature Reserve**, a fantastic way-marked woodland ablaze in season with anemones, bluebells, gentians, helleborines and several varieties of orchid. Managed by the Berks, Bucks & Oxon Wildlife Trust, the Visitor Centre (01491 642001, www.bbowt.org.uk) provides details of what you're likely to spot where and when. Superb views open up from Maidensgrove, with the green space of **Russell's Water Common** and the Five Horseshoes (*see p32*) worth seeking out beyond. Worth pressing on a mile or so westwards to see is the simple 11th-century church of St Botolph's at **Swyncombe**, set in a delightful dell on the Ridgeway long-distance footpath.

Three miles south of Henley, on the Berkshire bank of the Thames, is the pretty village of **Wargrave**. The church, burned down by suffragettes in 1914, was rebuilt in 1916, when Norman masonry was discovered beneath the 17th-century brick casing of the tower. Further upstream, the charming village of **Sonning**, where the playwright Sir Terence Rattigan lived in the Red House from 1945 to 1947, has a church with eight 15th- to 17th-century brasses. Sonning Lock, just west of the bridge, is one of the prettiest on the river. William Penn – of Pennsylvania fame – died in **Ruscombe**, near **Twyford**, in 1718. The B-road towards Windsor from Twyford passes through **White Waltham**, where the church built in 1337 at beautiful Shottesbrooke Park, headquarters of the Landmark Trust (01628 825925, www.landmark trust.org.uk), has some good tombs and a fantastic spire, and was much copied by Victorian church-builders. The park and church can be reached pleasantly, with fine views of the house, along a short footpath past woodland, off to the right on the back road to Waltham St Lawrence.

River & Rowing Museum
Henley *Mill Meadows (01491 415600/www.rrm.co.uk). Open May-Aug 10am-5.30pm daily. Sept-Apr 10am-5pm daily. Admission £7; £5 reductions.*
This large purpose-built museum makes a thoroughly entertaining wet-weather option. The Schwarzenbach International Rowing Gallery displays Matthew Pinsent's triumphant coxless boat from the 2000 Sydney Olympics, as well as a variety of other Olympic memorabilia, with lots of interactive displays and stirring soundtracks. On the ground floor, there's a walk-through *Wind in the Willows* attraction for kids, complete with smells and accompanying audio storybook. The Henley Gallery is the local history section, home to informative displays on the development of the town and its regatta. The Thames Gallery explores the history of the river from source to mouth.

Stonor Park
Henley *Stonor (01491 638587/www.stonor.com). Open Apr-June, Sept 1-5pm Sun & bank hol Mon. July, Aug 1-5pm Wed, Sun & bank hol Mon. Admission £8; £4 reductions.*
Home to the Stonor family for the past 850 years, Stonor Park has a magical position beneath a wooded Chiltern escarpment, where deer roam and red kites were first re-introduced. Parts of the house date back to the 12th century, and there are objets d'art, drawings, fine furniture and antiques, though the highlight of a visit is likely to be the exhibition on the life and work of recusant Catholic martyr Edmund Campion, who took sanctuary here in 1581, or the medieval chapel in regular use throughout the years of Catholic repression.

Eat

A good lunchtime stop in Marlow is the **Two Brewers** (St Peter Street, 01628 484140, www.twobrewersmarlow.com), reached through Church Yard and down an alleyway. Many of the hotels listed in the Stay section also have restaurants open to non-residents, serving good-quality food.

Black Boys Inn
Hurley *Henley Road (01628 824212/www.blackboys inn.co.uk). Open noon-2pm, 7-9pm Mon-Fri; noon-2.30pm, 7-9.30pm Sat; noon-2.30pm Sun. ££££. Modern European.*
Bang on the main road between Hurley and Henley, but only a short walk from the river, the Black Boys Inn is a 16th-century building that has won a wide-reaching reputation for its organic and home-grown ingredients, served in a comfortable pub conversion complete with wood-burning stove. With strong local support – booking is essential – the kitchen produces the kind of proven classics that might once have been dubbed 'country fare'. The bedrooms are impeccably clean and pretty.

> "The Fat Duck is a huge success, attracting dizzying quantities of food-lovers, reviewers and column inches."

Caldesi in Campagna
Bray *Old Mill Lane (01628 788500/www.campagna. caldesi.com). Open noon-2.30pm, 6.30-10.30pm Tue-Sat; noon-2.30pm Sun. ££££. Italian.*
A refreshing, marginally lower-key but hardly less accomplished alternative to Bray's Michelin star performers, this excellent Italian was opened in October 2007 by Giancarlo Caldesi and his wife Katie, branching out from their Tuscan caffè and cookery school in Marylebone. The menu majors on recipes from Tuscany, Liguria and Sicily – pan-fried calf's liver with butter and sage and sautéed spinach, perhaps, or baked fillet of John Dory with Sicilian caponata and mint dressing – served in the setting of a well-proportioned Georgian-looking house, decorated in muted Tuscan tones. The owners are particularly proud of their wood-burning oven in the sunny garden.

Chequers Brasserie
Cookham Dean *Dean Lane (01628 481232/ www.chequersbrasserie.co.uk). Open noon-2.30pm, 6.30-9.30pm Mon-Thur; noon-2.30pm, 6.30-10pm Fri, Sat; noon-9.30pm Sun. £££. Modern European.*

Hand & Flowers.

White Hart Nettlebed.

Hugely popular with the locals, especially for its £10 two-course lunches, this long-established gastropub can be quite hard to find – it's at the bottom of Winter Hill – but it's worth the effort. It looks like a doll's house and does a hearty menu based on seasonal ingredients, with a French and Mediterranean accent. Lamb might come with a truffle and pumpkin purée, or salmon with a brown shrimp and asparagus risotto. As well as the busy main dining areas, efficiently catered with considerable good cheer, there are quieter corners, including a bright little conservatory.

Fat Duck

Bray *High Street (01628 580333/www.thefatduck. co.uk). Open noon-2pm, 7-9.30pm Tue-Sat; noon-2pm Sun. ££££. Modern European.*
Health scare hiccups of early 2009 aside, the Fat Duck is a huge media and foodie success, attracting dizzying quantities of food-lovers, restaurant reviewers and column inches, bolstered by chef patron Heston Blumenthal's gathering celebrity. Essentially, dining here is all about high drama and high prices (à la carte £98, tasting menu £130). Expect a strange but uncannily appealing world of wacky flavours and combinations – roast scallops with caviar and white chocolate velouté, salmon poached in liquorice gel, mango and Douglas fir purée – as well as the restaurant's signature snail porridge. It's all memorable stuff and favours the brave.

Five Horseshoes

Henley *Maidensgrove (01491 641282/www.thefive horseshoes.co.uk). Open noon-2.30pm, 6.30-9.30pm Mon-Fri; noon-3pm, 6.30-9.30pm Sat; noon-4pm Sun. £££. Gastropub.*
The perfect place to find before or after a refreshing stroll around Maidensgrove or Russell's Water Common, the Five Horseshoes is a rambling old country pub with tremendous views of the Chilterns from its back garden and conservatory. From the kitchen come various classics – burgers, shepherd's pie, bangers and mash, and fish and chips – as well as marginally more adventurous (and more expensive) recipes such as butternut risotto, haunch of venison or coq au vin. The important thing, though, is that they're all very competently accomplished, and served up in an atmosphere of convivial appreciation.

Hand & Flowers

Marlow *126 West Street (01628 482277/www.thehand andflowers.co.uk). Open noon-2.30pm, 7-9.30pm Mon-Sat; noon-3pm Sun. ££££. Modern European.*
An acclaimed pub conversion on the main road from Henley into Marlow, the Hand & Flowers was opened in 2005 by Tom and Beth Kerridge. With low beams, brick walls, heavy wooden tables and high-backed chairs, it now makes a snug setting for some serious food: starters might include a terrine of Old Spot pork and bacon with hot pickled pineapple or moules marinière with warm stout, followed by honey-roast black leg chicken with Savoy cabbage or a saddle of Thames Valley lamb with bacon, pearl barely and laverbread. The menu focuses on doing local and seasonal ingredients simply and well, and it certainly succeeds in distracting from some of the faintly

dubious artwork on the walls. Since 2008, the place has also offered a few rooms in a tiny terraced cottage next door: these have wooden floors, huge beds and various decidedly quirky features, like a free-standing round copper bath in one corner.

Hinds Head

Bray *High Street (01628 626151). Open noon-2.30pm, 6.30-9.30pm Mon-Sat; noon-4pm Sun. £££. Gastropub.*
Heston Blumenthal's gastropub is almost as busy, and as difficult to book, as his fine dining restaurant the Fat Duck round the corner. It's a large Tudor building on a prominent corner of the village, and the food is indeed well above the average: signature tea-smoked salmon with soda bread or powdered goose with fig chutney might be among the starters, along with seasonal specials and seven or so fish and meat dishes plus one veggie option. The triple-cooked chips to go with the three different cuts of Aberdeen steak are world-famous.

Vanilla Pod

Marlow *31 West Street (01628 898101/www.thevanilla pod.co.uk). Open noon-2pm, 7-10pm Tue-Sat. ££££. Modern European.*
Beyond the tiny street-front reception area, the dining room here is a softly lit and intimate affair, though regularly pretty lively, largely due to the wonders being wrought in the kitchen. The three lunchtime courses might include an appetiser of beetroot salad with bleu d'auvergne cheese, followed by pan-fried gilt-head seabream with quinoa and Madeira jus, finishing up perhaps with an apple tarte tatin and ice-cream. Things get even more ambitious in the evenings, with a seven-course gourmand menu featuring the likes of seared scallops with vanilla poached pear purée and red wine shallots, halibut fillet with salsify, hazelnut emulsion and red wine sauce, and a bitter chocolate fondant with a deliriously silky, elusively fragrant tonka bean parfait. Gorgeous food, incredible value.

Waldo's

Taplow *Cliveden (01628 668561/www.cliveden house.co.uk). Open 7-9.30pm Tue-Sat. ££££. Modern European.*
Recently reopened under Chris Horridge, formerly of the Bath Priory, Cliveden's fine-dining restaurant is a thoroughly intriguing adventure into the art of nutritional balance. The menu divides into two halves, entitled With and Without. The latter avoids all use of creams, sugars and flours in a brave bid to prove that that is not the only way that flavour lies: hence a succulent Anjou pigeon might come with cep-cinnamon sauce and watercress, or the scallops might be poached in coconut oil, with whipped shallot and capers. The With menu is more traditional; both are presented with consummate attention to detail. Inspired.

Waterside Inn

Bray *Ferry Road (01628 620691/www waterside inn.co.uk). Open Feb-May, Sept-Dec noon-2pm, 7-10pm Wed-Sat; noon-2.30pm, 7-10pm Sun. June-Aug 7-10pm Tue; noon-2pm, 7-10pm Wed-Sat; noon-2.30pm, 7-10pm Sun. ££££. French.*

Accept the sommelier's invitation of a champagne aperitif, because you'll need something sustaining while you absorb the Waterside Inn's setting, and to take in the six-page menu. This is no place to be in a hurry. It was closed for a complete refurbishment at the time of writing, though no doubt the atmosphere of imperturbable serenity will remain. Past experience suggests that consistency is the Waterside's strength, in the kitchen's superb – and justly renowned – re-creation of classic French recipes. The three-course menu gastronomique usually includes canapés, petits fours and water, and the restaurant, founded in the early 1970s and now run by Gilbert Roux's son Alain, is the only one in the UK to have held three Michelin stars since the mid '80s.

White Oak
Cookham *The Pound (01628 523043/www.thewhite oak.co.uk). Open noon-2.30pm, 6.30-9.30pm Mon-Fri; noon-3pm, 6.30-9.30pm Sat; noon-3.30pm Sun. £££. Gastropub.*
Opened in November 2008 by Terry Wogan's daughter, Katherine Cripps and her husband Henry, who also the run the Greene Oak gastropub in Oakley Green, between Bray and Windsor, the White Oak is the latest toast of Cookham town. Inside, it goes for a clean, vaguely Scandic but definitely rather rustic look, and the acoustics are not ideal, but the menu is likely to please most comers, ranging from Welsh Rarebit with poached duck egg or wild mushroom ravioli to braised pork belly with crackling or a twice cooked blade of beef. There are plenty of vegetarian options, and the wine list from Corney & Barrow strides confidently around the New World without forgetting the French.

Stay

It comes as little surprise that hotels in the area are generally quite expensive, but all those listed below can offer their guests something out of the ordinary. In addition, the Five Horseshoes' website, www.thefivehorseshoes.co.uk, has a good list of recommended and more affordable B&Bs in its local area. The **Hand & Flowers** (*see p35*) has several quirky rooms in a separate cottage for diners who don't want to drive home. The **Olde Bell** in Hurley (*see p30*) and the **Black Boys Inn** (*see p32*) also have good rooms.

Cliveden House
Taplow *Cliveden (01628 668561/www.cliveden house.co.uk). ££££.*
Cliveden has been entertaining guests for almost 350 years. Unique among luxury hotels, this National Trust property (*see p29*) continues a tradition of glamorous hospitality that reached its zenith under the Astor family for much of the 20th century. Sweep up the wide front drive past the massive marble sea shell of the Fountain of Love and it's still easy to appreciate the welcome the place afforded sundry politicos, pundits, aristos and writers down the years. The drama continues inside, in the Great Hall, adorned with 18th-century Brussels tapestries, suits of armour and a mighty 16th-century mantelpiece, and in the French Dining Room, panelled with gilt and eau-de-nil rococo 'boiseries' from Louis XV's mistress Madame de Pompadour's Château d'Asnières. These can be enjoyed by anyone on a passing visit for tea, but the bedrooms are equally sumptuous, especially those overlooking the parterre, which include Nancy Astor's with its own terrace, monumental fireplace and gigantic bed. Cliveden's glory days as a centre of political influence in the world may have passed, but it remains impeccably well-run and grand times are still rolling here for anyone lucky enough to be able to afford it.

Compleat Angler
Marlow *Marlow Bridge, Bisham Road (0844 879 9128/ www.macdonaldhotels.co.uk/compleatangler). ££££.*
Easily the best hotel in Marlow, and one of the best on the Thames, the Compleat Angler occupies a tremendous site on the south bank of the river between the old suspension bridge and the wide waterfall of the weir. It boasts 64 bedrooms, some with four-posters – no.8 was formerly the manager's office and is closest to the water – all done up in a restrained, traditional style, some with amusing touches of purple. The Aubergine restaurant, with its capacious comfy chairs and pretty etched windowpanes on the river, has garnered accolades for its menu gourmand (£65 for seven courses), which might feature the likes of tortellini of lobster, seared foie gras or saddle of Lune Valley lamb, as well as its three-course lunches. Bowaters restaurant also overlooks the water and has a more traditional menu.

> ## "Sweep up the wide front drive past the massive marble sea shell of the Fountain of Love and it's still easy to appreciate the welcome the place afforded."

Danesfield House
Marlow *Henley Road (01628 891010/www.danesfield house.co.uk). ££££.*
A great white fin-de-siècle folly of a place in an extraordinary position high up on a ridge above the river, Danesfield has in its time been used as a school, an RAF signals group HQ and the head office of Carnation Foods. It's been a country house hotel since 1991, with a modern spa and swimming pool added more recently. The terraced gardens, with their amazing views, magnolias, topiary bushes and rockeries, are a wonder in themselves, while inside the decor goes for a sumptuous pastiche of baronial splendour – tapestries on the wall of the bar, scrubbed panelling in the Oak Room restaurant, and a monumental fireplace in the great hall. The 84 bedrooms are perfectly

comfortable, though some without the benefit of those great views don't quite deliver on the promise of the public areas. Dining in the Oak Room is a theatrical treat, as befits the kitchen's accomplished delivery of a gourmand's menu featuring the likes of a lager and lime soup amuse bouche and venison with coffee polenta and prune jus.

French Horn
Sonning, 5 miles S of Henley *(0118 969 2204/ www.thefrenchhorn.co.uk). ££££.*
Another hotel that's really all about its location on the river, but in a very different style from the Compleat Angler, the French Horn has exquisitely polite, ultra-conservative public areas, complete with leather button-backed armchairs, old wallpaper and indeed, a variety of French horns. The rooms are not quite as special, generally, but the dining room overlooking the river, or the garden in summer, are splendid places to enjoy the broadly French a la carte menu (starters £7.50, mains £16.50), which in winter might include snails roasted in garlic butter or poached eggs Hollandaise to start, followed by whole roast pheasant or pan-fried fillet of dover sole with banana and mango chutney sauce.

Hotel du Vin & Bistro
Henley *New Street (01491 848400/www.hotel duvin.com). ££££.*
A particularly successful four-year-old conversion of Henley's Brakspear brewery, this du Vin has 43 stylish and comfortable rooms, all different. Yolumba, named after an Australian wine, features a thunderbox loo; Laroche is the old office of Mr Brakspear; and the Comtes de Champagne has stained-glass windows and a superb free-standing bath on its balcony, as do the other River Suites. The snug bar occupies the old brick-arched off-licence, complete with humidor and outside, for smokers, the hotel chain's signature Cigar Shack – affectionately dubbed the 'cigloo'.

Milsoms
Henley *20 Market Place (01491 845789/www.milsoms hotel.co.uk). £££.*
Milsoms is the hotel arm of the Loch Fyne seafood restaurant chain. This one is right above the restaurant, in a fine old townhouse, and has seven simple bedrooms – all with showers and one with a bath – all done up in various shades of beige and taupe and all perfectly clean and comfortable. Visitors are allowed to ask for individual rooms, so we recommend the one in the roof, with its exposed rafters and Market Place views; it's a bit bigger than some of the others.

Stag & Huntsman
Hambleden, 4 miles N of Henley *(01491 571227/ www.stagandhuntsman.co.uk). ££.*
Location is everything here: the three cosy double rooms available above the three bars of this rambling old pub in the middle of lovely Hambleden make a good base for walks up into the Chiltern hills. The rooms are nothing special, but the pub does reasonable food and is still very much part of the village community.

White Hart Nettlebed
Nettlebed, 4 miles N of Henley *(01491 641245/ www.whitehartnettlebed.com). £££.*
Bought four years ago by Robyn Jones's Charlton House, corporate caterers to HM Treasury and RIBA, among many others – the White Hart occupies an old coaching stop on the Henley–Wallingford road. It has six rooms in the main house, plus six in a quieter annexe round the back, and all beds have very nice cotton sheets. In the latter, Caramel is a superior double; Spearmint is in the attic under the eaves, painted pale blue, with a bath and proper shower. A standard double called Coco in the main house has exposed beams and some rather extraordinary furnishings, including an enormous furry bed.

Factfile

When to go
April to October are undoubtedly the most rewarding months in this part of the country, so all the interesting houses are open, the beech woods are in full leaf or turning golden brown, and the riverside towns are at their jolliest. Henley's Literary Festival (September, www.henleyliterary festival.co.uk) sees a further boost to numbers. Not surprisingly, though, these are also the region's busiest months, meaning that places at those gourmet tables are even harder to book and the roads considerably more jammed up.

Getting there
Cookham Rise, Marlow and Henley all have train stations, as befits their top commuterland status, and are quickly and easily reached from London. Both the M4 and the M40, the latter usually marginally less congested,

make beelines past the area, connected by the hectic A404, a kind of mini M25.

Getting Around
The Chilterns are really best explored on foot or bike, though a car is undeniably the most convenient way of getting around. The Thames Path follows the river bank through the region, which is also crossed by the Oxfordshire Way long-distance footpath, and north of Henley, the ancient track of the Ridgeway. Boats can be hired in Marlow's Higginson Park and also in Henley, but not in Cookham.

Tourist information
Henley Visitor Information Centre King's Arms Barn, Kings Road (01491 578034/www.visit henley-on-thames.co.uk). Open Summer 10.30am-4.15pm Mon-Sat. Winter 10am-3pm Mon-Sat.

Peak District.

Peak District

Rolling hills, wide green moors and acres of forest.

Under ever-changing Derbyshire skies, the jutting crags and river-cut valleys of the Peak District are as dramatic as the literature they have inspired. Jane Austen had Elizabeth Bennet coquetting her way through its sunlit estates, while Mr Darcy proved as solemn and brooding as its low, blackening clouds. The endless moors, hidden villages and characteristic gritstone houses made a suitably rural Gothic setting for Charlotte Brontë's *Jane Eyre*.

This was Britain's first national park, created in 1951 after decades of campaigning by ramblers. The hills in the south, as gentle as a ruffled duvet, contrast with the saw-tooth summits of the northern Peak District. Autumn and winter, when the low sun shines its golden light across the frosty farmland, are perhaps the most spectacular seasons to walk the deserted footpaths. Enticing country pubs, many originally coaching inns dating from the 16th and 17th centuries, offer welcome respite from the crisp chill, providing well-kept local ales to be supped by the fireside. During spring and summer, the Peak District bristles with festivals and events, celebrating anything from its wonderful food to its ancient heritage. Among the best-known of these are well dressings, where village wells are decorated with collages of flowers and locals follow a route between them. Today the ceremony is Christian, with hymn singing, but its roots are pagan.

Explore

This chapter concentrates on the Hope Valley region, from Castleton to Bakewell, as well as Chatsworth and the lesser-visited areas of the Derbyshire Dales, Buxton and Matlock.

HOPE VALLEY

The rivers Derwent, Noe and Peak Water carved their way through the local gritstone to form Hope Valley, which connects quaint and tourist-friendly Castleton with Hope, Bamford, Hathersage and Grindleford. Trains on the Hope Valley line still chug through the area too, on their route between Manchester and Sheffield.

At the north-west head of the valley is the mighty **Mam Tor** peak, standing at 1,696 feet. It is known as the Shivering Mountain because of the unstable shale layers around its base. The remains of the Sheffield to Chapel-en-le-Frith road can still be seen under the peak; after repeated landslides the authorities gave up rebuilding it. Mam Tor is a magnet for walkers and is worth the hard journey to its summit – the views are magnificent. To the north and west, the heather-cloaked moors of High Peak and Dark Peak stretch into the horizon, dotted with derelict farmhouses. Below is the village of **Edale**, best known as the beginning of the 270-mile Pennine Way, which runs all the way to the Scottish Borders. It's a common starting point for hiking and biking.

Looking to the south and east from Mam Tor, you'll see silver threads of water trickling through the Hope Valley, heading towards Bakewell. During the spring, red grouse, golden plover and occasionally short-eared owls and merlins can be spotted. The area is also home to the only population of mountain hares in England. No wonder Iron Age man chose the peak to build a fort, the mounds of which can still be seen. There are countless paths and bridleways sprawling in all directions from Mam Tor. Whether you want an all-day hike, an hour-long stroll or some of the best mountain biking in the country, you'll find it here. One particularly lovely three-hour hike climbs Mam Tor and twists over the moors to **Peveril Castle** (*see p43*) in the middle of Castleton.

At the foot of the Tor is one of the area's most famous caves: **Blue John Cavern** (01433 620642, www.bluejohn-cavern.com) – the only place in the world where Derbyshire Blue John stone can be found; tours of the cavern are available. Jewellery made from the blue-yellow fluorite can be found in the surrounding villages and in a shop at the cavern entrance.

Castleton is the principal tourist village in the Hope Valley. The superb visitors' centre (Buxton Road, 01629 816572, www.peakdistrict.gov.uk) can provide maps of the area, and its small museum, charting the history of this formerly remote mining village, is genuinely fascinating. A stone head dating back 1,000 years is on display, after being discovered in a garden wall.

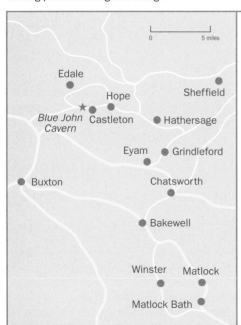

0   5 miles

Edale
Hope
Sheffield
Blue John Cavern
Castleton
Hathersage
Eyam
Grindleford
Buxton
Chatsworth
Bakewell
Winster
Matlock
Matlock Bath

Peak District

Historic sites
● ● ● ● ●

Art & architecture
● ● ● ● ●

Hotels
● ● ● ● ●

Eating & drinking
● ● ● ● ●

Scenery
● ● ● ● ●

Outdoor activities
● ● ● ● ●

Around Castleton.

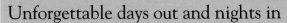

A riverside walk past old miners' cottages brings you to **Peak Cavern** (01433 620285, www.cavern.co.uk), otherwise know as the Devil's Arse because of the sounds akin to flatulence emanating from its depths (the name was changed to the polite version in time for a visit from Queen Victoria). The cave has a damp and imposing entrance. Just inside are remains of the homes of some of Britain's last troglodytes; people lived here until the early 20th century, making a living from rope-making. Tours of this part of the cave, along with its deeper chambers, are available, but even if you're claustrophobic, it's worth making the walk to the entrance.

Castleton is a pretty little place, full of warm pubs, outdoors shops and several B&Bs. Visitors descend on the area to begin hikes, and finish in one of the pubs. The best of these are **Ye Olde Cheshire Cheese Inn** (How Lane, 01433 620330, www.cheshirecheeseinn.co.uk), which has been serving local ales since 1577, and the **George Hotel** (Castle Street, 01433 620238, www.georgehotelcastleton.co.uk).

The largest village in Hope Valley is **Hathersage**, five and a half miles east of Castleton and less touristy. Popular with wealthy commuters to Sheffield or Manchester, it's a pretty place with gritstone houses and a high street containing a reasonable number of shops and some pubs. Hathersage is perhaps best known as the last resting place of Little John (of Robin Hood fame); his gravestone, added in 1935, can be seen in the graveyard of the 12th-century St Michael's Church. Charlotte Brontë is also thought to have stayed in the vicarage here and to have based the village of Morton in *Jane Eyre* on Hathersage. Above the village is a four-mile escarpment, the **Stanage Edge**, which attracts climbers of all levels. This is also the spot where, during her Derbyshire sojourn, Keira Knightley's Elizabeth Bennet brooded over Mr Darcy (Matthew Macfadyen) in the film adaptation of *Pride and Prejudice*.

Close to Hathersage, **Grindleford** (2.7 miles to the south) and **Bamford** (2.3 miles to the north-west) are also quaint villages worth a browse.

Towards the southern end of Hope Valley is the village of **Eyam**. In 1665 it went into voluntary quarantine after the bubonic plague arrived from London in a flea-infested parcel of cloth sent to the village tailor. The plague ravaged Eyam for 14 months, but thanks to the self-imposed isolation of the villagers the disease remained largely contained. Outsiders left food and supplies beside Mompesson's Well, and the money for payment was disinfected in the well's water. The well remains, as do the gravestones of the victims in the graveyard of St Lawrence's. The selfless villagers are remembered in a service on the last Sunday of August. Eyam Museum (Hawkhill Road, 01433 631371, www.eyam.org.uk) gives a comprehensive overview of the village's history.

Peveril Castle

Castleton *(01433 620613/www.english-heritage. org.uk). Open Apr, Sept, Oct 10am-5pm daily. May-Aug 10am-6pm daily. Nov-Mar 10am-4pm Mon, Thur-Sun. Admission £3.60; £1.90-£2.90 reductions.*

At the summit of an unscalably steep cliff, this castle was built after the Norman conquest by William Peverel, one of William I's most trusted knights, to increase French influence and control the hunting and the lead mining industry. Henry II sought shelter here during the 1173-74 rebellion instigated by his three sons and the French king. From the 13th century, Peveril Castle became a popular lodge for monarchs hunting in the Royal Forest of the Peak, but retained its role as a strategic fortress and a prison (legend has it that Robin Hood was once imprisoned here). Much conservation work has taken place on the square keep, built in 1176. There are lovely views from the castle, especially from the first-floor rooms.

BAKEWELL, CHATSWORTH & HADDON HALL

The delightful market town of **Bakewell** is the nearest hub for the impossibly grand Chatsworth, and older, but no less interesting, Haddon Hall. Take time to wander around the distinctive gritstone buildings of Bakewell and, of course, to try the famous pudding – call it a bakewell tart at your peril. This tea-time staple was reputedly invented at the White Horse Inn, now the grand Rutland Arms Hotel (01629 812812, www.rutlandarmsbakewell.co.uk), when a cook poured egg over the jam instead of mixing it in the pastry. Jane Austen reputedly stayed here while researching *Pride and Prejudice*; Lambton was based on Bakewell. Every bakery in town claims to have the original recipe, but we like the treats at the Old Original Bakewell Pudding Shop (The Square, 01629 812193, www.bakewellpuddingshop.co.uk).

There are several good pubs in Bakewell, but for lunch take the half-hour country walk to the Bull's Head (*see p46*) in the gorgeous village of **Ashford-in-the-Water**. The tourist information centre on the Square can provide maps and information for walks in the area, including the 12-mile Monsal Trail that follows part of the former Midland Railway line, passing several old mills.

Bakewell borders the 54-square-mile Chatsworth Estate, which extends over two counties and encloses several villages, hamlets and mills. The centrepiece is, of course, the 'Palace of the Peak', **Chatsworth**, the home of the Duke and Duchess of Devonshire. Within the estate you'll also discover marvellous walks to village pubs and tearooms. The 1,100-acre park around the house is open to the public and to the large herds of red and fallow deer. Although the park seems wild, most of it was landscaped by 'Capability' Brown in the 1760s. More modern additions include the 'Art in the Park' displays: a rolling series of sculpture curated by the forward-thinking duchess. Across the valley from the house is the hamlet of Edensor, with a church and tearoom. A pleasant walk south

Chatsworth House.

along the River Derwent is the village of **Beeley** (buildings with blue-painted trim belong to the estate) and the Devonshire Arms (see p46).

Game and fish hunted on the estate can be bought at the farm shop in **Pilsley**, on the B6048 towards Bakewell. The butchery, bakery, dairy, grocery and delicatessen specialise in local high-quality products, which you can taste in the reasonably priced farm-shop restaurant next door.

Buildings were first constructed around Chatsworth in 1552, but most of what can be seen is from a later, more opulent period. **Haddon Hall**, two miles south of Bakewell, is older and simpler.

Chatsworth House

3 miles NE of Bakewell *(01246 565300/ www.chatsworth.org). Open Mar-Nov 11am-5.30pm daily. Admission £16; £10-£12.50 reductions.*

In a majestic Derbyshire setting above the River Derwent, Chatsworth is perhaps Britain's finest stately home. Despite all the TV and film shots of the house, nothing quite prepares you for the approach down the drive, past herds of deer, to the building itself. Under the house's 1.3-acre roof are 297 rooms, 3,426 ft of passages, 18 staircases, 7,873 panes of glass and 56 lavatories. The indomitable Bess of Hardwick and her second husband Sir William Cavendish, one of Henry VIII's commissioners, built the first structure, Chatsworth Manor, in 1552. Her son was made Earl of Devonshire in 1618 and the house has remained in the family ever since. Between 1569 and 1584 Mary, Queen of Scots was imprisoned here by Elizabeth I. It was the fourth Earl in the late 17th century who expanded the house, including the additions of the State Apartments, East Front, Painted Hall, the Library and part of the incredible gardens (featuring a very difficult maze). Each successive duke has added something to produce what we see today. Only part of the house is open to the public but take time to explore the gardens and shops, then take high tea in the Cavendish Rooms.

Haddon Hall

2 miles SE of Bakewell *(01629 812855/www. haddonhall.co.uk). Open Apr, Oct noon-5pm Mon, Sat, Sun. May-Sept noon-5pm daily. Admission £8.75; £4.75-£7.75 reductions.*

Like Chatsworth, Haddon Hall has had its share of film and TV appearances, but tends to feature in dramas set in an earlier period. William Peverel, who also built Castleton's Peveril Castle (see p43), constructed the original hall in the 11th century, but it is in the Tudor age that Haddon firmly belongs; this is one of the most complete buildings dating from the era. The hall became the family home of the Earls of Rutland, and the current Duke of Rutland (the dukedom was created in the early 18th century) still resides here. Between 1703 and the 1920s the building gradually fell into a state of disrepair, until the ninth Duke and Duchess of Rutland restored the house and gardens. Original furniture survives, and the Tudor ambience has been retained. The 14th-century banqueting hall contains a minstrel's gallery; the frescoes in the chapel are also a highlight, as are the gardens (spectacular in summer). There's a gift shop and restaurant too. Events are held here throughout the year.

WHITE PEAK, BUXTON & MATLOCK BATH

Extending over the southern portion of the Peak District is the vast and sparsely populated limestone **White Peak**. Most tourists head directly for the Hope Valley access to High Peak, but the White Peak offers even more solitude and equally spectacular countryside. You could easily spend an entire day walking totally alone. White Peak also has probably the best mountain biking in the district – though few cyclists come here. Villages in the area, such as the lovely **Longnor**, **Youlgreave** and **Flash** (the highest village in England at 1,518 feet), can feel as isolated as they must have been centuries ago. All make great places to relax with a pint of creamy local ale after a bracing walk.

The area's most popular destination is **Arbor Low**, the finest stone age 'henge' north of Stonehenge. It is located near Parsley Hey on the A515 between Buxton and Ashbourne. The 50 limestone blocks form a circular bank, with monoliths at the two entrances. No one knows the exact purpose of the Neolithic henge monument, but it certainly points to there being human settlements in this area from 2500 BC.

At the top of White Peak is the largest town in the area, **Buxton**. For its relatively small size, Buxton has a remarkably vibrant cultural scene. The town is located in a little pocket out of the Peak District National Park, yet goes a long way towards confirming its self-proclaimed title of 'Capital of the Peaks'. As a spa town, Buxton has attracted tourists since Roman times, but most notably during the Georgian and Victorian periods. The fifth Duke of Devonshire, residing in Chatsworth, began to expand the town in the late 1700s with the now-famous Crescent – a striking example of Georgian architecture. By the time the railway arrived in 1863 Buxton was a vibrant place, and five years later the enormous Palace Hotel (see p49) was built. The Buxton Opera House (0845 127 2190, www.buxtonoperahouse.org.uk) today has a packed schedule, especially during its season that runs alongside the Buxton Festival in July. The building was restored to its former Edwardian glory in 2001. Equally impressive is what is known locally as 'the Dome'. Located next to the Palace Hotel, the former Devonshire Hospital is now a University of Derby campus, but is open for a wander around. The 23-acre Pavilion Gardens (01298 23114, www.paviliongardens. co.uk) is another landmark and makes for a lovely couple of hours' walking. Arts and crafts fairs or farmers' markets are held most weekends.

Like Buxton, **Matlock** and the adjoining **Matlock Bath** are just outside the Peak District borders, but remain an important destination. Although Matlock is a pleasant enough, it is Matlock Bath that dominates in terms of tourism – it's been a spa destination for 200 years. Sited at the bottom of a gorge carved out by the River

Derwent, it can feel enclosed and secluded; Lord Byron even compared it to Alpine Switzerland. Many visitors remark on its similarity to a seaside town, given the proximity of the River Derwent speeding past. At weekends, Matlock Bath is a popular canoeing destination. Its main tourist attraction, however, is the **Heights of Abraham** (01629 582365, www.heightsof abraham.com), a cable car that rises 450 feet above the Derwent, with fabulous views.

Hardwick Hall
Doe Lea, 2 miles E from junction 29 of M1 *(01246 850430/www.nationaltrust.org.uk/hardwick). Open Mar-Nov noon-4.30pm Wed-Sun. Dec 11am-3pm Sat, Sun. Admission £10; £5 reductions.*
Bess of Hardwick, who built this magnificent mansion, was an Elizabethan superstar. A ginger-haired beauty, she was born to a lower-end aristocrat, but through her four marriages she rose to become an influential figure. The Virgin Queen herself said of Bess, 'I can assure you there is no lady in the land I better love'. During her second marriage she persuaded her husband, Sir William Cavendish, Treasurer of the King's Chamber, to buy Chatsworth. When she was widowed for the third time, she became one of the wealthiest people in Britain. The hall was designed for Bess in the late 1500s, and was one of the first stately homes built without fortifications. Bess demanded lots of windows – the building's unique feature, which even led to a popular rhyme 'Hardwick Hall, more glass than wall' – and her true initials ES (Elizabeth, Countess of Shrewsbury) can be found all over the house, inside and out. She also accumulated an outstanding collection of tapestries and embroideries, many of which remain in the house. Opposite the building are the substantial ruins of Hardwick Old Hall, Bess's birthplace.

Eat

There's no shortage of great places to eat in the Peak District. Below we've listed a couple of the top gastropubs, but some of the best food can be had in hotels, particularly East Lodge (*see p49*). The food at the Maynard (*see p49*) and Callow Hall (*see below*) is also recommended.

Bull's Head
Ashford-in-the-Water, 3 miles NW of Bakewell, *Church Street (01629 812931). Open (restaurant) noon-2pm, 6.30-9pm Mon-Sat; noon-2pm, 7-9pm Sun. ££. Gastropub.*
A 1669 coaching inn on the Manchester to Derby route, the Bull's Head is one of the area's gastronomic highlights. Primarily, it's a lovely pub, with low beams, roaring log fires, authentic memorabilia on the walls, and two original bars. Family photos from three generations of the Shaw family overlook the bar. Today, Debbie and her chef husband Carl run proceedings but the place isn't wholly devoted to food: drinkers can enjoy fine ales from local brewers Robinson's. The high-quality menu changes seasonally. All meat comes from renowned butcher's Critchlows of Bakewell. Robust dishes include the likes of beef and Guinness sausages with celeriac mash and red wine gravy, and steak and Old Stockport (Robinson's ale) pie with braised cabbage and dripping-roasted potatoes – divine.

Devonshire Arms
Beeley, 5 miles N of Matlock, *Devonshire Square (01629 733259/www.devonshirebeeley.co.uk). Open (restaurant) noon-9.30pm Mon-Sat; noon-3pm Sun. £££. Gastropub.*
Built in 1747, this delightful pub on the Chatsworth estate – now a thoroughly modern gastropub – lies in the village of Beeley, a mile from the House. The Duchess of Devonshire's love of contemporary arts can be seen throughout the old pub, in the new glass-walled and colourful brasserie wing and in the well-appointed rooms. Purists will appreciate the well-kept beers from Peak Ales, including Chatsworth Gold, brewed using honey from the estate. The food is fabulous. Chef patron Alan Hill's starters might include a warm salad of Chatsworth Old Spot crispy belly pork with porter cheese, while main courses could be Chatsworth shoulder and neck of lamb, or estate pheasant. The Devonshire ploughman's is big enough to share. The wine list is of astonishing quality for a gastropub. The eight colourful cottage bedrooms are equipped with iPod speakers and DVD players.

Peacock at Rowsley
Rowsley, 3 miles S of Bakewell *(01629 733518/ www.thepeacockatrowsley.com). Open noon-2pm, 7-9pm Mon-Sat; noon-2pm, 7-8.30pm Sun. ££££. Modern European.*
The Peacock is as much a hotel as a restaurant – Keira Knightley, Scarlett Johansson and Kristin Scott Thomas have stayed in the sumptuous surroundings while filming in the area – but it is food that has made the place famous. Lord Edward Manners, owner of nearby Haddon Hall, recently refurbished the house (built in 1652) and appointed as head chef Daniel Smith, who learnt his trade with Tom Atkins. Modern European is the angle, and the seasonally changing dishes might include warm rabbit salad, or venison with pancetta, sweet potato and blackcurrant sauce. Prices are certainly A-list, but the Peacock remains one of the most renowned restaurants in the Peak District. There's also a small bar, private dining rooms and a large garden.

Stay

Callow Hall
Mappleton, 2 miles NW of Ashbourne *(01335 300900/www.callowhall.co.uk). ££££.*
On the southern border of the Peak District, this grand Victorian house, little changed since it was completed in 1852, dominates a 44-acre estate that comes complete with a bountiful trout stream. Inside, you'll find a homely atmosphere rather than the priggishness often associated with such establishments. Furnishings in the house and bedrooms favour the traditional over the modern. Enjoy a gin and tonic in the bar, overlooked by portraits of the mansion's

Top: Peacock at Rowsley.
Bottom: Bull's Head.

Peacock at Rowsley.

former residents, or relax in the lounge by the fire. The 16 bedrooms are comfortable and have views across the countryside. Superb local game (in season) is served in the restaurant, as well as plentiful fish dishes (highlights being the own-smoked salmon and herring). Everything is made on the premises, including the breakfast preserves. Nearby Ashbourne is a lovely old market town (its charter dates back to 1252; market days are Thursday and Saturday), with a fine choice of antiques shops, bistros and pubs. Callow Hall also makes a great base for exploring the White Peak.

East Lodge
Rowsley, 3 miles S of Bakewell *(01629 734474/ www.eastlodge.com). ££££.*
A couple of miles from Chatsworth, this 17th-century hunting lodge has been given a modern makeover, yet retains key historic ingredients. In the 12 bedrooms, comfy surroundings are boosted by flatscreen TVs (including one at the end of the bath) and iPod docks. A new disabled-access room has its own car parking space. The superior rooms contain four-poster beds, perfect for slumping in after dinner. Head chef Simon Bradley uses local seasonal ingredients to stunning effect, creating delights as Derbyshire black pudding baked in savoy cabbage, followed by belly pork with pan-fried terrine of trotters, sweetbreads and pig's ears. The less carnivorous may prefer the likes of roasted acorn squash and garlic chips, but no one should miss the crème brûlée take on bakewell pudding. Breakfasts are superb too. Awards have unsurprisingly been heaped on the family-owned East Lodge.

Maynard
Grindleford *Main Road (01433 630321/ www.themaynard.co.uk). £££.*
Since its refurbishment in 2008, the 100-year-old Maynard has been thoroughly modernised and become one of the finest hotels in the Peak District. Abstract art hangs in the bar, lounge area and restaurant, but it's the superb views over Hope Valley that attract most eyes. The rooms are large, with super king-size beds, huge plasma TV screens and free wireless internet. The attention to detail is superb, from the lovely bathroom fittings to the in-room amenities and quality of the linen. Some suites have free-standing baths and all have waterfall showers. The restaurant serves modern European cuisine, often using local ingredients. It isn't cheap, but the quality is high, and lunch is good value.

Palace Hotel Buxton
Buxton *Palace Road (01298 22001/www.barcelo-hotels.co.uk). £££.*
When the Palace first opened in 1868, Buxton was fast becoming an important tourist destination for Victorians. It was once the Peak District's finest hotel, and walking into the lobby of the 122-roomed premises is still an experience, though 'faded grandeur' might best describe the surroundings. Spanish Hotel chain Barceló took over a couple of years ago and has begun to improve the facilities – there's a modern gym, a spa and a swimming pool that's free to guests, and the bedrooms have new linen and bathrooms. Superb-value mid-week prices make it worth considering.

Factfile

When to go
Weather in the Peak District is notoriously variable at any time of year, but even during the bleaker moments, the snug country pubs provide a precious space to keep warm and meet the locals. When the sun shines the countryside is simply gorgeous. In late summer, the heather flowers on the moorland to stunning effect. Meteorological conditions can turn at any time, and the oft-repeated mantra for walkers and cyclists is 'never predict the weather'.

Getting there
The area lies between the major urban areas of Manchester, Sheffield, Chesterfield and Derby. The first two cities are the most convenient for High Peak and the Hope Valley. Derby and Chesterfield are better for accessing the White Peak.

The M1 is the best route from London. Trains regularly leave London to all the hub destinations. East Midlands Trains (www.eastmidlands trains.co.uk) connect London and Sheffield.

Getting around
A car is the best method for travelling across this area. However, public transport is certainly feasible if you're flexible. Trains connect destinations (www.northernrail.org), and all attractions mentioned in this chapter are served by regular buses, including Chatsworth and Haddon Hall. See www.visitpeakdistrict.com to download a timetable. Bakewell is the main hub for travel to most destinations.

Tourist information
The official tourist website, full of information, is www.visitpeakdistrict.com. There is also information on topics such as well dressing at www.derbyshireuk.net.
Bakewell Visitor Centre The Old Market Hall, Bridge Street (01629 813227). Open Summer 9.30am-5.30pm daily. Winter 10am-5pm daily.
Buxton Tourist Information Centre Pavilion Gardens, St John's Road (01298 25106). Open 9am-5pm daily.
Castleton Visitor Centre Buxton Road (01629 816572). Open Apr-Oct 9.30am-5.30pm daily; Nov-Mar 10am-5pm daily.
Matlock Tourist Information Centre Crown Square, Matlock (01629 583388). Open Mar-Oct 10am-5pm daily. Nov-Feb 10.30am-4pm daily.

Top: Victoria Bridge;
bottom: Wenlock Edge.

Shropshire Hills

Isolated English hills on the Welsh Marches.

'That is the land of lost content', wrote A E Housman in the 19th century. It seems that even then there was something about the Shropshire Hills, and the towns, villages and hamlets in their folds and valleys, that lent an air of an Edenic, prelapsarian England. Today, certainly, visitors to Shropshire come searching for a glimpse of a lost golden age. Standing on Wenlock Edge, wind in your hair and rustling through the trees, it's easy to feel a deep sense of history, or even prehistory. For this is an old land, its age conveyed in the rolling syllables of its semi-mythical place names. As you walk the ridge of the Long Mynd, seeing the devil take his chair on the Stiperstones as clouds descend, while sunlight ripples over Caer Caradoc and the Wrekin, it's impossible not to feel the deep pull of the past.

But this patchwork of field and wood, hill and stream is somehow timeless and definitive too, encapsulating a sense of England that trends and dogmas, even history and religion, cannot. Nothing expresses this otherness better than the silence and stillness that settles 'in valleys of springs and rivers'. The quietness can seem ironic when you remember that this is border country, its many ruined castles giving testament to the raiders, marauders and armies that passed back and forth across the Marches of England and Wales for centuries. But wars end: the noise and the gore have long gone; the land remains the same.

Explore

The Shropshire Hills cover a relatively small area and it's possible to use any of the district's towns and villages as a base, although Church Stretton is the most central. For Ludlow, *see p320.*

WROXETER AND THE WREKIN

The Wrekin (1,335 feet) is the first of the Shropshire Hills you'll see when driving into the county along the M54, and from the Telford side it doesn't look that impressive: a tree-covered hump with a radio mast stuck on its summit. But swing around to its south side and you'll see the Wrekin rising proud of the plains. Most people climb to the summit from the east, but the walk to the top from the west is better, as the Shropshire landscape unfolds with the climb. From the Wrekin the more distant hills – Clee, Long Mynd, Caer Caradoc – expand in a great panorama, separated from you by the flat, fat pastures bordering the River Severn.

A couple of miles west of the Wrekin, on the bank of the Severn, is **Wroxeter** (also called Viroconium), the fourth city of Roman Britain.

Wroxeter Roman City

Wroxeter *(01743 761330/www.english-heritage. org.uk). Open Mar-Oct 10am-5pm daily (last admission 4pm). Nov-Feb 10am-4pm Wed-Sun (last admission 3pm). Admission £4.10; £2.10-£3.30 reductions.*

The excavated remains of the public baths, and the reconstructions of the complete city in the informative museum, give a vivid impression of life in Roman Britain. Among the most impressive sights is the 'Old Work', one of the largest sections of free-standing Roman wall left in the country and a testament to classical civil engineering. Not so apparent, but ultimately more breathtaking, is the realisation that those rows of circles on the ground mark out the pillars of the bath's basilica. Look back and forth along the length of the rows and you'll realise just how big the building was. The city remained inhabited when the Romans left, but was eventually abandoned.

MUCH WENLOCK & WENLOCK EDGE

Wenlock Edge is a solidified ripple of limestone some 15 miles long. Woods that the Roman soldiers of Viroconium would have recognised still cloak the ridge's leading edge as it plunges down into the vale of the River Severn below. This is rich fossil-hunting territory, for the limestone formed some 425 million years ago when Shropshire lay beneath the waters of a shallow, tropical sea. Thus any walk along the Edge should be made with an eye on the rocks, for even an amateur can spot fossilised brachiopods, which look like a modern cockle, and maybe a trilobite or crinoid. Keeping that eye on the ground can be a problem, however, as the views over Corve Dale to Long Mynd are beautiful. Much of Wenlock Edge is owned by the National Trust, and the Jack Mytton and Shropshire ways both follow it for much of its length.

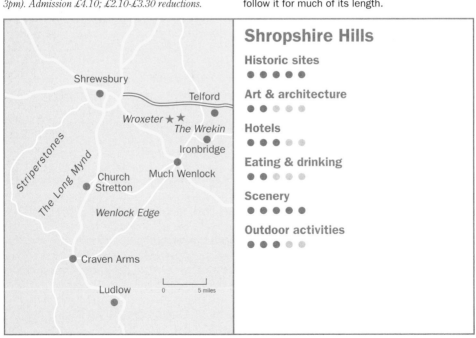

Shropshire Hills

Historic sites
● ● ● ● ●

Art & architecture
● ● ◉ ◉ ◉

Hotels
● ● ● ◉ ◉

Eating & drinking
● ● ◉ ◉ ◉

Scenery
● ● ● ● ●

Outdoor activities
● ● ● ◉ ◉

Map labels: Shrewsbury • Telford • Wroxeter ★ ★ • The Wrekin • Ironbridge • Stiperstones • The Long Mynd • Church Stretton • Much Wenlock • Wenlock Edge • Craven Arms • Ludlow • 0 5 miles

Wenlock Edge.

Wenlock Edge;
Shropshire Hills.

Nestled on the lee side of the Edge, **Much Wenlock** is about as pretty a town as you could wish for. Foremost among its buildings is the Guildhall (Wilmore Street, 01952 727509, www.muchwenlockguide.info), the lower section of which is still used as a market, although most of the shops, houses and businesses are charming. The Copper Kettle Tearooms & Restaurant (61 High Street, 01952 728419) serves delicious cakes, and the town has a couple of bookshops, a butcher and a good delicatessen. Colourful Ippikin (59 The High Street, 01952 728371, www.ippikin.co.uk) is stuffed with vivid balls of wool and bottles full of bright buttons. The owner, Lesley Butler, employs local spinners to spin the wool of rare breeds of sheep and then colours the wool with natural dyes, making textiles that are much in demand.

To the south-east is the Severn Valley preservation steam railway, much beloved of enthusiasts, and the spectacular **Victoria Bridge** that spans the river itself.

Wenlock Priory

Much Wenlock *Bullring (01952 727466/www. english-heritage.org.uk). Open Mar, Apr, Sept, Oct 10am-5pm Wed-Sun. May-Aug 10am-5pm daily. Nov-Feb 10am-4pm Thur-Sun. Admission £3.40; £1.80-£2.70 reductions.*
Once a grand Cluniac establishment, Wenlock Priory went the way of many others following the Dissolution, but much remains, particularly of the north and south transept, and nave. It was a huge church in its day, some 350 feet long, and the well-tended grounds, with a collection of lovingly clipped topiary, are a gorgeous place to spend an hour on a sunny summer's afternoon.

IRONBRIDGE

The ten museums that put the World Heritage Site of **Ironbridge** into context as the birthplace of the Industrial Revolution are a refuge if the weather turns, but they, and the town, are too good to relegate to a rainy-day outing. The museums' website says it takes two days to see them all, and it's not exaggerating.

At the **Museum of the Gorge**, films explain the importance of the site, and a giant scale model shows what the area was like in 1796. From here, it's a long but picturesque walk uphill to **Coalbrookdale** (at weekends from Easter to October there are shuttle buses connecting the widely spaced museums, which are free to Museum Passport holders) for the Museum of Iron, Enginuity and the Darby houses. The **Museum of Iron** does exactly what it says on the cast-iron plaque, telling the story of the early iron industry through its Victorian heyday to the Aga cookers of today (still made in Ironbridge at the factory you pass on the way up to the museums). **Enginuity** is a marvellous, hands-on celebration of engineering, with enough wheels, knobs and pulleys to entertain even the most blasé child. The series of dams, complete with floodgates that you open and close to regulate water flow, generate power and prevent buildings flooding, is a particular favourite. Aprons are available to stop over-enthusiastic hydraulic engineers getting waterlogged. A little further up the hill are **Rosehill** and **Dale** houses, where the Darbys lived. These offer a fascinating insight into the life of a pioneering Quaker family.

Heading back to the river, and downstream (you'll need to cross the river via either the Iron Bridge itself or Jackfield Bridge), you'll reach the **Jackfield Tile Museum** set in a Victorian industrial complex, while the adjacent Fusion is home to contemporary tile designers. Back over the Severn via the Jackfield Footbridge, it's time to go underground. The **Tar Tunnel**, 100 yards long, still has bitumen oozing from its brick-lined walls, more than 200 years after miners first discovered a spring of natural bitumen. It's quite an eerie experience. In vibrant contrast, the nearby **Coalport China Museum** is home to displays of wonderfully colourful china.

The final two museums are a fair distance apart. The **Broseley Pipeworks** once made millions of clay pipes, but it was abandoned in the 1950s and left virtually untouched. Now restored, it's a time capsule of our industrial past. But if you really want to travel back in time, head to **Blists Hill Victorian Town**. This 52-acre site is home to a re-creation of a 19th-century town, with shopkeepers, craftsmen, workers and home-owners – all in period costume, at work throughout. It's an extraordinary experience; on arrival, you can exchange your money at the bank for its Victorian equivalent – a collection of farthings, ha'pennies, pennies and thrupennies before heading for the shops. As you head down the street, you'll pass a sweet shop, a butcher's, a baker's, a candlestick maker's (the smell of tallow is rather overpowering), plus a pub, a plaster-maker, a tinsmith and a printing shop. John Edmunds, the bearded printer, is a fount of information concerning the various phrases that have entered the language from compositors.

Ironbridge Gorge Museums

Ironbridge *(01952 884391/www.ironbridge.org.uk). Open 10am-5pm daily (some museums have restricted hours in winter). Admission £19.95; £12.95-£15.95 reductions; admission to single sites varies.*
If you think ten museums seem excessive for such a small town, think again. In 1709, Abraham Darby smelted iron with coke at Coalbrookdale and began the Industrial Revolution. Nothing's been the same since. The tercentenary of iron production will be marked in 2009 by events through the year. You could easily spend a couple of days working your way through the various museums and exhibits, but perhaps the best way to start is with a walk along the banks of the River Severn to the Iron Bridge itself. The elegance

of this structure serves as a mute rejoinder to the ugly utilitarianism of so much modern civil engineering. There's a display on the bridge's history in the adjoining Tollhouse.

CRAVEN ARMS

Shropshire is full of delightful towns, but Craven Arms isn't one of them. It is, however, the home of the Shropshire Hills Discovery Centre and just up the road from Stokesay Castle and a whole lot of chickens at the Wernlas Poultry Collection.

Shropshire Hills Discovery Centre

Craven Arms *Ludlow Road (0845 678 9024/www. shropshirehillsdiscoverycentre.co.uk). Open Summer 10am-5.30pm daily. Winter 10am-4.30pm daily. £4.50; £3-£4 reductions.*
The exhibition takes you through the history of the hills. Highlights include the Iron Age house, dressing up in Celtic clothes, and a film of the Shropshire countryside, taken from a hot-air balloon. Inside, there's a café, gallery and shop, and outside some lovely walks down to the River Onny.

Stokesay Castle

Craven Arms *(01588 672544/www.english-heritage. org.uk). Open Apr-Sept 10am-5pm daily. Mar, Oct 10am-5pm Wed-Sun. Nov-Feb 10am-4pm Thur-Sun. Admission £4.90; £2.40-£3.90 reductions.*
If there's one historic property you visit in south Shropshire, make it Stokesay Castle. This medieval moated manor house has been scarcely altered, and almost all of it survives, including the spectacular cruck-built timber roof of the great hall. The only major addition is the Jacobean gatehouse, but that serves if anything to enhance the beauty of the place. Standing atop the north tower, on one side you can see (but not hear) the traffic on the A49, on the other the railway line to Ludlow – which often carries steam trains in summer – but you could be in a different world. If you've time, take the audio tour; it really helps bring the building, and those who cared for it, back to life.

Wernlas Poultry Collection

Green Lane, Nr Onibury, 2 miles S of Craven Arms *(01584 856318/www.wernlas.com). Open Mid July-mid Sept 10.30am-5.30pm daily. Mid Sept-mid July 10.30am-5.30pm Tue-Sun. Admission £3; £1.50-£2.65 reductions.*
For chickens, head this way. There are 70 breeds, over 700 busily crowing and laying residents, and some 15,000 eggs hatched each year. The birds are kept in coops arranged in rows over the flank of a Shropshire vale, with expansive views. Invest in a couple of cups of chicken feed (10p each) and you can feed the birds and get your feet muddy. We confess a fondness for the Transylvanian naked neck, a sort of vampire chicken, which is clothed in jet-black feathers, apart from its bare, and blood-red, head and neck. You can even take a (live) chicken home with you to start a coop.

THE STIPERSTONES

The ridge of the **Stiperstones** cuts across the landscape, the jagged tors that mark its spine looking like broken teeth. In fact, they were formed during the last Ice Age, when the ridge stood above the glaciers and the extreme temperatures shattered the quartzite into the scree outcrops we see today. The area is now a National Nature Reserve, and the five-mile Stiperstones Stomp along the ridge provides some of the best walking in Shropshire, taking you to the second-highest point in the county atop **Manstone Rock** (1,759 feet). However, the best-known and most dramatic of the tors is **Devil's Chair**. Local legend has it that when the clouds descend and cover the rocks, the devil himself is sitting upon his throne. It's hard to believe now, when the only sound you're likely to hear is the wind, and the only movement is a raven's wing as it takes to the air, but this area was once raucous with the sounds of industry. Mines honeycombed the countryside, and in the 1870s one tenth of the nation's lead came from here. Abandoned mine workings litter the district, and escapees like laburnums and lilacs from the miners' smallholdings make incongruously colourful splashes in the hedgerows.

Taking the road from the **Bog Visitor Centre** to Bridges, you'll come across a car park after the road crests the ridge, and a broad and relatively easy path up to the high ridge. This is the start of the Stiperstones Stomp and even if you don't have time to complete the whole trail (there's a shuttle bus back from its termination in Habberley at weekends in summer, see www.shropshirehillsshuttles.co.uk, or phone 01743 251000 for details), it's worth setting off uphill to the tors visible from the car park. The first outcrop is Cranberry Rock, the more distant Manstone Rock, with the Devil's Chair beyond.

Bog Visitor Centre

Stiperstones *(01743 792484/www.bogcentre.co.uk). Open Early Apr-Oct 10am-5pm Wed-Sun. Admission free.*
Once the school for the neighbouring mining community, the Bog is now run by local volunteers. Fans of Malcolm Saville's *Lone Pine* adventures (set on the Stiperstones and Long Mynd) should look for details of the locations in the books, including the house called Witchend. The kitchen supplies home-made cakes and there's a selection of local crafts and produce for sale.

LONG MYND AND CHURCH STRETTON

'Westward on the high-hilled plains, Where for me the world began,' AE Housman wrote in 'A Shropshire Lad'. The world itself might echo his words, as it had scarce begun when the sedimentary rock of the 'long mountain' was formed. The only fossils to be found in the **Long Mynd** are those of raindrops falling on a shore that no living thing had seen, some 575 million years ago. These rocks were folded vertically and thrust upwards to make the rolling ridge of plains that constitute the Long Mynd. Its eastern side is threaded with deep valleys, of which the best

Stokesay Castle.

known is **Carding Mill**, beloved of day-trippers. But an escape from the tea and cake crowd can easily be made; take to the high ground and walk the Port Way, now part of the Shropshire Way but in its origin a Bronze Age track that ran along the ridge of the Mynd, skirting its highest point at **Pole Bank** (1,693 feet).

On the eastern flank of the Long Mynd is **Church Stretton**, the only town within the Shropshire Hills Area of Outstanding Natural Beauty and thus a centre for walking. The Outdoor Depot (Sandford Avenue, 01694 724293, www.theoutdoordepot.co.uk) has walking gear, leaflets and maps, and knowledgeable staff. To the north-east of the town, and defining the other side of the valley in which the town lies, is lonely **Caer Caradoc**, which was possibly the site of Caractacus's last stand against the Roman invaders. At its summit is an Iron Age hill fort that once covered some six acres behind steeply banked ditches and banks. Standing in a lonely but pivotal position amid the Shropshire Hills, Caer Caradoc has one of the best views in the whole county.

Acton Scott Historic Working Farm
Acton Scott, 2.5 miles S of Church Stretton *off B4371 (01694 781306/www.go2.co.uk/for/acton scott.html). Open Apr-Oct 10am-5pm Tue-Sun. Closed Nov-Mar. Admission £3.50; £1.50-£3 reductions.*
Familiar to viewers of BBC2's *The Victorian Farm*, Acton Scott (signposted from the A49) is a re-creation of a late-Victorian upland farm. It has helped preserve many of the skills and crafts of pre-intensive agriculture, when heavy horses ploughed the fields, scythes cut the corn, and seed was sown by hand. The farm is also home to many rare breeds, including Tamworth pigs, Longhorn and Shorthorn cattle, and Shropshire sheep.

Eat

Outside Ludlow there's a handful of pubs serving food that's a cut above the norm. Among them are the Crown Country Inn (Munslow, near Craven Arms, 01584 841205, www.crowncountry inn.co.uk) and the more modern Roebuck Inn (Brimfield, nr Ludlow, 01584 711230, www.theroebuckludlow.co.uk).

Consider a detour to the delightful town of Bishop's Castle, which boasts not one but two pubs with breweries: the Three Tuns (Salop Street, Bishop's Castle, 01588 638797, www.thethree tunsinn.co.uk) and the Six Bells (Church Street, Bishop's Castle, 01588 630144).

Bell Inn at Yarpole
Yarpole, 7 miles SW of Ludlow *Green Lane (01568 780359/www.thebellinnyarpole.co.uk). Open (restaurant) noon-2.30pm, 6.30-9.30pm Tue-Sun. £££. Gastropub.*

Mark Jones's menu applies a number of appealing twists – some of them quite substantial – to traditional English cuisine, ending up with a menu that's two-thirds gastropub and one-third French restaurant. Starters include the likes of twice-baked cheddar soufflé with tarragon mousseline; among the mains, the pork belly is decent, but the steak and ale pie is a real knockout. There's also a list of more straightforward food on the blackboards: soups, baguettes, even a ploughman's lunch. Local ales make a splendid accompaniment.

Crown at Hopton
Hopton Wafers, 10 miles E of Ludlow *Cleobury Mortimer (01299 270372/www.crownathopton.co.uk). Open (restaurants) noon-2.30pm, 6.30-9.30pm daily. ££. Pub.*
An ivy-covered, 16th-century coaching inn, the Crown is a real sight for travellers' sore eyes. On sunny days, visitors can enjoy its marvellous setting in the heart of Shropshire's rolling countryside. At night, the glowing, firelit windows are a truly cheerful prospect. There are 18 agreeable bedrooms (seven in the homely original building, 11 in the new 'coach house' extension), but the Crown is perhaps best approached as a countryside inn, notable for its superior pub grub alongside its ranges of ales, wines and whiskies. It is child friendly and pet friendly.

Rocke Cottage Tea Rooms
Clungunford, 2.5 miles SW of Craven Arms *(01588 660631/www.rockecottagetearoom.co.uk). Open 10am-5pm Wed-Sun. £. Café.*
This quaint tea room is housed in a half-timbered building, with old advertising on the walls and proper tablecloths and lace doilies. If you're worried this sounds too twee for its own good, one taste of the scones or cakes will put your mind – and stomach – at rest; they are fantastic and all made on the premises. There's a lovely cottage garden (with tree house) where you can take tea on a summer's day, and a wood-burning stove within to keep things cosy in winter. The adjacent cottage is available for self-catering accommodation.

Waterdine
Llanfair Waterdine, 5 miles SE of Craven Arms *nr Knighton (01547 28214/www.waterdine.com). Open noon-4pm (last food orders by 1pm), 7-11.30pm (last food orders by 9pm) Tue-Sat. £££. Modern European.*
In the mid 1990s, chef Ken Adams garnered an excellent reputation at the Oaks restaurant in Ludlow. After selling up, Adams and wife Isabel moved out to this old pub, constructed in the 16th century as a drovers' inn, and set about converting it into a restaurant with rooms. The three cosy bedrooms are pleasant and countrified, but the cooking is the real draw. The menu changes daily, with many of the vegetables grown by Isabel in the grounds of the pub. On a recent visit, we enjoyed melt-in-the-mouth veal sweetbreads with a gentle apple and hazelnut sauce; perfectly pitched venison accompanied by celeriac remoulade; a hearty yet not overwhelming rack of lamb; and a treacle and walnut tart with freshly made kumquat ice-cream.

Ward Farm.

Jinlye Guest House.

Stay

In addition to accommodation below, take a look at the Ludlow chapter (*see p320*), the **Crown** at Hopton (*see p58*) and **Waterdine** (*see p58*).

Birches Mill
Nr Clun, 5 miles NW of Craven Arms *(01588 640409/www.birchesmill.co.uk). ££.*
Boasting a secluded, postcard-perfect setting in a lush valley, this stone mill house (closed Nov-Feb) is one of the area's most appealing accommodation options. The oldest parts of the house date from 1640, but beautiful old furniture is complemented by tasteful hints of modernity. Birches Mill is popular with walkers, as the Shropshire Way and Offa's Dyke paths are nearby. Be sure to pick up a jar or two of the moreish, own-made jams and chutneys before you leave.

Bridges Long Mynd Youth Hostel
Nr Ratlinghope, 2.5 miles NW of Church Stratton *(01588 650656/www.yha.org.uk). £. No credit cards.*
This former village school became a youth hostel in 1931. Present owners Mick and Gill Boulton bought it in 1990 and have devoted themselves to its running ever since. A full catering service is available, including packed lunches and evening meals. The Shropshire Way passes the hostel's front door, there's a large garden, and Mick bought the stream some years ago. With 37 beds, including two family rooms. Watch out for the Natterer's bats that live in the attic.

Jinlye Guest House
Castle Hill, All Stretton, 1 mile N of Church Stretton *(01694 723243/www.jinlye.co.uk). ££.*
Enticing in summer and dramatic in winter, the Jinlye's location could scarcely be bettered, offering amazing views and terrific walking opportunities. The stone guest house, built as a crofter's cottage in the 18th century, does a fine job at living up to its location. All six rooms are individually decorated, with handsome antique furniture: The Wild Moor room has a 17th-century bed complete with intricately carved headboard.

Raven Hotel
Much Wenlock *Barrow Street (01952 727251/ www.ravenhotel.com). £££.*
The oldest parts of the Raven date from the 15th century, the newer bits were a 17th-century coaching inn, so there's no lack of character to the place. A glass-covered hole in the floor of the new conservatory is a well that was revealed during the building work. Most of the rooms look over a shared courtyard, while the newly completed Forge annexe has six guest rooms that manage to pull off the trick of being modern yet characterful.

Ward Farm Bed & Breakfast
Nr Westhope, 3 miles NE of Craven Arms *(01584 861601/www.wardfarm.co.uk). ££.*
Set among beautifully peaceful countryside is 120 acres devoted to organically rearing beef, sheep, pigs, chicken and goats. The Batemans, who also run the B&B, will show guests around and let you pat the friendlier Herefords (cattle) and admire the handsome Gloucester Old Spot and Berkshire pigs. The three guestrooms are light, airy and spotless, the atmosphere friendly, and the milk is free. It's a delightful place to stay. There's also a small campsite.

Wilderhope Manor
Nr Longville in the Dale, 10 miles SW of Much Wenlock *(0845 371 9149/www.yha.org.uk). £. No credit cards.*
This unspoilt Elizabethan manor house (built in 1585) is a youth hostel as well as a National Trust property. Set in grounds below Wenlock Edge, the building is largely unaltered and features a wonderful oak spiral staircase, a grand dining room and original garderobes (no longer in use). There are five family rooms and four dormitories, plus a bar serving local beers and wines. An unforgettable place to stay.

Factfile

When to go
Some attractions close during the winter, but the hills are wild and empty then. Of course, in Britain it's a mistake to rely on the weather at any time of the year, particularly up on the hills.

Getting there & around
A train service, run by Arriva Trains Wales, stops at Church Stretton, Craven Arms and Ludlow. The Shropshire Hills shuttle bus runs at weekends in summer (01743 251000, www.shropshirehillsshuttles.co.uk), connecting Craven Arms, Clun and Bishop's Castle to the Stiperstones, the Long Mynd and Church Stretton. The Shropshire Hills is wonderful cycling country: try Wheely Wonderful Cycling (Petchfield Farm, Elton, Ludlow, 01568 770755, www.wheely wonderfulcycling.co.uk) for bike hire or cycling holidays. Alternatively, explore on horseback (www.shropshireriding.co.uk).

Tourist information
Church Stretton County Branch Library, Church Street (01694 723133). Open Summer 9.30am-5pm Mon-Sat. Winter 9.30am-12.30pm, 1.30-5pm Mon-Sat.
Ironbridge The Iron Bridge (01952 884391). Open 9am-5pm Mon-Fri; 10am-5pm Sat, Sun.
Much Wenlock The Museum, High Street (01952 727679). Open Summer 10.30am-5pm daily. Winter 10.30am-1pm, 1.30-4pm Tue, Fri; 10am-noon Sat.

Top: Cotswolds countryside; others: Minster Lovell.

South Cotswolds

Upmarket indulgences and picture-postcard villages.

It may be archetypal English countryside, but the Cotswolds isn't just any English countryside. Just a couple of hours' journey from London, the area has long been synonymous with wealth, sophistication and celebrity – as well as bucolic landscapes and quaint cottages. The good news is that while stars and second-homers may have ushered in a slice of metropolitan living, they haven't killed off the Cotswolds' distinct brand of rural charm.

The Cotswolds sit between four historic towns – Bath, Stratford on Avon, Oxford and Cheltenham – and it is in the southern tract that you'll find the prettiest and most tranquil spots: an imagined England of empty and rolling landscapes that beg to be walked on (there are over 3,000 miles of public footpaths), villages made from the local honey-coloured stone, winding leafy lanes, medieval churches and imposing stately homes. It was the wool trade that enabled many of them to be built. Cotswold wool first gained its reputation for superior quality in Roman times, and the trade reached its peak in the Middle Ages, sowing the seed for the region's long-term prosperity.

While it costs nothing to wander over hill and dale by foot or bike, if your pockets are deep, you'll find plenty of pleasant ways to empty them. Nearly every village seems to have its own great pub serving well-kept real ale and posh food. Many also boast traditional tearooms, gift and antique shops, restaurants and places to stay, from chintzy B&Bs to designer hotels. The Cotswolds have also garnered a gastronomic reputation; there's keen interest in locally produced, traditional and organic food here. Small producers have seen demand soar: orchard apple juice, locally smoked trout, organic vegetables and meat, and rural cheeses fill the farmers' markets and delis, and feature on restaurant menus.

Explore

WOODSTOCK & AROUND

The historic market town of Woodstock lies eight miles north of Oxford, and is best known for two trades – glove-making and decorative steel work. You can find out more about the area's heritage at the wide-ranging **Oxfordshire Museum** (Park Street, 01993 811456, www.oxfordshire.gov.uk), but you won't see many signs of artisan life in the streets, which are filled with cars bringing custom to the classy pubs and restaurants. Woodstock makes an excellent base for visiting the twin monuments to extravagance, **Blenheim Palace** (*see below*) and **Bicester Village**. The former is the country seat of the Duke of Marlborough and birthplace of Sir Winston Churchill; the luxury and splendour of Sir John Vanbrugh's design is breathtaking, and its sheer size will stop first-time visitors in their tracks. The same could be said of Bicester Village (50 Pingle Drive, 01869 323200, www.bicester-village.co.uk), a massive outdoor shopping mall that sells name brands at large discounts. The crowds are daunting; visit early.

Garden lovers should make a detour north of Woodstock to **Rousham House** (01869 347110, www.rousham.org), near Steeple Aston. The imposing – if rather gloomy – Jacobean mansion was remodelled in Tudor Gothic style by architect and landscape gardener William Kent, a predecessor of 'Capability' Brown, in the 18th century. But the real highlight here is his outstanding garden, inspired by Italian landscape painting. Rousham itself is determinedly and delightfully uncommercialised, with no shop or tearoom; you're encouraged to bring a picnic and wander the grounds.

Blenheim Palace

Woodstock *(0870 060 2080, www.blenheim palace.com). Open Palace & Gardens 10.30am-5.30pm daily (last admission 4.45pm). Park 9am-4.45pm daily. Admission Palace & Gardens £14.40 (winter), £17.50 (summer); £7.80-£14 reductions. Park £7.70 (winter), £10 (summer); £2.70-£7.50 reductions.*

Designed by Sir John Vanbrugh with the assistance of Nicholas Hawksmoor and set in 2,100 acres of grounds landscaped by 'Capability' Brown, Blenheim is the only non-royal residence in the country that is grand enough to be given the title 'palace'. Outside and in, it's awe-inspiring. It's worth enduring weekend crowds to see the remarkable long library, gilded state rooms and distinguished paintings and tapestry. A permanent exhibition is dedicated to Winston Churchill, who was born here. Another, Blenheim Palace: the Untold Story, uses innovative technology to bring the past of the palace to life, as seen through the eyes of servants.

MINSTER LOVELL & AROUND

As you head west from Woodstock to Burford, stop for a stroll around the village of Minster Lovell. Quiet and remarkably unspoiled, it boasts a gorgeous 15th-century church and the romantic

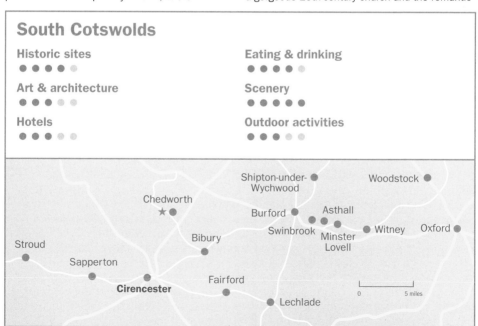

South Cotswolds

Historic sites
● ● ● ● ◦

Art & architecture
● ● ● ◦ ◦

Hotels
● ● ● ◦ ◦

Eating & drinking
● ● ● ● ◦

Scenery
● ● ● ● ●

Outdoor activities
● ● ● ◦ ◦

Shipton-under- ● Wychwood
Woodstock ●
Chedworth ★●
Burford ● Asthall ●
Swinbrook ● ● ● Witney ● Oxford ●
Bibury Minster Lovell
Stroud ●
Sapperton ●
Fairford
Cirencester ●
● Lechlade
0   5 miles

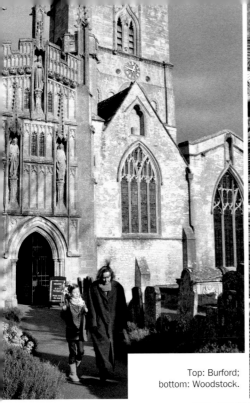

Top: Burford;
bottom: Woodstock.

Experience the beauty of the Cotswolds and the best of British at

BIBURY COURT

Set in 6 acres of stunning landscaped gardens, within the village of Bibury, once described by William Morris as *'the most beautiful village in England'* is Bibury Court Hotel.

Dating back to the 16th Century, Bibury Court is a stunning Jacobean Mansion, offering the best of all worlds – the perfect place to get away from the pressures of daily life, a wonderfully romantic hideaway, a great base for leisurely walks and an ideal place for families.

Bibury boasts a two rosettes award winning recently refurbished restaurant. Head Chef and his team are passionate about using local, seasonal ingredients and producing exquisite food. You can enjoy a two or three course lunch in the conservatory or fine dining in the restaurant. Afternoon tea is served by the roaring log fire in the oak-panelled drawing room, or outside on the sun terrace by the river Coln in the warmer months.

Only 7 miles from the historic market town of Cirencester, and 20 miles from the fashionable boutiques of Cheltenham, Bibury Court is a haven of traditional luxury in the Cotswolds in which to relax, dine and explore.

For more information please call us on 01285 740 337
or visit our website at www.biburycourt.com

BIBURY, CIRENCESTER, GLOUCESTERSHIRE, GL7 5NT, TEL: 01285 740337, FAX: 01285 740660
EMAIL: INFO@BIBURYCOURT.COM   WWW.BIBURYCOURT.COM

ruins of Minster Lovell Hall. Dating from the 1440s, the hall and its restored medieval dovecote make an imposing sight on the banks of the River Windrush, and the thatched cottages are some of the prettiest around. It's worth making further detours to visit picturesque **Asthall** and the Roman ruins at **North Leigh**, which include some wonderful mosaics now kept under shelter.

WITNEY

Also between Woodstock and Burford is Witney. Despite being one of the largest towns in the Cotswolds, it offers fewer tourist attractions than its neighbours. Famous for manufacturing blankets, its sights include the first medieval marketplace in England, attractive almshouses and the magnificent St Mary's church. For more local history, drop by the charming **Cogges Manor Farm Museum** (Church Lane, 01993 772602, www.westoxon.gov.uk, closed Sept-Mar), which aims to re-create rural Victorian Oxfordshire with costumed guides and a 20-acre working farm, complete with traditional breeds of livestock. In the activities room, children can try on Victorian clothes and play with replica toys.

BURFORD & AROUND

The elegant, historic coaching town of Burford makes a delightful, if pricey, base from which to explore the surrounding countryside. The broad High Street comprises a host of pretty buildings clinging to the slope leading down to the River Windrush. It's smattered with gift and antiques shops, as well as England's oldest pharmacy, an excellent delicatessen and a few beauty salons for those vital post-walk pedicures. For much of the year, the town is chock-full of traffic; visit in early spring or winter to get the best out of it.

Among the attractions is **Burford Garden Company** (Shilton Road, 01993 823117, www.burford.co.uk), a mammoth garden centre that is a huge draw all year round, while **Cotswold Wildlife Park** (01993 823006, www.cotswold wildlifepark.co.uk) has stunning gardens, set out around a listed Victorian manor house. Spacious paddocks house big cats, zebras, red pandas and monkeys, with separate buildings for reptiles, bats and insects.

Burford also has one or two less commercial claims to fame. Nell Gwynn visited a number of times, and the fruit of her liaisons with Charles II, Charles Beauclerk, was created Earl of Burford. In May 1649, at the end of the Civil War, Oliver Cromwell and his men imprisoned 340 Levellers in Burford's Norman church; carvings made by the incarcerated soldiers and bullet holes from the ringleaders' executions can still be seen. Insights into Burford's history can be found in the **Tolsey Museum** (126 High Street, 01993 823196).

To the north of Burford, there are paintings and fragments of Roman mosaics in the tiny church at **Widford**. The petite village of **Shipton-under-Wychwood** also boasts a pretty church, with some Pre-Raphaelite archangels and a stained-glass window designed by the William Morris Company. To the east is the village of **Swinbrook**, where Nancy Mitford is buried.

To see how the Cotswolds earned their crust before the tourist invasion, visit **Cotswold Woollen Weavers** (01367 860491, www.natural best.co.uk) in Filkins. At this working mill and museum, you can watch fleece being woven into fabric, then purchase a wide range of clothes, rugs and cushions from its shop.

Kelmscott Manor

Kelmscott, nr Lechlade, 8 miles S of Burford *(01367 252486/www.kelmscottmanor.co.uk). Open Apr-Sept 11am-5pm Wed, 1st & 3rd Sat of mth. Admission £8.50; £4.25 reductions.*
The country home of William Morris – writer, socialist and innovator in the Arts and Crafts movement. Built in 1570, the house is large but not ostentatious, and is now primarily a showcase for the work of Morris – tapestries, fabrics and wallpapers, plus examples of his printing, painting and writing – and his wife Janey, who helped to revive traditional embroidery techniques.

BIBURY

The gorgeous village of Bibury, ten miles north-east of Cirencester, is worth a visit, particularly out of season, when it's far quieter. William Morris's claim that this is 'the most beautiful village in England' has become a cliché, but you can certainly see what he was on about. Across the bridge from the Swan Hotel (*see p73*) is the one paying attraction of the village – **Bibury Trout Farm** (01285 740215, www.biburytrout farm.co.uk), where kids can feed fish. Near here you'll find **Arlington Row**, a perfect, typical row of Cotswold cottages, owned by the National Trust. When Henry Ford visited in the 1920s, he liked them so much he tried to take them back to America with him, but was stopped. The walk from here along the river to Coln St Aldwyns is particularly recommended.

CIRENCESTER & CHEDWORTH

Anyone with an interest in Roman history should take in both Cirencester (Roman Corinium) and the Roman villa at Chedworth, to the north. Corinium was one of Roman Britain's most important settlements, and its heritage is brought to life in the town's enjoyable **Corinium Museum** (01285 655611, www.cirencester.co.uk/coriniummuseum) and the remains of Corinium's amphitheatre, still visible on the western edge of the modern town. Near to Chedworth are the excavated remains of one of the UK's largest Roman villas (01242 890256, www.national

Perfect pampering

The southern Cotswolds has a plethora of spas where you can be truly pampered and detoxed – for a price. Many of these are attached to the luxury hotels dotted across the region, such as historic **Barnsley House** (*see p72*), whose contemporary spa sits in its beautiful gardens. Elegant, tranquil and comfortable, the spa is a must for celebrities – Liz Hurley and Kate Moss are regulars. Local stone, British hardwoods, floor-to-ceiling glass and B&B Italian furniture give it a stylish edge. The heated outdoor pool, relaxation room and sauna and steam rooms are superb; electronic beds have iPods and speakers, and guest numbers are kept low, so you'll be spoiled. The Signature Treatment (£155) is a decadent two-hour package including body exfoliation, facial, aromatherapy massage followed by a hot-stone treatment.

At **Cowley Manor** (*see p72*), the **C.Side Spa** is an ultra-modern, minimal building – a striking contrast to the stately Victorian mother ship. This is a peaceful and luxurious beauty oasis that's best enjoyed in the warmer months, when you can while away the hours around the heated outdoor pool gazing at the surrounding countryside. In colder months you can make use of an indoor pool, faced on two sides by floor-to-ceiling windows so you can enjoy the woodland views as you swim. The signature treatment is Cloud 9 (£107), an aromatherapy massage that will leave you right up there.

On a slightly more modest scale, but nevertheless still delightful, is **Calcot Manor**, near Tetbury (01666 890391, www.calcotspa. co.uk), a medium-sized country house hotel set in 220 acres of meadowland. Attractively designed around a central courtyard, its **Calcot Spa** blends sympathetically with the bucolic surroundings and features a glorious 52-foot indoor pool, sauna, steam room, outdoor spa pool, exercise studio, tennis courts, seven treatment rooms and a crèche. You'll find a good range of beauty and alternative treatments, with mini spa packages starting at £59.

Le Spa in Cirencester (01285 653840, www.lespa.com) is first and foremost a health/fitness club and spa as well as a hotel (although the nine bedrooms in the pretty Edwardian manor house are well thought out and plush). It's a pleasant place to relax and unwind, with beautifully landscaped grounds, outdoor treatment rooms and hot tubs, two gymnasia, a fitness studio and an 60-foot indoor pool. There is a choice of day spa packages that include facials, massage treatments, reiki and reflexology. The signature

treatment is the Lomi Lomi (£75), an 80-minute massage using exotic oil. Two guests can enjoy an overnight break from £129.

At **Preen** in the **Feathers Hotel** in Woodstock (*see p72*), you can take your perch in the eaves of the cosy upmarket hideaway for a relaxing treatment of your choice. Here, you can be massaged and manicured, body-brushed and balanced, acupressured and exfoliated. Preen specialises in Babor products, with the emphasis on natural ingredients. Prices are reasonable, with massages starting at £29.

In stark contrast to the historic surroundings of other neighbouring establishments, **Spa 6** at the **Four Pillars hotel** (0845 500 6666, www.cotswoldwaterparkhotel.co.uk) is rather functional and characterless, but clean and modern. The setting, overlooking a lake, is lovely and, as part of the Cotswold Water Park (*see p69*), there is access to plenty of land and water-based activities. The signature treatment is the Orange Blossom Sheer Indulgence Face & Body Treatment (£130), with exfoliation and full body massage, body mask and face massage. Other tempting treats include the moisturising Chocolate Delight (£90), dry flotation sessions, (£30) and rasul room (from £45).

trust.org.uk). The site includes more than a mile of walls, mosaics, two bathhouses and hypocausts (the Romans' version of central heating). Cirencester has some reasonable shops and frequent markets, but if you crave a more metropolitan buzz head to elegant Cheltenham, 24 miles to the north.

Garden-lovers are well served in this part of the country. In addition to the charming **Cerney House Gardens** (Cerney Lodge, North Cerney, 01285 831300, www.cerneygardens.com), there is the impressive **Misarden Park Gardens** at Miserden, between Cirencester and Cheltenham (01285 821303, www.gardens-guide.com, closed Oct-Mar), where the 17th-century, 12-acre gardens overlook the Golden Valley. The site contains a walled garden, an arboretum, a yew walk and topiary, including some designed by Lutyens.

Spreading out around Shorncote (about three miles south of Cirencester), more than 140 lakes over an area of 40 square miles make up the **Cotswold Water Park** (Keynes Country Park, Spratsgate Lane, 01285 861459, www.waterpark.org). On the main sports lakes visitors can indulge in sailing, canoeing, waterskiing, windsurfing and jetskiing, and hire watercraft or stick to land-based activities such as cycling and horse riding. Elsewhere nature has the upper hand, with two country parks (one with a children's beach) offering fine walking (including guided wildlife walks) and birdwatching. A programme of children's activities is run in the school holidays. To quote David Bellamy: 'It's a blooming marvellous place!'

Eat

The southern Cotswolds is teeming with charming gastropubs, but these tend to be pricey. If you want to cook your own food, there are plenty of farm shops in the area. One of the best is **Butts Farm Shop** (01285 862224, www.thebuttsfarm shop.com), near South Cerney, just south of Cirencester. Cirencester's **Abbey Home Farm** (01283 640441, www.theorganicfarmshop.co.uk) stocks organic meats, eggs, fruit and veg.

Hotel restaurants in the area, not listed below, which serve outstanding food and welcome non-residents include **Barnsley House** (see p72), the **Bay Tree Hotel** (see p72).

Allium
Fairford, 8 miles E of Cirencester *1 London Street, Market Place (01285 712200/www.allium. uk.net). Open 7-9pm Tue; noon-2pm, 7-9pm Wed-Sat; noon-2pm Sun. £££. Modern European.*
Modern restaurants (that aren't in pubs) are rare indeed in this part of the world – Allium is one of this uncommon breed. Its stark white interior, proactive service and discreet

local art mark it out as an ambitious operation, and the food largely lives up to its billing. The lunch menu changes daily, the evening selection seasonally, and both make creative use of the wealth of excellent local suppliers to produce dishes such as Claydon crayfish with cauliflower cream, venison with pear and parsnips, and puddings such as lavender parfait with white chocolate and lime. The special lunch menu at £10 offers good value.

Angel at Burford
Burford *14 Witney Street (01993 822714/www.the angelatburford.co.uk). Open noon-2pm, 7-9pm Tue-Sat; noon-2pm Sun. ££££. Gastropub.*
This 16th-century coaching inn has an appealing bricks-and-beams interior for winter dining and a narrow garden for when the weather's on form. Order at the bar (seating is limited if you're just in for an Adnams) and then you'll be taken to one of the various dining areas. Smoked haddock rarebit or fish cakes might be on the lunch menu; at dinner, when booking is essential, you'll find heartier fare such as venison steak, pan-fried calf's liver or seafood risotto; it's all well presented and competently cooked, if a touch pricey. Top marks for desserts, especially the warm sticky toffee pudding with date purée and vanilla ice-cream. Three en suite rooms are available if you've overindulged in pint or plate.

Bell at Sapperton
Sapperton, 4 miles W of Cirencester *(01285 760298/www.foodatthebell.co.uk). Open noon-2.15pm, 7-9.30pm Mon-Sat; noon-2.15pm, 7-9pm Sun. ££££. Gastropub.*
For some years now, the Bell has enjoyed a deserved reputation for its food. Outside, the pub is a typical Cotswold stone hostelry; inside, pine furniture and contemporary prints decorate a series of interlinking rooms, and tables are well spaced. The menu makes imaginative use of local ingredients, and might include hearty fare like pressed terrine of Old Spot pork with piccalilli or home-made burger of Copsegrove Farm Welsh black beef with dill pickles.

Cowley Manor
Cowley, 12 miles N of Cirencester *(01242 870900/www.cowleymanor.com). Open 12.30-2.30pm, 7-10pm Mon-Thur; 12.30-2.30pm, 7-11pm Fri; 12.30-3pm, 7-11pm Sat; 12.30-3pm, 7-10pm Sun. ££££. British.*
Ultra-cool Cowley Manor offers an enticing combination of modern design and facilities within an imposing Victorian neo-classical mansion. Its lofty-ceilinged dining room, clad in elaborately carved wood panelling, is an elegant and glamorous space, but far from overbearing – and service is attentive but thoroughly relaxed. The dinner menu offers an eclectic selection of bistro dishes, which are cooked with aplomb and the emphasis firmly on traditional British. You'll find a 28-day aged Butts Farm shorthorn beef steak dish at one end of the main-course menu, and a more modest Scottish girolles and spring onions with welsh onion cake at the other. Hearty accompaniments include bubble and squeak and mashed carrot and neeps. Desserts come with iconic labels such as burnt Trinity cream and Bakewell pudding. See also p72.

Feathers Hotel

Woodstock *16-20 Market Street (01993 812291/ www.feathers.co.uk). Open 12.30-2.30pm, 7-9.30pm daily. ££££. Modern English.*
Feathers offers an intimate fine dining experience in its antique, oak-panelled dining room. Head chef Russell Bateman uses his international experience to produce sophisticated fare such as Bayonne ham with houmous, spring onion, basil, chickpea and red onion salad; breast of guinea fowl with Jerusalem artichoke, and bitter chocolate mousse with black cherry parfait. The lunchtime menu is good value at £19, offering hearty dishes such as citrus-cured salmon with fennel and cresses or Kelmscott pork belly with carrot and spinach. The Feathers will also prepare you a luxury picnic hamper complete with cutlery, crockery and napkins for a gourmet day out. *See also p72.*

Fleece

Witney *11 Church Green (01993 892270/www.fleece witney.co.uk). Open 8am-10pm daily. £££. Gastropub.*
An unexpectedly modern Cotswolds find, the Fleece wouldn't look out of place in Islington, thanks to its contemporary decor of light wood and leather banquettes. It's certainly a popular spot with Witney's twenty- and thirtysomethings. The front bar can get rather crowded; head for the quieter back restaurant or dine outdoors if the sun's out. You can snack on sandwiches, go larger on fish cakes, mushroom risotto or tagine, or bust it with 21-day dry-aged Aberdeenshire rump steak or braised venison. Real ales on tap include Greene King IPA, Black Sheep and Old Speckled Hen, and the wine list is short and sensibly priced.

Jesse's Bistro

Cirencester *The Stableyard, Blackjack Street (01285 641497/www.jessesbistro.co.uk). Open noon-2.30pm Mon-Wed; noon-2.30pm, 7-9.30pm Wed-Sat. £££. British.*
Cirencester has a decent range of ethnic eateries but one of the best spots to dine is unassuming Jesse's Bistro, tucked down an alleyway off Blackjack Street in the centre of town. The focus within the atmospheric stone-floored restaurant is the wood-fired oven, where most of the cooking is done. The menu is compact and firmly British-skewed: try the steamed mutton and apricot suet pudding with savoy cabbage, bacon and potatoes, or roasted Suffolk duck breast with fennel and orange. Prices may be more restaurant than bistro, but the quality is similarly high. All the excellent meat is supplied by neighbouring Jesse Smith Butcher's, and Jesse's empire also includes a cheese shop and fish slab (you'll find five or so fish dishes on the menu – and there's always a good veggie option too). The wine list is tempting and comprehensive, with more than 20 available by the glass.

Lamb Inn

Shipton-under-Wychwood *High Street (01993 830465). Open noon-2.30pm, 7-9.30pm Mon-Sat; noon-2.30pm Sun. £££. Gastropub.*
You'll still find locals supping Abbot Ale in this picturesque Cotswold-stone inn, but there's also a big emphasis on food and wine. The dining area has a welcoming lounging space, equipped with a comfy, cushion-laden sofa; a fine spot for

a cappuccino or glass of shiraz. The menu has also successfully moved from old-fashioned pub grub standards to gastro favourites like duck breast, rack of lamb, roast chicken and steak, and puddings such as crème brulée, lemon tart and caramelised apple tart.

Lamb Inn & Restaurant

Burford *Sheep Street (01993 823155/www.lambinn-burford.co.uk). Open 7.30-9.30am, noon-2.30pm, 7-9.30pm daily. ££££. English.*
The Lamb's restaurant is reached via a distinctive stone-flagged corridor leading from the cosy pub, where you may also dine. While formal, it isn't fusty, with business people and families rubbing shoulders with the locals. The menu is uncomplicated and seasonal, drawing from local produce where possible: plenty of fresh fish and seafood, and heartier fare such as trio of beef (mini rib-eye, meatloaf, and mini shank) or roast pheasant. The wine list is comprehensive if pricey, with a good selection by the glass.

Seven Tuns

Chedworth *Queen's Street (01285 720242). Open noon-2.30pm, 6.30-9.30pm Mon-Fri; noon-3pm, 6.30-9.30pm Sat; noon-3pm, 6.30-9pm Sun. ££. Pub/English.*
You're spoiled for choice at this large, friendly 17th-century pub in the lovely village of Chedworth. The small bar area, with log fire, wooden booths and tables, has a homely bar menu (filled baguettes, baked potatoes, ploughman's, house salad of warm chicken, bacon and avocado). Out back is a modern restaurant (where you can sample the likes of Old Spot sausages, fish pie and pan-fried breaded camembert), and there's another, more up-to-date bar too. In summer, the revolving South African barbecue in the garden comes into its own. You'll always find some good cask ales on tap.

Swan

Southrop, 10 miles E of Cirencester *(01367 850205/www.theswanatsouthrop.co.uk). Open noon-3pm Mon-Sat; noon-3pm Sun. £££. Modern European.*
Right on the village green, the classy and upbeat 17th-century hostelry is a characterful, low-ceilinged, modern art-bedecked affair offering first-rate pan-European fare at London restaurant prices. Main courses from the evening menu might be Southrop lamb rump, creamed potato, a fricassée of pea, mint, bacon and wood sorrel, or wild sea bream fillet with pea purée, girolles mushrooms, spinach and pecorino.

Village Pub

Barnsley, 4 miles NE of Cirencester *High Street (01285 740421/www.thevillagepub.co.uk). Open noon-2.30pm, 7-9.30pm Mon-Thur; noon-2.30pm, 7-10pm Fri; noon-3pm, 7-10pm Sat; noon-3pm, 7-9.30pm Sun. £££. Gastropub.*
From pre-dinner beers to postprandial chocolates and coffee, the Village Pub really delivers. Diners have a choice of five rooms, each decorated in a different style; subtle paint effects, wood panelling and flagstones are a common theme. The menu – now presided over by Michael Davies, previously soups chef at Barnsley House just over the road

Top: King's Arms Hotel;
bottom: Lamb Inn.

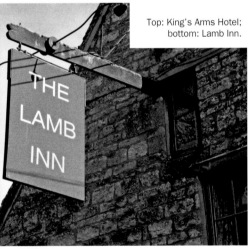

– makes a virtue of simplicity in flavour and presentation, but there's still plenty of scope for imagination: witness, for instance escalope of guinea fowl with rocket and fennel salad or roasted halibut with artichokes, potatoes and steamed cockles. And when in Gloucestershire… you have to try the twice-baked double gloucester soufflé.

Wild Duck Inn

Ewen, 3 miles S of Cirencester *Drakes Island (01285 770310/www.thewilteduckinn.co.uk). Open noon-2pm, 6.45-10pm Mon-Sat; noon-2pm, 6.45-9.45pm Sun. £££. Gastropub.*

Dark red walls, low beams and irreverently encased and beheaded wildlife upon the walls give the busy 16th-century Wild Duck a groovy charm. Diners spill through a series of interconnecting rooms with ample nooks and crannies, and there's a lovely tree-shaded garden (complete with giant chess set) out back. Prices aren't low, but neither is the quality of the likes of wok-fried rib-eye steak with ginger, spring onion and special fried rice, or grilled sea bass with vegetables and pesto dressing.

Stay

Accommodation is also offered at the **Angel at Burford** (*see p69*) and the **Lamb** (*see p70*) in Shipton-under-Wychwood, also home to traditional farmhouse B&B Court Farm (01993 831515, www.courtfarmbb.com). Barnsley's **Village Pub** (*see p70*), has six pleasing rooms above it. The **Wild Duck** in Ewen (*see p72*) is another excellent gastropub and offers good rooms. An affordable B&B is the **Old Rectory** in Rodmarton (01285 841246, www.rodmarton.com, from £70 double), parts of which date from the 16th century.

In Bibury, the **Bibury Court Hotel** (01285 740337, www.biburycourt.com, £170-£210 double) has a decent restaurant and is set in six acres of lovely gardens.

Barnsley House

Barnsley, 4 miles NE of Cirencester *(01285 740000/www.barnsleyhouse.com). ££££.*

The 18 bedrooms in this historic hotel are the height of contemporary luxury, decorated in subtle tones and equipped with Bose sound systems, plasma-screen and LCD TVs (including one in the bathroom), huge beds with Egyptian cotton sheets, artworks individually chosen for each room, and complimentary drinks. The fabulous spare-no-expense bathrooms have free-standing baths and are stocked with desirable smellies. Many of the house's 17th-century features remain: exposed beams, fireplaces and staircases. This mix of old and new continues throughout the hotel: public areas include a modern reading room and a clean-lined dining room, where decent poshed-up bistro dishes are served, a luxury spa and a cinema. In the 1950s, celebrated gardener Rosemary Verey transformed the garden into a classic small-scale English country-house garden.

Bay Tree Hotel

Burford *Sheep Street (01993 822791/www.cotswold-inns-hotels.co.uk). ££££.*

Sprawling over three ancient buildings, which between them offer 14 rooms and seven suites of differing character, the accommodation here boasts heritage colour schemes, tasteful antiques and first-rate facilities. Some rooms face the charming garden, while others overlook picturesque Sheep Street. Period features such as leaded windows, flagstone floors and cosy fireplaces combine harmoniously with flat-screen TVs and top-notch bathrooms, so character isn't sacrificed to modern comforts. A pleasantly laid-back bar and excellent restaurant are further draws. Staff and service are top-notch.

Burford House Hotel

Burford *99 High Street (01993 823151/www.burfordhouse.co.uk). £££.*

At this informal and intimate townhouse hotel, staff strike a perfect balance between providing top-quality service and making guests feel at home. Eight well-sized and beautifully decorated bedrooms occupy the 17th-century listed building, all with their own bathrooms (one has a decadent tub for two). Communal areas include a courtyard garden and two inviting sitting rooms (with an interestingly stocked honesty bar). Lunch is served Monday to Saturday, and dinner at weekends, with the emphasis on home-made and local produce.

Cowley Manor

Cowley *(01242 870900/www.cowleymanor.com). ££££.*

The neo-classical 19th-century manor house is stately on a manageable scale, and affords fine views over the attractively landscaped grounds and picture-postcard perfect lake. The tone is stylish but unfussy – the staff uniform is a variation on jeans and T-shirts – but absolutely professional. Each of the 30 rooms is individual in size and layout but all are decorated with strong, appealing splashes of colour and striking pieces of furniture; bathrooms are tranquil havens in neutral shades. You'll also find state-of-the-art hardware such as Loewe TVs and quality music systems. The public rooms are grand but groovy (the papier-mâché animal heads in the spacious bar can't fail to raise a smile). The billiards room is an intimate, chocolate leather-panelled refuge, while the carved floor-to-ceiling wood panelling in the dining room and dramatic dangling light fittings infuse the space with glamour. The modernist C.side spa (*see p68*) offers a range of desirable indulgences in its treatment rooms, plus a gym, sauna, steam room and two pools (indoor and outdoor). *See also p69.*

Feathers Hotel

Woodstock *16-20 Market Street (01993 812291/www.feathers.co.uk). ££££.*

Made up of seven interconnected 17th-century houses, and named by a stuffed bird-collecting former hotelier, the Feathers is a snug maze of corridors and 20 elegantly furnished bedrooms, the best of which is equipped with its own private steam room. Despite a certain air of faded glory, it remains Woodstock's most prominent hotel; service is smoothly professional but never lofty. The garden is pleasant on balmy afternoons; in winter, the wood-panelled lounge with huge fireplace is perfect for relaxed drinks. There's also a beauty salon, Preen (treatments must be pre-booked), and a fine-dining restaurant (see p70) and less formal bistro on site.

King's Arms Hotel
Woodstock *19 Market Street (01993 813636/ www.kings-hotel-woodstock.co.uk). £££.*
A comfortable, contemporary hotel, this listed Georgian building has been painstakingly renovated to retain its character, but is carefully balanced with neutral tones and modern furnishings. The only dark furniture you'll find here are the leather chairs in the restaurant, a converted billiards room. The 15 bedrooms – all named after kings – are simply, stylishly and individually appointed, with Wi-Fi and good en suites. There's decent bistro fare (with appealing vegetarian options) in the restaurant, while the bar is popular with Woodstock's youth – so expect a bit of noise on your way up to bed. No children under 12 are allowed in the hotel.

Lamb Inn & Restaurant
Burford *Sheep Street (01993 823155/www.lambinn-burford.co.uk). ££££.*
A few doors down from the Bay Tree (see p73), the Lamb makes an equally appealing period place to stay. The 17 well-equipped rooms are full of warmth and character, with nice personal touches such as proper leaf tea-making facilities and own-made biscuits awaiting as you flop into your room. Many of the rooms overlook a sheltered courtyard, where guests can lunch in summer. There are intimate bar and lounge areas in which to settle by the fire with a drink, and a well-regarded restaurant, serving uncomplicated, seasonal food, rounds off this pleasantly laid-back operation.

Macdonald Bear
Woodstock *Park Street (0844 879 9143/ www.macdonaldhotels.co.uk/bear). ££££.*
Owned by the Macdonald Hotels chain, Woodstock's largest hotel comprises an impressive 13th-century coaching inn

and an adjoining glove factory. There are still plenty of winding corridors, creaky wooden floors, oak beams and fireplaces for atmosphere, and a snug little bar for quiet drinks. Richard Burton and Elizabeth Taylor once famously holed up here and, rather spookily, the ghosts of a young woman and her baby son are said to haunt two of the rooms in the main building.

No.12
Cirencester *12 Park Street (01285 640232/www.no12 cirencester.co.uk). ££.*
Boutique hotels might be relatively commonplace these days, but boutique B&Bs are far more unusual. However, the best place to stay in Cirencester is just such an establishment – within a Grade II-listed Georgian townhouse in the centre of town you'll find four large, immaculately groomed bedrooms with extra long beds (maybe a French bateau lit or antique leather sleigh bed), feather pillows and sleek, contemporary bathrooms (equipped with Molton Brown toiletries and bathrobes). Friendly service and a good breakfast included in the price are further attractions.

Old Post Office
Southrop *(01367 850231/ www.theoldepostoffice.org). £.*
This 14th-century cottage has been tastefully refurbished as a B&B, with three comfortable bedrooms that are reasonably chintz free.

Swan Hotel
Bibury *(01285 740695/www.cotswold-inns-hotels.co.uk). ££££.*
The Swan is superbly located alongside the River Coln and right next to Bibury's beautiful old bridge. The former 17th-century coaching inn has 22 bedrooms, floral-heavy but perfectly comfortable. All have great bathrooms, five with jacuzzis and some with four-poster beds. Outside, the lovely landscaped garden is an ideal place to relax. The hotel bottles its own spring water, which you'll also find in the starched-to-the-hilt restaurant.

Factfile

When to go
Spring is ideal for walking, especially when the wild flowers and hedgerows come into bloom. Autumn sees swathes of golden colour and gorgeous fresh local produce. Winter's the time for roaring open fires and a pint of real ale in a country pub after a frosty tramp. Summer can get hectic, but all main sites are reliably open, and there are those inviting pub gardens to enjoy.

Getting there & around
The southern Cotswolds are served by trains going into Oxford, Cheltenham, Kemble and Stroud. Various bus services run from these

towns into the area. You can find timetables and more information at www.cotswoldsaonb.org.uk.

Tourist information
Burford The Brewery, Sheep Street (01993 823558). Open Mar-Oct 9.30am-5.30pm Mon-Sat; 2-7pm Sun.
Woodstock The Oxfordshire Museum, Park Street (01993 813276). Open Mar-Oct 9.30am-5.30pm Mon-Sat; 2-7pm Sun.

Internet
CLIX Internet Café (42 High Street, Stroud, 01453 766422).

Clockwise from top:
Bolton Abbey;
Malham Tarn;
Ingleborourgh.

Yorkshire Dales

Up hill and down dale in the wild north country.

Yorkshire is blessed with an unfair share of England's best high ground – it has the North York Moors, the Wolds, the Hovingham Hills, the millstone belt of the Pennines – but the 680 square miles of the Yorkshire Dales National Park accounts for most people's idea of Yorkshire's defining landscape.

From the high peaks and moorland wildernesses to the rivers that tumble down ice age valleys then meander through gentle meadows and unspoiled villages, the beauty appears timeless. Even the dominant man-made features are centuries old – the 5,000 miles of drystone walls and the countless stone field barns.

The palette of limestone grey and pasture green is easy on the eye but there is infinite variety to be found in the detail, in rare wildlife like the red squirrel and black grouse, in the wild flower meadows and the ferns in the fissures or grikes of the limestone pavements, in surprise waterfalls and monstrous boulders.

Exploration is essential. You can horse-ride on Roman roads or mountain bike on medieval green lanes; you can paddle down England's fastest flowing river, pothole its biggest cave system, or free-climb its toughest rock routes; you can ride over the monumental viaducts of the Settle-Carlisle Railway; you can even float over it all in a hot air balloon. But the sanest way to absorb the Dales is still at walking pace.

Even in the most popular villages a short climb will free the walker from the madding crowd. Keep climbing. The views get better and better, the sky gets bigger, and the world left behind becomes miniature.

Explore

WHARFEDALE

Wharfedale is most people's first sight of the Dales. It was the great escape from the industrial cities of Leeds and Bradford long before National Parks were invented and still is at weekends and in summer as the masses flock to the honeypots of Bolton Abbey, Burnsall, Grassington and Kettlewell.

Don't be deterred. Most of the crowds stay in the car parks and picnic areas and within ten minutes of walking Wharfedale's beauty belongs to you, and it is undoubtedly a most beautiful dale: great walking amid rivers, waterfalls and high moorland wildlife; wonderful drystone walls and calendar-cover villages; superior places to stay and eat; and notable detours to Littondale, Malhamdale, Nidderdale and Langstrothdale.

The **Bolton Abbey Estate** (www.boltonabbey. com, admission £5.50 per vehicle, free to visitors travelling by public transport) marks the southern boundary of the National Park. The Duke of Devonshire's estate village is kept in pristine condition and its pleasures range from a Michelin-starred restaurant (*see p85*) and a semi-ruined 12th-century priory to a surrounding natural playground that embraces the 57 Stepping Stones that cross the Wharfe, untouched woodlands, the dramatic Strid where the river forces itself through a narrow and dangerous gorge, and 80 miles of footpaths leading to Barden Moor, the Valley of Desolation and the vantage point of Simon's Seat.

Burnsall, framed by river, bridge, pub, church and the now-rising hills is a draw for day-trippers. Here you can paddle in the Wharfe's rocky pools, enjoy an ice-cream, and tell the kids how mammoth once roamed over nearby Elbolton Hill.

There is tourist shopping at **Grassington**, and **Stump Cross Caverns** beyond (www.stumpcross caverns.co.uk, open 10am-6pm daily, admission £6, £3.95 reductions). To the west, **Linton** is a ridiculously pretty village enhanced by the grandeur of Linton Hall and the 18th-century Fountain Hospital, but overrun by weekend cars.

Kilnsey is another magnet for its famous summer agricultural show and fell race, its fish farm, but especially for the roadside Kilnsey Crag, a 170-foot-high lump of ice-age rock with a 40-foot overhang that invariably has an intrepid climber perilously attached to it. This is also the place to join the medieval drovers' road of Mastiles Lane for a walk up to Malham Tarn. It's a lovely, high, green road with monastic stone crosses, lapwings and curlews for company (even peregrine falcons in summer, www. yorkshiredales.org.uk/peregrines.htm), and the most dramatic prizes at the end: the fierce gorges and waterfalls of **Gordale Scar**, the finest limestone pavements in Britain, and the show-stopping **Malham Cove**, a sheer 250-foot cliff formed at the end of the ice age.

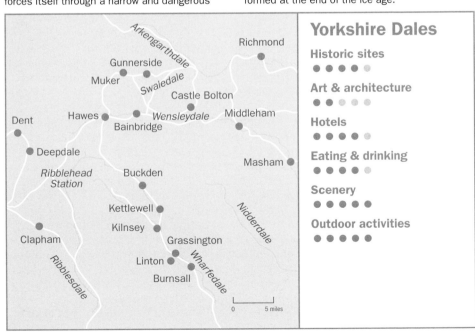

Yorkshire Dales

Historic sites
● ● ● ● ◉

Art & architecture
● ● ◉ ◉ ◉

Hotels
● ● ● ● ◉

Eating & drinking
● ● ● ● ◉

Scenery
● ● ● ● ●

Outdoor activities
● ● ● ● ●

Muker meadow;
a typical haybarn.

Get the local experience

Over 50 of the world's top destinations available.

TIME OUT GUIDES
WRITTEN BY
LOCAL EXPERTS
visit timeout.com/shop

Wharfedale's little tributary valley of **Littondale**, to the north-east, is a more soothing byway. By the time you reach the village of **Arncliffe** the cars have all but gone and you're left with a fine village green and a legendary pub, the Falcon (*see p85*).

By now the route from Kilnsey to Kettlewell, Upper Wharfedale has narrowed to a single lane hemmed in by high fells. **Kettlewell** is a good base for climbing the 2,311-foot Great Whernside (not to be confused with Whernside in Ribblesdale, one of the 'three peaks') and Buckden Pike, at 2,303 feet, which has a sad memorial on its summit, to the Polish air crew who were killed when their Wellington bomber crashed during a blizzard in 1942; the lone survivor found his way off the mountain by following the tracks of a fox.

Finally, beyond Starbotton and Buckden, lies the hamlet of **Hubberholme**. JB Priestley, whose ashes were scattered here by the lovely old church, thought Hubberholme 'one of the smallest and pleasantest places in the world'. The fabulously varied circular walk from Hubberholme to Cray and Yockenthwaite makes his point.

WENSLEYDALE

Broad and wide, Wensleydale lacks the immediate upfront beauty of other Dales, but it has a deep history and is rich in attractions. These range from England's highest waterfall to splendid castles and ruined abbeys, thoroughbred racehorses and rare red squirrels – along with guaranteed breathtaking vistas from its high points.

The Romans made a fort at **Bainbridge** and stayed for 400 years; it still makes a handy base today. From the network of local Roman roads, try walking the Cam High Road, which marches uncompromisingly for four miles straight up to the 2,014-foot peak of Wether Fell. Or branch off for the shores of remote and lonely Semer Water. It's no great size for the largest lake in Yorkshire, but is very atmospheric.

Bainbridge is close to **Askrigg**, the photogenic setting for Darrowby in *All Creatures Great and Small*. It is also an easy drive or bus ride to the rainy-day attractions of **Hawes**, where you can watch cheese-making at the Wensleydale Creamery (01969 667664, www.wensleydale.co. uk) or rope-making in Outhwaite's traditional workshop (01969 667487, www.ropemakers. com). Next door in the old Hawes railway station is the Dales Countryside Museum and National Park Centre (01969 666210, open 10am-5pm daily, admission £3 adults, free children), with neat displays on Dales life. The museum can also connect you to the 21st century via the high-tech craze of **geocaching**. As pioneered by the Yorkshire Dales National Park, GPS receivers are hired out by information centres at Hawes, Reeth, Grassington and Malham. With map and sat nav, participants search for distinctly low-tech treasure – a plastic box with log book and Dales literature. (www.yorkshiredales.org.uk).

Hardraw Force, England's highest unbroken waterfall (and more impressive for its height than its volume) is in a wooded ravine just outside the hamlet of Hardraw, near Hawes. A walk along Hardraw Beck from the Green Dragon Inn (www. greendragonhardraw.com) will bring you to the falls.

Aysgarth Falls, also near Hawes, comes in three bites, Upper, Middle and Lower, as the Ure pours impressively over broad limestone terraces. Park at the Hawes National Park Centre and follow the easy paths to the falls. One leads into Freeholders Wood, an ancient hazel coppiced woodland, where a detour will reward you with bluebells and wood anemones in spring and the rare chance of spotting a resident red squirrel.

There are far better odds of seeing red squirrels at **Widdale**, in a quiet woodland where artist and conservationist Hugh Kemp and the National Park are protecting an emerging population. A 9.5 mile, mostly linear, walk takes you to a feeding station viewpoint. Pick up details from the National Park Centre at Hawes or download the walk from www.yorkshiredales.org.uk/snaize holme-red-squirrel-trail.htm.

East from Hawes and Bainbridge, at Castle Bolton, is the menacing **Bolton Castle** (01969 623981, www.boltoncastle.co.uk, open Apr-Oct 10am-5pm Tue-Sun, admission £6.50, £4.50 reductions) with its tableaux and exhibits. Mary Queen of Scots was held captive here in 1569. Sir Nikolaus Pevsner's *Buildings of England* calls it 'a climax of English military architecture'.

Middleham has a castle, too, where Richard III lived, but it's better known as Yorkshire's racehorse capital, the 'Newmarket of the north', with 15 yards and some 550 horses in training. Arrive early morning at the gallops on **Middleham High Moor**, where it's said Richard III exercised his chargers, to experience the thrill of seeing sleek thoroughbreds thundering past. Horse-lovers can book a stable tour or even a two-day break (over-16s only) from 07775 568374, www.middlehamracingbreaks.co.uk.

Horse breeding has a long history in Wensleydale. The monks at nearby **Jervaulx** (www.jervaulxabbey.com) were renowned horse and sheep breeders. Today the grounds of this ruined 12th-century Cistercian abbey are a good place for a tranquil stroll, ending at the tearoom (01677 46039, open mid Mar-early Nov) and plant shop.

At the junction where Wensleydale meets Coverdale is a weird and amazing garden attraction, the **Forbidden Corner** at Coverham (01969 640638, www.theforbiddencorner.co.uk). Within the four-acre garden is an underground labyrinth of dead-end passages, false doors,

Aysgarth Falls.

surprise fountains and kitsch follies. Part *Alice in Wonderland*, part *Harry Potter*, it will beguile most kids. Pre-booking is required.

Finally, at the end of the dale, **Masham** has a massive market square, able to accommodate the huge flocks of sheep that were driven here from Jervaulx and Fountains monasteries for the sheep sales, now commemorated with a sheep fair at the end of September. Masham has two breweries, Theakston's (01765 680000, www.theakstons.co.uk), with its unique Old Peculier, or the subversive Black Sheep (Wellgarth, Masham, 01765 680101, www.blacksheepbrewery.com), established in 1992 after Theakston's sold out to Scottish & Newcastle. Both run brewery tours.

SWALEDALE AND ARKENGARTHDALE

There is a haunting beauty to these two smaller Dales on the National Park's northern rim. Shaped millions of years ago when the ice reached the highest peaks, their tumbling becks and steep-sided hills are topped by purple heathered moorland, making it prime habitat for merlin, golden plover, curlew, lapwing and prized red grouse.

Swaledale is textbook Dales countryside. Its bathtub valley passes through unspoilt villages to the wildflower meadows at Muker and the remote village of Keld. Nearly every field has its sturdy stone haybarn, and pastures are bounded by a network of drystone walls, built centuries ago.

Richmond is the principal entry point for Swaledale. Testament to the fortunes made here by stocking-makers during the Georgian era include the handsome houses in Newbiggin and Frenchgate and the jewel box of the still-active Georgian Theatre (Victoria Road, www.georgiantheatreroyal.co.uk). An impressive 21st-century enterprise is the former railway station (www.richmondstation.com), transformed by community effort into a cinema, art gallery, café and shops. It's an easy walk along the riverbank to the 12th-century ruins of **Easby Abbey**, or to scale the 100-foot-tall keep of the Norman **castle** (www.english-heritage.org.uk, open Apr-Sept 10am-6pm daily, Oct-Mar 10am-4pm daily, admission £3.90, £2-£3.10 reductions) for a panoramic view of the town and the mouth of the dale.

From Richmond, the old turnpike road winds its way into Swaledale. At **Grinton**, St Andrew's church is one of the oldest and loveliest churches in the Dales. **Reeth** is the centre of Swaledale and the start or finish of a detour into Arkengarthdale. Its handsome green is bordered by pubs and shops and overlooked by the dramatic scar of Fremington Edge. Also on the Green is Hudson House National Park Information Centre.

Carrying along up Swaledale, there is the opportunity to learn about Dales farming at **Hazel Brow** organic farm at Low Row (01748 886224, www.hazelbrow.co.uk). A less bucolic side of Dales life is visible at **Gunnerside**, where barren wastelands of old tippings and ruined smelt mills recall the days when lead was painfully hauled from rich seams of ore discovered deep in the hills.

The **Muker meadows** on Swaledale's western fringes were farmed traditionally for generations and are now a Site of Special Scientific Interest. In June and July they bloom with a technicolour show of buttercups, clover, bistort, eyebright, woody cranesbill and melancholy thistle. In August the meadows are cut down for fodder. Once commonplace, such land is now a precious part of our natural heritage. Footpath criss-cross the meadows.

Take a detour along the Hawes road for the strange roadside spectacle of the **Buttertubs**, a collection of weirdly shaped limestone sink holes close to the road. And set aside time for what is possibly Swaledale's defining walk, the six-mile circular from **Keld** to Muker and back. The first half is a stiff climb over Kisdon Hill on the old Corpse Way, the ancient footpath along which wicker coffins were carried to the nearest consecrated ground at Grinton 12 miles away.

After stunning high-level views, drop down to Muker for refreshment and a gentler return along the River Swale through meadows, more abandoned mine workings, and a worthwhile detour to Kisdon Force.

Tan Hill is 1,732 feet above Swaledale and the Tan Hill Inn (www.tanhillinn.com) is the highest pub in England. From here, take the high road to Arkengarthdale through a wild, windswept moorland plateau with views to Rogan's Seat and Water Crag in the distance.

Arkengarthdale, on the northern rim of Yorkshire, delivers a captivating descent as it slices through rocky outcrops, limestone farmsteads, the feeder streams and waterfalls of Arkle Beck and lonely settlements like **Booze** and **Whaw**. There are 1950s petrol pumps and a homely pub at **Langthwaite**, and more sophisticated comforts at the whitewashed roadside CB Inn (*see p85*), commemorating Charles Bathhurst, the 18th-century lord of the manor and wealthy lead mine owner. Its only 11 miles from Tan Hill before the road reaches Reeth but little Arkengarthdale is a dale apart, little visited, but much loved.

RIBBLESDALE AND THE CRAVEN DALES

This is the big country of the Dales National Park. Here are Yorkshire's highest mountains and its deepest caves, beloved of fell runners, serious climbers and expert potholers. There is stunning geology too, from ice age boulders to limestone scars, and the awesome engineering of the Settle-Carlisle railway.

The landscape is dominated by the **Three Peaks**: Pen-y-Ghent (2,276 feet), Ingleborough (2,372 feet) and Whernside (2,415 feet). The traditional challenge is to climb all three within a gruelling 12 hours.

Twice a year, on the May and August bank holidays, members of the public can descend 360 feet by bosun's chair into the cathedral-like chamber of **Gaping Gill**, Britain's largest cavern, so vast that York Minster could supposedly fit inside. Queues start forming at dawn.

Clapham offers an easy walk along the Reginald Farrer Nature Trail, named for the Victorian plantsman whose daring expeditions to the Himalayas and the Far East brought back the seeds and plants that created the English rock garden. Lake and woodland paths lead to **Ingleborough Cave** (www.ingleboroughcave. co.uk). **White Scar** (www.whitescarcave.co.uk) is another show cave in the Ingleborough area. Clapham is also a starting point for the weird **Norber Boulders**, great lumps of Silurian slate broken up by ice 12,000 years ago and carried here to perch incongruously, some on plinths, on the hillside.

Easier still is the half-hour hike to Castleberg Crag, with its panoramic views of Settle. **Settle**, the 'capital' of Ribblesdale, has its charms. The Folly, a Grade 1 listed 17th-century manor house, is home to the Museum of Northern Craven Life (Victoria Street, www.ncbpt.org.uk/folly). The Yorkshire Dales Falconry & Wildlife Conservation Centre (Crows Nest Road, 01729 822832, www.dalesfalconry.f9.co.uk) puts on displays and runs falconry courses. But, above all, Settle is the place to board Ribblesdale's most stellar man-made attraction, the **Settle–Carlisle railway**.

Building 72 miles of track through England's most inhospitable high terrain was an epic Victorian feat and the journey matches it, through 14 tunnels and over 20 viaducts. Six thousand navvies lived in shanty towns riddled with violence, drunkenness and countless deaths during the seven years it took to build this historic line. A long campaign happily saved it from British Rail's axe in 1989. The views along the line are spectacular. For a station by station commentary, download the MP3 guide from www.settle-carlisle.co.uk. **Horton** in Ribblesdale, the first stop on the line, is best for Pen-y-Ghent climbers, who can use the famous clocking-in machine at the Pen-Y-Ghent Café where, if you fail to return, staff will alert the emergency services.

Ribblehead, the next stop, is unmissable. Here the bleakest moorland stretch is spanned by the mighty 24-arch Ribblehead Viaduct. You can't actually see it from the train; you'll need to break your journey to be amazed by its million-plus blocks weighing up to eight tons each. Friends of the Railway run guided walks from the station. Alternatively, download an MP3 self-guided walk

or cycle. The company Off the Rails (www.offtherails.org.uk) will meet you with a bike to cycle round Ribblehead and back to Settle.

Dent, at 1,150 feet, is the highest railway station in England and it's available to rent (www.dentstation.co.uk). Rather inconveniently it's also four miles from Dent Town. Pre-book a taxi from Dale's Travel (01539 625555).

After so much rugged country, **Dent Town** is a sweet haven, with whitewashed cottages, a cobbled main street, neat shops, tearooms and galleries. In the 18th century everyone here knitted stockings; now they look after walkers and cyclists. The big granite water fountain in the village is dedicated to Victorian geologist Adam Sedgwick.

Leaving Dent, the narrow lane up Deepdale to Kingsdale is one of the most scenic in all the Dales. You rarely see another car, much less human habitation. The road climbs until you are almost level with Whernside, with only crows and kestrels for company. Suddenly, Kingsdale reveals itself, straight and true as a bowling alley, with a shiny, meandering beck at its heart and wild limestone escarpments on its flanks. The odd windswept tree sprouts miraculously from the rock. And still the dry-stone walls march up the highest fells.

Eat

Good food is also available for non-residents in some hotels listed in the Stay section, including **Austwick Hall** (*see p88*) and **Yorebridge House** (*see p89*).

Angel Inn

Wharfedale *Hetton (01756 730263/www.angel hetton.co.uk). Open (Brasserie) Winter noon-2.15pm, 6-9pm Mon-Fri; noon-2.15pm, 6-10pm Sat; noon-2.30pm, 6-8.30pm Sun. Summer noon-2.15pm, 6-9.30pm Mon-Fri, Sun; noon-2.15pm, 6-10pm Sat. (Restaurant) 6-9pm Mon-Fri; 6-9.30pm Sat; noon-1.45pm Sun. ££££. Gastropub.*
Around 25 years ago Denis Watkins began serving proper food and lovingly selected wine at this country pub between Wharfedale and Skipton. and unwittingly created what is generally recognised as the first gastropub in Britain. It is still up there with the best, doing great food in the ever-popular squeeze of the bar or the panelled dining room, with dishes like little bags of seafood and lobster sauce, local pheasant and Yorkshire beef. There are full-blown vegetarian and kids' menus too. Accommodation is available in stylish suites, with their own sitting rooms, in a series of converted barn buildings.

Black Sheep Brewery

Wensleydale *Wellgarth, Masham (01765 680101/ www.blacksheepbrewery.co.uk). Open 10.30am-4.30pm Mon-Wed; 10.30am-4.30pm, 6.30-9pm Thur-Sat; 10.30am-3pm Sun. £££. British.*

Angel

Say cheese

On every truckle of 'Real Yorkshire Wensleydale' that comes out of the **Wensleydale Creamery** at Hawes Dairy (www.wensleydale.co.uk) is the image of a dalesman with a trilby hat and a clay pipe. That's Kit Calvert who died in 1962 and is the man credited with saving Wensleydale cheese from extinction. When Hawes Dairy was threatened with closure, Calvert, a dairy farmer himself, galvanised local farmers and together they persuaded the creditors to keep it open.

English farmhouse cheesemaking made a striking recovery after wartime rationing and Milk Marketing Board diktats effectively killed it off. Today, after a perilous era, the Yorkshire Dales are once again synonymous with quality cheeses. Wensleydale cheese, like Cheshire or Lancashire, is one of our nine 'territorials': a classic English cheese. Add in Swaledale, Ribblesdale, Cotherstone and Yorkshire Blue, and North Yorkshire has a cheese board to shout about.

The standard bearer for the revival was the Richard II Wensleydale, made by Suzanne Stirke on her Bedale farm. Now that it's sourced in Lancashire the strong contender for the most traditional Dales cheese is **Lacey's** (www.laceyscheese.co.uk), made by the hyper-purist Simon Lacey. You can watch him make it by hand in his creamery at the impressively regenerated Richmond railway station (*see p81*). Using hand-cranked machinery to cut the curds and stones to press it, he freely admits that he doesn't obtain the consistency of commercial cheese. Sometimes it's softer, sometimes it's saltier – but that's the point, the human dimension.

Lacey learned cheesemaking with the **Swaledale Cheese Company** (www.swaledale cheese.co.uk) in Richmond – the traditional cow's milk Swaledale is its flagship cheese. Further north, Teesdale is the home of **Cotherstone** cheese. Joan Cross only makes a small amount but it's worth the search because it's soft, buttery and delicious, a unique cheese. To the west, the reliable **Ribblesdale** goat's and ewe's milk cheeses are made high up in the Pennines by the Hill family at Horton in Ribblesdale.

Yorkshire Blue comes from a different tradition to the moist, creamy white cheese that Kit Calvert championed. When the French Cistercian monks set up in Wensleydale in the 12th century at Jervaulx Abbey they bred sheep and made soft blue-veined cheese. Those origins are echoed by Judy Bell's excellent range of blues from her family enterprise,

the **Shepherd's Purse Creamery** (www. shepherdspurse.co.uk), near Thirsk.

You can find several of these cheeses in London food halls but of course they're best discovered in a Dales pub or bought from a village shop.

Where to buy Yorkshire cheese
Campbell's 4 Commercial Square, Leyburn (01969 624391/www.campbellsofleyburn.co.uk)
Elijah Allen & Son Market Place, Hawes (01969 667219)
Joneva's 7 Market Place, Masham (01765 689021/www.joneva.com)
Lacey's The Station, Richmond (01748 828264/www.laceyscheese.co.uk)
Lewis & Cooper 92 High Street, Northallerton (01609 772880/www.lewisandcooper.co.uk)
Post Office Barnard Castle, Cotherstone (01833 650255)
Village Store Muker (01748 886409/ www.mukervillage.co.uk)
Wensleydale Creamery Gayle Lane, Hawes (01969 667664/www.wensleydale.co.uk)
West End Stores 1 Reeth Road, Richmond (01748 822305)

Brewery tour aside, be sure to check out the bistro and bar – or the baa..r as they wittily call it – for good solid British fare and Black Sheep beer on tap. Lamb shanks in beer or pork fillet and black pudding come at lunch; tea and cakes are available morning and afternoon; and from Thursday to Saturday the bistro opens for dinner, with more elaborate dishes like crispy duck confit in port and plum sauce, or chicken stuffed with wensleydale cheese.

Blue Lion

Wensleydale *East Witton, nr Leyburn (01969 624273/www.thebluelion.co.uk). Open noon-2.15pm, 7-9.15pm daily. £££. British.*
Once a cobwebbed old boozer, now a charming country inn, with a cosy vibe reinforced by terrific food. Local meat, game and fresh fish dominate the blackboards. Steaming broths and crisp-topped venison pies come whizzing out of the kitchen on to mismatched oak tables to be enjoyed with a selection from the grown-up wine list or Black Sheep on tap. The dining rooms and little back bar are fine, but for atmosphere and gossip bag a Windsor chair by the fire in the homely main bar and tuck in. *See also p88.*

Burlington Restaurant

Wharfedale *Devonshire Arms Country House Hotel, Bolton Abbey (01756 718111/www.devonshire hotels.co.uk). Open noon-9.30pm Mon-Sat; noon-3pm Sun. £££. Modern European.*
Long established as one of Yorkshire's top-rated, Michelin starred restaurants. Be prepared for a smooth-as-silk operation at the Burlington, from the masterly front of house performance to Steve Smith's precise, intensely flavoured dishes. If elaborate, seven-plus-course menus are your thing try the Menu Prestige tasting menu. Sister operation, the Devonshire Arms has a world-famous cellar too *(see below).*

CB Inn

Arkengarthdale *Langthwaite (01748 884567/ www.cbinn.co.uk). Open noon-2pm, 6.30-9pm daily. £££. Modern European.*
The menu, written up daily in the bar, is enticingly ambitious. Rabbit consommé or wild mushroom ravioli, perhaps, followed by lamb shank with fondant potatoes, savoy cabbage and confit of garlic and juniper jus. Occasionally the truffled edges are too much, but the warm vibe more than makes up for it. The lovely long bar has exposed beams, Dales history on the walls and a log fire. This inn was once failing and forgotten; now it thrives again. *See also p88.*

Cavendish Pavilion

Wharfedale *Bolton Abbey (01756 710245/ www.cavendishpavilion.co.uk). Open Winter 10am-4.30pm daily. Summer 10am-5pm daily. ££. Café.*
It's hard to beat this lovely Victorian tea pavilion down by the Wharfe when it comes to location and value. It's self-service, with meals, sandwiches, tea and cakes. You can eat beneath the rafters inside or alfresco on the terrace. After paddling in the Wharfe a visit to the ice-cream parlour is essential.

Devonshire Brasserie

Wharfedale *Devonshire Arms Country House Hotel, Bolton Abbey (01629 733259/www.devonshire hotels.co.uk). Open noon-9.30pm daily. £££. Brasserie.*
The polar opposite of the finesse dining and formality of its sister restaurant, the Burlington *(see above)*, the sunny and easygoing Brasserie is perfect for a family lunch or dinner: popular dishes include the likes of confit of pork belly, moules marinière, Goosnargh chicken, local sausage and chive mash, risotto and fish and chips. Decor is vibrant and bright, defined by Howard Hodgkin prints. *See also p88.*

Devonshire Fell Hotel & Restaurant

Wharfedale *Burnsall (01756 729000/www. devonshirefell.co.uk). Open noon-2.30pm, 6.30-9pm daily. ££££. Modern European.*
Originally a club for gentlemen mill owners, the fusty old Fell was transformed by the Duchess of Devonshire into a stylish hotel and restaurant. The conservatory dining room exploits brilliant Wharfedale views of limestone fells, the River Wharfe and Burnsall's five-arched bridge. Soak them up with Dan Birk's exceptional cooking. Wood pigeon breast on Bury black pudding with celeriac purée, or local venison with glazed root vegetables, are delicately – even minimally – presented. Those after heartier dishes can find the likes of gammon and eggs and bangers and mash in the bar. *See also p88.*

Falcon Inn

Wharfedale *Arncliffe (01756 770205). Open noon-2pm daily. £. No credit cards. Pub.*
This untouched time-warp pub overlooking the village green is a Dales inn, pure and simple. Nothing's ostensibly changed in 50 years, through four generations of the Miller family; even the beer is poured from porcelain jugs.

Fountaine Inn

Wharfedale *Linton (01756 752210/www.fountaineinn atlinton.co.uk). Open noon-9pm daily. £££. International.*
This popular dining pub has a long, family-friendly menu featuring just about everything from garlic mushrooms to duck in orange sauce, via lasagne, fish and chips and tasty sandwiches.

Frenchgate Hotel

Swaledale *59 Frenchgate, Richmond (01748 822087/ www.thefrenchgate.co.uk). Open noon-2pm, 7-9.30pm daily. ££££. Modern British.*
The dining room revels in mismatched furniture, idiosyncratic lighting and a short, interesting menu that on our visit produced excellent roast cod served with cockles and mussels in a sherry and wild garlic vinaigrette and a vanilla bean and gin pannacotta dessert.

Muker Village Stores & Teashop

Swaledale *Muker (01748 886409/www.muker village.co.uk). Open Winter 11am-5pm Mon-Fri. Summer 11am-5pm Mon, Wed-Sun. £. Tearoom.*
A near obligatory stop on the Keld circular walk. Nothing fancy, just sandwiches, home-made cakes, pots of tea and a blessed fire in winter.

Old Hill Inn

Ribblesdale *Chapel-le-Dale, Ingleton (01524 241256/ www.oldhillinn.co.uk). Open noon-2.30pm, 6.30-8.45pm Tue-Fri; 6.30-8.45pm Sat; noon-3pm, 6-8.45pm Sun. £££. Pub.*

Sitting in the daunting shadows of Ingleborough and Whernside, this ancient inn has long given sanctuary to walkers descending Yorkshire's two highest peaks. Reviving comfort comes from big fires, hot chocolate and hearty dishes of steak pie and lamb shank served at rough-hewn tables in the bar or in the low, cosy dining room. Wherever you eat, local Dent Brewery bitter makes a great accompaniment. Dessert invariably comes with an elaborate spun sugar creation – the chef is an award-winning sugar sculptor. There are also two clean and simple bedrooms with en-suite bathrooms.

Overton House Café

Swaledale *Reeth High Row, Reeth (01748 884332/ www.overtonhousecafe.co.uk). Open 11am-3pm Wed; 11am-2.30pm, 6-10pm Thur, Sat; 10am-2.30pm, 6-10pm Fri. £££. Café/modern European.*

Prettily decorated, set by the village green, and much more than a mere café. By day seafood chowder and scallop gratin sit alongside bacon sarnies and smoked salmon scrambled egg. Evenings gear up with roast cod and mussels, sea bass in hazelnut butter, and assiette of pork with apple and chorizo and more. A private dining room caters for pre-booked tables of eight.

Punch Bowl Inn

Swaledale *Low Row, Richmond (01748 886 233/ www.pbinn.co.uk). Open noon-2pm, 6.30-9pm daily. £££. Pub.*

A long bar with simple scrubbed tables, the menu written up on a mirror, tables outside in summer and the emphasis on modern Yorkshire food: the Punch Bowl is a proto-gastropub for these parts, not perfect but raising the bar amid many Dales pub kitchens that are still in the dark ages. The convivial bar is a hub for visitors and locals. Upstairs, there's accommodation in the form of fresh, smart bedrooms with sweeping views over Swaledale.

Red Lion

Arkengarthdale *Langthwaite (01748 884218). Open 11am-3pm, 7-11pm daily. £. Pub.*

'Will gentlemen please remove their caps at the bar' reads the sign on the door of this time-warp village pub. Inside are swirly red carpets, lace curtains and a bar that stocks Riggwelter ale, honey, maps, ice-cream, confectionery and books of stamps. It has featured in various films and in the *All Creatures Great and Small* TV series. Bar snacks are also available.

Samuel's Restaurant

Wensleydale *Swinton Park, Masham (01765 680900/ www.swintonpark.com). Open 7.30-10am, 12.30-2pm, 7-9.30pm Mon-Thur, Sun; 7.30-10am, 12.30-2pm, 7-10pm Fri, Sat. ££££. Modern European.*

It will come as no surprise, given the rarefied surrounds of Swinton Park, that this restaurant offers high-end dining.

Menu descriptions like 'brill and Asian spiced belly pork' or 'braised beef, mushrooms and foie gras' hardly do justice to Simon Crannage's highly wrought, technically proficient dishes. Lunch is £24, the three-course à la carte starts at £42; prices are higher for the tasting and signature menus. Top-class ingredients are sourced locally and fruit and vegetables come from the restaurant's own walled garden. This is food to inspire. Rosemary Shrager's excellent cookery school also operates here.

Sandpiper Inn

Wensleydale *Market Place, Leyburn (01969 622206/ www.sandpiperinn.co.uk). Open noon-2.30pm, 6.30-9pm Mon-Fri; noon-2.30pm, 6.30-9.30pm Sat; noon-2pm, 6.30-9.30pm Sun. £££. British.*

This lovely stone-built inn in the centre of town has a cosy interior for warm winter evenings and a sunny terrace for summer. Old-school fish and chips, ham and eggs and sandwiches are served at lunch; there's the likes of pheasant, fish pie, steaks and stuffed aubergine at dinner: simple robust food that fits the bill after a day's Dale walking. There are a couple of bedrooms too.

Seasons Restaurant & Café Bar

Swaledale *The Station, Station Yard, Richmond (01748 850123/www.restaurant-seasons.co.uk). Open 9am-11pm Mon-Sat; 9am-7pm Sun. ££. Modern European.*

The dramatically restored railway station has an all-day café serving sandwiches, pizzas, plates to share, salads and simple dishes like sausage and mash. The evening menu reflects the seasons – wintery dishes include slow-braised shin of beef or barley broth with melted cheese croutons, and Lacey's excellent cheese.

Stoneclose Tearoom & Guest House

Dentdale *Main Street, Dent (01539 625231). Open noon-5pm Tue-Sun. £. No credit cards. Tearoom.*

A long-established tearoom in the centre of the village of Dent, serving good tea and home-made cakes and occasional special dinners. Cyclists and walkers can collect packed lunches. There are also B&B facilities.

Vennells

Wensleydale *7 Silver Street, Masham (01765 689000/www.vennellsrestaurant.co.uk). Open 7.15-11.30pm Tue-Sat; noon-2pm Sun. ££. Modern European.*

The modest shopfront belies the classy goings-on inside this smart, little family operation just off the market square. Jon Vennell's short, elegant menu has beef carpaccio or scallop ravioli to start followed by fish of the day or his signature soft and succulent roast belly of pork on mustard mash. The three-course menus at around £17.50 are outstanding value.

White Swan Hotel & Restaurant

Wensleydale *Middleham (01969 622093/www.white swanhotel.co.uk). Open 8am-9.30pm daily. £££. Pub.*

Sister to the Blue Lion at East Witton (*see p85*), this is even more informal – and cheaper. There's a cosy flagstoned bar with wood-burning stove and Black Sheep and Theakston's

Devonshire Arms,
Wharfedale.

on tap. Next door the brasserie is quietly contemporary with a menu to match: pizzas, pasta dishes as well as Blue Lion favourites like slow braised leg of lamb and a fabulous liquorice terrine for pud. *See also p89.*

Yorke Arms
Nidderdale *Ramsgill (01423 755243/www.yorke-arms.co.uk). Open noon-1.45pm, 7-9pm Mon-Sat; noon-1.45pm, 7-8pm Sun. ££££. Modern European.*
In the kitchen, proprietor and Michelin-starred chef Frances Atkins puts together sophisticated dishes crammed with seasonal Yorkshire produce. There's Yorkshire game, Whitby crab, Nidderdale mallard, leg of hare, beignet of Yorkshire blue cheese, and vegetables and herbs from the garden. This beautiful 18th-century coaching inn also has luxurious rooms, with four-poster beds, elegant bathrooms, beamed ceilings and fabulous views.

Stay

Good-quality accommodation is also available in some inns listed in the Eat section, including the **Angel Inn** (*see p82*), the **Punch Bowl Inn** (*see p86*) and the **Yorke Arms** (*see above*).

Austwick Hall
Ribblesdale *Austwick, Settle (01524 251794/www.austwickhall.co.uk). £££.*
For an over-the-top blow-out, it's hard to beat this gorgeous country house in 12 acres of superb garden (it's a member of the National Garden Scheme). Five large, individually furnished, indulgent bedrooms are stuffed with antiques. And there are various kinds of beds: four posters, half testers, old oak. Bathrooms are equally glamorous. Downstairs, curl up on comfy sofas with log fires, stone-flagged floors and scattered Turkish rugs. Michael Pearson cooks hearty breakfasts and elegant five-course dinners. No children.

Blue Lion
Wensleydale *East Witton, nr Leyburn (01969 624273/www.thebluelion.co.uk). £££.*
This handsome ivy-covered house in an immaculately manicured village is much loved – a model country pub with 15 en-suite rooms that are comfortable and homely without affecting glam or pretensions. Downstairs are dining rooms and an atmospheric old bar where stone-flagged floors, oak settles and a log fire guarantee a glow in the cheeks even before tucking into the excellent food, wine and beer. *See also p85.*

Burgoyne Hotel
Swaledale *On the Green, Reeth (01748 884292/www.theburgoyne.co.uk). £££.*
A sturdy traditional hotel overlooking the village green. There are nine plush bedrooms, of which Redmire and Marrick are the most luxurious. Warm fires and comfy lounges – and on sunny evenings the lovely lawned garden to the front – provide the right backdrop for relaxing before working through the daily changing four-course dinner menu.

CB Inn
Arkengarthdale *Richmond (01748 884567/www.cbinn.co.uk). £££.*
The Charles Bathurst is a charming old roadside inn with 19 en-suite rooms furnished country-style with brass bedsteads, old pine and bits of antiquery. Informal, comfortable and popular, the lively bar is the best of a string of dining areas on the premises, with an extensive menu. *See also p85.*

Dales Bike Centre
Swaledale *Fremington (01748 884908/www.dalesmountainbiking.co.uk). £.*
Warm, clean and simple two- and four-bunk bedded rooms for cyclists are housed in two newly restored barns. There's a shop, a café, bike hire, bike repair, cycle holidays, even showers for day visitors.

Devonshire Arms Country House Hotel
Wharfedale *Bolton Abbey (01756 718111/www.devonshirehotels.co.uk). ££££.*
The Devonshire Arms is country house hotel living *par excellence*: the ultimate in comfort and luxury, from the helicopter pad to the art collection, from fishing rods to flat-screen TVs. Guests can borrow a mountain bike, work out in the pool and spa, or sink into the sofas as armies of staff glide around with drinks, menus and trays of fine china tea. *See also p85.*

Devonshire Fell Hotel & Restaurant
Wharfedale *Burnsall (01756 729000/www.devonshirefell.co.uk). £££.*
Sister hotel to the swankier Devonshire Arms (*see above*), the Fell is more modest, more relaxed, but equally well located. Positioned high above the village of Burnsall, it has magnificent views and ten contemporary, smartly styled rooms with all the usual comforts. Food is good too: be sure to order Dan Birk's one hour 'poached' egg with Parma ham and truffle oil. Guests have free use of the spa and pool at the Devonshire Arms to work it off. *See also p85.*

George Inn
Wharfedale *Hubberhome (01756 760223/www.thegeorge-inn.co.uk). ££.*
A long-revered cosy inn by the river crossing in the tiny hamlet of Hubberholme. Whitewashed outside, it has rough stone walls inside with log fires, and tankards and horse brasses aplenty. By tradition a candle burns in the window whenever the bar is open. Bedrooms are clean and simple and food is unpretentious pub grub.

Grinton Youth Hostel
Swaledale *Grinton, Richmond (0845 371 9636/www.yha.org.uk). £.*
A handsome old shooting lodge set above the village sleeps 59 in a variety of family bunk rooms. The Salt House annexe takes 12. Both can be hired for exclusive use.

Littlebank House
Ribblesdale *Rathmell, Settle (01729 822330/www.littlebankbandb.co.uk). ££.*

They'll even stable your horse at this beautiful stone-built B&B tucked away in a wooded valley south of Settle. Thickly carpeted bedrooms, rich drapes, chandeliers, and roll-top baths make for sumptuous relaxation after walking, cycling or riding on the nearby ten-mile Settle Loop.

Millgate House
Swaledale *Millgate (01748 823571/ www.millgatehouse.com). £££. No credit cards.*
An upmarket Georgian B & B with spacious rooms stuffed with antiques, stylish bathrooms, a pretty garden and delicious breakfasts. The self-catering Garden Apartment sleeps two and the Coach House (book through English Country Cottages, 0845 268 0788, www.english-country-cottages.co.uk, reference KTN) sleeps ten.

Swinton Park
Wensleydale *Masham (01765 680900/ www.swintonpark.com). ££££.*
Amid sweeping lawns, castellated Swinton Park is fit for a Hollywood feature film. The castle has 200 acres of landscaped grounds, including a falconry centre, a deer park and lakes with swans. Indoors, 30 rooms provide every comfort – from the merely grand to suites fit for royalty, fitted out with everything from turreted bathrooms to dog beds. All this luxury comes at a price of course.

Wensleydale Heifer
Wensleydale *West Witton (01969 622322/ www.wensleydaleheifer.co.uk). £££.*

They like a joke at the Heifer – which turns out to have a fish restaurant. The nine bedrooms in this jolly country inn are all themed – so the Chocolate room is full of chocolate bars, the Black Sheep room has bottles of Black Sheep beer, the Middleham racing room gets the *Racing Post,* and so on. Happily, the rooms are also smart and comfortable, with Molton Brown toiletries, Egyptian cotton sheets and soft white towels.

White Swan Hotel & Restaurant
Wensleydale *Middleham (01969 622093/ www.whiteswanhotel.co.uk). ££.*
Sister to the Blue Lion at East Witton (*see p85*), this forgotten old pub in the centre of Middleham has been cleverly whipped into contemporary shape. There are 17 rooms, all with en-suite bedrooms. The food is recommended. See also p86.

Yorebridge House
Wensleydale *Bainbridge (01969 652060/ www.yorebridgehouse.co.uk). ££££.*
For a totally glamorous stay, book yourself into the lovely Yorebridge House, a former schoolhouse converted into a boutique hotel with seven ultra-smart rooms done out in shades of white and taupe. The hot tubs are particularly welcome to soothe those aching limbs after those arduous walks in the hills. A five-course gourmet dinner is offered every night; excellent local beef and lamb and good fish feature on the menu, but vegetarians can challenge the kitchen.

Factfile

When to go
Any time of year is a good time to visit the Dales as they are beautiful all-year-round. Summer is the busiest time to visit but also gives you the opportunity to attend a village agricultural show or one of the many arts festivals. June to mid-July is the prime time for viewing the wildflower hay meadows in flower. Grassington's Dickensian Festival runs for three Saturdays before Christmas.

Getting there
Public transport times and routes are limited in the Dales. Dales Bus (www.dalesbus.org) puts on additional services in the summer. The wonderful Settle–Carlisle railway is well worth taking, just for the journey. Combine it with bikes, taxis and car. The most practical way to reach the Dales is by car via the Dales 'gateways': Ilkley to explore the southern dales, and Richmond for Swaledale and the northern dales. Useful websites are www.travel dales.org.uk and www.yorkshiretravel.net.

Getting around
The best way to enjoy the Dales is to be out among the hills and dales either on foot, by bike or on horseback, using some of the 500 miles of bridleways and green lanes. There are numerous guides and maps available from the National Park information centres. Walks can also be downloaded from the National Park website www.yorkshiredales.org.uk. They also provide information for wheelchair users and less mobile visitors includes barrier-free trails and viewpoints.

Tourist information
There are five Yorkshire Dales National Park Information Centres: at **Aysgarth Falls** (01969 662910), **Grassington** (Hebden Road, 01756 751690), **Hawes** (Dales Countryside Museum, 01969 666210), **Malham** (01969 652 380) and **Reeth** (The Green, 01748 884059). **All** open Winter 10am-4pm daily. Summer 10am-5pm daily.
  The following organisations also have useful information on their websites: Yorkshire Dales National Park (www.yorkshiredales.org.uk); Yorkshire Dales & Harrogate Tourism Partnership (www.yorkshiredales.org); Yorkshire Tourist Board (www.yorkshire.com); Out of Oblivion (www.outofoblivion.org.uk); The Dales Way (www.dalesway.org.uk).

Top & left: Habourside;
top right: Clifton
Suspension Bridge;
bottom right:
Cabot Circus.

Bristol

Laid-back port city with a gritty trading past and a bright cultural future.

From Clifton's Georgian elegance to the edgy street art of Stokes Croft and the bustle of modern Harbourside – there are several Bristols. None are as picture-perfect as Bath, its chocolate-box neighbour upriver, but Bristol is a different deal: a complete, diverse city, with a big commercial (slavery-stained) and maritime history.

At the same time it is a city whose greatest asset may be its laid-back vibe. Stroll through north Bristol, say, and you'll be rewarded with delights as varied as Brunel's magnificent suspension bridge in Clifton, Banksy's famous *Mild Mild West* graffiti (recently voted Bristol's favourite alternative landmark) and the sight of dozens of hot air balloons drifting lazily over the tops of ice-cream-coloured houses, or across the hills beyond the city. Down at the docks, meanwhile, you'll find bars, restaurants and contemporary art alongside the twin stars of Bristol's maritime past: the reproduction of John Cabot's ship *The Matthew*, and Brunel's SS *Great Britain*.

This is Bristol's public face. But if you have time, venture east or south of the river to the vibrant suburbs of Easton, Totterdown, Windmill Hill and Southville: all have lively local scenes, with music gigs in many of the pubs, cool cafés and galleries and, as always, street art in abundance.

Explore

Although the city is compact, Bristol's many hills and the serpentine nature of the Avon can make orientation a challenge. Joining one of the many sightseeing tours (www.visitbristol.co.uk or Bristol Sightseeing Tours 0870 444 0654, www.city-sightseeing.com) is an excellent way to get a sense of the city's geography as well as its history.

HARBOURSIDE

A stroll or ferry trip around Bristol's Harbourside will give you a real sense of the city's maritime past. Start at the **Arnolfini** (*see p103*), a leading arts centre with a bar, gallery, cinema and shop. Outside sits a pensive-looking statue of the Genoese explorer John Cabot, who set out from Bristol in 1497 and discovered Newfoundland. From here, either cross the narrow swing bridge and follow the tracks of the old steam railway along the docks, past new designer apartment complexes, to the **SS Great Britain** (*see p94*), or hop on a **Number Seven Boat Trip** ferry (0117 929 3659, www.numbersevenboat trips.co.uk) for a chance to see the city from the water.

Unaccompanied adults may find the super-abundance of levers, buttons, screens and pulleys at **Explore-At-Bristol** more than a little overwhelming, but for families this place is a rainy day godsend, and educational too. Afterwards, cross the river and take a stroll among the water features, skateboarders and statues in **Millennium Square**.

Explore-At-Bristol

Harbourside *Anchor Road (0845 345 1235/www.at-bristol.org.uk). Open 10am-5pm Mon-Fri; 10am-6pm Sat, Sun, school & bank hols. Last entry 1hr before closing. Admission £10.80; £7-£9 reductions.*
Explore-At-Bristol has done much to engage young minds with science and is hugely popular with local children, many of whom have membership and pop in after school. In 2009 the museum's excellent permanent collection is expanding, with the arrival of 30 new hands-on science experiments from the USA, including a turbulent orb, a cloud chamber and best of all a giant soap bubble big enough to encase an adult. Once you're done with the experiments, head to the planetarium and marvel at the wonder of the winter sky at night.

SS Great Britain & Matthew

Harbourside *Great Western Dockyard, Gas Ferry Road (0117 926 0680/www.ssgreatbritain.org). Open Apr-Oct 10am-5.30pm daily. Nov-Jan 10am-4pm daily. Feb, Mar 10am-4.30pm daily. Admission £10.95; £5.95-£8.50 reductions.*
Designed by Isambard Kingdom Brunel, the SS *Great Britain* was the first ocean-going ship to be constructed of iron and driven by a propeller (rather than paddles). It is now housed in a dry dock – visitors can descend under the glass 'sea' for a view of the ship's formidable hull. The

0   50 miles

Bristol

Bristol

Historic sites
● ● ● ● ●

Art & architecture
● ● ● ● ●

Hotels
● ● ● ● ●

Eating & drinking
● ● ● ● ●

Nightlife
● ● ● ● ●

Shopping
● ● ● ● ●

Top: Millenium Square; left: Ashton Court; right: Avon Gorge.

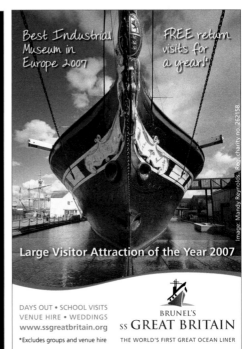

museum houses an excellent, and at times moving, exhibition that charts the ship's story from its construction and launch in 1843 to near decay. Aboard the ship, passengers' living quarters, from first class to the cramped steerage section, are preserved. Moored alongside the *Great Britain* is a life-size and working replica of John Cabot's boat, the touchingly small and fragile-looking *Matthew* (0117 927 6868, www.matthew.co.uk). Built in 1997 to commemorate the 500-year anniversary of Cabot's Atlantic crossing, the *Matthew* now offers a range of harbour cruises including the popular two-hour trip, with fish and chips thrown in.

PARK STREET & CITY CENTRE

Standing on College Green, at the bottom of Park Street, **Bristol Cathedral** (College Green, 0117 926 4879, www.bristol-cathedral.co.uk) is one of the most magnificent examples of a hall church – one with nave and side aisles of around equal height – anywhere in the world, and the only one of its kind in the UK. Founded in 1140 as part of an Augustinian monastery, the Cathedral has been slowly added to over the centuries, the abstract stained-glass windows depicting the Holy Spirit being the most recent additions.

A walk up Park Street – where the sight of skateboarders hurtling downhill through the traffic is not uncommon – leads to Great George Street, which runs along the bottom of Brandon Hill, the oldest park in Bristol. Here you can step back in time at the **Georgian House** (7 Great George Street, 0117 921 1362; open 10am-5pm Mon-Wed, Sat, Sun; admission free), and explore one of the best preserved interiors of this period. Continue along Great George Street to **Brandon Hill Park** and **Cabot Tower**. Built in 1897 to mark the 400th anniversary of Cabot's voyage to Newfoundland the tower is 105 feet tall and visible from many parts of the city. Not surprisingly the view from the top is breathtaking, and well worth the arduous climb. The formal flower beds and pretty ponds that surround the tower are a good place to picnic on summer days.

In Queen's Road is the towering **Wills Memorial Building**, built in 1915 by Sir George Oatley in grand Gothic Revival style, and now part of Bristol University. Next door is the **City Museum & Art Gallery**, home to an interesting permanent collection including Egyptian mummies, dinosaurs and old masters; there is also a decent café and shop. The **Royal West Of England Academy** (*see p103*) is nearby and has a permanent art collection as well as some small temporary exhibitions, such as the BP Portrait Show and the British Art Show.

On Park Row, the **Red Lodge** (0117 921 1360; open 10am-5pm Mon-Wed, Sat; admission free) is a wonderful Elizabethan house with oak-lined rooms and a Tudor knot garden.

Bristol's City Museum & Art Gallery

West End *Queen's Road (0117 922 3571/ www.bristol.gov.uk/museums). Open 10am-5pm daily. Admission free.*
Housed in a magnificent Edwardian building, a gift to the city from Sir William Henry Wills in 1905, the museum comprises 19 galleries on three floors, with collections spanning areas from prehistory to local history and natural history, and including Egyptology, European art, silver and ceramics. It also runs an impressive programme of temporary exhibitions, including touring shows from important national collections. Small World, next to the café, is a godsend for parents: you can relax with a coffee and watch from a comfortable distance while your children play, read or dress up in an enclosed area.

CLIFTON

With its grand crescents and elegant Georgian architecture, it's easy to see why Clifton remains one of Bristol's most desirable neighbourhoods. **Royal York Crescent**, perched high above the Avon Gorge, stretches in a wide arc for a quarter of a mile, making it the longest Georgian crescent in the UK. At the heart of the district, picturesque **Clifton Village** is filled with bijou boutiques, traditional shops, cafés, restaurants and pastel-coloured terraces.

Close by is Brunel's **Clifton Suspension Bridge** (0117 974 4664, www.clifton-suspension-bridge.org.uk), which spans the gorge 245 feet above the Avon. The **Camera Obscura** (0117 974 1242) on Clifton Down offers spectacular 360-degree views of the bridge, the gorge, the downs and the city. For those feeling brave enough, a tunnel leads from the Camera Obscura to **St Vincent's Cave**, also known as the Giant's Cave, which opens out on to a viewing platform suspended 250 feet up the cliff face.

On the other side of the bridge, Ashton Court and Leigh Woods offer opportunities for walks and cycling. A Sunday walk in Ashton Court is not complete without a visit to the **Ashton Court Estate Miniature Steam Railway** (0117 946 7110, www.bristolmodelengineers.co.uk, Apr-Oct noon-5.30pm Sun), surely the best fun to be had anywhere for 60p, and guaranteed to raise a smile in adults and children alike.

OTHER AREAS

To the north of the city centre, **Stokes Croft** and **Montpelier** have a reputation for being arty, alternative and bohemian. Stokes Croft is certainly the hub of the city's graffiti movement (*see p98*).

Traditionally a working-class area, **Southville**, south of the River Avon, has undergone some regeneration since the 1980s. **Redcliffe** is to the west of **Temple Meads station**, bounded by the Floating Harbour to the north (the River Avon's original course) and the man-made River Avon (New Cut) to the south.

Wall art

Bristol's come a long way since youth worker John Nation offered up the bare walls of Barton Hill Youth Club to novice spray painters in the early 1980s. As the brick walls played host to artists like Cheo and Inkie, a movement that was already gaining momentum in the US started to take hold in the UK.

Initially hampered by growing police interest in the illegal works, especially those of the infamous TUB (The United Bombers) crew, the scene remains as vibrant today as it did back then, and the media and celebrity interest (Brangelina recently shelled out around £200,000 for three Banksy pieces) suggests the south-west's spray painted walls are here to stay.

Stokes Croft is now the hub of the city's activity, with quality graffiti on most hoardings and abandoned buildings in the area. However, it is threatened by the city's regeneration drive – which started with new super-dooper shopping mall Cabot Circus and is quickly spreading from the city to the outskirts, threatening to swallow up one paint-splattered brick at a time.

Local group the People's Republic of Stokes Croft (www.prsc.org.uk) has declared the area 'Bristol's Cultural Quarter' and is trying to encourage sustainable development and improvement through street art. The group's Peephole Gallery is a set of hoardings at 27-33 Jamaica Street, which are whitewashed over every month, so that budding artists have a space on which to express their new ideas.

To tick off some of the city's key pieces, stand opposite the Jamaica Street/Cheltenham Road junction for a glimpse of Banksy's *Mild Mild West* (anarchic teddy threatens the plod with a Molotov cocktail), or head out of the area to Park Street for *Window Lovers* (naked adulterer hangs from a window ledge) next to uber-cool skate shop Fifty Fifty. Take a stroll along Gloucester Road and you'll soon spot 45RPM's trademark owls, or the domed temples and acid brights of Sickboy.

For your own personal (and permanent) piece visit Friend & Co (8 The Promenade, Gloucester Road, www.friend-and-co.blogspot.com), a small independent gallery set up by Portishead's Geoff Barrow, which sells canvases and prints by local artists Mr Jago and 45RPM, or venture online to www.art-el.co.uk or www.1loveart.com to find work by Milk and Dora – Bristol's burgeoning female artist contingent.

For news on fresh pieces, the web blog http://bristolgraffiti.wordpress.com browses

the city's boards for overnight activity, photographs it for prosperity and apportions praise/blame to the artist responsible. It's also a good resource for upcoming events listings or information on art sales. And to learn more about a movement that has helped invigorate parts of the city previously deemed untouchable, search out Felix Braun's *Children of Can: 25 Years of Bristol Graffiti*, an encyclopaedic tome complete with glossy pictures of works that have since been sprayed over time and time again.

Eat

Bell's Diner
Montpelier *1-3 York Road (0117 924 0357/www.bells diner.com). Open 7-10pm Mon; noon-2pm, 7-10pm Tue-Sat. £££. Global.*
Established in 1976 by chef Christopher Wicks, this tasteful bistro in a former grocer's has quite rightly been lauded by every restaurant guide and broadsheet worth the paper it's printed on. The relaxed and intimate atmosphere belies the fact that not a single corner has been nudged, let alone cut – evident in everything from the crisp white tablecloths to the sort of impeccable, unobtrusive service that makes you understand that there's so much more to waitressing than slapping down someone's dinner without spilling it. Food-wise, it's cutting-edge combinations of the highest-quality ingredients with influences from across Europe, Asia and beyond. Visit Monday to Thursday and you can give your tastebuds the time of their lives with the £45 tasting menu, which includes such Blumenthal-esque items as hot potato foam and vinadaloo ice-cream.

Budokan
Clifton *Clifton Down Shopping Centre, Whiteladies Road (0117 949 3030/www.budokan.co.uk). Open noon-2.30pm, 5.30-10pm Mon-Sat. ££. Oriental.*
A more intimate take on Asian communal-style dining, this culinary tour of Japan, Thailand, Malaysia, Indonesia and Singapore still has the picnic-style benches of the high street chains but also has enough space so you don't elbow a fellow diner when slurping on your noodles. Combine this with low lighting and a panoramic second-floor window that looks over busy Whiteladies Road (there's also a city centre branch on Colston Street), and you've got a cheap and cheerful alternative to the Italian dinner-à-deux first date stalwart. Menu-wise, it's a cut above average too – with reliable takes on teriyaki, salt and pepper squid, and a warming Malaysian curry that could easily become your new favourite comfort food.

Casa Mexicana
North Bristol *31 Zetland Road (0117 924 3901/ www.casamexicana.co.uk). Open 6.30-10pm daily. £££.*
A cosy candle-lit Mexican with continental-style seating outside, as well as the obligatory potted cacti and Inca-style gurning face masks once you get through the doors. The menu is inspired by the owner's regular trips to the Yucatan peninsula, so in between the bean-filled burritos and smoked chicken chimichangas you'll find spinach and aubergine tostadas as well as inventive mix and match tapas dishes priced between £2.50 and a fiver.

Fishers
Clifton *35 Princess Victoria Street (0117 974 7044/ www.fishers-restaurant.com). Open noon-2.30pm, 6-10pm Mon, Sun; noon-2.30pm, 6-10.30pm Tue-Sat. £££. Seafood.*
Nautically decked out, this fish restaurant (the clue's in the name) pays homage to the many edible wonders of the sea. Pull up a pew amid the ventilator pipes and portholes for

some of the finest seafood in the city – whether a light bite of pan-fried sardines or a large hot shellfish platter of garlic-slathered langoustines, mussels, clams and king scallops. The place is pretty popular, and despite two floors to play with space is at a premium, so tables are quite closely packed.

Old India
City Centre *34 St Nicholas Street (0117 922 1136/ www.oldindia.co.uk). Open noon-2pm, 6pm-midnight Mon-Sat. ££. Indian.*
The decor's the draw at this colonial-style Indian housed in what was once Bristol's stock exchange. The Victorian-influenced design includes ornate carvings, high ceilings, and toilets with more intricate tiling than a Grecian mosaic. Not to say there's anything wrong with the food – you'll find a good mix of standards alongside more experimental dishes like lamb chops smoked with pomegranate juice, and whole sea bream in a Bengali-style sauce. If you like it hot it's a good plan to mention this while ordering, as the default spice setting is tailored to the more cautious palate.

One Stop Thali Café
Montpelier *12 York Road (0117 942 6687/www.one stopthali.co.uk). Open 6pm-midnight daily. ££. Indian.*
Now sprinkling its exotic mix of Indian spices over Totterdown and Easton, the original branch of this cute and colourful curry cupboard is still turning foolish non-bookers away on a daily basis. There's no dress code, the decor is a jumble of mismatched furniture, hot pink paintwork and glitzy ethnic clutter, and there are only two main courses to choose from (one veggie). But opt for either the southern or northern thali and you'll discover a mixture of authentic dishes inspired by the roadside cafés of India and served on a compartmentalised platter reminiscent of your school dinner tray. Cheap, cheerful and a million times better than whatever you've been ordering from your local takeaway all these years.

River Station Bar + Kitchen
Harbourside *The Grove (0117 914 4434/www.river station.co.uk). Open noon-2.30pm, 6-10.30pm Mon-Thur; noon-2.30pm, 6-11pm Fri-Sat; noon-3pm, 6-9pm Sun. ££££. Modern European.*
A two-storey edifice of light and space, with a dock-side terrace that was made for summer dining, the jutting glass and steel here has won as much praise from aesthetics and architecture fans as the food has racked up industry awards. From the team behind Bell's Diner (*see right*), the carte dishes up similarly experimental concoctions, but this time with a Mediterranean influence – ox cheek ravioli, roast quail with risotto, fillet of wild sea bass – while lighter bites like fish cakes, risotto and mezze platters are available in the bar. Prefer a liquid lunch? Even the cocktail menu shows flare – fig and vanilla daiquiri anyone?

Rocatillos
Clifton *Queens Row, Triangle South (0117 929 7207). Open 8am-5pm Mon-Wed; 8am-11pm Thur-Sat; 10am-5pm Sun. ££. American.*
So the US may have pipped us at the post as far as theme parks and child obesity are concerned, but this '50s-style

diner is working hard to beat America at its own game where milkshakes are concerned. From old classics like strawberry and vanilla, to calorific concoctions such as Dime Bar, peanut butter and mint choc chip, there are over 12 varieties of the dairy delight to choose from, and the true connoisseur can ask for their order thick, extra thick, or with a hearty squirt of whipped cream on top. In between overdosing on the shaky stuff, you can treat your tummy to a 100%-English fry-up, or Scottish smoked salmon and scrambled eggs, or just admit defeat to our cousins across the pond and order up the biggest burger and fries your gut can stomach.

Taste

City Centre *1-3 Exchange Avenue, St Nicholas Market (0117 927 2988/www.taste.gb.com). Open 8am-5pm daily. ££. Café/British.*

When they're not barbecuing squirrel on local news programmes, the Taste team are sourcing similarly unusual fare for their down-to-earth gastro-café with picnic-style tables on the edge of St Nicholas Market. The on-site fishmonger, butcher and deli supply tasty cuts and experimental chutneys to local foodies, but also to top restaurants like Heston Blumenthal's the Fat Duck and the Ivy. The changing chalkboard is testament to the fresh and seasonal nature of the menu, but you can generally expect breakfast treats like porridge with Drambuie, and heartier fare like spider crab bisque or salt beef with mustard mash for lunch. No squirrel though – yet.

Shop

Bristol has several shopping hubs including a number of old-style high streets serving its many suburbs. Try **Park Street** for studenty club and skate gear; **Clifton** for chic boutiques, and **Whiteladies Road** and its side streets for a mix of independent and specialist shops. The **Gloucester Road** and **Cotham Hill** draw those who like to trawl thrift shops for treasure, while **Upper Maudlin Street**, **Colston Street** and **Christmas Steps** are where you'll find the best craft shops and galleries.

Blaze Gallery

City Centre *84 Colston Street (0117 904 7067/ www.blazestudio.co.uk). Open 10.30am-5.30pm Tue-Sat.*

Established as a co-operative in 2002 by a group of ceramicists, Blaze is studio, shop and gallery space. These days the works on show (and for sale) include textiles and jewellery as well as ceramics and space is given over to up and coming local talent.

Cabot Circus and Broadmead

City Centre *Cabot Circus (www.cabotcircus.com); Broadmead (www.bristolbroadmead.co.uk). Open 9.30am-8pm Mon-Sat; 11am-5pm Sun.*

Cabot Circus, the gleaming £500-million extension to Bristol's drab Broadmead shopping centre, opened its doors

in November 2008 to much excitement. It is here that you will find all the top-end highstreet names such as All Saints and Kurt Geiger, and a sprinkling of designer boutiques such as Ghost and most thrillingly for Bristol's fashionistas, a pocket-size Harvey Nichols (www.harvey nichols.com, 0117 916 8888). When you've finished designer shopping, have lunch at Brasserie Blanc (0117 910 2410, www.brasserieblanc.com), Carluccios (0117 933 8538, www.carluccios.com) or Yo Sushi (www.yosushi.com, 0117 321 3161). The development brought with it a much needed £11-million facelift for Broadmead itself.

Clifton Arcade

Clifton *Boyces Avenue (07831 166979/www.clifton arcade.co.uk). Open 10am-5.30pm Mon-Fri; 9.30am-5.30pm Sat; 11am-4pm Sun.*

Clifton's Victorian shopping arcade, built in 1878, is lined with an interesting mixture of gift shops, antique dealers and quirky designers. An excellent place for an afternoon's window shopping, be sure to visit Bees & Graves (0117 973 8448), for its glorious vintage and contemporary costume jewellery, and Soma (www.somagallery.co.uk, 0117 973 9838), a funky little gallery specialising in contemporary prints, ceramics, textiles and jewellery.

Diana Porter Contemporary Jewellery

West End *33 Park Street (0117 909 0225/ www.dianaporter.co.uk). Open 10.30am-6pm Mon-Sat; 11.30am-4.30pm Sun.*

Having made her name with award-winning wedding and engagement rings, Bristolian designer Diana Porter has recently opened this flagship store in which she also show-cases the work of up-and-coming designers.

Friend & Co

North Bristol *8 The Promenade, Gloucester Road (www.friend-and-co.com). Open 11am-5pm Sat.*

There's barely space to swing a magic marker – never mind a spray can – but this miniature gallery (set up by Tom Friend and Portishead's Geoff Barrow) displays some of the finest graffiti art in town. Recent shows have included works by 45RPM, Mr Jago and Horrors front man Faris Badwan.

Grace & Mabel

Clifton *17 Regent Street (0117 974 3882). Open 10am-5.30pm Mon-Sat; noon-5pm Sun.*

Bright and cheery, like a vintage thrift store, this lovely quirky shop offers a lot of fun in working through its racks. Clothes by the likes of Tara Jarmon, Marlene Birger, Sonia Rykiel and Paul Smith, along with fabulous tweedy Hope & Benson handbags and coin purses designed by the shop's co-owner, Daniela Benson.

Kitestore

Clifton *39A Cotham Hill (0117 974 5010/www. kitestore.co.uk). Open 10am-6pm Mon-Fri; 9.30am-5.30pm Sun.*

If you are planning a trip to the downs, stop here and choose something from the fabulous array of stunt, beginners, and sport kites. Staff are friendly and generous with advice.

Top and right:
Tobacco Factory;
below: Pieminister;
bottom right: Arnolfini.

River Station.

Rag Trade

West End *2 Upper Maudlin Street (0117 376 3085/ www.ragtradeboutique.co.uk). Open 10am-6pm Mon-Sat.*
Owner Cree Jones buys, sells and trades what she describes as 'pre-loved' designer womenswear. Her chic boutique is filled with an ever-changing selection of clothes and accessories by such designers as Vivienne Westwood, Nicole Farhi, D&G and Biba, as well as the likes of Whistles and LK Bennet.

St Nicholas Market

City Centre *Corn Street. Open (Main market) 9.30am-5pm Mon-Sat. (Farmers' market) 8.30am-2.30pm Wed. (Clothes) 10am-5pm Thur. (Crafts & gifts) 10am-5pm Fri, Sat. (Slow food) 10am-3pm 1st Sun of mth.*
It may be just a stone's throw from Broadmead, but St Nick's market is a world away in every other sense: recently voted the UK's greenest market and winner of a 2009 award for speciality markets for its weekly and monthly farmers' markets. Weave your way through the uninspiring crystals, candles and tie-dye to the middle section to find foodie heaven: lots of little restaurants including Pie Minister (www.pieminister.co.uk) are housed in what can only be described as huts alongside excellent food stalls such as The Real Olive Co (0117 954 7480, www.therealolivecompany.co.uk). Indulge your sweet tooth and wallow in nostalgia at Treasure Island Sweets (0117 967 9752, www.treasureislandsweets.co.uk). No trip to the market is complete without popping in to Taste (*see p99*) where you can stock up at the deli counter, have a coffee or better still, lunch.

Snap Gallery

City Centre *20-21 Lower Park Row (0117 376 3564/ www.snapstudio.org.uk). Open 10am-6pm Tue-Sat.*
A charming little gallery space run by a co-operative of excellent print makers or, as they like to say, print-centric artists. Studio space above the gallery is occasionally made available for print-making courses open to the public. Prints are sold both framed and unframed, and artists include Simon Tozer, Tortie Rye and Lucie Sheridan.

Arts

Arnolfini

Harbourside *16 Narrow Quay (0117 917 2300/ www.arnolfini.org.uk). Open 10am-6pm Tue-Sun. Admission free.*
This Harbourside edifice won't win any awards for space-saving – the seemingly endless span of whitewashed gallery space often feels like its crying out for some attention. Having said that, when the walls are covered, it's with thought-provoking stuff such as investigations into how we play or the noises of everyday life. There's a hands-on ethos, too, which might encourage visitors to take glue guns in hand to create their own masterpiece out of broken crockery and abandoned doll heads. The ground-floor bookshop has one of the best alternative reading selections in the city –

with academic and pictorial tomes on everything from Hieronymous Bosch to the *Big Lebowski* jostling for shelf space with that month's art and design mags.

The Royal West of England Academy

West End *Queen's Road (0117 973 5129/www.rwa. org.uk). Open 10am-5.30pm Mon-Sat; 2-5pm Sun. Admission £4; £2.50 reductions.*
If you like your artwork old skool, soak up the sketches and watercolours at this Grade II listed building. This focus point for fine art hosts free temporary exhibitions downstairs and has galleries upstairs displaying a changing selection of works from the permanent collection. There are also events such as artist-led gallery tours, workshops and lectures that run alongside the exhibitions.

Spike Island

Harbourside *133 Cumberland Road (0117 929 2266/ www.spikeisland.org.uk). Open 11am-6pm Tue-Sun. Admission free.*
Despite the seafaring location and a name that sounds like the working title of the next *Pirates of the Caribbean* sequel, this contemporary art and design centre is a bit of an architectural eyesore from the outside, and just that bit too far out of the city centre to attract passing trade – swashbuckling or otherwise. However, nestling inside the smog-sodden brickwork of this former Brook Bond tea packing factory you'll find 80,000sq ft of exhibition, studio and office space dedicated to contemporary local artists. The suitably minimalist ground floor canteen/bar serves up Rainforest Alliance coffee, freshly made cakes, daily papers and free Wi-Fi access. Right on.

Tobacco Factory

Southville *Raleigh Road (0117 902 0344/www. tobaccofactory.com). Open (box office) 10am-6.30pm Mon-Sat. Tickets £5-£20.*
A slice of the city's nicotine-tinged history, this survivor from the Imperial Tobacco site was designed in 1912 by the city's lord mayor Sir Frank Mills (he also did the flamboyantly baroque City Museum & Art Gallery) and saved from demolition by Bristol architect George Ferguson. Now a multi-use arts venue, the slick set-up combines a small theatre, creative industry work space, café bar and oriental bistro, showcasing a much-praised programme of Shakespearean tragedies, intelligent stand-up, engaging children's shows, and performing arts workshops.

Watershed

Harbourside *1 Canons Road (0117 927 5100/ www.watershed.co.uk). Open (box office) 9am-start of final film Mon-Fri; 10am-start of final film Sat, Sun. Tickets £3.50-£6; £4.50 reductions.*
Three screens of alternative cinema with a nice sideline in animation, shorts and the occasional workshop. With such a varied programme, runs for individual films are often short – one to two weeks – so you'll need to get in quickly to see the latest Allen or vintage Kubrick on the big screen, because you're unlikely to find it on

elsewhere in the city. The first-floor café is a fine spot for discussing the merits of Mamet afterwards – that's if you can navigate your way through the pushchair-wielding mob feeding strips of toasted foccacia to the film critics of tomorrow.

Nightlife

Tube

Park Street *1 Unity Street (0117 930 4429/ www.tubebristol.com). Open 10pm-3am Mon, Tue; 10pm-4am Fri, Sat. Admission £3-£10.*
Waving goodbye to the rat race doesn't mean you have to fill your days kicking empty Coke cans around the streets and watching Jeremy Kyle. Just look at DJ Derek, a regular fixture at this basement club tucked off the Park Street thoroughfare. Pushing 70 and resplendent in beige, the Newkie Brown sipping disc spinner jacked in his job as an accountant at Cadbury's to deliver old skool reggae medleys with a sideline in Jamaican patois, despite never having been further south than Bermondsey. The rest of the month, the soundtrack here careers from all things house, to a smattering of hip hop and a soupçon of DnB, all served up in a lounge-like interior with red leather sofas and a postage stamp-sized dancefloor.

Thekla

Harbourside *East Mud Dock, the Grove (0117 929 3301/www.theklabristol.co.uk). Open/admission varies, check website or phone for details.*
All aboard! As if a bar on a boat – which hosts club nights seven days a week – isn't reason enough to visit this Harbourside haven to decadent party behaviour, the eclectic array of events should suit music-lovers of almost every genre (except perhaps country & western). For *Skins*-style debauchery, see Monday's Gorilla Audios, when UWESU's Hub Radio delivers cheap drinks and indie anthems, or get your electro boogaloo on at Thursday's CSS-inspired Death from Above Club. Stood on the deck enjoying a crafty coffin nail? If you lean precariously over the side of this old Baltic coaster you can glimpse the Banksy on the hull – a typically cheery hooded skeleton.

Comedy Box @ Hen & Chicken

Southville *210 North Street (0117 922 3686/ www.thecomedybox.co.uk). Open 7.45-11pm Fri, Sat. Admission varies, check website or phone for details. No credit cards.*
Ricky Gervais and Russell Brand may be able to sell out a stadium in 3.24 seconds, but a draughty auditorium is no match for a candlelit attic room where the stand-up is fresh, raw and so in your face you can see literally see the sweat dripping down the forehead of the unlucky soul whose last gag resulted in a room full of dead air. Not that that often happens here at the Comedy Box, where a considered line-up of circuit stalwarts delivers rapid fire entertainment for the bargain price of a tenner. Booking is a must – and arrive early to sample the excellent pub grub downstairs beforehand.

Dojo Lounge

Clifton *12-16 Park Row (0117 925 1177). Open 10pm-3am Wed, Thur; 11pm-7am Fri, Sat. Admission £5 (may vary according to event).*
A quick poll of anyone who's ever set foot in this late-night den of deep and dirty beats is that it's a 'go hard or go home' kind of place where music and messiness go hand in hand. In fact, stumble out of its doors any time between midnight and 6am and you'll still find a queue of late-night revellers clambering to get in and continue the carnage. The thumping sound system more than fills the limited square footage, and the sweat-sodden walls reverberate to the sounds of DnB, dupstep, progressive, tribal and techno house from high calibre disc-spinners like Fergie, Anil Chawal, Greg Wilson and the Bugged Out crew. Not one for wallflowers.

Start the Bus

City Centre *7-9 Baldwin Street (0117 930 4370/ www.startthebus.tv). Open noon-midnight Mon-Wed, Sun; noon-3am Thur-Sat. Admission varies, check website for details.*
Bounding on to the city centre scene like an energetic toddler, this laidback bar with a serious music policy has an old skool vibe in both the decor – doodle-strewn walls and '70s-style lounging, and the soundtrack – electro, indie and big beats from the likes of Ladyhawke, Andy Votel, and Mr Ouizo. Current highlights include new night No Need To Shout – a showcase of up-and-coming bands and DJs, and Monday's bi-weekly music quiz – the perfect way for musos to start the week.

Stay

Berkeley Square Hotel

Clifton *15 Berkeley Square (0117 925 4000/ www.cliftonhotels.com). £££.*
Located on an imposing Georgian square, the Berkeley Square Hotel enjoys fine views over the city from its upper floors. The open-plan reception area and lounge, with its stuffed peacock and customised projections, is bright and good-humoured if eccentric. Adjoining is the more restrained Square restaurant, which is open to the public until 9pm but reserved for hotel guests and members later in the evening. The same applies to the hotel's basement bar. The executive suites are smallish, considering the price, but have a contemporary vibe, CD and DVD players and minibars; the complimentary decanter of sherry is a nice touch.

City Inn Hotel

Temple *Temple Way (0117 925 1001/ www.cityinn.com). £££.*
Close to Temple Meads station but backing on to the leafier surrounds of Temple Gardens, this sleek hotel is very much a corporate hangout during the week. However, its attention to detail and guest-focused ethos make it a good option for weekend visitors too. The contemporary rooms avoid the anonymity of the

larger chains thanks to bright decor, large windows and excellent facilities: air-conditioning, 24-hour room service, CD/DVD player, satellite TV and broadband internet access are standard, with free Wi-Fi in the public areas. Rooms are also well soundproofed against noise from the busy main road. Classy modern British food is served in the City Café.

Hotel du Vin & Bistro

City Centre *The Sugar House, Narrow Lewins Mead (0117 925 5577/www.hotelduvin.com).* £££.

A sheltered courtyard leads from the busy main road into a haven of sensitive restoration and thoughtful styling. Converted from an 18th-century sugar warehouse, this branch of the Hotel du Vin features exposed brickwork, wooden floors and metal joists – a soft industrial-chic setting for spacious bedrooms and loft suites with stand-alone baths and enormous walk-in showers. On the ground floor, the comfortable lounge bar has a gentlemen's club vibe, with carefully distressed leather sofas, low lights and the du Vin chain's signature cigar humidor. Beyond is a formal dining room where excellent bistro-style cuisine is accompanied by an exemplary wine list. Regular tastings and wine masterclasses are held throughout the year.

IBIS

City Centre *Explore Lane (0117 989 7200/ www.ibishotel.com).* ££.

What this bright and breezy, no-nonsense budget hotel may lack in little luxuries it more than makes up for with its brilliant location: just off Millennium square, the Harbourside and city centre are a short walk away and Explore@Bristol is on the doorstep. The Ibis has 182 rooms all of which are clean and modern in design with en-suite bathrooms and air-conditioning. The hotel's restaurant serves meals from 6am-10pm, and the bar is open 24-hours. Guests may use the secure public car park nearby at a reduced rate.

Mercure Brigstow Hotel

Harbourside *Welsh Back (0117 929 1030/ www.mercure.com).* £££.

The harbourside Brigstow is both practical and good-looking, and is ideal for the centre of town and the docks. It has 116 rooms – you'll pay around £10 extra for a river view – kitted out in a subtle palette of beige, red and green, with air-conditioning, internet access and a plasma TV screen in the bathroom. Shiny wooden floors and overhanging mezzanine balconies impart a hint of cruise-ship styling to the sleek reception area and open-plan Ellipse bar and restaurant on the ground floor. Other facilities include a business centre, conference rooms and 24-hour room service. Weekend B&B is good value.

Mercure Holland House

Redcliffe *Redcliffe Hill (0117 968 9900/ www.mercure.com).* £££.

One of Bristol's newest hotels, Holland House is rapidly becoming one of its most popular, so booking is essential. All 275 rooms are sleek and well appointed, with flat screen televisions and spacious bathrooms. But the hotel's real treat is the Spa Naturel, which offers a wide range of relaxation and beauty treatments including facials, Aroma Stone Therapy, Swedish massage and reflexology. There is also a mini-gym with cycling, rowing and step machines and a 14m pool. The hotel's restaurant serves modern European cuisine with a mediterranean twist, while the stylish Phoenix Lounge Bar is a great place to meet friends or relax with an after-dinner drink. Other facilities include conference suites, free wifi in all business and public areas, satellite and cable television and 24-hour room service.

Factfile

When to go

Any time is a good time to visit Bristol, but having said that, the city does seem particularly appealing in summer, especially if you fancy a boat trip on the Avon followed by drinks beside the Avon Gorge. A spectacular balloon festival, the Bristol International Balloon Fiesta, (www.bristolfiesta.co.uk) is held every August. Following the success of the first Bristol Festival in 2008 a second festival is being organised for September 2009 (www.thebristolfestival.org), featuring music, performance and food.

Getting there & around

There is a direct train line from London to Bristol, operated by First Great Western (www.firstgreatwestern.co.uk), with trains leaving from Paddington Station. Journey time is around one hour, 45 minutes. By car from London, take the M4 and then the M32.

Bristol is a reasonably compact city and walking is the easiest way to get around it – especially given that the city's public transport is not great. There is a bus service run by FirstGroup (for details of routes see www.firstgroup.com/ukbus/ southwest/bristol) and a local train line also runs a roughly hourly service from Temple Meads through the city to Severn Beach.

Tourist information

Bristol Visitor Information Centre
Explore@Bristol, Anchor Road, Harbourside (0333 321 0101/www.visitbristol.co.uk).
Open 10am-5pm Mon-Sat; 11am-4pm Sun.

Internet

Dottel Communication Internet Café 110 Stepleton Road, Easton (0117 955 8033).
The Flow Internet Café 108A Stokes Croft (0117 924 1999/www.flowbusinesssupport.co.uk).

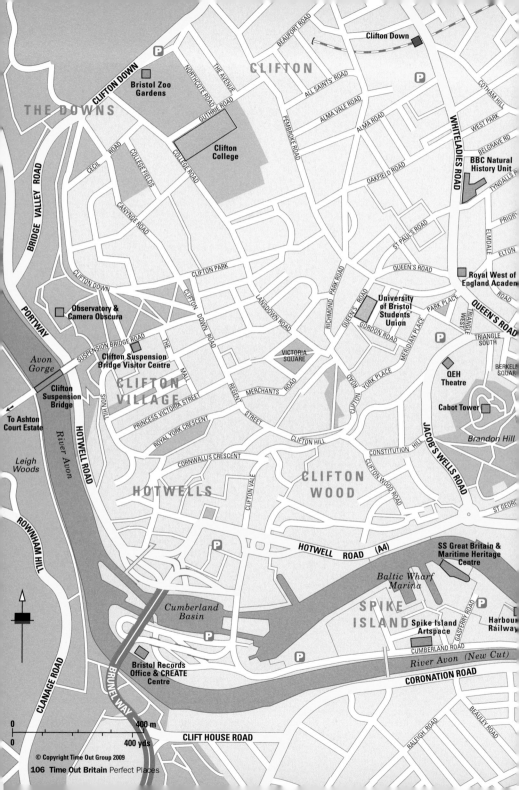

BEAUFORT ROAD

Clifton Down

CLIFTON

P

CLIFTON DOWN

Bristol Zoo
Gardens

THE DOWNS

ALL SAINT'S ROAD

ALMA VALE ROAD

ALMA ROAD

COTHAM HILL

WEST PARK

WHITELADIES ROAD

BELGRAVE RD

BBC Natural
History Unit

NORTHCOTE ROAD

THE AVENUE

GUTHRIE ROAD

PEMBROKE ROAD

OAKFIELD ROAD

TYNDALL'S PK

Clifton
College

Clifton College

BRIDGE VALLEY ROAD

CECIL ROAD

COLLEGE FIELDS

COLLEGE ROAD

CANYNGE ROAD

ST PAUL'S ROAD

QUEEN'S ROAD

PRIORY

ELMDALE

ELTON

Royal West of
England Academy

PORTWAY

CLIFTON DOWN

Observatory &
Camera Obscura

CLIFTON PARK

CLIFTON DOWN ROAD

LANSDOWN ROAD

RICHMOND PARK ROAD

QUEEN'S ROAD

University
of Bristol
Students'
Union

PARK PLACE

TRIANGLE WEST

QUEEN'S ROAD

Avon
Gorge

SUSPENSION BRIDGE ROAD

Clifton Suspension
Bridge Visitor Centre

THE MALL

GORDON ROAD

MERIDIAN PLACE

TRIANGLE
SOUTH

BERKELEY
SQUARE

P

Clifton
Suspension
Bridge

CLIFTON
VILLAGE

SION HILL

PRINCESS VICTORIA STREET

REGENT STREET

MERCHANTS ROAD

VICTORIA
SQUARE

CLIFTON ROAD

YORK PLACE

QEH
Theatre

Cabot Tower

To Ashton
Court Estate

ROYAL YORK CRESCENT

CLIFTON HILL

Brandon Hill

ST GEORG

Leigh
Woods

River Avon

CORNWALLIS CRESCENT

CLIFTON VALE

CLIFTON WOOD

CONSTITUTION HILL

CLIFTON WOOD ROAD

JACOB'S WELLS ROAD

HOTWELLS

HOTWELL ROAD

ROWNHAM HILL

P

HOTWELL ROAD (A4)

SS Great Britain &
Maritime Heritage
Centre

Baltic Wharf
Marina

P

P

Cumberland
Basin

SPIKE
ISLAND

Spike Island
Artspace

GASFERRY ROAD

P

Harbour
Railway

CUMBERLAND ROAD

P

Bristol Records
Office & CREATE
Centre

River Avon (New Cut)

CLANAGE ROAD

BRUNEL WAY

CORONATION ROAD

RALEIGH ROAD

BEAULEY ROAD

0   400 m
0   400 yds

CLIFT HOUSE ROAD

© Copyright Time Out Group 2009

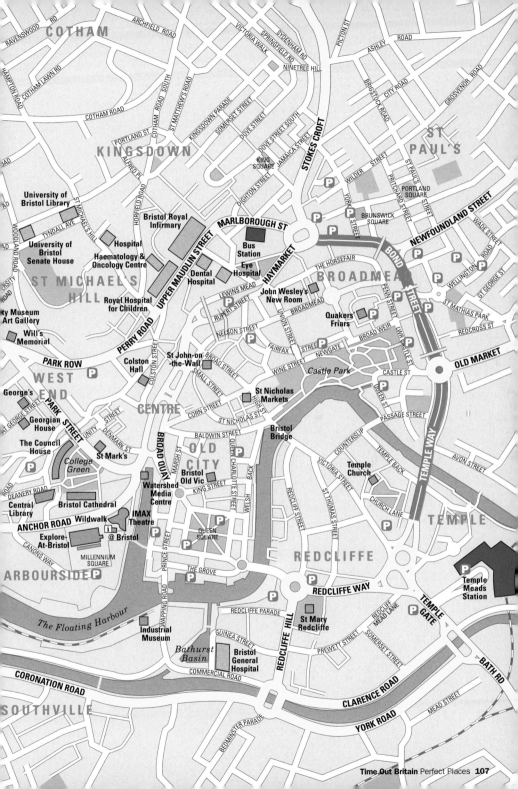

Top: Marchmont; bottom left: Edinburgh Zoo; Beltane; bottom right: Edinburgh Castle.

Edinburgh

A superb natural setting for a striking capital city.

Millions of years ago, the Earth's natural processes threw up a precipitous landscape of rare beauty on the site that we today call Edinburgh. Weathered and eroded over subsequent aeons, it featured an easily defensible whaleback hill topped out at its western extent with a fist of implacable rock, a much larger volcanic remnant nearby, sentinel crags, fertile land and river courses. On to this remarkable physical geography humans made their very distinctive marks: in the 11th century, Malcolm III strengthened an already ancient fortification up on the rock to create the forerunner of the Castle. His son, David I, founded Holyrood Abbey at the eastern foot of Edinburgh's ridge, neatly creating a Royal Mile between the two, forming the spine of the medieval Old Town. Viewed from the air, the Old Town resembles some ancient leviathan, running from the castle down to Holyrood, the ribs of the beast splaying out to the north and south, taking in both major thoroughfares and tiny, atmospheric passageways known locally as closes. The contrast with the elegant New Town, neatly ordered and regimented in its Georgian grids, couldn't be more dramatic. Today, both the Old Town and New Town are World Heritage Sites.

But Edinburgh is no historical theme park. Acclaimed restaurants, an annual arts jamboree that makes Edinburgh the world's cultural epicentre every August, plus major galleries and museums as befits a national capital add up to a vibrant city that brims with life. Welcome to Edinburgh.

Explore

OLD TOWN

The **Royal Mile** – the Old Town's undulating spine – is a strip of adjoining streets: Castlehill, Lawnmarket, High Street and Canongate. It is the central thoroughfare from which the major roads and small passageways of the Old Town branch out. On the ground, it translates into a compact, sloping walk that swings by more historic attractions and key sites than any other pocket of land in Scotland. Politics, religions, lives and loves were forged, betrayed and destroyed here. With much of the commerce centred on the tourist industry it's hardly surprising that the Old Town is like a huge open-air museum, with around 900 years of architecture on show.

The most iconic and most visited venues are the **Castle** (see p110) of course, the **National Museum of Scotland** (see p113), the **High Kirk of St Giles** (see p110) and the **Palace of Holyroodhouse** (see p113). Between them, they not only explain the history of Edinburgh, and Scotland, but also provide illustrative examples of that history. More modern attractions around Holyrood also spark interest thanks to the visitor centre at the **Scottish Parliament** (see p113) and the interactive science museum approach at **Our Dynamic Earth** (see p113). The list could go on, but the real excitement of the Old Town is the opportunity for random investigations and decisions made on impulse to explore nooks and crannies, happening across odd pubs, shops and other attractions. During such wanderings, you can be alternately stunned by sudden open views to the countryside and the Firth of Forth, or drawn by the drama of detail. The vagaries of scale are so outlandish and engaging as to be almost intemperate – whether in time or in sheer space. From the grandiose to the singular, however, the Old Town is never less than fascinating.

Edinburgh Castle

Castlehill (0131 225 9846/tickets 0131 668 8800/ www.edinburghcastle.gov.uk). Open Apr-Sept 9.30am-6pm daily. Oct-Mar 9.30am-5pm daily. Admission £9.79; £4.89-£6.85 reductions.

Military barracks, prison, royal residence, murder scene, birthplace of kings and queens… Edinburgh Castle has served a variety of purposes during the centuries it has stood high above the city. The buildings are the main attraction – the Scottish National War Memorial is highly affecting, while St Margaret's Chapel beguiles with its simplicity – but it's also worth keeping your eyes peeled for more ephemeral bits and pieces: the graffiti scrawled by Napoleonic and American prisoners of war who were imprisoned here, for example.

High Kirk of St Giles (St Giles Cathedral)

High Street (0131 225 9442/www.stgilescathedral. org.uk). Open May-Sept 9am-7pm Mon-Fri; 9am-5.30pm Sat; 1-5pm Sun. Oct-Mar 9am-5pm Mon-Sat; 1-5pm Sun. Admission free (suggested donation £3).

0 50 miles

Edinburgh

Edinburgh

Historic sites

● ● ● ● ○

Art & architecture

● ● ● ● ●

Hotels

● ● ● ○ ○

Eating & drinking

● ● ● ● ●

Nightlife

● ● ● ○ ○

Shopping

● ● ● ○ ○

Top: Palace of
Holyroodhouse;
Royal Scottish Academy;
bottom: a close;
Stockbridge Market.

Scottish Parliament.

There has been a church on the site of St Giles since 854. Nothing remains of the earliest structures, but the four pillars that surround the Holy Table in the centre of the church have stood firm since around 1120, surviving the desecration of marauding armies during the Reformation. Numerous memorials and statues pay tribute to such famous characters as John Knox, but perhaps the most notable features of the interior are the magnificent stained-glass windows and the ornate Thistle Chapel, which dates from 1911.

National Museum of Scotland
Chambers Street (0131 225 7534/www.nms.ac.uk). Open 10am-5pm daily. Admission free.
Formerly known as the Museum of Scotland before administratively merging with the adjacent Royal Museum, this is now a grand complex with thousands of artefacts on display. You can trace Scotland's entire story here, from its geological origins through prehistory to the headline-grabbing moments of past centuries, and ultimately the modern era. Simply brilliant.

Our Dynamic Earth
112 Holyrood Road (0131 550 7800/www.dynamic earth.co.uk). Open Apr-June, Sept, Oct 10am-5pm daily. July, Aug 10am-6pm daily. Nov-Mar 10am-5pm Wed-Sun. (Last admission 90mins before closing.) Admission £9.50; £5.95-£7.50 reductions.
Our Dynamic Earth is located near the former home of Edinburgh-born James Hutton, the so-called 'Father of Geology'. It's anyone's guess what he'd make of its ultra-modern, tent-like exterior, but he'd surely approve of its educational aims: to take visitors back to the creation of the universe nearly 14 billion years ago, then bring them forward to the present day. Aimed primarily at school-age children, it's a science museum that combines natural history with simulated natural disasters, and attempts to make geology fun.

Palace of Holyroodhouse
Holyrood Road (0131 556 5100/www.royal collection.org.uk). Open Apr-Oct 9.30am-6pm daily (last admission 5pm). Nov-Mar 9.30am-4.30pm daily (last admission 3.30pm). Closed 16 May-6 June, 22 June-3 July & during royal visits. Admission £10; £6-£9 reductions.
The Palace of Holyroodhouse has its origins in the Abbey of Holyrood (now picturesque ruins), established in 1128 by David I. When Edinburgh was confirmed as the nation's capital city, royal quarters were built adjacent to the abbey and have been gradually upgraded and renovated over the years. It's still used by the Queen as an official residence. When she's elsewhere, parts of the building are open to the public; an audio tour details the history of a series of plush bedrooms, galleries and dining rooms.

The adjacent Queen's Gallery hosts a changing programme of exhibitions from the Royal Collection, with a focus on works from the Royal Library at Windsor Castle.

The café in the mews courtyard will take care of all your sustenance requirements in the form of drinks, light snacks and lunches, served all day.

Scottish Parliament
Canongate (0131 348 5200/www.scottish. parliament.uk). Open Apr-Sept 10am-5.30pm Mon, Fri; 9am-6.30pm Tue-Thur; 11am-5.30pm Sat. Oct-Mar 10am-4pm Mon, Fri; 9am-6.30pm Tue-Thur; 11am-5.30pm Sat. (Times & days subject to change.) Admission free. Tours (Mon, Fri, Sat when parliament in session; Mon-Sat when in recess) £5.85, £3.50 reductions.
Edinburgh had a long wait to see the building that houses the Scottish Parliament – created by the late Catalan architect Enrico Miralles – but when the scaffolding and coverings were removed, a confident, dynamic and innovative complex was revealed, utterly different to any other such building in the UK. At least, that's one view. Others saw it as a hard-to-maintain, overpriced and ugly carbuncle: the debate is ongoing. If you have time, make up your own mind by taking the tour, which explores areas that are not accessible to the casual visitor.

NEW TOWN & STOCKBRIDGE
The New Town could be said to have two distinct personalities. At its southern reaches, on George Street and Princes Street, it's a shopping hub with crowds of people, big hotels and major attractions like the **National Galleries Complex** (*see p114*), Princes Street Gardens or the soaring Gothic monument to Sir Walter Scott. Around here you can find all kinds of places to eat, drink and party late into the night. Venture a little further north however – beyond Queen Street and Queen Street Gardens – and another, more reserved side of the New Town comes into play.

There may be independent art galleries down Dundas Street, and the odd pub or restaurant to discover, but here the New Town is resolutely residential. The façades are beautiful but also perhaps a little forbidding – somehow managing to draw a veil of privacy over the homes of Edinburgh's establishment and monied middle classes behind, just as they have done for around two centuries. The sense of history is all-pervading here, making the planned, cobbled streets of the New Town an attraction in their own right, with a very particular atmosphere. It's almost as if you might see a frock-coated gentleman emerge from behind a black-painted door at any moment and stride off into the night; only the parked cars and electric street lights betray the illusion.

Less Georgian, less patrician, but interesting all the same is **Stockbridge** to the north-west of the New Town. With its bustling village atmosphere and array of shops, pubs and restaurants it was a kind of bohemian centre for Edinburgh back in the day. Although this reputation has long since faded, it's still an engaging area to browse. The major attraction is the restful expanse of the **Royal Botanic Garden** nearby (*see p114*).

National Galleries Complex

*The Mound (0131 624 6200/www.nationalgalleries.org).
Open 10am-5pm Mon-Wed, Fri-Sun; 10am-7pm Thur.
Admission free; charges for special exhibitions.*
Royal Scottish Academy *(0131 225 6671/www.royal
scottishacademy.org). Open 10am-5pm Mon-Sat; noon-
5pm Sun. Admission varies.*

Edinburgh has a wealth of institutions serving the visual
arts but perhaps none quite as grand as the National Gallery
of Scotland, built in 1848, and its neighbour the Royal
Scottish Academy (RSA). The former boasts an excellent
collection of painting and sculpture and the sheer wealth of
great work is undeniable, from Byzantine-like Madonnas
through works from the Northern Renaissance, the High
Renaissance and right on into the 20th century. The RSA,
meanwhile, is effectively a large-scale temporary exhibition
space in classical premises dating from 1826. It hosts
blockbuster touring shows but also annual displays devoted
to Scottish artists, particularly the official RSA Exhibition
every spring. In 2004 the basement-level Weston Link was
added, physically joining the two institutions and providing
a restaurant and shops.

Royal Botanic Garden

*20A Inverleith Row (0131 552 7171/www.rbge.org.uk).
Open Mar, Oct 10am-6pm daily. Apr-Sept 10am-7pm
daily. Nov-Feb 10am-4pm daily. Admission Garden free.
Glasshouses £3.50; £1-£3 reductions.*

Acres of plants, trees and peace. Possibly Edinburgh's most
placid attraction, this is also a noted centre for botanical and
horticultural research and houses the oldest botanical
library in Britain. The gardens are continuously remodelled
and improved so there's usually something new to see. The
Rock Garden Stream is a highlight, along with the Chinese
Hillside which focuses on intrepid Scottish plant hunters of
the past. In summer, particularly August, art installations
and exhibits are often set up around the grounds, but there's
a pond with ducks too – keeping both culture vultures and
toddlers happy. The Terrace Café will provide sustenance,
while the late 18th-century Inverleith House has been an art
gallery since 1960 and mounts some absorbing exhibitions.

CALTON HILL & BROUGHTON

Just past the east end of Princes Street, lording
it over the city centre, Calton Hill affords all-
round views, including the classic panorama
of Edinburgh back towards the clock tower of
the Balmoral Hotel with the Old Town skyline
and Castle behind. Around its summit you can
find the original **City Observatory**, dating from
1774, and the **Nelson Monument**, which was
completed as a memorial to the legendary
admiral in 1816. Modelled on the Parthenon,
this was begun in 1822 as a memorial for the
dead of the Napoleonic Wars but was never
completed as the city ran out of money.
The incomplete National Monument, as it's
officially known, turned into something of
an embarrassment, nicknamed Edinburgh's
Disgrace. Today it just looks suitably grand,
neoclassical and stoic.

The elevation, sense of space and accessibility
makes Calton Hill something of a magnet for
visitors but also for celebrations. In the run-up
to Hogmanay the annual torchlight procession
concludes at the summit, while late in the
evening on 30 April every year the top of the hill
is again covered in revellers. Edinburgh's **Beltane
Festival** is officially the modern revival of a pre-
Christian celebration to welcome in the spring.
To the casual observer it looks much more like
an excuse to bang drums, paint your body, dance
around the firelight, and generally go a bit pagan-
crazy with iconic figures like the May Queen, the
Green Man, and their ilk.

Immediately north of Calton Hill is **Broughton**.
As Leith Street morphs into Greenside Place, this
is where you find the modern mall-style delights
of the **Omni Centre**, with its comedy club, bars,
restaurants and a multiplex cinema, making the
Playhouse Theatre just a bit further down
Greenside Place look almost austere.

Broughton has two real claims to fame: as
a good-time quarter, especially thanks to all the
bars and eateries down Broughton Street itself,
but also as the centre of the city's gay scene.
Delve a little deeper though and there's more to
Broughton than leisure and lifestyle. In 1685, a
colony of French Protestants fled their native land
and came to settle around the area, earning their
keep as silk weavers. The short street opposite
the Omni Centre is still called Picardy Place.

LEITH

A docks area that had seen better days, things
started to improve in Leith in the 1980s when
a few intrepid entrepreneurs and restaurateurs
took the plunge and set up here, encouraging
others to follow. Things started to move even
more quickly when the local port authority was
privatised and its derelict land was put to more
profitable use. That saw the launch of some
ambitious projects: the **Scottish Executive
building** at Victoria Quay was completed in
1995, followed in short order by the Royal Yacht
Britannia in 1998 *(see p117)* and the opening
of the gargantuan **Ocean Terminal** shopping
mall in 2001. The arrival of the first ever
Malmaison Hotel *(see p123)* here in 1994,
bringing boutique chic, didn't hurt either.

These days the formerly independent
burgh has an additional feather in its cap –
as a centre for fine food. The area immediately
around **the Shore**, the very heart of old Leith,
has enjoyed an elevated reputation for
restaurants and pubs since those openings
in the 1980s. However, with the arrival of
Restaurant Martin Wishart (1999, *see p119*),
the **Kitchin** (2006, *see p119*) and the **Plumed
Horse** (also 2006, *see p119*), Leith can now
say that it has the highest concentration of
talented chefs anywhere in Scotland.

Top: Lochrin Basin;
Barclay Church; bottom:
Princes Street.

Glasgow: the rival

It is quite possible to jump on a train at Edinburgh's Waverley Station at noon, be in central Glasgow less than an hour later, grab a bite of lunch, check out a gallery and still be back in Edinburgh before 5pm. So visitors to Edinburgh really have no excuse not to check out its larger, western cousin for at least a few hours – whether you want to do culture, shopping (Glasgow is more of an orthodox retail centre than the Scottish capital), or to stay on later to experience the city's famous bars and restaurants.

Although the city has genuine Dark Age roots, the real energy here burned brightest during the mercantile and industrial eras, which is why the grandest neighbourhoods or buildings date to the 18th and 19th centuries: the **Merchant City** south-west of George Square for example, or the ostentatious and Italianate **City Chambers** on George Square itself. The **Necropolis** (Cathedral Square, open 24hrs daily), on a hill just east of the city's cathedral, is an affecting and tumbledown Victorian cemetery modelled on Père Lachaise in Paris. This place tells a lot about the ambitions of those who helped build the city: from 1832, Glasgow's great and good were interred here beneath monuments and mausoleums of increasingly deliberate grandeur.

The city centre immediately west of George Square is laid out on a very rational grid pattern, like a mini New York, and hosts untold numbers of restaurants and bars. For a taste of Glasgow's more bohemian side you have to jump on the cutesy underground service (Buchanan Street underground is adjacent to Queen Street railway station) and aim for the **West End**, specifically the Hillhead stop on Byres Road. Just behind the underground station is Ashton Lane, with raffish pubs and café-bars, as well as the highly regarded Scottish restaurant the **Ubiquitous Chip** (no.12, 0141 334 5007, www.ubiquitouschip.co.uk) while Byres Road has a selection of decent restaurants too, including **No.16** (no.16, 0141 339 2544, www.number16.co.uk).

Although people come here for the nightlife and the general buzz, Glasgow's number one attraction – over 2.2 million visitors a year – is the **Kelvingrove Art Gallery & Museum** (Argyle Street, 0141 287 2699, www.glasgow museums.com, open 10am-5pm Mon-Sat; 11am-5pm Sun). Reopened in 2006 after a multi-million pound refurbishment, it's now one of Scotland's must-see venues – and it's free. The impressive atrium sparkles in the light that floods in through its windows, the ground floor exhibitions cover every subject under the sun – architecture to war – while the first floor houses masterpieces by Dalí, Rembrandt, Van Gogh and Botticelli. Tempted? Trains to Glasgow leave Edinburgh every 15 minutes.

People come to Leith to eat and drink, to walk by the old docks, to shop and to see *Britannia*. It's not merely a nostalgic leisure experience – for all its ups and downs, Leith is still Scotland's largest enclosed deepwater port and that means a certain authentic saltiness remains alongside the luxury apartments and cauliflower velouté...

Royal Yacht Britannia
Ocean Terminal (0131 555 5566/www.royalyacht britannia.co.uk). Open Apr-June, Sept, Oct 10am-5.30pm daily. July 9.30am-5.30pm daily. Aug 9.30am-6pm daily. Nov-Mar 10am-5pm daily. (Last admission 90mins before closing.) Admission £10; £6-£8.75 reductions.
Launched in 1953, the year of Queen Elizabeth II's coronation, the Royal Yacht *Britannia* was used by the royal family for more than four decades. It was decommissioned at the end of 1997 and now resides permanently in Leith.

SOUTH & WEST
Edinburgh's south and west are largely suburban in nature but do offer the odd gem. Backing on to to the green space of the **Meadows** in the south is the Franco-Venetian Gothic extravaganza of **Barclay Church** (Bruntsfield, www.barclay church.org.uk). The **Marchmont** district, south of the Meadows, is composed almost entirely of baronial-style tenement buildings, built between 1876 and 1914.

You have to venture deep into the west of the city to visit the legendary **Edinburgh Zoo** (*see p117*) a good two miles from Princes Street. West Edinburgh is also home to Scotland's national rugby stadium at Murrayfield, but perhaps its most surprising feature is the **Union Canal**, which has its modern terminus at **Lochrin Basin** – with a couple of café-bars – just off Fountainbridge. Restored thanks to the Millennium Link Project, the once-derelict waterway was officially reopened in 2002 and it is again possible to travel all the way across central Scotland by boat. Alternatively, you can walk or cycle on the towpath all the way from Lochrin Basin to the city limits (four miles), the pleasant Bridge Inn pub at the village of Ratho (seven miles), or beyond.

Other waterside walks in west Edinburgh include the bucolic path beside the River Almond at **Cramond** and the shore of the Forth from Cramond back towards **Granton** – a wide open space with views over to Fife. Meanwhile, where south Edinburgh adjoins the Old Town, you can find **Surgeons Hall Museums** (18 Nicolson Street, 0131 527 1649, www.rcsed.ak.uk) – with a morbidly fascinating pathology collection – and the unmissable **Holyrood Park**, with the volcanic plug of **Arthur's Seat** soaring high over everything between the Pentlands and the sea.

Finally, in the deep south you come to **Blackford Hill**, a countryside patch of trees and greenery. Walkers can either amble by the stream that runs through the glen on the south side of

the hill, or climb to the summit, which not only has drop-dead gorgeous views over Edinburgh but also hosts the twin-teacake structure of the **Royal Observatory**, completed in 1896.

Edinburgh Zoo
Corstorphine Road (0131 334 9171/www.edinburgh zoo.org.uk). Open Apr-Sept 9am-6pm daily. Oct, Mar 9am-5pm daily. Nov-Feb 9am-4.30pm daily. Admission £12.50; £8.50-£10.50 reductions.
Opened in 1913 on the side of Corstorphine Hill, Edinburgh Zoo is now home to over 1,000 different species. Principally a family-oriented attraction, albeit one that puts an emphasis on conservation, its penguin parade is one of the most enchanting sights in the city whatever your age; check with zoo staff for times. Wow factor animals such as lions, polar bears and gorillas are among the other inhabitants.

Eat

David Bann
Old Town *56-58 St Mary's Street (0131 556 5888/ www.davidbann.com). Open 11am-10pm Mon-Thur, Sun; 11am-10.30pm Fri, Sat. £££. Vegetarian.*
There are Indian vegetarian venues in Edinburgh, and illustrious establishments with meat-free menus, but when it comes to modern, European-style and completely vegetarian eateries, David Bann is the market leader. The approach is flexible; it's fine for a quick coffee and a light snack, but also for a full lunch or dinner. Try parmesan and basil polenta to start, followed by spinach and smoked cheese strudel. The wine list is short and affordable.

Forth Floor
New Town *Harvey Nichols, 30-34 St Andrew Square (0131 524 8350/www.harveynichols.com). Open (brasserie) 10am-5pm Mon; 10am-10pm Tue-Sat; 11am-5pm Sun. (Restaurant) noon-3pm Mon; noon-3pm, 6-10pm Tue-Fri; noon-3.30pm, 6-10pm Sat; noon-3.30pm Sun. £££. Modern European.*
Even the anti-fashion brigade has had to admit that Harvey Nicks' fourth-floor restaurant and brasserie are pretty good. The views over the Forth are tremendous, the decor is funky, and the kitchen operates at an elevated standard. During the day it caters for shoppers, but at night there's a real buzz. The restaurant has a slightly more elaborate menu than the brasserie, but it's all effectively one space with a discreet partition.

La Garrigue
Old Town *31 Jeffrey Street (0131 557 3032/www. lagarrigue.co.uk). Open noon-2.30pm, 6.30-9.30pm Mon-Sat. £££. French.*
The quality rustic decor of Edinburgh's specialist Languedoc restaurant – tables and chairs are by the late, great furniture-maker Tim Stead – are in keeping with chef Jean Michel Gauffre's food philosophy. Highlights include 'three meat cassoulet' with pork, lamb and duck (plus Toulouse sausage, of course), but there are meat-free options for vegetarians.

Top: Number 1;
left: Malmaison;
right: the Kitchin.

The Kitchin

Leith *78 Commercial Quay (0131 555 1755/www.the kitchin.com). Open 12.30-1.45pm, 6.45pm-10pm Tue-Thur. 12.30-2pm, 6.45-10.30pm Fri, Sat. ££££. Scottish/French.*
A simple story: a chef (Tom Kitchin) with an illustrious CV decided to have a go with his own place; his wife (Michaela Kitchin) also had bags of experience front of house. They opened in summer 2006 and by early 2007 had a Michelin star, catapulting them into the city's list of 'best eats'. A deceptively simple menu with interesting combinations (like a starter of duck with salsify, pear and toast soldiers) is allied with seriously good cooking and service.

"Wishart's has retained a Michelin star since 2001, and the food is sublime."

Number One

New Town *The Balmoral, 1 Princes Street (0131 557 6727/www.restaurantnumberone.com). Open 6.30-10pm daily. ££££. Modern European.*
An enviable address, a keen reputation and a very talented kitchen brigade all combine to make this a first-class dining experience, one of only four venues in Edinburgh with a Michelin star. The spacious dining room is at once contemporary and classic, and the menu brings you into the heady territory of foie gras roulade with pineapple chutney, followed by poached beef sirloin with horseradish gratin.

Plumed Horse

Leith *50-54 Henderson Street (0131 554 5556/ www.plumedhorse.co.uk). Open noon-1.30pm, 7-9pm Tue-Sat. ££££. Modern European.*
Tony Borthwick ran a Michelin-starred restaurant in Dumfriesshire but opted to move to Edinburgh at the end of 2006. His new venture confounded expectation. Foodies and critics looked for immediate excellence; he provided something small, low-key and well crafted, but it took a while to find its feet. There is no big front-of-house crew or kitchen brigade here, but Tony and company still do a grand job. Odd location, likeable venue.

Restaurant Martin Wishart

Leith *54 The Shore (0131 553 3557/www.martin-wishart.co.uk). Open noon-1.30pm, 6.30-10pm Tue-Fri; noon-1pm, 6.30-10pm Sat. £££££. Scottish/French.*
Located in the historical heart of Leith, Wishart's establishment has retained a Michelin star since 2001, and the food is sublime: the likes of subtle frothy pumpkin purée with vegetable shavings, served in a small glass vase as an amuse-bouche; intense jerusalem artichoke soup as a starter, with a dainty bouillabaisse to follow, perhaps. Then, for dessert, achingly good almond and pear tart with Armagnac ice-cream. The sommelier is brilliant, the front of house staff are approachable and efficient, and the kitchen crew are the best in the city. Marks out of ten? Eleven.

Roti

New Town *73 Morrison Street (0131 221 9998/ www.roti.uk.com). Open (restaurant) noon-2.30pm, 6-10.30pm Mon-Sat. £££. Indian.*
The brainchild of Tony Singh at Oloroso, Roti opened in 2005 but proved such a success that it moved to this larger space in 2007. The Indian-influenced menu goes way beyond curry clichés – beef vindaloo is marinated for 24 hours then braised for eight, or try duck breast with marrow and ginger. The alternative tiffin menu offers a tapas-like taste of various dishes, in the restaurant or bar.

Witchery by the Castle

Old Town *352 Castlehill (0131 225 5613/www.the witchery.com). Open noon-4pm, 5.30-11.30pm daily. ££££. Scottish/International.*
One 16th-century venue, two dining rooms and tons of ambience. James Thomson opened the Witchery back in 1979, its wood panelling, red leather and candlelit interior immediately lending it a reputation for destination dining. The possibly even more romantic Secret Garden followed in 1989. Neither is cheap, and some critics grumble that the cooking (whole grilled Dover sole and roast loin of Scottish deer are typical mains) isn't always top class, but it's still of a high standard, served with a legendary wine list. Try a post-theatre supper to experience the Witchery without breaking the bank.

Shop

I J Mellis

Old Town *30A Victoria Street (0131 226 6215/ www.mellischeese.co.uk). Open 10am-6pm Mon-Fri; 9am-6pm Sat; noon-5pm Sun.*
Although you might associate Edinburgh with whisky or kilts, would you associate it with cheese? Maybe not, but Mellis runs one of the very best cheese shops not just in Scotland but also in the entire UK. His Victoria Street branch is like a small cavern of fromage, an homage to its artisan possibilities.

Kinloch Anderson

Leith *4 Dock Street (0131 555 1390/www.kinloch anderson.com). Open 9am-5.30pm Mon-Sat.*
A family business since 1868, this is perhaps the city's most renowned kilt maker – none of your tourist tat here, but serious tailoring. The store in Leith also has a small heritage museum where you can follow the progress of Highland dress over the years.

Royal Mile Whiskies

Old Town *379 High Street (0131 225 3383/www.royal milewhiskies.com). Open July-mid Sept 10am-8pm Mon-Sat; 12.30-8pm Sun. Mid Sept-June 10am-6pm Mon-Sat; 12.30-6pm Sun.*
Japanese whisky? American bourbon? Irish whiskey with an 'e'? Yes, it's all here along with more varieties of single malt Scotch than you can shake a stick at: all the usual names plus a large choice of rare and limited edition expressions.

Arts

Edinburgh International Festival

Various venues. Information & tickets: The Hub, Castlehill (tickets 0131 473 2000/www.eif.co.uk).
The world's premier arts festival, inaugurated in 1947 runs for three weeks every year in the late summer, usually from August into the first few days of September. It has an incredible programme of classical music, theatre, opera and dance, with major international companies visiting the city. Edinburgh in August has a number of administratively separate festivals – this is the daddy, culturally speaking.

Edinburgh Festival Fringe

Various venues. Information & tickets: Fringe Office, 180 High Street (tickets 0131 226 0000/www.edfringe.com).
The Fringe started as a kind of unofficial retort to the Edinburgh International Festival back in 1947, but the tail now wags the dog as it has more shows, more performers and is just bigger in every sense. All life is here: theatre, comedy, children's shows, dance, all genres of music, exhibitions and events – performed by everyone from enthusiastic amateurs to well known faces from film and television. It also runs for around three weeks in August, largely overlapping with the International Festival; together, they make the city simply unique at this time of year.

Nightlife

Bow Bar

Old Town *80 West Bow (0131 226 7667). Open noon-11.30pm Mon-Sat; 12.30-11pm Sun.*
A small and simple one-room pub in the heart of the Old Town, but one offering a good selection of cask ales and a fantastic range of single malt Scotch, including very rare examples. Some nights it can get so busy that you'll have to stand; catch it on a quiet winter midweek evening and you can sit for a couple of hours, learning just why Scotch whisky has such an elevated reputation.

"A nightclub and gig venue, the aim here is 'breaking the boundaries in music'."

Cabaret Voltaire

Old Town *36 Blair Street (0131 220 4638/www.the cabaretvoltaire.com). Open (club) 11pm-3am daily; gig nights from 7pm. Admission free-£10.*
A nightclub and gig venue, the self-proclaimed aim here is 'breaking the boundaries in music'. Housed in atmospheric cellar-like premises, suitable for its Old Town location, some of the city's longest running and most successful club nights

are based here; stage acts range from local unknowns to internationally acclaimed niche performers like Kristin Hersh.

Dragonfly

South Edinburgh *52 West Port (0131 228 4543/www.dragonflycocktailbar.com). Open 4pm-1am daily.*
Combining cocktail culture with a pre-club atmosphere, Dragonfly makes the best of both worlds, spanning that part of the evening between going out and the clubs opening. The drinks here are decent too – not teeny-bubble confections in shocking pink, but actual cocktails that you will want to linger over. The decor is almost ironic, your Hemingway daiquiri is not.

Stay

Balmoral

New Town *1 Princes Street (0131 556 2414/www.thebalmoralhotel.com). ££££.*
A kilted doorman welcomes you to 'Scotland's most famous address' where the trappings are all you would expect from a five-star hotel. Exterior rooms offer panoramic views, while the quieter interior rooms overlook the chandeliered Palm Court where a famous afternoon tea is served in serene splendour before the space morphs into the Bollinger Bar at the Palm Court. Hadrian's Brasserie does a fair imitation of cosmopolitan Milan, but the real jewel in the crown is the Michelin starred Number One restaurant (*see p119*).

Caledonian Hilton

New Town *4 Princes Street (0131 222 8888/www.hilton.co.uk/caledonian). ££££.*
The Caledonian Hilton's imposing red sandstone façade has made this hotel an Edinburgh landmark. Modern but restrained decor in the rooms blends well with its Edwardian origins although the stand-out feature of the interior may well be the fabulously rococo Pompadour dining room. High service standards has made 'the Caley' a favourite with luminaries from Nelson Mandela to Sean Connery.

George Hotel

New Town *19-21 George Street (0131 225 1251/www.principal-hotels.com). ££££.*
If the Balmoral and the Caledonian Hilton are the king and queen of Edinburgh's hotel scene, this is the prince. EH2 Tempus is its huge bar-restaurant with a 'modern aristocrat' feel, while all of the 116 rooms in the contemporary wing have had a complete makeover in recent years. The north-facing deluxe double rooms on floors five to seven boast eye-popping 180 degree views of the Forth shore and Fife, while others look to the Castle.

Glasshouse

Calton Hill *2 Greenside Place (0131 525 8200/www.theetoncollection.com). ££££.*
From the same group as the Scotsman, the Glasshouse lies behind the façade of the former Lady Glenorchy church at the foot of Calton Hill. Its USP is in the name – floor-to-ceiling windows in every room offer impressive views over the two-

acre, lavender-scented roof garden or the city skyline; even the bathrooms are glass (with screening, of course). Clean, modern lines throughout make for a stylish boutique hotel.

Howard
New Town *34 Great King Street (0131 557 3500/ www.thehoward.com). ££££.*
Built in 1829, the Howard is a perfect example of how to combine Georgian style with modern luxury. All the terraced basement suites have their own separate entrances and are particularly popular with honeymooning couples. Large bathrooms and state-of-the-art showers and roll-top baths are luxurious bonuses. Service is exemplary; a butler checks in guests in the lavishly decorated drawing room.

"The quieter interior rooms overlook the chandeliered Palm Court, where a famous afternoon tea is served in serene splendour."

Malmaison
Leith *1 Tower Place (0131 468 5000/ www.malmaison.com). ££££.*
The first ever Malmaison (opened in 1994), this hotel set new service standards in Edinburgh and helped push along the resurgence of Leith. Its Arthur's Suite penthouse has views of Arthur's Seat from the bed and the bath. Downstairs, the brasserie serves a modern European menu while the adjacent café-bar is a watering hole for the local creative industries and suits from the Scottish Executive nearby.

Prestonfield
South Edinburgh *Priestfield Road (0131 225 7800/www.prestonfield.com). ££££.*
Prestonfield was always a prestigious hotel but when local restaurateur James Thomson took it over in 2003 and turned it became a kind of Jacobean wonderland. To say it's a plush affair would be an understatement – the core of the hotel is 17th century, set in parkland under the shadow of Arthur's Seat. Outside in the grounds don't be surprised to see peacocks and Highland cattle.

Scotsman
Old Town *20 North Bridge (0131 556 5565/ www.thescotsmanhotel.co.uk). ££££.*
The former offices of the *Scotsman* newspaper house the state-of-the-art Escape Health Club, the hyper-chic Cowshed Spa with stainless steel swimming pool, and the North Bridge Brasserie – not to mention individually decorated rooms with estate tweeds and original art, plus a well-stocked wine bar and privacy hatch for delivering room service.

Tigerlily
New Town *125 George Street (0131 225 5005/ www.tigerlilyedinburgh.co.uk). £££.*
This sumptuous and ambitious hotel, which opened in 2006, offers more than rooms. It also has a restaurant, cocktail bar and nightclub, within a five-storey townhouse bang in the city centre. Each of the 33 bedrooms and suites is decorated differently but all combine classic and contemporary influences, smooth and textured surfaces plus masculine and feminine appeal. In the main stairwell, giant disco balls splash the walls with sparkle.

Factfile

When to go
Although this is a year-round tourist city, visitor numbers tend to pick up after Easter, then reach a crescendo with the slew of cultural festivals in August. This is liveliest and most interesting month, but also the busiest and – perversely – often the rainiest. A maritime, temperate climate means that winters are cold and wet rather than snowy and sub-zero, while 26°C constitutes a warm summer's day. On average, June offers maximum sunshine, below average rain and a temperature range of 12-23°C.

Getting there & around
Edinburgh Airport is around 10 miles west of the city centre. The main railway station is Waverley, at the east end of Princes Street. This is on the UK's east coast mainline. First Scotrail runs trains all over Scotland, while the First TransPennine Express runs to Manchester Airport. National Express and Virgin provide the main cross-border services to London and other major cities.

The main bus station is at St Andrew Square, with Scottish Citylink buses serving Scotland, National Express buses heading cross-border.

Within Edinburgh, congestion and parking charges mean that cars are not the best option. Black cabs can be hailed in the street or at taxi ranks while Edinburgh also has a comprehensive bus service thanks to Lothian Buses.

Tourist information
Edinburgh & Scotland Information Centre above Princes Mall, 3 Princes Street EH2 2QP (08452 255 121/www.edinburgh.org).

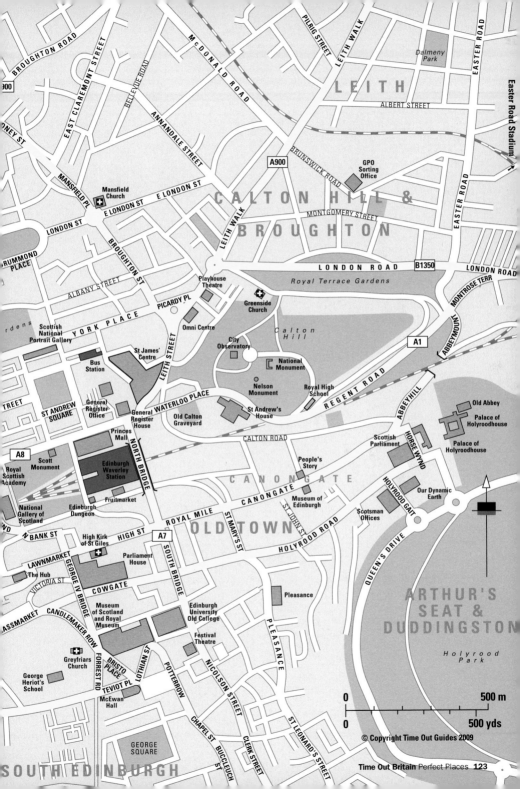

BROUGHTON ROAD

A900

SIDNEY ST

EAST CLAREMONT STREET

BELLEVUE ROAD

ANNANDALE STREET

McDONALD ROAD

PILRIG STREET

LEITH WALK

LEITH WALK

EASTER ROAD

Easter Road Stadium

Dalmeny Park

LEITH

ALBERT STREET

MANSFIELD PL

Mansfield Church

E LONDON ST

E LONDON ST

A900

BRUNSWICK ROAD

GPO Sorting Office

EASTER ROAD

CALTON HILL & BROUGHTON

LONDON ST

DRUMMOND PLACE

ALBANY STREET

BROUGHTON STREET

MONTGOMERY STREET

LONDON ROAD

B1350

LONDON ROAD

MONTROSE TERR

Royal Terrace Gardens

dens

Playhouse Theatre

PICARDY PL

Greenside Church

Omni Centre

Calton Hill

A1

ABBEYMOUNT

Scottish National Portrait Gallery

YORK PLACE

LEITH STREET

City Observatory

National Monument

St James' Centre

Bus Station

Nelson Monument

ABBEYHILL

Old Abbey

STREET

ST ANDREW SQUARE

General Register Office

Royal High School

REGENT ROAD

Palace of Holyroodhouse

General Register House

WATERLOO PLACE

St Andrew's House

ABBEYHILL

HORSE WYND

Palace of Holyroodhouse

A8

Scott Monument

Princes Mall

Old Calton Graveyard

CALTON ROAD

Scottish Parliament

Royal Scottish Academy

NORTH BRIDGE

Edinburgh Waverley Station

People's Story

HOLYROOD GAIT

Our Dynamic Earth

National Gallery of Scotland

Edinburgh Dungeon

Fruitmarket

CANONGATE

Museum of Edinburgh

Scotsman Offices

N BANK ST

High Kirk of St Giles

HIGH ST

CANONGATE

QUEEN'S DRIVE

ROYAL MILE

ST MARY'S ST

ST JOHN'S ST

HOLYROOD ROAD

OLD TOWN

A7

LAWNMARKET

SOUTH BRIDGE

The Hub

Parliament House

ARTHUR'S SEAT & DUDDINGSTON

VICTORIA ST

GEORGE IV BRIDGE

COWGATE

CANDLEMAKER ROW

Museum of Scotland and Royal Museum

Pleasance

GRASSMARKET

Greyfriars Church

BRISTO PLACE

LOTHIAN ST

Edinburgh University Old College

PLEASANCE

Holyrood Park

FORREST RD

TEVIOT PL

Festival Theatre

NICOLSON STREET

George Heriot's School

McEwan Hall

POTTEROW

ST LEONARD'S STREET

CHAPEL ST

CLERK STREET

BUCCLEUCH

GEORGE SQUARE

0   500 m

0   500 yds

© Copyright Time Out Guides 2009

Top left: Manchester at night; right: Manchester Art Gallery; bottom: Salford Lads Club.

Manchester

A city of grit, glamour and hard graft.

Manchester today is unrecognisable from the post-industrial city of 20 years ago. Home to grand relics of the industrial revolution, the modern city is also studded with independent boutiques and top-flight shops, cool bars and snug pubs. Not only do its museums house some of the UK's finest historic collections, but Manchester has a contemporary cultural pulse that puts other British cities to shame. At first glance, Manchester doesn't look half as impressive as it actually is. Architecturally, it's a mishmash. The city centre is better, saved from post-war shabbiness by the 1996 IRA bomb, which, though it ripped the heart out of the city, also supplied an unprecedented opportunity to right its architectural wrongs. The Royal Exchange got a £30-million facelift. New public squares were unveiled. A glass twist of a footbridge now connects Selfridges to the Arndale. Below it sits the post box that became a symbol of the city's determination to recover from the blast: despite its proximity to the explosion, it survived intact.

The kind of tenacity symbolised here is what makes Manchester tick. The city that was crucial to the industrial revolution and the history of the Labour Movement – and was also a hub of the free trade movement – is determined to regain its place at the global table. The sense of civic pride here is almost tangible, and it is this that fuels Manchester's attempts to position itself as a pioneer in fields as diverse as culture, sport, science and technology. An old saying has it that: 'What Manchester does today, London does tomorrow.' That might not be objectively true in the 21st century, but the fact remains that Manchester is one of Britain's most richly rewarding, and forward thinking, cities. If you put in a little effort, Manchester offers an experience you'll not find anywhere else. Pack your brolly, roll your sleeves up and get stuck in.

Explore

CITY CENTRE

Manchester's compact and bustling city centre is easy to get around. The glorious, neo-Gothic **Town Hall** (and the contrasting neo-classical **Central Library** close by) speak volumes about Manchester's sense of self and are fine introductions to this industrious city. Nearby, **Manchester Art Gallery** is also housed in an imposing neo-classical building, designed by Charles Barry in 1824.

Heading north along **Deansgate** will take you past the **Spinningfields** complex (all steel and glass façades and top-name designer outlets) before opening out on to the smaller, older charms of **St Ann's Square**, home to the Royal Exchange Theatre. Further north lies **Exchange Square** and the retail delights of Selfridges and nearby Harvey Nichols; the square's concentric benches make it a pleasant place to rest up if the sun's out. It's also close to **Urbis**, Manchester's museum of urban culture, whose vertiginous glass façade opens directly on to the pleasantly undulating green slopes of **Cathedral Gardens**, often colonised by skateboarders.

Slotted between Victoria Station and the Triangle, a corner of medieval Manchester lives on in the form of **Chetham's Library** (Long Millgate, 0161 834 7961, www.chethams. org.uk), a stunning fragment of the 15th century that has survived more or less intact, open to visitors (it's still a functioning library, so phone to check that all rooms are open). Within its impressive walls Karl Marx and adopted Mancunian Friedrich Engels met in the reading room to research their ideas of communist theory. Not far away is **Manchester Cathedral**: a church has stood on this site since the first millennium. The current structure was rebuilt following damage caused during the Civil War and World War II, and by the IRA bomb of 1996.

Manchester Art Gallery

Mosley Street (0161 235 8888/www.manchester galleries.org). Open 10am-5pm Tue-Sun. Admission free.
The city's municipal gallery is home to some stunning Pre-Raphaelite art. Highlights of the permanent collection include Rossetti's *Astarte Syriaca* as well as notable pieces by Turner and Modigliani. There's also a changing programme of prestigious exhibitions on the top floor. The building had an extensive extension and refit in 2002, which brought a new wing and an interactive children's gallery.

Town Hall

Albert Square (0161 234 5000/www.manchester.gov.uk). Open 9am-5pm Mon-Fri. Admission free.
Alfred Waterhouse's building, completed in 1887, remains a proud symbol of the city. Its imposing halls are usually, but not always, open to the public – ring in advance to check. Visitors are normally free to visit the ground floor Sculpture Hall and, on the first floor, the Great Hall, which features a noted series of 12 Ford Madox Brown murals.

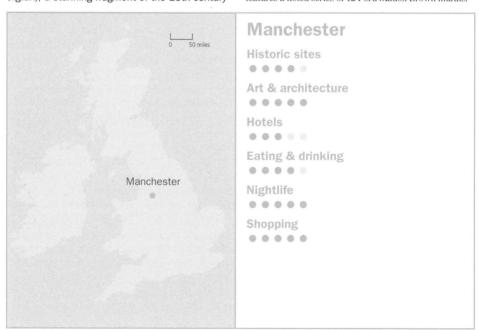

0   50 miles

Manchester

Manchester

Historic sites
● ● ● ● ●

Art & architecture
● ● ● ● ●

Hotels
● ● ● ● ●

Eating & drinking
● ● ● ● ●

Nightlife
● ● ● ● ●

Shopping
● ● ● ● ●

Urbis

Cathedral Gardens (0161 605 8200/www.urbis. org.uk). Open Galleries 10am-6pm Tue-Sun. Admission Galleries free.

For several years after it opened in 2002, no one really knew what Urbis was all about. It remained unloved and unpopular until a new director was brought in to shake things up – to good effect. This museum of urban culture now puts on a changing display of thought-provoking and edgy shows on subjects as diverse as street art, hip hop, civil rights, sustainability and high fashion. It also runs some of the best guided tours of the city. On the top floor, the Modern restaurant serves some mean cocktails and does a brisk trade in British food.

NORTHERN QUARTER

To find Manchester's self-styled creative quarter, follow the stream of skinny-jean-clad kids heading up **Oldham Street**, with its defiantly independent vintage boutiques, galleries, cafés and record shops. Part of the Northern Quarter's charm is its architecture – a ramshackle collection of 18th- and 19th-century warehouses. Some have been beautifully restored (such as the building housing the Buddhist Centre), while others are falling into disrepair. At the heart of the district is the neo-Romanesque façade of the former **Smithfield Market**. Now surrounded by rather ugly flats, it fronts on to a pocket-sized square. The market's sister building can be found on Oak Street, now the **Craft & Design Centre** (see p133).

> "Let's get one thing straight: Salford isn't in Manchester. There's nothing likely to rile the locals more than mistaking the two."

PICCADILLY, CHINATOWN & THE GAY VILLAGE

Strolling down **Canal Street** can feel a bit like walking on to the set of *Queer as Folk*, the 1990s TV show that propelled the area into the national consciousness. Bars, clubs and restaurants cluster around the canal, and it's a treat to grab a seat on this traffic-free street and watch life's parade pass by. **Tribeca** (50 Sackville Street, 0161 236 8300, www.tribeca-bar.co.uk), **Taurus** (1 Canal Street, 0161 236 4593, www.taurus-bar.co.uk) and **Manto** (46 Canal Street, 0161 236 2667) are good places to start the night, while the choice of clubs means you won't stop until sunrise (see pp135-136).

Close by is **Piccadilly Gardens**. Tadao Ando's concrete 'bunker' at its foot provides a barrier from the fuming buses at the interchange beyond, making for a more pleasant open-air experience. A series of splashy walk-though fountains attract kids, while bars and cafés have improved the ugly office block that lies to the east.

A few minutes' walk away, the multi-tiered **Chinese Imperial Arch** marks the start of **Chinatown**. Built in 1987 as a gift from the Chinese people, the arch was the first of its kind in Europe. Chinatown is lively all year round, but Chinese New Year is celebrated with particular vigour: expect lavish fireworks, food and an enormous dancing dragon.

OXFORD ROAD & AROUND

Infamous for its thundering traffic, Oxford Road nevertheless packs in so many galleries, museums and theatres that locals talk of it as Manchester's 'cultural corridor'. At the northern end of the main arterial route connecting the centre to south Manchester is **Cornerhouse** (see p132), the city's acclaimed contemporary art complex, while at the other is the red-brick **Whitworth Art Gallery** (see p135). In between are theatres, the **Manchester Museum** (University of Manchester, Oxford Road, 0161 275 2634, www.museum.man.ac.uk) and the University of Manchester's collegiate campus, a quadrangle of Gothic buildings designed by Alfred Waterhouse.

CASTLEFIELD & DEANSGATE LOCKS

With its railway arches, vast viaduct, cleaned-up canals and impressive supply of cobblestones, **Castlefield** is one of the city's loveliest outdoor spots. Though it can be quiet on weekdays, Castlefield offers something that the rest of the city often overlooks: peace and tranquillity. In summer, it is the perfect place to sit in the sun and sup a decent pint. Closer to town, **Deansgate Locks** is home to a collection of bars frequented by the short-skirted and shirt-and-booted brigade; each bar is located within a railway arch and faces on to the canal.

Museum of Science & Industry in Manchester

Liverpool Road (0161 832 2244/www.msim.org.uk). Open 10am-5pm daily. Admission free.

A family-friendly playground of vintage technology, set amid the remains of Liverpool Road's 1830s railway station. Highlights include a huge Power Hall of thrusting, steaming turbines and an Air and Space Hall that features airborne greats such as a colossal Shackleton bomber.

SALFORD & SALFORD QUAYS

Let's get one thing straight: Salford isn't in Manchester. There's nothing likely to rile the locals more than mistaking the two cities. Salford and Manchester are two separate cities that just

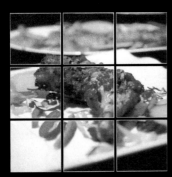

happen to share a border (and, arguably, a city centre). Salfordians are proud of their industrial heritage and tight-knit communities, while the Smiths' *The Queen is Dead* album cover (shot in front of Salford Lads Club) put Salford on the musical map. The **King's Arms** (*see p135*) is testament to Salford's eclectic independence; a regular theatre and gig venue, it's one of the hosts of the **Sounds From The Other City** music festival in May.

Salford Quays boasts one thing its sister city doesn't: a spectacular waterfront. A 15-minute tram-hop west of the city centre, the **Lowry Arts Centre** (*see p135*) lies by the **Manchester Ship Canal**, surrounded by the made-for-footballers deluxe apartments and a designer-outlet shopping mall. It's also smack bang opposite **Imperial War Museum North**. Come 2011 it will have a brand new neighbour: Media City, the new northern home of the BBC.

Imperial War Museum North

Salford Quays *The Quays, Trafford Wharf (0161 836 4000/www.iwm.org.uk). Open Mar-Oct 10am-6pm daily. Nov-Feb 10am-5pm daily. Admission free.*
The brain-boggling design of the Imperial War Museum is based on renowned architect Daniel Libeskind's concept of a shattered globe (representing a world divided by conflict). Inside, the floors and doors gently slope and disorientate. The place works hard – and mainly succeeds – at being an entertaining and educational multi-media-led venue. Its permanent displays – which include artillery, audio-visual shows and interactive exhibits such as the Trench – are supplemented by regular temporary exhibitions. The tower, meanwhile, gives an impressive, if vertigo-inducing, view across the Ship Canal.

NORTH MANCHESTER

Sometimes overlooked in favour of south Manchester's more affluent suburbs, the north races ahead of its southern sister when it comes to sports. Two miles from the centre, **Sportcity** is a sprawling complex that houses the National Squash Centre, the Regional Tennis Centre and Manchester Velodrome. It's part of the legacy of the 2002 Commonwealth Games, an event that single-handedly reversed economic decline in north-east Manchester. No tour of Sportcity would be complete without visiting Manchester City's ground – the **City of Manchester Stadium**.

SOUTH MANCHESTER

Heading south along **Oxford Road** takes you towards the Curry Mile at **Rusholme**, a riotous strip of neon lights, booming bhangra tunes and tightly packed curry houses. Further south, **West Didsbury** and **Chorlton** are stuffed with enough independent boutiques, delis, cafés and bars to satisfy the most discerning of urbanites. Comfy boozers abound, and it's easy to lose an afternoon downing pints of local and organic beer;

Chorlton's Marble Beer House (57 Manchester Road) is a good bet. Although not quite as spectacular as the north, this slice of Manchester also enjoys decent sports venues: **Old Trafford** is home to Manchester United and Lancashire County Cricket Club.

Eat

Good food is also available for non-residents in some hotels listed in the Stay section, including **Abode** (*see p136*, winner of Restaurant of the Year in the 2008 Manchester Food & Drink Festival), **Obsidian** at the Arora International (*see p136*), and **Podium** at the Hilton (*see p139*). See also **Deaf Institute** (*p135*), the **Modern** in Urbis (*p127*), and **Harvey Nichols** (*p132*).

Greens

South Manchester *43 Lapwing Lane, Didsbury (0161 434 4259/www.greensdidsbury.co.uk). Open 5.30-10.30pm Mon; noon-2pm, 5.30-10.30pm Tue-Fri; 11am-4pm, 5.30-10.30pm Sat; 12.30-3.30pm, 5.30-10.30pm Sun. £££. Vegetarian.*
A visit to Greens has many carnivores avowing 'I loved it, and I'm not even vegetarian'. The 'Inclusive Menu' (two courses for £13.95 from 5.30pm to 6.45pm Monday to Friday, Sunday and Sunday lunch) is a real bargain. The carte, meanwhile, offers adventurous dishes such as deep-fried oyster mushrooms with plum sauce and Chinese pancakes, followed by a 'black pudding' kedgeree of rice, lentils and egg with curry spices. Pudding might be apple and blueberry crumble with caramel coconut sauce.

Isinglass

South Manchester *46 Flixton Road, Urmston (0161 749 8400/www.isinglassrestaurant.co.uk). Open 6-10pm Tue-Sat; noon-10pm Sun. ££.*
Suburban Urmston is the unlikely home of Isinglass, one of Manchester's most impressive restaurants. The name refers to the gelatin-like substance made from fish bladders used to clarify beer and wine – but don't let that put you off. This idiosyncratic establishment takes the oft-empty promise of only using local ingredients, and shows what can be achieved: salad leaves from Chat Moss, rich Dunham Massey ice-cream, meat from Knutsford. The menu pays homage to traditional British dishes, with the likes of venison toad-in-the-hole, wilted kale, Cumberland gravy and mash, but there's nothing old-fashioned about the cooking. Prices are impressively low.

Ithaca

City Centre *36 John Dalton Street (0870 740 4000/ www.ithacamanchester.com). Open noon-3pm, 6-10pm Mon-Wed; noon-3pm, 6pm-11pm Thur-Sat. ££££. Japanese.*
One of Manchester's most sumptuous and long-awaited (two years and £4 million in development) eateries, Ithaca's

high-voltage interior (glossy black tables, statement chandeliers) more than matches the quality of its contemporary Japanese cuisine. The Wagyu beef carpaccio is exquisite, though the à la carte sushi menu gives it a run for its money. This is fine dining with a side order of bling – and all the better for it.

Lime Tree

South Manchester *8 Lapwing Lane, Didsbury (0161 445 1217/www.thelimetreerestaurant.co.uk). Open 5.30-10.15pm Mon, Sat; noon-2.30pm, 5.30-10.15pm Tue-Fri, Sun. £££. French.*
Patrick Hannity's refined operation has loyal customers bordering on the evangelical in their enthusiasm, but their fervour is well placed. This place wears its French influences lightly, so dishes of calves liver are served with a delicious bubble and squeak.

Market Restaurant

Northern Quarter *104 High Street (0161 834 3743/ www.market-restaurant.com). Open noon-10pm Tue-Sat; noon-5pm Sun. £££. Modern British.*
The unprepossessing decor may underwhelm but, as is so often the case in Manchester, looks should not be read as an indicator of quality. The Market has racked up a quarter of a century of excellent cooking and has now refined its modern British style to perfection, with the likes of pan-fried plaice with oxtail tortellini, roasted cepes and red wine reduction meeting macaroni cheese with wild mushrooms and spring onion fricassée. The beers also come highly recommended, with a fine list of Belgian brews.

River Restaurant

Salford *Lowry Hotel, 50 Dearmans Place (0161 827 4041/www.theriverrestaurant.com). Open 7-10.30am, noon-2.30pm, 5.30-10pm Mon-Fri; 7.30-11am, noon-2.30pm, 5.30-10.30pm Sat; 7.30-11am, 12.30-3pm, 5.30-10pm Sun. ££££. British.*
Eyck Zimmer – a chef who honed his talent at the Dorchester and the Ritz, and originally put the River Restaurant on the foodie map – was always going to be a hard act to follow. Luckily, the fast-rising Oliver Thomas ensures that this waterfront restaurant continues to delight, with subtle treatments of British ingredients (ham hock with yellow split peas and dandelion, say, followed by Welsh salt marsh lamb cutlets with kidney and bubble and squeak). Views over the Irwell aren't that inspiring, but the seafood is excellent, particularly the straight-from-the-deep oysters.

Room

City Centre *81 King Street (0161 839 2005/ www.roomrestaurants.com). Open noon-10pm Mon-Wed; noon-11pm Thur-Sat. ££. International.*
Taking its inspiration from the now infamous dishes of the 1970s, Room's mission is to put the kitsch back to the kitchen. Don't be put off; Room takes old retro favourites like prawn and avocado cocktail or chicken Kiev and delivers them kicking and screaming into the 21st century, thus proving that old-fashioned doesn't necessarily mean bad.

Sam's Chop House

City Centre *Chapel Walks (0161 834 3210/www. samschophouse.co.uk). Open noon-3pm, 5.30-9.30pm Mon-Sat; noon-8pm Sun. £££. British.*
If you fancy some truly traditional British cooking, Sam's is your place. It's a beautiful old pub with Victorian green tiling and curved lead windows. Menu highlights include brown onion soup, dumplings, roast beef, corned beef hash and steak and kidney pudding. Don't forget to leave room for dessert: steamed lemon sponge with custard will leave you weak at the knees. Its sister establishment, Mr Thomas's Chop House, is located nearby at 52 Cross Street (0161 832 2245).

Tampopo

City Centre *16 Albert Square (0161 819 1966/ www.tampopo.co.uk). Open noon-11pm Mon-Sat; noon-10pm Sun. ££. Oriental.*
In spite of its subterranean location, Tampopo has a pleasantly airy feel, and the shared tables lend the place a buzz when it's busy. The menu incorporates tastes from Japan, Malaysia, Indonesia and other Eastern destinations to deliver a Most Wanted of the region's cooking: the tasty noodle dishes are especially recommended.

Vermilion

North Manchester *Lord North Street, Hulme Hall Lane (0161 202 0055/www.vermilionrestaurant.co.uk). Open noon-2.30pm, 6-10pm Mon-Thur; noon-2.30pm, 5-11pm Fri; 5-11pm Sat; noon-4pm, 6-10pm Sun. £££. Thai.*
The fringes of an industrial estate may not be the most salubrious of locations, but Vermilion is certainly a sumptuous affair. From the lifts that whisk you up to the bar, with its gigantic coconut-shaped seating pods, to the display of Buddha heads that runs throughout the restaurant, it's easy to see where the £4.5-million fit-out budget went. The restaurant is headed up by Chumpol Jangprai, once named Bangkok's best chef; his menu presents an accessible selection of Thai dishes.

Yang Sing

Chinatown *34 Princess Street (0161 236 2200/ www.yang-sing.com). Open noon-11pm Mon-Thur; noon-midnight Fri, Sat; noon-10.30pm Sun. £££. Chinese.*
This fantastically glamorous Chinese restaurant has had a tumultuous 30-year history: a fire and a reality TV show being just two of its events. Through it all, the kitchen has remained admirably consistent. Don't bother with the menu: simply explain to your waiter what you like and don't like, agree a price per head, and leave it to the kitchen to prepare you a feast.

Shop

The best shopping in Manchester can be found at either end of the retail spectrum. For a high-end, big-brand experience, head for **King Street** and its environs: if you're in search of more quirky

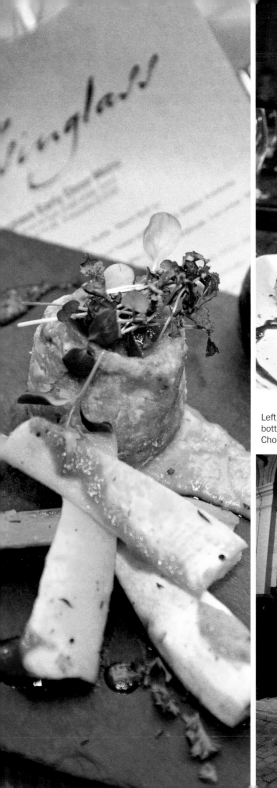

Left & top: Isinglass;
bottom: Sam's
Chop House.

Manchester International Festival

The government-backed regeneration of Manchester following the IRA bomb of 1996 transformed what was once a moribund city centre into something vibrant, dynamic and indubitably modern. Old buildings were renovated and repurposed; gleaming new towers now pierce the sky above them. Visitors returning to the city after a couple of decades away may not recognise it.

However, the changes haven't been limited to the city's appearance. Manchester has a famous musical heritage, of course, and its theatre scene has been strong for a number of years. But the cultural regeneration of the city really picked up speed in 2007 with the launch of the Manchester International Festival, a daring enterprise – held every two years in summer – that quickly grabbed both press headlines and public attention.

Cultural festivals are ten a penny in the UK these days, but the MIF has been careful to carve for itself a unique selling point. Billed as 'an artist-led festival', the MIF concentrates on commissioning brand new works from artists hailing from home and abroad, covering everything from rock music to visual art. It's a bold initiative – and one that could run the risk of embarrassing everyone concerned. However, backed by funding from the city council and a host of big-ticket sponsors, festival director Alex Poots and his team have wasted no time in putting the event on the country's cultural map.

Not everything in the 2007 festival was a roaring success, but there were more hits than misses. And nothing hit bigger than *Monkey: Journey to the West*, an opera created by director Chen Shi-Zheng with the Gorillaz

team of Damon Albarn and Jamie Hewlett, which won rave reviews before going on to extended sell-out runs in London and Paris. Other highlights in 2007 included *Il Tempo del Postino*, a controversial show that premièred stage works from visual artists such as Matthew Barney; and *Interiors*, staged in a Chorley house and starring Johnny Vegas as a man on the edge of a breakdown.

The line-up for the 2009 festival was every bit as impressive. Some shows featured artists who'd first appeared in 2007: Albarn worked with documentarian Adam Curtis and theatre director Felix Barrett on a haunted house-inspired show about America's rise to global pre-eminence in the '60s; Neil Bartlett, who directed *The Pianist* in 2007, devised a bingo-themed show for the Royal Exchange; and dancer Carlos Acosta returned with a new show paying tribute to some of the greats of classical ballet. However, other events shone the spotlight on artists who were new to the festival: the world première of singer-songwriter Rufus Wainwright's debut opera, for instance, and two sold-out concerts by Elbow with the city's Hallé orchestra.

The challenge for all cultural festivals is to retain the attention of their audiences from year to year, which can only safely be done by topping what's gone before. The challenge for the Manchester International Festical, in particular, is to maintain its momentum: for all its early success, it's still a young festival fighting for attention in a crowded cultural calendar. However, after such a strong launch, it's hard to bet against the 2011 event building further on the festival's strong foundations.

For more information see www.mif.co.uk.

finds, try the one-off independent boutiques that cluster around the **Northern Quarter**. In between, along **Market Street** and in the **Arndale**, you'll find more run-of-the-mill high-street shops that do the job (just not as expensively or as lovingly).

Afflecks Palace

Northern Quarter *52 Church Street (0161 839 0718/ www.afflecks.com). Open 10.30am-6pm Mon-Fri; 10am-6pm Sat.*
The building used to be Affleck & Brown's – Manchester's premier department store – and at weekends, this four-floor alternative shopping mecca heaves with disaffected teens. You'll find new designers, clubwear, vintage, fancy dress, records and cute and kitsch gifts. For a leisurely browse visit midweek and, with careful purchasing, you can still emerge with gorgeous items at teenage prices.

Craft & Design Centre

Northern Quarter *17 Oak Street (0161 832 4274/ www.craftanddesign.com). Open 10am-5.30pm Mon-Sat.*
This long-established creative hub continues to draw the best local talent. Each floor is lined with small shops and studios, and many traders sell direct from their workshops. Products include one-off bags, jewellery, photographic prints, paintings and sculpture. There's also a pleasant café, and changing exhibitions throughout the year.

Flannels

City Centre *4 St Ann's Place (0161 832 5536/ www.flannelsgroup.com). Open 10am-6pm Mon-Sat; 11am-5pm Sun.*
A Manchester-based independent chain, Flannels stocks the cream of each season's fashion crop. Adored by footballers and their wives, the labels lean towards high-glamour; think Versace, D&G, Gucci and Cavalli. This is the flagship branch, with more formal styles for men and women – a second branch, for women only, is on King Street and stocks casual designer wear such as Juicy Couture. Take your gold card, or an understanding partner.

Harvey Nichols

City Centre *Exchange Square (0161 828 8888/ www.harveynichols.com). Open 10am-7pm Mon-Wed, Fri; 10am-8pm Thur; 9am-7pm Sat; noon-6pm Sun.*
A beacon of luxury with three floors of beauty products, shoes and breathtakingly expensive womenswear. There's a floor of choice menswear morsels, and the small jewel of a food department offers a sublime browsing experience. There's also an absolutely fabulous handbag department featuring the season's most gorgeous arm-candy. The second-floor restaurant is recommended.

Rags to Bitches

Northern Quarter *60 Tib Street (0161 835 9265/ www.rags-to-bitches.co.uk). Open 11.30am-6pm Mon-Sat; 1-5pm Sun.*
This upmarket vintage boutique is decorated like a Victorian jewellery box, and offers carefuly-sourced one-offs, designer and customised pieces from the 1940s to the '80s. It also stocks a fabulous selection of costume jewellery,

handbags and shoes. Regular events, such as clothes swap parties and Dansette disco nights, are held in the '30s-speakeasy-style basement.

Ran

City Centre *7 & 8 St Ann's Arcade (0161 832 9650/ www.ranshop.co.uk). Open 9.30am-6pm Mon-Sat; 11am-5pm Sun.*
This hard-to-find shoe shop rewards perseverance. Its diminutive premises house an eclectic mix of shoes and clothes for men and women, including cutting-edge and rare labels such as Love from Australia, Princess Katrina and Dr Denim. Friendly, personal service and a comfy leather sofa are further draws.

Arts

The first **Manchester International Festival** (*see p134*), held in 2007, gave Manchester a cultural shot in the arm: now the city's galleries, theatre and music events aspire to equally high creative standards. Music festivals **In The City** (October, www.inthecity.co.uk) and **Sounds From The Other City** (May) are a chance to see the UK's hottest up-and-coming bands.

Bridgewater Hall

City Centre *Lower Mosley Street (box office 0161 907 9000/www.bridgewater-hall.co.uk). Open Box office 10am-6pm (8pm performance nights) Mon-Sat; noon-8pm Sun (performance nights only). Tickets £7-£35.*
With impressive musical accoutrements such as a 5,500-pipe organ and a programme of 300-plus events every year, there's no better place to tune into classical, jazz, pop and world music. The decade-old £42-million concert hall is also the performing home of the Hallé and the BBC Philharmonic orchestras.

Cornerhouse

Oxford Road *70 Oxford Street (box office 0161 200 1500/www.cornerhouse.org). Open Box office noon-8pm daily. Admission prices vary.*
At one time the only place in Manchester where you could get a decent cappuccino, Cornerhouse has long been a hip place for hanging out. With three arthouse cinemas, an equal number of galleries and two bookshops, it remains a hub of cutting-edge culture. Weekend nights feature DJs, while the film programme, with regular festivals, talks and indie selections, is the best in town.

Library Theatre

City Centre *Central Library, St Peter's Square (0161 236 7110/www.librarytheatre.com). Open Box Office 10.30am-8pm Mon-Fri; noon-8pm Sat. Tickets £10-£20.*
How does one of the city's smallest theatres garner so much critical acclaim? It's age (50-plus) might help, and the fact that it's the only rep theatre in the country that is funded by a city council means it can maintain its own unique ethos.

But what really sets it apart is the passion with which it stages its productions. The blend of drama, modern classics and regional premières keeps the plaudits rolling in.

Lowry Arts Centre
Salford Quays *Pier 8 (0870 787 5780/www.the lowry.com). Open Galleries 11am-5pm Mon-Fri, Sun; 10am-5pm Sat. Admission Galleries free.*
As the name might suggest, this landmark waterside building at Salford Quays houses an extensive collection of LS Lowry's art. Lowry is only half of the story, however, as the centre also brings together an impressive variety of visual and performing arts. As well as a changing programme of painting, sculpture and photography, the steel-clad wonder has also hosted more award-winning theatre productions than any other regional venue. Its two theatres also host blockbuster musicals, dance, opera, comedy, ballet, jazz and folk.

Whitworth Art Gallery
Oxford Road *Whitworth Park (0161 275 7450/ www.whitworth.manchester.ac.uk). Open 10am-5pm Mon-Sat; noon-4pm Sun. Admission free.*
The Manchester arts scene has seen some sweeping changes to this Victorian gallery since the arrival of a new director in 2006. Expect cutting-edge contemporary art displayed alongside some of the finest historical collections of textiles, wallpaper, watercolours and historic painting in the country.

Nightlife

An evening out in Manchester can be an eclectic experience. From the venues favoured by the skimpily-clad lovelies and their admirers in **Deansgate Locks** (*see p127*), and the footballer hangouts around **Deansgate** (*see p126*), to the painfully hip bars that cluster around the **Northern Quarter** (*see p127*) and the lively bars and clubs of the **Gay Village** (*see p127*), there really is something for everyone.

As well as the venues listed below, see also **Rags to Bitches** (*see p132*) and the **Podium** restaurant-bar at the Hilton (*see p139*).

Briton's Protection
City Centre *50 Great Bridgewater Street (0161 236 5895). Open 11am-11pm Mon-Thur; 11am-midnight Fri; noon-midnight Sat; noon-10.30pm Sun. No credit cards.*
The red neon sign over the door at Briton's Protection draws drinkers like moths to a flame. The roomy interior is pub perfection: brass fixtures and fittings, and paintings commemorating the 1819 Peterloo Massacre. At lunchtime, punters are mostly business people; later on, Bridgewater Hall concertgoers sneaking in a pre-show quickie take over the tables. No-nonsense brews from Jennings and Robinson's are the staples, but the real attractions are the 150-plus whiskies and bourbons.

Cruz 101
Gay Village *101 Princess Street (0161 950 0101/ www.cruz101.com). Open 11pm-5am Mon, Thur, Sun; 11pm-3.30am Tue; 11pm-6am Fri, Sat.*
Really two clubs in one, with a large main room and smaller lower level, Cruz is Manchester's oldest gay club – but the (mostly) bright young things on its dancefloor keep its appeal fresh. Though it started as a gay disco (think Chic and Donna Summer), the music policy has since evolved, and now features a more varied mix of funky house, pop, trance and R&B.

Deaf Institute
Oxford Road *Grosvenor Street (0161 276 9350/ www.thedeafinstitute.co.uk). Open 10am-2am Mon-Thur, Sun; 10am-3am Fri, Sat (closing times may vary).*
The Deaf Institute stands out from the bar-and-clubbing pack by virtue of its location. Set in glorious neo-Gothic surrounds, the three-storey building has a communal-benches-and-tables café, cosy boutique bar and a dome-shaped music hall, complete with tiered seating and glittering mirror ball. This latter space has put the Institute on the musical map, as it has played host to nights as diverse as Chips With Everything and Akoustik Anarkhy. Complete with cute/cool/quirky interior, the Deaf Institute is the hot ticket south of the city centre.

Essential
Gay Village *8 Minshull Street (0161 236 0077/www. essentialmanchester.com). Open 11pm-4am Thur, Sun; 11pm-5am Fri; 11pm-7am Sat.*
Run by Take That's former manager and de facto king of camp Nigel Martyn Smith, Manchester's first gay superclub took the city by storm when it burst on to the scene about a decade ago. Visits by gay deities like Kylie Minogue kept the buzz going, and on a scene defined by the new and fresh, the longevity of the biggest gay superclub outside the capital now seems assured.

King's Arms
Salford *11 Bloom Street (0161 832 3605/www.studio salford.com). Open noon-11pm Mon-Thur; noon-midnight Fri, Sat; noon-6pm Sun.*
The King's Arms is a real gem; an alcopop-free zone, sitting pretty in the no-man's-land between Manchester and Salford (it's an easy stroll from the city centre). Beers include offerings from Bazens and Flintshire beer-meisters Facers, with Timothy Taylor a staple. The menu promises hearty grub sourced from local suppliers, while the fantastic vaulted room upstairs (home to Studio Salford, a collective of theatre groups) plays host to regular band nights and plays. All told, it's hard to fault this pub – even the jukebox has won awards.

Matt & Phred's Jazz Club
Northern Quarter *64 Tib Street (0161 831 7002/ www.mattandphreds.com). Open 5pm-1.30am Mon-Thur; 5pm-2am Fri, Sat.*
Set up by two musicians, Matt & Phred's is a much-loved Northern Quarter staple, and Manchester's only live jazz music club. The cosy interior is the perfect setting for the

Great John Street Hotel.

musical entertainment provided by local and international acts. Legendary pizzas and meticulously-mixed cocktails add to the appeal.

Modern

City Centre *Levels 5 & 6 Urbis, Cathedral Gardens (0161 605 8200/www.themodernmcr.co.uk). Open noon-midnight Mon-Thur, Sun; noon-2am Fri, Sat..*
Perched on the top floors of Urbis, Manchester's very own museum of urban life, this restaurant and bar is good for three things. First, the view from up top isn't half bad. Second, its menu – unpretentious modern British – is fabulous (and fantastically good value). And third, the cocktails are arguably among the best in the city.

Night & Day Café

Northern Quarter *26 Oldham Street (0161 236 4597/www.nightnday.org). Open 10am-2am Mon-Sat (occasional Sun).*
Dingy but full of character, Night & Day is perfectly situated among Oldham Street's record shops: first do some crate-digging, then head on over for a relaxed beer and catch tomorrow's big act or cult faves hanging out, having fun and – if you're lucky – playing intimate sets. Relaxed café-bar by day, world-class rock 'n' roll bar by night: no self-respecting music fan can claim a 'proper' trip to Manchester without a visit here.

A Place Called Common

Northern Quarter *39-41 Edge Street (0161 832 9245/ www.aplacecalledcommon.co.uk). Open noon-midnight Mon-Wed; noon-1am Thur; noon-2am Fri; 1pm-2am Sat; 2pm-midnight Sun.*
A sure-fire bet in the Northern Quarter for friendly staff, quality drinks and lively environment: Common doesn't sacrifice service for boho charm. There's an ever-changing mix of street art on the walls, DJs spinning records and own-made food being served up until closing time.

Warehouse Project

Piccadilly *Store Street (underneath Piccadilly Station) (0161 835 3500/www.thewarehouseproject.com). Open/ admission Sept-1 Jan times & prices vary, call or check website for details. No credit cards.*
Dubbed the 'biggest thing to happen to clubbing in Manchester this decade', the Warehouse Project is an annual season of underground parties of epic proportions. Running for 12 weeks (September to New Year's Eve), the Project features some of the biggest names in dance and electronica alongside smaller, edgier acts. With an up-for-it-crowd, as well as the old-school vibes of its 'secret' underground location, it's little wonder tickets regularly sell out. If you're in Manchester in the autumn, this is one not to be missed.

Stay

Abode

Piccadilly *107 Piccadilly (0161 247 7744/ www.abodehotels.co.uk). £££.*

A recent-ish addition to the hotels in the city (it opened in 2007), Abode is notable for its location, a stone's throw from Piccadilly Station, and its basement restaurant. The latter is masterminded by the Michelin-starred chef, Michael Caines, and it shows: it scooped Restaurant of the Year in the 2008 Manchester Food & Drink Festival awards with a menu that is as stylish as its sophisticated champagne bar. Rooms are comfortable and contemporary.

Arora International

City Centre *18-24 Princess Street (0161 236 8999/ www.arorainternational.com). £££.*
Cliff Richard isn't a name you'd normally associate with cutting-edge design. Yet the holy rock 'n' roller is part owner of one of the hippest hotels in the city. Set in the city centre, the Arora is a vision of contemporary cool, with sleek, modern rooms and funky furniture (though unless you're a fan, you might want to avoid the five Cliff-themed rooms). A visit to the hotel bar and fine-dining restaurant, Obsidian, is a must.

Britannia Manchester

City Centre *35 Portland Street (0871 222 0017/ www.britanniahotels.com). ££.*
The Britannia's main selling points are its location – right on Piccadilly Gardens – and its reasonable rates. The ostentatious building and decor will not be to everyone's taste, but it's perfect for those who like a bit of faded grandeur, with a sweeping gold staircase and huge chandeliers. A recent refurbishment has spruced up the traditionally furnished rooms.

Great John Street Hotel

City Centre *Great John Street (0161 831 3211/www.greatjohnstreet.co.uk). ££££.*
This Eclectic Collection hotel pulls out all the stops to deliver a truly luxurious boutique experience. Housed in an old Victorian school, all the accommodation is in the form of duplex suites, each uniquely designed. Hand-carved furniture, roll-top baths and super-sexy fabrics and fittings lend the place a modern-vintage feel. The absence of a restaurant and guest parking is made up for by a butler's tray for breakfast, a chi-chi ground-floor bar and a rooftop hot tub.

Hatters

Northern Quarter *50 Newton Street (0161 236 9500/ www.hattersgroup.com). £.*
A short walk from Piccadilly Station, Hatters offers hostel accommodation for budget travellers. Rooms are basic, but added extras such as complimentary tea, coffee and toast and quality mattresses on the bunk beds make a stay here more comfortable. An open kitchen and canteen area gives guests somewhere sociable to warm up their soup. Friendly staff lead regular pub crawls and tours around the area.

Hilton Manchester Deansgate

Castlefield & Deansgate Locks *303 Deansgate (0161 870 1600/www.hilton.co.uk). £££.*
There may be a set of swanky apartments above, but for 23 impressive floors the Beetham Tower belongs to the Hilton,

as witnessed by the unmissable branding. Rooms are kitted out with all the latest technology (ergonomic workstations, laptop access). Cloud 23 bar, at the top of the hotel, is straight out of *Lost in Translation*. The ground floor Podium restaurant-bar doesn't have the impressive views, but does great food.

Holiday Inn Manchester West

Salford *West Liverpool Street (0161 743 0080/ www.holidayinn.co.uk). ££.*
What the Holiday Inn lacks in character it makes up for in reliability. You know what you're getting at this straightforward chain in sunny Salford: a mid-range option with 82 modern looking rooms and a bar and restaurant. A refurbishment has given the place a clean, fresh feel.

Lowry

Salford *50 Dearmans Place, Chapel Wharf (0161 827 4000/www.thelowryhotel.com). ££££.*
The hotel of choice for visiting actors, politicians and Premiership footballers, the Lowry is Manchester's original five-star hotel. The address may be Salford, but it's located right on the city centre's edge, on the banks of the murky River Irwell. Everything is as it should be – huge, hip rooms with super-sized beds, original modern art, discreet service and clued-up staff. A swanky spa and the serene River Restaurant are further draws.

Malmaison

Piccadilly *(0161 278 1000/www.malmaison-manchester.com). ££££.*
A favourite with visiting bands and celebs, the Malmaison is a first choice for those who like to think of themselves as arbiters of taste. The old Joshua Hoyle textile mill now sports a theatrical dark-toned red, brown and black colour scheme in many of the suites. The star of the line-up, though, has to be the seriously sexy Moulin Rouge room; the free-standing bath in the lounge takes around 30 minutes to fill, such is its depth.

Midland Hotel

City Centre *Peter Street (0161 236 3333/ www.qhotels.co.uk). £££.*
This grand old dame of Manchester hotels opened in 1905. It has had its fair share of high-profile visitors over the decades (Winston Churchill, Princess Anne) and is famous as the place where Charles Stewart Rolls and Frederick Henry Royce met. After a few years in hotel-world wilderness, the Midland is back on glamorous form after a massive £15 million makeover by new owners Q Hotels. The feel is modern classic throughout, from the marble-floored reception to its richly furnished rooms.

Palace Hotel

Oxford Road *Oxford Street (0161 288 1111/ www.principal-hotels.com). £££.*
This well-loved, characterful hotel, housed in the Grade II-listed Refuge Assurance Building, was acquired by the Principal Hotels group and received a £7-million facelift in 2005. The restored glass dome over the vast reception makes for an impressive entrance, while the Tempus bar combines original marble flooring and Victorian tiles with cool design. The stylish, understated bedrooms have undergone a recent revamp.

Radisson Edwardian

City Centre *Free Trade Hall, Peter Street (0161 835 9929/www.radissonedwardian.com). ££££.*
Some may say that turning the historically important Free Trade Hall into a hotel is criminal, but the Radisson has made real efforts to do so sympathetically, retaining many of the building's original features. A new extension houses 263 deluxe bedrooms, each with an inviting king-size bed, plenty of sleek technology (including Bang & Olufsen entertainment systems) and gleaming marble bathrooms. Suites are named after illustrious figures who have performed or spoken at the hall, with Dylan and Fitzgerald making penthouse appearances, and Gladstone and Dickens patronising the meeting rooms.

Factfile

When to go

Let's face it: you won't be going to Manchester for the weather – and, although the city's reputation as one of Britain's wettest is undeserved (it doesn't even make it into the top five of the country's soggiest), it's worth packing your waterproofs. The best time to visit is late summer and early autumn, with Manchester International Festival held every other July and the city's festival, live music and clubbing season In The City getting into full swing in October.

Getting there & around

Piccadilly Station is the main railway station; the Metrolink shuttle (www.gmpte.com) operates a free bus service connecting this, and the other

city railway stations, to the City Centre. Buses run every 5-10 minutes. Manchester Airport is to the south of the City Centre and well served by a regular rail connection to Piccadilly Station. Getting around the city is easy, thanks to its network of trams and buses; exploring on foot is also straightforward, as the city is pretty compact.

Tourist information

Visitor Information Centre Lloyd Street (0871 222 8223/www.manchester.gov.uk). Open 10am-5.30pm Mon-Sat; 10.30am-4.30pm Sun.

Internet

Intercafe Debenhams, 123 Market Street (0161 832 8666).

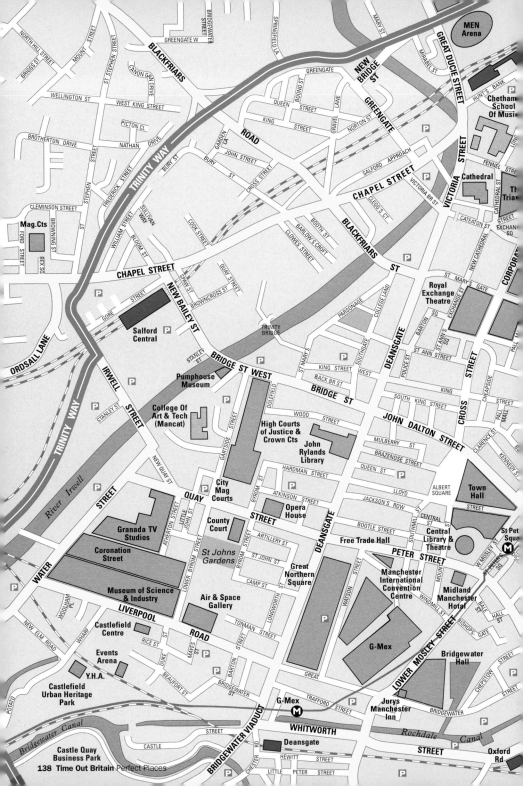

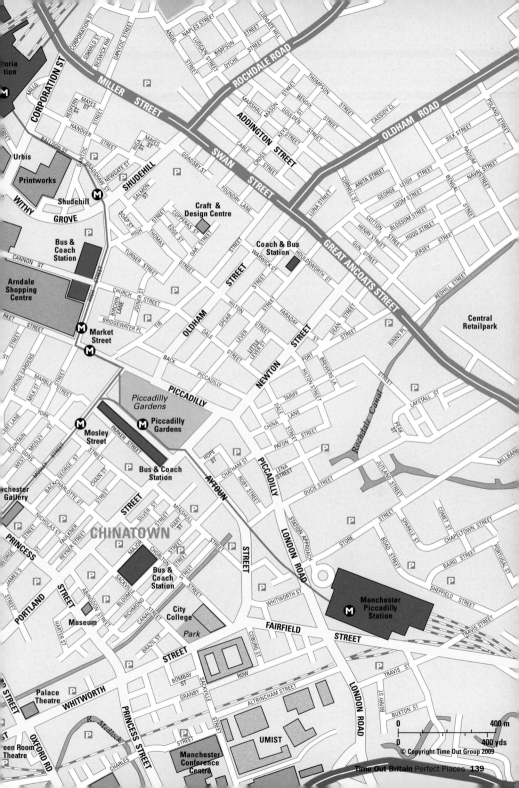

Urbis

Printworks

WITHY

GROVE

Shudehill

Bus &
Coach
Station

Arndale
Shopping
Centre

Market
Street

Craft &
Design Centre

Coach & Bus
Station

Central
Retailpark

Piccadilly
Gardens

Piccadilly
Gardens

Mosley
Street

Bus & Coach
Station

...chester
Gallery

CHINATOWN

PRINCESS

Bus &
Coach
Station

Museum

City
College

Park

Manchester
Piccadilly
Station

FAIRFIELD STREET

Palace
Theatre

WHITWORTH

...een Room
Theatre

OXFORD RD

PRINCESS STREET

R. Medlock

UMIST

Manchester
Conference
Centre

CORPORATION ST

MILLER STREET

SWAN STREET

ROCHDALE ROAD

ADDINGTON STREET

OLDHAM ROAD

GREAT ANCOATS STREET

OLDHAM STREET

NEWTON STREET

PICCADILLY

Rochdale Canal

LONDON ROAD

LONDON ROAD

PORTLAND STREET

0   400 m
0   400 yds

© Copyright Time Out Group 2009

Top: Canary Wharf station; Brick Lane; right: Tower Bridge at night; Tooting Underground station; left: an aerial view.

London

Old city, new heart.

London is the definitive city – not just within Britain, but across the globe. After all, from the Greenwich Prime Meridian it defines time itself. Even the Romans, who founded Londinium in a nothing-much bend of the River Thames in AD 43, cannot have imagined the scale of the empire that London would find itself controlling by the 19th century. Through disasters like the Great Fire of 1666 and the total destruction of huge swathes of the city during the Blitz, London has renewed itself over and over again: now you'll discover a combination of ancient fragments and brand-new buildings, a sometimes baffling mish-mash of neighbourhoods and architectural styles, of wealth and poverty, of beauty and filth. In the midst of it you'll find museums that are the envy of the world, leading performers of dance, classical music and opera, cutting-edge fashion and bleeding-edge music of all types and origins. Here too are representatives of all the world's cultures – the most visible effect of which is the opportunity to dine all round the globe, pretty much without setting foot outside Soho. Of course, London's dominance comes at a price: hotels and restaurants can be eye-wateringly costly. However, many of the city's pleasures are discovered by happenstance on an idle wander through the streets, rather than by booking the hot table a month in advance – and paying through the nose for the privilege. So when the interminable refurbishment of our creaking Underground rail system gets in the way of your day's itinerary, when your bus breaks down or your taxi becomes snarled up in traffic, perhaps Old Father Thames is telling you to get out, explore, see where this ancient, eccentric city wants to take you. London is a fabulous, complex metropolis – be sure to pack your inquisitive spirit.

Explore

THE SOUTH BANK

To walk along the South Bank of the Thames is at once the most unimaginative tourist cliché of modern London and a delight that even the locals find hard to deny themselves. Many of the city's headline sights are packed into a curve of broad riverbank walkway that stretches little more than a mile and a half. At Westminster Bridge, you're opposite the Houses of Parliament and have at your shoulder the populist attractions of the grand **County Hall** (Dalí Universe, the Aquarium, the Movieum) and the **London Eye** (*see below*). Follow the river eastward and you pass the concrete expanse of the **Southbank Centre** (*see p153*), the **National Theatre** (*see p153*), **OXO Tower**, **Shakespeare's Globe** (21 New Globe Walk 020 7902 1400, www.shakespeares-globe.org) – the painstaking reconstruction of a Tudor theatre, and eventually **Borough Market** (*see p153*). Those interested in more idiosyncratic attractions can begin their riverside stroll a little sooner and take in the fully refurbished **Garden Museum** (Lambeth Palace Road, 020 7401 8865, www.gardenmuseum.org. uk), or finish it later in the converted 1930s banana warehouse of the **Design Museum** (Shad Thames, 0870 833 9955, www.designmuseum.org).

London Eye

Westminster Bridge Road (0870 500 0600/www. londoneye.com). Open Oct-May 10am-8pm daily. June, Sept 10am-9pm daily. July, Aug 10am-9.30pm daily. Admission £15.50; £7.75-£12 reductions.
Only intended to turn for five years, this giant wheel beside the Thames proved so popular that it's now scheduled to keep spinning for another 20 years. The 443ft frame, whose 32 glass capsules each hold 25 people, takes you on a half-hour 'flight', allowing plenty of time to ogle the Queen's back garden and study the snake of the Thames.

Tate Modern

Bankside (020 7887 8888/www.tate.org.uk). Open 10am-6pm Mon-Thur, Sun; 10am-10pm Fri, Sat. Admission free; temporary exhibitions prices vary.
This powerhouse of modern art is awe-inspiring for its industrial architecture as much as its exceptional collection of modern (post-1900) international art. Designed by Sir Giles Gilbert Scott, Bankside Power Station shut down in 1981 – to be reborn as an art museum in 2000. It has enjoyed spectacular popularity ever since. The main entrance (tucked to the side, rather than facing the river) leads straight into the cavernous Turbine Hall, used to jaw-dropping effect for large-scale, annual installations (Oct-Apr). The permanent displays feature such heavy-hitters as Matisse, Bacon and Rothko, supplemented by superb blockbuster temporary exhibitions. The Tate-to-Tate boat service (020 7887 8888, £4.30 adults) – decor by Damien Hirst, bar on board – runs every 20 minutes to Millbank and the gallery's equally illustrious predecessor Tate Britain (Millbank, 020 7887 8888), which has a broader and more

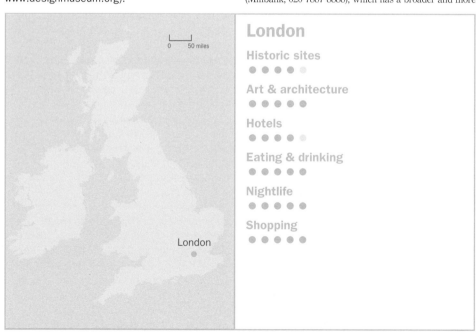

0   50 miles

London

Historic sites

● ● ● ● ○

Art & architecture

● ● ● ● ●

Hotels

● ● ● ● ○

Eating & drinking

● ● ● ● ●

Nightlife

● ● ● ● ●

Shopping

● ● ● ● ●

London
●

Top: Regents park;
bottom: Hyde Park.

inclusive brief: its historical collection includes Hogarth, Constable and Turner, plus modern art from the likes of Stanley Spencer and Lucian Freud.

WESTMINSTER & ST JAMES'S

Trafalgar Square is the literal and symbolic centre of London. Tourists come in their thousands to pose for photographs in front of the lions at the foot of **Nelson's Column**, while locals pile in for frequent festivals (www.london.gov.uk/trafalgar square has an events link) and occasional political protests. Once isolated by busy roads, the square was improved markedly in 2003 by pedestrianisation of the North Terrace, in front of the **National Gallery** (see p145). South down Whitehall, past the shiny-helmeted, mounted sentries outside **Horse Guards** (020 7414 2390, www.householdcavalry.co.uk), is the country's political heart: **Big Ben** and the **Houses of Parliament**, as well as **St Margaret's Church** and **Westminster Abbey** (20 Dean's Yard, 020 7222 5152, www.westminster-abbey.org; admission £12, £9 reductions), site of the coronation of every British monarch (with two exceptions) since William the Conqueror in 1066. The most haunting memorial is the Grave of the Unknown Warrior, but Poets' Corner is another draw. From here, **St James's Park** is just north, with a central lake full of ducks and pelicans (fed at 3pm daily). The bridge over the lake offers very snappable views of **Buckingham Palace** (The Mall, 020 7766 7300, www.royal collection.org.uk), home to British rulers since Queen Victoria and now open for visitors during the summer. The broad, straight road leading east from the palace is the Mall, on which the **ICA** (Institute of Contemporary Arts; 020 7930 0493, www.ica.org.uk) tries to define a forward-looking London of arthouse cinema, performance art and esoteric music.

National Gallery

Trafalgar Square (020 7747 2885/www.national gallery.org.uk). Open 10am-6pm Mon-Thur, Sat, Sun; 10am-9pm Fri. Admission free; temporary exhibitions prices vary.

Founded in 1824 to display just 36 paintings, the National Gallery today houses more than 2,000 works. There are masterpieces from virtually every European school of art, from austere 13th-century religious paintings to the sensual delights of Caravaggio and Van Gogh. In the West Wing are Italian Renaissance masterpieces by Correggio, Titian and Raphael, while the East Wing shows some of the gallery's most popular paintings: French Impressionists and post-Impressionists, including a Van Gogh *Sunflowers* and Renoir's lovely *Les Parapluies*.

SOUTH KENSINGTON & CHELSEA

South Kensington was once known as 'Albertopolis', in honour of the prince who, using profits from the 1851 Great Exhibition, oversaw the inception of its three world-class museums (see pp145-147), colleges and the vast **Royal Albert Hall** (Kensington Gore, 020 7589 3203, www.royalalberthall.com). Albert's contribution is celebrated in the dimensions of the overblown **Albert Memorial**, facing the Albert Hall in Kensington Gardens, its 180-foot spire inlaid with semi-precious stones. Serenely adjacent to both cultural must-sees are the green acres of both **Kensington Gardens** and **Hyde Park** (020 7298 2000, www.royalparks.gov.uk), the division between them now marked only by the Long Water and London's oldest boating lake, the Serpentine. With the park, the small **Serpentine Gallery** (020 7402 6075, www.serpentine gallery.org) shows compelling contemporary art, while the insanities and inanities of political and religious ranters at **Speakers' Corner** (close to Marble Arch tube) continue to entertain passers-by, as they have done since the right to free speech was formalised on this spot in 1872.

For many tourists, London means shopping and shopping means one district: **Knightsbridge**; and one store: **Harrods** (87-135 Brompton Road, 020 7730 1234, www.harrods.com), with its green-coated doormen and showbiz glitz. Here too, glam department store **Harvey Nichols** (109-125 Knightsbridge, 020 7235 5000, www.harveynichols.com), sits on the corner of Sloane Street and heads the parade of expensive designer shops – Gucci, Prada, Chanel – that leads all the way to **Sloane Square**, where blondes with manicured accents sip rosé on brasserie terraces. Nearby, **Duke of York Square** is an enclave of glass-fronted boutiques and eateries, and now the vast new **Saatchi Gallery** (Duke of York's HQ, 020 7823 2363, www.saatchi-gallery.co.uk). **King's Road** itself, hippest of the hip in the Swingin' Sixties, is these days an insipid mix of trendier-than-thou fashion houses and high-street chains, enlivened by a few gems like the **Shop at Bluebird** (350 King's Road, 020 7351 3873). For a break from the bustle, enjoy the gorgeous seclusion of **Chelsea Physic Garden** (66 Royal Hospital Road, 020 7352 5646, www.chelseaphysicgarden.co.uk).

Natural History Museum

Cromwell Road (020 7942 5000/www.nhm.ac.uk). Open 10am-5.50pm daily. Admission free; temporary exhibitions prices vary.

The Natural History Museum opened in a magnificent, purpose-built, Romanesque palazzo in 1881. Now, the vast entrance hall is taken up by a cast of a Diplodocus skeleton, the Blue Zone has a 90ft model of a Blue Whale, and the Green Zone displays a cross-section through a giant sequoia tree – as well as an amazing array of stuffed birds, among which you can compare the fingernail-sized egg of a hummingbird with an elephant bird egg as big as a football. Some 22 million insect and plant specimens are housed in

Eagle.

the new Darwin Centre, where the brand-new eight-storey 'cocoon' enables you to watch the museum's research scientists at work.

Science Museum

Exhibition Road (0870 870 4868/www.sciencemuseum. org.uk). Open 10am-6pm daily. Admission free; temporary exhibitions prices vary.

The Science Museum celebrates the wonders of technology in the service of our daily lives. On the ground floor, the shop – selling wacky toys – is part of the revamped Energy Hall, with its impressive 18th-century steam engines. In 'Exploring Space', rocket science and the lunar landings are illustrated by dramatically lit mock-ups and models, before the museum gears up for its core collection in 'Making the Modern World'. Introduced by the world's oldest steam locomotive, the gallery also contains Stephenson's Rocket and the Apollo 10 command module.

Victoria & Albert Museum

Cromwell Road (020 7942 2000/www.vam.ac.uk). Open 10am-5.45pm Mon-Thur, Sat, Sun; 10am-10pm Fri. Admission free; temporary exhibitions prices vary.

The V&A is one of the world's finest museums, a superb showcase for applied arts from around the world. Some 150 galleries on seven floors contain around four million pieces of furniture, ceramics, sculpture, paintings, posters, jewellery, metalwork, glass, textiles and clothes. Highlights include the seven Raphael Cartoons from 1515, the finest collection of Italian Renaissance sculpture outside Italy, the Great Bed of Ware, Canova's *Three Graces* and the Ardabil carpet. The Fashion galleries run from 18th-century court dress up to contemporary chiffon.

THE WEST END

The modern centre of London is, confusingly, referred to as 'the West End' – a historic hangover from the days when this district was just outside the western City walls. **Covent Garden Piazza** is more warmly looked on by tourists than locals: it's choked by crowds, but buskers and silly shops make it fun if you've some time to kill. Serious shoppers head north to the excellent boutiques that radiate from **Seven Dials**, while serious sightseers can visit the **London Transport Museum** (*see p148*) or, on the north side of the fountain court of **Somerset House** (020 7845 4600, www.somersethouse.org.uk), the surprisingly brilliant modern art (Gauguin, Manet, Cézanne) in the eccentric **Courtauld** (020 7848 2526, www.courtauld.ac.uk/gallery).

A counter-sign to squeaky-clean Covent Garden is the seamy reputation of **Soho**. It is one that is barely deserved these days, although some prostitution and grim strip joints linger. Soho is about different kinds of gratification nowadays: food and booze for the media types that populate the area. Wander the maze of alleys to get a feel for the place, refuelling at characterful cafés like **Maison Bertaux** (28 Greek Street, 020 7437 6007) or **Fernandez & Wells** (73 Beak Street,

020 7287 8124, www.fernandezandwells.com). Soho also has London's longest-established gay scene, its central axis the theatrically cruisey Old Compton Street.

The occasionally earthy and tirelessly exuberant pleasures of Soho are separated from the dignified delights of **Mayfair** only by the grand sweep of Regent's Street. Window-shop exclusive galleries and super-expensive shops before taking on the city's major commercial thoroughfare, **Oxford Street**, with department stores like **Selfridges** (*see p151*) and chain flagships like fashion leader **Topshop** (Oxford Circus, 0844 984 0264, www.topshop.com).

Cross to the north for the boutiques of **Marylebone** and the esoteric delights of the **Wallace Collection** (Hertford House, Manchester Square, 020 7563 9500, www.wallace collection.org): 18th-century furniture, fine painting (Titian, Velázquez) and medieval weaponry. At Marylebone Road, streams of humanity jostle excitedly for the chance to take pictures of each other planting a smacker on the waxen visage of fame at **Madame Tussauds** (0870 999 0046, www.madame-tussauds.co.uk); a bit further north, the slebs are furry – in Regent's Park, **London Zoo** (020 7722 3333, www.zsl.org/london-zoo) has everything from a family of gorillas to a giant anteater.

North of Covent Garden, among the green squares of **Bloomsbury**, is the West End's keynote attraction: the stellar **British Museum** (*see below*). Here too you can visit the coming area of **King's Cross**, where the splendidly refurbished Victorian station **St Pancras International** and bibliographic treasures of the **British Library** (96 Euston Road, 020 7412 7332, www.bl.uk), from the Magna Carta to Beatles lyrics, are free to visit. The macabre medical and anthropological curios and contemporary art of the **Wellcome Collection** (183 Euston Road, 020 7611 2222, www.wellcomecollection.org) are also free.

British Museum

Great Russell Street (020 7323 8000/www.british museum.org). Open Galleries 10am-5.30pm Mon-Wed, Sat, Sun; 10am-8.30pm Thur, Fri. Great Court 9am-6pm Mon-Wed, Sun; 9am-11pm Thur-Sat. Admission free; temporary exhibitions prices vary.

The British Museum occupies a wonderful neoclassical building, built in 1847 but enhanced in 2000 by Lord Foster's impressive glass-roofed Great Court, said to be 'the largest covered public square in Europe'. This £100m landmark surrounds the domed Reading Room, where Marx, Dickens and Darwin once worked. Star exhibits include ancient Egyptian artefacts (the Rosetta Stone, the mummies) and Greek antiquities (the Elgin Marbles – friezes from the Parthenon), but there are any number of less famous pieces to enjoy. The Celts gallery upstairs has Lindow Man, killed in 300 BC but preserved in peat, while the Wellcome Gallery of Ethnography holds an Easter Island statue and regalia from Captain Cook's travels.

London Transport Museum
The Piazza (020 7379 6344/www.ltmuseum.co.uk). Open 10am-6pm Mon-Thur, Sat, Sun; 11am-6pm Fri. Admission £10; £6-£8 reductions.
Reopened in 2007, after a massive refurbishment of its lovely old flower market building, the museum traces the city's transport history from the horse age to the present day. The collections begin with a replica of Shillibeer's first horse-drawn bus service, from 1829, and proceed more-or-less chronologically through a superb array of preserved buses, trams and trains. The museum also raises interesting and important questions about the future of public transport.

THE CITY
The City of London – the self-governing 'square mile' of tall offices and expense-account restaurants that remains England's financial heart – has kept to much the same boundaries as the Romans gave it. This was the original Londinium and is crammed with historic buildings, monuments and alleys with strange, old-fashioned names. Wren's **St Paul's Cathedral** (*see below*) and **Monument** (Monument Street, 020 7626 2717, www.themonument.info), 202 feet of free-standing stone column that marks the seat of the Great Fire, are here, as well as London's original tourist attraction, the **Tower** (*see below*), squatting beside the distinctive twin towers of **Tower Bridge** (020 7403 3761, www.towerbridge.org.uk). Towards the West End, among the legal profession's ancient Inns of Court, you'll find most Londoners' favourite small museum – the cunningly adapted house and eccentric archaeological collection of **Sir John Soane's Museum** (13 Lincoln's Inn Fields, 020 7405 2107, www.soane.org) – while neighbouring **Clerkenwell** is today a foodie heartland; it was here that the **Eagle** (159 Farringdon Road, 020 7837 1353) pioneered the wild idea of serving restaurant-quality food in a boozer, inventing the now ubiquitous gastropub. Many City businesses close at the weekend; although the handsome **Millennium ('Wobbly') Bridge** connecting St Paul's and Tate Modern across the river has made things busier, this is still a low-key part of town at weekends.

Just outside where the old City walls once were, under the severe spire of Christ Church Spitalfields, **Old Spitalfields Market** (*see p153*) is a modern London must-visit. To the north, **Hoxton Square** still has the pioneering contemporary art of White Cube (48 Hoxton Square, 020 7930 5373, www.whitecube.com), to which the reconstructed, chronologically displayed domestic interiors of the **Geffrye Museum** (136 Kingsland Road, 020 7739 9893, www.geffrye-museum.org.uk) provide a charming contrast.

Museum of London
150 London Wall (020 7001 9844/www.museumof london.org.uk). Open 10am-6pm daily. Admission free.
Opened in 1976, this museum shares the job of recreating London's history with east London's Museum of London Docklands (No.1 Warehouse, West India Quay, Hertsmere Road, 0870 444 3856, www.museumindocklands.org.uk). Here, the chronological displays begin with 'London Before London': flint axes from 300,000 BC found in Piccadilly; bones from an aurochs; a replica of the Bronze Age Dagenham idol. 'Roman London' includes an impressive reconstructed dining room, with a fine mosaic floor. Sound effects and audio-visual displays illustrate the medieval city and the Great Fire of London. From Elizabethan and Jacobean London, heyday of the Globe Theatre, comes the Cheapside Hoard of jewellery. The downstairs galleries reopen after extensive remodelling in 2010.

St Paul's Cathedral
Ludgate Hill (020 7236 4128/www.stpauls.co.uk). Open 8.30am-4pm Mon-Sat. Special events may cause closure; check before visiting. Admission Cathedral, crypt & gallery £11; £3.50-£10 reductions.
A £40m restoration project has painstakingly removed the Victorian grime from the 300-year-old walls and magnificent façade of London's most famous cathedral. The vast open spaces of the interior contain grandiloquent memorials to national heroes, but the dome justly attracts most attention: the Whispering Gallery (where the acoustics are so good a whisper can be heard clearly the other side of the dome) is reached by 259 steps from the main hall, then further steps take you past the Stone Gallery and, finally, to the giddying views of the Golden Gallery. The crypt has an impressive memorial to Nelson and Wren's own modest tombstone: 'Reader, if you seek a monument, look around you', his epitaph reads.

Tower of London
Tower Hill (0875 482 7777/www.hrp.org.uk). Open 10am-5.30pm Mon, Sun; 9am-5.30pm Tue-Sat. Admission £17; £9-£16 reductions.
Despite exhausting crowds and long, slow climbs up narrow stairways, the Tower is one of Britain's most enjoyable historical attractions. The buildings span nine centuries, the bastions and battlements now housing interactive displays on the lives of monarchs and often painful deaths of traitors, as well as the resident Yeoman Warders ('Beefeaters'). Along with the Crown Jewels (get there early to avoid the long queue), the other big draw to the tower is the Royal Armoury, with its swords, armour and morning stars (spiky maces). Kids are entertained by swordsmanship games, coin-minting activities and even a child-sized long bow.

FURTHER AFIELD
You'll have plenty to keep you busy in central London, but there are some must-sees a little further afield. In north London, the highlights couldn't be more different. In **Camden**, teenagers and wannabe indie-rockers slouch around the resolutely popular series of markets spread out around Chalk Farm Road and the Regent's Canal.

Nightlife confidential

London's nightlife scene saturated? Sure. But there are still plenty of great nights out to be had in Shoreditch, Spitalfields and Soho: you just need to know which unmarked doors to turn to.

In Shoreditch, **Lounge Bohemia** (1E Great Eastern Street, 07720 707000, www.lounge bohemia.com) is often referred to, in whispers, as 'the bar with no name'. The door is unmarked, but it's one of the first on Great Eastern Street (Bishopsgate end) – it looks as though you're entering someone's flat rather than a decadent, picture-perfect basement lounge bar full of enviable retro furniture and a killer cocktail list. Book a table before you go – there's no standing here – and don't bother if you look like you've stepped out of the City or are in a lairy group: it's strictly Shoreditch cool or vintage vamp. And what ever you do, please don't tell anyone else about this place... Further up Great Eastern Street, **Favela Chic** (no.91-93, 020 7613 4228, www.favelachic.com) is a long-running ode to shabby Brazilian cool, with beachcomber finds and palm trees towering over the ample seating. DJs play ace, globe-spanning tunes, and it's strictly dancefloor-filling, rather than chin-stroking, stuff. Over in Hoxton, the **Electricity Showrooms** (39A Hoxton Square, 020 7739 6934, www.electricity showrooms.co.uk) is hard to miss, with its Broadway-sized neon-lit sign. This two-floored

day-and-nightspot is one of the best in the area. The downstairs holds a wonderful secret: a 1970s disco dancefloor. But for pure East End cool, you can't beat a drink at the legendary **Golden Hart** (110 Commercial Street). Tracy Emin's fave boozer is a haven for local creatives, just don't expect to get a seat.

In the West End, meanwhile, the gems are vastly outweighed by the tosh. Still, it's worth heading to Soho for a night out at **Madame JoJo's** (8-10 Brewer Street, 020 7734 3040, www.madamejojos.com), a sleazy dive of a club, all red hues and broken toilet seats. Burlesque strippers and cabaret performers hustle for centre stage most nights of the week before the likes of Keb Darge's Deep Funk every Friday and rockabilly White Head every Saturday take over. Over on Soho Street, **Punk** (no.14, 020 7734 4004, www.punksoho.co.uk) is one of Soho's most popular clubs, and it pays to get here early. DJs, such as perennial party favourites Queens of Noize, play fillers not killers. Finally, for speakeasy Soho, make for the **Black Gardenia** (93 Dean Street). Way beyond shabby, this chipped, paint-peeling retro basement bar has a strict 'no jeans' rule – think vintage cool rather than smart casual, though – and serves red wine in chipped tumblers. Blues and jazz bands squeeze on to the tiny dancefloor, and burlesque girls work the bar. You'll never want to leave.

Potter through the world-food stands and craft stalls of **Camden Lock Market** (www.camden lockmarket.com) into gentrified **Stables Market** (020 7485 5511, www.stablesmarket.com), where vintage clothing and clubwear shops are tucked into the rail arches. Directly north are the wonderfully wild woods, hills and ponds of **Hampstead Heath**, as well as the substantial art collection (Rembrandt, Vermeer) at **Kenwood House** (Hampstead Lane, 020 8348 1286, www.english-heritage.org.uk). Only a little further, **Highgate Cemetery** (Swains Lane, www.highgate-cemetery.org) is a dramatic and spooky boneyard, the last resting place of Karl Marx and George Eliot.

At Greenwich, in south-east London, the **Old Royal Naval College** (020 8269 4747, www.oldroyalnavalcollege.org.uk) has a superb collection of buildings, with a rococo chapel and the Painted Hall, a tribute to William and Mary that took 19 years to complete. The College's broad colonnades beautifully frame the older **Queen's House**, which adjoins the expansive **National Maritime Museum** (*see p150*). Behind the museum in Greenwich Park, the **Royal Observatory & Planetarium** (020 8858 4422, www.rog.nmm.ac.uk) and **Prime Meridian Line** look down from the top of the hill.

National Maritime Museum
Greenwich *Romney Road (020 8858 4422/ www.nmm.ac.uk). Open 10am-5pm daily. Admission free.*
The NMM is the world's largest maritime museum. Galleries include 'Passengers', a delightful exploration of the 20th-century fashion for cruise travel; 'Explorers' and 'Oceans of Discovery', on great sea expeditions and world exploration; and 'Maritime London', looking at the city as a port. Upstairs, 'Nelson's Navy' exhibits more than 250 pieces of memorabilia, including the undress coat worn by the admiral at the Battle of Trafalgar. There are interactives too: 'The Bridge' has a ship simulator and 'All Hands' lets children load cargo and practise Morse Code.

Royal Botanic Gardens (Kew Gardens)
Kew *Kew Road (020 8332 5655/www.kew.org). Open Jan, Sept-Dec 9.30am-4.15pm. Feb, Mar 9.30am-5.30pm daily. Apr-Aug 9.30am-6.30pm Mon-Fri; 9.30am-7.30pm Sat, Sun. Admission £13; £12 reductions.*
The unparalleled collection of plants at Kew was begun by Queen Caroline, wife of George II, with exotic plants brought back by voyaging botanists (Darwin among them). In 1759, 'Capability' Brown was employed by George III to improve on the work of his predecessors, setting the template for a garden that today attracts thousands of visitors every year. Head straight for the 19th-century greenhouses, filled to the roof with tropical plants, and next door the Waterlily House's quiet, gorgeous indoor pond (closed in winter). Capability Brown's Rhododendron Dell is at its best in May, while

the new Xstrata Treetop Walkway, almost 60ft above the ground, is fun among the falling leaves of autumn.

Eat & drink

Albion at the Boundary Project
City *2-4 Boundary Street, Shoreditch (020 7729 1051/ www.albioncaff.co.uk). Open noon-2pm, 6.30-10.30pm Mon-Fri; 6.30-10.30pm Sat; noon-4pm Sun. ££. British.*
Boundary Project is an astonishingly professional operation in otherwise dishevelled-looking Shoreditch. Albion is the ground-floor 'caff' (their description), food shop and bakery; Boundary is the smarter French restaurant in the basement; a rooftop bar-grill and hotel rooms top off the operation. Albion's room is a looker – wholesome, traditional and, from stools made from tractor seats to Brown Betty teapots in hand-knitted cosies, knowingly chic – and everything served from British nostalgia-revival menu delicious, from a little appetiser of perfect crackling to a proper Irish stew.

L'Autre Pied
West End *5-7 Blandford Street, Marylebone (020 7486 9696/www.lautrepied.co.uk). Open noon-2.45pm, 6-10.45pm Mon-Fri; noon-2.30pm, 6-10.45pm Sat; noon-3.30pm, 6.30-9.30pm Sun. ££££. French.*
Opened in 2007, with talented chef Marcus Eaves at the helm, L'Autre Pied won an award from us in 2008 – and in 2009 a Michelin star. The cooking is accomplished and precise, with imaginative taste combinations, and the food looks stunning: perhaps a translucent poached egg sitting on a vibrant green bed of crushed peas and broad beans, the flavours brought together by a smoked butter emulsion. The surroundings have a vaguely oriental feel, with cloisonné-like screens. One of the capital's best places to dine.

Connaught Bar
West End *16 Carlos Place, Mayfair (020 7499 7070/ www.theconnaught.com). Open 4pm-1am Mon-Sat. Cocktail bar.*
The Connaught is one of London's most properly old-fashioned luxury hotels, with sharp-suited, engagingly well-mannered staff – but this is one hell of a sexy bar, with attentive staff and a sleek, black-and-chrome, cruise-liner style David Collins interior. The range of spirits covers every desirable and fashionable drink you can think of – 13 Islay single-malt whiskies, more than 40 tequilas – and the cocktails are risk-taking and irresistible. Across the corridor, the sibling Coburg Bar specialises in more traditional mixed drinks. It doesn't come cheap, but this is the bartender's craft as an art.

Giaconda Dining Room
West End *9 Denmark Street, Covent Garden (020 7240 3334/www.giacondadining.com). Open noon-2.15pm, 6-9.45pm Mon-Fri. £££. Modern European.*
The simple black-and-white dining room belies the esteem in which chef Paul Merrony is held in his native Australia,

and his brilliant dishes belie the modest setting (we've seen bigger beach huts). We loved the hot pillow of ham hock hash with fried egg and lightly dressed mixed leaves, off a reasonably extensive menu where the short descriptions tend to undersell the imaginative, attractive dishes that arrive at the tables. A generous, egalitarian spot where the unpretentious food is the star.

Hakkasan

West End *8 Hanway Place, Fitzrovia (020 7907 1888/ www.hakkasan.com). Open noon-12.30am Mon-Wed; noon-1.30am Thur-Sat; noon-midnight Sun. ££££. Chinese.*
When Alan Yau opened this glamtastic take on the Shanghai teahouse in 2001, he redefined Chinese dining in Britain. Its moody, nightclub feel, lounge music and high-ticket dining still draw one of the liveliest, sleekest crowds in London. Descend the stairs to a warm, incense-filled space where you can choose from impeccable, hearty Chinese braises or superior Imperial-style soups. To enjoy the Hakkasan experience for less, visit for the brilliant lunchtime dim sum.

Hummus Bros

West End *88 Wardour Street, Soho (020 7734 1311/ www.hbros.co.uk). Open noon-10pm Mon-Wed, Sun; noon-11pm Thur-Sat. £. Middle Eastern.*
Hummus Bros – self-proclaimed 'first hummus bar in London', and now with a second location in Bloomsbury (37-63 Southampton Row, 020 7404 7079) – woos harried office workers with creative houmous-based lunches and Med-inspired sides, to eat in or takeaway. Choose your toppings from moreish, gravy-rich braised chunks of beef to smokey chargrilled veg and mop the lot up with warm pitta, washed down with refreshing ginger and mint lemonade. The food is nutritious and good value.

LAB

West End *12 Old Compton Street, Soho (020 7437 7820/www.lab-townhouse.com). Open 6-11pm Mon-Sat; 6-10.30pm Sun. ££. Cocktail bar.*
As the painstakingly conceived sections of its encyclopaedic drinks menu suggest, LAB is streets ahead: 'high and mighty', as well as being 'short and sexy'. Certainly small and sexy, its two-floor space is invariably packed with Sohoites fuelled by London's freshest mixologists. Straight out of the LAB (London Academy of Bartending), graduates are aided by colleagues of considerable global experience, and can fix some 30 original concoctions (most around £7) or 50 classics, using high-end spirits and fresh ingredients. Contemporary retro decorative and aural touches do the rest.

Lamb & Flag

West End *33 Rose Street, Covent Garden (020 7497 9504). Open (food served) noon-3pm Mon-Fri, Sun; noon-4.30pm Sat. ££. Pub.*
Character is in short supply around Covent Garden, but the unabashedly traditional Lamb & Flag has bags of the stuff. A pub for over 300 years and a fixture on this site for longer, it is always a squeeze, but no one seems to mind.

There's fine ale on tap and a daily menu that runs from ploughman's to a choice of roasts. The afternoon-only bar upstairs is 'ye olde' to a fault, and pictures of passed-on regulars ('Barnsey', Corporal Bill West) give the place a great local feel.

St John

City *26 St John Street, Smithfield (020 7553 9842/ www.stjohnrestaurant.com). Open noon-3pm, 6-11pm Mon-Fri; 6-11pm Sat; 1-3pm Sun. ££££. British.*
For a leading light of the 'British revival', St John is a remarkably austere-looking and modest place, opened in a former Smithfield smokehouse by architect and chef-patron Fergus Henderson in 1995. The focus is entirely on seasonal and unusual British ingredients, simply cooked and presented. Some dishes, such as roast bone marrow with parsley, have become classics. Others, such as pig's head and radishes, are more challenging. Despite St John's reputation for offal, there are usually some interesting meat-free dishes, perhaps fennel and berkswell cheese. The cheaper, no-reservations bar is livelier but serves a pared down version of the menu.

Wild Honey

West End *12 St George Street, Mayfair (020 7758 9160/www.wildhoneyrestaurant.co.uk). Open noon-2.30pm, 6-11pm Mon-Sat; noon-3pm, 6-10.30pm Sun. £££. Modern European.*
It takes seconds after entering this sister of Soho's Arbutus (63-64 Frith Street, 020 7734 4545, www.arbutus restaurant.co.uk) to be won over by its charm and professionalism. The oak-panelled walls are lightened by modern art, and the place's popularity means a happy buzz is inevitable – even the counter seats are much in demand. The reasonably priced menu (£16.95 for three courses at lunch) mixes the best of the UK and Europe: Cornish gurnard alongside Limousin veal, lamb from the Pyrenees or Elwy Valley. Mains and puddings are equally well made, and there's a terrific cheeseboard. The wine list gives the option of 250ml carafes.

Shop

For many visitors, London's department stores are a highlight: try the recently refurbished but still splendidly old-fashioned **Fortnum & Mason** (181 Piccadilly 7734 8040, www.fortnumandmason.co.uk); idiosyncratic **Liberty** (Regent Street, 020 7734 1234, www.liberty.co.uk), stocking up-to-the-minute labels in its 1920s mock Tudor structure; and the cutting-edge concession boutiques and themed events at century-old **Selfridges** (400 Oxford Street, 0800 123400, www. selfridges.com). Bringing in the new is the 46-acre, 265-shop, £1.6 billion **Westfield London** mall (Shepherd's Bush, www.westfield. com/london), which opened in the teeth of recession in late 2008.

Top left: Hoxton Hotel;
right: Andaz Hotel;
bottom: Fox & Anchor.

Borough Market

South Bank *Southwark Street, Borough (020 7407 1002/www.boroughmarket.org.uk). Open 11am-5pm Thur; noon-6pm Fri; 9am-4pm Sat.*
The foodie's favourite market occupies a sprawling site near London Bridge. Gourmet goodies run the gamut from Flour Power City Bakery's organic loaves to chorizo and rocket rolls from Brindisa, plus rare-breed meats, fruit and veg, cakes and all manner of preserves, oils and teas – head out hungry to take advantage of the numerous free samples. Thursdays tend to be quieter than the mobbed weekends.

Burlington Arcade

West End *Piccadilly, St James's (www.burlington-arcade.co.uk). Open 8am-7pm Mon-Sat; 11am-5pm Sun.*
In 1819, Lord Cavendish commissioned Britain's very first shopping arcade and the Burlington is still London's most prestigious. It is also still patrolled by 'Beadles' decked out in top hats and tailcoats. Highlights include collections of classic watches, Luponde Tea and outlets for such iconic British brands as Mackintosh and Globe-Trotter.

Dover Street Market

West End *17-18 Dover Street, Mayfair (020 7518 0680/www.doverstreetmarket.com). Open 11am-6pm Mon-Wed; 11am-7pm Thur-Sat.*
Comme des Garçons designer Rei Kawakubo's ground-breaking six-storey space isn't, in fact, a market. Instead, it combines the edgy energy of London's indoor markets – concrete floors, tills housed in corrugated-iron shacks, Portaloo dressing rooms – with some pretty rarefied labels. All 14 of the Comme collections are here, alongside exciting exclusive lines such as Azzedine Alaïa and Veronique Branquinho.

Old Spitalfields Market

City *Commercial Street, Spitalfields (020 7247 8556/ www.visitspitalfields.com). Open 10am-4pm Thur, Fri; 11am-5pm Sat; 9am-5pm Sun.*
Recent redevelopment has given a new lease of life to this East End stalwart. The market now comprises the refurbished 1887 covered market and an adjacent modern shopping precinct. Around the edge of Old Spitalfields Market, stands sell grub from around the world. The busiest day is Sunday, when a short walk to the east takes you to Brick Lane Market and Sunday (Up)Market in the Old Truman Brewery, a buzzy collection of 140 stalls selling vintage gear and edgy fashion from fresh young designers.

Arts

Certain West End shows seem unstoppable – *Chicago*, *Les Misérables*, *The Mousetrap* – but others disappear suddenly without trace in the face of new arrivals from Broadway. Visit the Leicester Square tkts booth (Clocktower Building, www.officiallondontheatre.co.uk; open 10am-7pm Mon Sat; noon 3pm Sun) for half-price tickets on the day of performance, and check the website www.timeout.com/london/theatre/ for reviews of the hottest current shows.

Barbican Centre

City *Silk Street (020 7638 4141/box office 020 7638 4141/www.barbican.org.uk). Open Box office 9am-8pm daily. Admission varies, check website for details.*
The Barbican is a prime example of 1970s brutalism, softened by rectangular ponds of friendly resident ducks. The complex houses a cinema, theatre, concert hall and art galleries, a labyrinthine array of spaces that isn't all that easy to navigate. The programming, however, is first class. At the core of the classical music roster, performing 90 concerts a year, is the brilliant London Symphony Orchestra (LSO), supplemented by top jazz, world-music and rock gigs. The annual BITE season cherry-picks exciting theatre and dance from around the globe, and the cinema shows art-house, mainstream and international films.

National Theatre

South Bank *(information 020 7452 3400/box office 7452 3000/www.nationaltheatre.org.uk). Open Box office 9.30am-8pm Mon-Sat. Admission varies, check website for details.*
The concrete-clad, 1960s modernist grandmother of them all: no theatrical tour of London is complete without a visit to the National, whose three auditoriums and rolling repertory programme offer a choice of several productions in a single week. Artistic director Nicholas Hytner has programmed a canny mix of crowd-pleasers and more esoteric fare. He's picked some fine directors too: among them the Donmar's Michael Grandage, Deborah Warner and man-of-the-moment Rupert Goold.

Southbank Centre

South Bank *Belvedere Road (0871 663 2501/ box office 0871 663 2500/www.rfh.org.uk). Open Box office In person 90mins before performance. By phone 9.30am-8pm daily. Admission varies, check website for details.*
The 3,000-capacity Royal Festival Hall reopened in 2007 after a £90m renovation that improved access and brilliantly refurbished the acoustics. Showcase annual events include Meltdown, guest-curated each year by intriguing stars such as Ornette Coleman and Patti Smith, and the Shell Classic International Season, but you'll get major dance, music and theatre performances all year. Next door to the RFH are the 900-seat Queen Elizabeth Hall and 250-capacity Purcell Room, which host everything from chamber concerts and low-key pop gigs to poetry readings. A little further along the South Bank, three-screen BFI Southbank (020 7928 3535, www.bfi.org.uk) is London's premier repertory cinema.

Nightlife

Comedy Store

West End *1A Oxendon Street, Soho (0844 847 1728/ www.thecomedystore.co.uk). Open 8-11.30pm Mon;*

8-10.15pm Tue; 8-10pm Wed, Sun; 8-10.30pm Thur; 8pm-2.15am Fri; 8pm-2.30am Sat. Admission £15-£18. Dubbed 'Comedy's Unofficial National Theatre', the Comedy Store was founded in 1979. Through the 1980s, it became the home of alternative comedy: the Comedy Store Players improv group, now including Paul Merton and Josie Lawrence, continues to shine on Wednesdays and Sundays. The venue is purpose-built for serious punters, with seats arranged in a gladiatorial semicircle.

O2 Arena & IndigO2

North Greenwich *Millennium Way (020 8463 2000/box office 0871 984 0002/www.theo2.co.uk). Open Box office In person noon-7pm daily. By phone 24hrs daily. Admission varies, check website for details.*
This conversion of the national embarrassment that was the Millennium Dome has been a huge success. It now comprises a state-of-the-art, 23,000-capacity enormodome with good acoustics and sightlines, hosting big acts like Stevie Wonder and Michael Jackson, and two substantial subsidiary venues: Matter and the 2,350-capacity IndigO2, itself one of London's bigger concert venues. There are also temporary blockbuster shows (Tutankhamun, Body Worlds) and, since early 2009, the permanent British Music Experience (www.britishmusicexperience.com). Although there's a tube stop, the 20-minute Thames Clipper boat ride back to London Bridge or Waterloo is more fun.

Roundhouse

Camden *Chalk Farm Road (0844 482 8008/ www.roundhouse.org.uk). Open Box office In person 11am-6pm Mon-Sat. By phone 9am-7pm Mon-Sat; 9am-4pm Sun. Admission varies, check website for details.*
Once a railway turntable shed, the Roundhouse was used for experimental theatre and hippie happenings in the 1960s, for rock concerts in the '70s and then fell dormant. Reborn a few years back, it now mixes arty gigs with dance, theatre and multimedia events. Sightlines can be poor, but the acoustics are good.

Stay

Andaz Liverpool Street

City *40 Liverpool Street (020 7961 1234/www.london. liverpoolstreet.andaz.com). ££££.*
A faded railway hotel until its £70-million Conran overhaul in 2000, the Great Eastern became the first of Hyatt's new Andaz portfolio in 2007. The approach means out go gimmicky menus, closet-sized minibars and even the lobby reception desk, and in come down-to-earth, well-informed service and eco-friendliness. The bedrooms still wear style-mag uniform – Eames chairs, Frette linens – and are minimalist to a point quite close to underfurnished, but free services (breakfast, local calls, movies, internet, healthy minibar, laundry) and the management's savvy efforts to connect with the vibey local area are appreciated, as are a number of buzzy bar-restaurants and a pub on the premises.

City Inn Westminster

Westminster & St James's *30 John Islip Street (020 7630 1000/www.cityinn.com). ££.*
There's nothing particularly flashy about this new-build hotel, but it is well run, neatly designed and obliging: the rooms have all the added extras you'd want (iMacs, CD/DVD library for your in-room player, free broadband, flatscreen TVs) and the floor-to-ceiling windows mean that river-facing suites on the 12th and 13th floors have superb night views – when the businessmen go home for the weekend you might be able to grab one for £125. With half an eye on near neighbour Tate Britain (Millbank, 020 7887 8888), the owners have collaborated with the Chelsea College of Art to provide changing art through the lobbies and meeting rooms.

Covent Garden Hotel

West End *10 Monmouth Street, Covent Garden (020 7806 1000/www.firmdale.com). ££££.*
On the ground floor of the Covent Garden Hotel, the 1920s Paris-style Brasserie Max and its retro zinc bar have been cunningly expanded – testament to the continuing popularity of boutique hotel queen Kit Kemp's snug and stylish establishment. It opened in 1996 and hasn't made a misstep since. The location, downstairs screening room and lovely panelled private library and drawing room for guests ensure it continues to attract starry customers. In the rooms themselves, Kemp's distinctive style mixes pinstriped wallpaper, pristine white quilts and floral upholstery with contemporary elements; each room is unique, but each has the trademark upholstered mannequin and granite and oak bathroom.

Fox & Anchor

City *115 Charterhouse Street, Smithfield (0845 347 0100/www.foxandanchor.com). £££.*
What's not to like about a handful of well-appointed, atmospheric and surprisingly luxurious rooms above a bustling and historic Smithfield pub? Each en suite room differs, but the high-spec facilities (big flatscreen TV, clawfoot bath, drench shower) and quirky attention to detail (bottles of ale in the minibar, the 'Nursing hangover' signs to hang out for privacy) are common throughout. Expect some clanking market noise in the early mornings, but proximity to the historic meat market also means a feisty fried breakfast in the handsome dark wood and pewter tankards pub below. The pub is where you check in, but you do have a key to the separate entrance door.

Hoxton Hotel

City *81 Great Eastern Street, Hoxton (020 7550 1000/ www.hoxtonhotels.com). ££££.*
Ah, the Hoxton… everything you've read about it is true. First, the hip Shoreditch location. Then the great design values (the foyer is a sort of postmodern country lodge, complete with stag's head) and well-thought-out rooms (Frette bed linens, free internet, free fresh milk in the mini-fridge). But, above all, it's the budget-airline style pricing system, by which the early bird catches a very cheap worm – perhaps even one of those publicity-garnering £1 a night rooms, still released in small numbers every few months.

No.5 Maddox Street

West End *5 Maddox Street, Mayfair (020 7647 0200/ www.living-rooms.co.uk). ££££.*
This bolthole just off Regent Street provides deliciously discreet and chic apartments. You can shut the brown front door, climb the stairs and flop into a home from home with all contemporary cons, including new flatscreen TVs and iPod docks. The East-meets-West decor is classic 1990s minimalist, but very bright and clean after a gentle refurbishment. Each apartment has a fully equipped kitchen, but room service will shop for you as well as providing the usual hotel services. There's no bar, but breakfasts and snacks are served, the Thai restaurant Patara is on the ground floor and all the bars of Soho lie just across the road.

Park Plaza County Hall

South Bank *1 Addington Street (020 7021 1800/ www.parkplaza.com). £££.*
Approach along the grubby streets from Lambeth North and you'll wonder why we've brought you here, but this is an enthusiastically – if somewhat haphazardly – run new-build. Each room has its own kitchenette with microwave and sink, and room sizes aren't bad across the price range (the floor-to-ceiling windows help them feel bigger). There's a handsomely vertiginous atrium, enabling you to peer down into the central restaurant from the frustratingly infrequent glass lifts, and the ground-floor bar is buzzy with business types after work. There's a downstairs gym too, soothingly decorated. But it is the views from the expansive penthouses that are the real knock-out.

Trafalgar

Westminster & St James's *2 Spring Gardens (020 7870 2900/www.thetrafalgar.com). ££££.*
The Trafalgar is a Hilton – but you'd hardly notice. For all that the chain's first 'concept' hotel is housed in an imposing edifice, the mood is young and dynamic. To the right of the 'open' reception is the Rockwell Bar, serving mixes both cocktail and DJ, while breakfast downstairs is accompanied by gentle live music. Yet it is the none-more-central location that's the biggest draw – the few corner suites look directly into Trafalgar Square (prices reflect location), but those without a room view can, in season, avail themselves of the small rooftop bar. The good-sized rooms have a masculine feel, with white walls and walnut furniture.

Factfile

When to go

Summer (June, July and August) is the busiest time in London, with the heaviest concentration of open-air festivals and events, but humidity and pollution can make the city uncomfortably hot. May is usually very pleasant, and the weather can still have a mild, summery feel into September.

Getting there

London is served by five principal airports, all with good public transport connections: Gatwick (0870 000 2468, www.baa.co.uk/gatwick), Heathrow (0870 000 0123, www.baa.co.uk/heathrow), London City (020 7646 0000, www.londoncityairport.com), Luton (01582 405100, www.london-luton.com) and Stansted (0870 000 0303, www.stanstedairport.com). Coaches run by National Express (0870 580 8080, www.nationalexpress.com) arrive from all over Britain at Victoria Coach Station (164 Buckingham Palace Road, SW1W 9TP, 020 7730 3466, www.tfl.gov.uk), and the major train stations are Euston (West Midlands, north-west and Scotland), King's Cross (north, north-east and Scotland), Paddington (West Country, south-west and south Wales) and Waterloo (south and south-west). St Pancras, the new Eurostar terminal, serves the East Midlands and Yorkshire.

Getting around

London's public transport is neither cheap, nor particularly efficient (especially with major refurbishment work in preparation for the 2012 Olympics), but almost everywhere is easily accessible by a combination of Underground, Docklands Light Railway, rail and bus. Riverboats too are increasingly efficient. For details of services (including how to save money by using the pre-pay Oyster card), visit www.tfl.gov.uk or phone 020 7222 1234. Many of London's key sights are surprisingly close to each other, so get a good map and walk when you can.

Tourist information

City of London Information Centre
St Paul's Churchyard (020 7332 1456, www.cityoflondon.gov.uk). Open 9.30am-5.30pm Mon-Sat; 10am-4pm Sun.
This new office has information on sights and events within the City, as well as offering specialist guided walks. There are also tourist offices in Leicester Square and Tate Modern (*see p142*).

Internet

For proper cafés with wireless access try: Benugo Bar & Kitchen (BFI Southbank, Belvedere Road, South Bank, 020 7401 9000, www.benugo.com), Hummus Bros (88 Wardour Street, Soho, 020 7734 1311, www.hbros.co.uk) and the Wellcome Collection's Peyton & Byrne (183 Euston Road, Bloomsbury, 020 7611 2138, www.peytonandbyrne.com).

Coast & Country

Top: Pittenweem; left: Anstruther Fish Bar & Restaurant; right: Crail.

...oley – from well managed fi
Hot-Smoked Mackerel fu
sustainable seas
£7.9
ENJOY SEAFOOD
TWICE A WEEK
www.

The East Neuk

Ragged coastline, atmospheric fishing villages, fabulous views.

Fife is a forgotten place. The 'dog's head' sticking out from Scotland's blasted east coast is defined by the wide estuaries of the rivers Forth and Tay. It may not be remote enough to have the thrill of the Highlands, nor as cultured as Glasgow or Edinburgh. But East Neuk ('neuk' meaning corner), made up of the string of villages punctuating Fife's coast – from Earlsferry to Kingsbarns – is an overlooked treasure. The ragged coastline has created natural harbours with thick-set villages characterised by steep, narrow wynds and cheerful gabled cottages. It has been described as a place where the clock stands still and (by King James VI) as the fringe of gold on a beggar's mantle. Integral to its charms are the sweeping views across the Firth of Forth to North Berwick, the Isle of May, the mysterious Bass Rock, and, in the far distance, the twinkling lights of Edinburgh.

Beauty aside, these are working villages, inhabited by families who have lived here for generations. The pretty fishing boats are worked by tough, weather-worn men ekeing out a living in a diminishing industry. Soulless housing estates are congealing on the edges of historic stone burghs. Inland, corn and rape are cultivated on softly undulating hills, with charming untouched hamlets – Kilconquar, Arncroach, Kilrenny – tucked in among the fields.

There are still traces here of Fife's heady days as a seaside resort – dwindling caravan parks, outdoor swimming pools filled by the tide (but sadly no longer maintained by the council), golfing links, ice-cream shops, and the best fish and chips in Scotland. But the seaside cottages have since been snapped up by second-homers and artists drawn by the unique quality of the light, creating a new dynamic for this corner of the ancient Pictish kingdom.

Explore

ELIE & EARLSFERRY

Rather than the jagged rocks that give the rest of the coastline its character, Elie and Earlsferry benefit from sweeping sandy beaches, designated Blue Flag quality.

The two towns flow together, forming one long, linear parade of large stone houses. At the western end is Earlsferry Beach and **Elie Golf House Club** (Golf Course Lane, 01333 330301, www.golfhouseclub.co.uk) – the popular course was laid out in 1895, though golf has been played on the site since the 16th century. Walkers should watch out for flying balls.

Beyond the beach to the west are foreboding cliffs that lead round Kincraig Point to Shell Bay, where McDuff is said to have once hidden when fleeing from Macbeth. These can be explored using the **Chain Walk** – a series of steel chains and steps carved into the rock that take you past caves, basalt columns and volcanic rock pools. Many of the local outdoor centres organise accompanied climbs.

The Lady's Tower, the ruin that stands on the eastern point of Elie Bay, was built as a summer house for Lady Janet Anstruther, wife of the local laird, in the 18th century, and is now a sheltered viewpoint. Beside it is Ruby Bay, so called for the garnets that are occasionally washed up on the sands.

ST MONANS & PITTENWEEM

St Monans and Pittenweem are two real workaday villages where the area's ancient fishing traditions are most in evidence.

The St Monan's town motto, 'mare vivimus' (we live by the sea) still holds true. Boats are built here, crab and other shellfish are landed, haddock smoked, and the town even sustains a top-class fish restaurant (*see p164*).

A stone windmill along the coastal path to Pittenweem harks back to the turn of the 18th century, when it was used for salt production. There are atmospheric ruins at **Newark Castle**, an old doocot (dovecot) – its inhabitants supplied fresh meat in winter and the **Auld Kirk**, the closest church to the sea in Scotland, with sections predating the Reformation.

The big local commercial fish market is at Pittenweem harbour, which has been expanded in recent years to try to keep up with competition from larger harbours operating on a more industrial scale further up Scotland's east coast.

Along Pittenweem's West Shore are picturesque 17th-century fishermen's cottages. Outdoor stone steps lead up to the front door and first-floor sitting rooms, with bedrooms downstairs – a sensible precaution on exposed stretches prone to storm flooding. The charming High Street, reached via steep wynds (narrow streets and passages), is dominated by the old kirk, tollbooth and historic Kellie Lodging, where Charles II was once a house guest. It has also

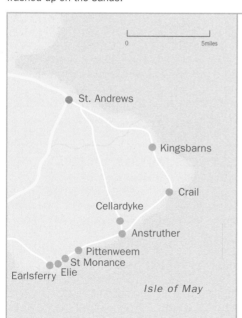

The East Neuk

Historic sites
● ● ● ● ○

Art & architecture
● ● ○ ○ ○

Hotels
● ● ● ● ○

Eating & drinking
● ● ● ● ○

Scenery
● ● ● ● ○

Outdoor activities
● ● ● ○ ○

Top: Anstruther Fish Bar & Restaurant; bottom: Golf Hotel.

sprouted several bijou art galleries and become the hub of the annual local arts festival (*see* *p165* **When to go**).

Halfway up Cove Wynd is **St Fillan's Cave**, a consecrated Christian shrine where, legend has it, the sixth-century Irish missionary worked and prayed by the light of his luminous left arm, attempting to convert the local Picts (key available from the Cocoa Tree, 9 High Street, 01333 311495, www.thecocoatreeshop.com). Pittenweem, in fact, means 'place of the cave'.

Kellie Castle & Gardens
Pittenweem *(0844 493 2184/www.nts.org.uk). Open Apr-May 1-5pm Mon, Tue, Fri-Sun. June-Aug 1-5pm daily. Admission £8.50; £5.50 reductions.*
Three miles inland is Kellie Castle, a National Trust for Scotland property surrounded by tranquil gardens. Though its oldest sections date from 1360, its most interesting features are the ornamental plaster ceilings, panelled rooms, Victorian nursery, walled garden, woodland walks and children's adventure playground.

ANSTRUTHER & CELLARDYKE
Anstruther (pronounced by locals as Ain-ster) is the largest, busiest (and, consequently, least attractive) town along this stretch, but the one with all the amenities. In season, the seafront car park here is full of visiting families enjoying Italian ice-cream and fresh fish suppers. Boats leave from the harbour for the **Isle of May**, once the site of a monastery, now a bird sanctuary. Cellardyke harbour, by contrast, is all but deserted, too shallow to be of use any more, but out along the braes, at the **East Neuk Outdoors Centre** (01333 311929, www.eastneuk outdoors.co.uk), families can learn climbing, abseiling, canoeing and kayaking.

The bands of black rocks that stride round to Crail make excellent climbing and rock-pooling territory. They are also a good spot for fossils, with tracks of giant millipedes visible in the cliffs and boulders, and a discernable tree stump on the foreshore just before you reach Crail.

Isle of May boat trips
Anstruther Harbour *May Princess (01333 310103/ www.isleofmayferry.com). Open Apr-Sept times vary, check website for details. Tickets £18; £9-£16 reductions.*
The Isle of May is an intriguing landmark out in the Firth of Forth, owned and managed by Scottish National Heritage. The island was the site of a 12th-century monastery and Scotland's oldest lighthouse, both ruined but still standing; now it is uninhabited save for a few scientists and a lot of seabirds. The island is the UK's biggest puffin colony, and it is also possible to spot seals, porpoises, dolphins and even the occasional whale. In season, the *May Princess* sails daily from Anstruther harbour, according to the tide, with time for visitors to explore the island.

Scottish Fisheries Museum
Anstruther *St Ayles, Harbourhead (01333 310628/ www.scotfishmuseum.org). Open Apr-Sept 10am-5.30pm Mon-Sat; 11am-5pm Sun. Oct-Mar 10am-4.30pm Mon-Sat; noon-4.30pm Sun. Admission £6; £5 reductions.*
A vignette of life in the East Neuk before intensive fishing and high-tech equipment. As well as several historic boats, old-fashioned tools and fascinating photographs, there are life-size sets re-creating everyday scenes: herring lassies gutting fish, a sail loft, a 1900 fisherman's cottage.

CRAIL & KINGSBARNS
Just before the East Neuk reaches the 'dog's nose' (or Fife Ness as it is officially called) and turns the corner towards St Andrews, things take on a far more genteel air. Possibly the prettiest of all the villages, Crail has a broad high street and elegant marketplace, as well as cobbled streets and an unspoilt harbour.

On the way through town and down to the sheltered harbour, there are many welcoming attractions: **Jerdan Gallery & Sculpture Garden** (42 Marketgate Sout, 01333 450797, www.thejerdangallery.com), **Crail Potteries** (75 Nethergate, 01333 451212, www.crail pottery.com), **Crail Gallery** (22 High Street, 01333 450316, www.crailgallery.com), and the bijou **Crail Harbour Gallery & Tearoom** (01333 451896, www.crailharbourgallery.co.uk) for a brew with a view. Though fishing seems more of a hobby than an industry here, a tiny hut by the harbour, **Reilly's** (01333 450476, noon-4pm Tue-Sun) caters for passing trade by selling freshly caught and cooked crab and lobsters. Walk back up along the walls of Crail Castle to enjoy the best views of the Isle of May.

Just over three miles north of Crail is **Kingsbarns**, a village long associated with golf, and worth a visit for the lovely **Cambo Gardens**.

Cambo Gardens
Kingsbarns *Cambo Estate (01333 450054/www. camboestate.com). Open 10am-5pm daily. Admission £4.*
Romantic Victorian gardens two miles from Crail at Kingsbarns. The landscaping is set around Cambo Burn and features weeping willows, wrought-iron bridges, follies, rambling roses, a lilac wall and a waterfall. Its snowdrops cause a sensation every spring.

Eat

Anstruther Fish Bar & Restaurant
Anstruther *42-44 Shore Street (01333 310518/ www.anstrutherfishbar.co.uk). Open 11.30am-9.30pm daily. ££. Fish & chips.*
Consistently voted among the best fish and chip shops in Scotland (in 2009 it was voted UK fish and chip shop of the year) and a favourite with Prince William when he was studying at St Andrews. Portions are big (two pieces of fish

equal one fish supper) and the haddock is so fresh that they can even tell you which boat has just brought it in. Adjoining the fish restaurant is a Luvians ice-cream concession, offering a great selection of unusual flavours. Eat in or sitting by the harbour, but in high season be prepared for a long queue.

Cocoa Tree
Pittenweem *9 High Street (01333 311495/ www.thecocoatreeshop.com). Open 10am-6pm daily. £. Chocolatier/Café.*
Exquisite French and Belgian chocolates are sold loose, or enjoyed in the opulent café at the rear of the shop. Indulgent hot chocolates have their own menu, which includes white, hazelnut and 70% dark varieties, as well as the 'caliente', an espresso-sized cup of dark chocolate with a chilli kick. More conventional tearoom fare includes milkshakes, infusions, panini, crêpes, cakes and freshly baked scones.

Seafood Restaurant at St Monans
St Monans *16 West End (01333 730327/ www.theseafoodrestaurant.com). £££. Seafood.*
Award-winning seafood restaurant, and the closest you'll get to fine dining in the East Neuk. The emphasis is on delicate, simply cooked fish dishes and locally caught shellfish, accompanied by parfaits, veloutés and citrussy couscous. St Monans is an unlikely location for an upmarket restaurant, but the vantage point, overlooking the harbour, is a joy.

Ship Inn
Elie *The Toft (01333 330246/www.ship-elie.com). Open Apr-Oct noon-2.30pm, 6-9pm Mon-Thur; noon-2.30pm, 6-9.30pm Fri, Sat; 12.30-3pm, 6-9pm Sun. Nov-Mar noon-2pm, 6-9pm Mon-Thur; noon-2pm, 6-9.30pm Fri, Sat; 12.30-3pm, 6-9pm Sun. ££. Pub.*
The East Neuk is well served with cosy pubs serving food, but the home cooking, summer barbecues and waterfront location of the Ship marks it out. There are gourmet sandwiches (tomato salsa and goat's cheese; avocado, smoked salmon and crayfish) and chef Jill Phillips' legendary Cullen Skink (Scottish soup). There's a friendly guesthouse next door.

Stay

The villages above are full of small, friendly guesthouses and B&Bs, as well as self-catering holiday lets. See www.eastneukholidays.com.

Cambo Estate
Kingsbarns *Cambo House (01333 450054/ www.camboestate.com). ££.*
Indulge in some country house grandeur by sleeping in a four-poster bed in the Victorian mansion on the Cambo Estate. As well as three sumptuous bed and breakfast suites, there are five self-catering apartments in the main house, and three self-catering cottages by the main gate. Tennis courts, basketball, a games room and a children's play area are also available.

Crusoe Hotel
Lower Largo, 5 miles NW of Earlsferry *2 Main Street (01333 320759/www.crusoehotel.co.uk). ££.*
It's old-school Scottish but has the advantage of being right at the water's edge. This is no longer the East Neuk proper, but a convenient halfway point en route from the bright lights of Leven and Kirkaldy. The crepuscular bar and restaurant are popular with locals.

Golf Hotel
Crail *4 High Street (01333 450206/ www.thegolfhotelcrail.com). ££.*
An 18th-century coaching inn with a decent, if rather retro, restaurant and sun terrace. Expect pleasant, comfortable and unpretentious rooms (two doubles and three twins) and a friendly welcome. Golf packages are available.

Symphony Craw's Nest Hotel
Anstruther *Bankwell Road (01333 310691/ www.crawsnesthotel.co.uk). £££.*
East Neuk's three-star hotel has 50 rooms and is comfortable, well-equipped and modern. Some character was lost following conversion from a family-run enterprise to part of a mini-chain.

Factfile

When to go
The East Neuk is 'in season' from Easter to the end of September; outside these months you'll find many attractions closed. The Pittenweem Arts Festival (www.pittenweemartsfestival.co.uk) is held during the first week in August.

Getting there & around
The nearest railway stations are **Leuchars** (from where there is a bus, changing in St Andrews) and **Kirkaldy**. There are airports in Edinburgh and Dundee, but it will still require multiple modes of transport to get you from there to the East Neuk. Details of the local bus service can be found by visiting www.fifedirect.org, while bus timetables

for the whole of Scotland are available from traveline (0871 200 2233, www.traveline.org.uk). The council has also introduced a taxi-like service for more isolated communities, called Go-Flexi (01592 583223, www.go-flexi.org), which operates within limited time periods and can be booked up to an hour before you want to travel.

As with all remote places, it is still far easier to explore by car or bicycle.

Tourist Information
Scottish Fisheries Museum (Harbourhead, Anstruther, 01333 311073/www.visitfife.com/ guide/5663931). Open seasonally; call for details.

COAST PATH
West Porthhead 2 cm

COAST PATH
Public Footpath
Nare Head 2¾
Carne Beach

S.T MAWES
TREGONY 10½
LONDON 263¼
SAFETY FIRST

Shell

2/3d gallon

Left: Falmouth Harbour;
top: Coast Path; middle:
St Mawes; bottom:
River Fal.

Falmouth & the Roseland Peninsula

Peaceful natural escapes and a colourful maritime heritage.

The surf lessons, blustery cliffs of the north coast, and stag-do image of holidays in Cornwall may dominate the headlines, but the area around Falmouth and the Roseland Peninsula is another world – quietly beautiful, wildly romantic and largely untouched. The merging of river estuaries, protected from the relentless Atlantic swell by the vast granite bulk of the Lizard Peninsula, has created endless watery escapes: silent wooded creeks, secluded beaches and rolling green hills that dip gently into the sea. The Carrick Roads, the wide waterway dividing Falmouth and the Roseland Peninsula, is the world's third largest natural harbour (after Rio de Janeiro and Sydney) – and countless ships and sails, vestiges of a long and prosperous maritime history, still dot the horizon. Meanwhile, a fleet of top restaurants, idyllic inns and small luxury hotels are signs of a newer burgeoning trade – in upmarket tourism.

Famously favoured by holidaying surrealist artists (Lee Miller, Roland Penrose, Max Ernst, Man Ray et al) in the 1930s, the glamorous yachting set in the 1950s and '60s, and a string of A-lister celebs in recent years, the beauty of the Roseland Peninsula could hardly be described as an insider secret. But even in busy summer months, it somehow manages to feel like one. It's easy to escape the crowds and the area offers a delightfully quiet brand of tourism: row your boat up a quiet creek, take a water taxi to the jetty of a thatched pub, learn how to sail, or curl up with a book and bucolic view.

A short ferry ride across the mouth of the estuary takes you to the bustling port town of Falmouth. Put on the map by its historic docks, a colourful maritime heritage and highly acclaimed art college, Falmouth is still a working dock town, these days with bucketloads of bohemian charm and an active yachtie scene.

Explore

ST MAWES

St Mawes has been a swanky holiday destination since Edwardian times. Neat white cottages and smart townhouses cling to the hillside above the small, sheltered harbour, with the dramatic shapes of dark Monterey pine trees framing the skyline on the brow of the hill behind. Across the clear, sheltered mouth of the Percuil River, the views of **St Anthony's Head Lighthouse** have graced the covers of many a glossy holiday magazine citing comparisons with the South of France. The gloss of this exclusive retreat was given further polish in 1999 by the renovation of the **Hotel Tresanton** by celebrated interior designer Olga Polizzi.

St Mawes has two beaches: both are thin strips of sand revealed at low tide, with sheltered clear bathing water and sunny south-facing stretches. A short walk along the narrow road up to the headland leads to **St Mawes Castle** (*see below*).

Running 15 long miles from the main road between Truro and St Austell, the A3078's sharp bends wind across the Roseland, through open fields framed with pretty Cornish hedges and dipping down through wooded valleys. Attractive as it undoubtedly is, a couple of return trips to Truro or Falmouth along this road are usually enough to make you take the boat or King Harry Ferry next time (shortening the journey by at least 40 minutes). The only vehicular crossing of the Fal, the **King Harry Ferry** (01872 862312, www.kingharryscornwall.co.uk) is one of only five remaining chain ferries in the country. It takes just five scenic minutes to cross this narrow section of the Fal, flanked by thick woods.

The ferry crossing between St Mawes and Falmouth takes around 25 minutes. There's a year-round ferry service.

St Mawes Castle

St Mawes *Castle Drive, Upper Castle Road (01326 270526/www.english-heritage.org.uk). Open Apr-June, Sept 10am-5pm Mon-Fri, Sun. July, Aug 10am-6pm Mon-Fri, Sun. Oct 10am-4pm daily. Nov-Mar 10am-4pm Mon, Fri, Sat, Sun. Admission £3.90; £2-£3.10 reductions.*

Like its larger sister across the water, Pendennis Castle (*see p173*), St Mawes Castle was built between 1539 and 1543 to defend against attacks from the French and Spanish that never came. When the castle was finally threatened with some serious action in the Civil War, its occupants quickly surrendered it to Parliamentarian forces, hence preserving its immaculate state (it is one of the finest, most complete examples of Henry VIII's chain of south-coast forts).

It has the same clover-leaf design as Pendennis, but the three semicircular bastions that surround the four-storey central tower make it the more architecturally distinguished of the two. It also enjoys the benefits of a remote location; where Pendennis Point sees ice-cream vans, day trippers and canoodling teenagers crowding the car park day and night, St Mawes enjoys exposed rocks and panoramic seascapes.

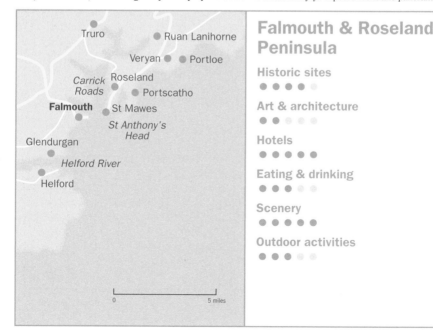

Falmouth & Roseland Peninsula

Historic sites
● ● ● ● ○

Art & architecture
● ● ● ○ ○ ○

Hotels
● ● ● ● ●

Eating & drinking
● ● ● ○ ○

Scenery
● ● ● ● ●

Outdoor activities
● ● ● ● ○ ○

Truro
Ruan Lanihorne
Veryan ● Portloe
Carrick Roseland
Roads ● Portscatho
Falmouth St Mawes
St Anthony's Head
Glendurgan
Helford River
Helford

0   5 miles

Top: St Anthony-in-Meneage; left: St Anthony's Head Lighthouse; right: Pendennis Castle.

Time Out

timeout.com/travel
Get the local experience

Lifeguards keep watch over Lummus Park beach, **Miami**

© Russ Tomlinson

FURTHER UP THE CARRICK ROADS

There are plenty of beautiful spots to explore from a base in St Mawes. If you take the coastal path around from the castle and head inland/north up the shore, the views west across the Carrick Roads towards Mylor, Feock and Trelissick are superb. Head slightly eastwards up St Just Creek to reach **St-Just-in-Roseland Church**, set in steep subtropical gardens on the side of the creek, with its sandbar and moored yachts. The granite church was consecrated in 1261, but evidence suggests there was a building here as far back as 500. It is a breathtaking spot: 'to many people the most beautiful on earth', as John Betjeman gushed.

Further north, the Carrick Roads divides into the River Fal and the Truro River, the latter being the wider and deeper of the two (navigable all the way to Truro at high tide). The River Fal, with its muddy floodplains of tufty grass, meanders through woods and fields (a bird lovers' paradise) up to the tranquil village of **Ruan Lanihorne**. This area grew rich on the pilchard boom and naval patronage in the 19th century – although it's hard to imagine it as anything other than the beautiful, sleepy backwater it is today. Near here, the **King's Head** (Ruan Lanihorne, 01872 501263, www.kingsheadruan.co.uk) is a popular gastropub that comes with glowing local recommendations.

It's worth taking the time to pay a brief visit to **Veryan**, a pretty village made famous for its curious thatched and crucifix-topped roundhouses, built in the 19th century by a local minister for his five daughters. Constructed without any corners, these houses apparently ensured that the devil would have nowhere to hide. There are also a couple of good local craft shops and galleries in the village.

A few miles on, follow the signs for **Portloe** and take the narrow lane down to this pristine fishing village, with its whitewashed and pastel-painted granite cottages tightly packed around a steep rocky inlet and harbour. Although the local fishermen still sell the day's catch on the small pebbly beach here, the smart four-wheel drives and Mercedes parked up the hill tell a very different story of the village's full- and part-time inhabitants. The coastal path heading westwards from here gives yet more stunning coastal views back towards the Roseland and nearby Gul Rock; poking dramatically out of the sea, this is a nesting ground for an array of seabirds.

AROUND ST ANTHONY'S HEAD

The striking **St Anthony's Head Lighthouse** was built in 1834, although a coal beacon burned at this crucial location for hundreds of years beforehand. Playing a critical part in guiding ships to safety both in the Carrick Roads and on the perilous Manacles Reef to the south, this lighthouse was also the set for the 1980s television series *Fraggle Rock*. The many defensive batteries around this point demonstrate its strategic importance throughout World War I and II. These days, it's a delightful spot to potter around and take in the coastal views to either side of this narrow finger of land, with benches conveniently placed along the path.

In the summer (1 Apr-30 Oct), you can take the St Mawes to Place Ferry (07791 283884, daily every 30 mins, 9.30am-5pm) across the Percuil River, then follow the pretty coastal path around to the lighthouse. Alternatively, the journey takes around 20 minutes from St Mawes by road.

Just above the lighthouse, the South West Coast Path skirts around the top of the cliffs towards the old pilchard port of **Portscatho**, commanding wonderful views all the way over the broad sweep of Gerrans Bay. Along the Coast Path just past Portscatho is **Porthcurnick Beach**, a sheltered and delightfully undeveloped sweep of sand; a mile or so further is the larger stretch of the lovely **Pendower Beach**, which extends a couple of miles, backed by dunes and low cliffs.

FALMOUTH

Thriving, lively Falmouth has many more accommodation, eating and drinking options than the peninsula opposite, and it's the perfect base if you want to do more than simply hole up for the weekend. Its buzzing arts scene, which has grown up around the acclaimed University College Falmouth, pushes the boundaries further than Cornwall's mainstream watercolour seascapes and lends the town a more cosmopolitan, progressive edge.

South of Pendennis Point, a string of sandy beaches – interspersed with classic rock-pooling territory at low tide – face out over calm blue waters, often dotted with the white sails of yachts or large tankers taking shelter in the bay. Backed by a number of hotels (including the grand, imposing Falmouth Hotel, which was the town's first purpose-built tourist accommodation when it opened in 1865), Falmouth's beaches may lack the peaceful natural beauty of the Roseland, but are a pleasant counterpoint to the busy town. The water is also incredibly clear – Gyllyngvase Beach boasts a European Blue Flag.

Until the 17th century, Falmouth was little more than a fishing village; Penryn to the north-west was the main town, with Pendennis Castle proudly protecting the mouth of the river. Established in 1689 as the chief base for the Packet Ships, which took the first international mail to the Continent and the colonies, Falmouth developed quickly, and its huge natural harbour – the first or last stop before heading out or back across the Atlantic, and a safe haven in bad weather – ensured the town's fortunes.

Heading into town from the modern piazza-like **Discovery Quay** and **Events Square** (home to the **National Maritime Museum,** (*see p173*), the road

Top: Pandora Inn;
bottom: Three Mackerel.

narrows into charming Arwenack Street, with its pretty pastel-coloured Georgian façades and a number of funky shops, cafés and restaurants. At the dog-leg corner by the attractive granite **Church of King Charles the Martyr** (whose palm-framed square tower overlooking the harbour features on many a postcard), Arwenack becomes Church Street. Along this cobbled street – again flanked by handsome Georgian façades – is the **Poly** (01326 212300, www.thepoly.org), a buzzing hub of creativity comprising three exhibition spaces and an art-house cinema, with regular theatre, dance and live music performances.

At the far end of town, after the inevitable chain shops, is the charismatic old High Street. Here you can browse the galleries, antiques and second-hand shops, grab a coffee and catch some rhythms at **Jam** (32 High Street, 01326 211722, www.jamrecords.co.uk), or head for lovely **Old Brewery Yard** a little further up, where you'll find **Cinnamon Girl** (01326 211457, www.cinnamon girl.co.uk), a friendly organic café with great food, and outside tables in the cobbled yard.

Near the top of the High Street stands the old town hall, originally a Congregational chapel presented to the town by Martin Lister Killigrew in 1725. It was also used as the courthouse and was the scene of a famous trial in 1884, when two sailors were acquitted on a charge of cannibalism, having eaten the cabin boy while adrift in the Atlantic after their ship sank. The friendly **Star & Garter pub** (52 High Street, 01326 318313), opposite, has lovely harbour views.

On the Moor, an attractive large continental-style square that serves as both marketplace and bus terminal, is another testament to the town's solid artistic identity – the award-winning **Falmouth Art Gallery Municipal Buildings** (01326 313863, www.falmouthartgallery.com). No average town gallery, it contains original works by major 19th- and 20th-century artists – including Alfred Munnings, HS Tuke, JM Waterhouse and Henry Moore – and also features upbeat and unusual contemporary art exhibitions. It's very family-friendly, with automata, a papier mâché show and children's workshops.

Opposite are the 111 steps of **Jacob's Ladder**, which ascend the large hill above the town. The steps have no real biblical association – they were installed by Jacob Hamblen, a builder and property owner, to facilitate access between his business (at the bottom) and some of his property (at the top). Once you get your breath back, follow the road around the brow of the hill for a fabulous panorama over the town and out across the bay. Take it all in over a quiet pint at the Seaview Inn (Wodehouse Terrace, 01326 311359, www.seaviewfalmouth.co.uk).

Out on the promontory stands **Pendennis Castle** (*see below*), built at the same time (1543) as its twin, St Mawes (*see p168*), a mile across

the estuary. Just below, a road runs all around the point, taking in the mighty docks on the way. In 1860, the foundation of Falmouth Docks created a focus for maritime industries, and an extensive ship repair and maintenance industry developed. An observation platform on the Pendennis Road makes for absorbing viewing. Beneath the road that leads around the point, a number of narrow paths weave between the rocks, trees and remains of defensive batteries.

The beachside road below the castle takes you to the town's three main sandy beaches: family-friendly Gyllyngvase is the nearest to town, with Maenporth and Swanpool stretching to the south.

Carrick Roads is the last remaining oyster fishery in Europe that is still dredged under sail and oar, with traditional working boats on duty between October and March. The beginning of the season is celebrated every October with the **Falmouth Oyster Festival** (01872 224367, 01326 312300).

National Maritime Museum
Falmouth *Discovery Quay (01326 313388/ www.nmmc.co.uk). Open 10am-5pm daily. Admission £8.75; £6-£7 reductions.*
Housed in an impressive teaked wooden building, the five-year-old NMM features a huge collection of impeccably restored small boats suspended from the ceiling in the main hall, as well as hands-on interactive displays, audio-visuals, talks and special exhibitions, covering all aspects of maritime life, from boat design to fascinating tales of survival at sea, and an exhibition on the history of diving. One highlight for all ages is the Tidal Zone, a natural underwater viewing gallery (one of only three in the world apparently); another is the 360° views over the harbour and town from the top of the 95-ft viewing tower. One ticket buys you annual unlimited access – and, given the vast scope of the museum, it's worth considering a second visit. There is a stylish glass-fronted café on the first floor looking out over the water.

Pendennis Castle
Falmouth *Castle Drive (01326 316594/www.english-heritage.org.uk). Open Mar-June, Sept 10am-5pm Mon-Fri, Sun; 10am-4pm Sat. July, Aug 10am-6pm Mon-Fri, Sun; 10am-4pm Sat. Oct-Mar 10am-4pm daily. (Last admission 1hr before closing). Admission £5.40; £2.70-£4.30.*
A crucial defensive garrison from Tudor times to World War II, Pendennis is somewhat larger than St Mawes across the water, having been extended by Elizabeth I at the end of the 16th century. During the Civil War, the young Prince Charles (who later became Charles II) hid here before escaping to the Continent – only just avoiding a siege of the castle by Parliamentarian forces. Visitors can explore the castle's fascinating history at the Discovery Centre, which also contains interactive displays and an exhibit on Tudor battles. In the summer, battle re-enactments take place on the gun deck, and a number of open-air concerts and events are held on the lawn.

THE HELFORD RIVER

No visit to Falmouth is complete without a boat trip up the enchanting Helford River, a few miles south of the town. Its stunning landscape of gentle hills, dense woods, sandy beaches, yachts and picture-postcard villages makes it an idyllic retreat.

At the mouth of the river, on the bank of Gillan Creek, is **St Anthony-in-Meneage** church (www.kerrierdeanery.co.uk/stanthony.html). Two excellent National Trust Gardens, Trebah and Glendurgan, overlook the river from Mawnan Smith on the north bank. **Trebah** (01326 252200, www.trebah-garden.co.uk) is a dramatic 26-acre ravine garden tumbling down to a sheltered beach, containing all manner of subtropical and native plants. In season, you can take the small ferry across to **Glendurgan** (01326 250906, www.nationaltrust.org.uk), another impressive garden – and great fun for kids, with its restored laurel maze and the Giant's Stride rope swing.

At Helford Passage, the **Ferry Boat Inn** (01326 250625, www.staustellbrewery.co.uk) sits right on the water's edge, and is a great spot for a beer and pub grub in the sunshine. Across the water on the south bank (accessible via a short ferry ride), Helford Village, with its granite thatched cottages (mostly converted into luxury second homes), is incredibly picturesque and makes for a pleasant amble, rounded off by a pint in the **Shipwright's Arms** (Helford Village, 01326 231235) – which also has a prime waterside location, and a garden stretching down to just above water level. Boat trips (closed winter) depart from Falmouth's Prince of Wales Pier (for timetable information, call 01326 212939 or visit www.boattrips-falmouth.co.uk).

Eat

Good food is also available for non-residents in the **Hotel Tresanton** (*see p176*).

Gylly Beach Cafe

Gyllyngvase Beach *Cliff Road (01326 312884/ www.gyllybeach.com). Open 10am-3pm Mon-Wed; 10am-3pm, 6-9pm Thur, Fri; 9am-4pm, 6-9pm Sat, Sun. ££. Café.*
This slick bar-restaurant right on Gyllyngvase Beach, has been popular from day one. The serving staff are bright young things who have perfected the art of slick but informal service and despite the chic surroundings – lots of white, blond woods and trendy white plastic chairs (actually very comfortable) – prices are perfectly reasonable: £7.95 for a gourmet burger with chunky skin-on chips on the side, or £6.50 for posh fish and chips. But the wide wraparound beachside terrace out front, giving far-reaching views of the estuary, is the real catch. Gylly attracts a mix of well-heeled tourists and locals of all ages – as well as art school students (particularly for 'curry and a drink for a fiver' night on Sunday).

Hunkydory's

Falmouth *46 Arwenack Street (01326 212997/ www.hunkydoryfalmouth.co.uk). Open 6-10pm daily. ££££. Modern European/Seafood.*
This airy blue-and-white restaurant on Falmouth's main drag is a favourite for its stellar array of local seafood – crab, clams, mussels and prawns are all present – and daily-changing fresh fish specials such as line-caught sea bass, monkfish and john dory. The frequently changing menu takes a predominantly modern European stance, with occasional Asian accents (as well as a sushi tasting plate). The crowd-pleasing dessert menu takes its inspiration from closer to home, with a crème brûlée, chocolate brownies and a platter of Cornish cheeses. Choose between the cosy wooden-beamed front room or the brighter steamship-style back room with its big booths. It's advisable to book in the summer months.

Miss Peapod's Kitchen Café

Penryn *Jubilee Wharf (01326 374424/www.miss peapod.co.uk). Open 10am-2.30pm Tue-Sat; 11am-4pm Sun. ££. Café.*
Eco chic haven Miss Peapod's occupies an enviable position in Penryn's new wind- and sun-powered Jubilee Wharf development. The Med-inspired menu demonstrates considerably more than a passing interest in sustainable practices: eggs come from Penryn's own Boswin farm, meat from the Lizard, coffee from Constantine and beer from a local boutique brewery. All of Miss Peapod's china and furniture is recycled, and even the floor once graced a London nightclub, so you can pull up a chair out on the decking (made of sustainably sourced timber, naturally), order a glass of organic wine and feel a warm, worthy glow. There's an eclectic live music and DJ programme at weekends.

Pandora Inn

Mylor, 2 miles NE of Penryn *Restronguet Creek (01326 372678/www.pandorainn.com). Open noon-3pm, 6.30-9pm Mon-Thur, Sun; noon-3pm, 6.30-9.30pm Fri, Sat. £££. Pub.*
This impossibly pretty thatched 13th-century inn has a glorious setting on the water at Mylor. A warren of interconnected rooms, vaulted with low beams, dark wooden panels, benches and fireside tables, the pub has two floors, with the restaurant upstairs serving the same food in a more upmarket setting. In summer, though, most people try to bag a table on the jetty looking out over Restronguet Creek. Rather romantically, you can take the Aqua Cab from the pier in Falmouth (07970 242258, www.aquacab.co.uk) right on to the Pandora jetty.

Three Mackerel

Falmouth *Swanpool (01326 311886/www.thethree mackerel.com). Open noon-2.30pm, 6.30-9.30pm daily. £££. Modern European.*
The dreamy location of the Three Mackerel – with a blue parasol-strewn large deck perched above the clear blue waters of Swanpool Beach – means people would probably flock here even if they were serving baked beans on toast. The fact that the menu is an alluring mix of well-executed Mediterranean and modern British cuisine, with the emphasis on local meat and super fresh fish, makes this one of the stars

Driftwood Hotel.

of the Falmouth restaurant scene. There is a pleasantly informal feel, particularly on the decking, and the tapas barbecues in summer are incredibly popular. Recommended.

Victory Inn
St Mawes *Victory Hill (01326 270324/www.victory-inn.co.uk). Open Winter noon-2.30pm, 6.30-9pm daily. Summer noon-2.30pm, 6-9.30pm daily. ££. Pub.*
Formerly a fishermen's haunt, the Victory sees more chinos and blazers than yellow fishing overalls these days. Its beamed interior retains an intimate old world vibe, while the restaurant upstairs – serving the same food – is fresh, airy and modern with a small outdoor terrace. Serving up a number of real ales and lagers, as well as innovative pub food that includes lots of fresh seafood (using as much local and organic produce as possible – dishes include locally caught and picked crab risotto, beer-battered cod and chips, fish pie), this is a great place to while away carefree holiday hours. Bookings recommended in high season.

Stay

Budock Vean
Falmouth *Helford Passage, Mawnan Smith (01326 252100/www.budockvean.co.uk). £££.*
Sitting proudly on the beautiful north bank of the Helford River, a short drive from nearby Falmouth, this is a lavish four-star resort boasting its own golf course, tennis courts, pool and spa, and extensive, organically managed gardens leading down to a private foreshore on the river, complete with private sun lounge. It's all about luxury, although the emphasis is less on innovative interior design and more on the traditional values of exclusive hotel-keeping. Highlights include multi-course dinners at the elegant restaurant (jacket and tie requested, gentlemen) and sumptuous teas.

Driftwood Hotel
Portscatho *Rosevine (01872 580644/www.driftwoodhotel.co.uk). ££££.*
This enchanting privately owned beach house is set in seven acres of gardens leading down to the sea. Catering to families (there's a small separate games room for children) as well as couples, the Driftwood is all about carefully considered comfort. Design is stylish and crisp but informal, with lots of driftwood (believe it or not), natural fabrics and stone. The smart white restaurant, which serves up the best locally sourced produce cooked in imaginative modern European and fusion styles, is another big pull, as are after-dinner drinks watching the moon on the water from the decking area. The restored weather-boarded cabin down in the gardens, with two bedrooms and a living room, is worth booking if you possibly can.

Falmouth Town House
Falmouth *Grove Place (01326 312009/www.falmouthtownhouse.co.uk). ££.*
Given its arty air, Falmouth was long overdue a hotel with design flair – and with the arrival of Falmouth Town House, crafted with care from an incredibly handsome

double-fronted Georgian house, it finally has one. The ten rooms at this retro-styled hotel are artfully scattered with vintage modernist design classics, original art and bespoke furniture, amassed with care by the owners, as well as equipped with king-sized beds, spacious luxury bathrooms (with toiletries from natural specialists Korres) and an unbeatable location in the centre of town – right opposite the harbour and the National Maritime Museum. The cool little bar in the reception rooms serving tapas, wines and cocktails is a neat addition.

Greenbank Hotel
Falmouth *Harbourside (01326 312440/www.greenbank-hotel.com). £££.*
Dating from 1640, the Greenbank is the oldest hotel in Falmouth and has an impressive history to go with it, boasting Florence Nightingale and Kenneth '*Wind in the Willows*' Grahame as former guests. Aside from the display cases in the lobby, which proudly highlight this point, history is evident all around you, with high ceilings, sweeping staircases and tasteful but traditional decor. Situated on the Falmouth harbour front with unrivalled views of Flushing – and its own 16th-century private quay to boot – the hotel is popular with the yachting crowd, but is also a great base for anyone wanting a touch of class within a stone's throw of the town centre. Modern British cuisine, with the emphasis on fish and seafood, and twinkling harbour views, are the order of the day at the hotel's Harbourside restaurant.

Hotel Tresanton
St Mawes *Lower Castle Road (01326 270055/www.tresanton.com). ££££.*
Arguably one of the UK's best country hotels, renowned interior designer Olga Polizzi's Hotel Tresanton has become synonymous with waterside chic, and has played host to a stellar cast of celebrities since it opened in 1999. Polizzi spent two years and a cool £2 million renovating and restoring it, adding personal touches to every room (guests are even provided with wellies). Nevertheless, it has a friendly, intimate and homely atmosphere that will make mere mortals feel welcome. Originally created in the 1940s as a yachtsmen's club, the hotel became a popular and well-known haunt for yachties and tourists in the 1950s and '60s. A cluster of houses built into the hillside on different levels, the Tresanton has 27 (out of its 29) rooms with views out to sea and St Anthony's Lighthouse on the headland beyond. Nautical patterns influence the design of some rooms, while others blend natural hues of cream and beige with dark wood and richly coloured fabrics. Original works of art adorn the hallways and lounge areas, with pieces by Terry Frost, Barbara Hepworth and acclaimed St Mawes sculptor Julian Dyson in the collection.

Tresanton is a hotel for all seasons: spend a day aboard the *Pinuccia* (a 48ft classic racing yacht built to represent Italy in the 1938 World Cup), followed by dinner on the terrace in summer; or try the yoga, bridge and treatment weekend packages, and the cosy lounge, in the winter. (Sarah Key, a physio who treats the royal family, hosts programmes in November and April.) A great selection of books, magazines and DVDs is available all year round.

The upmarket restaurant is superb: everything from the cut-above waiting staff to the thick starched napkins, smart decor and elevated prices is a statement of serious gastronomic intent. And the food delivers – choose from a daily-changing modern European menu of exquisite fresh fish dishes, classic meat selections or imaginative vegetarian fare, all executed with flair and precision. Summer sees cocktails and dinner on the terrace, while winter is a cosy candlelit affair in the dining room. Non-residents can also enjoy light lunches and cream teas. For food and service of this quality, the Tresanton has few peers.

Lugger Hotel

Portloe *(01872 501322/www.luggerhotel.com). ££££.*
Elegantly simple and tastefully contemporary, the Lugger is ideal for anyone looking for a peaceful retreat in the lap of luxury. Nestled into the cliffs above the tiny fishing village of Portloe on the Roseland peninsula, the historic 17th-century inn (one landlord was hanged for smuggling in the 1890s) and fishermen's cottages that now collectively form the 21-room hotel have been given a stylish 21st-century facelift. The spacious interiors are decorated in cream and chocolate with sumptuous leather sofas and white wicker chairs – and there are pretty views across the harbour from the excellent restaurant. For post-prandial lingering, there's a stoked log fire to sit by in winter and a terrace in summer.

Nare Hotel

Veryan-in-Roseland, 1 mile W of Portloe *Carne Beach (01872 501111/www.thenare.com). ££££.*
Standing proud above Carne Beach on Gerrans Bay, the Nare is an elegant, traditional affair. First opened in 1925, the extended 37-room hotel still retains much of its original character, with winding corridors, roaring log fires and rooms bursting with antiques. The individually decorated bedrooms add to the sense of old-world charm, from the comfortable countryside-view rooms to the luxurious sea-view suites, with carriage clocks, floral fabrics and high-backed armchairs throughout.

The four-star Nare has justly won a slew of awards for its facilities, service and atmosphere. From the indoor and outdoor pools, subtropical gardens leading down to the beach, sauna, hot tub, gym, beauty salon and billiards room, to fine dining with views, it has everything you would expect of a premium country hotel. It's the finishing touches that really make it special, though: a decanter of complimentary sherry (in deluxe rooms), fresh milk, hot-water bottles provided just before bedtime in the winter and a lovingly selected 500-strong wine list. Special activities also keep guests entertained, from wine- and cheese-tastings to theatre trips.

St Mawes Hotel

St Mawes *The Sea Front (01326 270266/www.st maweshotel.co.uk). £££.*
This friendly establishment on the waterfront in the centre of town has five simple but attractively decorated rooms. Warm yellows, natural wood and superb sea views create a relaxed mood and prices are incredibly reasonable for this well-heeled town. The brasserie and bar downstairs are extremely popular, so be warned that this may not be the most serene of retreats in the busy summer months.

St Michael's Hotel & Spa

Gyllyngvase Beach *(01326 312707/www.stmichaels-hotel.co.uk). £££.*
Less prominent than the imposing Falmouth Beach Hotel, St Michael's has the advantage of being situated right opposite Gyllyngvase Beach (and ten minutes' walk from town). Set back from the main road by award-winning subtropical gardens (including a children's play area and an outdoor massage pagoda), St Michael's has a host of extra features including an indoor pool, sauna, jacuzzi, steam rooms, gym and sundeck. The fresh, nautical-inspired interior is light and airy but not too gimmicky (where else would you find a boat for a reception desk and beach hut-style toilets?), and the comfortable rooms are amply equipped. There are a number of scenic lounges and outdoor terraces where you can enjoy a sunset drink.

Factfile

When to go
Go in summer for boating, strolling and outdoor events – but empty beaches and lower hotel rates make a spring or autumn trip attractive. The celebrated Falmouth Oyster Festival takes place in October.

Getting there & around
Falmouth is accessible by train via a connecting branch line from Truro. Those wanting to explore remote corners or find deserted beaches will do much better by car, but it is perfectly possible (not to mention pleasurable) to explore the town on foot and take the ferry across to St Mawes, up to Truro and south to the Helford River (though off-season some ferries are less frequent or stop altogether).

Tourist information
Falmouth 28 Killigrew Street (01326 312300/ www.acornishriver.co.uk). Open Jan-Mar, Nov, Dec 9.30am-5.15pm Mon-Fri. Apr-July, Sept, Oct 9.30am-5.15pm Mon-Sat. Aug 9.30am-5.15pm Mon-Sat; 10.15am-1.45pm Sun.

St Mawes Roseland Visitor Centre, The Square (01326 270440/www.acornishriver.co.uk). Open Jan-May, Oct-Dec 10am-2pm Mon-Fri. June-Early July, Sept 10am-4pm Mon-Sat. Late July-Aug 10am-4pm Mon-Sat; noon-2pm Sun.

Internet
Falmouth Library Municipal Buildings, The Moor (01326 314901).

Top: Ilfracombe Quay;
bottom: Saunton Sands

North Devon & Exmoor

Remote landscapes of wide sands, dense woods and moorland.

North Devon is out there. Rebellious and strange, it's suffused with an enquiring, obstinate independence. Yes, this is the south-west, but north Devon somehow feels northern and Welsh, rather than southern and soft. There's some fairly severe economic hardship too. Second-homers have snapped up smallholdings, and in parts there's a sense of decay.

Then again, this is also the land of scrumptious clotted-cream teas, a superb coastline largely protected by the National Trust, and some of Britain's best surfing. There's space here too, with magnificent strands of sandy beach and the UK's largest UNESCO biosphere reserve. The Devon greensward descends close to the sea; in the more sheltered coastal combes, you could imagine yourself deep inland.

The thickly wooded cleaves, romantic coves and steep cliffs of the Exmoor coast make a spectacular introduction to the region. Exmoor itself is great walking and pony-trekking country, as well as being good for hunting, shooting and fishing. Further west, beyond the decaying splendour of Ilfracombe, famous surfing beaches punctuate the coastal scenery, sweeping into the amazing sand dunes of Braunton Burrows and the marshes of the Taw and Torridge estuaries. These two rivers are bridged respectively at doughty Barnstaple and mazy Bideford. And, on its far western shore, north Devon breaks up and goes wild with the fearsome rocks of Hartland.

Explore

EXMOOR

One of the less visited of the UK's National Parks, Exmoor is often bypassed in favour of its south Devon neighbour, Dartmoor. But in many ways, it's more charming. Covering 250 square miles, the moor is endearingly small in scale, like its most famous resident, the Exmoor pony. These stubborn little nags rarely stand taller than 12 hands (four feet) and are possibly the most ancient equine type in existence. You're bound to spot some grazing – they're privately owned, yet best not approached, and wander the moor as they please. As do England's last herds of wild red deer, a rarer sight, which have survived here since prehistory. Exmoor was enclosed as a Royal hunting forest in 1204. High beech hedges now line the roads, planted as windbreaks by the moor's Victorian landowner; they obscure views from the car but are a beautiful sight, especially in May and autumn.

Dulverton, on the River Barle, is the 'gateway' to the moor from the south, offering scope for organising outdoor activities. **Winsford**, to the north, is a prettier village. The road there passes close to the Caractacus Stone, on Winsford Hill, likely to be a sixth- or seventh-century boundary marker erected by someone linked with the Welsh court of King Caractacus. Wales often feels surprisingly close in north Devon.

Exford is a farming village in the heart of the moor. The road north from here over the hills to Porlock gives fantastic views of coast and sea. It runs past the foot of Dunkery Beacon, Exmoor's highest hill at 1,704 feet (popular with mountain bikers). Superb walks begin at Webber's Post. The hanging sessile oak woods around Horner and Cloutsham are wonderfully mysterious, and an important wildlife habitat. Nearby, the tiny church of Stoke Pero, Exmoor's highest, stands in an isolated spot down winding sunken lanes. A picture on the wall commemorates Zulu, a donkey who carried timber here from Porlock for the church's Victorian restorers.

Five miles west of Exford, **Simonsbath** sits on the edge of Exmoor Forest, the bleakest almost tree-less part of the moor where its four rivers rise in desolate wilds known as the Chains. A beautiful two-mile walk (part of the Two Moors Way long-distance path, a fragment of Exmoor's 650 miles of footpath) heads south-east from Simonsbath down the peaceful valley of the Barle, passing England's highest beech woodland, confusingly called Birch Cleave, to the striking conical hillock of Cow Castle, an Iron Age fort.

Seven or so miles north of Simonsbath, across the moor, lies the coast. From Dunster and Porlock in the east to Combe Martin in the west, the Exmoor Coast is one of the most surprising and romantic in England, but its beauty is well-known and the A39 coast road gets severely congested in summer. In the 19th century,

Exmoor & North Devon

Historic sites
● ● ● ○ ○ ○

Art & architecture
● ● ○ ○ ○ ○

Hotels
● ● ● ○ ○ ○

Eating & drinking
● ● ● ○ ○ ○

Scenery
● ● ● ● ● ○

Outdoor activities
● ● ● ● ● ○

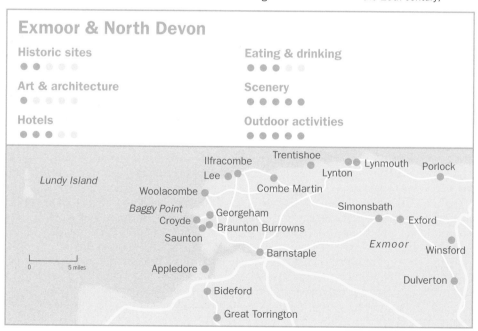

Woolacombe.

Make the most of London life

Strand magazine publisher George Newnes developed **Lynton** as a resort, linking it to the lovely riverside harbour town of Lynmouth below with a hydraulic cliff railway, still in operation. Sadly the Lynton & Barnstaple Railway no longer runs, but a mile or so has been restored for fun at Woody Bay. Near Lynton, Outovercott Riding Stables (01598 753341, www.outovercott.co.uk) is a widely recommended pony-trekking centre.

> "Sherrycombe is so remote that German U-boats are said to have refreshed their water supplies here in World War II."

Beyond, the mossy woods round **Trentishoe** are a treat, their steep roads giving glimpses of the sea shining below through the trees. The craggy gulch of Heddon's Mouth Cleave (with the famous Hunter's Inn at its head) is the best trodden of a series of paths down to the sea between here and Ilfracombe. **Holdstone Down** is renowned for UFO sightings, and also, probably coincidentally, for comedian Bill Bailey and his Glass Box bungalow. **Sherrycombe** below is so remote that German U-boats are said to have refreshed their water supplies here in World War II. Nearby, Great Hangman's cliffs are England's highest.

ILFRACOMBE

The perfect setting for a B-movie, Ilfracombe is a dilapidated Victorian seaside resort that could do with some A-list treatment from the likes of David Lynch. Instead, it's lucky enough to have Damien Hirst, whose Quay Restaurant & White Hart Bar (*see p189*) on the harbour quayside has divided local opinion but remains a draw for visitors. Among Ilfracombe's quirks is the fact it doesn't have a proper seafront. The views from the back of Hirst's gaff are about as close as it gets.

Just inland, the town's grand old High Street sports wrought-iron balconies above the shop-fronts. At the end of the street, valetudinarians would once have sallied forth to the segregated tidal pools of the **Tunnels Beaches**. Welsh miners burrowed through the cliffs to reach the beaches in 1823, and these remain a major attraction today. Ilfracombe harbour is a popular departure point for day-trips on MS *Oldenburg* to **Lundy Island**, a whale-shaped granite outcrop in the Bristol Channel famous for puffins and pricey accommodation (Mar Oct, for more details see www.lundyisland.co.uk).

In 1986, the island was designated as the UK's first Marine Nature Reserve.

A couple of miles west of Ilfracombe, directly accessible on foot via the clifftop Torrs Park, the tiny village of **Lee** is famous for fuchsias (and has an excellent pub). Its green, pleasant cosiness edges right up against the rocky, storm-battered shoreline. The coast path becomes even more rewarding beyond Lee, rounding Bull Point and skirting the aptly named Rockham Bay. **Mortehoe** village, only two miles from Lee by the coast path (several more by road), snuggles beneath a gorsey bluff occupied by a Memorial Park and cemetery, tapering out on to the slate cliffs of Morte Point where seals can sometimes be seen.

South from here, Devon's west coast lets rip. By way of prelude, **Barricane Beach** is a sheltered little shell bay, with a great café doing takeaway snacks in summer. **Woolacombe** still looks good from a distance, though up close it's overwhelmed by holiday builds and bungalows. Most people are here for the beach: two miles of glorious, clean sand where windsurfers, surf boarders and anyone else can usually find room to enjoy themselves. The family fun continues at the south end, in **Putsborough**, also very popular with surfers, especially when their favourite beach at **Croyde Bay**, just round Baggy Point, fails to deliver. Being surfers' first choice, **Croyde** can become impossibly crowded in summer. Just inland is **Georgeham**, where Henry Williamson retreated to write *Tarka the Otter* in 1921. His writing hut in a field at Ox's Cross, just above the village, has been preserved by the Henry Williamson Society (www.henrywilliamson.co.uk).

The coast road from Croyde to Saunton hugs the cliffs, to arrive at the three-mile sweep of **Saunton Sands**, one of north Devon's most extraordinary sights, backed by the unearthly landscape of Braunton Burrows. The dunes form the heart of the north Devon UNESCO Biosphere Reserve (www.northdevonbiosphere.org.uk), designed to promote an ecologically sustainable economic future for the area. An astonishing variety of flowering plants thrives here, many of them unique to the Burrows.

BARNSTAPLE

Known as 'Barum' to the natives, and north Devon's principal town, Barnstaple boasts a fine old High Street. Don't miss the **Pannier Market**, a great arcaded space constructed in 1855, and, of the same date, Butchers Row, a series of butchers, fishmongers and delis (Ballantyne's at No.15 is good for picnic materials) facing one side of the market hall. Antiques take preference in the market on Wednesdays, while Tuesdays, Fridays and Saturdays are best for general goods and local produce. St Peter's Church nearby has a bizarrely twisted spire. The free Museum of Barnstaple & North Devon (The Square,

Board room

North Devon has something for every level of surfer. From point and reef set-ups to mellow beach breaks, there's a huge variety of surf in an area that just happens to be one of England's prettiest. If the swell goes flat, you won't be short of other delights along a coastline that combines moorland, golden sands and ancient harbours.

The focal point for surfing has always been Croyde, described by Alf Alderson in *Surf UK* as 'one of the best beach breaks in Britain, with fast, hollow waves common around low water, especially on spring tides,' but there's a number of other quality breaks, not least Speke's Mill and Lynmouth. The former is an all-but-inaccessible reef break for experts only, while Lynmouth is a left-hand point break set at the foot of a village that's the quintessential Devonian idyll (Percy Bysshe Shelley honeymooned here in 1812).

In Saunton Sands, a few miles from the town of Braunton (which contains all the main surf shops and brands), north Devon has one of the most perfect beginners' surfing beaches. Here, waves peel slowly over a gently sloping beach; there's a healthy longboarding scene too.

One of Europe's largest surfing companies has its base in Braunton. Tiki, set up in 1970 by Tim Heyland, has become a byword for quality surfboards and associated gear. From here it's a short drive to the area's principal surfing beaches at Saunton, Woolacombe, Putsborough and Croyde. There are other spots too. Try Westward Ho! if you're looking to escape the crowds, while Downend Point and Bucks Mills have challenging waves suitable for experienced surfers only.

Several top surfers have made an impact in north Devon. They include Totnes-bred Eugene Tollemache, a highly rated big-wave rider and ex-Rick Stein chef, as well as Andrew Cotton, Scott Rannochan and Adam Thornton. But perhaps the area's most notable endorsement comes from Olympic rower James Cracknell. The gold medal winning oarsman loves surfing at Croyde so much, he named his son after the village.

01271 346747, www.devonmuseums.net/ barnstaple, open 9.30am-5pm Mon-Sat), in an imposing brick building on the main town square, contains an amusing Tarka Gallery featuring illuminated dioramas and models of local wildlife, reached through a short corridor of mothballed creepy-crawlies wall-mounted in glass cases. A room on the first floor is dedicated to an exhibition on the late-Victorian and Edwardian art potters of Barnstaple. Thanks to the railway still running from Exeter, the Tarka Line, Barnstaple is also the main jumping-off point for explorations of Tarka Country (*see below* Tarka Trail).

"Owned by the Countess of Arran, Castle Hill is the perfect picture of an 18th-century country seat."

Arlington Court
Arlington, 9 miles N of Barnstaple *(01271 850296/www.nationaltrust.org.uk). Open (house/ museum) Late Feb noon-4pm daily. Mar-Sept 11am-5pm daily. Admission £8.20; £4.10 reductions.*
This severe grey-stone neoclassical house was formerly the home of the Chichester family. It's set in the middle of a huge National Trust estate, which includes a heronry. Many visitors are drawn by the collection of some 50 horse-drawn carriages, ranging from a grand state coach to a simple hearse. Inside the house, treats include Miss Chichester's shell collection and 18th-century Beauvais tapestries.

Beaford Archive
Beaford, 22 miles S of Barnstaple *Beaford Arts, Greenwarren House, Winkleigh (01805 603201/ www.beaford-arts.org.uk). Open (by appointment) 9am-5pm Mon-Fri. Admission free.*
The oldest rural arts centre in the UK, founded in 1966, the Beaford Archive is an amazing photographic record of old Devon. Pride of the collection are some 80,000 images captured by James Ravilious from 1972 to 1989, revealing the rural scene of 'deep Devon', now almost extinct. Visitor facilities are very limited, but appointments can be made to view the collection on computer and order digital prints.

Broomhill Sculpture Gardens
Barnstaple *Muddiford Road (01271 850262/ www.broomhillart.co.uk). Open July, Aug 11am-4pm daily. Sept-June 11am-4pm Wed-Sun. Admission £4.50; £3.50 reductions.*
Since 1997, Rinus and Aniet van de Sande have been filling up the steep 10-acre hillside garden of their hotel (*see p190*) with a huge variety of sculpture (some 300 at the last count). A wander here is likely to provoke and entertain. We particularly liked *Fat Boy* by Lucy Kinsella, an

Exmoor pony rolling on its back. The gallery in the hotel is free to visit and often mounts eye-catching exhibitions.

Castle Hill
Filleigh, 9 miles SE of Barnstaple *(01598 760336/www.castlehilldevon.co.uk). Open (gardens) Apr-Sept 11am-5pm Mon-Thur, Sun. Admission £4; £3.50 reductions.*
Owned by the Countess of Arran, Castle Hill is the perfect picture of an 18th-century country seat. The Palladian house is painted a gorgeous deep yellow, and overlooks a wide landscaped park, complete with a tributary of the River Bray contained within a series of terraced cascades.

TARKA TRAIL
The Tarka Trail, all of which can be followed on foot, and parts also by bike or train, runs for almost 200 miles in a figure of eight round 'Tarka Country', roughly tracing some of the locations in Henry Williamson's novel. It's one of the best things about north Devon. The bike trail between Barnstaple and Bideford passes through Fremington Quay, looking across to Chivenor airstrip and the church of Heanton Punchardon, with the magical light of the Braunton Burrows biosphere off in the distance to the west.

BIDEFORD
A quietly crumbling old place on the banks of the Torridge, **Bideford** achieved fame in the 19th century as the 'Little White Town'. It was dubbed this by the clergyman Charles *Water Babies* Kingsley in his 1855 novel *Westward Ho!*, which was so popular that the title was given to a nearby resort. Recent suggestions that Bideford be re-branded an 'Elizabethan Maritime Town', capitalising on its history of migration to the New World, have met some resistance. Still, the warren of lanes around Mill Street and the High Street are pleasant to explore, while the riverside along the Quay is enhanced by the sleek, modern lines of the new Lundy Shore Office.

The town's **Burton Art Gallery** has two large rooms housing a remarkable collection based on the watercolours of Hubert Coop, including *Lake Nemi* by Richard Wilson, landscapes by Mark Fisher and the American E Aubrey Hunt, and crayons by George Belcher, who taught at Bideford Art School. Upstairs, the **Bideford Museum** has an exhibition on local man Sir Richard Grenville, who brought one of the first native Americans, of the 'Wynganditoian' tribe (actually an Algonquian), back to England from Virginia in 1586. It also has a display on the Abbotsham Hoard: coins buried in 1653 during the Civil War, and discovered in 2001.

A mile downriver of Bideford, high up on the east bank of the Torridge, is **Tapeley Park** (www.tapeley-park.co.uk), a dilapidated old mansion that has become a venue for a variety of way-out events and is home to an esoteric gift shop, Olde Ways (www.whichkraftshop.com). From the grounds, there are superb views over the river to **Appledore**, the shipbuilding village at the mouth of the Torridge. Hocking's ice-cream is a Devon delicacy made there. Farther upstream, **Great Torrington** is a sturdy market town, home to Dartington Crystal's glass factory (well worth a look on a rainy day), and the thriving Plough Arts Centre (9-11 Fore Street, 01805 624624, www.plough-arts.org).

North Devon Maritime Museum
Appledore *Odun Road (01237 474852/422064/ www.devonmuseums.net). Open Easter-Apr, Oct 2-4.30pm daily. May-Sept 11am-1pm, 2-4.30pm Mon-Fri; 2-4.30pm Sat, Sun. Admission £1.50; 30p-£1 reductions. No credit cards.*
A tremendous, old-fashioned museum in a large Georgian mansion, run by volunteers. Here you'll get an engaging insight into Appledore and Bideford's shipbuilding history. Models include the *Nonsuch*, which in 1776 helped to found the Hudson Bay Company, and a replica of Drake's *Golden Hinde*, built in Appledore. A display describes the trade with Newfoundland. Framed in a porthole is the museum's mascot: Albert Ross the Albatross.

RHS Garden Rosemoor
Great Torrington *(01805 624067/www.rhs.org.uk/ rosemoor). Open Apr-Sept 10am-6pm daily (last admission 5pm). Oct-Mar 10am-5pm daily (last admission 4pm). Admission £6.50; £2 reductions.*
Lady Anne Berry gave her eight-acre garden to the Royal Horticultural Society in 1988, along with 32 acres of pastureland. Lady Anne's Garden, with its Mediterranean garden, croquet lawn and stone garden, is reached through a tunnel under the main road beyond the rockery. Part of her house is now the Wisteria Tea Room (closed in winter). There are also formal and wild gardens around the lake, some 68 acres in total. In summer, the roses are the thing. In May, it's the rhodies in Lady Anne's Garden, while in autumn the fruit and veg gardens come into their own. Everything is neatly signposted and labelled.

HARTLAND
The wildest, most remote part of north Devon, **Hartland** is the county's true Atlantic seaboard. Wonderful coastal walks can be made right around the peninsula of Hartland Point (www.hartlandpeninsula.com), but highlights are the waterfall at Speke's Mill, treks from Hartland Quay, strolls to the sea from Hartland Abbey, and also Clovelly's Gallantry Bower.

Everyone has heard of **Clovelly**, the impossibly quaint 'waterfall' of cottages tumbling down to a tiny old harbour, pub and lifeboat station. A visitor centre deals with the coach tours, but less crowded pleasures are the walks through the woods along the cliffs. The next big thing at Clovelly is apparently going to be sea sculling.

In Hartland's hinterland, **Bradworthy** is more lively than the town of Hartland, but both have good independent shops and a strong community spirit. The Gnome Reserve (West Putford, 01409 241435, www.gnomereserve.co.uk) lures punters into a four-acre wild flower garden full of the little blighters that were first introduced to Britain from Germany in the 1840s. The Big Sheep adventure park near Bideford may be even more of a hit with your little nippers.

Near **Welcombe**, the forward-thinking Yarner Trust (Welcombe Barton, 01288 331692, www.yarnertrust.org) runs respected courses for all-comers in sustainable, creative living and rural crafts; you can stay in a yurt here if you like. Just over the border into Cornwall, **Morwenstow** is a must: for the extraordinary church of St Morwenna and its association with R S Hawker, the vicar who, against local custom, buried shipwrecked sailors in the graveyard here rather than on the beach. A replica of the wrecked *Caledonia*'s figurehead, startlingly white, now stands in the churchyard; the original was moved into the church for safekeeping in 2008.

Eat

There are many places where you can find great food in north Devon, but they take some tracking down and in high season must be booked in advance. Full justice is done to seafood, especially crab and lobster, in several coastal resorts. Further inland, ingredients from 'deep Devon' are a highlight: superb lamb, game and beef. Surprisingly, given the area's New Age credentials, vegetarians are likely to find fairly slim pickings.

"The long, low-beamed saloon gets into its stride on Saturday folk-music nights, and there's pool, darts and board games."

In addition to the venues listed below, other useful places in **Ilfracombe** include: the Gurkha (12-13 Belgrave Promenade, 01271 863287, www.devongurkharestaurant.co.uk), for its Nepalese dishes and oriental buffet; the Gendarmerie brasserie (63 Fore Street, 01271 865984); and the more upmarket No.6 St James (6 St James's Place, 01271 866602, www.no6st james.co.uk). In **Mortehoe**, the estimable B&B at Rockleigh House (The Square, 01271 870704, www.rockleighhouse.com) has a good restaurant.

Saunton Sands.

Southcliffe Hall.

Barnstaple has 62 The Bank (62 Boutport Street, 01271 324446, www.brend-hotels.co.uk), which boasts an amazing Jacobean ceiling and is run by the people behind the Saunton Sands Hotel (*see p191*). In **Parracombe** (13 miles to the north-east of Barnstaple), the rustic Fox & Goose (01598 763239, www.foxandgoose-parracombe.co.uk) is a fine pub, as is the Bush Inn in **Morwenstow** (01288 331242, www.bushinn-morwenstow.co.uk). Of the hotel restaurants, Northcote Manor (*see p191*) is worth a special trip.

Decks

Instow, 3.5 miles NE of Bideford *Hatton Croft, Marine Parade (01271 860671/www.decksrestaurant.co.uk). Open 7-9.30pm Tue-Sat. £££. French.*
With 50 covers on two levels, both enjoying fine views overlooking the Torridge estuary, Decks has become a local institution with a lively following. The menu specialises in Anglo-French cooking, perhaps not at the cutting edge of culinary fashion, but with careful attention to detail. Starters might be Cornish scallops and salami, or confit duck leg with risotto, while mains deal confidently with local fish, meat and fowl, and include at least one vegetarian dish.

Docton Mill

Lymebridge Nr Milford, 3 miles SW of Hartland *(01237 441369/www.doctonmill.co.uk). Open (tearoom) Mar-Oct 10am-5.30pm daily. ££. Café.*
In an enchanting wild garden hidden in a secluded valley, Docton Mill serves perhaps the world's best cream teas. Most ingredients are own-made or locally sourced, even the Italian-style ice-cream, and there can be few more idyllic places to enjoy them than this medieval mill house, inside or out. The seafood platters and hearty soups are the stuff of legends.

Grampus Inn

Lee Bay, 3 miles W of Ilfracombe *(01271 862906/ www.thegrampus-inn.co.uk). Open (food served) noon-3pm, 7-9pm daily. ££. No credit cards. Pub.*
Bill Harvey, a champion fiddle player and experienced smallholder, runs this amiable establishment. It's a proper pub with guest ales and some decent wines: just the thing to accompany the locally sourced food. Dishes are good value, freshly prepared and uncomplicated. Our request for quince jelly to go with a pheasant fricassee was met with the welcome alternative of home-made medlar jelly. The long, low-beamed saloon gets into its stride on Saturday folk-music nights, and there's pool, darts and board games.

Hobbs

Croyde *6 Hobbs Hill (01271 890256). Open Mar-Oct dinner only. Times vary, phone for details. £££. Modern European.*
The food here isn't going to revolutionise your appreciation of fine dining, but it's probably the best offered in Croyde. Hobbs's decidedly modern European menu incorporates the likes of beef wellington, lamb tagine or whole baked sea bass. The place is usually packed, and the jolly atmosphere and happy holiday revelry are the main reasons for booking a table. The breakfasts are pretty good too, apparently.

Lathwells

Bideford *4 Cooper Street (01237 476447/www.lathwells.com). Open 7-10.30pm Wed-Sat. £££. Modern European.*
Small and spotless Lathwells opened on one of Bideford's quaint old sidestreets in 2004. Owner John Emms maintains that 70% of his food comes from within 25 miles of the town. Rustic cuisine of considerable flair is created here: duck, pear and walnut salad as a starter, for instance, perhaps followed by pan-fried sea bass or slow-roast lamb shank in redcurrant and port sauce. Smiling staff are efficient.

> ## "The Atlantic Room is stunning, with a boat's-hull ceiling and superb views over the breakers."

Mortehoe Shellfish

Mortehoe, 6.5 miles SW of Ilfracombe *North Morte Road (01271 870633/www.mortehoeshellfish.co.uk). Open Easter & Summer noon-3pm, 6-9pm daily. £££. Fish.*
This gloriously eccentric spot is run by a local fishing family. Visitors are guided inside by an arrow on a plastic lobster on the lawn; the interior looks like a suburban front room. The menu is short and sweet, majoring in fresh crab and lobster. Opening hours vary ('on quiet days we may be skiving, on busy days you may be disappointed,' states the website), so phone ahead to check. The family also runs a shellfish van that tours campsites.

Quay Café

Fremington, 2.5 miles W of Barnstaple *Fremington Quay (01271 378783/www.fremington quaycafe.co.uk). Open Feb half-term-Oct half-term 10.30am-5pm Tue-Sun (also open Mon school & bank hols). Nov-Feb 10.30am-4.30pm Tue-Sun (also open Mon school & bank hols). £££. British.*
On the Tarka Cycle Trail, the Quay Café occupies the old Fremington Quay railway station and has fabulous views from its outside tables over the estuary. Lunch (served noon-3pm) isn't cheap, as the café tag might suggest, but it's likely to be very good. On our visit, a fiver bought a modest bowl of scrummy winter vegetable soup, with a crust, and £10.50 a steaming plate of fantastic Taw mussels marinière. Old bicycles hang from the ceiling inside, along with big black and white photos depicting the quay's history. Deservedly popular.

Quay Restaurant & White Hart Bar

Ilfracombe *11 The Quay (01271 868090/www.11the quay.co.uk). Open noon-3pm, 6-9pm Thur-Sat; noon-3pm Sun. £££. Modern European.*
Opened in 2004, Damien Hirst's restaurant on Ilfracombe's quayside was being refurbished as we went to press. It offers an burst of sophistication among the local chippies and tourist-tat. The trendy bar is decorated with Hirst's artwork,

and we gather the first-floor Atlantic Room is stunning, with a boat's-hull ceiling and superb views over the breakers. Local seafood, game (in season) and cheeses feature, and there are plans to open for coffee and waffles.

Rectory Farm & Tea Rooms

Crosstown Nr Morwenstow, 10.5 miles S of Hartland *(01288 331251/www.rectory-tearooms.co.uk). Open Apr-Oct 11am-5pm daily. £. Café.*
OK, so it isn't in Devon, but just over the border in Cornwall, Rectory Farm (by the church) is idyllic enough to merit the trip. A brook babbles through the garden, while inside, high-backed settles and sepia photos set the mood. The tearoom is part of a working farmhouse and purveys good honest cooking. The generous ploughman's includes an impressive choice of local cheeses. As well as great cream teas, you might also find fruit cake or bakewell tart.

Rock Inn

Georgeham *Rock Hill (01271 890322/www.croyde-bay.co.uk/Business/rockinn.htm). Open (food served) noon-2.30pm, 6-9pm Mon-Thur; noon-2.30pm, 6-10pm Fri, Sat; noon-3pm, 6-9.30pm Sun. £££. Pub.*
Now the only pub in Georgeham, this low-beamed, 17th-century free house sits on top of the village, just up from the church. There are tables outside, cosy log fires within, and a choice of up to eight real ales. Dogs are welcome, and there's a family seating area. Food is locally sourced, freshly prepared and of a high quality. Lunchtime mains (around £12) could be a bowl of fresh tagliatelle with a choice of toppings, fish pie or a less pricey three-egg omelette with chips and salad. The evening menu is a bit more ambitious: a sea bass, crayfish and rocket risotto (£17), for example.

Squires Fish

Braunton *Exeter Road (01271 815533). Open Summer 11.45am-9.30pm Mon-Sat; 11.45am-8pm Sun. Winter 11.45am-9.30pm Mon-Sat. ££. Fish & chips.*
Of all north Devon's many chippies, Squires is the one that keeps attracting locals and tourists. It's not hard to see why: the fish is always fresh, and the service friendly and efficient. This is a surprisingly modern outfit, given that it has been around for 25 years or so. There are sit-down and takeaway sections, though you may have to queue at peak times. Round off a meal with a knickerbocker glory.

Stay

Broomhill Art Hotel

Barnstaple *Muddiford Road (01271 850262/www.broomhillart.co.uk). ££.*
In a mildly forbidding Victorian mansion on a steep wooded hillside enlivened by curious open-air artworks (*see p185*), the hotel isn't the *raison d'être* of Broomhill, but it's perfectly serviceable accommodation and pretty good value. There are only six rooms and so long as you're not expecting luxury – the shower rooms are tiny and the beds aren't the best – you'll appreciate the adventurous vibe established by the welcoming Dutch owners and curators Rinus and Aniet van de Sande. The mellow Terra Madre restaurant espouses the 'slow food' philosophy, and features a menu with a faintly incongruous Mediterranean slant. The sitting room gallery is just the place to enjoy a Somerset apple brandy digestif.

Exmoor White Horse Inn

Exmoor *Exford (01643 831229/www.exmoor-hospitality-inns.co.uk). £££.*
Bang in the middle of Exmoor, overlooking the bridge at Exford, the White Horse is a rambling, creeper-clad place that's been a jolly, family-run, hunting, shooting and fishing hotel for generations. The manager, Peter Hendrie, a landscape photographer, showcases his work here. He's a knowledgeable host, being a guiding spirit behind the Exmoor Safaris based at the hotel. The bar, which stocks numerous whiskies as well as guest ales, is a firm favourite with the locals. The 28 bedrooms are varied in character and price, all absolutely clean and comfortable, including some with four-posters. Breakfasts are of the buffet variety.

> ## "A rambling, creeper-clad place that's been a jolly, family-run, hunting, shooting and fishing hotel for generations."

Ford Mill

Nr Umberleigh, 10 miles S of Barnstaple *(01769 540326/www.fordmill.uniquehomestays.com). ££.*
Anthony and Sandy Sharpe's welcoming home could hardly be more secluded (just north of the B3227). It's an old mill-house nestling in a hidden valley near the confluence of two streams, with a wonderful orchard garden. This B&B is strictly for animal lovers (the Sharpes keep three Labradors and several cats), but guests get their own wing of the house, with three bedrooms on the first floor and a sitting/dining room at ground level. Goose-down duvets and superior cotton sheets make for a blissful night's rest. Breakfasts feature fabulous porridge or eggs done any which way. Anthony will happily regale you with local information.

Hartland Quay Hotel

Hartland *(01237 441218/www.hartlandquayhotel.com). ££.*
A quirky establishment on the farthest-flung outpost of Hartland. The location is unmatchable, and the hotel's strongest reason for recommendation. Vast waves lash at the fantastic jagged rocks of the coast just a hundred yards from the door. Rooms are basic and functional, and only those on the upper storey have good views. Corridors and stairs are decorated with an alarming white and pea-green colour scheme. The Wreckers Retreat bar, with its log-cabin look and plastic fish on the walls, is a spirited place, featuring an awe-inspiring chart of where ships have foundered on the terrifying coast. This is not such a bad place to have washed up in.

Northcote Manor

Nr Umberleigh, 13.5 miles S of Barnstaple
(01769 560501/www.northcotemanor.co.uk). ££££.
Climbing the long, steep and narrow drive through the conifers from the A377 (opposite Portsmouth Arms train station), you know you're heading somewhere special. Northcote Manor is a grand old Victorian grey-stone pile, hidden in a fabulous spot on a hill above the Taw Valley. The tennis court and croquet lawn boast superb views. Once you're inside the heavy old front door, the welcome is honest and charming. There are only 11 bedrooms, each with its own unassuming but comfortable style. The restaurant (with a colourful mural) has garnered plaudits; food is British, expertly sourced and prepared, and quite rich, featuring seasonal fish, flesh and fowl. Breakfasts in the conservatory are first class too.

Red Lion Hotel

Clovelly *The Quay (01237 431237). £££.*
A stay here at the Red Lion Hotel is one of the best ways to experience the famous yet occasionally over-subscribed charms of Clovelly. The handful of bedrooms above the cosy old harbourside pub have been done up comfortably, in restrained shades of ochre and duck-egg green, but aren't as dreary as that might sound. Most only have a shower, not a bath. Room No.3 is especially snug, with a full sea view from its tiny window. The larger Rous Room has its own terrace overlooking the harbour. There are also a couple of family rooms and a ground-floor room suitable for the elderly or disabled.

Saunton Sands Hotel

Saunton Sands, 11 miles SW of Ilfracombe
(01271 890212/www.sauntonsands.com). ££££.
Probably the most famous (and expensive) hotel in north Devon, the Saunton Sands occupies an amazing position overlooking Braunton Burrows and the wide expanse of the sands. It's rather an eyesore architecturally, unless you're a fan of bright white, art deco functionalism. Inside, the colour scheme is a subtle symphony of beige, camel, brown and blue, but you come here for the views. Staff are friendly and buzzy, maintaining a smart holiday-making ambience. The rooms (there's a multitude) are all perfectly comfy and differ slightly from each other (of those sea-facing, we can recommend No.124, but were less impressed with No.125). There's an outdoor swimming pool too.

Southcliffe Hall

Lee, 3.5 miles W of Ilfracombe *(01271 867068/ www.southcliffehall.co.uk). £££.*
An idyllic Edwardian mansion, Southcliffe Hall stands on the choicest spot in the picturesque coastal village of Lee. Kate and Barry welcome you into their home with tea and cake. The house has inspiring views down to the sea, but is just as remarkable inside as out. Antiques abound in the bathrooms; all the old cisterns are locally made. The huge four-poster room even has an old Cabinet bath. A refreshing absence of TV, dinners in a panelled dining room cooked by Kate (book in advance), delicious breakfasts, and perfect peace and quiet (grown-up children only) make this superior B&B a fabulous find.

Factfile

When to go

On average, Exmoor gets more than twice as much rain or snow as the surrounding area. The beech hedges and bluebells of the moors are a wonderful sight in May, as is the heather in autumn. The beach resorts are at their brightest and busiest in summer, though surfing has become a year-round sport. The vibrant North Devon Arts Festival is a bonus in June and July, and Appledore has a good visual arts fest in the spring. Early or late season often provide the best combination of fine weather and fewer crowds, while winter on the coast has a desolate charm.

Getting there

By car from the M5, the Exmoor coast is best reached via junctions 23 or 24 at Bridgewater for the A39 to Barnstaple (often a very slow road in summer). A quicker approach to the moor, Barnstaple and Ilfracombe is via the A361 North Devon Link Road from junction 27. By train, Barnstaple can be reached via the pretty Tarka Line from the London mainline station at Exeter.

Getting around

To get the best from the area, a car is essential, but a bicycle or pony could prove rewarding. The Tarka Trail (*see p185*) is a great car-free coastal bike route, and Exmoor provides ample space for pony treks. Countryside explorations from the small stations along the Tarka Line railway between Barnstaple and Exeter can be great fun.

Tourist offices

Exmoor National Park Offices (www.exmoor-nationalpark.gov.uk): Dunster (01643 821835, open Summer 10.30am-5pm daily, Winter 10.30am-3pm Sat, Sun), Dulverton (01398 323841, open Summer 10.30am-5pm daily, Winter 10.30am-3pm daily), Lynmouth (01598 752509, open Summer 10.30am-5pm daily, Winter 10.30am-3pm Sat, Sun).
Ilfracombe The Landmark, The Promenade (01271 863001). Open Summer 10am-5pm daily. Winter 10am-5pm Mon-Fri; 10am-4pm Sat.
Woolacombe The Esplanade (01271 870553/ www.woolacombetourism.co.uk). Open Summer 10am-5pm Mon-Sat; 10am-3pm Sun. Winter 10am-1pm Mon-Sat.

Brancaster.

North Norfolk

Big sands, big skies.

Yes, it's true: many of Norfolk's 2,067 square miles lie below sea level, but that's exactly what makes England's fifth-largest county so spectacular. Nowhere else in Britain offers such huge skies, such extraordinary light. Here, you'll discover scores of unspoilt villages and myriad acres of untrampled countryside dotted with glorious echoes of Norfolk's prosperous past. The county holds some of England's finest examples of ecclesiastical architecture; almost all its villages boast a church that's worth a second look.

Some of the country's wildest, most exhilarating scenery is to be found on the north Norfolk coast, much of which has been designated an Area of Outstanding Natural Beauty. The winding A149 links Thornham in the west with Cromer in the east, passing through gorgeous harbour villages and tranquil seaside retreats like Holkham, Wells-next-the-Sea, Blakeney and Cley on its seaward side, as well as inland enticements such as Burnham Market, the bustling country town of Holt, quiet hamlets and rolling countryside – even some hills. Further east, the resorts of Sheringham and Cromer exude a faded Victorian charm. In summer, visit them at low tide for two hundred yards of castle-builder's sand; in winter venture forth at high tide for an awe-inspiring windswept walk, scored to the crashing of waves against the sea defences. Then watch the sun descend through the vast East Anglian skies. It may take a while, but in time you'll find yourself perfectly attuned to Norfolk's unhasty pace of life.

Explore

The best of the north Norfolk coast is broadly made up of three areas: Brancaster Bay; Holkham Bay as far as Wells-next-the-Sea; and the coastal stretch from Wells to Blakeney Point and the village of Cley-next-the-Sea. Locals and Norfolk's regular twitchers, golfers and walkers could probably distinguish one stretch of coastline from the other, heading from the wide sweep of Brancaster in the west to the rising cliffs of Cromer in east, but new visitors might be hard-pressed to find the distinctions unless they take things at a good old Norfolk – in other words, very leisurely – pace. Take the time to discover this beautiful coast as a whole and you'll be rewarded in (perfect sand-filled) buckets and spades.

BRANCASTER BAY (HUNSTANTON TO BURNHAM MARKET)

The wild stretch of coastline along Brancaster Bay makes a terrific introduction to north Norfolk. As with most of the western half of this coast, the salt marshes, creeks and windswept sandy beaches are renowned for bird life, and draw spotters and walkers from across the UK and beyond. Wildlife, rural strolls and coastal hikes predominate, and fortunately there are some great bases from which to start. In **Thornham**, a typical village of the area, small cottages of clunch, reddish-brown carstone and knapped flint can

be seen on the High Street (the A149), but a little lane north soon brings you to the Norfolk Coastal Path, an ancient route that can be followed west for a two-and-a-half-mile hike along the salt marshes (with the sea visible in the distance) to the little village of **Holme-next-the-Sea**. Continuing along the A149, you next encounter the village of **Titchwell**, home of the **Titchwell Marsh Nature Reserve** (*see p137*).

The coastal path can be picked up at many villages east of here. Beach-lovers might want to start at **Brancaster**, where you should turn north down Broad Lane until you reach a car park (charge payable). Brancaster beach – a huge expanse of sand past a hotel, beach kiosk and golf course – is one of Norfolk's best, and even in summer you don't have to walk far to have the place virtually to yourself. The currents, however, can be treacherous.

Brancaster is famous for its mussels, and during the season (when there's an 'r' in the month) bags of tender little bivalves are sold from fishermen's cottages in Brancaster Staithe. Small boats litter the silted-up inlets of the harbour; only at high tide can they make their way out to sea. The coastal path runs along the pretty harbour, and you can walk across the marshes a mile to **Burnham Deepdale**. From here it's worth making a detour a couple of miles inland (by car) to **Burnham Market**. In the 13th century, the River Burn was navigable by seagoing boats as far as Burnham Thorpe, now almost three miles inland.

North Norfolk

Historic sites
● ● ● ○ ○

Art & architecture
● ● ● ● ○ ○

Hotels
● ● ● ○ ○

Eating & drinking
● ● ● ● ○ ○

Scenery
● ● ● ● ●

Outdoor activities
● ● ● ● ○

Bracaster Bay   *Holkham Bay*   *Blakeney Point*

Titchwell Marsh Nature Reserve ●   Brancaster   Burnham Market   Wells-next-the-Sea   Morston   Cley-next-the-Sea

Thornham   Burnham Deepdale   Stiffkey   Blakeney

● Hunstanton   Burnham Thorpe

● Great Walsingham

0   5 miles

Blakeney.

Holkham.

Silting of the river led to a decrease in the commercial importance of the clutch of villages known as the Burnhams, but in the past 20 years there has been a curious and profound transformation in the fortunes of the largest of these villages, Burnham Market, a handsome old place with a long, tree-lined green at its centre. Perhaps encouraged by the success of the area's first gastropub, the Hoste Arms (*see p201*), affluent newcomers – many from London and the Home Counties – started buying up Burnham's beautiful old houses for use as second homes. The consequences of this invasion of the Chelsea set have been mixed for the area. Here, more than anywhere else in the county, locals have been priced out of the market and the Norfolk accent is rarely heard. Yet the newcomers' money has allowed some of the area's most interesting shops to flourish. High-quality food is a highlight. Gather the ingredients for a picnic at the first-class deli Humble Pie (Market Place, 01328 738581), the traditional baker's Grooms (Market Place, 01328 738289, www.groomsbakery.co.uk) and Satchells Wines (North Street, 01328 738272, www.satchellswines.com). Gurneys Fish Shop (Market Place, 01328 738967) is great for smoked fish, while non-food treats include two bookshops – Brazen Head (Market Place, 01328 730700) for second-hand books and White House (Market Place, 01328 730270) for new books and maps – plus clothes, antiques and gift shops.

Titchwell Marsh Nature Reserve

Titchwell *(01485 210779/www.rspb.org.uk).*
This wetland reserve run by the Royal Society for the Protection of Birds is utterly absorbing, whatever your level of knowledge (or binocular power). On the lagoons and foreshore, winter visitors include dunlins and bar-tailed godwits, Brent geese, teals and widgeon, while avocets, sedge warblers and marsh harriers can be spotted in summer. The RSPB runs a visitor's centre, shop (stocking bird-watching paraphernalia) and a café; there's a charge for parking.

HOLKHAM BAY TO WELLS-NEXT-THE-SEA

Just east of Burnham Market is a little village that seems thoroughly unremarkable, and so it is, but for one thing. **Burnham Thorpe**, a mile and a half inland of Burnham Market, was the birthplace of Horatio Nelson. There's little here to mark the fame of this local boy made good, though Nelson held a farewell party at the village pub (now called the Lord Nelson, *see p201*) before returning to sea in 1793. If you make a detour here to pay homage, follow his example and call in at the pub, then take the B1155 to rejoin the coast road, which you reach just west of **Holkham**. The land for miles around this area is owned by the Coke family, the Earls of Leicester. **Holkham Hall** (01328 710227, www.holkham.co.uk), their stately pile (rebuilt in the Palladian style during

the 18th century), is open on selected days in summer, though the gardens stay open longer. Holkham also has a gorgeous beach, reached on foot from the car park through pine woods. If you've ever seen a picture of a north Norfolk beach it's likely to be this one. At high tide the scene is perfect: a wide, sandy shore, backed by lovely pine woods. And there's a great place to stay and eat close by in the Victoria (*see p203*).

Less than two miles east of Holkham is the little town of **Wells-next-the-Sea**, which manages to cram in a beach resort, fishing port, picturesque shopping street and leafy green (the Buttlands) within its small circumference. The 'Burnham Market effect' has only recently had an impact here, so although there's posh dining at the Crown Hotel (*see p198*) and Italianate foodstuffs at the Wells Deli by the quay (15 the Quay, 01328 711171, www.wellsdeli.co.uk), there are also old-fashioned independent shops – a butcher's, a baker's, a fishmonger's and a hardware store – along the Staithe, a narrow high street that runs uphill from the quay. Crab fishing from the quay is a popular pastime; buy the kit (line, bait, bucket and net cost less than £5) from M L Walsingham & Son (78 Staithe Street, 01328 710438), about 100 yards up from the quay (this shop also hires out bicycles). While on the quay, take a look at the *Albatross* (07979 087228), a large sailing vessel built in Holland in 1899. Below decks you'll find a snug (if rough round the edges) bar where savoury and sweet Dutch pancakes are served alongside Norfolk ales. On-board accommodation is available too.

The sandy beach is a mile away from the town. Come at high tide or you'll have a long walk to the water. Wells Beach dramatically shrinks when the tide comes in (sirens sound to warn bathers against being cut off on the dunes), while crabbing boats flood into the harbour to unload their cargo.

The other main local attraction is the **Wells & Walsingham Light Railway** (01328 711630, www.northnorfolk.co.uk/walsinghamrail) which operates a narrow-gauge steam locomotive to the beautiful village of **Little Walsingham** (30 minutes). Walsingham has been an important place of Christian pilgrimage for nigh-on 1,000 years; members of the Anglican, Catholic and Orthodox churches are still drawn to shrines of **Our Lady of Walsingham**. Half-timbered medieval buildings are plentiful along the narrow streets, and there are enough tearooms, gift shops and pubs to fill an afternoon before you catch the train back to Wells, not to mention the impressive **Walsingham Farms Shop** (*see p198*). Eat fish and chips or something more adventurous at the excellent **Norfolk Riddle** (*see p202*) and, to walk off your meal, explore the ruins and peaceful gardens of Walsingham Abbey; they're particularly popular in February for snowdrop walks (*see* Walsingham Tourist Information Office *p203*).

Walsingham Farms Shop

Walsingham *Guild Street (01328 821877/ www.walsinghamfarmshop.co.uk). Open 9am-6pm Tue-Fri; 9am-5pm Sat; 10am-1pm Sun.*
The Walsingham Farms Shop deserves special mention. Stocked as much as possible with goods from local producers and farmers, it holds a bewildering array of fresh and prepared food, including salami from Suffolk, veg from local allotment-holders, honey from Walsingham bees and a mouth-watering range of picnic goodies made in the shop's kitchen. Where produce travels farther, it's often from producers with local links; Tim and Simone Pringle have olive groves in Spain and run their business from Suffolk.

WELLS TO CLEY

East of Wells, the coast road narrows as it goes through the little villages of **Stiffkey** (pronounced 'Stukey' by locals) and **Morston**, reflecting the move away from the out-of-towners' pace and wealth to a more rural, homely feel; look out for seasonal produce sold from roadside cottages, along with more exotic comestibles like mussels, oysters, honeycomb and samphire. Stiffkey's pub, the Red Lion (44 Wells Road, 01328 830552, www.stiffkey.com) is worth a look-in for its beers (Woodforde's Wherry, straight from the barrel), its food (featuring local ingredients), and its views across to the River Stiffkey. Pub-lovers could also make a small detour inland to the west of Stiffkey to pay homage to the Three Horseshoes at Warham (69 Bridge Street, 01328 710547), which has a classic old interior as well as well-kept ales, decent food (pies a speciality), and accommodation. Others will want to head on to Blakeney or out to sea for a very special encounter. Seals can be seen in a number of places along Britain's coastline, but the beauty of those at **Blakeney Point** is in their proximity. At high tide, motor boats run from Morston quay (contact Bean's Boats, 01263 740038, www.beansboat trips.co.uk); or Temple's Seal Trips (01263 740791, www.sealtrips.co.uk) take visitors out to a spit of land where a sizeable colony of seals can be viewed at surprisingly close quarters. Carry on to the lovely coastal village of **Blakeney** and you can go out to the Point on foot, taking a desolate but wonderful two-and-a-half-mile hike along the coastal path and back inland to Cley.

While a visit to the seals is a must, leave yourself plenty of time to explore the quay at Blakeney and the two narrow streets running off it, where you'll find a handful of shops, pubs and restaurants, including a deli and a fishmonger's. It's a nice place to while away a few hours before heading east along the A149 to lovely **Cley-next-the-Sea**, where a delicatessen, a smokehouse, an endearing bookshop, a brace of pubs and two galleries create a wonderfully relaxing away-from-the-world bolt-hole – and a great base for hikes. Two walks in particular stand out; the energetic should take the lane east of the village down to the shingle beach (about half a mile) and from there it's possible to trek to **Blakeney Point** (four miles return trip). Keep a seaward eye out for seals along the way. A more leisurely stroll starts from Church Lane (off the A149 by Picnic Fayre delicatessen) and runs past Cley's impressive church. This was built in the 13th century when the village was a prosperous port; don't miss the stunning south porch, with its traceried battlements and fan-vaulted roof. Whichever walk you choose, be sure to stock up at Picnic Fayre first (the Old Forge, 01263 740587, www.picnic-fayre.co.uk) and pick up presents for your foodie friends from the Cley Smokehouse (High Street, 01263 740282, www.cleysmokehouse.com).

Eat

There's more than one advantage to an isolated location. North Norfolk's out-of-the-way situation means that its hostelries need to strive hard for custom, and they've risen to the challenge admirably. In the past decade the quality of both food and drink has soared – whether it be beer brewed from Norfolk barley (try Woodforde's prize-winning ales), Cromer crab with samphire freshly picked from the salt marshes, Brancaster mussels or locally smoked North Sea herring. In winter there's a wealth of game, with hare, pheasant and venison making frequent appearances. Many of the hotels we list have noteworthy restaurants too. Also worth a visit are the **Crown** (The Buttlands, Wells-next-the-Sea, 01328 710209, www.thecrownhotelwells.co.uk), which has an imaginative global menu, the White Horse (Main Road, Brancaster Staithe, 01485 210262, www.whitehorsebrancaster.co.uk), and the Old Bakehouse in Little Walsingham (33 High Street, 01328 820454) which serves Anglo-French cuisine in a lovely historic building.

The Blakeney White Horse

Blakeney *4 High Street (01263 740574/www.blakeney whitehorse.co.uk). Open noon-2.15pm, 6-9pm Mon-Thur; noon-2.15pm, 6-9.30pm Fri, Sat; noon-2.30pm, 6-9pm Sun. £££. Gastropub.*
A rabbit warren of a place, the White Horse is a friendly and unpretentious spot for a drink, a meal or an overnight stay. You can eat in the bar or airy conservatory, or (at dinner only) in the yellow-walled restaurant in the former stables. The à la carte menu – a definite notch above pub grub – features inventive takes on traditional dishes (pork belly with oriental broth and pak choi as a starter, pan-fried halibut with saffron potatoes and roast squash, or rib-eye steak with red kale and own-made black pudding as mains). Fish and shellfish are a forte, and there's an emphasis on local produce (Norfolk lamb, Morston mussels, prawns from the Cley Smokehouse, pâté from local game). An appealing snack menu at lunchtime is equally fish-oriented (fried local whitebait, fish pie, or Cley

The Neptune.

Victoria.

Smokehouse smoked prawns, for example). Leave room for desserts: cinnamon pannacotta, maybe, or pumpkin tart. Upstairs are nine bedrooms (all recently refurbished), simply decorated in cream and blue, with striped blinds and large beds. The Harbour room is the biggest, with the best views.

Deepdale Café
Burnham Deepdale *Main Road (01485 211055/ www.deepdalecafe.co.uk). Open 7.30am-4pm daily. £. Café.*

This interesting daytime-only eaterie on a new parade of shops off the A149 offers great-value food ranging from enticing sandwiches (BLTs through to ripe camembert with rocket and plum chutney) to specials such as fig, parmesan and red onion frittata, or a selection of tapas. Chef Jeremy Tagg is largely self-taught, though a spot of training with seafood celeb chef Rick Stein has ensured a healthy interest in fish dishes, like poached locally smoked haddock and egg. The Sunday lunch roasts come highly recommended too. A nice touch is the choose-your-own breakfast; pay for three, four or five items from a wide range including black pudding, veggie sausages, field mushrooms and hash browns. And feel free to bring your own champagne too.

Hoste Arms
Burnham Market *The Green (01328 738777/ www.hostearms.co.uk). Open (restaurant) 7.30-10.30am, noon-2pm, 6-9pm daily. £££. Gastropub.*

Often credited (or blamed, depending on your viewpoint) with being the inn that brought Londoners to north Norfolk, the Hoste produces food that's likely to keep them returning time and again. From the lavish breakfast (the porridge with honey is recommended) to the extensive dinner menu, everything served in the wood-panelled dining room is beautifully prepared. Local ingredients predominate (Brancaster mussels, Burnham Creek oysters, Holkham Estate venison). Homely dishes (steak and kidney pud, burger and chips) share menu space with more international flavours (swordfish sashimi, pad thai chicken), all cooked on a huge Aga, designed for the inn by the owner Paul Whittome and one-time head chef Andrew McPherson. A 300-bin wine list completes this impressive restaurant's appeal.

King's Arms
Blakeney *Westgate Street (01263 740341/www. blakeneykingsarms.co.uk). Open (food served) noon-9pm Mon-Sat; noon-8.30pm Sun. ££. Pub.*

The Chelsea set has had little impact on this wonderful old pub. Norfolk accents resound throughout the three tiny low-ceilinged rooms, especially after the consumption of a few pints of Theakston Best, Marston's Pedigree or Old Speckled Hen. Yet newcomers are welcomed, and the King's Arms is especially popular with walkers fresh from the salt marshes. Slow-roasted brisket of beef or local mussels might be on the bar menu, or perfectly cooked scampi and chips. As if to complement the other-worldliness of this old-fashioned boozer, a bizarre collection of *Black and White Minstrel Show* posters decorates the walls (souvenirs of owners Marjorie and Howard, who toured Australia with the B&WMS before opening the pub in 1976). There's accommodation upstairs, a real fire in the grate, and a family room out back.

Lord Nelson
Burnham Thorpe *Walsingham Road (01328 738241/ www.nelsonslocal.co.uk). Open (restaurant) noon-2.30pm Mon; noon-3pm, 6-9pm Tue-Sun. ££. Pub.*

Nelson memorabilia adorns this whitewashed classic boozer in Horatio's home village. Built in 1637, it boasts high-backed wooden settles, stone-flagged flooring, a brick fireplace and comfortable snugs that create the ideal setting to enjoy a pint of Nelson's Revenge – served straight from the cask and delivered to your table by friendly staff – or a tot of Nelson's Blood (spiced brandy). Food is of higher quality (and price) than your average pub grub; you could tuck into Brancaster moules marinière or smoked duck salad, followed by solid standards like rump steak or guinea fowl, and a most superior bread and butter pudding with marmalade. A good bar menu includes an impressive scampi, anchovy, calamares and garlic prawn platter, and a nicely varied vegetarian platter featuring stuffed vine leaves and feta cheese. There's a range of roasts for Sunday lunch, and outside a large sunny garden in which to enjoy them on warmer days.

Morston Hall
Morston *The Street (01263 741041/www.morston hall.com). Open 7.30pm Mon-Sat; 12.30pm & 7.30pm Sun. ££££. Modern European.*

The Hall is a fine place to stay (*see p202*), but it's the hotel's gastronomic credentials that are the real draw; the restaurant has been booked almost solidly since chef Galton Blackiston (who runs the hotel with his wife Tracy) appeared on the *Great British Menu* TV series in 2006. The dinner menu is fixed – no choices – so phone in advance with any dietary requirements. For a Michelin-starred chef, Galton is disarmingly keen to get feedback on the food, which focuses on local produce cooked simply but exquisitely. The creaminess of lightly seared foie gras, atop toasted brioche, is offset by a rhubarby jus; pearly white, herb-crusted cod comes with tomato fondue and a lemony beurre blanc. This might be followed by pink-tinged fillet of roast (locally reared) beef or roast tail of monkfish on peperonata with white lemon butter. To finish, there's a pudding (champagne jelly with strawberry ripple ice-cream on our visit) or an array of British cheeses, plus petits fours and coffee. Thankfully, it's only a short stagger upstairs to bed if you're staying (if you're not, book ahead). Afternoon cream teas are also available to both residents and non-residents.

The Neptune
Old Hunstanton *85 Old Hunstanton Road (01485 532122/www.theneptune.co.uk). Open 7-9pm Tue-Sat; noon-2pm, 7-9pm Sun. (Lunch Mon-Sat by appointment.) ££££. Modern European.*

In a further sign that north Norfolk is becoming a magnet for the food cognoscenti, Kevin and Jacki Mangeolles took over this 18th-century pub in 2007 and converted it into a first-rate restaurant with rooms. The small dining area is cosy, woody and understated, in a New England sort of way, with an adjacent lounge and bar. Kevin, who held a Michelin star at his previous Isle of Wight post, creates an inventive collection of modern European dishes on his regularly changing menu (which includes amuses bouche and pre-desserts). Smoked haddock, pumpkin seeds and apple salad, might precede hare with bitter chocolate sauce, potato purée, glazed carrots and savoy cabbage, then chestnut parfait with caramel sauce, yoghurt, porridge and honey sorbet for pudding. The results can verge on the over-complex, but rare technical expertise usually produces happy marriages of high-quality ingredients. Prices are justifiably high. Front of house is managed with affable informality by Jacki.

The Norfolk Riddle

Walsingham *2 Wells Road (01328 821903/www. walsinghamfarmshop.co.uk). Open (restaurant) noon-2pm, 6-9pm Wed-Sat; noon-2.30pm, 6-8.30pm Sun. (Fish & chip shop) 11.30am-2pm, 4.30-8.30pm Wed, Thur; 11.30am-2pm, 4.30-9.30pm Fri, Sat; 11.30am-2.30pm, 4.30-8.30pm Sun. £££. British/fish & chips.*
There's no question about it: this Riddle is a great chippie. But next to the takeaway, the restaurant also serves some adventurous meat dishes. It is owned by the same group of farmers who run the Walsingham Farms Shop (*see p198*), they supply potatoes for the chips, and much of the meat. Inside, a woodburner makes the modern dining room cosy and cheerful, and a riddle (a device for sifting potatoes) hangs on the wall. For the rare warm days there's a decking area. Chef Hervé (from Alsace) serves a daily changing menu, including a vegetarian special, plus pies, pâtés and puddings made here or in the kitchens of the Farms Shop – as well as battered cod or haddock. Specials might feature ox kidney and mushroom casserole, slow-roasted belly pork with sage jus, or fresh local game. Most drinks are locally sourced too, including apple juice, cider and beer, and there's fabulous bread and butter pud for afters.

Stay

Sleepy Norfolk contains a surprising range of places for resting your head, from tiny pubs with snug accommodation to stately piles that could fit an entire pub into each of their rooms. Across the region standards are high, and locations often delightful. Many of the pubs and restaurants featured in **Eat** (*see p198*) also offer rooms.

Cley Mill

Cley-next-the-Sea *(01263 740209/www.cleymill. co.uk). £££.*
The spectacular views alone would make this converted windmill a terrific place to stay. The location on the marshes, away from the main road (but just a short walk from the shops) ensures an expansive vista from most of the ten rooms, though the circular Wheel room on the third and fourth floors might be the best choice if you're bringing your binoculars; accessed by a ladder, it has four windows enabling a 360-degree view of the countryside and distant sea. The second-floor Stone room features huge oak beams from which the grinding stones once turned. All the mill rooms have access to the balcony that runs around the mill, and some have private galleries. Other rooms are in out-buildings by the mill and have vaulted ceilings, prettily painted tongue and groove walls, and access to the garden. Newspapers

aren't delivered to this out-of-the-way spot, but there is a man in Cley who sells them from his sitting-room window.

George Hotel

Cley-next-the-Sea *High Street (01263 740652/ www.thegeorgehotelatcley.co.uk). ££.*
Delightfully idiosyncratic Cley is a great place to hole up for a night or two, and this pretty country inn makes an appealingly calm base. All 12 rooms are unfussy, furnished in neutral colours and delicate fabrics. Rooms 3, 4 and 5 offer glorious views and plenty of space, the attic rooms are cosier but have the same expansive views across the marshes. Food in the understated, modern restaurant ranges from sandwiches to an à la carte menu of simply cooked and reasonably priced dishes.

Hoste Arms

Burnham Market *The Green (01328 738777/ www.hostearms.co.uk). £££.*
Paul and Jeanne Whittome bought this yellow-fronted 17th-century inn on Burnham Market's green in 1989, paving the way for the village's subsequent gentrification and reputation as a holiday hotspot. The acquisition of two other high-quality hostelries (Vine House and the Railway Inn) followed, as well as a number of self-catering cottages including a refurbished railway carriage. All the accommodation exhibits Jeanne's love of exuberant decor, light, space and art (works by local artists are scattered around the public spaces, and there's even a small gallery). Each of the 35 beautifully appointed rooms is individually furnished with boldly patterned fabrics; beds include a tartan four-poster and a canopied faux-Georgian. In its time the Hoste has been a coaching inn, a livestock auction house and an assizes; it's now also a pub and restaurant (*see p201*), where the atmosphere is convivial and professional.

The Lifeboat Inn

Thornham *Ship Lane (01485 512236/www.life boatinn.co.uk). ££.*
On its ground floor, this pleasantly ramshackle 16th-century country pub serves crowd-pleasing bar meals (bowls of mussels, fish and chips) alongside a full restaurant menu and real ales to an appreciative wide-ranging clientele (dogs and children welcome). Upstairs and in the adjacent building, the Lifeboat offers 14 light-filled, pine-furnished rooms prettily decorated with patchwork quilts and bright fabrics and featuring big comfy beds. Some have views over the marshes and across Thornham harbour to the sea, but the pub's location (away from the main road) means all the rooms have decent views. Free Wi-Fi is included, and the huge hearty breakfast should send you on your way sated and happy.

Morston Hall

Morston *The Street (01263 741041/ www.morstonhall.com). ££££.*
You get the feeling Agatha Christie would feel right at home among the flowery curtains and cosy armchairs (perfect for curling up with a good book) of this award-winning hotel. Yet Morston Hall isn't overbearingly old-fashioned; think English country house rather than Gothic mansion. Each of the rooms comes with a bath and shower, toiletries, bathrobes

and CD players – some even have tile TVs in the bathrooms. The large flint building is grand enough to provide a sense of occasion, but small enough to feel welcoming: just seven rooms and space for 40 in the dining rooms. Six new suites, housed in a separate building at the rear of the garden, exhibit the same attention to detail including ultra-modern comforts such as walk-in wetrooms, as well as private garden terraces with table and chairs. The hotel's restaurant is top notch (*see p201*) and while room rates (£145-£170 per person) might seem pricey, a night here includes an excellent four-course dinner (though you pay extra for wine) and breakfast.

Rose & Crown
Snettisham, 5 miles S of Hunstanton *Old Church Road (01485 541382/www.roseandcrown snettisham.co.uk). ££.*
Part village pub, part smart restaurant and part boutique hotel, the Rose & Crown makes a lovely base from which to explore nearby Sandringham and Hunstanton. The setting, on the edge of the large village of Snettisham – near the church and opposite the cricket pitch – is serene. Three snug bars are at the centre of the pub, the oldest part of which dates from the 14th century. The 16 bedrooms are more modern and pleasingly varied, from oak-panelled spaces to contemporary, pastel-hued rooms in the extension. All are bright and pretty, with a note of luxury provided by power showers, Molton Brown toiletries, bottled mineral water and Wi-Fi, magazines and books. There's ample choice for breakfast, including a vegetarian assembly, a whole kipper (with poached egg and spinach) as well as a hefty full English.

Titchwell Manor
Titchwell *(01485 210221/www.titchwell manor.com). £££.*
Overlooking the marshes of the RSPB reserve and just steps away from the main coastal path, Titchwell Manor is in a lovely location. A long windswept walk will leave you deeply appreciative of the comfy leather sofas and an afternoon pint (or evening aperitif). The 31 rooms are spread throughout a number of buildings, chief of which is the main hotel, where rooms at the front have views over the coast road and the marshes to the sea. Herb-garden rooms and those in an annexe cottage look out over rural scenes, and many rooms have original open fires and period features. Beech and oak, wicker and white linen give a feeling of luxury and space. Good food featuring local produce (Norfolk lamb, Holkham venison, Brancaster mussels and oysters) is served in two dining rooms. The hotel is family- and pet-friendly, but not to the detriment of other guests.

Victoria
Holkham *Park Road (01328 711008/www.victoria atholkham.co.uk). £££.*
In vibrant contrast to the neutral colours of most boutique hotels, the Victoria stands out like a technicolour dream. Walls are painted in gorgeous greens, rich purples and deep ochres, there are Arabic bird cages, woven Indian textiles, and furniture from Rajasthan – all combined with modern TVs and gleaming bathrooms to create a sense of style and comfort. No two rooms are the same; there's a choice of ten, including an attic suite. The hotel is set back from the A149 on the Earl of Leicester's Holkham Estate, just across the road from the lane leading to the beach. For extra privacy, book one of the three estate follies that have been converted into two-bedroom 'lodges'. A big fire in the lounge, together with squashy, lived-in sofas and a bar, add to the feeling of warmth and bonhomie. Meals are served in the ground-floor dining room and in the bar, with both menus making use of local produce: Holkham steaks, organic chickens and, in winter, game from estate shoots. Prices are a little steep given the deluxe-pub nature of the enterprise, but that doesn't deter the Victoria's many fans – the place is regularly fully booked.

Factfile

When to go
Any time. The North Sea will rarely be sunbathers' heaven, and you'll just as likely find a bright, warm sunny day in November as you will in June. What you'll get throughout the year, though, are big skies, light that seems to go on forever, and windswept coastal scenery where little interrupts the sound of sea birds and the distant waves.

Getting there and around
National train services run to King's Lynn (from London King's Cross, via Cambridge, see www.firstcapitalconnect.co.uk), Cromer and Sheringham (from London Liverpool Street, via Norwich, see www.nationalexpresseast anglia.com). An extensive network of **buses** serves the area and smaller towns; get details at www.travelineeastanglia.co.uk. Most useful are the No.35 King's Lynn to Hunstanton route and the Coasthopper buses that idle along the A149 coast road from Hunstanton to Wells, and from Wells to Cromer – all run by the Norfolk Green company, see www.norfolkgreen.co.uk.

Tourist information
Shirehall Museum Common Place, Walsingham, Norfolk NR22 6BP (01328 820510/www.visit norfolk.co.uk). Open Apr-Sept 10am-4.30pm daily. Oct-Mar 10am-4pm daily.
Wells Staithe Street, Wells-next-the-Sea, Norfolk NR25 7RN (01328 710885/www.visitnorth norfolk.co.uk). Open phone for details.

Internet
Wells Library Station Road, Wells-next-the-Sea, Norfolk NR23 1EA (01328 710467/www.norlink. norfolk.gov.uk). Open 2-7pm Mon; 9am-1pm Tue, Sat; 9am-6pm Wed, Fri.

Top: Druridge Bay;
left: Bamburgh Castle;
right: high tide at Holy
Island causeway.

Northumberland Coast

Beaches , castles and a myth-steeped centre of Celtic Christianity.

Drive north on the A1 out of Newcastle, and some time after passing Morpeth you'll begin to notice something. It might take a while to realise what it is, but wind down the window, breathe deep and look around. After Alnwick it should become clear: space. Northumberland's 1,936 square miles are the most sparsely populated in England, with 161 people spread over each mile (compared to London's 12,300). In England's most northerly county, there's room for everyone to find, if not a place in the sun (after all, that's the North Sea rolling grey to the east), at least a beach to themselves.

But what makes the stretch of coast between Holy Island in the north and Warkworth in the south truly unique is the other expanse that overwhelms you in this Border country: time. Along some 50 miles of coast you'll find the cradle of English Christianity on Holy Island; Bamburgh, the finest castle anywhere in this country and a site continuously inhabited since the Iron Age; the Farne Islands, where St Cuthbert sought retreat from human demands but found one of the great wildlife spectacles in Britain; the ruins of huge Dunstanburgh Castle, lowering on their headland above the sea; and Warkworth Castle, where the 'kings of the north', the Percy family, proclaimed Henry Bolingbroke king of England, making him Henry IV.

Should the history not inspire, take comfort in the fact that at least it serves to provide the most dramatic backdrop to the country's finest coastline. From Warkworth northwards, tide-exposed expanses of sand stretching impossibly far out to sea alternate with slabs of wave-gouged granite, perfect for rock pooling. And coming right up to date, Alnwick is home to a new and spectacularly modern grand garden, as well as being the hub of a vibrant community of artists.

Explore

The A1 and the East Coast railway line run north roughly parallel to each other and the sea. The area we're looking at starts with Holy Island in the north and ends at Warkworth in the south, but Berwick-upon-Tweed and Druridge Bay down to Newbiggin-by-Sea are worthwhile extensions towards Scotland and Newcastle respectively.

HOLY ISLAND

From the A1, the road to Holy Island (known as Lindisfarne) winds through a mile of countryside, going past the Barn at Beal (01289 381477, www.barnatbeal.com, open 15 Feb-Apr, Sept-Dec 10am-4pm daily. May-Aug 10am-7pm daily), a working farm, visitor and wild bird centre, which has a restaurant specialising in locally produced food. After the Barn, the road swings down and you come to what is, depending on the time of day, either a narrow strip of tarmac cutting across an expanse of mud and sand, or a sheet of water, glittering or sullen grey. For Lindisfarne is a tidal island, cut off from the mainland twice a day by the incoming North Sea. At either end of the causeway are notice boards with the crossing times; don't try running the tide. Each year the local paper shows a hapless tourist perched on his car roof waiting for the lifeboat. Driving across to Holy Island, if you look to the right you can see the old (11th-century) pilgrim route, visible as a line of poles.

Those pilgrims first started coming to the island when St Aidan, with 12 other monks from Iona, founded a monastery here in AD 635 after being invited by King Oswald of Bamburgh. The monks set about preaching the Gospel and building a civilisation. The luminous result of this flowering of Celtic Christianity is now in the British Museum, but a facsimile of the Lindisfarne Gospels is on show at the Lindisfarne Centre (Marygate, 01289 389004, www.lindisfarne-centre.com) as well as a 'virtual' version that allows you to turn the pages. The centre also has exhibitions on the Vikings (who in AD 793 killed most of the monks of Lindisfarne Priory), and on the flora, fauna and people.

Visible from the priory is Lindisfarne Castle. Much of the island is a National Nature Reserve, with some 14 square miles protected. The tidal flats and sand dunes are an important over-wintering area for birds. Even a casual drive over the causeway will often reveal oystercatchers sieving the mud for shellfish. For guided walks on Lindisfarne and the rest of Northumberland, contact Northern Experience Wildlife Tours (01670 827465, www.northernexperiencewildlifetours.co.uk) or Walk Northumbria (0191 257 2601, www.walknorthumbria.co.uk).

Lindisfarne Castle

Holy Island (01289 389244/www.nationaltrust.org.uk). Open Feb 10am-3pm daily. Mar-Nov Tue-Sat times vary, phone for details. Late Dec 10am-3pm Mon, Tue, Sun. Admission £6.30; £3.10 reductions.

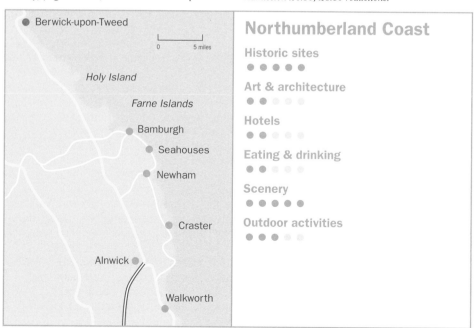

Berwick-upon-Tweed

0   5 miles

Holy Island

Farne Islands

Bamburgh

Seahouses

Newham

Craster

Alnwick

Walkworth

Northumberland Coast

Historic sites
● ● ● ● ●

Art & architecture
● ● ● ● ●

Hotels
● ● ● ● ●

Eating & drinking
● ● ● ● ●

Scenery
● ● ● ● ●

Outdoor activities
● ● ● ● ●

Low tide at Holy Island
causeway.

Top & right: Alnwick Garden; bottom & left: Dunstanburgh Castle.

Lindisfarne Castle is, like the Priory, an iconic image of Holy Island. It's located a mile's walk from the village. There's a shuttle bus in season, but the walk along the coast is spectacular, with views towards Bamburgh and the Farne Islands. The castle is perched on Bexlome Crag, part of the Great Whin Sill (a layer of rock formed 295 million years ago, which covers 1,500 square miles of north-east England).

The castle was built in Tudor times, using stone from the dissolved monastery, as a defence against Scottish raiders. After the union of thrones under James (I of England, VI of Scotland) the threat diminished, although the Borders remained wild country into the 17th century, and a reduced garrison manned the castle until the mid 19th century. Given its exposed position, the castle feels surprisingly cosy. This is due to its conversion in 1903 by Edwin Lutyens into a country retreat for Edward Hudson, founder of *Country Life*. A few hundred yards away is a glorious walled garden, designed by the great horticulturalist Gertrude Jekyll in 1911 – a visit on a windy day soon reveals the necessity of the walls.

Lindisfarne Priory

Holy Island *Church Lane (01289 389200/www.english-heritage.org.uk). Open Apr-Sept 9.30am-5pm daily. Oct 9.30am-4pm daily. Nov-Jan 10am-2pm Mon, Sat, Sun. Feb, Mar 10am-4pm daily. Admission £3.90; £2-£3.10 reductions.*

What we see today of Lindisfarne Priory was first erected when Benedictine monks reclaimed the island in 1080. The destruction is due to Henry VIII rather than the Northmen, who had caused the monks to abandon Lindisfarne in 875 after further Danish depredations, taking with them the mortal remains of the man who had cemented the island's reputation for sanctity: Cuthbert. If only a tenth of the things said about him were true, Cuthbert would still be one of the most remarkable men ever: a saint (although an irascible and antisocial one), miracle worker, ascetic, orator, visionary, soldier, missionary and conservationist. He came to Lindisfarne in 664 and stayed for 12 years before attempting to find even greater seclusion on the Inner Farne Islands. English Heritage has an excellent museum, explaining the history of the priory from founding to dissolution.

SOUTH TO BAMBURGH

Leaving Holy Island, unless you have a boat, there's no alternative to travelling a short way south on the A1. West of the main road is the small town of **Belford**, once on the coach route to Edinburgh, which contains the Wooden Toy Shop (Market Place, 01668 213101) and the equally descriptive Belford Craft Gallery (2 Market Place, 01668 213888). Taking the B6349 west will bring you to **Wooler**, a gateway town to the Cheviot Hills. **Chatton**, just off the B6349, is the home of Chatton Gallery (Church House, New Road, 01668 215494, www.chatton-gallery.co.uk), a fine art and sculpture gallery, specialising in contemporary landscapes by such artists as Robert Turnbull and Peter Hicks . Turnbull owns the gallery and is often on hand to chat or dole out blank canvases to young artists wanting to paint. There's a branch in Bamburgh too (Bamburgh Gallery, 9 Lucker Road).

If you cross back over the A1, the road leads to **Budle Bay**, the southern extension of the Lindisfarne National Nature Reserve. There can be few more convenient tidal estuaries for birdwatchers, as the road skirts the edge of the bay and there are parking bays with displays explaining which birds visit the area, thus allowing your car to double as a hide – an advantage when a north-easterly is blowing.

Further along the B1342 is **Bamburgh**. You may have seen photographs, but nothing prepares you for the jaw-dropping reality as you top a rise and there, squatting above an outcrop of the Great Whin Sill, is the magnificent **Bamburgh Castle**. The castle dominates the village, but many visitors come simply for the beach.

Getting to the beach involves a walk over sandy paths through the marram grass-covered **Bamburgh Dunes** (Site of Special Scientific Interest). Most visitors yomp across, but nature lovers might like to investigate the rare plant and insect life. Emerging from the dunes, you'll see the finest beach in the world. As far as the eye can see, to north and south, fine golden sand inclines gently down to the sea. What you won't see is too many people. Even in summer there'll only be a few hundred visitors, so it's easy to find an uncluttered patch of sand. At other times you'll have the beach virtually to yourself. When the tide is out the sand reaches a good three to four hundred yards further, making the beach a safe place for children to paddle (although the sea is never going to get hot, the retreating tide leaves shallow lagoons that warm up quickly in the sun and are ideal for wading). Apart from the sand, it's the setting that makes the beach exceptional. Look to shore: there's Bamburgh Castle; look north: Holy Island and Lindisfarne Castle; look out to sea: the Farne Islands and their lighthouses. And because the area is protected and – let's be honest – often cold and windy, there's no ribbon of ugly apartment developments sealing off the sea from the land. Your fantasy of a wild and lonely coast comes to salty, sandy life here.

Returning to Bamburgh, taking the Wynding will bring you to a truly spectacular golf course, the 18-hole Bamburgh Castle Golf Club (The Wynding, 01668 214378, www.bamburghcastlegolfclub.co.uk, green fees £37.50-£40). Bamburgh is as perfect an English village as you might wish to find, with the parish church of St Aidan worth visiting for its serenity and the views from its graveyard (final resting place of Victorian heroine Grace Darling, *see p210*). For local produce and sandwiches, try the tiny Pantry Deli (13 Front Street, 01668 214455, www.thebamburghpantry.co.uk).

Bamburgh Castle

Bamburgh *(01668 214515/www.bamburghcastle.com). Open Mar-Nov 10am-5pm daily. Admission £7.50; £3.50-£6.50 reductions.*

Romantic ruins are all very well, but nothing beats an intact, inhabited castle that could still, at a pinch, provide a bastion in times of strife. We owe the castle's present state of repair to 19th-century industrialist, Lord Armstrong, who bought it from a Dr John Sharp. Sharp had begun restoration by founding a school for girls and a hostel for shipwrecked mariners (who probably couldn't believe their luck). There is written evidence for Bamburgh being an important stronghold in the sixth century, but archaeological excavations suggest the site was already inhabited in the Iron Age. Ongoing work by the Bamburgh Research Project shows that the Romans were here too (*see p211* **Dig it!**). The castle reached the zenith of its power during the Northumbrian golden age of the late seventh and eighth centuries, when it was the centre of a kingdom ruling much of northern England and southern Scotland. Following the Conquest, and an unsuccessful rebellion by Earl Robert de Mowbray, the castle passed into royal ownership. In 1464 it became the first fortress to fall to artillery fire when it was captured by Edward IV during the Wars of the Roses.

RNLI Grace Darling Museum

Banburgh *1 Radcliffe Road (01668 214910/www.rnli. org.uk/gracedarling). Open Easter-Sept 10am-5pm daily. Oct-Easter 10am-4pm Tue-Sun. Admission free.*
This excellent small museum tells the story of Grace Darling, following her part in the rescue of survivors of the *SS Forfarshire*. The daughter of William Darling, keeper of Longstone lighthouse on the Farnes, Grace spotted the wreck of the *Forfarshire* at 4.45am on 7 September 1838. It had foundered during the night, but nine survivors were clinging to the rocks. William and Grace set off in the family cobble boat and rowed to the rescue. The boat is preserved in the museum; looking at it you can only marvel that the pair weren't swamped. News soon spread and Grace became a Victorian superstar, with even William Wordsworth writing a poem about her. Examples of Grace Darling Victoriana are on show in the museum, demonstrating the evolution of her image into 'the girl with windswept hair': an idea fixed forever in the public imagination following her death from consumption only four years after the rescue.

SOUTH TO SEAHOUSES

The B1340 runs south beside Bamburgh Dunes to Seahouses. About halfway along is the historic Monks House, which features in Robert Westall's fine children's novel *The Wind Eye*. **Seahouses** itself is not particularly attractive, but it is the largest town on this stretch of coast and a good place to do some basic shopping (there's a Co-op and bakery). You'll also find plenty of shops that will kit you out with buckets, spades, cricket bat and balls, and windbreaks for a day at the beach. The meat pies from the butcher's George Scott & Son (53 Main Street, 01665 720367) are excellent, and Seahouses has at least two claimants to the title of best fish and chips in the north-east: Pinnacles (19 Main Street, 01665 720708) and Neptune (3 Seafield Road, 01665 721310). The lifeboat station (Seafield Road, 01665 720370, www.seahouseslifeboat.org.uk)

is open to the public; here you can see the *RNLB Grace Darling* and records of past rescues, including apparently annual retrievals of tourists stranded on the Holy Island causeway. Apart from the practicalities of holiday-making, however, the main reason to visit Seahouses is to catch a boat to the Farne Islands.

FARNE ISLANDS

Between May and July the **Farnes** are the site of one of the great wildlife spectacles in the world, when more than 200,000 sea birds and their chicks nest among the guano-splattered rocks. The islands themselves, the easternmost outcrop of the Great Whin Sill, are split into the Inner and Outer Farnes, divided by Staple Sound. Exactly how many islands there are depends on the tide: at high water the usual count is 15, but there are as many as 28 visible at low tide. Unsurprisingly, the area is dangerous to shipping, and various beacons and lighthouses have been built. The many wrecks, and a colony of 5,000 inquisitive grey seals, make the Farnes popular with divers. If you fancy a dip, try Farne Island Divers (01327 860895, www.farneislanddivers.co.uk).

A trip to the islands is worthwhile at any time, but try to come during the May to July breeding season. **Boats** leave from Seahouses hourly in season, although check that your trip includes a landing on either Inner Farne (May-July 1.30-5pm daily; Apr, Aug, Sept 10am-6pm daily; £5.80 adults, £2.90 children) or Staple Island (open May-July 10.30am-1.30pm daily, £5.80 adults, £2.90 children). The sail-around trips are interesting, but to experience the reality of hundreds of thousands of nesting birds you have to land. The noise will be the first thing to hit you, sounding something like a high-amplitude Geiger counter, likely to be closely followed by a dive-bombing arctic tern (which is why visitors are told to wear hats). The tern won't actually strike, but be careful not to fall into a puffin burrow in surprise. These most personable of birds take over the burrows of the resident rabbits when they arrive – those beaks aren't just for show – leaving the bunnies scampering outside while they raise their chicks in safety underground. Apart from terns and puffins, about 50,000 guillemots, 5,000 kittiwakes and smaller numbers of eider ducks, sandwich terns, cormorants, shags, razorbills and fulmars nest on the islands. A word of warning – even if it's warm on land, take a coat. Many a T-shirt clad tourist has returned, shivering, to shore, surprised by the cold of the sea breezes. Note that landing charges are in addition to the fees paid to the boatmen (whose booths are on the harbour wall in Seahouses).

CRASTER & AROUND

Craster is a small fishing village that retains the atmosphere of a working seafaring community, as evidenced by the smell of roasting herring. It's the

Dig it!

Visitors to Bamburgh Castle will see archaeologists busily digging, unearthing the castle's medieval and Anglo-Saxon past. They are part of the Bamburgh Research Project (www.bamburghresearchproject.co.uk), which has featured on *Time Team* and *Meet the Ancestors*. We interviewed Paul Gething, project director, to find out what they're doing, and how visitors can join in.

What is the Bamburgh Research Project?
The BRP is an archaeological research project that digs in Bamburgh Castle and the surrounding grounds each year, from mid June to the end of August. We specialise in teaching accessible archaeology to anyone who has a genuine interest. Part of the ethos of the project is that archaeology belongs firmly in the public domain and should be available to everyone. You can sign up for a taste of real, practical archaeology, or take part as an extra credit towards a degree, or do it just for fun and interest.

Do you have to be an archaeology student to take part in the project?
No, the BRP is open to anyone. Most come from a university, but we have people from all over the world, from all walks of life and all ages. We've trained more than 1,000 people so far.

Is there anywhere else that does this?
No, we're unique!

Where do applicants come from?
Anywhere and everywhere. Bamburgh village, Northumberland, UK, mainland Europe, USA, Australia, Asia, Africa.

What's the age range?
From ten to 75. But that isn't writ in stone. Under-16s have to be accompanied, though. We also have a trench set up for children, where they can dig, get themselves thoroughly dirty and discover bits of pottery, pieces of bone, lots of things. Parents love us!

Why are you digging in Bamburgh Castle?
Because people have lived here probably as long as there have been people in the north of England. Its prominent location made it an ideal spot for watching migrating herds. Bamburgh has been defended as a fortress at least since the sixth century.

What's your most important find?
Probably the gatehouse in Trench 1. It gives a wonderful window into the life of the Anglo-Saxon castle.

What's your most interesting find?
The most interesting find for me, is the seventh/eighth-century pattern-welded sword from the West Ward. It is one of the greatest feats of weapon-smithing ever undertaken. It was almost certainly the pride and joy of a very important warrior and has seen hard use. It has sparked a personal exploration into its creation that led me to learn how to smelt iron, pattern weld, forge and smith. Hard work, but incredibly rewarding.

What do guide books miss when writing about Northumberland?
I personally am a dyed-in-the-wool, card-carrying Yorkshireman and extremely proud of that. Northumberland is the only place I have ever been that comes close. It has a very real, down-to-earth beauty, which borders on the hostile occasionally. Winters in Bamburgh are staggering, but still have an amazing quality to them.

The thing people often overlook about Northumberland is that in the Anglo-Saxon period, it was one of the principal centres of the known world. Bamburgh housed the kings of England and Lindisfarne was a tremendous seat of learning and religious activity. The stones of Northumberland still resonate with history. It is a very magical place.

Alnwick Treehouse.

home of Craster kippers, beloved by foodies: L Robson & Sons (Haven Hill, 01665 576223, www.kipper.co.uk) has four generations of experience in preparing the fish and they can be delivered to your home, should you not fancy driving back with them.

One of the best things about **Dunstanburgh Castle** is that there's no car park outside. Instead, leave the car outside Craster and set off on the mile and a half walk.

Dunstanburgh Castle

1.5 miles NW of Craster *(01665 576231/ www.nationaltrust.org.uk). Open Apr-Sept 10am-5pm daily. Oct 10am-4pm daily. Nov-Mar 10am-4pm Mon, Thur-Sun. Admission £3.50; £1.80 reductions.*

You get some indication of the sheer scale of Dunstanburgh Castle on the walk to it along the coast from Caister. The trip at first looks like being a short stroll to the headland, from where the ruined but still magnificent gatehouse glowers at you. Ten minutes later, when the castle hardly seems any closer, you realise just how big it is. Ruined curtain walls seal off 11 acres of headland from raiders, with sheer cliffs providing unbreachable ramparts to seaward. The scale of the architecture would have impressed the most megalomaniacal emperor. Quite appropriate, for the place was built (starting in 1313) by a man who would be king, at least of the north: Thomas, Earl of Lancaster. He had been one of the main participants in the army that the barons led against King Edward II's exiled favourite and alleged lover, Piers Gaveston. Today, both in location and appearance, Dunstanburgh is the archetypal romantic ruined castle.

Howick Hall Gardens

Howick, 1 mile S of Craster *(01665 577285/ www.howickhallgardens.org). Open Feb, Mar noon-4pm Wed, Sat, Sun. Apr-mid Nov noon-6pm daily. Admission £5; £4 reductions.*

The grounds and arboretum of Howick Hall are for serious gardeners, placing plants and flowers to the fore rather than the whims of fashion. The display is at its most magnificent in spring, when the collection of rhododendrons springs into incandescent life. After a stroll, you can have a cuppa in the Earl Grey tea house, named after the hall's former owner.

Mick Oxley Gallery

Craster *17 Haven Hill (01665 571082/www.mick oxley.com). Open Summer 10am-5pm Tue-Sat; 11am-5pm Sun. Winter 10am-4pm Wed-Sat; 11am-5pm Sun. Admission free.*

Artist Mick Oxley works and shows here. Acrylics and watercolours of dramatic seascapes are interposed with more textural works, plus jewellery and sculpture from other local artists. Mick was a PE teacher until ME incapacitated him. He remains wheelchair-bound, but painting has provided a lifeline and then a career for him.

ALNMOUTH & WARKWORTH

Alnmouth is an attractive seaside resort, with a beach some claim to be Northumberland's best, and another fine golf course (Alnmouth Golf Club,

Foxton Hall, Foxton Drive, 01665 830231, www.alnmouthgolfclub.com, green fees £20-£40). Some four miles south, on a loop of the River Coquet within sight of the sea, is the ancient town of **Warkworth** and its castle.

Warkworth Castle

Warkworth *Castle Terrace (01665 711423/www. english-heritage.org.uk). Open Apr-Sept 10am-5pm daily. Oct 10am-4pm daily. Nov-Mar 10am-4pm Mon, Sat, Sun. Admission £3.90; £2-£3.10 reductions.*

If you're known, unofficially at least, as the 'kings of the north', then one castle simply won't cut it, so the Percys developed Warkworth into another stronghold along with Alnwick Castle. The still largely intact remains stand on a commanding hill over the river. It was here that Henry, first Earl of Northumberland, and his son, Harry 'Hotspur' began to plot against the man they'd helped make king, Henry IV. Deposing a second monarch proved beyond them, and Hotspur died at the battle of Shrewsbury in 1403.

ALNWICK

Inland from Alnmouth, Alnwick was rated the best place in the country to live in a 2002 survey by *Country Life* magazine; it's beginning to recover from the unwanted attention. The busy town centre is home to the bright, airy Bakehouse Gallery (Prudhoe Street, 01665 602277, www.thebakehousegallery.com, open 10.30am-5pm Tue-Sat), which exhibits paintings, sculpture, jewellery and glass-work by some excellent local artists. To find out more about Northumberland's thriving art scene, see www.networkartists.org.uk.

The town is dominated by the Percy family: Earls of Northumberland, owners of Alnwick Castle since 1309, and creators of the strikingly modern Alnwick Garden. But bibliophiles may want to stop a while at Barter Books too.

Alnwick Castle

01665 510777/www.alnwickcastle.com. Open Apr-Oct 11am-5pm daily. Admission £11.95; £4.95-£9.95 reductions.

The Percys have lived here for 700 years, and the length of their tenure has a striking ability to move with the times. Their castle is an intact medieval fortress, a family home for the five months when it's closed to the public, an oft-seen backdrop in films (most famously *Harry Potter and the Philosopher's Stone*) and a great, if pricey, venue for a day out. There are exhibitions in some of the perimeter towers, as well as interactive exhibits to show children the life of a medieval knight (they can dress up and bash each other with foam swords). Admission doesn't include Alnwick Garden.

Alnwick Garden

Denwick Lane (01665 511350/www.alnwickgarden.com). Open Summer 10am-6pm daily; Winter 10am-4pm daily. Admission £10; 1p-£7.50 reductions.

We visited Alnwick Garden when it first opened in 2001, and subsequent visits have confirmed our initial impression: Jane, Duchess of Northumberland (the inspiration behind the plan developed by Belgian designers Jacques and Peter Wirtz) has created something special. What strikes you first on entering is the Grand Cascade, an arrestingly modern water feature falling in steps down the hill, with water jets along its length. At the top of the hill is a more traditional walled garden, and at the bottom a bamboo maze. There are also 3,000 varieties of bloom in the Rose Garden, and intriguing water sculptures in the Serpent's Garden. The Poison Garden, behind locked gates, can be entered only with a guide, who will explain the properties of the plants therein (including cannabis and coca plants grown under Home Office licence). Alnwick Garden is great for children on hot days, when they can get wet and cool down; admission for under-17s is just 1p. The garden is hugely popular and its success is deserved. Not to be missed.

Barter Books

Alnwick Station, Broadgate Without (01665 604888/ www.barterbooks.co.uk). Open Apr-Sept 9am-7pm daily. Oct-Mar 9am-5pm Mon-Wed, Fri-Sun; 9am-7pm Thur.
This most civilised shop contains one of England's largest stocks of second-hand books. Housed in the old Alnwick railway station (the line closed in 1968), it includes a newly opened tiled café in the old waiting room, with a coal fire in winter. There are separate tea, coffee and cake supplies near the entrance, with an honesty box for payment. There's a model train running on the track above the bookcases.

Eat

Even its partisans couldn't claim Northumberland as a great gourmet destinations. There's good local produce available – at the **Pantry Deli**, for instance (*see p209*), and Craster kippers of course (*see p212*) – but not much of a local dining scene (the Treehouse restaurant at Alnwick Garden is an exception). Don't despair, though, as the pubs serve decent food and you'll rarely go wrong if you're after an honest meal. Seahouses is excellent for fish and chips.

Alnwick Treehouse

Alnwick *Denwick Lane (01665 511852/www.alnwick garden.com). Open 11.30am-2.45pm Mon-Wed; 11.30am-2.45pm, 6.30-9.30pm Thur-Sun. ££. Modern European.*
This is no ordinary treehouse, but then neither is it an ordinary restaurant. Built around some huge trees in the grounds of Alnwick Garden, and reached via walkways, the venue is a large part of the reason for eating here, with the arboreal theme completed by rough-hewn wooden furniture within. The regularly changing menu might feature goat's cheese stack with white bean purée followed by halibut with garlic mash and mushroom sauce, then turkish delight crème brûlée, perhaps. For a breath of fresh air between courses, take a walk through the tree-tops on the bouncy rope bridges.

Blackmore's of Alnwick

Alnwick *Bondgate Without (01665 602395/ www.blackmoresofalnwick.com). Open noon-2.30pm, 5.50-9.30pm daily. ££. British.*

The best bet for a slap-up meal in the area is probably Blackmore's. The chef and owner, John Blackmore, gives British classics a local twist. Craster smoked salmon could be followed by steak and Alnwick IPA ale pie. Furnishings in the dining room are contemporary. There are also 13 guest rooms, individually designed in earth tones, making this one of the few boutique hotels in the area.

Copper Kettle Tea Rooms

Bamburgh *21 Front Street (01668 214315/www. copperkettletearooms.com). Open 10am-6pm daily. ££. No credit cards. Café.*
Once cottages housing castle labourers, this row of six properties has been converted into one of the prettiest tearooms in the county. Food is prepared in-house, with a range of light meals, sandwiches and salads served, as well as a wide selection of teas. The garden is delightful in good weather.

Links Hotel

Seahouses *8 King Street (01665 720062/www.links hotel-seahouses.co.uk). Open (restaurant) 6.30-9pm Mon-Sat; noon-2pm, 6.30-9pm Sun. £££. Pub.*
Just off the main street in Seahouses, the Links provides a varied (and occasionally startling) pub menu in slightly nondescript surroundings. There are steaks aplenty, but devil-may-care diners might chance the chicken stuffed with haggis on a Drambuie sauce with black pudding mash. Staff are friendly, you can eat either in the bar or restaurant area, and the food is good value. Local people rate it highly.

The Ship Inn

Low Newton-by-the-Sea, 12 miles N of Alnwick *(01665 576262/www.shipinnnewton.co.uk). Open (restaurant) noon-2.30pm Mon-Wed, Sun; noon-2.30pm, 7-8pm Thur-Sat. £££. Pub.*
Ask locals for a recommendation of a place to eat and you'll be told about the Ship. Owner Christine Forsyth is committed to using local producers, so the simple but well-prepared food is always fresh. The pub also serves a good range of real ales, and is about to begin brewing its own beer. There's an attached self-catering flat too.

Stay

Most visitors to the coast stay either in self-catering cottages and apartments, or B&Bs. There's a large choice of properties to rent, with many having great facilities or a location in characterful buildings. Try Northumbria Coast & Country Cottages (01665 830783, www. northumbria-cottages.co.uk), Northumberland Coastal Retreats (0191 285 1272, www. coastalretreats.co.uk) and Doxford Cottages (01665 589393, www.doxfordcottages.co.uk). Blackmore's of Alnwick (*see above*) has rooms too.

Blue Bell Hotel

Belford *Market Place (01668 213543/ www.bluebellhotel.com). £££.*

St Cuthbert's House.

Doxford Hall.

The vine-covered Blue Bell is a coaching inn dating from the 18th century; it once looked after travellers on the long haul to Edinburgh. These days the Great North Road (or A1) bypasses Belford, making the town much quieter. The hotel is traditionally decorated, with superior rooms having four-poster beds; rooms in the annexe are more modern but less interesting. The restaurant serves Modern European food. Outside is a large garden with countryside views and children's play equipment.

Crown & Anchor
Holy Island *Market Place (01289 389215/ www.holyislandcrown.co.uk). ££.*
The Crown & Anchor's guest rooms – at least three of the four – have the best views available to anybody staying on Holy Island, with outlooks over priory, castle and bay. Rooms are simply furnished and clean, and the proprietors, islander Keith Shell and all-but-islander wife Rachel, are good hosts. The pub, decorated with old photos of fishermen, has an open coal fire and serves good pub food.

Doxford Hall
Nr Chathill, 10 miles N of Alnwick *(01665 589700/www.doxfordhall.com). £££.*
There was a dearth of top-class hotel accommodation along the coast until Doxford Hall opened in late 2008, in this rural spot a mile south of Chathill. A mark of owner Brian Burnie's achievement is that it's difficult to tell where the original hall, built in 1818 by John Dobson, ends and the new hotel begins. The whole enterprise bears evidence of attention to detail, from the grand oak staircase through the paintings of Northumbrian historical scenes in the basement to Molton Brown toiletries in the bathrooms. Red squirrels scamper around the grounds.

Joiners Shop Bunkhouse
Preston, Nr Chathill, 10 miles N of Alnwick *(01665 589245/www.bunkhousenorthumberland.co.uk). £. No credit cards.*
You don't expect luxury in a bunkhouse, but you hope for somewhere clean, well run and welcoming, and that's just what proprietors Wal and Annie Wallace provide. There are 18 bunks, arranged in curtained-off dormitories. The bunkhouse has self-catering facilities, but meals and packed lunches are provided if requested in advance. You can either bring a sleeping bag or rent them here. Joiners is in a rural area, with easy access to the A1 and coast, and a nearby railway stop at Chathill.

Pot-a-Doodle Do
Scremerston, 3 miles S of Berwick-upon-Tweed *Borewell Farm (01289 307107/www.northumbrian wigwams.com). £.*
Think of this as camping in a solid structure. The accommodation is in prism-shaped wood constructions called wigwams, with heat and light, and a fridge. Bring your own sleeping bag, and either use the kitchen or eat at the on-site restaurant. The tipis and yurts are more basic, with no electricity, so are good for those wanting a back-to-nature experience within easy reach of a shower block. The shop can provide basics as well as beach necessities. There are enjoyable walks in the vicinity, although the beach is a car drive away. It's basic, but if the weather's good, fun. If it's wet, those wigwams might soon feel rather small.

St Cuthbert's House
Seahouses *192 Main Street (01665 720456/ www.stcuthbertshouse.com). ££.*
Jeff and Jill Sutheran took a semi-derelict Presbyterian church and turned it into an exemplary modern B&B. Here you'll find all the comfort and most of the refinements of a major hotel, but also the personal service and human contact of the best B&Bs. The cooked breakfast is excellent. Guest rooms are clean and well thought out, but the highlight is the communal area, with natural light flooding through the arched windows of the old church, and the old lectern repositioned in the overlooking gallery. It's a glorious space, ideal for relaxing in at day's end. Jeff and Jill are musicians, and if you ask, Jill might play the Northumbrian small pipes.

Victoria Hotel
Bamburgh *Front Street (01668 214431/ www.thevictoriahotelbamburgh.co.uk). ££.*
The Victoria looks over the village green in Bamburgh. Only three new additions to its 37 rooms have views towards the castle; the rest look towards the parish church, the sea beyond, or inland to the Cheviots. Superior rooms have four-poster beds, and are decorated in earthy colours in keeping with the pleasing Victorian feel of the hotel. The ambience is enhanced by winding staircases leading up to some rooms.

Factfile

When to go
Anytime. Don't expect good weather and you might get it.

Getting there & around
By car via the A1 or **train** to Newcastle or Berwick-upon-Tweed, changing to local lines. Arriva (www.arrivabus.co.uk) runs local **bus** services, but a car or bicycle is useful if you want to explore – Northumberland is quite spread out.

Tourist information
The official, and useful, tourist site is www.visitnorthumberland.com. In the area covered by this chapter, there are tourist information offices at **Alnwick** (2 The Shambles, 01665 511333); **Berwick-upon-Tweed** (106 Marygate, 01289 330733); **Seahouses** (Seafield Car Park, Seafield Road, 01665 720884); and **Wooler** (Cheviot Centre, 12 Padgepool Place, 01668 282123).

Top: Barafundle Bay;
middle: Tenby;
bottom left: beach;
bottom right: Newport.

Pembrokeshire Coast

Hidden beaches, dramatic landscapes and pretty towns.

Stereotypes are made to be shattered – and Pembrokeshire is a good place to start. This is not the Wales of mining towns, leeks, strident nationalism and soggy climate. This wild and beautiful coastal playground has been rebranded in recent years, variously christened as the new Cornwall, the California of Wales or Little England. All the monikers are true to a degree. With its craggy coastal scenery and abundance of sugary beaches and secret coves, it could double for Cornwall, but without the crowds and commercialisation. The California comparisons are also apt, with crashing waves, surfer dudes and a benign climate (Pembrokeshire is one of the three sunniest places in the UK, and the waters are warmed by the Gulf Stream), while the dramatic coastal roads near places like Freshwater West or Newgale could be snapshots from the Pacific Coast's Highway 1. As for the Little England nickname, in fact, Pembrokeshire has been known as 'Little England beyond Wales' for centuries. Even though the county is far from the English border, it is English speaking in the large majority. Despite this, there is plenty of wonderful Welsh culture and history present, including the cathedral city of St Davids (birthplace of Wales's patron saint), megalithic monuments and medieval castles. There is also a burgeoning Welsh confidence and sense of style, reflected in a sprinkling of cool new hotels and restaurants that possess a modern outlook while staying true to the area's cultural roots. But most people come to Pembrokeshire for the natural wonders: the magical coastal walks, the wildlife (birds, whales, dolphins and seals) and, above all, those magnificent beaches.

Explore

TENBY

Once a booming Victorian resort, today Tenby is an irresistible slice of faded seaside grandeur, combining elegance and beauty with a salty, jaunty British seaside feel. The clifftop promenade by **South Beach** is classy and old school: a string of smart Georgian buildings painted in pastel shades, complemented by old-fashioned street lamps, wrought-iron railings and tasteful landscaped gardens. The beaches are impeccable – long, firm and golden – and the harbour is handsome. There's history, too, in the form of old city walls, a ruined castle and an ancient monastery across the water on **Caldey Island**. Despite its pedigree, Tenby has no airs and graces: it's unpretentious and slightly behind the times, so foodies and boutique-hotel divas should look elsewhere.

BARAFUNDLE BAY & AROUND

One of Wales's most cherished beaches, **Barafundle** is the stuff of fairy tales. The entrance is through a dainty stone archway, followed by a sweeping stone staircase down to the sea. The beach is small, secretive and golden – perfect for childhood memories and family picnics (*Country Life* magazine recently named it Britain's best beach for picnics). Nestled snugly between two limestone headlands, it's a true safe haven.

The beach is sheltered from south-westerly winds and the surf is gentle. There's even an enchanting woodland path above – you almost expect to bump into a fairy here.

If you venture into the open, along the **Pembrokeshire Coast Path**, things get more exciting. Suddenly the landscape becomes exposed, windswept and dramatic. But soon there's another charm offensive: the golden **Broad Haven South** beach (like a bigger, meatier Barafundle) and the **Bosherton Lily Ponds** (an hour's walk west from Barafundle). Built in the 18th century by a local aristo, these real-life landscape paintings evoke images of frogs and princes, ugly ducklings and swans. As you drift dreamily along the paths, look out for otters, toads, dragonflies and birdlife (swans, kingfisher and herons).

Serious twitchers will have to go further west to **Stack Rocks**, which jut out of the sea near **Castlemartin**. In the spring and summer, the rocks swarm with nesting guillemots, razorbills, kittiwakes, fulmars and gulls. The mysterious Green Bridge of Wales, a limestone arch seen from a viewing platform, is as mesmerising as the birds.

Climbers head for the majestic sea cliffs at nearby **St Govan's Head**. So do religious pilgrims, who make a beeline for **St Govan's Chapel**, a 13th-century hermit's dwelling hidden in the cliff face at the bottom of 74 steps. The wishing well adds to the storybook feel.

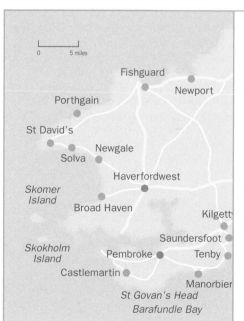

0   5 miles

Fishguard

Newport

Porthgain

St David's

Newgale

Solva

Haverfordwest

Skomer Island

Broad Haven

Kilgetty

Saundersfoot

Skokholm Island   Pembroke   Tenby

Castlemartin

Manorbier

St Govan's Head

Barafundle Bay

Pembrokeshire Coast

Historic sites
● ● ● ○ ○

Art & architecture
● ● ○ ○ ○

Hotels
● ● ● ○ ○

Eating & drinking
● ● ● ○ ○

Scenery
● ● ● ● ●

Outdoor activities
● ● ● ● ○

Top: Barafundle;
middle: Newport;
bottom: Pembrokeshire
landscape.

Marina.

The Great British Take Away

Freshwater West is only a 20-minute drive from Barafundle Bay, but the contrast couldn't be greater. The gentle ripples of Barafundle turn into giant swells here – the picnicking families give way to serious surfer dudes and the cute cove is replaced by a sweeping strand. There's no lifeguard, and no peace: the roar of the surf is relentless.

ST DAVIDS & AROUND

Isolated on the western tip of Pembrokeshire, **St Davids** is on the edge literally and figuratively: they do things differently out here. It's officially Britain's smallest city, according to the *Guinness World Records*, but it feels more like a village; indeed, it's only a city by dint of its magnificent medieval cathedral. A cathedral was first built here in 550 AD by St David, the patron saint of Wales, who was born and died here. The ornate, beautifully aged cathedral you see here today dates from the 12th century, a time when the Pope declared that two visits to St Davids were the equivalent of one to Rome; if you made three visits, you could skip Jerusalem. But although this is the holiest spot in Wales, and history oozes from every cobblestone, St Davids town has a strangely progressive, contemporary vibe. The quaint high street is dotted with surf and outdoor shops and frequented by sporty, eco-minded adventurers; local restaurants emphasise organic food and sophisticated cuisine (there's even a funky café in the cathedral) and there is a sprinkling of art galleries here and in surrounding villages.

Whitesands Bay, on the outskirts of the town of St Davids, is one of Pembrokeshire's best beaches: it's a mile long, wide and white, and the surf is good. And what's more, it can hold its own in a beauty contest: it was recently placed 18th out of 250, ahead of Copacabana in Brazil and Koh Phi Phi in Thailand, in a survey of the world's best beaches. And if you only have time for a one-day coastal walk, the stretch from **Caerfai**, south of St Davids, to Whitesands Bay, is vintage Pembrokeshire: rugged, windswept and camera-friendly.

South of St Davids, there are three highlights: Solva, Newgale and Broad Haven. **Solva** is a snug fishing village-cum-artist's colony, with a couple of decent pubs. **Newgale**, further south, is a jaw-dropping beach: long, sweeping, and pounded by breakers that sweep in from America. Surfers are in their element here, as are photographers – you'll be stopping your car at every bend in the scenic coastal to try and get the money shot. **Broad Haven**, not to be confused with Broadhaven South near Barafundle Bay, is another poster child for Welsh pulchritude, framed by craggy rocks that are so dramatic they make Cornwall look tame by comparison. Unfortunately, the magnificent beach is backed by a slightly tacky seaside town; in summer, this is pure bucket and spade territory.

North and west of St Davids, **Porthgain** is a bit of a one-fish town. But this remote and lonely little coastal village attracts the hordes for two reasons: the **Sloop Inn** (*see p227*) and the local seafood at the irresistible **Shed** bistro (*see p227*).

THE ISLANDS

In summer, the islands near St Davids attract birdwatchers, whale-watchers, dolphin-lovers and seal-stalkers. There are frequent boat trips to **Ramsey Island** from St Davids. The island is an RSPB reserve for choughs and also famous for grey seals, and you'll be likely to spot marine mammals frolicking along the way. Three other islands, further south, are similarly beloved of wildlife enthusiasts: **Skomer Island**, **Skokholm Island** and **Grassholm** are swarming with puffins, Manx shearwaters, gannets and storm petrels. The islands' distinctly Nordic names are a remnant of Viking invasions. For Ramsey Island trips, contact **Thousand Island Expeditions** (from St Justinians, 01437 721721, www.thousandislands.co. uk), **Voyages of Discovery** (01437 720285, www.ramseyisland.co.uk), or **Aquaphobia** (01437 721648, www.aquaphobia-ramsey island.co.uk). For the other islands, there are boat trips from April to October from **Martin's Haven** (Dale Sailing Company, 01646 603107, www.dale-sailing.co.uk).

NEWPORT & AROUND

Not to be confused with the grim industrial Newport near Cardiff, this Newport is pastel pretty with narrow streets and cute cottages. Though smaller than nearby Fishguard, it is the belle of the north coast, and has recently come to the attention of foodies, thanks to restaurants like **Llys Meddyg** (*see p224*) and **Cnapan** (*see p224*). The village is sandwiched between **Carn Ingli**, one of the Preseli Hills, and **Newport Sands**, yet another stellar strand. There's also a Norman castle (now a private residence) and **Carreg Coeltan**, a neolithic burial chamber, but the main attraction is a lookout point at the top of the hill – the sweeping panorama of the north Welsh coast is laid out before you.

Fishguard is synonymous with ferries to Ireland, but it's also a bustling and, in places, handsome town. The old lower town, by the harbour, is particularly atmospheric; it was the setting for the 1971 film version of Dylan Thomas's *Under Milk Wood* starring Richard Burton and Elizabeth Taylor. Fishguard, as locals will tell you, was also the site of the last foreign invasion of Britain, in 1797, when the French landed here and were defeated, with the help of local women, according to legend. Their surrender is commemorated in a tapestry on display in the **Town Hall** and in the

Royal Oak Inn, a historic pub. **Seaways** (12 West Street, 01348 873433), a surprisingly good bookshop, suggests the locals are an extremely literary crowd.

West of Fishguard, **Strumble Head** is a wild and windswept headland topped by a working lighthouse, where the coast path is strewn with heather, gorse and dramatic black rocks. It is another scenic lookout *par excellence*, and Wales's nearest point to Ireland.

East of Newport, **Pentre Ifan** is the largest dolmen in Wales. To the layman, that's a neolithic burial chamber, dating from 4500 BC. It looks a bit like a mini Stonehenge; in fact, the stones used to build that famous circle came from this area. Nearby, **Castell Henllys** (01239 891319, www.castellhenllys.com; open Apr-Oct 10am-5pm daily, Nov-Mar 11am-3pm; admission £3.50, £2.50 reductions), is a reconstruction of an   village on the site of a neolithic hill fort.

Eat

See also **Druidstone** (*p228*) and the **Stackpole Inn** (*p229*).

Bench

St Davids *11 High Street (01437 721778/www.bench-bar.co.uk). Open noon-3pm, 6-9pm Mon-Sat; noon-3pm Sun. £££. Italian.*
The Bench is a family-run restaurant in which dining feels rather like eating in your neighbour's front room. The Italian owner and his British wife and children do the cooking and wait the tables. The decor mixes rustic (warm woods, slate floors), quirky (arty plastic Italian chairs, knick-knacks galore, twinkly lights) and contemporary (black leather sofa, framed photography). Like the ambience, the cuisine is hearty and unpretentious. An array of pizzas and pastas is complemented by more sophisticated dishes: pigeon bruschetta, pheasant wrapped in bacon and stuffed with chestnuts, game terrine with red-onion marmalade. (All the game here is local.) For pudding, the obvious choice is own-made Italian ice-cream from the adjoining parlour.

Cambrian

Solva *6 Main Street (01437 721210). Open 8am-10pm daily. £££. Pub.*
A pleasing mix of cosy and quirky: the low beamed ceilings and stone walls are vintage country pub, as are the twee knick-knacks (of the china ducks ilk), but there are cute touches like the *Carry On…* posters, framed saucy seaside postcards and black and white photographs of vintage Hollywood starlets. There's also a funky purple café area. But the main chalkboard menu is pure comfort: Welsh rarebit, ham hock with mash, and slow-roasted pork belly. Fresh local seafood may include lobster. In short, a cut above your average pub grub.

Cnapan

Newport *East Street (01239 820575/www.cnapan. co.uk). Open 6.30-9pm Mon, Wed-Sun. £££. Restaurant/tearoom.*
Opened in the mid 1980s, Cnapan is still going strong. A cross between a tearoom and restaurant, it holds wide appeal. Behind the pink frontage is a light and airy dining room with comfortably practical furniture and knick-knacks. Lunches tend to be light, with lots of salads, or local crab and lobster. In the evening, the food is more ambitious. Try roast peppers and tomatoes, capers, basil and olive oil topped with good local goat's cheese or crab and smoked salmon tart, or local seafood chowder. Next, there's local Welsh beef and lamb served in a variety of ways. Guinea fowl also makes an appearance in interesting guises and sauces. Presentation is simple and cooking has a light touch. Puddings are rich; service is informal, efficient and friendly.

Cwtch

St Davids *22 High Street ((01437 720491/www.cwtch restaurant.co.uk). Open Apr-July, Sept, Oct 6-9.30pm Tue-Sun. Aug 6-9.30pm daily. Nov-Mar 6-9.30pm Wed-Sat. £££. British.*
Cwtch, pronounced Cutsh, means cosy in Welsh. And the name reflects the menu, which is heavy on good, wholesome British comfort food – fans of St John, the 'best of British' London restaurant, will be in their element here. The formula is familiar: local ingredients prepared with minimum fuss and pretension, and nostalgic flavours, all served by bright young things in a rustic-minimalist setting, in this case, wood and slate floors, beamed ceilings and chalkboard menus. Starters might include St Brides Bay potted crab with remoulade and toast, Pembrokeshire ham hock terrine with piccalilli, and duck liver pâté with port and juniper granary toast and walnut chutney. Mains are equally local and hearty: Pembrokeshire venison with Penlon chocolate stout casserole and Yorkshire pudding, say, or St Brides Bay halibut with Penclawd cockles fish cake and sauce vierge.

Llys Meddyg

Newport *East Street (01239 820008/www.llys meddyg.com). Open 7-9pm Tue; noon-2pm, 7-9pm Wed-Sat. ££££. Modern British.*
Newport's only boutique hotel (*see p228*) has a quietly hip restaurant to match. You can eat in the simple teal blue dining room or the cool basement bar. Both possess the style and quality of a London venue, minus the attitude. The aesthetic is understated and chic, but rustic too. Downstairs, grey walls, slate floors and artful lighting are mixed with chunky wood tables and beamed ceiling (the building is an 1850s coach house). The crackling fire adds cosiness, but tasteful art keeps things cosmopolitan. So does chef Scott Davis, a local boy who earned his chops in London under chefs like Marco Pierre White and Nobu Matsuhitsa. The menu merges playful fusion techniques with local ingredients, in dishes such as Newport Bay crab cakes with papaya mustard, roast Bethesda pork belly with coffee and prunes, and poached blackberry soup served with buttermilk sorbet and vanilla shortbread.

St Brides Spa Hotel.

Llys Meddyg Hotel.

Marina

Saundersfoot *The Harbour (01834 813598). Open 10am-7pm Mon-Thur, Sun; 10am-8pm Fri; 10am-8.30pm Sun. ££. Fish & chips.*
The local chippie has gone all chic. On a pearl of a Pembrokeshire beach, Saundersfoot, the Marina is blessed with a gorgeous location. But the interior makes the biggest impression. The regulation chippie uniform – cheap linoleum flooring and Formica tables – has been replaced by glossy black and white tiles and handsome oak tables; the plastic signage has been swapped for chalkboard menus; and the deathly fluorescent lights ditched for flattering halogen pot lights. But the biggest transformation is on the menu. In addition to the usual cod or haddock, you can choose from hake, mackerel, plaice, black bream, sea bass or salmon. You can order your fish skinless and grilled. But even the deep-fried version comes with a whiff of worthiness: the batter is made from real ale. The fresh cut chips are made from Pembrokeshire potatoes and come with a choice of garlic mayonnaise, chutney or grated cheese. If you've never tried chips with champagne, crack open a mini bottle at the Marina – yes, it's licensed. But if you want a 'proper' restaurant, walk down the beach to its bigger sister, the Mermaid on the Strand (www.stbridesspahotel.com), which offers a more formal alternative. Both are owned by the sleek St Brides Spa Hotel (*see p229*).

Morgan's

St Davids *20 Nun Street (01437 720508/www. morgans-restaurant.co.uk). Open Summer 6.30-9.30pm Mon, Wed-Sun. Winter 6.30-9.30pm Mon, Thur-Sun. ££££. Modern European.*
Morgan's is one of a couple of St Davids 'destination' restaurants, and it's emblematic of the city as a whole: a little bit trad, but cool and contemporary too. The setting is an old stone Welsh house, but the interior is modern and modish. The menu is a very St Davids mix of farm-fresh, locally sourced ingredients, but prepared with sophistication. Fish is a forte – Turbot fillet comes with braised oxtail, red wine sauce and tempura cockles; fillet of sea bass is accompanied by leek foam, Solva lobster sauce and truffle oil. Local meat is another strength.

Old Sailors

Pwllgwaelod Beach *Sailors Safety, Dinas Cross (01348 811491). Open Summer noon-2.30pm, 7-8.30pm Tue-Sun. Winter noon-2.30pm Tue-Thur, Sun; noon-2.30pm, 7-8.30pm Fri, Sat. ££. Pub.*
The Old Sailors is something of a local legend. Back in the 1940s, when it was a ramshackle old inn, Dylan Thomas made special trips all the way from Carmarthen just for the lobster – no doubt he washed it down with copious amounts of beer. Today, locals and tourists also make a special trip here, but not so much for the food. The big hook is the spectacular seafront location: a sleepy cove, framed by wild beaches and cliffs. Sadly, the pub's interior – with a bland, faux rustic look – pales in comparison to the natural wonders outside. Still, the dining room offers front-row views of the crashing waves. And if you don't set your gastronomic hopes too high, you can have a satisfying

lunch or dinner, provided you order the fruits of the sea you are looking at (lobster, scallops, crab or sewin).

Refectory at St Davids

St Davids *St Davids Cathedral, The Close (01437 721760/www.stdavidscathedral.org.uk). Open Summer 11am-8.30pm daily. Winter 11am-4pm daily. ££. Café.*
The Refectory at St Davids is so good that even atheists are flocking to the cathedral for lunch. It's not buried in some spooky crypt either: the medieval hall has been modernised with sleek blond wood furniture, flattering halogen lighting, a rotating collection of art and a dazzling white balcony structure that resembles a sailboat. The food is inspiring too: home-made soups, quiches and salads; sandwiches using local foodstuffs like Pembrokeshire chipolata sausage and Welsh cheddar and sinfully good desserts such as Welsh cakes and bakewell tarts.

Shed

Porthgain *(01348 831518/www.theshedporthgain. co.uk). Open 5.30-9pm Mon; 6.30-9.30pm Fri; 11am-5pm, 6.30-9.30pm Sat; 11am-5pm Sun. ££££. Seafood.*
If you only eat at one restaurant in Pembrokeshire, make it the Shed. It has a romantic and atmospheric setting, perched on the seafront next to the ivy-covered ruins of a Victorian brickworks. The interior is pleasingly rustic, without being twee. The seafood menu is simple, local and authentic, without trying too hard. It doesn't have to, as the chefs have plentiful catches of the day at their disposal. The sea bass – line-caught, pan-fried and served with a herbed beurre blanc cream and roasted tomato – is subtle, flavourful and perfectly prepared. The grilled local mullet fillet comes marinated in chilli, ginger, garlic and lemongrass. Service is faultless and friendly (staff are all family or friends). Booking is essential in summer and at weekends – and with good reason.

Sloop Inn

Porthgain *(01348 831449/www.sloop.co.uk). Open 9.30-11am, noon-2.30pm, 6-9.30pm daily. ££. Pub.*
Hidden in the secret cove of Porthgain, a minuscule fishing village, the Sloop Inn reflects its coastal, weather-beaten location: the rustic and cosy decor is a sea of nautical touches (anchors, model ships, compasses), fishing paraphernalia, and local art (landscape paintings and nostalgic photographs). And though it is a local institution – it's been going since 1743 – a gastropub it is not. True, the menu is ambitious and varied – minted lamb chop with fondant potato in red wine and redcurrant sauce, say, followed by vanilla pannacotta with Belgian waffles – but the execution is uneven. You're better off sticking to a beer and a freshly made crab sandwich.

Stone Hall

Welsh Hook, 7 miles S of Fishguard *(01348 840212/www.stonehall-mansion.co.uk). Open 7-9pm daily. ££££. French.*
Pembrokeshire may be known as Little England, but Stone Hall flies the flag for France. Owner Martine Watson relocated from France 20 years ago, and turned this idyllic country house into an elegant restaurant with rooms. Her Gallic roots dominate the menu, which attracts serious

gourmands. It's classic stuff: starters like escargots with garlic butter, twice-baked gruyère cheese soufflé or chicken liver terrine read like dishes from a 1970s edition of the *Joy of Cooking*. The rotating cast of mains is similarly traditional: you might be offered filet de boeuf with port sauce and Dijon mustard or duo of canard with apple compote. Desserts are also straight from a disco era dinner party: crème brûlée, profiteroles au chocolat, Hazelnut meringue with cream. This is French cooking for purists, and thank goodness for that.

Stay

See also **Stone Hall** *(p227).*

Cefn y Dre
Fishguard *(01348 875663/www.cefnydre.co.uk). ££. No credit cards.*
High above Fishguard, Cefn y Dre has bucolic views of the Preseli Hills, framed by an acre of gardens and mature ash, sycamore and yew trees. It's also got history: the house dates back to the 15th century, and more recently, Lloyd George stayed in. Though the house has classically proportioned rooms and handsome Regency and Victorian touches, it has an unpretentious and informal feel. Rooms are comfortable and mumsy – lots of beige, with the odd piece of antique furniture handed down from the family of owner Gaye Williams. Indeed, Cefn y Dre's biggest selling point is the personal touches offered by Williams and her husband Geoff Stickler: there are family heirlooms and oil paintings, but more importantly, personal advice on where to go walking and birdwatching, and where to eat in Fishguard and Newport. They know it all, and will tell you as you sip tea by one of the crackling fires in the homely drawing room or elegant dining room.

Crug Glas
Abereiddy, 3 miles E of St Davids *(01348 831302/www.crug-glas.co.uk). £££.*
If *Gone with the Wind* had been set in Wales, Crug Glas could have been Tara. It's an epic Georgian house that has been in the same family for generations, and there are stunning sunsets across the farmers' fields. Proprietor Janet Evans works hard to keep the family home ticking over. In addition to running the hotel, she does all the cooking for the restaurant, plays gracious hostess, and has filled the stately bedrooms with grand family heirlooms, from four-poster beds to oak wardrobes and gracious armchairs. It's a pleasing mix of formality and feminity: damask wallpaper meets floral bedspreads with a few frilly lampshades thrown in. There's a palpable sense of history, and you can read all about the house's ancestors in documents and books in the drawing room. Outside, the grand avenue of mature trees leading up to the house adds to the cinematic feel.

Druidstone
Broad Haven *(01437 781221/www.druidstone. co.uk). £££.*
A bohemian version of a country house hotel, the Druidstone is a curious mix of new age and old money – the posh flower

child of Pembrokeshire. It's perched on the edge of a cliff overlooking the sea, and crammed with paintings and photographs by local artists. There's a whiff of blue blood in the rambling 1850s stone house, with its draughty corridors and Persian rugs. Owner Jane Bell, who grew up here, is a combination of earth mother and grand dame, presiding over a keen but casual staff of local youths. Her decorative style is tasteful yet eccentric. There are 11 bedrooms, four with private bathrooms, but the penthouse rooms are the best: newly decked out with pine panelling and crisp white bedding, they are both rustic and smart. But the biggest draws are the ocean-view balconies and sound effects: on a stormy night, the sound of the whistling wind is deeply atmospheric; in summer, a gem of a beach cries out for walks. There's also an eco cottage on the property, powered entirely by the elements. But the main house is the place to be in the evenings. In the basement bar, guests and locals drink to a soft soundtrack of 1960s tunes. In the dining room, top-notch local and organic food dominates the menu.

Grove
St Davids *High Street (01437 720341/www.grove stdavids.co.uk). ££.*
Not too long ago, the Grove would have been a simple chain pub where you could grab a cheap room for the night in St Davids. Nowadays, Welsh pub chain Brains is trying to take it more upmarket. The menu has gastropub aspirations, and if you wanted to be trendy you could call it 'a restaurant with rooms', though the whole place still feels chainy and slightly middle of the road. Upstairs, the seven bedrooms are going for a boutique look, with white duvets, flat-screen TVs and free Wi-Fi access. It's all very comfortable, if not memorable, and offers very good value for money.

Llys Meddyg
Newport *East Street (01239 820008/www.llys meddyg.com). £££.*
This funky and fashionable 'restaurant with rooms' has put the sleepy fishing village of Newport on the tourist and foodie map. Its owners recently relocated from London, and they have brought some urban style and modern comfort to a Georgian coaching inn. The bedrooms are simple, bold and striking, with an emphasis on colour and texture. Think tasteful Farrow & Ball shades, crisp white duvets, stylishly patterned Welsh woollen blankets from Melin Tregwynt, and flooring that judiciously mixes sisal matting and white shag rugs, warm wood and Welsh slate. Eye-popping abstract paintings by Peter Daniels and Wallpaper*-esque lamps add to the contemporary feel, as do the flat-screen TVs and monsoon showerheads in the bathrooms. Period fixtures like beamed ceilings remind you of the building's roots. The dark basement bar and acclaimed restaurant are bonuses. The sea is a 10-minute walk from here.

Old Smithy
Merrion, 3 miles W of Castlemartin *7 Merrion Village (01646 661310). £. No credit cards.*
The Old Smithy B&B lives up to its characterful name. It's a 200-year-old cottage in a sleepy hamlet, with low beamed ceilings, exposed brickwork and antique furniture, complemented by shiny modern bathrooms. Barafundle

Bay, one of Wales's most treasured beaches, is a short drive away, but so are a range of other supreme strands, including Freshwater West, Broadhaven, and a little further afield, Tenby and Manorbier. Other attractions include birdwatching at Stack Rocks and the nearby Bosherton Lily Ponds.

St Brides Spa Hotel

Saundersfoot *St Brides Hill (01834 812304/ www.stbridesspahotel.com). ££££.*
A little touch of Miami luxury transplanted to the craggy Welsh coast. Hovering dramatically on a cliff overlooking a sweeping beach, St Brides is vintage Pembrokeshire in terms of location. But the aesthetics are more tropical and glossy. The landscape is dotted with palm trees, and the building has shades of art deco with its peach colour, ocean-liner railings and sea-view decks. The spa treatment rooms are truly sensual: with tropical rain showers, herbal steam rooms and an outdoor infinity pool that seems to float over the ocean, they take the edge off any wild Welsh weather. So does the sunny and stylish decor, which is faithful to the world of glossy interior mags. There's an emphasis on rich textures: suede headboards, limestone bathrooms, polished oak furniture and plush taupe carpets with sisal patterns. The shell and nautical motifs say beach resort, but the Melin Tregwynt wool blankets remind you this is Wales. Downstairs, the sea-view restaurant and bar are a showpiece – all blond wood, white walls and huge windows.

Stackpole Inn

Stackpole *Jasons Corner (01646 672324/www. stackpoleinn.co.uk). ££.*
The main attraction of Stackpole Inn is its proximity to Barafundle Bay and the Pembrokeshire coastal path. But it has plenty of other charms. With its ivy-covered stone walls, gabled windows and sweet garden, the 17th-century inn is the epitome of quaintness. Yet the four bedrooms are cool and contemporary (and two have pullout sofas for family stays). The area's best local grub is offered downstairs. Served in a modern rustic setting, the food comprises classy gastropub fare – such as Welsh Black beef steaks, Welsh cheeses, Tenby crab, Pembroke sausages – and a selection of real ales.

Warpool Court Hotel

St Davids *(01702 720300/www.warpoolcourt hotel.com). ££.*
Some say that Pembrokeshire is like Cornwall was 40 years ago. The Warpool Court Hotel could make a similar claim: there's a distinct whiff of the '70s about this country house hotel. The decor is formal but fusty, comfortable but forgettable. It's the views, however, that will linger in the mind. Built majestically on the edge of a cliff, the hotel boasts vintage Atlantic vistas, complemented by formal, statue-filled gardens that open on to the coastal paths. The hotel attracts a seasonal cast of regulars, of the type who prefer tradition to trendiness and scenery to style, who might enjoy a game of croquet before dining amid the white tablecloths, chandeliers and frilly drapes of the retro dining room. Still, the glass-covered, heated indoor swimming pool is a unique selling point in these parts. And those amazing views trump designer makeovers any day.

Waterings

St Davids *Anchor Drive, High Street (01437 720876/ www.waterings.co.uk). ££.*
A retro American-style motel in traditional St Davids? It sounds unlikely, but the Waterings is more 1960s motorway than 1860s cobblestone – a sprawling one-storey building with rooms that open on to a courtyard, and a deliciously kitsch lobby filled with conch shells and shark's teeth. The marine paraphernalia is a nod to the Waterings' former incarnation, as a tourist aquarium. Back in 1989, it was converted into a motel, but the family held on to its heritage, hence the pond of koi carp. All the fishy stuff goes well with the motel's nautical motif (buoys flank the entrance and the rooms have cute names like First Mate, Cabin Boy, and so on). Rooms are done up in pine furniture, all have a double and a twin, and many possess skylights. And, in contrast to its American counterparts, this is one motel where the car isn't king: you can walk into the centre of St Davids in ten minutes.

Factfile

When to go
The best weather is in the summer (June to September). The rainiest season is from October to January. From February onwards, there is generally less rain and you can have good winter walking.

Getting there & around
With its remote beaches and villages, the Pembrokeshire coast is most easily explored by car. However, there are train services to Pembrokeshire stations including Haverfordwest, Fishguard and Tenby, run by Arrive Trains Wales (www.arrivatrainswales.co.uk).
Ask about the coastal shuttle bus between beaches and coastal paths (seasonal) and the West Wales Rover bus, 01437 776313, www.pembrokeshiregreenways.co.uk. For other bus services, see Firstcymru.co.uk.

Tourist information
Tenby Upper Park Road (01834 842404/ www.pembrokeshire.gov.uk). Open Winter 10am-4pm Mon-Sat. Summer 9.30am-5pm Mon-Sat; 10am-4pm Sun.
Newport John Frost Square (01239 820912/ www.pembrokeshire.gov.uk). Open 9.30am-6pm Mon-Thur; 9am-6pm Fri; 9am-5pm Sat.
St David's The Grove (01437 720392/www.st davids.co.uk). Open Winter 10am-4.30pm daily. Summer 9.30am 5.30pm daily.

Square & Compass;
Corfe Castle.

Poole & the Isle of Purbeck

Limestone cliffs, grassy heaths and a huge natural harbour.

Welcome to the lost world – if not quite the land that time forgot. Purbeck delights in being one end of the UK's World Heritage Jurassic Coast, partly, perhaps, because it's just about impossible to revel in any more distant past. In fact, everything pertaining to this small corner of Dorset seems to hark back to a lost age of innocence: from Hardy's characters roaming the local landscape, to Enid Blyton's Toyland, via Baden-Powell's boy scouts and the idealism of T E Lawrence, the sense of the past is all-pervasive. Yet Purbeck somehow avoids being twee or cloyingly nostalgic. That must have something to do with the solid rock on which it's founded, famously providing much of the stone for the streets of London, a prominent army presence, and – lest we forget – the sea.

Poole Harbour, one of the largest natural anchorages in the world, was the setting-off point for some of the ships that took part in the D Day landings; more recently it has launched at least a thousand luxury yachts. On the other side of the harbour from Poole, Wareham is the doughty old town on the Frome that must be wondering why its neighbour got all the dosh. Elsewhere, the area is defined by its limestone sea cliffs, chalk downlands, grassland heaths and sandy beaches. Not really an island, Purbeck nevertheless remains oddly off the beaten track, though it's actually only just over a couple of hours by train from London. Some 8,500 acres of its countryside and coast are in the care of the National Trust, including the wonderful beaches around Studland. There's a huge amount to explore: for geologists and historians; for rock-climbers, swimmers, windsurfers and hikers too. And it can even satisfy the most demanding sandcastlers. Happy days.

Explore

POOLE AND WAREHAM

Poole is a confusing place to approach by car, and unless you're careful, the one-way system will propel you into Bournemouth or beyond. At its core, alongside Poole Quay, is a charming old harbour town, currently caught somewhere between being a working port and ferry terminal – with services to the Channel Islands and France – and what locals like to call the 'Sandbanks Effect'. They're referring to the chi-chi spit of land at the mouth of Poole Harbour, effectively an extension of Bournemouth's beaches, where property values have apparently rivalled Manhattan's. The 'effect' has been developers' and estate agents' consequent attempts to turn Poole into St Tropez. No doubt these efforts will prove an early casualty of the credit crunch, and meanwhile there's much else here for visitors to enjoy: a stroll along the harbourside; a boat trip out to Brownsea island, where Baden-Powell founded the Scouting movement in 1907, or to the Isle of Wight, or up the river to Wareham; or even just following the unusually interesting Cockle Trail, a series of numbered scallop shells set in bronze on the pavements of the old town with an accompanying historical leaflet-guide (www.pooletourism.com).

The quay itself has been enhanced by a public art commission called Memory and the Tide Line, featuring landscaped pavements and quotations inscribed on the bollards: 'Twenty boys, mixed up like plums in a pudding,' said B-P of his early days with the Scouting movement on Brownsea Island in Poole Harbour, now a National Trust nature reserve with a population of endangered red squirrels.

The Cockle Trail leads past the grand old Custom House, down Thames Street, to the revamped **Poole Museum** (4 High Street, 01202 262600, www.boroughofpoole.com/museums). Here you'll find a logboat from 295 BC, the largest ever found in the south of England, and, on the first floor, displays about the town's ships and trade, the wildlife of the harbour.

Four miles west by water, eight by road, **Wareham** bills itself as a 'Saxon Walled Town'. It is indeed a fine old market town (the market is on Thursday). It is also notable for the beautiful Saxon church of **St Martin-on-the-Walls**, founded by St Aldhelm in the seventh century (services on Wednesday at 11am), and home to an effigy of TE Lawrence in Arab dress, sculpted by Eric Kennington. It was donated by Lawrence's brother in 1939, and was originally intended for Salisbury Cathedral. On the chancel wall is a 12th-century painting of St Martin of Tours, as a mounted Roman officer. There's more on Lawrence in the **Wareham Museum** (East Street, 01929 553448, www.warehammuseum.fsnet.co.uk, open summer only). Many visitors will also want to explore the town's lovely riverbank along the Frome.

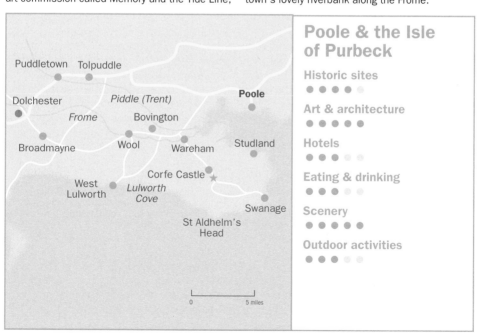

Poole & the Isle of Purbeck

Historic sites
● ● ● ● ●

Art & architecture
● ● ● ● ●

Hotels
● ● ● ● ●

Eating & drinking
● ● ● ● ●

Scenery
● ● ● ● ●

Outdoor activities
● ● ● ● ●

Map labels: Puddletown, Tolpuddle, Dolchester, Piddle (Trent), Poole, Frome, Bovington, Broadmayne, Wool, Wareham, Studland, Corfe Castle, West Lulworth, Lulworth Cove, Swanage, St Aldhelm's Head

0   5 miles

ISLE OF PURBECK

South of Wareham to the sea stretch the beautiful chalk downlands of the **Purbeck Hills**. A straight road leads across the gorsey heaths of Stoborough, Middlebere and Creech. From the Stoborough roundabout, a minor road makes for **Furzebrook** and the charming 1930s tearooms beside the **Blue Pool** (01929 551408, www.bluepooltearooms.co.uk, open Mar-Oct). The Pool is an old clay pit; a fine clay suspension in the water is responsible for the pool appearing in shades from green to turquoise according to the light. Once back on the main road, it's a straight route towards a gap in the hills that's guarded by the mighty medieval ruins of **Corfe Castle**, teetering atop their earthen mound. The village itself, a higgledy-piggledy, stone-built place, partly thanks to having cannibalised its castle after the Civil War, is very popular and makes a good gateway to the limestone uplands of the Isle of Purbeck proper.

Just before the village, the B3351 ducks under the **Swanage Railway** (see p234) and skirts the northern foot of the Downs for some five miles to **Studland**, where some of the best sandy beaches on the entire south coast can be found around Studland Bay. **Knoll Beach**, with its tasteful National Trust log cabin of a café, is the most typical. Studland village, supposedly the inspiration for Enid Blyton's Toyland in the Noddy books, is not much to look at, though the Norman chancel arches of its church of St Nicholas are well worth a look and the Manor Farm Tea Rooms (Ringwood Road, 01929-450411) does a brisk trade with walkers in the summer. Beyond the village, the sandy lakes of **Studland Heath** pull in thousands of migratory birds and the way-marked tracks only marginally fewer mountain bikers. An old chain ferry clanks its car-loads across to Sandbanks and Poole. And it's also here that the **South West Coast Path** begins, at South Haven Point, eventually leading all the way round Dorset, Devon and Cornwall to Minehead in Somerset on the Bristol Channel. The less ambitious could happily settle for its first few steps from here, entrancing walks leading round the Foreland or Handfast Point via the foaming chalk sea-stacks of Old Harry into the expanse of Swanage Bay.

Accessible, most appropriately, by steam train (see p234), at first glance **Swanage** itself could almost have just stepped out of the 1950s. In fact this charming old seaside resort has recently picked up the pace a little without losing very much of its dignity or independent character. The pier remains mercifully free of amusements, instead offering punters the opportunity to contribute to its upkeep and immortalise their visit with a commemorative plate on one of its planks – yours for about £40. It's also home to Divers Down (01929 423565, www.diversdown swanage.co.uk), the oldest scuba school in the UK, established in 1958, and the gents' loo comes complete with timeless marine sound effects. The pier overlooks the town's long sandy beach; visitors might also want to pop their heads into Jane Ramsay and Keith Roker's Quarr Gallery (17 High Street, 01929 475719, www.quarr art.com) to see some work by local artists, or the Art Hut (opposite the Stone Quay, Pier Approach, 07947 613430) for individual works by Antonia Phillips or Nina Camplin. The Owl Pottery (108 High Street, 01929 425850) is an attractive old house showcasing the hand-painted earthenware of Leslie Gibbons.

> "T E Lawrence, whose cottage can be visited at Clouds Hill, opined that 'the army is loathsome, Dorsetshire beautiful'."

A mile or so west of Swanage, the B3069 heads up through Langton Matravers, where a left turn down Durnford Drove (just before the Langton Matravers Scout and Guide HQ) leads to the car park for the lovely **Dancing Ledge**, a flat area of rock at the bottom of small cliff, from where quarrystone was once shipped: there's a tidal sea-swimming pool, blasted out of the rock of the raised beach by the quarrymen. It's about a mile from the car park, via **Spyway Barn**. A fairly arduous but wonderful walk leads on from here along the coast path via Seacombe and Winspit – where quarrying ceased as recently as 1960 – with their rocky little beaches, to **St Aldhelm's Head**, where there's a lonely Norman chapel and a coastguard lookout. The history of the local quarries, fossils and stone-carving is well illustrated and explained at the small museum of the **Square & Compass** pub in the idyllic village of Worth Matravers (see p238). The coast path, meanwhile, continues down steep steps to the eerie calm of **Chapman's Pool**, a proper little cove that often seems to be strangely full of seaweed, until it reaches **Kimmeridge Bay**, providing some of the most exciting windsurfing opportunities on the south coast, though really for experienced surfers only.

Corfe Castle

The Square, East Street (01929 481294/www. nationaltrust.org.uk). Open Summer 10am-6pm daily. Winter 10am-4pm daily. Admission £5.90; £2.95 reductions.

Huge fun to go scrambling around, Corfe Castle is a proper old ruined fortress and one of the most spectacularly sited in Britain. Built shortly after the Norman conquest in order to police the royal hunting forests of the Isle of Purbeck, it was extended by King John in the early 13th century. Bought by Sir John Bankes in the early 17th century, it was successfully held by his wife against parliamentarian forces during a first siege in the Civil War, and then fell through subterfuge in a second, whereupon it was dismantled. The Bankes family gave it to the National Trust, as part of the Kingston Lacy estate, in 1981.

Swanage Museum & Heritage Centre

Swanage *The Square, High Street (01929 421427/ www.swanagemuseum.co.uk). Open Easter-Oct 10am-1pm, 2-5pm. Admission free.*
A delightful little local museum with displays that focus on the landforms of the Jurassic Coast, on some of the local bigwigs that put Swanage on the map in the 19th century, and on the remarkable bits of London memorabilia that have ended up here, such as the bollards from London boroughs that were apparently carried as ballast in ships arriving to pick up Purbeck stone. There's also a small exhibition on the top secret Telecommunications Research Establishment at Worth Matravers during World War II, where pioneering progress was made in radar technology.

Swanage Railway

Swanage *Swanage Station, Station Road (01929 425800/www.swanagerailway.co.uk). Open Apr-Oct daily. Nov, Dec, Feb, Mar Sat, Sun & school holidays. Fares from £9 day return; £7 reductions.*
The railway provides a useful and very enjoyable ride on antique Southern Railways rolling stock, steaming through beautiful scenery from Norden, near Corfe Castle, to Swanage, calling at Corfe Castle, Harmans Cross, Herston Halt and Swanage. There's a bus link to Studland and Bournemouth, and the railway hopes eventually to link up a full service with the London mainline at Wareham. The Thomas the Tank Engine days are a very big hit with kids.

LULWORTH

From **Kimmeridge Bay** to **Lulworth Cove**, the Jurassic Coast really gets into its stride, though for some of the year it's out of bounds during the week, being used by the Ministry of Defence for target practice. The Lulworth Range Walks are some of the most beautiful in the south of England, thanks partly to the variety of flora and fauna left relatively undisturbed by the activities of soldiers compared to those of farmers. The walks are usually open at weekends throughout the year, and on weekdays during school holidays (at the MOD's discretion; observe the red warning flags). Particularly well worth the trek are **Worbarrow Tout**, beyond the deserted village of Tyneham, requisitioned during World War II and never given back, and **Bindon Hill** beyond, overlooking Mupe Bay.

 Lulworth Cove is one of the most famous beaches on the south coast, and in summer that can show: the lanes can be jammed and the car park full. But it's always worth the struggle to

reach this luminous crescent of a beach, sheltered beneath crumbling cliffs. You can embark at the Cove with White Motor Boats (01305 785000, www.whitemotorboat. freeuk.com) at 11.30am and be in Weymouth for lunch by 12.15pm. Also here, **Stair Hole** is a great lump of Portland stone that has been pounded by the sea over the centuries, creating a couple of sea caves at the bottom and a blow hole at the top, scooping out a trio of tiny cove-lets behind.

"The valleys inland from Lulworth are a treat to explore, full of strange surprises and bucolic villages with absurdly quaint names."

Further along the coast, and often appreciably less crowded, is the beach facing the limestone sea arch of **Durdle Door**, a surging portal beckoning strong swimmers to brave a circumnavigation. Dogs are welcome throughout the year, but must be kept on a lead.

Lulworth Castle & Park

East Lulworth *(0845 450 1054/www.lulworth.com). Open Apr-Sept 10.30am-6pm Mon-Fri, Sun (last admission 5pm). Oct-Mar 10.30am-4pm Mon-Fri, Sun (last admission 3pm). Admission £8.50; £4-£7 reductions.*
A castellated Jacobean hunting lodge built in 1608 where King Charles X of France stayed after landing in Weymouth, fleeing the July Revolution of 1830. The castle went up in smoke during a dramatic fire in 1929. Painstakingly restored by English Heritage, it now stages a wide variety of events throughout the year and is a fascinating place to explore, with fantastic views from the battlements. In the grounds is St Mary's Chapel, the first Roman Catholic church to be built since the Reformation, completed in 1789 on the condition, as George III put it to Cardinal Thomas Weld, that it was 'a mausoleum, furnished inside as you wish'. And sumptuous enough it is too.

FROME AND PIDDLE VALLEYS

The valleys inland from Lulworth are a treat to explore, full of strange surprises and bucolic villages with absurdly quaint names, notably the 'puddles' of the Piddle Valley: Turners Puddle, Briantspuddle, Affpuddle, Tolpuddle, and finally **Puddletown**, where the church of St Mary the Virgin has splendid old box pews (1634) and the marble tombs of the Martyns of Athelhampton. Hardy's grandfather backed up the choir with

St Aldhelm.

Square & Compass.

his cello here, and the church gets the novelist's full treatment in *Far From the Madding Crowd*, as the setting for the wedding of Gabriel Oak and Bathsheba. And you can see where Hardy wrote the novel, if you like, a short way west at Higher Bockhampton.

Tolpuddle is also redolent of those turbulent times: at a time of considerable unrest among agricultural labourers in the southern counties – the widespread 'Captain Swing' riots of 1830 had involved much machine-wrecking and even several deaths – it marks a very significant milestone in labour relations: the six men from here that were convicted of 'taking illegal oaths', though not the first trade unionists, aroused such popular sympathy that their deportation sentences were eventually commuted. Only one returned to England; the others quite reasonably preferred to try their luck in Canada, which they did with considerable success, as attested to by the number of their descendants who have visited Tolpuddle.

"Its wonderful clear-glass windows were beautifully engraved by Laurence Whistler after the originals were blown out by a stray Luftwaffe bomber."

The Frome Valley is wider and less cute than that of the Piddle, though less disturbed by the thunder of the A35. Instead, it's the thunder of tank fire, or of their engines, that is most likely to impinge on your day around here. T E Lawrence, whose cottage can be visited at **Clouds Hill** (*see below*), opined that 'the army is loathsome, Dorsetshire beautiful', and you might be tempted to agree. A Lawrence of Arabia Trail has been mapped out around these parts, taking in **Bovington** (where he worked) with its Tank Museum, and also **St Nicholas's Church** in Moreton, with its wonderful clear-glass windows beautifully engraved by Laurence Whistler over several decades after the originals were blown out by a stray Luftwaffe bomber. The grave of TE Lawrence can be found in the small cemetery beside the road in Moreton; on the advice of his mother, his last resting place makes no mention of Arabia, quoting instead the motto of Oxford University, in his home town, his student days being those that apparently filled her with most pride. The road where he came off his Brough

Superior motorbike and suffered fatal injuries in 1935 connects Bovington with Clouds Hill. A memorial stone has been placed in the Lawrence Memorial Car Park, where a viewing platform overlooks tanks on training exercises. Another memorial stone, deeper into the woods on the same side of the road, may be closer to the actual scene of the crash, but nobody seems to agree: yet another twist in the enigma surrounding the man.

Athelhampton House & Gardens

Athelhampton, 1 mile E of Puddletown *(01305 848363/www.athelhampton.co.uk). Open Mar-Oct 11am-4.30pm Mon-Thur, Sun. Nov-Feb 11am-4.30pm Sun. Admission £8.75; £5.75-£6.75 reductions.*

Called Athelhall by Hardy, Athelhampton has a tremendous 15th-century Great Hall and a Tudor Great Chamber in the west wing. The north wing was designed in sympathy with older parts of the building in the early 1920s, later receiving illustrious guests like Noel Coward and Douglas Fairbanks. The gardens are beautiful: the octagonal Cloister Garden, with its pleached lime tree 'pillars', has a central fountain that inspired the one in New Palace Yard, Westminster; the Pyramid Garden features extraordinary topiary obelisks. And the sound effects in the old dovecote are worth the price of admission in themselves.

Clouds Hill

Bovington *(01929 405616/www.nationaltrust.org.uk). Open Mar-Oct noon-5pm Thur-Sun. Closed Nov-Feb. Admission £4.50; £2 reductions.*

Here is the tiny tumbledown cottage where TE Lawrence retreated, under the pseudonyms of Ross or Shaw, with only partial success, from the glare of publicity that was the inevitable result of his being the only acceptable 'hero' of World War I. His efforts in Arabia were abortive in his opinion, and over the door he carved an ambiguous motto from Herodotus: OU ØPOVTIS or 'don't care'. Inside, a sanitised version of his domestic arrangements can be seen, including some of his old records and a gramophone player. Sleeping bags for himself and his eminent guests were labelled 'meum' and 'tuum'. Outside, the cottage is hidden behind thick laurel hedges.

Monkey World

Longthorns, 1 mile E of Bovington *(information 0800 456600/01929 462537/www.monkeyworld.org). Open July, Aug 10am-6pm daily (last entry 5pm). Sept-June 10am-5pm daily (last entry 4pm). Admission £10.50; £7.25-£8.75 reductions.*

As seen on TV, Monkey World has become one of the area's most popular attractions. Opened in 1987 by the late Jim Cronin with just nine chimps, there are now more than 160 primates living here in a 65-acre park, most of them rescued from much worse lives as photgraphers' props in Spain, lab experiments, or drug testers. Some still carry the scars: Cindy 'smokes' twigs because she was once worked in a nightclub. Others were drugged with heroin and had their teeth knocked out. But let's not frighten the children: if you don't mind the fact that it's still just a zoo, there's much to warm the heart here. The scatter feed is an amazingly gentle and considerate occasion, and big-eared baby Bart is quite frankly adorable. Kids also go a bundle on the Great Ape Adventure play area.

Tank Museum
Bovington *(01929 405096/www.tankmuseum.org).* *Open 10am-5pm daily. Admission £11; £7-£9 reductions.*
A £16 million refurb over the last five years has created much more space here, the first major capital investment ever in the Museum of the Royal Armoured Corps. Bovington is the country's only tank training centre, and this place honours the achievements of a very British invention. The Trench Experience recreates the first ever tank attack, on 15 September 1916, as a setting for the last surviving Mark I, complete with a soundtrack of fairly ludicrous German reactions and a soldier sobbing from shell shock. The Discovery Centre marshalls a huge variety of vehicles, from the oldest Sherman in the world to Cold War Chieftains and Centurions in the Tamiya Hall. The most exciting part of the collections is the Tank Story: showcasing 35 key tanks, antique and modern, from Little Willy in the corner, through British, German – yes, there's a Tiger – Russian and American machines to the Challenger 2. Particularly popular are the tanks in action outside, especially during June's Tank Fest, and some insights are provided into what a hellish job crewing these beasts must be.

Tolpuddle Martyrs Memorial Museum
Tolpuddle *(01305 848237/www.tolpuddle martyrs.org.uk). Open Apr-Oct 10am-5pm Tue-Sat; 11am-5pm Sun. Nov-Mar 10am-4pm Thur-Sat; 11am-4pm Sun. Admission free.*
The museum occupies a room in the memorial cottages built for the poor and needy in 1934 by the TUC, who at the same time brought electricity to the village. The story of the Tolpuddle Martyrs and their role in the history of the trades union movement is celebrated with wall displays providing a wealth of interesting information. In the village itself, the sycamore tree under which the labourers are said to have to have met can still be seen, as can several of their original cottages, now rather desirable private homes.

Eat

Surprisingly perhaps, considering the ample opportunity afforded by its local produce and the potential knock-on effect of Hugh Fearnley-Whittingstall's celebrated activities not much further west, near Bridport, Purbeck has yet fully to grasp the gourmet nettle. That said, all the restaurants listed below are well worth seeking out and there are quite a few decent enough fall-back options. For good snacks and cocktails in a buzzy atmosphere, head for the **Beach Point Snackbar** (10 High Street, Swanage, 01929 421253, www.snackbarswanage.co.uk), specialising in pizzas and cocktails. Also worth

a look is the **Ship Inn** (07932 819609, theship-swanage.co.uk) on the town's main square. In Puddletown, the **Blue Vinny** (12 The Moor, 0971 917 0007) does very decent pub grub that's reasonably priced.

Clavell's Café & Farm Shop
Kimmeridge, Isle of Purbeck *(01929 480701). Open Summer 8.30am-8.30pm daily. Winter 9am-5pm daily. £. British.*
Relaunched in early 2008 after a thorough refurbishment, the shop and café-restaurant in Kimmeridge's old post office stocks plenty of goodies to take away and cooks up a great lunch too. It's a long, low stone-built old cottage, with several tables outside. Dorset produce on offer includes Forest Products' range of jams and preserves, and honey from Field Honey Farm's hives near Swanage. In the café-restaurant, the owners serve up their own beef, and source lamb and pork from local farms.

Kemps Country House
East Stoke, 3 miles W of Wareham *(0845 862 0315/www.kempscountryhouse.co.uk). Open 7.30-9.30am, 6.30-9pm Mon-Fri; 8-10am, 6.30-9pm Sat, Sun. £££. Modern European.*
A restaurant that accomplishes very well what it sets out to do, in the capable hands of chef Max Allen. On a recent visit, a large group of businessmen was being capably served a full set dinner in the conservatory while the remainder of the restaurant, admittedly relatively quiet of a Monday night, continued to function perfectly normally. Deliciously tender roast shoulder of local lamb and a fantastic chocolate fondant dessert are typical culinary highlights; service is smiling. Good acoustics, too, for a relatively small dining room, and very comfortable, which obviously pleases regular punters, many of whom are over 60. *See also p240.*

Ocean Bay
Swanage, Isle of Purbeck *2 Ulwell Road (01929 422222/www.oceanbayrestaurant.com). Open 9-11.30am, noon-3pm, 7-9.30pm Mon-Thur, Sun; 9-11.30am, noon-3pm, 6.30-9.30pm Fri, Sat. £££. Modern European.*
Right on the beach, at the far end from the town, Ocean Bay has carved out a reputation for itself as one of Swanage's most accomplished restaurants. Dishes might include Swanage Bay dressed crab with toast or Dorset game pâté, followed by the likes of a superior fish and chips, a venison burger, or roast salmon fillet niçoise. All the tables have views of the sea, and children are happily accommodated. It becomes more sophisticated in the evenings (but still good value at £25 for three courses).

Olivers
Corfe Castle, Isle of Purbeck *5 West Street (01929 477111/www.oliverscorfecastle.co.uk). Open June-Sept 10am-9pm daily. Oct-May 10am-9pm Tue-Sat; 10am-5pm Sun. ££. Bistro.*
A pleasant little café, bistro and restaurant, in the old stone terrace of West Street, Olivers has a cheerful atmosphere in winter, thanks to its open fire, and remains fairly calm, cool and collected in summer, at the height of the season. The

Priory Hotel.

evening menu changes monthly, but is likely to feature seasonal local produce done simply and well, while during the day there's a wide choice of salads, 'gourmet sandwiches', baguettes and jacket potatoes. Definitely a useful place to have up your sleeve.

Square & Compass
Worth Matravers, Isle of Purbeck *(01929 439229). Open (food served) noon-3pm, 6-11pm Mon-Fri; noon-11pm Sat, Sun. £. No credit cards. Pub grub.*
Surely everyone's idea of a perfect country pub, the Square and Compass does everything that matters very well, in its own inimitable way, as it has done for more than a century under the ownership of the Newman family. It has fantastic views; a friendly collie dog; an exceptional variety of ciders and a few ales, pasties, and pies, all served through a hatch; two warm, dimly lit rooms in which to enjoy them; and an impressive museum of local fossil finds gathered together by the current landlord, Charlie Newman. There's a stone-carving festival held here most summers, with several works on display around the outside seating area.

Storm Fish
Poole *16 High Street (01202 674970/www.stormfish. co.uk). Open May-Oct noon-2.30pm, 7-9.30pm Mon-Fri; noon-2.30pm, 6-10pm Sat; 7-9.30pm Sun. Nov-Apr 7-9.30pm Tue-Sat (phone for lunch). ££££. Seafood/modern European.*
Bare brick walls, wooden tables and stripped floorboards create a loft-like but quite cosy effect in this popular local restaurant. As the name suggests, a lot of fish features on the menu, and it's all freshly caught and prepared, much of it apparently by the patron himself. The cooking aims to emphasise the freshness of the ingredients by avoiding over-complicated flavours and spicing. Vegetables are home-grown as often as possible, and the puddings have a loyal following among regulars. Starters nudge £10 and mains are almost twice as much.

Weld Arms
East Lulworth *(01929 400211/www.weldarms.co.uk). Open (food served) noon-2.30pm, 6-9.30pm daily. £££. Pub grub/modern European.*
With its hop-decorated old beams, tankards above the bar, old copper kettles on the shelves and model yacht on the mantelpiece, the Weld Arms is a warming and traditional old country pub that does above-average grub: sausage and mash, fish and chips, ham and eggs, as well as superior salads and the odd slightly more risky recipe are standard; the specials menu moves things up a notch, often with considerable success. Most importantly, though, the kitchen uses fresh produce from the surrounding area whenever possible. The beer's well kept and there's a huge garden, with plenty of room to eat outside. A further half-panelled dining room is furnished with simple pine furniture.

Yalbury Cottage
Lower Bockhampton, 3 miles E of Dorchester *(01305 262382/www.yalburycottage.com). Open 7-9pm Tue-Sat; 12.30-2pm Sun. (Dinner Sun, Mon for residents only). £££. Modern European.*

Ariana and Jamie Jones took over this tidy, quiet little cottage in 2007 and have transformed it into an accomplished restaurant with rooms. Jamie has worked with the Four Seasons hotel chain and knows how to get the best out of local, seasonal ingredients: the dinner menu might feature a 'cannon of Tolpuddle lamb' with local white pudding, swede cream, roast potatoes and garlic and rosemary sauce, or an organic pearled spelt and Dorset Down mushroom pie with celeriac purée and Dorset camembert fondue. Breakfasts are also pretty special; the rooms, some with field views, are cosy, comfortable and clean; and the Joneses also welcome dogs.

Stay

Burngate Farmhouse
West Lulworth *(01929 400783/www.burngate farm.co.uk) ££.*
Half an hour's walk inland from the coast at Durdle Door, close to Lulworth Camp, Burngate is a sturdy, stonebuilt old farmhouse, in part dating back to the Middle Ages. The chosen HQ of Rob da Bank and his crew for the first Camp Bestival at Lulworth Castle in 2008, it has three very comfortable first-floor double bedrooms – French beds, cotton sheets, plenty of books – all with their own bathrooms. Guests are also welcome to use the large sitting room downstairs, with its wood-burning stove, mags, TV and generous sofas, where they might even be joined by Guinness, the cheerful pointer belonging to proprietors Sophie and David Weld-Davies. Lifts to the pub are all part of the service, though not after midnight, wedding guests should take note. Exceptionally good breakfasts are served in the dining room: homemade bread, kippers from Bideford, and Dorset oats in the porridge.

Hotel du Vin & Bistro
Poole *Thames Street, the Quay (01202 785570/ www.hotelduvin.com). £££.*
The du Vin & Bistro hotels have successfully developed a style that appeals to a wide variety of folk: this one, relatively new, occupies a grand old mansion built in the late 18th century for Newfoundland cod traders Isaac and Benjamin Lester. The site is fairly cramped, so don't expect wonderful sea views. Instead, the 33 rooms are all modern and comfortable, with French beds and Plasma TV/DVDs. Those designated deluxe have free-standing roll-top baths in the bedroom, possibly not to everyone's taste, though the beauty mirror on the wooden soap racks is a nice touch. All rooms have monsoon showers. Downstairs, the bar has both snug and breezy areas, cunningly conceived outdoor seating – in the car park, though it's not that obvious – along with the du Vin brand's signature Cigar Shack.

Kemps Country House
East Stoke, 3 miles W of Wareham *(0845 862 0315/www.kempscountryhouse.co.uk). £££.*
At first glance it may look like a souped-up motel, but it's worth giving Kemps some time. The rooms in the annexe,

largely responsibly for that first impression, are all completely inoffensive and extremely comfortable. The six rooms on the ground floor have large bathrooms and underfloor heating; those above, designated Purbeck View, are smaller, but hardly less well appointed. In the old house, the Champagne Room is a symphony in white, and comes complete with a variety of added extras. The bar is an old-fashioned sort of place, boasting a 45rpm Wurlizter jukebox that's big on Roy Orbison, Elvis Presley, Bill Haley and the Beatles. It all may appeal largely to those of more advanced years, but then again, as we all know, they appreciate the good things in life. *See also p238.*

Longthorns Farm Campsite
Longthorns, 1 mile E of Bovington, Wareham
(01929 401539/www.longthornsfarm.co.uk). £.
Close to Monkey World and the Tank Museum, meaning that you might well be woken in the morning by the hoot of gibbons or the rumble of tanks, this friendly campsite has a great atmosphere, partly thanks also to the presence of its 18ft tipis. They can sleep up to six, though four might be more comfortable, complete with futons, a fully equipped cookhouse and basic honesty shop. In fact, you're only expected to need to bring your own bedding, food and drink for a tipi stay. Tents and caravans are also welcome and it's a working farm, which is lots of fun for the children.

Park Lodge
East Lulworth *(01929 400546/www.park-lodge.co.uk). ££.*
This extraordinary old stone tower of a house on the edge of Lulworth Castle's park – you can just see the castle's chapel over a distant ridge – probably dates from the 17th century. It has been both a farmhouse and a gamekeeper's house in its time but looks as though it was destined to be part of something much more impressive. Guests get to stay in the roof, up a steep and wide old wooden staircase, where there are two rooms, simply furnished and perfectly clean, one with a free-standing roll-top bath in the corner. There's a quirky little sitting area on the landing, while breakfast is served downstairs in the dining room, with its huge fireplace, log-burning stove, and stone-mullioned windows. All in all, Park Lodge has got a lot of character, and Hennie Weld runs the place with enthusiasm and charm.

Priory Hotel
Wareham *Church Green (01929 551666/ www.theprioryhotel.co.uk). ££££.*
A defiantly old-fashioned, family-run hotel that does things in a way that was once much more normal. Guests are expected to dress up for dinner, no children are allowed, a piano tinkles away on Saturday nights and there'll probably be sherry on the lawn. It occupies a superb position right next to Wareham's church, with a south-facing terrace and garden sloping down to its own river frontage. A recently refurbished annexe in the old stone-walled boathouse features upstairs rooms fitted with jacuzzi baths. In Mallard, guests have their own back door. It's generally blissfully quiet – bar the odd church bell or several – with a real fire, baby grand, and comfortable sofas in the sitting room. The smart restaurant in the old cellar manages to maintain the illusion of those glory days of yore, not always for entirely the right reasons when it comes to the cooking.

Factfile

When to go
Summer is much the busiest time in Purbeck, with prices and crowds reflecting that fact. Between 15 March and 30 September, for example, the double yellow lines prohibiting parking in the quieter country lanes are strictly enforced. Dogs are unrestricted on the beaches, too, from October through April; they must be kept on leads in May, June and September in order to protect nesting birds; and are banned from several beaches in July and August. At Lulworth Cove, car parking charges apply from 7am to 7pm, and they're pricey: £2.50 for up to two hours, £4 for up to four, £5 for longer, with no overnight parking except at Durdle Door, where it's £20. Weather is generally fairly dry, often blissful in spring and autumn, hot in summer, and wild, with any luck, in winter.

Getting there
Poole is a two-hour express train ride from London Waterloo. By road, take the M3 to Southampton, then the M27 and A31 towards Bournemouth and Poole; the journey usually takes about three hours. Swanage is more like four hours from London.

Getting around
Though a car is undeniably the most convenient way to explore Purbeck, the area is actually quite well served by public transport, with mainline train stations at Wool, Wareham and Poole, and regular bus services serving Poole, Wareham, Swanage and Corfe Castle.

Tourist offices
Poole Tourist Information Poole Welcome Centre, Enefco House, Poole Quay, Poole (01202 253253/www.pooletourism.com). Open 10am-5pm Mon-Sat (plus 10am-4pm Sun in summer). Recorded information at other times.

Internet
Southcoast Cafe 345 Ashley Road, Poole (01202 741090).

Left: Amberley; right: Arundel Cathedral; bottom: Arundel Wildfowl & Wetlands Trust.

West Sussex

Lush downland, gentle beaches – a dose of southern comfort.

When William Blake wrote his preface to *Milton a Poem* in 1804, he had no idea that 117 years later his lines would become the hymn 'Jerusalem'. It was his West Sussex home of Felpham that inspired the words: 'And did those feet in ancient time/Walk upon England's mountains green/And was the holy Lamb of God/On England's pleasant pastures seen.' West Sussex is still the epitome of 'pleasant', a part of England that makes even hardened city dwellers go misty-eyed with quasi-nostalgia for the quaint old villages hidden among the lush folds of the South Downs, the 16th-century coaching inns and the well-preserved Norman churches. Over on the sheltered coastline, the sands of West Wittering are as popular with children and holiday-makers as with the abundant bird-life. And the area has more than 2,500 miles of public footpath, traversing countryside cluttered with wild flowers, dry-stone walling, flint cottages and fine pubs. Despite the large amount of grass downland, this is one of the most heavily wooded counties in England. More than half of it, including Chichester Harbour, the Sussex Downs and the High Weald to the north, is designated an Area of Outstanding Natural Beauty.

   While history suffuses the landscape in the shape of fine cathedrals, castles and stately homes, modern wealth has brought a very 21st-century kind of luxury, in the form of spas, five-star hotels and Michelin-starred restaurants, all of which make West Sussex's green and pleasant land a prime getaway destination – less than a couple of hours from London.

Explore

CHICHESTER AND AROUND

In many ways **Chichester** is the archetypal English cathedral city, but as the cry of seagulls will remind you, the water is not far away. The Romans founded the settlement in AD 70, and laid out the street plan with impeccable logic: North, South, East and West Streets slice the city neatly into four areas. The cathedral dominates the south-west sector, while the finest of the Georgian buildings are in the south-eastern district known as the Pallants. The fine Pallant House Gallery (*see p249*) holds a well-curated collection of 20th-century art.

By the cathedral and the main shopping area is a Tudor-era market cross surrounded by seats for weary shoppers. Much of the town's Georgian style has been maintained in the tasteful façades of the usual high street shops, but there are still plenty of small boutiques, sumptuous chocolate shops and some excellent restaurants and cafés. During June and July, the Chichester Festival Theatre (Oaklands Park, 01243 781312, www.cft.org.uk) hosts the prestigious Chichester Festival. The theatre also programmes a range of ballet, opera and drama throughout the year. Just west of Chichester is **Fishbourne** Roman Palace, the largest Roman residence unearthed in Britain.

One of the most attractive places in the area is the picturesque village of **Bosham** (pronounced 'Bozzum'), four miles west of Chichester. It extends right down to the water's edge and the road here is passable only at low tide. Many of the houses have a high step to the front door, evidence of past floods. Bosham's history as a fishing port dates back to Roman times, when the Emperor Vespasian allegedly had a residence here. Today, traces of this history can be found in the simple Saxon church, which includes stones from the original Roman basilica along with a truly beautiful arched chapel in the crypt. A stone coffin discovered in the church in the 19th century contained a child's body, thought to have been the daughter of the Viking king, Canute. This, legend dictates, is the spot where he tried to turn back the tide, although some say it was at Hamwich, near Southampton.

From Bosham there is a pleasant walk around to Bosham Hoe, where a short ferry ride has, for centuries, saved travellers a 13-mile walk around the coast to the pretty village of West Itchenor. South from here are the coastal towns of the Witterings (*see p250*).

North of Chichester, the flat coastal plain rises gently into the **South Downs**, perhaps the most beautiful part of West Sussex. Walkers, riders and mountain bikers rhapsodise about the 100-mile South Downs Way, the oldest long-distance footpath in Britain, stretching from Winchester to Eastbourne. The 30-mile section that passes through West Sussex, from South Harting to Storrington, would take two or three leisurely

West Sussex

Historic sites
● ● ● ● ○

Art & architecture
● ● ● ● ●

Hotels
● ● ● ○ ○

Eating & drinking
● ● ● ○ ○

Scenery
● ● ● ● ○

Outdoor activities
● ● ● ○ ○

(Map labels: Midhurst, Petworth, Singleton, Charlton, Amberley, Goodwood, Burpham, Chichester, Arundel, Bosham, Fishbourne, Littlehampton, Itchenor, Felpham, West Wittering, Bognor Regis)

0   5 miles

Left & bottom: West
Wittering; right: Bosham.

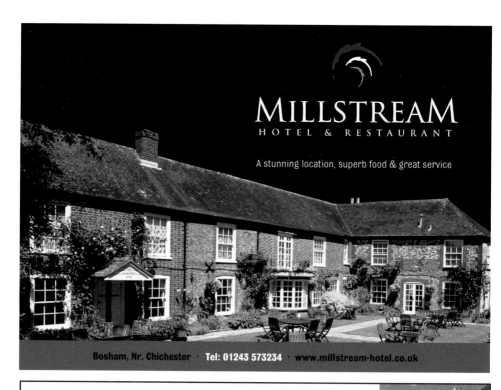

days to walk, but there are plenty of shorter routes to give a taste of the sweeping views and captivating woodland (see the *South Downs Way National Trail Guide* by Paul Millmore).

Spreading out from the main (but still narrow) road north towards Midhurst are several notable attractions, impossibly quaint villages and some of the best pubs in Sussex, such as the Fox Goes Free (*see p251*) and the Duke of Cumberland (*see p250*).

"The highlight is a stained-glass window made by the Russian modernist Marc Chagall in 1978."

Singleton houses the Weald & Downland Open Air Museum (01243 811363, www.weald down.co.uk), an unusual collection of 40 historic buildings on 40 acres of land that have been rescued, rebuilt and restored to offer a fascinating journey through life in the region over the past 500 years. Nearby are the West Dean Gardens (01243 818210, www.westdean.org. uk), enjoyed by those with a horticultural bent. The kitchen garden here includes Victorian greenhouses with fig and peach trees and grapevines; there's also a long pergola in the 35 acres of ornamental grounds, an arboretum and a restaurant. To the east is the village of **Charlton**, home of the Fox Goes Free pub.

From here it is only a couple of miles to **Goodwood**, where Goodwood House and Goodwood Racecourse (01243 755022, www.goodwood.co.uk) are set in an Area of Outstanding Natural Beauty. The red-letter race days are 'Glorious Goodwood', five days of racing heaven in July. The Glorious Goodwood Festival is just one part of a race season that starts in May and runs until October (course opens 11am, racing begins 12.15pm, and seven races are scheduled each day). However, it is without question the calendar's highlight. Goodwood's edge is its unique relaxed atmosphere. Where other racing events call for a strict dress code, the vibe here is very much panamas and linen suits, and while everyone makes an effort, ladies don't have to wear hats, even on Ladies Day. Meanwhile, the Goodwood Revival weekend in September sees a rally of the world's finest vintage vehicles. There's vintage clothing too: if you like your fashion from the 1950s or '60s, this is the place to show it off. Thousands flock to Goodwood for the weekend, dressed to the nines in stunning period outfits. Starting from 9am on

Friday and 10am on Saturday and Sunday, races run until around 6pm; there's the added bonus of a free shuttle bus from Chichester station.

East of the agreeable little market town of **Midhurst** is the 17th-century mansion Petworth House (*see p249*). JMW Turner was a regular guest here, and the artistic collection is still the main reason to visit, although 700 acres of gorgeous park inhabited by deer is a major bonus.

Chichester Cathedral
Chichester *West Street (01243 782595/www. chichestercathedral.org.uk). Open Summer 7.15am-7pm daily. Winter 7.15am-6pm daily. Admission free.*
The magnificent cathedral was built by the Normans and consecrated in 1108. Since then, numerous buildings have been added, including the cloisters, which now house a café. Volunteers are on hand around the cathedral to answer questions about its turbulent 900-year history, and free tours are provided at 11.15am and 2.30pm Monday to Saturday. Informative plaques explain the most important pieces. The cathedral is known for artistic works, such as the fabulous stained-glass windows, John Skelton's stone and copper font, Graham Sutherland's painting *Noli Me Tangere* and a tapestry designed by John Piper in 1966. The highlight is a stained-glass window made by the Russian modernist Marc Chagall in 1978. The Shrine of St Richard (canonised in 1262) was venerated by pilgrims until Henry VIII destroyed it in 1533, but pilgrims have returned in recent times. The cathedral holds a forward-thinking series of concerts, exhibitions and talks.

Fishbourne Roman Palace
Fishbourne, 2 miles W of Chichester *Salthill Road (01243 785859/www.sussexpast.co.uk). Open Jan 10am-4pm Sat, Sun. Feb, Nov, Dec 10am-4pm daily. Mar-July, Sept, Oct 10am-5pm daily. Aug 10am-6pm daily. Admission £7.30; £3.80-£6.50 reductions.*
Fishbourne Roman Palace was probably once the finest residence north of the Alps. Only rediscovered in 1960 by Professor Sir Barry Cunliffe, it was constructed in the first century AD for King Tiberius Claudius Togidubnus and contained around 100 rooms. The foundations of a quarter of them can still be seen, partly protected in the north wing. There are at least 20 marvellous mosaics, including the well-known *Cupid on a Dolphin*. The garden has been replanted, and contains a museum of gardens. The Collections Discovery Centre houses a large archaeological hoard.

Goodwood House
Goodwood, 4.5 miles NE of Chichester *(01243 755040/www.goodwood.co.uk/house). Open Apr-July, Sept 1-5pm Mon, Sun. Aug 1-5pm daily. Admission £9; £4-£7.50 reductions.*
The beautifully restored Regency mansion is on the immense Goodwood Estate. The house is still the home of the Dukes of Richmond, who have lived on the site for 300 years, but is often open to the public. The State Apartments include paintings of London by Canaletto, pieces from the horse artist George Stubbs and several Van Dyck portraits. One highlight is Napoleon Bonaparte's campaign chair. The

Duke of Cumberland.

public are allowed to walk around the estate, which includes a sculpture garden (01243 538449, www.sculpture.org.uk, closed Dec-Feb), and visit the famous racecourse.

Pallant House Gallery
Chichester *9 North Pallant (01243 774557/ www.pallant.org.uk). Open 10am-5pm Tue, Wed, Fri, Sat; 10am-8pm Thur; 12.30-5pm Sun, bank hols. Admission £7.50; £2.30-£4 reductions.*
This modern gallery has an outstanding collection of 20th-century British art, hosting works by Henry Moore, Peter Blake, Bridget Riley, Lucian Freud, Walter Sickert and Graham Sutherland. The gallery was voted Museum of the Year in 2007 for its ample permanent collection and exciting contemporary art shows. The extensive bookshop specialises in modern British art and has a large selection of rare out-of-print books. There's a restaurant too; Field & Fork serves high-quality cakes, snacks and meals, all using regional and seasonal ingredients.

Petworth House & Park
Petworth, 6.5 miles E of Midhurst *(01798 342207/www.nationaltrust.org.uk). Open (house) Mar-Oct 11am-5pm Mon-Wed, Sat, Sun. Admission £10.40; £5.20 reductions.*
Petworth House holds the National Trust's finest collection of art and sculpture. The third Lord Egremont was an art lover and in the early 1800s often invited JMW Turner and William Blake to the estate. There are 19 of Turner's paintings, many depicting the mansion and surrounding landscape, including the celebrated *Egremont Sea Piece* and a view of the new Chichester Canal. The collection, which includes scores of other old masters, provides one of the best insights into Regency taste in art, architecture and landscaping. The Countess of Egremont was a patron of William Blake, whose incredible illustration for Milton's *Paradise Lost, Satan Calling up his Legions* hangs here.

ARUNDEL AND AROUND
Seen from across the river, **Arundel**, with its castle and church at the top of the hill and the river along the bottom, looks more like a stage set for a medieval period drama than a real town. Even the town centre, with its refreshing lack of high street stores (kept out by antiques shops, fashion boutiques and tea shops), seems to hark back to another age. It's easy to understand why visitors in search of Ye Olde Englande are so drawn to the place. During the summer, coach parties descend on the small town, but it somehow manages to retain a laid-back charm, and in the off-season (when the castle is closed) the streets seem almost empty. It's hard to imagine that as late as the 1920s Arundel was still a working port with large ships steaming up the river.

The main attraction is the truly beautiful **Arundel Castle**, and the fascinating and informative exhibits within its walls. But a wander around the locality reaps other delights. The Catholic Arundel Cathedral (Parsons Hill,

01903 882297, www.arundelcathedral.org) was built in 1873 and is Joseph Hansom's take on French Gothic. It somewhat overshadows St Nicholas's (London Road, 01903 882262, www.stnicholas-arundel.co.uk) across the road, but this gorgeous church (which according to the sign was rebuilt in 1380) is certainly worth a look around.

> "The castle is definitely worth exploring for its fine collections of paintings by Van Dyck, Gainsborough and Reynolds among others."

The other notable attraction in the area is the **Arundel Wildfowl & Wetlands Trust** (Offham, South Stoke, 01903 883355, www.wwt.org.uk), which extends over 60 acres of parkland and lakes and is visited by thousands of migratory birds. It is best seen on a boat safari.

From Arundel, it's only a short drive to **Amberley**, also accessible via the river courtesy of Arun Cruises (Arundel Boat Yard or Town Quay, 01903 882609, www.riveraruncruises.com). The village is home to the 36-acre Amberley Working Museum (01798 831370, www.amberley museum.co.uk), which traces the working heritage of the region with the help of numerous craftsmen who demonstrate everything from blacksmithing to clay-pipe making. Exhibits include a narrow-gauge railway and a vintage bus collection.

South-west of Arundel is the town of **Littlehampton**. *Vogue* may have hailed it as the 'coolest British seaside resort' in 2007, but many who visit struggle to believe the hype; the place still has some way to go before it becomes the Sussex equivalent of Kent's Whitstable. Yet herein lies the appeal for many: with its pretty coastline, faded promenade, colourful beach huts and old-school fairground, the place has held on to a ramshackle charm. Add in the East Beach and West Beach cafés – a pair of architecturally striking, and, in the case of the East Beach Café (*see p252*), gastronomically lauded seafront eateries, and Littlehampton has the makings of a foodie destination. Traditionalists need not fret however; there are still plenty of retro chippies in town.

Further west along the coast is the village of **Felpham**. Felpham's most famous former resident is William Blake, who penned his epic work *Milton a Poem* during the four years he spent here between 1800 and 1804. In his preface to *Milton* (1804) Blake wrote what became the hymn 'Jerusalem'. He described Felpham as the 'sweetest spot on earth' and 'more spiritual than London'. His thatched cottage can be seen on what is now known as Blake's Road.

Arundel Castle

Arundel *(01903 882173/www.arundelcastle.org). Open Apr-July, Sept, Oct 10am-5pm Tue-Sun (last admission 4pm). Aug 10am-5pm daily (last admission 4pm). Admission £7-£15; £7-£12.50 reductions.*

The imposing castle was built in the 11th century by Roger de Montgomery, but massively remodelled in the 18th and 19th centuries. Now the seat of the Duke of Norfolk and Earl of Arundel, the castle is definitely worth exploring (despite the high admission price) for its fine collections of paintings by Van Dyck, Gainsborough and Reynolds among others, as well as its tapestries and furniture, and the gorgeous Fitzlan Chapel. The fabulous gardens were opened by the Prince of Wales in 2008 and are a tribute to Thomas Howard, 14th Earl of Arundel (1585-1646), known as 'the Collector'. An organic kitchen garden has been re-created, but the over-the-top decorations are based on what 'the Collector' is thought to have enjoyed at Arundel House in London. Guided tours of the castle and gardens can be organised in advance, but there are guides in most rooms.

"The pub used to be popular with World War II Hurricane pilots based nearby."

WEST WITTERING & AROUND

Around eight miles south-west of Chichester, the twin villages of **East** and **West Wittering** offer basic facilities, but the attraction for most visitors is the long sandy beach. The gently shelving sands and shallow, sun-warmed tidal pools make an ideal destination for families. The area is sheltered by the Isle of Wight and the South Downs, and so enjoys a benign microclimate that earns it the sobriquet 'God's pocket' among locals (who include the Rolling Stones' guitarist Keith Richards). The beaches in this area are popular no matter what the weather, and the coast has become a top destination for windsurfers, kite surfers (West Wittering Windsurf Club, 01243 513077, www.2xs.co.uk) and wind-pulled sand buggys (www.westwitteringsbuggyclub.co.uk).

Despite the adventure sports, the main sandy Blue Flag beach is tranquil. During summer, bathers potter about at the edge of the sea: a vast, shimmering expanse, broken only by the yacht sails on the Solent. Even on blustery days,

there's a chance the sun will be shining, and if not, you can celebrate your solitude with fortifying cups of hot chocolate from the beach café. At low tide, a quarter of a mile of fine, softly sloping sand emerges, along with shallow tidal pools and a sandbar-sheltered lagoon. In warm weather, children paddle and drift in dinghies in the smaller pools, while the bigger tidal lagoon is ideal for a sedate (and warmer) swim.

Inviting as West Wittering's clean sands and calm waters may be, that's only half the story. At the western end of the beach is **East Head**, where shifting sand dunes, salt marshes and a shingle spit marks the entrance to Chichester Harbour. The area possesses a desolate beauty and is a haven for wildlife, including Harper seals that swim across to Thorney Island to bask in the winter sun. Coastal foragers here will find pearl-lined slipper limpet shells, razor clams, cockles and whelks too.

Thanks to a group of enterprising locals, who pooled resources and bought the beach and surrounding grassland in 1952 to save it from developers, the inland vista is unspoilt. Behind a row of colourful beach huts, the wide sloping dunes and a 20-acre swathe of grassland are occupied by a vast array of bird-life (such as ringed plovers that nest among the spiky marram grass) and, in early summer, purple lavender. The grassland is also home to silver spiny digger wasps – one of the reasons the area has been designated a Site of Special Scientific Interest (SSSI), protected by the National Trust.

The beach's sole concession to commercialism is a beach shop (with windsurf hire), the café, and takeaway hatches. Most people bring a picnic or spark up a barbecue. In West Wittering village, about half a mile inland, is the Old House at Home pub (01243 511234, www.oldhouse pub.co.uk), which has a large pub and seafood menu. The Beach House (01243 514800, www.beachhse.co.uk) is a bright B&B (with spacious rooms) and restaurant. Claim a table on its wooden veranda and order some local marine life: English Channel black bream or beer-battered fish and chips.

Where East Head meets the mainland, a footpath meanders along the edge of the marshland and around the harbour to the sailing village of **Itchenor**. Along the way is the green triangle of Snow Hill Common and the diminutive, white-painted row of old coastguard's cottages, built to deter 18th-century smugglers. Setting out from Itchenor, summer boat trips explore the harbour. The footpath stretches onwards to **Chichester Marina**. Here the red-brick Ship Inn (The Street, 01243 512284, www.theshipinn.biz) beckons, with its locally brewed real ales and its local fish and chips and seafood dishes. The pub used to be popular with World War II Hurricane pilots based nearby.

Sparkling Sussex

English wine is no longer a joke, and – with English sparklers bubbling their way to the top in international competitions – that's official.

'English sparkling wines are among the best in the world, and the dry whites are also excellent, says Ben Furst, tour manager with English Vine Tours. 'They are competing with French champagnes and winning... regularly.'

Indeed, in the prestigious International Wine Challenge in 2008, England won 22 medals including a gold for a sparkling rosé. That most of the English winners were from Sussex and Kent should come as no surprise: the chalk and subsoil strata from this area dips under the English Channel and emerges just around the Champagne region of France.

English Vine Tours (01323 732001/ www.englishvinetours.co.uk) is the first British company to offer tours taking in a variety of vineyards in Kent and Sussex. At each, visitors are given an insightful tour explaining the winemaking process and then plied with samples of the product. Producers who open their vineyards to the public include Bookers (www.bookersvineyard. co.uk), Carr Taylor (www.carr-taylor.co.uk), Nutbourne (www.nutbournevineyards.com) and Nyetimber (www.nyetimber.com), along with Kent producers Chapel Down(www. englishwinesgroup.co.uk) and Biddenden (www.biddendenvineyards.com). Many of these growers also offer their own tours and tastings.

The problem for British wine producers has historically been the weather, but with the climate becoming milder, eyes are on the south coast of England for the next generation of vineyards. Even French growers are beginning to buy up land here. It's hard to imagine this stood next to a bare vine on a wet, cold and blustery winter's day in deepest Sussex, but the British climate is almost perfect for growing sparkling wines.

'We produce only what the summer produces for us,' David Harrison of Carr Taylor Vineyard explains. 'But we have the right temperature and in the Wealden clay and sandstone, a mineral-rich soil.'

It is a climate suited only to white wines, but none of the grape varieties grown are easily recognisable, and Teutonic names such as schönburger, reichensteiner, müller-thurgau and huxelrebe lend a clue as to their provenance. Proven on the chilly banks of the Rhine, these crisp, fruity varieties have been

grown in England since the 1970s – although grape-growing in this country actually dates back to Roman times.

This is still an industry very much in its infancy. England is not a big-league producer on the world stage – we currently loiter in 63rd position, just below Ethiopia. But the small-scale nature of English winemaking does have its advantages, allowing producers to concentrate on quality. It has also been the mother of invention, as producers have found novel ways to diversify. Many of the wineries also make ciders and excellent fruit wines, but Carr Taylor has launched the first wine that has been blended specifically to go with curry and spicy foods. 'The sweetness and higher alcohol aids in cooling the heat of the curry and spice down whilst enhancing the flavours,' claims Ben Furst.

Eat

The food at **West Stoke House** (*see p255*) has earned a Michelin star.

Duke of Cumberland

Henley, 3 miles N of Midhurst *(01428 652280). Open (food served) noon-2pm, 7-9pm Tue-Sat; noon-2pm Sun. £££. Gastropub.*

This wonderfully isolated pub (just east of the A286) is well known for its fresh fish (sometimes from the trout stream out back) and pints of prawns, but the menu is more ambitious. Cauliflower and tuna choux pastry buns, and pan-fried salmon with cabbage parcels, is the sort of food that might feature. There is also a 'garden menu' of snacky lunch dishes like ploughmans and salads: the garden itself is a miniature wonderland of ponds and paths. Interesting puddings include Drambuie and oatmeal bavarois, or strawberry, elderflower and champagne terrine. English wines like the local Nyetimber are also sold. With a log fire in winter and many well-kept ales poured directly from their casks, the Duke is a perfect place to idle away an afternoon.

East Beach Café

Littlehampton *Sea Road (01903 731903/www.east beachcafe.co.uk). Open Summer 10am-5pm, 6.30-9pm daily. Winter 10am-2.30pm Mon-Wed, Sun; 10.30am-2.30pm, 6.30-8.30pm Thur-Sat.*

Designed by visionary architect Thomas Heatherwick, this striking, shell-like construction is home to a fresh and functional café. The exterior's organic, sculptural form is matched with an interior that is more boutique restaurant than beachside café, with a quirky curved white ceiling, smart navy decking and floor-to-ceiling windows with dramatic sea views. The menu runs from simple classics such as beer-battered fish to imaginative seafood dishes like mussel, gurnard and salmon saffron chowder, all made under the watchful eye of Ritz-trained head chef David Whiteside. The ambience is buzzing.

Fox Goes Free

Charlton *(01243 811461/www.thefoxgoesfree.com). Open (restaurant) noon-2.30pm, 6.30-10pm Mon-Fri; noon-10pm Sat, Sun. £££. Pub.*

A contender for the loveliest pub in West Sussex, this 300-year-old inn takes its name from William III's stopovers while on hunting trips to the Goodwood Estate that it borders. These days, the low dark-timbered nooks and large garden on the rolling hills of the South Downs play host to families and friends enjoying some locally produced pints (including a couple brewed by the pub), perhaps over a game of Trivial Pursuit by the log fire, or some excellent food. The menu features dishes such as South Down lamb shank with braised cabbage, wild mushroom risotto, or roast partridge, shot in the area; there's a bar menu of pub grub too. The Fox also has five rooms for B&B. .

George & Dragon

Burpham, 3.5 miles NE of Arundel *The Main Street (01903 883131/www.burphamgeorgeanddragoninn.com).*

Open (restaurant) noon-2pm, 6.30-9.30pm Mon-Fri; noon-3pm, 6.30-9.30pm Sat, Sun. £££. Gastropub.

Take a winding downland road from Arundel and you'll find this quaint little village (pronounced 'burfam'), complete with a rose-clad lychgate in front of the 12th-century flint church (writer and illustrator Mervyn Peake is buried in the churchyard). Just up the lane beyond the pub is a cricket pitch occupying an Anglo-Saxon hill fort that once guarded the Arun River. The pub – once used by smugglers to divide the spoils that came up the river – is 300 years old, and has an 18th-century spinning jenny set in its ceiling. In its food menu, the George & Dragon leans more towards a restaurant than a pub. Modern European dishes are served in the elegant dining room: the likes of grilled green-lip mussels with garlic, lemon and thyme crust as a starter, followed by pan-roasted lamb, or stilton- and celery-crusted cod fillet for main course. Excellent thick-cut sandwiches are available from the bar and there are several tables dedicated to drinkers (beers come from Arundel Brewery).

St Martin's Organic Tea Rooms

Chichester *3 St Martin's Street (01243 786715/www.organictearooms.co.uk). Open 10am-6pm Mon-Fri; 9am-6pm Sat. ££. No credit cards. Café.*

In a higgledy-piggledy medieval terraced house with an 18th-century façade, this highly popular tearoom and café is a delightful option for wholesome snacks and lunches. The building was renovated in 1975 by the current owners, yet remains a charming labyrinth. A range of carefully prepared, organic and mostly vegetarian dishes is served: soups, salads, quiches, risottos and the best welsh rarebit ever. A selection of tempting cakes and desserts (apple crumble, banana and walnut loaf) adds a sweet touch. There's a pleasant courtyard for sunny weather, but the peaceful vibe inside makes for an enjoyable hour or two over a pot of loose tea.

Stay

See also **Fox Goes Free** *above.*

Amberley Castle

Amberley, 5 miles N of Arundel *(01798 831992/www.amberleycastle.co.uk). ££££.*

This astonishing hotel is housed in a mansion within the crenellated walls and moat of a medieval castle. Buildings on the site date back to 1103, when Bishop Ralph de Luffa (who also oversaw the building of Chichester Cathedral) ruled over the area. Since then, Henry VII, Charles II and the Queens Elizabeth I and II have all stayed the night. As a royalist stronghold, Amberley Castle was high on Cromwell's list of places to destroy. Fortunately, though, much of the original fortifications remain. A sense of history charges the hotel's atmosphere. Tapestries, ancestral portraits, furniture and weapons hang from the walls, and suits of armour look as though they're about to walk away. The rooms are superb, featuring four-poster beds, roaring

West Stoke House.

Amberly House

fires in winter and antique furniture. Service is unobtrusive and flawless. The restaurant's talented head chef, James Duggan, creates modern twists on British classics. (You'll need to dress up – jacket and tie for men.) The grounds include a tree-house by the main gates – it can be hired for a dinner for two, a tennis court, an 18-hole putting green and strolling peacocks. To add to the overall effect, the portcullis is still ceremoniously raised and lowered daily.

Bailiffscourt Hotel & Health Spa
Climping, 2.5 miles W of Littlehampton
Climping Street (01903 723511/www.hshotels.co.uk).
££££.
Bailiffscourt is one of Sussex's more extraordinary hotel properties, a palimpsest of old English architectural styles occupying a secluded spot near the coast. In 1927, inspired by the small Norman chapel on his land, Walter Guinness (son of the first Earl Iveagh of Kenwood, part of the brewing clan) asked the antiquarian Amyas Phillips to construct a medieval-style manor house to go with it. Phillips used as many original pieces as possible, salvaged from ruined medieval buildings around the country. Within the set of buildings is, for example, a 15th-century oak front door from a church in South Wanborough and a gatehouse transported from Loxwood of the same era. In the main house there are 'feature rooms', many with four-poster beds and full of antique furniture, but with modern facilities. The maze-like building, with low ceilings and narrow stairs, also contains small meeting rooms and a well-equipped conference suite. There's a good (if pricey) restaurant with a notable wine list too. The most recent additions are a new wing of modern rooms, and a sumptuous spa with an indoor and outdoor swimming pool, steam room, sauna, treatment rooms and a jacuzzi. You can also take a stroll down to the beach, or through the grounds (shared by several peacocks).

West Stoke House
West Stoke, 5 miles NW of Chichester *Downs Road (01243 575226/www.weststokehouse.co.uk).*
££££.
Designed with relaxation in mind, West Stoke House describes itself as a 'restaurant with rooms', so the emphasis here is on the Michelin-starred cooking. Under the stewardship of Darren Brown, formerly of the Lanesborough Hotel and Monsieur Max in London, the restaurant serves British food with French touches – the likes of roasted loin of venison with butternut squash purée and oxtail ravioli, perhaps. Understandably, the Sunday lunches are incredibly popular. A rotating exhibition of mostly modern art adds to the contemporary feel, but the grandeur of the beautifully converted mansion remains intact. The eight rooms are extremely spacious and comfortable, marrying antique furniture with 21st-century art and facilities. The grounds extend to the Sussex Downs, and a nearby nature reserve offers a perfect place for a stroll (before heading back for a large G&T). An elegant country retreat without any pretensions.

Factfile

When to go
The weather in West Sussex (like the rest of Britain) can be dreary or stunning at any time of year. During spring and summer, the flowers are lovely along the South Downs and the beaches at the Witterings will be warmer. Yet the area also has its own charm in winter – the cold is a good excuse to huddle up in the gorgeous pubs. Remember that Arundel Castle closes from November until the beginning of April.

Getting there
Direct trains leave London about every half hour to Chichester and Arundel (the journey to both takes 90 minutes). A car is needed to get to many of the country pubs. Chichester and Arundel are on the main A27 road between Brighton and Portsmouth.

Getting around
A car is the best way to travel through the rural areas of West Sussex. West Wittering is seven miles south of Chichester on the A286. There is no train to West Wittering but the number 53 **bus** can be taken (0871 200 2233, www.stagecoachbus.com/south).

Chichester is an 11-mile **cycle** ride from the beach along the pleasant Salterns Way Cycle and Wheelchair Path (www.conservancy.co.uk/out/cycling.asp). Direct **trains** between Arundel and Chichester leave hourly and take 17 minutes.

Tourist information
Arundel 1-3 Crown Yard Mews, River Road (01903 882268/www.sussexbythesea.com). Open Apr-Sept 10am-5pm Mon-Sat. Oct-Mar 10am-3pm daily.
Chichester 29A South Street (01243 775888/ www.chichester.gov.uk). Open 10.15am-5.15pm Mon; 9.15am-5.15pm Tue-Sat; (Apr-Sept) 11am-3.30pm Sun.
West Wittering No office but lots of information at www.westwitteringbeach.co.uk

Internet
The visitor information centre at Arundel listed above has free public internet access.
Internet Junction 2 Southdown Buildings, Southgate, Chichester (01243 776644/ www.internetjunction.co.uk). Open 9am-8pm Mon-Fri; 11am-8pm Sat, Sun.

Islands

Top: coast at Bonchurch;
middle: New Inn;
bottom: beach.

Isle of Wight

England in miniature: hills, creeks, cliffs and coast.

The four miles of sea that lie between the Isle of Wight and Portsmouth might be the most expensive ferry crossing in the world, but it's worth every penny, offering a genteel vision of Little Britain that is rose-tinted in some ways, but resolutely modern in others. Villages, roadside shops, picturesque little towns and winding country roads could easily be from the 1950s, but the hotels and restaurants are definitely not, their superior menus and high-quality rooms and facilities firmly rooted in the here and now. This charming mix of old and new, combined with the natural beauties of this sweet island – crumbling chalk cliffs, gently rolling downs, pretty creeks, wizened groynes and dramatic landslips – create the perfect British getaway; 147 square miles of rolling farmland, marshy estuaries, castles, cliffs, vineyards, beaches, steam trains, Roman villas, dinosaur fossils, red squirrels and a whole clutch of manor houses.

During the 19th century, visitors poured on to the Isle of Wight to enjoy the water, the sea air and the balmy climate. Tennyson made his home here, Dickens worked on *David Copperfield* here and Queen Victoria loved it so much that she spent her summers here. Charles I had been a less willing visitor, held in the hill-top Norman Carisbrooke Castle (where kindly captors created a bowling green for him) before being taken back to London to be executed in 1649.

Today, the eastern resorts of Shanklin and Sandown are still pretty lively, but the rest of the island is a quiet delight. For unrivalled peace, visit in the winter when most of the attractions are closed and the 77-mile coastal path stretches out, empty to the distant horizon of the spectacular coastline. Head inland for walks, drives and days spent on the downs, in the woods and along the creeks, and you'll build a picture of paradise for walkers, cyclists and horse riders that is arguably unrivalled for its variety and perfect mix of country, coast and town.

Explore

The Isle of Wight boasts more footpaths per square mile than anywhere else in Britain, all meticulously signposted and maintained, so exploring the island on foot is an easy delight. The westernmost point is a lovely place to spend a day or two. Here, you'll find pretty Yarmouth harbour forming a triangle with Freshwater to the south and, at the western tip of the island, the Needles, a jagged chalk line of teeth soaring out of the sea just off the coast. Starting from the westernmost point, the Military Road heads south to the great crumbling sweep of Compton Bay and the sheer cliffs of Blackgang Chine, falling dramatically (and literally) into the Channel, before climbing north for a few miles to vertiginous Ventnor. The eastern half of the island is busier, with hordes of day-trippers from the mainland swarming along the tat-filled promenades at the East Wight resorts of Shanklin and Sandown. But continue straight past these, on to the eastern tip of the island to spend some time in the romantic and rural towns of Bembridge, St Helens and Seaview. Even Fishbourne, the nearest point to mainland Portsmouth, feels as though it's a million miles away from the tawdry concerns and activities of a modern-day port. If you can't bear to leave, hop on the Waverley paddle steamer for a fantastic circumnavigation of the whole island.

THE WESTERN TRIANGLE (YARMOUTH, FRESHWATER & THE NEEDLES)

Despite being the Wightlink Ferries' link to Lymington on the mainland, the 13th-century town of **Yarmouth** is utterly charming. Here, you can wander down tiny lanes, while away the afternoon in tearooms and galleries and walk to the end of the wooden pier to get a lovely view of the town and hotel. Guarded by the Yarmouth Castle, the harbour is a lovely spot for daydreaming, gazing or sunbathing, and a place to catch a boat out to sea for a spot of fishing. A singular pleasure of the town is how little there is to do in the way of 'attractions', leaving you free to meander along the promenade without feeling the pull of museums, historic houses and the like. Walk along the former railway track, the Causeway, following the banks of the Yar to Freshwater and you might get to see some of the island's red squirrels.

Freshwater is a town of two halves, both equally enjoyable in their own different ways. The town centre is a busy shopping hub for the whole area but retains an old-world charm that makes it a great base, particularly if you plan to explore the stunning coastline nearby: **Freshwater Bay**, Totland, **Colwell**, the **Downs at Tennyson** (named after the poet, who made his home at Freshwater's Farringford Hotel), **Alum Bay** and the Needles. Many of these have excellent beaches, and **Totland Bay**, with good sand, clean water and views across the Solent

Isle of Wight

Historic sites
● ● ● ● ●

Art & architecture
● ● ● ● ●

Hotels
● ● ● ● ●

Eating & drinking
● ● ● ● ●

Scenery
● ● ● ● ●

Outdoor activities
● ● ● ● ●

Cowes; Ventnor Down;
Freshwater Bay.

New Inn.

NEW INN

to Hurst Castle, is a lovely place to watch the sun go down, but it's **the Needles**, rising up like jagged white teeth from the sea, punctuated like a full stop by a lighthouse at their treacherous end, that are the *pièce de résistance*. If they seem familiar, it's because you'll have seen them on countless TV shows about Britain's coastline, and with good reason; they are quite possibly our most breathtaking coastal feature.

Take a walk to the **Needles Old & New Batteries** (*see below*) to get the most spectacular views of the Needles, and for a fascinating poke around what was the site of secret rocket-testing in the 1950s and '60s. All of the coastline in this south-west corner of the island is stunning, but its drama is created by the very thing that's destroying it; each winter more of the soaring chalk cliffs collapse inexorably and unstoppably, like a soufflé, on to the beaches below, leaving fences and steps suspended precariously in mid-air. Catch them while you can.

Dimbola Lodge Museum

Freshwater Bay *Terrace Lane (01983 756814/ www.dimbola.co.uk). Open Mar-Oct 10am-5pm Tue-Sun. Nov-Feb 10am-4pm Tue-Sun. Admission £4; £3.50 reductions.*

The Victorian portrait photographer Julia Margaret Cameron lived at Dimbola Lodge for 15 years, taking pictures of whoever she could persuade to sit still long enough and developing the results in her coal shed. The house is now a fascinating museum broken down into a number of permanent and temporary exhibition spaces – including the IOW Pop Festival Room, which is stuffed with memorabilia from all of the Isle of Wight Festivals. The Tearoom houses a permanent display of cameras through the ages. This place is definitely worth poking around for an hour or so; don't miss the sculpture of Jimi Hendrix in the garden.

The Needles Old Battery & New Battery

Alum Bay *West High Down (01983 754772/ www.nationaltrust.org.uk). Open Old Battery Mar-Oct 10.30am-5pm daily. New Battery Mar-Oct 11am-4pm Tue, Sat, Sun. Tearoom Mar-Oct 10.30am-4.30pm daily. Nov-Feb 11am-3pm Sat, Sun. Admission £4.85; £2.30 reductions.*

Even if it didn't offer one of the best possible views of the Needles, the 19th-century clifftop fort built to guard against the threat of French invasion would be worth a visit. A military history spanning 150 years, tunnels through cliffs, guns, secret rocket sites and a glorious position on the most western tip of the island make for a fun visit to the two batteries. The fact that you have to walk almost a mile from Alum Bay to get to them (the new one, built in 1895, is situated next to the bus turning point and contains a display about the secret rocket testing carried out in the 1950s and '60s) just adds to the pleasure here. Catch your breath at the Old Look-out Tower tearoom, but be careful – the expansive sea views might just take your breath away again.

VENTNOR & THE SOUTH COAST

The western tip is just the beginning of the Isle of Wight's southern splendours. Just a few miles south-east along the A3055, the southern half of the island's circular road, lies **Compton Bay**, a beautiful sweep of sand beneath collapsing cliffs, without a kiss-me-quick hat in sight. Here, surfers brave the waves, fossil hunters admire the casts of dinosaurs' footprints at low tide, kitesurfers leap and soar across the sea and paragliders hurl themselves off the cliffs. The clifftop Military Road winds along, past sweet villages with sweet names like Brightstone and Atherfield to arrive at **Blackgang Chine**, home to the dinky **Blackgang Chine Theme Park** (*see below*), and from there to **Ventnor**, one of the prettiest – and least British – towns on the island. Approaching the town, you could easily imagine yourself cruising the Côte d'Azur.

"Soaring chalk cliffs collapse inexorably and unstoppably on to the beaches below, leaving fences and steps suspended in mid-air."

As you clamber in a higgledy-piggledy fashion down the cliff face, you'll see hundreds of rooftops and gardens, their giant steps calling to mind the Mediterranean towns and villages tumbling down the slopes towards the sea on the Amalfi Coast. If you stay at a hotel near the top, you'll be rewarded with terrific views over the town and out to sea, and getting down is easy thanks to numerous staircases. Climbing back up after one too many at the Spyglass Inn (*see p267*) is another matter, but it's a great way in which to burn off the wonderful food that you'll find in this enjoyable town.

If you enjoy rambling, then take a walk to the nearby **Botanic Gardens** (*see p264*), or the longer but hugely enjoyable trek east out of town, past the harbour and Wheeler's Bay to the village of **Bonchurch**, the island's best-preserved Victorian village. This really does feel like a village that's been preserved from a much older, kinder time. At the large pond, huge carp rise from the deep when visitors throw them bread, ducks quack happily under the weeping willows and the feeling is one of sheltered cosiness, largely thanks to the stunning backdrop of **St Boniface Down**, the Island's highest point. Even if walking isn't your thing, take the superb path through **the Landslip**, a coastal woodland filled with ancient oaks perched on top of the cliffs, which has been fashioned into fantastic sculptural shapes by landslips and erosion. At the top of the deep stone gorge (the Devil's Chimney), reward yourself with a cream tea at the **Smugglers Haven** tearoom (01983 852992). Back in the village, pop into the tiny **Old Church of St Boniface**, which was built by Benedictine monks almost a thousand years ago.

Blackgang Chine Theme Park

Blackgang Chine *(01983 730052/www.blackgang chine.com). Open Apr-mid July 10am-5pm daily. Mid July, Aug 10am-6pm daily. Sept, Oct 10.30am-4.30pm Tue-Thur, Sat, Sun. Admission £9.50; £7.50 reductions.*

Spread over 40 acres of Victorian clifftop gardens, this cute theme park forgoes the humungous in favour of the humorous. Teenagers are likely to think its mix of goblins, cowboys, wizards, water gardens, hall of funny mirrors, animated shows, dinosaurs, pirate fort and smugglers' ship are all a bit underwhelming, but younger children and grown-ups with a nostalgic bent will love it; not least for the full-sized Cowboy Town, set within Frontierland and including goldpanning activities. There's so much to do you'll probably want to come back, so it's ace that your ticket allows unlimited free return within seven days.

"You can spend the day overlooking the airport and the coast, feeling there's no finer place in England."

Ventnor Botanic Gardens

Ventnor *Undercliff Drive (01983 855397/ www.botanic.co.uk). Open Summer 10am-6pm daily. Winter 10am-4pm daily. Admission free.*

There's not much in the way of things to do in Ventnor, but a must-see is this lovely outdoor attraction, where 22 acres, divided into 'continents', are filled with more than 10,000 plants, trees and shrubs spanning everything from medicinal herbs and tiny alpine delicacies to herbaceous borders and a steamy temperate glasshouse. Much of it is new planting after a vicious winter followed by the infamous 1987 storm destroyed many of the plants, but even as a largely new garden it's still a joy to wander round.

THE EASTERN TIP

Oddly, given its proximity to the tourist hubs of nearby Shanklin, Sandown and Ryde, the eastern tip of the Isle of Wight is surprisingly secluded. Without such draws as the southern coast's dramatic scenery, there's little to bring the tourists here, which of course makes it a laid-back

joy for walkers, nature-lovers and beach bums. Second to Cowes, the area around Bembridge, St Helens and Seaview is the island's main sailing hub, and is as upmarket as the yachties would expect. The shallow beaches at **Bembridge** offer safe bathing and hours of time for beachcombing and crabbing for the kids, with none of the tat or diversions of the nearby resort towns. The village's lovely harbour is filled with pleasure craft, fishing boats and house boats – some offering afternoon tea or accommodation. The village itself is charming, stuffed with quaint shops and heaps of good options for food and drink, and as with the rest of the island, there's plenty of great walking to be done along sweeping bays and clifftops. Head west out of town and you'll come to Bembridge's small airport, on the way towards St Helens and Sandown. Pack a picnic and from the top of **Bembridge Down**, you can spend the day overlooking the airport and the coast, feeling there's no finer place in England. Or go on to explore the **Duver**, a broad stretch of dunes, which bring you to **St Helens** and its gorgeous secluded beach, where you'll find one of the best lunches (or even better, dinners) at one of Britain's finest beach restaurants, Baywatch on the Beach (*see below*). Further north, **Seaview** again offers solitude and natural beauties, no more so than at **Priory Bay**, a small picturesque sandy bay backed by small cliffs, fronted by a perfect view out across the eastern Solent, and served by just a small café. With no car park nearby, it's always wonderfully quiet here – most visitors are guests at the nearby Priory Bay Hotel (*see p267*); treat yourself and join them.

Eat

Unsurprisingly, the Isle of Wight offers an excellent range of seafood and fish. What might be an unexpected pleasure is the quality; sleepy Isle of Wight is fast becoming a foodie heaven, with excellent food available across the whole island. The **Bonchurch Inn** (01983 852611, www.bonchurch-inn.co.uk), nestled under the steep cliffs of the village and centred on a cobbled courtyard, is definitely worth a visit too. As well as the coastal pubs and restaurants listed here, most inland pubs, such as the **Crown Inn** (01983 740293, www.crowninnshorwell. co.uk) in the pretty thatched village of Shorwell, are great places to stop for a wide-ranging menu. Nearby Newport's award-winning **New Inn** (01983 531314, www.thenewinn.co.uk) is a wonderfully atmospheric coaching inn dating from 1743.

Baywatch on the Beach

St Helens *Duver Road (01983 873259). Open Apr-Oct 10.30am-9pm daily. £££.*

Hambrough.

Priory Bay.

Rightly lauded in the British press as one of Britain's best seaside restaurants, the Baywatch hides its treasures in a slightly rickety wooden train carriage in attractive blue and white, with huge picture windows offering views out to sea. During the day, it's a sweet beach café serving top quality café lunches, such as crab and gruyère tartlet, Shetland Island mussels, a gourmet burger or simple seafood dishes: scampi, shell-on prawns, whitebait and so on. However, in the evening this gorgeously located place dons its tux to offer a full restaurant menu, including pan-fried garlic langoustines, whole sea bass or lobster and crayfish tails. The emphasis is on seafood simply cooked, and it's a winning proposition.

Buddle Inn

Niton, 4 miles W of Ventnor *St Catherine's Road, (01983 730243/www.buddleinn.co.uk). Open (food served) noon-2.45pm, 6-9pm daily. ££. Pub.*
The perfect place to take a break while walking the cliffs, or just to enjoy the stunning sea views from the garden. Built in the 16th century as a farmhouse, this quaint clifftop pub manages to retain a sense of cosy bonhomie thanks to a huge inglenook fireplace, ancient flagstones and beams and a wealth of old photographs. Close to St Catherine's lighthouse at the southern tip of the island, with stunning views across the channel, the inn offers largely pub grub – such as venison casserole, or an island game pie – served in pleasing portions and at reasonable prices, and there are always good real ales on tap.

Crab & Lobster Inn

Bembridge *32 Forelands, Field Road (01983 872244/ www.crabandlobsterinn.co.uk). Open (food served) noon-2.30pm, 6-9pm daily. ££. Seafood/modern European.*
Heaven for seafood-lovers, this pub offers such mouthwatering dishes as seafood mixed grills, crab cakes with fries, spicy baked local crab and tagliatelle seafood. There is also a respectable smattering of meat and vegetarian dishes. All these are served by amazingly efficient and welcoming staff in a pretty outdoor area on the low cliffs, or in the pleasant dining room, which adjoins a couple of cosy bar areas. The beer selection is as good as you might expect from an Isle of Wight pub.

George

Yarmouth *Quay Street (01983 760331/www.the george.co.uk). Open 8-10am, noon-3pm, 7-10pm daily. £££. Modern European.*
The light-filled brasserie at this lovely hotel has a small but nicely diverse menu that would satisfy most palates, courtesy of chef Jose Graziosi, who offers an inventive but not outlandish menu of modern European cuisine. For starters, there are dishes such as tempura salt and pepper squid or spiced goat's cheese truffles with pepperonata, while mains include hearty, traditional dishes – slow-cooked pork, braised pheasant, or whole Dover sole – using as much island produce as possible. Desserts like chocolate tart with pistaccio ice-cream are as delicious as they are stunning, and a range of great-value house wines rounds off a lovely meal in a beautiful setting.

Hambrough

Ventnor *Hambrough Road (01983 856333/ www.thehambrough.com). Open noon-1.30pm, 7-9.30pm Tue-Sat. £££. Modern European.*
At the smartest boutique accommodation on the island, chef patron Robert Thompson – awarded a Michelin star at the tender age of 23 – uses the freshest, best-quality produce to put together impeccable set menus of exceedingly good value (a two-course dinner is £38, three courses £45). Here you'll find starters such as risotto of local lobster with avocado crème fraîche or seared tuna with Charentais melon, followed by a nice variety of fish dishes and local game that make you want to opt for the tasting menu (£50), just so you get to sample more of this wonderful food. Portions are just large enough to satisfy, just small enough to leave space for the moreish puddings, which continue to stick to the local produce theme where possible – the likes of blackberry soufflé and local Ventnor Stout ice-cream. *See also p268.*

"Desserts are original in a way that would make Heston Blumenthal sit up and take notice."

Pond Café

Bonchurch *Bonchurch Village Road (01983 855666/ www.thepondcafe.com). Open noon-2.30pm, 7-9.30pm Mon, Thur-Sun. ££££. Modern European.*
This tiny, light-filled restaurant in the pretty village of Bonchurch offers a great counterpoint to the brooding, vertiginous setting of the village, and a creative, daily-changing menu with an emphasis on seasonal food. The Pond Café is that rare beast, a restaurant where everything sounds innovative but good, whether it be gnocchi of wild rabbit and wild mushrooms, warm salad of smoked eel, or calves' liver with cavalo nero and Castelluccio lentils. The range of desserts is likely to present you with an even greater dilemma; should it be baked lemon tart with blackcurrant sorbet or chocolate titanic? Espresso crème brûlée or chestnut and chocolate torte? Walk it all off with a lovely post-dinner wander through this atmospheric and fascinating village, and warm up in the Bonchurch Inn afterwards (*see p264*).

Priory Bay

Seaview *Priory Drive (01983 613146/www.priory bay.co.uk). Open 12.30-2pm, 7-9pm daily. £££. Modern European.*
At 'the country house hotel by the sea', dinner is an elegant, refined affair, from the sumptuous seascape frescoes that decorate the gold and azure Island Room dining room to the excellent (and good value) food served in it. Starters such as rabbit and crayfish or lobster cooked in fennel seed broth are delicate but full of flavour, while mains of halibut and squid, red deer and poached pear or a veal tasting plate are

a brave departure from the norm. Desserts are equally adventurous and original, making use of ingredients like cardamom and coriander in a way that would make Heston Blumenthal sit up and take notice. We'd advise the tasting menu at £45, Heston, although you may want to wander down to the less formal waterside Priory Oyster Bar & Grill first to look over the more brasserie-style (and priced) fare; a dozen rock oysters, perhaps, or grilled Bembridge lobster.

Spyglass Inn
Ventnor *The Esplanade (01983 855338/www.the spyglass.com). Open (food served) noon-9.30pm daily. ££. Pub.*
There are two good reasons to sample a beer or two from the extensive and impressive range on offer at the Spyglass – the brilliant beachside location and the surreal mass of seafaring objects and memorabilia that festoon every inch of the spacious unglazed floor-tiled interior. A huge patio means you can gaze at the lovely sea views while also enjoying reasonably priced traditional pub grub from an extensive menu with a focus on local seafood (Ventnor Bay crab and lobster); dishes like seafood stew, baked fisherman's pie, sausage and mash and seafood chowder won't win Michelin stars, but will please most with their home-cooked heartiness. If you're looking for a great spot in which to eat dishes to please everyone, this is the one.

Stay

George
Yarmouth *Quay Street (01983 760331/ www.thegeorge.co.uk). ££££.*
The unprepossessing exterior of this 17th-century townhouse – once home to the island's governor Sir Robert Holmes – hides what is undoubtedly one of the island's best hotels. Every wood-panelled inch and tapestried surface exudes the luxurious impression of a five-star hotel, yet creates the warmth and intimacy of a top-class guesthouse. The 17 roomsare small (number 12 was once occupied by King Charles I), but this only adds to the feeling of cosiness, and the two balcony rooms, with large private terraces that lead directly to a delightful garden running down to the sea, are stunning. When the weather's good, breakfast is served in the garden, which has a lovely view of the harbour and pier; and when it's bad, a roaring fire makes the bar a tempting place to have an aperitif before heading for dinner at the excellent and pretty brasserie (*see p267*).

Hambrough
Ventnor *Hambrough Road (01983 856333/ www.thehambrough.com). £££.*
The seven-room Hambrough Hotel introduced the concept of boutique hotels to island life a few years back, and it's proving a winning one. Flat-screen TVs, DVD players, espresso machines, mini bars and free Wi-Fi feature in all the rooms, which – as you'd expect – have stylish contemporary fittings in neutral tones, and cool greys

linking interior spaces with the vaguely art deco chic of the hotel's exterior. Bathrooms are gorgeous too, with underfloor heating and acres of space. If you're lucky enough to be able to book one of the two balcony rooms, it's quite possible that between the comforts of the room and the elegance of the balconies over the sea you'll never make it down to the famed restaurant. That would be a huge shame, because the Hambrough's attention to detail continues in the public spaces, and in the dedication of the staff to their craft. *See also p267.*

Old House
Chale *Gotten Manor, Gotten Lane (01983 551368/ www.gottenmanor.co.uk). ££.*
There are just two rooms in this charming B&B, situated in the early 14th-century annexe to 17th-century Gotten Manor on the rugged south of the island, but both are beautifully decorated, with limewashed walls, quality textiles and polished wooden floors. They are as luxurious as any first-rate hotel, housing rosewood double beds, sofas and huge cast-iron baths, with fluffy white robes, soft towels, crisp bedlinen, fresh flowers and candles completing the picture of loving care and attention to detail. Breakfast, served in either the walled garden or the former creamery, is as good as you would expect; local and organic produce features heavily, as do home-made jams, yoghurt and smoothies. Three attractive self-catering cottages in converted barns are also available to hire for weekends or whole weeks in this highly recommended, unique, discreet hideaway.

"The rooms are exotic and sensuous, with dark, rich furnishings and decor."

Priory Bay
Seaview *Priory Drive (01983 613146/ www.priorybay.com). £££.*
Taking a stroll around the 70 acres of this country hotel (which mixes medieval architecture with Tudor, Georgian and even 20th-century additions), or checking out the summer season oyster bar flanking the beautiful private beach, it's easy to imagine yourself living here in the lap of luxury. Playing the odd round of golf, taking a dip in the outdoor pool before breakfasting on the terrace, dozing happily in front of the fire in the drawing room and eating a delicious dinner in the frescoed dining room are all part of the good life at Priory Bay, and happily the 18 rooms easily live up to the expectations created by the public spaces. In the older part of the building, the cosy rooms are exotic and sensuous, with dark, rich furnishings and decor. The newer part of the building, by contrast, is filled with light, as huge windows flood pretty rooms with light and Georgian patterns, chaise longues and bright colours help to create a languid air of age-old charm. *See also p267.*

Royal Hotel

Ventnor *Belgrave Road (01983 852186/ www.royalhoteliow.co.uk). ££££.*
This grand old dame of the island hotels lacks the intimacy of the Hambrough or the Old House, but that's no bad thing if what you look for in a hotel is friendly, efficient service and luxurious anonymity. Fifty-five classically decorated rooms, many with wonderful views of the sea or perfectly tended gardens, along with numerous indoor and outdoor bars, lounges and seating areas, an outdoor unheated pool and a traditional restaurant menu, make this feel like a country hotel with all the benefits of a pretty, lively town on your doorstep.

Seaview Hotel

Seaview *High Street (01983 612711/ www.seaviewhotel.co.uk). £££.*
The award-winning Seaview is a small hotel situated in the centre of this popular sailing village, a minute's walk from the beach. It's surprisingly large, with 16 bedrooms, two bars and two restaurants serving excellent, fresh local produce. The Seaview gets booked up for long stays in the summer and is geared towards families, with food that should keep all your little ones happy. The children's menu includes dishes so sophisticated that they often tempt adults: mussels in cream and garlic, Seaview hot crab ramekin, macaroni cheese or fish pie, followed by summer berry eton mess or warm apple soup, ginger ice-cream and oat biscuits. Who needs nuggets? Dogs are welcome too. If there's no room in the hotel, a self-catering fisherman's cottage with space for a family of four is available.

Wellington Hotel

Ventnor *Belgrave Road (01983 856600/ www.thewellingtonhotel.net). £££.*
Perched almost at the highest point of vertiginous Ventnor, the Wellington Hotel has one of the best locations in this old-fashioned, pretty southern town. Walk into your contemporary, simply furnished room and your sightline is an uninterrupted view of the sea; step out on to the wrought-iron balcony and you're perched over the hotel's spacious, decked breakfast terrace (a steep flight of steps leads from here to the beach and the Spyglass Inn, *see p267*) and below that the town's rooftops. The sea views (in 99% of the rooms) lend a light, airy feel to the smallish rooms, which compensate for cramped corridors that lead to them. Fixtures and fittings are not always first rate, but the beds are comfy, the rooms quiet, and the view breathtaking enough to make you forget everything else.

Windmill Inn

Bembridge *1 Steyne Road (01983 872875/ www.windmill-inn.com). £.*
This refurbished inn isn't quite in the league of the Priory Bay hotel, the George or the Hambrough, but it's a great east island base, nestled in the centre of Bembridge village, and its 14 en-suite rooms are comfortable and pleasing to the eye. Fresh local fish and lobster, alongside a great range of ales and wine from a good list, are served in the cosy bar, or you can eat in the pretty garden room, where the warm colours and Mediterranean feel of the space, overlooking the patio and garden, will make you feel you're somewhere more exotic than England.

Factfile

When to go

Many attractions are closed between the end of October and Easter, so phone ahead to check when planning a visit. There are many seasonal events, including Britain's biggest walking festival in May, an international kite festival in July, a cycling festival in September and White Air, a festival of extreme sports, at the end of October.

Those looking for a quiet weekend might want to avoid Cowes in August as the town – and the island – become jam-packed. Also worth noting is the Isle of Wight Music Festival, which takes place in Newport in June (www.isleofwight festival.com), and the increasingly popular Bestival (www.bestival.net) in September.

Getting there

Wightlink Ferries (0871 376 4342, www. wightlink.co.uk) has a 24-hour service from Portsmouth to Fishbourne (car ferry, journey time, 30 minutes) and Ryde (FastCat foot passenger catamaran, journey time 18 minutes), and from Lymington to Yarmouth (car ferry, journey time 30 minutes).

Getting around

Once on the island, getting around is child's play. Roads are well signposted and extensive; a car is by far the best way to experience the quieter parts of the island. Children will love taking an Island Line train (www.island-line.co.uk) from Ryde Pier to Shanklin, via Ryde Esplanade, Brading, Sandown and Lake. Island-wide bus services are great for getting about and seeing the island, especially with a Southern Vectis Rover Ticket or 'go-where-you-please' passes. (0871 200 2233, www.islandbuses.info).

For information on cycling and walking, call Rights of Way (01983 821000, www.iwight.com).

Tourist information

All Isle of Wight tourist information centres (Cowes, Newport, Ryde, Sandown, Shanklin and Yarmouth) are contactable on 01983 813818; for the accommodation booking service call 01983 813813 or book online (www.islandbreaks.co.uk). Full addresses and opening hours details for all tourist information offices are listed on the official website www.islandbreaks.co.uk.

Left: St Agnes; right: Hugh Town harbour; bottom: Island Hotel, Tresco.

Isles of Scilly

Cosy teas, crazy sea captains and walks in the wild.

Small, wonderfully quiet and strangely beautiful, the Isles of Scilly are the kind of place people visit once on a whim – and end up returning to regularly for the rest of their lives. Located 28 miles out into the Atlantic Ocean from Land's End, the five inhabited islands – St Mary's and the 'off-islands' of St Martin's, St Agnes, Tresco and Bryher, each with white-sand beaches, clear waters and heather-covered headlands – bask in the warmth of the Gulf Stream. Around them, over a hundred unoccupied islets, rock formations, reefs, outcrops and ledges are a sanctuary for grey seals, puffins and shearwaters, migratory birds and passing dolphins. In winter, though, the islands show another face: when an Atlantic gale comes roaring in, the memory of more than 700 local shipwrecks is brought forcefully to mind.

The Scillies have been settled for at least 4,000 years, with even the Romans recognising them as 'Sun Isles' (the translation of their Latin name Sillinae insulae), and the continuity of life is richly evident in prehistoric burial chambers, standing stones and settlements. In legend, this is the Lost Land of Lyonesse, to which King Arthur's men retreated after their leader's last fatal battle.

With a total population of around 3,000 people, these are small islands; with an almost total absence of cars, the pace of life is an enjoyable stroll. There's a pleasing pragmatism about even the most deluxe accommodation: everything is set up to please posh grannies as much as sandy-footed surf-teens, and beardie birders as much as strung-out families. Don't expect theme parks, nightlife or a cutting edge on anything except a fisherman's knife, just the unflashy excitement of stunning views – Scilly was designated an Area of Outstanding Natural Beauty in 1975 – and the chance to walk, read and chat over a relaxed Ales of Scilly pint.

Explore

ST MARY'S

Although it's only two and a half miles across at its widest point, St Mary's is the largest of the Isles of Scilly, as well as the most populous – it even has a recognisable road system. Its centre, **Hugh Town**, is bustling if you've already spent time on the other islands, laid-back if you've come here first. On a narrow isthmus on the island's south-western side, the town is flanked to the south by pretty, sheltered **Porthcressa Beach**, and to the north by the less appealing **Town Beach** where the Penzance ferry and inter-island passenger boats come and go. In the harbour waiting room, the **Quay Visitors' Centre** (01720 422988, www.ios-wildlifetrust.org.uk) has information about nature walks and tours, and itineraries of tours and boats to the off-islands are chalked up on boards on the quay. From May to September the harbour is also the finish of gig races. The gigs – 32 feet of brightly painted wooden rowing boat, some of them more than 100 years old, crewed by six oarsmen and a cox – are raced on Wednesday and Friday evenings.

Above the harbour, west of Hugh Town, **Garrison Hill** offers brilliant views. It is dominated by the 16th-century, eight-pointed **Star Castle**, built as a defence against the Spanish Armada and now a hotel. In the other direction, Telegraph Road leads from Hugh Town towards the island's interior; passing Carreg Dhu (pronounced 'Crake Dew'; 01720 422404), a small, volunteer-run community garden that is quiet and pleasingly overgrown; a sign invites visitors to get stuck into some weeding. Here also begins a pleasant trail around the island's dozen galleries, open studios and craft shops, making a comfortable circuit south to the Old Town.

Heading east from Porthcressa Beach, a path loops south round jagged **Peninnis Head**, passing some intriguing geological formations such as the 'Kettle and Pans' close to the lighthouse. Beyond is the sheltered **Old Town Bay**, whose straggling settlement was, until the 17th century, the island's main port.

Near the airport, the small bay at Porth Hellick is overlooked by a monument to Rear Admiral Sir Cloudesley Shovell, who steered his fleet into the rocks off the island during a storm in 1707, losing 2,000 men. A mile north, **Pelistry Bay** is one of the most secluded and picturesque beaches on St Mary's, with the small licensed Carn Vean café providing sustenance after a bracing dip. At low tide a sand bar enables you to cross to the idyllic Toll's island (don't try and swim at high tide, since the sand bar causes vicious rip tides). Go north-west round the coast and you'll come to the most impressive prehistoric remains on the archipelago: **Halangy Down** has stone huts, a burial chamber and a standing stone that is thought to date to 2000 BC.

Tresco
Teän
St Martin's
Bryrher
New Grimsby
Higher Town
St Mary's
Hugh Town
Old Town
Middle Town
St Agnes
0   2 miles

Isles of Scilly

Historic sites
● ● ● ● ●

Art & architecture
● ● ● ● ●

Hotels
● ● ● ● ●

Eating & drinking
● ● ● ● ●

Scenery
● ● ● ● ●

Outdoor activities
● ● ● ● ●

Isles of Scilly Museum

*Church Street (01720 422337/www.iosmuseum.org).
Open Apr-Sept 10am-4.30pm Mon-Sat. Oct-Mar 10am-
noon Mon-Sat. Admission £3.50; £2.50 reductions.
No credit cards.*
There's no escaping the thread of disaster and loss,
primarily from shipwrecks, at the Isles of Scilly Museum,
but – alongside the cases of flotsam and jetsam – you'll
find curiosities like a Scilly shrew's nest in a discarded
can, Iron Age axeheads and a Napoleonic dagger stick.
Downstairs are stuffed birds and fish, including 6lb 2oz
of broad-nosed eel.

TRESCO & BRYHER

For some, a visit to the Scillies' privately run
and closely managed island estate (still leased
from the Duchy of Cornwall by descendents of
19th-century reforming landlord Augustus Smith)
is altogether too cosseted. For others, it's a life
of delicious simplicity: one pub, one hotel-
restaurant, one café and no cars. The scene
is set by the toy-town jollity of the tractor ride
between the heliport and your accommodation.

At two miles by one, it's the largest off-island.
The unassailable selling point is the **Abbey
Gardens** (*see below*). There's no denying the
unique atmosphere of this singular experiment
in horticulture, with fabulously exotic golden
pheasants strutting about and each section
screened off from others to provide new vistas
at every turn. But a walk around it also takes in
exquisite, barely populated beaches, peaceful
lakes, secluded woods and a heathered headland
with two defensive fortifications – the 1651
Cromwell's Castle and, above it, the earlier King
Charles's Castle. Most settlement on Tresco runs
across the island between **Old** and **New Grimsby**:
New Grimsby houses Gallery Tresco (01720
424925, www.tresco.co.uk/gallery), a single
room of local art and souvenirs overlooking the
sleepy little jetty, and the New Inn (*see p275*);
Old Grimsby is the location of the far grander
Island Hotel (*see p276*).

Just opposite New Grimsby, tiny **Bryher** feels
a place apart – even in Scilly. It takes its name
from the Celtic for 'place of hills' – to the north,
Shipman Head Down and **Watch Hill**; in the
south, **Samson Hill** – and is a beautifully wild
island, generally undeveloped and looking out
on stunning rock fortresses such as **Scilly Rock**,
Castle Bryher and **Maiden Bower**. On the
western shore, **Hell Bay** delivers all the name
suggests when a storm's up; the Hell Bay Hotel
(*see p276*), one of the most dramatically
positioned hotels in England, is just to the
south. Nearby, artist Richard Pearce (01720
423665, www.rpearce.net) has a similarly
startling outlook from an Atlantic studio barely
the size of a rowing boat (it is, in fact, a
converted gig shed). The considerably more
sheltered east shore has fine beaches, such

as **Green Bay**, and friendly boat hire from long-
time islanders, the Bennetts (01720 422411).

A circumambulation of Bryher takes little
more than an hour but is wonderfully invigorating,
with bees and birds literally at your feet in the
undergrowth and amazing views all around:
Gweal Hill offers the best sunset vantage in
the Scillies, while Samson Hill gives you the
whole archipelago.

Abbey Gardens

Tresco *(01720 424108/www.tresco.co.uk). Open
10am-4pm daily. Admission £10.*
There's no denying the unique atmosphere of this singular
experiment in horticulture, with fabulously exotic golden
pheasants strutting about the subtropical gardens. When
Augustus Smith arrived in 1834 to take on the lease of the
islands, Tresco was exposed to vicious winds and far from
sympathetic to the kind of vegetation now here. He had tall
windbreaks built around the remains of the 12th-century
Benedictine priory to shelter sloping terraces, and the
magnificent gardens now have over 20,000 plants from 80
countries, including succulents, palms, cacti and
eucalyptus. Italianate landscaping adds perspective and
ensures that, even if a cruise-ship load has just sailed up,
it's easy to lose your fellow visitors. Valhalla, the on-site
collection of salvaged ships' figureheads, is less thrilling
than the name suggests. The Garden Café (01720 424108)
is open to all-comers.

> "The island's main
> quay is on Par Beach,
> a slice of pure white
> sand lapped by
> translucent waters."

ST MARTIN'S

Growing flowers is the main industry here,
which accounts for the colourful fields, but
the island has attracted a number of sensitive
entrepreneurial operations, from the organic
smallholding and café at Little Arthur Farm to
the impeccable St Martin's Bakery in **Higher
Town**. Higher Town has few other attractions:
head instead for the stunning beaches and jaw-
dropping views, in particular from **St Martin's
Head** on the north-east coast. Sparsely inhabited
and virtually pollution-free, St Martin's is great
for diving; St Martin's Diving Services (Higher
Town, St Martin's, 01720 422848, www.scilly
diving.com) provides scuba equipment and
tuition for all levels of experience.

The island's main quay is on **Par Beach**, a
slice of pure white sand lapped by translucent
waters, with the St Martin's Vineyard & Winery

(01720 423418, www.stmartinsvineyard.co.uk) just east along the bay. On the southern coast, **Lawrence's Bay** is long, sandy and perfect for collecting shells. Further west, **Lower Town** enjoys terrific views across to the uninhabited islands of Teän and St Helen's – climb '111 steps to the best pub view', as the roadside sign rightly puts it, from the decked terrace of the Seven Stones (01720 423560, www.seven stonesinn.co.uk). On the north coast, **Great Bay** and **Little Bay** are secluded spots, the former frequently appearing on lists of the best British beaches. Climb across the boulders from the latter at low tide to wild **White Island** (pronounced 'Wit') to explore **Underland Girt**, a huge underground cave.

ST AGNES

Craggy St Agnes, set apart from the cluster of Bryher, Tresco and St Martin's, is the most south-westerly community in the British Isles. The simple lifestyle is fully embraced here: on St Agnes, bird- and butterfly-watching are about as energetic as it gets.

> ## "Also out west is the extraordinary Bishop Rock Lighthouse, a must-see miracle of Victorian construction."

Boats land and leave from **Porth Conger**, under the watchful eyes of the Turk's Head pub. There you'll also find St Agnes's most attractive beach, **Covean**. When the tide is right you can walk across the sand bar to the tiny island of **Gugh** (pronounced 'Goo'), where there are rocky outcrops, a Bronze Age burial chamber and a standing stone – or rather a crazily leaning stone. Inland, St Agnes is dominated by the squat, white form of the **Old Lighthouse**, which dates from 1680, making it one of the oldest in England. Near to **Periglis Cove** (on the western side of the island) is **Troy Town Maze**, laid out in large pebbles in 1729 by, it is said, the lighthouse keeper's bored son. Although since copied elsewhere in the Scillies, it was a layout unique in Britain.

The wild heathland of the wonderfully named **Wingletang Down** takes up much of the south of St Agnes, edged on its western side by impressive coastal scenery and on its eastern side by **Beady Pool**. This inlet takes its name from a haul of beads from a wrecked 17th-century Venetian trader that was washed up on the shores. Above the cove, two enormous boulders

indented with a three-foot-deep basin form the **Giant's Punchbowl**, the most extraordinary rock formation on Scilly.

UNINHABITED ISLANDS & BISHOP ROCK LIGHTHOUSE

Samson, the largest uninhabited island, was populated until the 1850s, when poverty and the threat of eviction by Augustus Smith forced the islanders to resettle. A beautiful beach lies at the foot of North Hill, while significant prehistoric remains dot the slopes above. At low tide look out for the Samson Flats, the remains of ancient field systems that show up in the sands between Samson and Tresco.

Just off St Martin's, **Teän** has large, crescent-shaped sandy beaches and **St Helen's**, just behind it, an interesting ruined church. On the other side of St Martin's, the milder Eastern Isles have fantastic beaches on **Great Arthur** and **Great Ganilly**. They are also home to puffins and grey seals – you can spend three hours snorkelling with them on a trip orgnaised by Island Sea Safaris (01720 422732, www.scilly online.co.uk/seasafaris.html). However, the best place to spot these captivating creatures is the storm-harried **Western Rocks** beyond St Agnes, site of many shipwrecks.

Also out west is the extraordinary **Bishop Rock Lighthouse**, a must-see miracle of Victorian construction that perches on a rock base little wider than its own circumference.

Eat

Several of the best dining options on Scilly are in hotels, especially on the off-islands: **Hell Bay Hotel** (*see p276*), the **Island Hotel** (*see p276*), **St Martin's-on-the-Isle** (*see p277*) and the **Star Castle** (*see p277*) all accept non-resident custom.

Deli

St Mary's *Hugh Street (01720 422734). Open Summer 8.30am-5.30pm Mon-Wed, Sat; 8.30am-7.30pm Thur, Fri. Winter 9am-2.30pm Mon-Wed; 8.30am-5pm Thur-Sat. Times may vary. £. Deli.*
A great place to put together a picnic from largely local produce, the Deli is in a converted butcher's shop – with the fixtures and fittings (hooks, chopping blocks) modishly retained to display parma hams and olives, as well as Scillonian delicacies. There are half a dozen tables for light lunches and drinks, with wireless internet available while you sit. The Deli also supplies the same owners' bistro, Dibble & Grub (01720 423719), in the Old Fire Station at Porthcressa Beach.

Fraggle Rock Bar-Café
Bryher *(01720 422222). Open Summer 10.30am-4.30pm, 6.30-9pm daily. ££. Pub.*

Hell Bay Hotel.

Situated in a little granite house with a beer garden out front, right down by the beach, this great little pub serves lunch (double-decker crab sandwiches) and evening meals (including a fine fish and chips), and pulls pints such as Sharp's Doom Bar or Timothy Taylor Landlord. The first floor has sea views, internet access and incongruously bright stripped pine decor, comfortable enough, but less cosy and pub-like than the downstairs.

Little Arthur Farm
St Martin's *Higher Town (01720 422457/www.little arthur.co.uk). Open times/days vary. ££. Café.*
Looking down the steady slope to Par Beach on St Martin's, this wholefood café offers excellent salads and rolls filled with own-grown organic ingredients, soups such as nettle and onion, freshly caught shellfish and lovely cakes, all served in a sweet black and white trellised conservatory or the garden. It runs a variety of specialist evenings: excellent local, sustainable fish and chips, a bistro night and so on. The enterprise is even powered by a wind turbine.

Mermaid Inn
St Mary's *Hugh Town (01720 422701). Open noon-2pm, 6-9pm daily. ££. Pub/café.*
The Mermaid is an atmospheric local right on the end of the quay, serving fine real ales downstairs, pub grub upstairs – and accommodating a snoozy dog on the steps to the quiet main street. The handsome café-bar upstairs, only a few years old, is more modern-looking, with flagged floor and a striking counter made out of a white gig. It serves wine, Guinness and light meals, such as lunchtime panini, and more substantial tucker after 6pm.

"Suites have exposed A-frame beams and jaunty portholes; most open on to private balconies or patios with a sea view."

New Inn
Tresco *(01720 422844/www.tresco.co.uk). Open noon-2pm, 7-9pm daily. £££. Pub.*
Tresco is at its liveliest in the New Inn's snug Driftwood Bar, lined with dark reclaimed wood. Sunny days seem to draw the entire population of the island to its shady outdoor terrace, where they are attended by cheekily well-fed sparrows and chaffinches. There's a fine selection of ales and wines, as well as food such as devilled whitebait and salmon fish cakes. An additional conservatory-style space (the Pavilion) serves ice-cream and pastries, while more full-blooded, traditional meals are available in the hotel restaurant.

St Martin's Bakery
St Martin's *Moo Green (01720 423444/www.stmartins bakery.co.uk). Open Mar-Sept 9am-5.30pm daily. Bakery.*

Toby Tobin-Dougan runs baking holidays off-season and, judging by the homity pie (an open pie of potato, garlic, onion and cheese) and upside-down pineapple sponge cake, there are some serious skills ready to be passed on. Sip own-made lemonade and tuck in at the trestle tables outdoors, leaving a few crumbs for the little chicken pecking about your ankles. The bakery uses local ingredients, including eggs produced on its own farm, and provides excellent gluten-free options.

Turk's Head
St Agnes *(01720 422434). Open Summer times/days vary. ££. Pub.*
The most south-westerly pub in the British Isles, the Turk's Head has a superb location looking out at the quay, perfect for enjoying a beer and local crab while taking in the view of St Mary's – or keeping an eye out so that you don't miss your boat home. Inside, it's model boats and maps, flagstone floors and a pint of the pub's own Turk's Head ale or comforting hot chocolate braced with a nip of something stronger.

Stay

Tourism here is carefully managed, which means there is only a relatively select range of accommodation options (especially on the off-islands and for short stays in peak season). This means occupancy levels and prices stay high, so it is essential to book in advance. There are plenty of decent, old-fashioned B&Bs on St Mary's, fewer on the off-islands: on St Agnes, try **Covean Cottage** (01720 422620); on St Martin's, the two sea-view rooms at **Polreath Guesthouse & Tearoom** (01720 422046, www.polreath.com) or **Little Arthur Farm's** eco-cabin (*see p275*), complete with wormery for 'waste'. Tresco's only pub, the **New Inn** (*see above*), is also a 'cheaper' option (£140-£210 double) for short-stay accommodation; a couple of rooms back on to the heated outdoor pool (open May-Sept).

Hell Bay Hotel
Bryher *(01720 422947/www.hellbay.co.uk). ££££.*
In an unbeatable position on the edge of the Atlantic, Hell Bay Hotel is a pioneer of contemporary if not quite cutting-edge style in the Scillies. The relaxed, spacious suites have exposed A-frame beams and jaunty portholes in the doors; most open on to private balconies or patios with a sea view. Small details are carefully attended to (an umbrella tucked behind the door, internet, water and fresh milk in the fridge, personal cafetière), encouraging you to overlook less appealing aspects (the profusion of branded goods for sale). There's impressive modern art in the expansive bar area, as well as sculptures dotted about the place. Food can be served on the heated patio as well as in the restaurant – the likes of black bream or duck, or local crab from the bar menu. Facilities include a heated outdoor pool, golf and a mini gym and spa.

Island Hotel
Tresco *(01720 422883/www.tresco.co.uk). ££££.*
The front lawn of the Island Hotel sweeps down to the sheltered sands of Raven's Porth on one side, while the other side gives wonderful views of rocky islands and a single line of surf breaking at the reef – though you'll need to fork out for the upper luxury suite, Menavaur, to get the best sight of it. This pleasantly weathered, 'colonial-style' hotel has a five-star location and a peculiar layout that provides most rooms with some kind of sea view. The restaurant serves a combination of locally caught seafood and well-rendered pub classics; salads and sandwiches can be eaten on the bar's large decked terrace. Work up an appetite on the tennis court in the heated outdoor swimming pool (May-Sept), or opt for a yoga break and table tennis in the games room.

St Martin's on the Isle
St Martin's *Lower Town (01720 422090/ www.stmartinshotel.co.uk). ££££.*
The only hotel on St Martin's is a rather angular building. Built of stern grey stone, it opened in 1989 and rather looks like it. The hotel overlooks gardens with incongruous Caribbean rush umbrellas (offset by a perky Union flag) and, beyond them, the quay and beautiful sandy beach. Many of the rooms have enviable sea views, but are otherwise lacking in character. Teän, the main restaurant, is on the first floor

and has one prized table perched right in the angled window looking over the channel to its namesake island. Even though they didn't retain their 2008 Michelin star, the menu remains serious – how about Scillonian fish with lemon-poached lobster and a red onion, mango and coriander salsa? The less formal ground-floor bistro-bar, albeit sleek and rather severe-looking, shows a willingness to move towards (if not quite with) the times. A swimming pool is tucked away indoors.

Star Castle Hotel
St Mary's *The Garrison (01720 422317/www.star-castle.co.uk). ££££.*
This star-shaped granite Elizabethan castle is wonderfully atmospheric. Despite steady refurbishments, the prevailing style remains traditional; stay on the first floor to be in a point of the star, or the second floor for even better views through mullioned windows. Most of the accommodation is in modern, spacious bungalows out back: old World War II barracks, they're simply furnished, light and airy. The patios of rooms on the western side look over the cliff path to the ocean, those to the east on to a lawn and green fields. There are two restaurants, serving veg from the kitchen garden – one is in the castle's original, stone-walled officers' mess room; the other (summer only), a bright conservatory that serves mostly fish under lovely vines. Facilities include a covered pool and grass tennis courts.

Factfile

When to go
Technically accessible all year, most of the islands are in practice closed off-season (usually Nov-Mar). Nearly all events and tours are geared to summer (especially the family rush in August), not even restarting for a flurry of Christmas visitors. Migration patterns ensure a glut of birders arrive each May and September.

Getting there
Transport is very much part of the island experience, but can add complications. There are no scheduled services to or from the islands on a Sunday, and adverse weather (especially fog) can lead to major delays and cancellations. Most hotels and B&Bs make sure you know about any alterations, but do check.

Most visitors pick up the *Scillonian III* at Penzance. The ferry (Isles of Scilly Travel, 0845 710 5555, www.ios-travel.co.uk, £70-£92) makes stately progress to St Mary's (taking the best part of three hours) but it's a real pleasure to sit up on deck in the breeze on a sunny day.

Isles of Scilly Travel operates flights to St Mary's. You can get a twin-prop Skybus from Southampton, Bristol, Exeter, Newquay or Land's End (£100-£298). St Mary's and Tresco are accessible by helicopter (01736 363871, www.islesofscilly helicopter.com, £75-£152) from Penzance.

Getting around
A variety of open boats bounce between islands. From St Mary's Quay, the St Mary's Boatmen's Association (01720 423999, www.scilly boating.co.uk) runs a daily connecting service to the off-islands – the off-islands also have their own services. There are also regular half-day excursions to Bishop Rock and the Western Rocks, various other trips that include sightseeing, and high-speed trips in a RIB – 'rigid inflatable boat'.

On land, walk or rent a bicycle if you can: even St Mary's has no more than nine miles of country lanes to navigate. On Tresco, you can hop on one of the twee golf carts or the heliport's tractor-pulled trailer.

Tourist information
St Mary's Hugh Town (01720 422536/ www.simplyscilly.co.uk). Open Apr-Oct 8.30am-6pm Mon-Sat; 9am-2pm Sun. Sept-Mar 9am-5pm Mon-Fri.

Internet
Public internet access is available at several locations on St Mary's (the tourist office and Buzza Street library are most convenient), with wireless internet at the Deli (*see p275*). On Bryher, the Fraggle Rock (*see p275*) has wireless throughout.

Top: Bla Bheinn;
bottom: Trotternish.

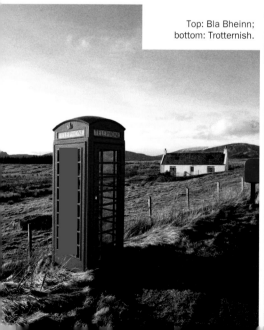

Skye

Mountains and mystique on a Scottish island.

Although Scotland's very name conjures up visions of hills and heather, today the vast majority of its people live in the urban heartlands of Glasgow, Edinburgh and the surrounding towns. But though Scotland's core 21st-century reality may be housing estate tenement and a congested bus ride to work, its self-image is closer to Skye.

With beauty, resonant history, wilderness, a hint of danger and an island sense of otherness, the island, with a population of barely 10,000 people, doesn't just hold out a hope of national self-esteem but embodies it. Like in many other parts of the Highlands and Islands, the landscape, light and sea lochs factor together to become an exemplar, an ideal of an imagined Scotland, unproblematic, layered through with authentic natural drama and a unique identity. Skye continues to claim a special place in Scotland's national psyche as a better and more elegant reflection of itself. The archaeology of nationhood aside, there need be no argument about its status as a perfect place: all its advocates have to do is stand below the Cuillin or among the twisted crags of Trotternish and gesture at the sublime made manifest.

Explore

SLEAT – SOUTH SKYE

One of the very few traditional Scottish airs that people can pluck from the depths of memory, the Skye Boat Song was actually written in the late Victorian period. It commemorated the escape of Bonnie Prince Charlie via Skye to France after the failed Jacobite insurrection of 1745-6.

There's a great deal of romance in the tale: the would-be Stewart monarch, defeated, the dream of his family dynasty finally extinguished – a dynasty that had been the kings of Scotland, then of Great Britain, since the 14th century.

For 20th-century visitors, it was almost impossible to take the ferry to Skye without humming a few bars of the song. Then in 1995, the most popular ferry service – and indeed the Skye Boat Song itself – became somewhat redundant as a bridge was completed from Kyle of Lochalsh to **Kyleakin** on the island. Despite a controversy over its funding, and spectacularly high tolls, from day one the bridge was good for the local economy; it carried more traffic than the ferry it replaced. Visitor numbers stepped up again when tolls were abolished at the end of 2004, and today you can still drive over to Skye for free.

All the same, it is still possible to reach the island the old-fashioned way. The vast majority of visitors setting foot here for the first time arrive on or around Sleat, Skye's southern peninsula.

Generally that means the bridge crossing, but there is also a ferry from Mallaig to Armadale and a summer-only ferry from Glenelg to Kylerhea.

Down at **Armadale**, the obvious attraction is the early 19th-century ruin of Armadale Castle set in 40 acres of well-tended grounds. The Museum primes you for your Skye experience by explaining 1,500 years of local history and culture.

Otherwise, Sleat may not be able to boast the topological splendour seen elsewhere on Skye but it can give you a sneak preview. There is a minor road that heads off in a loop through its hinterland, dropping you at its northern coast, where you get a bracing view across the water to the Cuillin with the furthest extent of its serrated ridge around 12 miles distant. It's a winding, single track but there are some obvious places to stop and take in the panorama, particularly at the hamlet of **Ord**.

Armadale Castle Gardens & Museum of the Isles

Armadale *(01471 844305/www.clandonald.com).*
Open Apr-Oct 9.30am-5.30pm daily. Closed Nov-Mar.
Admission £6; £4.40 reductions.
The gardens, planted just over 200 years ago, are a placid place to walk among mature trees and – in season – meadow flowers. Much of the castle dates from 1815, but it was abandoned in 1925 and exists now only as a shell, albeit a fairly grand one. The museum is housed in a modern building and telling the story of Skye and Ri Innse Gall, the medieval kingdom of the isles. Out of season the museum is closed but you can wander the gardens and see the castle ruins for free.

0   5 miles

Kilmuir

Staffin

Uig

Loch Dungevan

Trotternish

Dunvegan

Neist

Portree

Loch Bracadale

Talisker

Kyle of Lochalsh

The Cuillins

Loch Coruisk

Kyleakin

Ord

Elgol

Sleat Peninsula

Armadale

Skye

Historic sites
● ● ● ● ●

Art & architecture
● ● ● ● ●

Hotels
● ● ● ● ◐

Eating & drinking
● ● ● ● ◐

Scenery
● ● ● ● ●

Outdoor activities
● ● ● ● ●

Cuillin.

Whalespotting

The waters around Skye are home to all kinds of marine animals and a minor industry has grown up to accommodate the interest in these creatures, ranging from populist one-hour jaunts to much more adventurous trips further offshore. They are weather-dependent and usually operate from Easter to October only – no sailing is guaranteed.

Over the Skye Bridge at Kyle of Lochalsh, the rather delightful **Seaprobe Atlantis** (0800 980 4846, www.seaprobeatlantis.com) is a semi-submersible, glass-bottom boat with windows along the hull. It runs excursions that encounter seals, otters and a lot of kelp, although whales, dolphins and sharks have been spotted.

By contrast, **AquaXplore** at Elgol (the end of the B8083 on the Strathaird peninsula, 0800 731 3089, www.aquaxplore.co.uk) offers various options including trips around the minor isles to the south-west of Skye, seeking out sperm and minke whales, basking sharks, porpoises, various types of dolphin and rare seabirds. The company uses RIBs (rigid inflatable boats) that scoot along at 35 knots

or more, so wrap up warm. The more placid *Bella Jane* (www.bellajane.co.uk), also moored at Elgol, will take you over the open waters of Loch Scavaig and into Loch Coruisk, whether you want to get off and explore the Cuillin, or just see the view. Also at Elgol, **Misty Isle Boat Trips** runs a separate service up into Loch Coruisk (01471 866288, www.mistyisle boattrips.co.uk).

Down at Armadale, **Sea.fari Adventures** (01471 833316, www.whalespotting.co.uk) also uses an RIB to head out and look for cetaceans, successfully spotting the likes of minke and humpbacked whales, with trips ranging from one-hour to full-day affairs. See website for details.

Finally, for a more bespoke experience, **Fast-Boat** (0845 224 2219, www.fast-boat.net) asks a simple question on its website: 'Where do you want to go?' They will take you right round Skye in anything from two to four days, whizz out to nearby islands and sea lochs, offer simple day charters and more. It's their RIB but your agenda.

THE CUILLIN AND PORTREE – CENTRAL SKYE

Skye has Norse heritage. The Vikings first came here around 1,200 years ago and eventually settled rather than simply raiding the island for treasure and slaves. What followed on Scotland's western seaboard and in the Hebrides was a complex history of Norse overlordship, hybrid Gaelic-Norse culture and the emergence of an independent polity known as the Lordship of the Isles that only faded as a meaningful power in the 15th century.

All over Skye, place names have Gaelic and Norse roots, and the sea lochs cutting deep into the land are really just fjords, making it easy to imagine longships sailing unchallenged into sheltered waters all those years ago. In the ninth and tenth centuries, the visitors would not even have been Christian but adherents of the old Norse religion, tellers of tales involving Odin and Thor. When you look round Skye today, if there is one place where it's possible to visualise a home for these gods, it's surely the Cuillin.

More than a simple range of mountains, the Cuillin is a complex of peaks, at its most egregious where it clusters around **Loch Coruisk** – from the Gaelic Coire-Uisg, the Cauldron of the Waters – soaring, jagged and challenging. Here is the **Black Cuillin**, which can be traversed as a twisting and exposed ridge from Sgurr nan Eag in the south to Sgurr nan Gillean in the north, taking in 11 Munros – mountains over 3,000 feet – on the way.

The tenor of these hills can be deduced from the names that translate from Gaelic into phrases like the Executioner, the Peak of Torment, the Notched Peak or in plain old English, the Inaccessible Pinnacle. This is not a playground for the inexperienced. A few miles east, there is one more Munro called Bla Bheinn, completing a neat dozen for Skye in total. North of Bla Bheinn are the smaller hills of the **Red Cuillin**, geologically distinct from their near neighbours.

Some say that Skye's grandest panorama is actually from the minor hill **Sgurr na Stri**, not even 1,600 feet high, but positioned far from any road, above the southern end of Loch Coruisk and looking straight up the throat of the Black Cuillin.

Skye experiences a lot of rain. That means the mountains can often be obscured by heavy grey cloud rolling in from the ocean. Conversely, clear days should be all the more treasured; moments when you can cast your gaze along the fearsome Cuillin ridge and almost convince yourself you can see a monocular Norse god up there.

Whether you've been up the Cuillin, or just awed by looking at it, **Portree** provides an antidote. This is the biggest town on Skye, with around 2,500 people. In the compact town centre, between Somerled Square and the small fishing harbour, it's possible to pass an hour or two, browsing some craft shops, or grabbing a coffee.

TROTTERNISH – NORTH-EAST SKYE

Trotternish, the north-east finger of Skye, is home to a lengthy ridge that resembles nothing more than a huge, breaking wave of rock, twisted, complex and recursive, falling back on itself in places, around 15 miles from end to end. It seems to rise gently from sea level in the west at Loch Snizort to more than 2,300 feet at its highest, falling away, sudden and precipitous, a line of cliffs from the north end of the peninsula to the south.

The two main sites where people wander in among this geological insanity are the **Storr** and the **Quiraing**. The former, a becragged association of rock faces, pinnacles and stacks, is just a few miles north of Portree. For Quiraing, take the minor road across the north of Trotternish between Staffin Bay and Uig – there's an obvious parking place. Its name derives from the Norse phrase Kvi Rand, or Rounded Fold, and it's not hard to imagine Vikings sailing down the west coast of Scotland more than a thousand years ago, seeing the features of Trotternish resolve through the clouds: rounded folds of rock coursing away to the south. At the Quiraing, there are more pinnacles and stacks, some dubbed with names like the Needle or the Prison – also a flat grassy area called the Table, splendidly anomalous in context.

Both the Storr and the Quiraing have an insistent atmosphere of the supernatural and both are readily accessible from the road as long as you're willing to venture a mile or so up a rough track. The view from the Storr, to the mountains of Torridon and Wester Ross, also south to the Cuillin, more than repays the effort in reaching its summit. The Quiraing too has those mainland views, but since it stands at the northern end of the chaotic landslip that created all those miles of cliffs and precipices, it offers a south-facing perspective that gives the viewer pause. From here, the convolutions of the ridge seem anguished and painful: fractures and compressions in the Earth that set before they properly healed, trauma cast in stone.

Another part of Trotternish offers a different kind of escape: the small port of Uig is the embarkation point for ferry services to the Outer Hebrides. North from Uig you come to the **Skye Museum of Island Life** at Kilmuir (*see p284*) and, nearby, the memorial for Flora MacDonald, who memorably helped Bonnie Prince Charlie flee Scotland after his defeat at Culloden.

Skye Museum of Island Life

Kilmuir *(01470 552206/www.skyemuseum.co.uk). Open Easter-Oct 9.30am-5pm Mon-Sat. Closed Nov-Easter. Admission £2.50; 50p-£2 reductions.*
Up at Kilmuir north of Uig, this museum comprises a small township of thatched cottages, focusing on social history and the crofting that was prevalent on the island towards the end of the 19th century and the beginning of the 20th.

FURTHER AFIELD: NORTH-WEST SKYE

Skye throws up surprises. Take a trip to the **Talisker Distillery** (*see below*), for example, and you might just be inspired to drive the extra four miles 'over the hill' to **Talisker Bay**. Road access stops short of the shore, but a brisk 20-minute walk finally brings you to a pincer of land, around half a mile across, with a sea stack offshore, high cliffs on the north side and a beach made of shingle and black sand. In winter it can be haunting, in summer simply beautiful.

The north-west has its fair share of other natural wonders: **Loch Bracadale** perhaps, with its small isles and peninsulas; **Loch Dunvegan** and its castle (*see below*), or even Skye's westernmost point at **Neist**, beyond Glendale. There is a lighthouse here, and the Uists and Benbecula are only 15 miles away. You can look back to Waterstein Head and Moonen Bay, or west to the Outer Hebrides.

Dunvegan Castle

Dunvegan *(01470 521206/www.dunvegancastle.com). Open Apr-mid Oct 10am-5.30pm daily. 11am-4pm daily. Admission Castle & gardens £7.50; £4-£6 reductions. Gardens only £5/ £3-£3.50 reductions.*
The seat of the Clan MacLeod can boast continuous occupation by the same family for nearly eight centuries, give or take a few decades' absence here and there. Dunvegan Castle sits at the south end of Loch Dunvegan, cheek by jowl with the eponymous village, in gardens dating to the 18th century. The castle itself has been added to over the years, while the unmissable display item is the Fairy Flag. This has been scientifically analysed and found to be made of Middle Eastern silk, anything from 1,300-1,700 years old. Legend has it that the MacLeods can wave the flag to ward off ill fortune in times of severe crisis but it will only work three times. They have used it twice so far…

Talisker Distillery

Carbost *(01478 614308/www.taliskerwhisky.com/ www.discovering-distilleries.com). Open Apr-June, Sept, Oct 9.30am-5pm (last tour 4pm) Mon-Sat. July, Aug 9.30am-5pm (last tour 4pm) Mon-Sat; 12.30-5pm (last tour 4pm) Sun. Nov-Mar tours 10.30am, noon, 2pm, 3.30pm Mon-Fri. Admission £5, £2.50 reductions.*
At the village of Carbost on Loch Harpor, is the far-flung distillery where Talisker, the splendid single malt Scotch, is made. Standard tours conclude with a nip of whisky for adults. The more in-depth tasting tour (£15) needs to be booked in advance. In the well-stocked shop you can buy everything from the familiar 10-year-old Talisker to more mature expressions and limited editions.

Eat

Good food is also available for non-residents in the **Hotel Eilean Iarmain**; it's reviewed in the Stay section (*see p287*).

Café Arriba

Portree *Quay Brae (01478 611830/www.cafe arriba.co.uk). Open Summer 7am-10pm daily. Winter 8am-5pm daily. ££. International.*
This is a spacious and bohemian first-floor establishment in the middle of Portree – colourful and informal. It's where to come for some curried parsnip soup then Moroccan lamb perhaps, with a Black Cuillin ale. Alternatively, pop in for coffee or an echinacea and raspberry tea.

Chandlery Restaurant

Portree *Bosville Hotel, Bosville Terrace (01478 612 846/www.bosvillehotel.co.uk). Open Summer 6.30-9pm. Winter phone for details. ££££. Modern European.*
The Bosville Hotel's flagship restaurant – the Chandlery – is under the control of chef John Kelly; modern and smart without being starchy. The establishment overlooks the town's small harbour and seafood is a big feature. A typical menu might offer hand-dived scallops to start, poached halibut as a main. It's the best restaurant in Portree so it's prudent to book; also, in the very depths of midwinter opening hours are sometimes curtailed.

Kinloch Lodge Hotel

12 miles S of Skye bridge, Sleat *(01471 833 333/ www.kinloch-lodge.co.uk). Open 8.30-9.30am, noon-2.30pm, 6.30-9pm daily. ££££. Modern European.*
Kinloch has always been a foodie destination thanks to the reputation of cook and food writer Lady Claire Macdonald, who built its reputation from the 1970s. With her other commitments however, and an eye to the future, Marcello Tully, who had trained under the Roux brothers at La Gavroche – took the reins in the kitchen in 2007. Lady Claire says the menu has taken a leap forward with a professionalism and precision that could garner awards in years to come. The dining room is bedecked with antique Macdonald portraits, while Tully offers up a five-course dinner that could bring parsnip and Pernod soup, a complex salmon and sesame mousse, scallops on black pudding mousse, seared venison fillet, then lemon and vanilla chiboust: a very high standard indeed, accordingly priced.

Loch Bay Seafood

Stein, Waternish, 6 miles N of Dunvegan, North-west Skye *(01470 592235/www.lochbay-seafood-restaurant.co.uk). Open noon-2pm, 6.30-9.30pm daily. £££. Seafood.*
A small seasonal (open Easter to October) restaurant, Loch Bay Seafood is around six miles north of Dunvegan on the west side of the Waternish peninsula at Stein. A much-praised establishment, the premises are fisherman's cottage-style, with simple decor, and it's a great place to sample seafood fresh from local waters: oysters or mussels to start, grilled prawns or fish as a main, depending on the day's catch.

The Three Chimneys/House Over By

Dunvegan, North-west Skye *Colbost (01470 511258/ www.threechimneys.co.uk). Open Mid Mar-Oct 12.30-1.45pm, 6.30-9.30pm Mon-Sat; 6.30-9.30pm Sun. Nov-mid Mar 6.30-9.30pm daily. ££££. Modern European.*

Chandlery Restaurant.

Hotel Eilean Iarmain.

Kinloch Lodge dominates the fine dining scene on Sleat but up by Dunvegan, the Three Chimneys is its main competitor, and has provided an acclaimed dining experience since 1984. It's a smartened-up crofter's cottage with stone walls and cool furniture, offering a focus on local produce: Moonen Bay lobster to start, perhaps, then fillet of Limousin beef from Lochalsh. In 1999 the owners added the House Over-By, six rather fabulous en-suite bedrooms with a swish, modern design. It's a winner if you've just had dinner here and don't want to drive. The breakfasts are rather amazing too.

Stay

Good-quality accommodation is also available at the House Over-By at the **Three Chimneys** (*see p284*).

Bosville Hotel
Portree *Bosville Terrace (01478 612 846/www.bosville hotel.co.uk). £££.*
The Bosville offers comfortable, contemporary rooms that bring a metropolitan feel to your sleepover – until you look out the window and realise you're in the middle of Portree and a long, long way from Big City UK.

Hotel Eilean Iarmain
Sleat *(01471 833 332/www.eilean-iarmain.co.uk). £££.*
Great setting, brilliant views, a good pub, adjacent whisky shop and an art gallery that opens from April to October. Even before you get round to the accommodation, this affable 19th-century inn has a lot going for it. The rooms are more Edwardian and traditional than boutique-groovy, although four suites in the old stable block over the road

are much more up to date. The complimentary miniature of Té Bheag whisky in each room is a nice touch. The small dining room offers the likes of home-cured salmon with horseradish ice-cream and organic leaves to start; roast rump of lamb with olive oil mash to follow. The hotel bar, popular with locals, also does food, with most mains under a tenner – haddock and chips, perhaps, or venison burger.

Kinloch Lodge Hotel
12 miles S of Skye bridge, Sleat *(01471 833 333/ www.kinloch-lodge.co.uk). ££££.*
Sitting on a small inlet known as Loch na Dal looking across to Knoydart, the core of the original Kinloch Lodge has been here since the late 17th century, although much added-to in subsequent years. A second lodge was built in sympathetic style in 1998 and both offer accommodation. Kinloch is also a family seat – the Macdonalds – and both lodges are replete with antique portraits and memorabilia. General decor is in keeping with the history, contemporary comfort colliding with a traditional sensibility. Welcoming and hospitable, service is right on the button, cooking standards are Skye-high (*see p284*), breakfasts fabulous and a visit here is more of an experience than just a stayover in a country house.

Stein Inn
Stein, Waternish, 6 miles N of Dunvegan, Northwest Skye *(01470 592 362/www.steininn.co.uk). ££.*
Want to stay in a small and simple 18th-century inn? Thanks to some illustrious venues, Skye is often associated with the upper end of the hotel market, although a more economical bed for the night is a welcome addition to the island's hotel roster. The rooms at the Stein Inn, up on Loch Bay, are simple in decor, the seafood is fresh (weather permitting) and there's a decent bar with around 125 single malt whiskies to choose from, some cask ales too. No frills, good atmosphere.

Factfile

When to go
While the rest of Britain goes about its business, Skye could be battered by gale force winds but on days when Central Scotland is covered in snow, the island might enjoy blustery winter sunshine and blue skies – all subject to change in minutes. In general, Skye's location means it is rainy but temperate thanks to the Gulf Stream. Late spring and summer tend to have most sunshine, least wind and least rain although any day can be a wet day. Rainfall tends to get up a real head of steam in September however and stays pretty insistent through to January. Average top temperatures around Skye even in July are only in the 15-16°C range and anything over 20°C is 'hot'.

Getting there & around
The nearest airport is Inverness (www.hial.co.uk), which has scheduled flights to Edinburgh, Belfast, London and other English cities; it also has car

hire. The nearest train stations are Kyle of Lochalsh (with connections to Inverness) and Mallaig (connections to Glasgow) – see www.scotrail.co.uk. Regular buses run from Inverness via the Skye Bridge to Portree then up to Uig (www.citylink.co.uk). Caledonian MacBrayne runs the ferry from Mallaig to Armadale (www.calmac.co.uk) and its website also has details of the summer-only service between Glenelg and Kylerhea, and connections to Uig from the Outer Hebrides. There are local bus services around Skye, also on and off the island to Kyle of Lochalsh (08712 002233/ www.stagecoachbus.com) so it is possible to visit without a car, but it's a lot easier with one.

Tourist information
Bayfield House, Bayfield Road, Portree (01478 612 137/www.skye.co.uk). Open 9am-5pm Mon-Fri, 10am-4pm Sat.

Small Gems

Top: Royal Crescent; middle: Thermae Bath Spa; bottom: street scene, Parade Gardens.

Bath

Georgian England, perfectly preserved.

As England's most famous spa town, Bath has attracted visitors for some two thousand years. In many ways, the place was designed as a tourist destination, built as it was around the natural hot springs that gave the city its name. The Romans were the first to tap the waters properly, constructing a bathhouse that formed the gushing heart of 'Aquae Sulis'. The excavated Roman Baths remain one of the city's glories.

Bath enjoyed a surge of popularity in the 18th century, when bathing in thermal springs became increasingly fashionable, and legendary socialite Richard 'Beau' Nash soon established the city as high society's favourite watering hole. Most of Bath's landmark buildings – the stunning Royal Crescent, the Pump Room, the Circus, the Cross Bath and Hot Bath, the Assembly Rooms and Pulteney Bridge over the River Avon – date from the period. The city's gorgeous (and often steep) streets and squares, classically conceived and built with honey-coloured bath stone, lend the city its period film-set feel. Bath became a World Heritage Site in 1987, and conservation of this Georgian heritage is taken seriously.

Artists, writers and musicians inspired by Bath include Dickens, Scott, Gainsborough, Handel and Daniel Defoe, who once said: 'Bath is a spot of ground which our countrymen ought to esteem as a particular favour of heaven.' The most famous literary resident, however, was Jane Austen. 'Oh, who can ever be tired of Bath?' sighed the heroine of *Northanger Abbey*, echoing the sentiment of many a social butterfly who flitted from the Pump Room to the new Theatre Royal, between the promenades, balls and assemblies. It is the spirit of those times – along with its Roman heritage – that remains the main draws for visitors today. However, Bath's bright new Thermae Bath Spa, opened in 2006, has brought the city bang up to date as a 21st-century spa destination.

Explore

Bath is an easy city to navigate, being small and compact with lots of pedestrianised areas. There's an aura of classical decorum about the place, established by the Georgian streets and squares. **Abbey Church Yard**, home to both Bath Abbey and the Roman Baths, is a natural meeting point in the centre of the city. It is also the site of the main tourist information office. Another highlight is the **Royal Crescent**, an awe-inspiring spectacle of Georgian grace that affords sumptuous views of the city (although many of its houses appear to be unoccupied for much of the year). The Crescent was the work of John Wood the Younger, who along with his father was among the city's principal architects.

All the major stages in the history of England are well-represented in Bath; to learn more about the city's, and England's, heritage, take advantage of the free two-hour **walking tours** that take place every day (phone 01225 477411 or visit www.thecityofbath.co.uk). The tourist office can provide information on the many museums and attractions not listed here, such as the Theatre Royal, Museum of East Asian Art, the Victoria Art Gallery, Bath Postal Museum and the Jane Austen Centre.

Bath is also home to a number of annual festivals including the Bath Literature Festival in February/March, the Bath International Music Festival and the Bath Fringe Festival, both in May/June. For all, *see p388* **Festivals**.

Bath Abbey

Abbey Church Yard (01225 422462/www.bath abbey.org). Open Apr-Oct 9am-6pm Mon-Sat; 1-2.30pm, 4.30-5.30pm Sun. Nov-Mar 9am-4.30pm Mon-Sat; 1-2.30pm, 4.30-5.30pm Sun. Admission free.

Both the geographical and spiritual heart of the city, the Abbey Church of St Peter and St Paul (aka Bath Abbey) was the last Tudor church to be built prior to the Reformation. Work started on its construction in the late 15th century, but it incorporates parts of a once-massive Norman predecessor built in the late 11th century. This in turn stood on the remains of an Anglo-Saxon monastery dating from 757 (where Edgar, the first king of England, was crowned in 973), destroyed during the Norman Conquest. The building suffered at the hands of Henry VIII, but Elizabeth I ensured its reconstruction and called it the 'Lantern of the West'. Above the great west door of the abbey is a Latin inscription that translates as 'Behold, how good and pleasing it is'. A very true statement: enjoy the heavenly colours and spectacular vaulting, and explore the site's 1,600-year history in the vaults heritage museum. The abbey is also the city's largest concert venue, and home to the Klais organ.

Fashion Museum & Assembly Rooms

Bennett Street (01225 477173/www.fashion museum.co.uk). Open Jan, Feb, Nov, Dec 10.30am-4pm daily. Mar-Oct 10.30am-5pm daily. Admission £7; £5-£6.25 reductions.

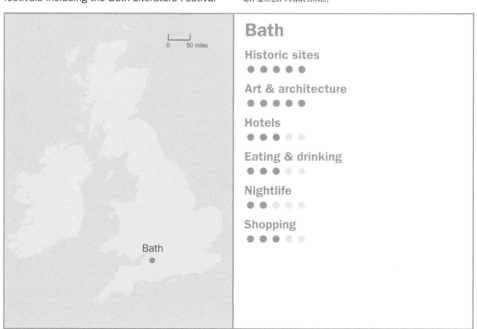

0 ⌞ 50 miles

Bath
•

Bath

Historic sites
● ● ● ● ●

Art & architecture
● ● ● ● ●

Hotels
● ● ● ● ○

Eating & drinking
● ● ● ● ○

Nightlife
● ● ○ ○ ○

Shopping
● ● ● ○ ○

Roman Baths.

Housed in the grand Georgian Assembly Rooms, this collection covers 400 years of fashion. The earliest complete costume in the museum is a very rare survival from the 1660s: a formal cream silk dress woven with silver thread. Interactive features include the chance to try on reproduction corsets and crinolines. Special exhibitions are held here too; recent shows displayed a collection of intricate 17th-century gloves, explored 30 years of punk and new wave bands in a photographic exhibition, and celebrated the work of 1970s fashion designer Bill Gibb.

"Apart from the steaming, photogenic Great Bath, surrounded by a 2,000-year-old pavement structure, there are complexes of indoor baths."

Roman Baths

Abbey Church Yard (01225 477785/www.roman baths.co.uk). Open Jan, Feb, Nov, Dec 9.30am-4.30pm daily. Mar-June, Sept, Oct 9am-5pm daily. July, Aug 9am-9pm daily. Admission £11-£11.50; £7.20-£9.50 reductions.

An excellent handset-guided tour (with additional Bill Bryson commentary, should you choose that option) takes you around the steamy bowels of the Roman Baths. The Romans constructed a temple here, next to England's only hot springs, in 60-70 AD (although the first to discover the site were the Celts, a few hundred years earlier). The baths flourished until the fifth century AD, when the complex becoming a place of pilgrimage. They were excavated some 1,400 years later, missing out on Bath's Georgian heyday as a spa destination.

Apart from the steaming, photogenic Great Bath, surrounded by a 2,000-year-old pavement structure, there are surprising complexes of indoor baths, the ruins of the temple of Minerva (goddess of the thermal spring) and bubbling King's Bath source. Also on display are great collections of temple sculpture, jewellery, pottery, wishing-spa coins and curses (bathers often left notes cursing fellow users for stealing their belongings, for example). Computer animations re-create Roman life, with projections of life-sized bathers using the Frigidarium (the cold plunge pool) a creative new addition in 2008. The water is, alas, no longer safe to swim in, but the nearby Thermae Bath Spa (*see below*) uses the same natural springs for the modern-day experience. The Baths are a must-see – although note that at busy times it can be a stressfully slow-moving experience due to the high numbers of visitors; allow about two hours to view everything. The most calming time to see the baths is on July and August evenings, by torchlight, when the complex is open until 10pm (last entry 9pm). Alternatively, complete an afternoon trip here with tea at the adjacent Pump Room (*see p297*).

Thermae Bath Spa

The Hetling Pump Room, Hot Bath Street (0844 888 0844/www.thermaebathspa.com). Open 9am-10pm daily. Admission from £22 (2hr session).

The open-air rooftop pool at 'Britain's original and only natural thermal spa' is the most relaxing way to soak up the beauty of Bath. Head straight to the top of Nicholas Grimshaw's slick glass cube, which finally opened to great fanfare in 2006, and submerge yourself in the warm, mineral-rich jets for an effortless view of the city skyline, Bath Abbey and the hills beyond. The vista is impressive at any time of day, but an evening visit is particularly magical, with well-considered lighting, twinkling streetlights and steam rising off the water's surface as you recline above the city. Additional watery facilities to relax mind, body and soul include the gentle currents and whirlpool jets of the lower floor's curvaceous Minerva bath, and, on the upper floor, four circular glass aroma steam rooms, foot baths and a huge waterfall shower. Take the de-stressing up a notch by booking one of the spa's treatments – everything from hot-stone massage to caviar facials is offered. Two-hour, four-hour and full-day spa sessions are available, alongside an array of packages including treatments, followed by refreshments in the stylishly minimal café-restaurant.

Eat

Bath is thought to have more restaurants per capita in the UK than any city outside London. The 'source locally, eat seasonally' ethos has been pursued with vigour by many of the city's restaurants, partly because this tends to be a middle-class preoccupation – and Bath isn't short of middle-class residents – and partly because the city is located close to some of England's best food producers. Somerset is famed for two culinary items: cheese (namely cheddar) and cider, and both can be found in abundance in the city. The **Fine Cheese Co** (*see p298*) is a particularly good source of the former, while the **Packhorse Inn** (01225 832060, www.packhorseinn.com) in Southstoke, just outside the city, is an excellent spot for a pint of the latter.

Bath is also close to excellent West Country suppliers of meat, game and seafood, so you're unlikely to go far wrong in the city's restaurants and pubs – unless, that is, you're looking for ultra-modish decor or highly innovative cuisine. Bath's rather conservative spirit extends to its British-focused dining scene. Some of the best places are listed below, but you'd also do well to check out the **King William** pub and dining rooms (36 Thomas Street, 01225 428096, www.kingwilliampub.com), with its award-winning gastropub food and excellent local beverages; **Bistro Papillon** (2 Margaret's Buildings, Brock Street, 01225 310064, www.bistropapillon.co.uk) for relaxed contemporary French cuisine; **No.5** (5 Argyle Street, 01225 444499, www.no5 restaurant.co.uk) for French bistro dishes with a modern twist, served in a homely spot; and, if you're looking for haute cuisine, the **Dower House** restaurant at the Royal Crescent Hotel (16 Royal Crescent, 01225 823333, www.royal crescent.co.uk, *see p301*).

Bell Inn

103 Walcot Street (01225 460426/www.walcot street.com). Open 11.30am-11pm Mon-Sat; noon-10.30pm Sun. £. Pub.

Set on Bath's bohemian Walcot Street, the Bell keeps it real with nine real ales (including Otter, Pitchfork, Bellringer, and Summer Lightning), proper pub banter, a real fire and regular bands (normally of the folk, acoustic and funk variety). It's definitely a locals' pub, but don't let that stop you putting your foot through the door, as the bar is usually packed with punters (of all ages) so squeezing in unnoticed is pretty easy. Other draws include a bar-billiards table, table football, vegan and vegetarian filled rolls, and rowdy events such as the popular open mic nights.

Demuths Vegetarian Restaurant

2 North Parade Passage, off Abbey Green (01225 446059/www.demuths.co.uk). Open 10-11.30am, noon-10pm Mon-Fri, Sun; 9-11.30am, noon-10pm Sat. £££. Vegetarian.

It may be over 20 years old, but Rachel Demuth's world-food vegetarian restaurant, near Bath Abbey, continues to keep diners on their toes. The cooking has garnered praise, as well as a string of accolades, and with Helen Lawrence now head chef, the menu is as exciting and tasty as ever. A meal might start with some labneh with lavash (cream cheese balls rolled in fresh herbs and seeds, served with sesame flatbread), or an eastern wrap filled with tofu, vegetables and tahini. The small number of mains are as diverse in scope as they are satisfying, with an Indian thali competing with sausages (vegetarian, natch) and mash, and an Italian vegetable-based roast. Vegetables, breads and cheese come from local suppliers, an organic and fair-trade ethos is upheld, and there are vegan and wheat-free dishes available. To finish, make sure you tuck into one of the indulgent desserts, such as tiramisu semifreddo. Those sold on the food might like to learn the recipes at Demuths Cookery School.

Jamie's Italian

10 Milsom Place (01225 510051/www.jamies italian.com). Open noon-11pm Mon-Sat; noon-10.30pm Sun. £££. Italian.

Bath's version of Jamie Oliver's new mini-chain was attracting queues in the months after it opened in 2008, and deservedly so. The concept is rustic Italian food served in a stylish, laid-back space – at accessible prices. You can't book, but you're well looked-after in the ground-floor bar area if all the tables are full when you arrive. The warm and light upstairs space is nicely decorated with sunflower-yellow walls, metal pendant lamps, patterned country tiled floors and a long wooden table in the centre, but the best tables are on the terrace, with great views of the city. Anyone who has bought a Jamie Oliver cookbook won't be surprised by the menu – lots of fresh pasta (sausage pappardelle, ravioli caramelle), chargrilled meat, superb side salads and 'pukka' Italian desserts. The food is excellent value, and the wine list strong. The only downside was the rather imposing background pop music, supposedly in keeping with the egalitarian vibe.

Marlborough Tavern

35 Marlborough Buildings (01225 423731/www. marlborough-tavern.com). Open (restaurant) 12.30-2.30pm, 6-9.30pm Mon-Sat; 12.30-4pm Sun. £££. Gastropub.

An upmarket gastropub in an upmarket part of town, the friendly Marlborough Tavern is a good bet for a pint of well-kept local ale or cider, along with some freshly prepared restaurant-quality British food made from locally sourced ingredients. The menu changes with the seasons, but might include the likes of pan-fried chicken livers with plum syrup for starters, then Cornish pollack with bouillabaisse sauce, or a rib-eye steak from a nearby farm for mains, and locally produced ice-cream or West Country cheeses for dessert. The wine list is exemplary and regular tasting sessions are held. The 'pub' element is kept alive by the pretty beer garden. This place is popular: it's a good idea to book.

"Something of a Bath institution, the Pump Room is an obligatory stop for brunch or afternoon tea."

Olive Tree Restaurant

Queensberry Hotel, Russell Street (01225 447928/www. thequeensberry.co.uk). Open noon-2pm, 7-10pm Mon-Sat; 12.30-2pm, 7-10pm Sun. ££££. Modern European.

The basement Olive Tree restaurant at the Queensberry Hotel (*see p301*) has fast become one of Bath's most esteemed dining-out venues. On any given night, you're likely to find as many locals as hotel guests here. Head chef Marc Salmon is committed to using local and seasonal ingredients, and both his menu and the nicely lit, artily decorated space (with colourful contemporary artwork) evoke strong modern European sensibilities (with the attendant Mediterranean influences). A la carte mains include the likes of wild sea bass with herb risotto, duo of beef with creamed potato and root vegetables, and roast chicken breast with purple sprouting broccoli, carrots and roast potatoes. Prices are high, so if you're on a tight budget, consider sampling the fixed-price lunch menu.

Pump Room

Abbey Church Yard (01225 444477/www.searcys.co.uk). Open 9.30am-4.30pm daily. ££. Café.

Something of a Bath institution, the Pump Room is an obligatory stop for brunch or afternoon tea of toasted Bath buns, between a trip to the Abbey and the adjacent Roman Baths. The huge, grand space – with columned walls, chandeliers and round tables bearing white tablecloths – was the social heart of the city for more than two centuries. A wide range of cakes, coffees, tea and smoothies is offered in addition to the British lunch and (in much of May, June and July, to coincide with Bath's International Music festival and the late opening of the Roman baths) dinner menus (field mushroom and squash stew, local rabbit and venison sausages, and fish pie are typical mains).

Same Same But Different

Bartlett Street (01225 466856). Open 8-11.45am, noon-3.30pm Mon-Fri; 9-11.45am, 12.30-4pm Sat; 10-11.45am, noon-4pm Sun. ££. Spanish.

Taken over a couple of years back by a young couple, this daytime-only fave on trend-setting Bartlett Street is a tapas bar with a difference, as the name implies. Creative flair is used to heighten the flavours of classic tapas dishes, often improving them in the process. Spanish chorizo comes glazed in Somerset cider, meatballs are cooked in a tomato and rosemary sauce, while calamares (that tapas bar staple) are flavoured with paprika and lime and served with aïoli. You'll also find sandwiches (pickled beetroot and Somerset cheddar, say), soups and main-course salads (hot salmon niçoise, for instance).

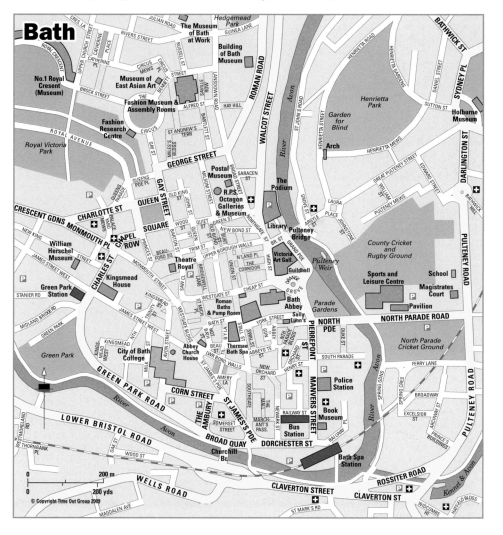

Shop

Bath may not be a centre for cutting-edge fashion, but if you're after an easily navigated layout (with plenty of pedestrianised areas) and lots of upmarket chains, as well as a high number of independent gift, beauty and food shops (plus an excellent musical instruments shop in the form of **Duck, Son & Pinker**, 9-12 Bridge Street, 01225 465975, www.duckson andpinker.co.uk), then you've come to the right place. To find more left-field items, head to bohemian Walcot Street, home to a host of second-hand clothing shops, as well as the excellent **Fine Cheese Co** (*see p298*).

Bath is one of only two places in the world to contain a bridge with shops incorporated into the original design (the other being in Florence); Robert Adam's Pulteney Bridge, built in 1773, is stuffed with tiny (and mainly tourist-orientated) shops selling antiques, souvenirs, fashions and, in the **Dolls House Miniatures of Bath** (01225 426161), thousands of scaled-down objects for dolls' houses.

Bath is a great place for **markets**. The **Guildhall Market** (open 9am-5pm Mon-Sat), located in a Grade II listed structure, is filled with around 30 independent traders selling a wide variety of goods, including food (the Nibbles Cheese Stall, Bath Bakery, Bath Humbug Shop), household goods, books, antiques and some crafts. Another fine covered shopping space is the **Green Park Station** (Green Park Road, 01225 787910, www.greenparkstation.co.uk), an attractive former Victorian railway station that now houses a variety of shops, a twice-weekly general market (selling everything from antiques and collectibles to clothing, books and crafts), and on Saturdays (8.30am-1.30pm) a farmers' market – it was the UK's first, opening in 1997. But the *pièce de résistance* has to be the Christmas market: 123 wooden chalet stalls selling handicrafts, original gifts, cards, decorations, luxury food and drink – all in a suitably festive setting between Bath Abbey and the Roman Baths.

Fine Cheese Co

29 & 31 Walcot Street (01225 483407/www.fine cheese.co.uk). Open 9.30am-5.30pm Mon-Fri; 9am-5.30pm Sat.

You may know this company from its upmarket cheese biscuits, which have been sneaking into posh delis around Britain. The shop specialises in artisan British cheeses, particularly West Country varieties. Tasting is encouraged, but it would be hard to sample all the cheeses, with over 100 British varieties available – from rediscovered gems like devon oke to the lord of the hundreds (an unpasteurised sheep's milk cheese in the style of a pecorino) – as well as a good choice of European imports. A range of biscuits,

chutneys and breads is also sold, and there's an on-site café. The Fine Cheese Co has made headlines for its alternative wedding 'cakes' consisting of three tiers of cheese.

Mee

9A Bartlett Street (01225 442250/www.mee boutique.com). Open 10am-5.30pm Mon-Sat; 11.30am-4.30pm Sun.

This 'women's fashion and lifestyle boutique' on cute Bartlett Street is where to go for an upmarket girly fix. Opened in 2003, the pretty shop stocks flouncy clothing, sexy but tasteful lingerie, handbags, shoes and sparkly jewellery. Labels include Traffic People, Heidi Klein, Johnny Loves Rosie and Tocca. Express your feminine and frivolous side with scented candles, hair accessories, Venetian mirror jewellery boxes, glass perfume bottles and cult beauty products and body oils.

Mr B's Emporium of Reading Delights

14-15 John Street (01225 331155/www.mrbs emporium.com). Open 9.30am-6.30pm Mon-Sat.

It's easy to see why Mr B's was recently awarded the accolade of Independent Bookshop of the Year at the British Book Industry awards; enthusiastic and knowledgeable staff are just the beginning. Within the two-storey Georgian premises, the creaky and old-fashioned are combined with the fresh and modern to create a 'proper bookshop' that's beautifully organised. Plenty of book notes, inviting seating arrangements and even complimentary coffee encourage long browsing sessions. The stock is exemplary (with a forte in contemporary literature and the arts), and frequent events are held (this was the official bookseller for Bath's prestigious Literature Festival). There's even a friendly shop dog. Highly recommended.

Stay

Bath has a good range of places to stay, ranging from a widening array of boutique-type townhouses and B&Bs, to luxury pads that wouldn't disappoint any American statesman who happens to be in town.

In addition to the venues listed below, it's worth checking out the **Town House** (01225 422505, www.thetownhousebath.co.uk). Meanwhile, those in search of aristocratic opulence might want to head for **Homewood Park** (01225 723731,www.homewood park.co.uk, a classically furnished luxury country house in the Limpley Stoke valley, just a short taxi ride from the city, set in ten acres of beautiful gardens and with a nationally acclaimed restaurant. Wherever you decide to rest your head, it's generally wise to book in advance; Bath is one of England's most popular tourist destinations, so rooms tend to fill up quickly, especially in the summer high season or during one of the many festivals.

Jamie's Italian.

Royal Crescent Hotel.

Bloomfield House

146 Bloomfield Road (01225 420105/www.eco bloomfield.com). £££.

This eco B&B/hotel is housed in an impressive Grade II listed Georgian dwelling on the outskirts of the city, once the home of Bath's Lord Mayor. Welcoming and friendly owners Karen and Robert Barnard-Weston were co-founders of Bath's farmers' market, the first of its kind in the country. They pride themselves on their full English breakfast, which uses locally sourced and organic ingredients. The sustainability credentials don't stop there: the hotel car runs on used, filtered vegetable oil, and the garden furniture is made from sustainably grown wood. Rooms have fine views of the city. They're a bit chintzy, but comfortable and filled with artworks and antiques.

Harington's Hotel

8-10 Queen Street (01225 461728/www.haringtons hotel.co.uk). £££.

Probably the best value of all the central hotels, Harington's is smack bang in the middle of things – on a quiet cobbled sidestreet a stone's throw from the Thermae Bath Spa, the main shopping street and a number of restaurants and bars. Its 13 en suite 'boutique' bedrooms are all decorated in a contemporary, clean-lined style and come complete with the requisite power showers, super-comfy beds (with Egyptian cotton bedding), and mod cons like Wi-Fi and LCD TVs. A hotel bar and top-notch breakfasts complete the experience.

Queensberry Hotel

Russell Street (01225 447928/www.the queensberry.co.uk). £££.

One of Bath's few boutique hotels, the Queensberry occupies four interlinking classic Georgian townhouses.

The drawing room, bar and 29 guest rooms are done out in tastefully muted tones (think plums, olives and slate greys) with smart mahogany furniture, flock wallpaper and warm carpets. Comfy beds, sophisticated lighting and modern amenities like flatscreen TVs and DAB radios in the guest rooms ensure a relaxing stay. To truly splash out, opt for Room Four, the hotel's signature suite, complete with a seven-foot custom-made bed and iPod docking station. For the hotel's well-regarded Olive Tree restaurant, *see p297*.

Royal Crescent Hotel

16 Royal Crescent (01225 823333/www.royal crescent.co.uk). ££££.

One should expect nothing but the best from a hotel with possibly the best address in Britain, slap bang in the centre of the 'world's finest crescent'. Both the properties making up the hotel are Grade I listed. The 45 bedrooms all overlook gardens or parkland. A stylishly unfussy entrance hall, with chequered flooring, leads into the hotel's impressive central gardens. The suites are all named after local personalities, such as Jane Austen, Sir Thomas Gainsborough and celebrated dandy Beau Nash, and boast handcrafted beds, stucco ceilings and huge bathrooms, as well as fluffy bathrobes and quality smellies. The Bath House spa and the award-winning Dower House restaurant are both big attractions. The spa is housed in a converted coach house and stables, with teak-lined jacuzzi and plunge pool, a warming relaxation pool, dry and steam saunas and fully equipped gymnasium, as well as a range of treatments. The restaurant offers Anglo-French cuisine (with all the appetisers, palate-refreshers and foams you'd expect at such a place) from a menu that changes seasonally. The wine cellar is exemplary too.

Factfile

When to go

Bath is a popular destination year-round, but particular highlights include December, when the Christmas Market is in full swing and the classical decorum of the city looks especially beautiful, and during one of the many cultural festivals held in the city: namely the nine-day, well-attended Bath Literature Festival (www.bathlitfest.org.uk) in February/March; the Bath International Music Festival (www.bathmusicfest.org.uk) and Bath Fringe Festival (www.bathfringe.co.uk, a lively Walcot Street-based party) both in late May/early June; and the Mozartfest (www.bathmozartfest.org.uk) in November.

Getting there and around

There are direct trains from London's Paddington Station to Bath Spa, the city's main railway station. The journey time is around 90 minutes. If travelling by **car**, leave the M4 at junction 18. Bath is an easy city to explore **on foot** and

is compact enough to make public transport redundant if you're staying fairly central. However, narrow streets and identical building façades make losing your bearings fairly easy. There are **taxi ranks** outside the station and near Bath Abbey.

Tourist information

Bath Tourist Information Centre Abbey Chambers, Abbey Church Yard (0906 711 2000/www.visitbath.co.uk). Open Oct-May 9.30am-5pm Mon-Sat; 10am-4pm Sun. June-Sept 9.30am-6pm Mon-Sat; 10am-4pm Sun. Free walking tours are run by the centre (*see p292*).

Internet

Many pubs and most hotels in the city have wireless internet access.
Bath Library 19-23 The Podium (01225 394041/www.librarieswest.org.uk).
Discover IT 7A York Street (01225 463030).

Top: St John's College (left); King's College Chapel; bottom: Trinity College (left); the Backs.

Cambridge

Small university city that packs a big visual and intellectual punch.

Cambridge is a ground-level city, as flat as the fenland it was first built upon 2,000 years ago. Sure, you can climb the bell tower of Great St Mary's to get your bearings or tramp up steep little Castle Mound – the chalk hill that is all that remains of the city's originary fort – but the attractions of this river town are not laid out for you to look on from above, like a tinker's blanket full of fripperies. Instead, they are glimpsed down alleys or through ancient gates. Perhaps on leaving the over-elaborate fan vaulting of cathedral-sized King's Chapel, you chance upon the loveliness of Clare's aligned arches. Maybe you're in brooding St John's chapel as the organist strikes up. Or you timidly push through a human-scale subsidiary door set into vast wooden gates – unsure you're even allowed in – only for it to swing open on a cloistered courtyard of such verdant grass you think it must be the gardeners, not the professors, who are the key college personnel. Chased out of the back of Trinity by gruff, bowler-hatted porters, you discover the narrow meadows of the Backs are resplendent in purple crocuses. Gingerly poled punts populate the Cam every sunny day with a traffic jam of squealing delight and splashy disaster, and everyone – mountain-bike hippies waggling straggly beards, girls in ra-ra skirts or saggy University tracks, tweedoids gravely wobbling on sit-up-and-begs – rides a bike (look over your shoulder, unwary newcomer!). Not even the tourist-choked days of high summer drown the echoes of intellectual achievement: Marlowe, Milton and the key Romantics were students, Newton and Darwin too. Crick and Watson unwound DNA and Turing laid the groundwork for modern computing in this tiny city. But Cambridge is as proud of breeding Monty Python and Sacha Baron Cohen as it is of its many Nobel laureates. It's a modest city, with very little to be modest about.

Explore

Cambridge's life as a university town began in 1209, when students, evicted from Oxford after a dicey prank involving a dead woman and an undergrad arrow, began scholarly activities here.

Their presence was formalised by the Bishop of Ely in 1284 with the foundation of **Peterhouse** (01223 338200, www.pet.cam.ac.uk), the first of 31 Cambridge colleges. Apart from the original hall, it is now mostly tobacco-coloured 19th-century buildings, so the excellent **Fitzwilliam Museum** (*see p305*), which stands next door behind a grand neoclassical façade, is likely to occupy more of your time.

The most impressive colleges are all handily clustered along a single quiet road through central Cambridge. It begins, off Trumpington Street, as King's Parade. **Corpus Christi** (01223 338000, www.corpus.cam.ac.uk) has an Old Court that dates to its foundation in 1352; it is linked by a gallery to the college's original chapel, 11th-century **St Bene't Church** (01223 353903), the oldest surviving building in Cambridge. Further up, the fussily grandiose **King's College** – founded by Henry VI in 1441 and renowned for its **chapel** (*see p306*) – is opposite a sweetly touristy parade of shops. At the end of the shops is the university church of **Great St Mary's** (Market Street, 01223 741716, www.gsm.cam.ac.uk). You can climb the steep stairs up the bell tower, but the views are rather utilitarian. Behind the church is the bustling market.

After the church, King's Parade becomes Trinity Street, leading you past **Gonville and Caius** (pronounced 'Keys'), **Trinity** (*see p307*) and **St John's** (*see p307*) before joining Bridge Street, where you'll find the 12th-century **Round Church** (01223 311602, www.christianheritage uk.org.uk), oldest of the country's few remaining round churches. Its current 'medieval' look owes much to its 19th-century restorers. Follow Bridge Street over the river for one of the city's real highlights: the delicious **Kettle's Yard** (*see p305*) with its fabulous collection of 20th-century art. Next door, the **Folk Museum** (*see p305*) is also surprisingly appealing.

The most impressive colleges are on King's Parade, but one of the prettiest is by the river down Silver Street. Most of the original, red-brick buildings of 15th-century **Queens' College** (01223 335511, www.queens.cam.ac.uk) are intact, including the half-timbered president's lodge. The inner courts are especially lovely, but the wooden Mathematical Bridge attracts most tourist attention. The tale is told of the bridge that, designed by Sir Isaac Newton to stand without nails or screws, it was taken apart by curious students eager to uncover the secret... who discovered they couldn't put it back together again. In fact, Newton was dead before the bridge was built.

0   50 miles

Cambridge

Historic sites
● ● ● ● ●

Art & architecture
● ● ● ● ●

Hotels
● ● ● ● ●

Eating & drinking
● ● ● ● ●

Nightlife
● ● ● ● ●

Shopping
● ● ● ● ●

Cambridge
●

Fans of eccentric and ghoulish museums will be in second heaven along Downing Street. In the courtyard on the south side of the street are both the **Museum of Archaeology & Anthropology** (*see p307*) and the fossils, rocks and scintillating gemstones of the **Sedgwick Museum of Earth Sciences** (01223 333456, www.sedgwickmuseum.org). On the north side of Downing Street, a few paces up Free School Lane, you'll find the strange scientific devices and grand orreries of the **Whipple Museum of the History of Science** (01223 330906, www.hps.cam.ac.uk/whipple), while through an arch a little further along Downing Street, beneath a suspended whale skeleton, are the hundreds of animal skeletons and stuffed birds of the **Museum of Zoology** (01223 336650, www.zoo.cam.ac.uk/museum). If those haven't thoroughly exhausted you, head west towards the landmark **Cambridge University Library** (01223 333030, www.lib.cam.ac.uk), a wonderfully stern brick building by Sir George Gilbert Scott, recognisably stylistic kin with London's Tate Modern. Although library's own exhibition room need hardly detain you, the nearby Museum of Classical Archaeology *(Sidgwick Avenue, 01223 330402, www.classics.cam.ac.uk/museum) – due to reopen after refurbishment in spring 2009 – is a terrific collection of casts of Greek and Roman sculpture, jostling together so that many a full-bearded Zeus gives the eye to sundry willowy Athenas. On the station side of town, the **Scott Polar Research Institute Museum** (Lensfield Road, 01223 336562, www.spri.cam. ac.uk/museum), also undergoing refurbishment until summer 2010, collects beautifully intricate scrimshaw carvings, a 1961 Polaris motor sledge, Shackleton's snow goggles and the fox-fur parka of a child who lived with his researcher family on Herbert Island in the early 1970s.

Behind the main run of colleges, the beautiful meadows bordering the willow-shaded River Cam are known as the **Backs**. This is idyllic for summer strolling or punting, and, among the trees behind John's and Trinity, carpeted with crocuses in spring. Punts can be hired – Scudamore's Boatyard (01223 359750, www.scudamores.com) is the largest operator – and, if you get handy at the surprisingly difficult skill of propelling them with an unwieldy long pole, you could boat upstream to the **Orchard Tea Room** at Grantchester (45-47 Mill Way, 01223 845788, www.orchard-grantchester. com). Rupert Brooke lodged here when he was a student – and got up to all manner of bohemian high jinks with a roll-call of intellectual stars that runs from Virginia Woolf to philosopher Bertrand Russell. There's a tiny museum dedicated to him (rather prosaically) in the car park outside.

The exploration of Cambridge does require a certain amount of this kind of brass neck: ducking into courtyards you think might only welcome students. Be brave, but also respectful – many students live within the rooms that surround these quiet, historic quadrangles.

Cambridge & County Folk Museum

2-3 Castle Street (01223 355159/www.folkmuseum. org.uk). Open Apr-Sept 10.30am-5pm Mon-Sat; 2-5pm Sun. Oct-Mar 10.30am-5pm Tue-Sat; 2-5pm Sun. Admission £3.50; £1-£2 reductions.

A museum of local history is probably filed in your brain somewhere fairly close to the word 'dull', but leave your preconceptions behind before entering the Folk Museum. Over the three floors of a 17th-century building that was for 300 years the White Horse Inn, the museum recreates domestic interiors and tells the history of both university folk and locals. But it is the 'Fens & Folklore' that most appeals: exhibits include fenland skates and a pair of mole's paws, kept as cure for rheumatism.

Cambridge University Botanic Gardens

1 Brookside (01223 336265/www.botanic.cam.ac.uk). Open Apr-Sept 10am-6pm daily. Oct, Feb, Mar 10am-5pm daily. Nov-Jan 10am-4pm daily. Admission £4; £3.50 reductions.

Cambridge isn't somewhere that's short of quiet, green spaces, but if the sound of bicycle bells and learned discourse gets too much, the Botanic Garden is a real treat. Opened to the public in 1846, the 40-acre garden holds more than 8,000 plant species, many of them in the tropical and alpine greenhouses. The layout is centred on a walk between huge evergreens, but there are woodland areas, a lovely lake and a fine limestone rock garden through which runs a little waterfall. Healthy Herbie explains what various plants do for us, and a descendant of Sir Isaac Newton's apple tree greets you near the entrance.

Fitzwilliam Museum

Trumpington Street (01223 332900/www.fitzmuseum. cam.ac.uk). Open 10am-5pm Tue-Sat; noon-5pm Sun. Admission free.

The city's most important museum has been displaying a superb collection of paintings, sculpture and ancient artefacts behind its broad neoclassical façade since 1848. It started life when the seventh Viscount Fitzwilliam of Merrion bequeathed his library and collection of 144 artworks to the University of Cambridge. His art included paintings by Veronese and Palma Vecchio as well as a series of Rembrandt's etchings, while his library included medieval manuscripts and music by Purcell and Handel. When you enter the museum, be sure to look up: the dome by the main staircase is quite wonderful. Upstairs, artistic highlights include masterpieces by Titian, Modigliani and Picasso, as well as pieces of furniture. Downstairs there are relics from Egypt, Greece and Rome (from curios like a third century Swiss Army-style penknife to impressive mummies and a granite sarcophagus), as well as ceramics, armour and manuscripts. There's a great programme of lunchtime talks, drop-in events and concerts.

Kettle's Yard

Castle Street (01223 748100/www.kettlesyard.co.uk). Open (House) Summer 1.30-4.30pm Tue-Sun & bank hol Mon. Winter 2-4pm Tue-Sun & bank hol Mon. (Gallery & bookshop) 11.30am-5pm Tue-Sun & bank holiday Mon. Admission free.

When former Tate curator Jim Ede lived here, he held an 'open house' each afternoon so visitors could enjoy his collection of early 20th-century artists – Miró, Brancusi, Hepworth and Moore among them. Ring the doorbell and you can do the same, as well as – delightfully – being allowed to settle yourself in a chair and read a book from the shelf. A tiny bookshop and gallery for temporary exhibitions of modern and contemporary art occupy a separate building (closed while exhibitions are set up). A living, lovely gallery.

King's College Chapel

King's Parade (01223 331100/www.kings.cam.ac.uk). Open Term-time 9.30am-3.30pm Mon-Fri; 9.30am-3.15pm Sat; 1.15-2.15pm Sun. Holidays 9.30am-4.30pm Mon-Sat; 10am-5pm Sun. Admission £5; £3.50 reductions.

Cambridge's most famous building, this vast chapel – built between 1446 and 1515 – was funded by many kings, among them Henry VIII, who was responsible for the ornate decoration of the antechapel and magnificent stained glass (sunlight through it plays intoxicatingly on the north wall late on a spring morning). Henry's initials (and those of his then-wife Anne Boleyn) are carved into the dark oak screen that divides the building in two. The narrowness of the chapel emphasises its height, as do the slender, linear

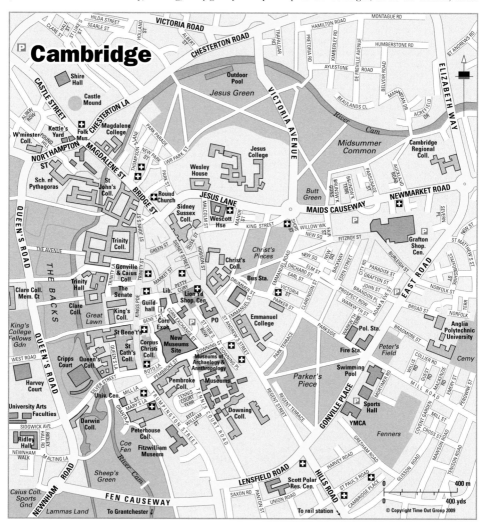

columns that stretch up to an extravagant botheration of fan vaulting – an example of Perpendicular Gothic excess that is unequalled in Britain. Rubens's *Adoration of the Magi* (1634) is at the altar, and a side chapel gives the tortuous history of the chapel's construction – along with interesting details about the making of stained glass. If you're visiting during term, be sure to attend a service: the choirboys' other-worldly voices provide a sublime counterpoint to the beauty of the building. The chapel backs on to Clare College – one of Cambridge's prettiest, with a lovely bridge and gardens through a mathematically neat sequence of arches.

Museum of Archaeology & Anthropology
Downing Street (01223 333516/www.maa-cambridge.org). Open 10.30am-4.30pm Tue-Sat. Admission free.
The ground floor (Clarke Gallery) of this sober but fascinating museum packs in everything from Albanian grave goods and a 4,000-year-old plank for crossing marshes to a tiny 'lime scoop' in the shape of a toucan. Displays detail neolithic hunting practices and reconstruct local farming and domestic life. Upstairs, however, the Maudsley Gallery is the real eye-opener, with Haida and Maori totem poles that reach easily up to the third mezzanine level. Other artefacts include samurai armour and an 18-foot 'qayaq' (kayak) brought back from an 1934 Arctic expedition.

St John's
St John's Street (01223 338600/www.joh.cam.ac.uk). Open Mar-Sept 10am-5pm daily. Oct-Feb 10am-4pm daily. Admission £3; £2 reductions.
One Cambridge's largest colleges, St John's was founded by Henry VII's mum, Lady Margaret Beaufort, in 1511. Although the crenellated entry gatehouse is rather charming, the river side of the college is the loveliest, with the famous neo-Gothic Bridge of Sighs a major attraction (or hazard, if you're among the punts beneath it). Across the river, manicured lawns stretch out behind college buildings that seem big enough to have been castles in a former life. By contrast, the huge chapel is a sombre place: designed by Sir George Gilbert Scott in 1829, it has a statue of alumnus William Wilberforce before the nave, and the dark-hearted palette of reds and golds suggests the Victorian God was master rather than friend.

Trinity
St John's Street (01223 338400/www.trin.cam.ac.uk). Open 10am-5pm daily. Admission Mar-Oct £3; £1 reductions. Nov-Feb free. No credit cards.
Founded in 1336 by Edward III, Trinity was refounded by Henry VIII in 1546. A fine crowd of Tudor buildings surround the justly named Great Court where, legend has it, Lord Byron bathed naked with his pet bear. Push through to the next – coolly colonnaded – court for the wonderful Wren Library (open noon-2pm Mon-Fri; in full term 10.30am-12.30pm Sat). The library is on the first floor, sat on top of the cloisters. Within, its black and white chequerboard floor and pristine, lofty white roof are a model of serene Enlightenment beauty, with busts of Spenser and

Locke facing off against Homer and Marcus Aurelius to underline the point. On either side, covered cases contain such treasures as a lock of Newton's hair, a Shakespeare first folio and Otto Robert Frisch's crisp and terribly moving account of the first atomic bomb test. Head out on to the Backs for great views of the lawns and bridges of St John's.

Eat

Generations of students have been sustained by the Chelsea buns from **Fitzbillies** (52 Trumpington Street, 01223 352500, www.fitzbillies.co.uk), made here since 1922, and fine ale at the touristy **Eagle** (8 Bene't Street, 01223 505020), which has graffiti from World War II air force personnel on a ceiling. The bistro at **Hotel du Vin** (*see p311*) is a good option, whether for breakfasts or more substantial fare.

Cambridge Chop House
1 King's Parade (01223 359506/www.cambscuisine.com/thechophouse). Open noon-10.30pm Mon-Sat; 10.30am-9.30pm Sun. £££. Bistro.
The Chop House is a great come-one-come-all option, with good people-watching possibilities if you can get one of the few ground-floor tables – picture windows look directly out at King's College from the sleek, wine-bar style room. Otherwise, head to the larger and less self-conscious white-washed cellar room beneath. The menu cheerfully offers British comfort food at reasonable prices, complemented by a few wines and a couple of excellent draught ales (Milton Pegasus ruby ale for our visit). The feel is relaxed and friendly, and – for all that the cooking don't hit the spot every time – suet pudding of the day, a range of sausage and mash, and Lincolnshire Poacher and ham hock macaroni cheese aren't going to miss too often.

Free Press
Prospect Row (01223 368337/www.freepresspub.com). Open noon-2pm, 6-9pm Mon-Fri; noon-2.30pm, 6-9pm Sat; noon-2.30pm Sun. ££. Pub.
Tucked away in a back alley north of the green grass of Parker's Piece, the Free Press is an excellent little corner pub, busy with locals and students rather than tourists. More than 100 years old, the pub's time hosting a printing press is reflected in the decor: *Punch* cartoons and printers' block trays full of eccentric memorabilia, passport snaps and, well, tat. The real ales are excellent (five on tap for our visit, including Abbot Mild), there are half a dozen wines each colour by the glass, and a snacky lunch menu and more substantial evening meals are served. A smoke-free pub decades before the ban, the Free Press is now also stalwart against mobile phones – which doubtless contributes to the bustling, chatty atmosphere around the crammed-in tables.

Midsummer House
Midsummer Common (01223 369299/www.midsummerhouse.co.uk). Open 7-9.30pm Tue; noon-1.45pm, 7-9.30pm Wed-Sat; ££££. Haute cuisine.

Occupying an enviable riverside spot on the northern edge of the common, Midsummer House produces high-profile French food that rises to the occasion. Service is as fussy as you'd expect but this is peripheral to the perfectly presented, painstakingly prepared food. Culinary extras (amuses-bouches and pre-desserts come even with the set lunch) punctuate the meal, and the combinations are never less than intriguing: perhaps ravioli of pigeon, sweet potato and chocolate or zander with onion and cinnamon purée, wilted nettles and smoked eel. Colourful arrangements of gelatinous cubes or smears of sauce give a sense of theatre, but there's no skimping on punchily direct combinations: a potato and smoked bacon soup, albeit poured at the table. The atmosphere can be too reverent and prices for wine get scary, but on food alone this is Cambridge's finest restaurant.

Pickerel Inn
30 Magdalene Street (01223 355068). Open noon-3pm, 4-8pm daily. ££. Pub (drinks).
This low-slung and atmospheric old pub serves a great selection of real ales – and is often less crowded than places closer to the centre of town. Grab a window seat to watch people stroll in and out of the pretty River Court of Magdalene (pronounced 'Maudlin') College, or take your pint through to the dimly lit, cosy backroom to take in the heavy beams. There's mulled wine and a fire in winter and a small courtyard for summer and year-round smoking.

Rainbow Café
9A King's Parade (01223 321551/www.rainbowcafe. co.uk). Open 10am-4pm Mon, Sun; 10am-9.30pm Tue-Sat. ££. Vegetarian.
This sweet little vegetarian eaterie, tucked away in a basement down an alley off King's Parade (it's the white door) delights die-hard vegans, gluten avoiders and just about anyone in need of a big feed. Everything is locally sourced and freshly prepared, from a huge plate of tofu-based Jamaican patties to mornay Italienne (a dolcelatte-topped potato and veg bake). The premises are licensed and the puddings brilliant – chocolate and blueberry vegan cheesecake a highlight among more than a dozen on the menu – should you be worried that you're being too virtuous. It's all a bit of a squeeze and you can expect to have to wait for a seat at lunchtimes, but just relax and enjoy the inevitable world music soundtrack until it's your turn.

Restaurant 22
22 Chesterton Road (01223 351880/www.restaurant 22.co.uk). Open 7-9.45pm Tue-Sat. ££££. Modern European.
A white Victorian terraced house, set beside a parade of shops where the ring road becomes aggressively one-way, 22 is in a lousy location. Once inside, though, the completely disarming, charmingly quirky house will soothe frazzled nerves with unpretentious service and delightful modern food, in a dining room that seats just 26 people. It's a justifiably popular place, noted for value and a surprising degree of variety within the confines of a set menu: try the likes of cauliflower velouté with goat's cheese, then a roast hake, cockles, avruga caviar and spring onion risotto, perhaps finished with a rhubarb assiette with buttermilk panna cotta.

Trockel, Ulmann & Freunde
13 Pembroke Street (01223 460923/www.trockel ulmannfreunde.co.uk). Open July, Aug 10am-3.30pm Mon-Fri. Sept-June 9am-4.30pm Mon-Fri; 10am-4.30pm Sat. £. Café.
This skinny café is perfect for a quick refuel after the Downing Street museums. The range of food is narrow – pastries for breakfast, baguettes and soups for lunch – but the German-style cakes are excellent. Perch yourself at the counter seats in the window to watch the scarved students rush past, or take in the uni digs decor of theatre and travel posters from behind a book and a green tea at one of the handful of tables. A pleasingly eccentric little place.

Shop

Despite the trumpeted arrival of a five-storey John Lewis, neither the shiny Grand Arcade (www.grandarcade.co.uk) and Christ's Lane (www.christslane.co.uk) opposite, nor the dated Lion Yard and Grafton Centre malls need detain you. Instead, for the best independent boutiques explore the tiny streets just off Market Square – **Rose Crescent** and **Green Street**, or the generously entitled 'Arts Quarter' around **Ben'et Street**. **Market Square** is full of lively stalls – books, flowers, fruit and veg most of the week, a farmers' market and arts and crafts on Sunday – and there's further entertaining browsing to be done in a sweet little craft market just opposite Trinity College on Saturdays (more frequently in July, August and the run-up to Christmas; www.cambridge-art-craft.co.uk). The tourist throng also have the right idea: the run of shops along King's Parade through to the cluster of charity shops past Magdalene bridge, passing the biggest colleges, is obvious – almost unavoidable, in fact – but can be rewarding if you don't try to rush through the camera-wielders.

Stay

There's a cluster of B&Bs nicely located just across the Cam from the centre of town, to the north of Midsummer Common. **Harry's Bed & Breakfast** (39 Milton Road, 01223 503866, www.welcometoharrys.co.uk, ££), **Worth House** (152 Chesterton Road, 01223 316074, www.worth-house.co.uk, £) and **Victoria Guest House** (57 Arbury Road, 01223 350086, www.victoria-guesthouse.co.uk, ££) are all good value.

DoubleTree by Hilton
Granta Place, Mill Lane (01223 259988/www.double treebyhilton.co.uk). £££.

A field full of folk

Item 1: 'Show some love'. Item 2: 'Bring your instruments!'. When a critically respected music festival survives four decades and still feels confident enough in its hippy heritage to put such advice on its website, you know you've stumbled across something special – although in reality it's unlikely that you'll 'stumble across' the **Cambridge Folk Festival** (www.cambridgefolkfestival.co.uk, 01223 357851) as the 10,000 tickets regularly sell out as soon as they are issued.

It all began in 1964, when the city council got in touch with local folk-club member, fireman and political activist Ken Woollard about setting up a music festival. Extraordinarily, Woollard remained chief organiser and artistic director until his death in 1993 – and his socialist conscience and insistence that the event remain true to folk's exploratory and human-focused legacy remain at the heart of the festival.

The line-ups are reliably eccentric, coupling the likes of Buffy Sainte-Marie, Oumou Sangare and the Zutons with out-and-out folkies such as the Waterson Family and Jon Boden. An effort is always made to present new music, rather than allowing the festival to become hidebound to some desiccated, preserved-in-aspic notion of folk authenticity. Through the years the list of performers has encompassed the Ukulele Orchestra of Great Britain, Jimmy Cliff, kd lang, Paul Simon, Rachel Unthank, Bo Diddley, Donovan, Joan Armatrading, Chas & Dave, Ry Cooder and Bill Wyman, and Martha Wainwright has in recent years been able to build on the huge affection her father Loudon Wainwright III built up through gigs here over many years. For a flavour of the sounds, look out a copy of the 2007 double album *Cool as Folk*, a compilation of recordings of many of the artists who appeared that year.

The feel of the festival is notably relaxed, communal and progressive. In the middle of the Cherry Hinton campsite, the Folknet Café provides internet access and munchies, while strolling players entertain the troops all through the site. The organisers also won a Greener Festival Award in 2008; proudly noting that they began recycling initiatives back in the mid-1990s, they continue to cut waste and increase recycling each year.

It is the biggest and best, but the Folk Festival is by no means the only music festival in Cambridge. Every three years there's classical and jazz at the **Cambridge**

Music Festival (www.cammusic.co.uk), while the annual volunteer-run **Strawberry Fair** (www.strawberry-fair.org.uk) attracts a younger crowd with four music stages of rock and dance music in early June. If you're not around for any of these, the city can be relied on for curious music gigs – after all, Syd Barrett of Pink Floyd lived here until his death and Radiohead's Colin Greenwood studied English at Peterhouse. Our most recent visit turned up local psych-popsters Scissors at the **Man on the Moon** (2 Norfolk Street, 01223 474144, www.man onthemoon.freeserve.co.uk), avant lapsteel/ drum improvising duo Flower-Corsano at the **Portland Arms** (129 Chesterton Road, 01223 357268, www.theportland.co.uk), jazz saxist Tim Garland at **Kettle's Yard** (*see p305*) and rock poet John Cooper Clarke at J2, one of the three venues that make up the **Junction** (Clifton Road, 01223 511511, www.junction.co.uk). The **Cambridge Corn Exchange** (Wheeler Street, 01223 357851, www.cornex.co.uk), meanwhile, was hosting Ray Lamontagne.

Top: Hotel Felix; middle right: Rainbow Café; left & bottom right: Hotel du Vin.

Hilton took over the former Cambridge Garden House in 2008, making it the first English hotel under the company's less corporate DoubleTree sub-brand. The central location could hardly be better – right on the Cam at Mill Pond – and rooms are clean, comfortable and inoffensively decorated, with those with private balconies overlooking the river understandably highly prized. In spite of its size (122 rooms), the hotel is often fully booked with business types, undergrad parents and grown-up returnees. The Riverside Brasserie has been recently refurbished as Hilton brings the premises up to date, and there's wireless internet throughout the hotel. The swimming pool and spa are another attraction.

Hotel du Vin
15-19 Trumpington Street (01223 227330/www.hotel duvin.com). ££££.
From the droll chandelier made of downturned cut-crystal wine glasses in the entrance to the trademark trompe l'oeil in the residents' library, this is at once comfortably part of the du Vin chain and thoroughly individual. It is also the best hotel in Cambridge, a cheerfully but carefully run place. The hotel premises are in listed terraced houses, and the layout takes some getting used to, but manager Denis Frucot has taken pains to make original features work for

each room, whether converting the annexe to one suite into a private screening room or leaving a well (covered by glass) in one corner of another. Sober colour tones and all mod cons (wireless internet, flatscreens, drench showers) keep things classy. A basement bar (with wine cellar) extends the whole length of the hotel, while the busy all-day restaurant occupies one end of the ground floor. The heated and covered cigar 'room' outside is another nice touch.

Hotel Felix
Whitehouse Lane, Huntingdon Road (01223 277977/ www.hotelfelix.co.uk). ££££.
The characterful central section of this hotel is a Victorian mansion, built for a surgeon in 1852, but on approaching it is rather overwhelmed by its two large modern wings. There are 52 decent-sized, simply furnished bedrooms and a penthouse junior suite with its own staircase, all with laptop, safes, TV, wireless internet and a CD player. There's also a quiet sitting room beside the entrance. The twinkly bar-restaurant (Graffiti) has a fabulous decked area outside, which looks into the garden and out over college playing fields, and some vigorous modern art gives a bit of edge to the otherwise muted, conference-friendly decor. Ample parking is a major plus as the hotel is a good half-hour stride from the main colleges.

Factfile

When to go
Early spring is a lovely time to visit, with the Backs in full flower and fewer tourists than in high summer. From mid-April to late June many of the colleges are entirely closed to the public, so that the students are not disturbed during their exams; at all times it is forbidden to walk on the lawns and to enter doors and staircases other than to the chapels and, in some colleges, the halls and libraries. Each college is an independent entity, so entry times (and, for some of the more famous ones, prices) vary considerably: check www.cam.ac.uk/cambuniv/ colleges.html for details.

Getting there
By car from London or Stansted airport (30 miles to the south), take the M11, exiting at Junctions 11, 12 or 13; if you're coming from the north of the country, take the A14 directly into the city from the M1 and A1. Parking in the city is at a premium, so day-trippers do well to use one of the five Park & Ride sites (01223 845561, www.cambridgeshire. gov.uk/parkandride). Frequent National Express coach services arrive from all over the country at the central Parkside depot, and the train station – with regular connections to Liverpool Street and King's Cross stations in London, or via Peterborough to the north of England – is a short taxi ride or 20-minute walk from the town centre.

Getting around
Pretty much everything you'll want to see in Cambridge is in the compact central area, and parking is a nightmare, so getting about on foot is by far the best option. Bicycles can be hired – staff at Cambridge Station Cycles (01223 307125, www.station cycles.co.uk) in the car park to the right out of the train station are very helpful (and will store luggage at a reasonable rate) – but, like getting a punt, you'll do so for the fun of it rather than out of any necessity. The tourist office can also provide walking and guided tour information.

Tourist information
VisitCambridge Visitor Information Centre The Old Library, Wheeler Street (0871 226 8006/www.visitcambridge.org). Open Oct-Easter 10am-5.30pm Mon-Fri; 10am-5pm Sat. Easter-Sept 10am-5.30pm Mon-Fri; 10am-5pm Sat; 11am-5pm Sun & bank hols.

Internet
There are plenty of internet cafés in Cambridge. The restaurant and performance venue CB2 (5-7 Norfolk Street, 01223 508503, www.cb2bistro.com) is surely the most fun, and has both wireless and plug-in points. There's also wireless access at the very central Starbucks off Market Square (18 Market Street, 01223 328575).

Top: Conwy Bay; left:
Conwy Mussels; top right:
Smallest House in Great
Britain; bottom right:
Conwy Castle.

The Smallest
House
IN GREAT BRITAIN

Y TY LLEIAF YM MHRYDAIN FAWR

Conwy

A picturesque town and harbour dominated by a classic castle.

More than 700 years ago the English king, Edward I, came to the banks of the Conwy river and ordered the fortification of the tiny town he found there. The magnificent, filmic castle he built still stands guard, rising from a giant rocky outcrop into eight mighty towers; the walls that spread from the castle to encircle the town weave between modern houses and roads, with 22 intact towers and three gates studding their perimeter. The level of preservation is astonishing – it's easy to see why it's a UNESCO World Heritage Site; the setting on the Conwy estuary is scenic; and the little town is picturesque, with well-preserved buildings from the medieval and Elizabethan eras.

In nearby Llandudno, it's the Victorians who have left the most lasting impact: this great sweep of a bay, bookended by rocky outcrops, became one of the great 19th-century seaside holiday towns. Grand hotels, a wide promenade and a 2,300-foot pier marked the transformation from a small village on an isolated stretch of coastline to accessible resort, a transformation made possible by the Victorians' creation of a nationwide rail system and by the introduction of paid holidays for workers, allowing working men and women the leisure time to explore the country and discover the joys of the seaside. Just beyond the town stretches the limestone headland of Great Orme, with stunning views of the coast. It was natural beauty of this order, as well as political troubles on the continent making the Grand Tour a less attractive prospect, that drew a different kind of Victorian visitor – young artists – to the area; the Royal Cambrian Academy in Conwy is their legacy.

Explore

It's not hard to find your way around the tiny walled town of Conwy. Most activity takes place on or just off the High Street: near one end is the train station, at the other the quay. But the real attraction here is the towering **castle** (*see p315*), and there's no missing that. Spanning the Conwy opposite the castle, the **Conwy Suspension Bridge** (0149 2573282/www.nationaltrust.org.uk) was built by Thomas Telford in 1826, designed to be in sympathy with the castle. The tollhouse is open to visitors between March and November. The town is home to two houses of keen historic interest. The 14th-century **Aberconwy House** (*see below*), the town's oldest, is on Castle Street, which runs inside and parallel to the walls. **Plas Mawr** (*see below*), on the High Street, dates from the Elizabethan era. Both are strikingly well-preserved. The 19th century, when the area saw an influx of artists, is represented in the Royal Cambrian Academy (*see p315*), established in 1881 and still home to the best in Welsh art.

One of the most pleasant ways of seeing the town is to walk the three-quarters of a mile circuit of the surviving walls. There is also an open-top bus service that also takes in nearby **Llandudno** (City Sightseeing, 0800 043 2452, www.city-sightseeing.com), a Victorian resort town known mainly for its dramatic setting on **Llandudno Bay**, overlooked by the headland of **Great Orme**.

Conwy lies on the border of Snowdonia National Park, and makes an excellent base for walking or cycling. The foot of Mount Snowdon lies just 27 miles from Llandudno. Leaflets with information about walking are available from the Conwy Countryside service (01492 575200, www.conwy.gov.uk/countryside) and further suggestions are available at www.alpine-travel.co.uk. Countryside highlights within easy reach of Conwy include the beautiful **Bodnant Gardens** at Colwyn Bay, and the **RSPB Conwy** reserve near Llandudno.

Aberconwy House
Conwy *Castle Street (01492 592246/www.national trust.org.uk). Open Apr-Oct 11am-5pm Mon, Wed-Sun. Admission £3; £1.50 reductions .*
This medieval merchant's house, now owned by the National Trust, dates back to around 1300. The half-timbered stone building is well-preserved, and the interiors re-create different eras in the house's history.

Bodnant Gardens
Tal-y-Cafn, nr Colwyn Bay, 5.5 miles NW of Conwy *(01492 650460/www.bodnantgarden.co.uk/ www.nationaltrust.org.uk). Open Mar-Oct 10am-5pm daily. Nov 10am-4pm daily. Admission £7.50; £3.75 reductions.*
Arguably the most beautiful gardens in Wales, Bodnant spans 80 acres, and commands views over the River Conwy and Snowdonia. The gardens were begun in 1874 by the Aberconwy family, who supervised experiments

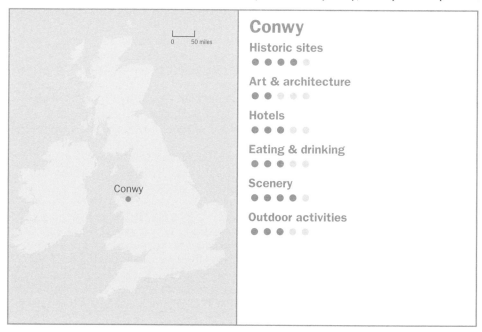

Conwy

Historic sites
● ● ● ● ○

Art & architecture
● ● ○ ○ ○

Hotels
● ● ● ○ ○

Eating & drinking
● ● ● ○ ○

Scenery
● ● ● ● ○

Outdoor activities
● ● ● ○ ○

0   50 miles

Conwy

with numerous exotic species of plant, including Chinese rhododendrons and Chilean fire bush. In addition to spectacular floral displays, look out for Pin Mill, an 18th-century garden house shipped here from Gloucester in 1939. The gardens are now run by the National Trust; there is a nursery, café and gift centre.

Great Orme Mines
Great Orme, Llandudno *(01492 870447/www.great ormemines.info). Open 10am-5pm daily. Admission £6; £4 reductions.*
Discovered in 1987 by a group of unsuspecting workmen, this Bronze Age cave and four-mile network of tunnels is a staggering 4,000 years old. You can don a hard hat for a trip down the mine, and marvel at one of prehistory's most important sources of bronze.

Conwy Butterfly Jungle
Conwy *Bodlondeb Park (01492 593149/www.conwy-butterfly.co.uk). Open Apr-Aug 10am-5.30pm Mon, Wed-Sun. Sept, Oct 10am-4pm Mon, Wed-Sun. Admission £5; £3.50 reductions.*
Just a few minutes' walk beyond the town walls, this impressive conservational project (2,000sq ft of greenhouse space) houses almost 50 species of butterfly and moth. Chinese water dragons (a kind of lizard), seed-eating finches and other ecological delights can also be spotted.

"Standing on a great slab of pure granite, the castle seems like an organic extension of the rock."

Conwy Castle
Conwy *(01492 592358/www.conwy.com). Open Apr-Oct 9am-5pm daily. Nov-Mar 9.30am-4pm Mon-Sat; 11am-4pm Sun. Admission £4.70; £4.20 reductions.*
Edward I's classic medieval castle totally dominates sleepy Conwy. Its eight giant towers reach skyward; the solid walls emanating from the structure encircle the entire town centre. The UNESCO-protected site has lost none of its visual impact, although its importance as a fortification diminished significantly after the Civil War, when the castle fell into disuse and disrepair.

Built between 1283 and 1287, it took 1,500 workers and £15,000 to realise the design of James of St George, the Savoy-born architect also responsible for Harlech, Caernarfon and Beaumaris castles. Conwy Castle was part of Edward I's 'iron ring' of Welsh defensive outposts, a massive network of castles built to maintain his subjugation of the Welsh in the face of frequent rebellion. Others in the 'iron ring' are Flint, Rhuddlan, Aberystwyth, Builth, Caernarfon, Criccleth, Harlech and Beaumaris. Edward invested a lot of resources in his Wales – an

investment made possible by the signing of an accord with France, England's old enemy, by his predecessor, Henry III, which meant that funds were no longer needed to fight the French. As building projects, the castles weren't cheap: in today's money, Conwy would have cost around £5 million to build. Standing on a great slab of pure granite, it seems like an organic extension of the rock. It remains one of the most impressive of the network, and most intimidating and impenetrable to potential enemies, with a design that would have forced an enemy into attacking in a narrow area of its perimeter. It features two barbicans, eight towers, four internal turrets and a long great hall. Royal apartments, a chapel, a granary and even a bakery are all still discernable. Guided tours explain more about the castle's layout and history.

Great Orme Tramway
Llandudno *Victoria Station, Church Walks (01492 879306/www.greatormetramway.co.uk). Open Jan,Feb, Apr-Sept, Nov, Dec 10am-6pm daily. Mar, Nov 10am-5pm daily. Admission £5.40; £3.70 reductions.*
This authentic Victorian tram system, built in 1902, has been spruced up with great care and affection. Beautifully restored cable-hauled cars take you some 679ft over the Great Orme headland; it's the only such system still in operation in Britain.

Llandudno Cable Car
Great Orme, Llandudno *Happy Valley Gardens (01492 877205/www.llandudnoattractions.co.uk). Open Mar-Oct 10am-5pm daily. Admission £6.50; £4.50 reductions.*
Along with the Great Orme Tramway (*see above*), this is one of the most enjoyable ways of surveying the glories of the Llandudno coastline. Cable-car trivia fans will be delighted to know that it's the longest passenger cable-car system in Britain.

Plas Mawr
Conwy *High Street (01492 580167/www.conwy.com/plasmawr). Open Apr-Sept 9.30am-5pm Tue-Sun. Oct 9.30am-4pm Tue-Sun. Admission £5.10; £4.70 reductions.*
Plas Mawr ('Great Hall') was built between 1576 and 1585 for Robert Wynn, a wealthy Welsh merchant. It is probably the best-preserved Elizabethan townhouse in Britain: fine ceilings with delicate plasterwork, elaborate friezes, and an impressive overmantle in the hallway, spruced up to restore the original colouring.

Royal Cambrian Academy
Town Centre *Crown Lane (01492 593413/www.rca conwy.org). Open 11am-5pm Tue-Sat; 1-4.30pm Sun. Admission free.*
The RCA was established in 1881, at a time when political unrest in Europe had made the Grand Tour too dangerous a prospect for the Young British Artists of their day, forcing them to explore Britain in their search for their inspiration. Some gathered in the Conwy area. Formerly housed in Plas Mawr (*see above*), it is still the place to see the best Welsh art, with 100 contributing members.

Top: Castle Hotel; bottom: Bodysgallen Hall.

RSPB Conwy

Llandudno *Llandudno Junction (01492 584091/
www.rspb.org.uk). Open Reserve 24hrs daily. Visitor
Centre 9.30am-5pm daily. Admission Reserve free.
Visitor Centre £2.50; £1-£1.50 reductions.*
Godwits and shelducks count among the 200 species spotted
at this 80-acre RSPB reserve, created in the early 1990s
when the estuary was drained to build the A55.

Smallest House in Great Britain

Conwy *Lower Gate Street (01492 593484). Open
Apr-Oct 10am-6pm daily. Admission £1; 50p reductions.
No credit cards.*
Novelty attractions are rarely as charming as this.
Measuring just 10ft by 4ft 2in, this tiny houselet was a
genuine dwelling once occupied, bizarrely enough, by a 6ft
3in-tall fisherman called Robert Jones. Its bright red
frontage is easily to spot as you wander along the pier.

Eat

A century ago, at the height of its economic
strength, Conwy boasted 48 public houses.
These days the pickings are slimmer; there
are a few take-'em-or-leave-'em pubs and a
couple of tolerable chippies, but the food lover
is best served slightly out of town, and in nearby
Llandudno. In addition to the following, the
Mulberry (Ellis Way, Conwy, 01492 583350) is
popular locally, though perhaps more remarkable
for its views over the harbour than its food.

Bodysgallen Hall

Llandudno *(01492 584466/www.bodysgallen.com).
Open 12.30-1.45pm, 7-9pm Tue-Sat; 12.30-2pm Sun.
££££. Modern European.*
For formal dining and the highest-quality food, Bodysgallen's
main restaurant is one of the few serious options in the region,
with three AA Rosettes and a formal dress code (ties aren't
necessary, but no trainers or T-shirts are allowed). Menus
centre on local, seasonal food, which might be a hand-dived
scallop paired with crisp pork belly, peas and truffle, followed
by Welsh beef accompanied by a braised oxtail, onion and
garlic risotto. It's all excellent, though it comes at a price; main
courses can reach the £30 mark (hotel guests are given a £39
allowance towards the cost of their meal).

Dawson's Cuisine

Conwy *Castle Hotel, High Street (01492 582800/
www.castlewales.co.uk). Open 10.30am-9.30pm
Mon-Thur, Sun; 10.30am-10pm Fri, Sat. £££. British.*
Under the sure hand of head chef Graham Tinsley, the
restaurant at the Castle Hotel (*see p318*) delivers
unpretentious, well-executed fare. Keen to promote Welsh
classics and local meat, Dawson's does particularly well
with the likes of a moist rump of lamb and a steamed steak
pudding with fine suet pastry. The restaurant's name refers
to the original John Dawson Watson paintings of scenes
from Shakespeare's plays that hang around the hotel.

Groes Inn

Ty-Ny-Groes, 3 miles S of Conwy *(01492 650545/
www.groesinn.com). Open noon-2.15pm, 6.30-9pm Mon-
Sat; noon-9pm Sun. ££££. Gastropub.*
Three miles out of Conwy lies the Groes. Food is decent and
reliable rather than dazzling, but the place is also worth a
visit just to taste the home-brewed ales. The beautiful
setting is a big draw too: you can gaze over the countryside
as you dine. The Groes is also a hotel, and a fine spot from
which to begin several walks.

Pen-Y-Bryn

Colwyn Bay, 5.5 NW of Conwy *Pen-Y-Bryn Road
(01492 533360/www.brunningandprice.co.uk/penybryn).
Open noon-9.30pm Mon-Sat; noon-9pm Sun. £££.
Gastropub.*
A short drive from Conwy and with the unprepossessing
look of a suburban bungalow, this gastropub serves some
of the best food in the area, majoring on robust dishes such
as braised pigeon faggot with bubble and squeak and
roasted shallots. The interior features polished wooden
floors, a solid fireplace and blackboard menus; there are
stunning views over Colwyn Bay. The pub is rightly
lauded by CAMRA for its frequently changing roster of
beers and ales.

"The gloriously decadent interior – wall-to-wall murals of north Italy's lake Como, tented ceilings, glittering chandeliers – is just the start."

Seahorse

Llandudno *7 Church Walks (01492 875315/www.the-
seahorse.co.uk). Open 4.30-9.30pm Mon-Sat; noon-4pm
Sun. ££££.*
This impressive seafood restaurant is set on two floors, in
a Grade II-listed Victorian building. The underground
bistro is imaginatively kitted out with old church
furniture; upstairs is a more formal, though unstuffy,
dining room decorated with Mediterranean murals. The
menu changes daily, according to the local catch, but
might include mussels, scallops thermidor, or monkfish
wrapped in pancetta.

Terrace Restaurant, St Tudno Hotel

Llandudno *North Parade, Promenade (01492 874411/
www.st-tudno.co.uk). Open 7.30-9.30am, 12.30-2pm,
7-9.30pm daily. ££££. French.*
The place for destination dining in north Wales. The
gloriously decadent interior – wall-to-wall murals of north

Italy's lake Como, tented ceilings, glittering chandeliers – is just the start. Significantly more adventurous than most of its Llandudno brethren, the Terrace uses local and seasonal ingredients (including crab, sea bass or Welsh Black Beef) to brilliant effect. Dishes on a recent visit included an original but highly successful gorau glas (a local cheese) crème brûlèe with crab-apple jelly and beetroot glaze, followed by an accomplished classic – Tournedos Rossini. The wine list is one of the best in Wales.

Shop

Visitors don't come to Conwy for the shopping, but if you're looking for a gift or some tasty takeaway food, check out the places below.

Conwy Antiques
Conwy *17 Bangor Road (01745 356904/www. conwyantiques.com). Open 11am-5pm Mon-Sat. No credit cards.*
A small antiques shop beneath the castle walls, for gifts that aren't mass-produced Welsh love spoons.

Conwy Mussels
Conwy *The Quay (01492 592689). Open 10am-5pm daily. No credit cards.*
Freshly caught mussels are sold at £4 per kilogramme from this seafront shack.

Edwards of Conwy
Conwy *High Street (01492 592443/www.edwardsof conwy.co.uk). Open 8am-5.30pm Mon-Sat.*
An excellent, award-winning butcher that doubles as a deli and purveyor of quality takeaway meals.

Stay

Conwy has plenty of guesthouses, although only a few are above average. Some of our favourite accommodation lies out of town within country houses, or in and around Llandudno (which is reputed to have one third of all the tourist bed space in Wales). **Groes Inn** (*see p317*) offers good country accommodation too. See also www.farmstaywales.co.uk.

Bodysgallen Hall
Llandudno *Pentywyn Road (01492 584466/ www.bodysgallen.com). £££.*
The acquisition of this 17th-century house by the National Trust in September 2008 should ensure its continuing high profile as a north Wales destination hotel. The Hall is filled with antique furnishings and paintings; log fires and deep sofas add to the traditional sense of country-house comfort. Bedrooms are bright and airy and sumptuously decorated, most with stunning views over the valley. It is set in 20 acres of grounds, with rose gardens and 17th-century box hedges,

and staff can direct you towards the best local walks. The building conceals a 13th-century watchtower designed to spot attacks on Conwy Castle: ask staff to show you to the top. The hotel's fine-dining restaurant (*see p317*) is one of the region's best places to eat, though newly-added restaurant 1620 is surprisingly uninspiring. In addition to the grounds, the food and the history, Bodysgallen houses a spa complex with a 50ft swimming pool, as well as a gym, sauna and steam room.

Carmen
Llandudno *Sylva Road (01492 876361/www.carmen llandudno.co.uk). ££.*
Probably Llandudno's best guesthouse, Carmen is affectionately tended and a pleasure to visit. All rooms are uniquely decorated and have en suite facilities. A major refurb and redesign in 2008 earned it Wales's four-star guest accommodation status, but it's the personal touches from the charming owners that make the place stand out.

"In the grounds is a series of luxury tents – safari-style canvas lodges fitted out to the same standard as hotel rooms."

Castle Hotel
Conwy *High Street (01492 582800/www.castle wales.co.uk). £££.*
As a 15th-century coaching inn, this hotel would have played an important role in Conwy's history as the main stopping point for travellers and a major communications hub. Over the years it has hosted such luminaries as William Wordsworth and Samuel Johnson, and it's still the best hotel in town, especially with the completion of a large-scale refurb in February 2008. All rooms have been fitted out with eye-catching furniture, paintings and mirrors: room 104 boasts a 16th-century bed, while boudoir-like room 112 is plush in purples and silks.

Crow's Nest Hall
Sychnant Pass, 1.5 miles W of Conwy *(01492 572956/www.crows-nest-hall.wales.info). £££.*
Just a mile or so outside Conwy, this 18th-century house is is set in three acres of bucolic gardens, with great views of the town's medieval walls and towers. There are four comfortable rooms (three of which are en suite), enlivened by fairytale touches including steep gables and hand-painted stained-glass windows.

Empire Hotel
Llandudno *Church Walks (01492 860555/ www.empirehotel.co.uk). £££.*

A well-situated Victorian pile at one end of the bay, with spacious rooms filled with period furniture and lovely views down Mostyn Street, Llandudno's main thoroughfare. All rooms are en suite. The large restaurant and lounge bar are rather retro, but the hotel has impressively up-to-date fitness facilities and a reasonably sized indoor swimming pool.

Escape
Llandudno *48 Church Walks (01492 877776/ www.escapebandb.co.uk). £££.*
This 'boutique B&B' brings a luxury contemporary approach to Victorian Llandudno. Leathers in chocolate and black, bold design lines and minimalist layouts feature in the hotel's aesthetic, though there are plenty of softer touches to be found in the nine individually decorated rooms, among which are 'the Boudoir' and 'French Fancy'. The latter is decorated with Sanderson flock wallpaper and has a roll-top bath. No children under ten are allowed.

Pentre Mawr Country House
Llandyrnog, Denbigh, 26.4 miles SW of Conwy *(01824 790732/www.pentremawrcountryhouse.co.uk). £££.*
Pentre Mawr, 30 minutes' drive from Conwy, has been in the Carrington-Sykes family for four centuries, and is full of wonderful old paintings and antique furniture, but manages to avoid being stuffy or museum-like. In the main house, sunny rooms (each named after one of TS Eliot's cats) have been sympathetically fitted with period furniture and quality touches like roll-top baths and the odd four-poster bed. An unobtrusive working farm occupies some of the grounds; some of the barns have been converted into suites decorated in a more contemporary style, each of which has a private outdoor hot tub. Also in the grounds is something unique in Britain: a series of luxury tents – safari-style canvas lodges fitted out to the same standard as hotel rooms. Dogs and walkers are particularly welcome at Pentre Mawr, and the owners will happily drive you to the best spots for a ramble.

Sychnant Pass Country House
Sychnant Pass, 1.5 miles W of Conwy *Sychnant Pass Road (01492 596868/www.sychnant-pass-house.co.uk). £££.*
A mile and a half out of Conwy, this fine country-house hotel is owned by the same people who run Pentre Mawr (*see above*), and is operated to the same high standards. The twelve rooms are of mixed sizes, and priced accordingly: some of the suites have private decks with their own hot tubs. If your room doesn't have one, try the tasteful indoor pool and sauna. The hotel is in the north-east corner of Snowdonia National Park, so many of the rooms have fabulous views; you can walk to the top of Conwy Mountain in about an hour, or just stroll around the grounds.

St Tudno
Llandudno, 4.5 miles N of Conwy *North Parade, Promenade (01492 874411/www.st-tudno.co.uk). ££££.*
St Tudno's was converted into a hotel in 1972. Continuous upgradings have ensured that it offers the most luxurious stay in town, enhanced by the opportunities of cream teas in the opulent, sea-view sitting room, a dip in the pool or dinner in one of its restaurants (*see p317*). Rooms are bright and kitted out with Egyptian cotton sheets and whirlpool baths. Owner Martin Bland goes out of his way to make guests feel welcome, and is happy to explain the hotel's curious (and curiouser?) connections with Alice Liddell, of *Alice in Wonderland* fame.

Factfile

When to go
Welsh weather is notoriously fickle, but possible seasonal closures of venues and hotels aside, any time is a good time to visit Conwy. You may wish to coincide with one of the town's festivals. The Royal Charter fairs – a seed fair (March) and a honey fair (September) – date back more than 700 years and are an important part of the town's identity; for details of both see www.conwy beekeepers.org.uk. The Conwy Classical Music Festival takes place in July (01492 592166), and the River Conwy becomes the centre of the action in August with the River Festival (01492 596253, www.conwyriverfestival.org) and Rock the River, a two-day wakeboarding event (www.rocktheriver.co.uk).

Getting there & Around
Conwy is on the North Coast Line, and its railway station is conveniently located for all the major sites. It connects with Llandudno Junction on the other side of the Conwy river in around three minutes. You'll need to change here for a train to Llandudno station, the main stop for the town; the journey can take up to 40 minutes.

If coming by car, the best approach from the south is by the A470 and then the A55. A A55 also approaches Conwy from west Wales. You'll find Vicarage Gardens (off Rosehill Street) short-stay car park useful. Another car park can be found just south of the town walls.

Tourist office
Conwy Castle Visitor Centre Conwy Castle (01492 592248/www.conwy.gov.uk). Open Summer 9.30am-6pm daily. Winter 9.30am-4pm daily.

Internet
Conwy Library Castle Street (01492 596242). Open 10am-5.30pm Mon, Thur, Fri; 10am-7pm Tue; 10am-1pm Sat.

Top: Ludlow Castle; others: street scenes.

D.W.WALL & SON

Ludlow

The perfect small town, with a penchant for good food.

'Oh I have been to Ludlow fair/And left my necktie God knows where/And carried half-way home, or near/Pints and quarts of Ludlow beer.' Thus wrote AE Housman in the 19th century, and if his ashes should rise from their rest beside St Laurence's Church, he'd likely notice little change in Ludlow at first glance. Castle and church still dominate the skyline, the River Teme still skirts the rocky base of the outcrop on which the town stands, and the same mix of butchers, bakers and grocers fills the high street (not for Ludlow the drift into the bland uniformity of chain-store domination). In fact, more than 500 of the town's buildings are listed, making even the most cursory stroll through its streets a cause of architectural wonder. Around virtually every corner is another beautiful, half-timbered building or mullioned window. No wonder John Betjeman lauded the place as the perfect historic town.

But there's one area in which Ludlow is defiantly up to date: food. Since the mid 1990s, it has become a prime destination for gourmets, chefs and those simply keen on good, local food. The town, with a population of less than 10,000, supports two Michelin-starred restaurants in La Bécasse and Mr Underhill's, and many other fine restaurants and pubs, as well as retailers selling locally produced meat, cheese, beer, fruit and veg, a bi-monthly produce market, and an annual food festival.

And once you've eaten your fill for lunch, there are few more beautiful places than Ludlow and its surrounding countryside to walk off your meal and work up an appetite for dinner.

Explore

The Normans, those masters of military architecture, planned well when they came to build an outpost in Ludlow. Their use of the local topography provides a handy basic rule for any visitor to the town: head uphill. **Ludlow Castle** (*see p325*) is set at the top, then the hill falls precipitously to a bend in the River Teme. The town spread downhill from the castle, with only the coming of the railway giving an impetus for building on lower ground. These days, the A49 loops east of the town, as the river meanders to its west. Ludlow is thus kept squeezed within the two boundaries, helping to make it such a rewarding place to wander around. There's a tangible sense of community here, and the pace of life is so unhurried that Ludlow was recognised by the international Slow Movement as Britain's first official 'Slow Town' (www.cittaslow.org.uk).

From the castle, crossing the square in front of Ludlow College takes you to the market on Castle Street. Carry on down the High Street then King Street and you'll pass many of the independent retailers that make shopping in Ludlow so interesting (*see p327*). You'll eventually come to the alley that leads to the other defining building of the town, **St Laurence's Church**. Dating back to 1199 but modified at various points since, St Laurence's (College Street, 01584 872073, www.stlaurences.org.uk)

combines Norman and Early English Gothic architecture to magnificent effect. Indeed, the building is often assumed to be a cathedral. The church's tower dominates the skyline; if you climb the 200 steps to the top, you'll be treated to the best views in Ludlow. The ashes of writer A E Housman are buried just outside the church. Listen for the carillon, which chimes a different tune each day of the week at 8am, noon, 4pm and 8pm.

While both church and castle are worth a visit, Ludlow truly rewards the wanderer. The centre of the town is small and very walkable, lined with roughly 500 listed buildings of various shapes, sizes, grades and ages. Pick up a copy of the 'Ludlow Town Trail' leaflet, available for £1.50 from a variety of spots around town. The fold-out map provides a little context for the history that's visible on every corner.

One of the best **walks** in the area starts from the very centre of Ludlow. From the castle, stroll downhill towards Dinham Bridge, but instead of crossing the bridge, follow the road around to the right. You'll soon come to the beautiful Linney Riverside Park, where you can rent a rowing boat in season and take to the idyllic River Teme that runs around the town.

Alternatively, head downhill from the castle past Dinham House, and then cross over Dinham Bridge. If you're only in the mood for a short amble (20 minutes or so), turn left along the river. The path soon rises and takes you to

0   50 miles

Ludlow
•

Ludlow

Historic sites

● ● ● ○ ○

Art & architecture

● ● ● ● ○

Hotels

● ● ● ○ ○

Eating & drinking

● ● ● ● ●

Nightlife

● ○ ○ ○ ○

Shopping

● ● ● ○ ○

Whitcliffe Common, which yields fine views of Ludlow, before leading downhill again to Ludford Bridge Road. Turn left and cross over the bridge, and you're back in town. For something more ambitious, turn right instead of left after the bridge and follow the path along the edge of the hill. The Mortimer Trail, a 30-mile walk, takes in Mortimer Forest (prime wildlife-watching territory) and ends in the village of Kington.

Guided walks help to put Ludlow into perspective. Run by the Ludlow Historical Research Society, walks start by the cannon at the castle entrance at 2.30pm every Saturday, Sunday and Bank Holiday Monday, from April to the end of October (daily during Ludlow Festival – late June to early July). They cost £2.50 for adults (children are free); for details, phone 01584 874205. For more information on walks in the Ludlow area, visit the Tourist Information Centre (Assembly Rooms, Castle Street, 01584 875053). And for cycling holidays – this is excellent bike country – contact Wheely Wonderful (01568 770755, www.wheely wonderfulcycling.co.uk).

Ludlow Castle

Castle Square (01584 873355/www.ludlowcastle.com). Open Jan, Dec 10am-4pm Sat, Sun. Feb, Mar, Oct, Nov 10am-4pm daily. Apr-July, Sept 10am-5pm daily. Aug 10am-7pm daily. Admission £4.50; £2.50-£4 reductions.
Ludlow Castle was built in the 11th century to assert Norman mastery over the Saxons and to protect England from attacks by the yet-to-be-conquered Welsh. It's undoubtedly one of the country's most magnificent castles. The roof has long since gone, but the proud limestone walls remain, turning various shades of pink and purple in the evening sun. The building is both architecturally significant (combining Norman, medieval and Tudor styles) and historically important. If you stand in the impressive bailey, it's easy to see how the owner could summon the political strength and personal courage to overthrow the reigning monarch.

Such was Roger Mortimer, 1st Earl of March, who fell foul of Edward II and, escaping from the Tower of London, fled to France in 1323. Taking refuge at the court of the French king, Charles IV, Roger renewed his acquaintance with Charles's sister (who was Edward's wife) Isabella, when she came to visit. Roger and Isabella became lovers and returned to England at the head of an army in 1326. Edward fled, but the rebels captured him and forced him to abdicate in favour of his young son. However, for three years Roger ruled as undeclared king and lover of the queen. As legend has it, Edward was disposed of with a red-hot poker, although some scholars now claim he was kept secretly alive on Roger's orders. Roger was himself captured, in a daring night-time raid, by knights loyal to Edward III, summarily tried and executed – slowly.

This was not the end of Ludlow Castle's importance, as it played a major part in the Wars of the Roses in the 15th century. There was also Tudor drama at the castle. In 1502 Prince Arthur died here on his honeymoon with Catherine of Aragon, allowing younger brother Henry VIII to marry Catherine and ascend to the throne.

Eat

With its first-rate market stalls, specialist food shops and restaurants, Ludlow wholly deserves its reputation as an unrivalled foodie destination. In addition to the restaurants listed below, there are a number of other options worth investigation. In a pleasingly secluded courtyard location in the centre of town the Courtyard Café Restaurant (2 Quality Square, 01584 878080, www.thecourtyard-ludlow.co.uk) offers simple, stylish cooking (risottos, steaks, tarts and the like) as well as being a good place for having coffee and home-baked cakes, and both Ye Olde Bull Ring Tavern (44 The Bull Ring, 01584 872311) and the Wheatsheaf Inn (Lower Broad Street, 01584 872980, www.wheatsheaf-ludlow.co.uk) are decent spots in which to enjoy a pint or two.

'The wine list is strong enough to keep pace with the food at what is arguably the best restaurant in this most food-oriented of towns.'

La Bécasse

17 Corve Street (01584 872325/www.labecasse.co.uk). Open 7-9pm Tue; noon-2pm, 7-9pm Wed-Sat; noon-2pm Sun. ££££. Haute cuisine.
When this restaurant was known as Hibiscus and owned by French chef Claude Bosi, it achieved two Michelin stars. Bosi left for London in 2007, but new owner Alan Murchison (of Berkshire's L'ortolan) has installed Will Holland as head chef and a coveted star has been reclaimed. A choice of oft-changing French-accented menus is offered in the oak-panelled dining room, including a vegetarian list (artichokes with caramelised garlic risotto and braised baby-gem lettuce, perhaps), a gourmand version (the likes of roast new season lamb loin and confit neck fillet with liquorice, pomme anna, spring vegetables and à wild garlic leaf), a more kindly priced lunch menu and an à la carte. Local produce and the occasional Asian twist add interest. Ludlow once again has two Michelin-starred restaurants (the other being Mr Underhill's, *see p327*). Phew!

Church Inn

The Buttercross (01584 872174/www.thechurch inn.com). Open (restaurant) noon-2.30pm, 6.30-9pm Mon-Fri; noon-3pm, 6.30-9pm Sat; noon-2.30pm, 6.30-8.30pm Sun. ££. Pub.

Top: La Bécasse;
bottom: De Grey's.

Ludlow's best pub is also its most pleasingly old-fashioned. Set in the shadow of St Laurence's Church, it offers more ales than most livers can handle (including many local brews, all kept in sparkling nick) and an agreeably straightforward menu of pub food classics. The Church is a local pub above all else, albeit one in which the many visitors are welcomed with cheery saloon-room banter. Keep an eye out for the fabulous nutcracker, permanently attached to the far side of the bar. There are also nine en suite rooms here (three with balconies), should you be unable to drag yourself away from the craic. A very easy place in which to lose track of an evening.

"The pies are excellent stomach fillers on a long ramble up nearby Clee Hill – especially the award-winning pork pies."

Clive Bar & Restaurant with Rooms
Bromfield, 2 miles NW of Ludlow *(01584 856565/ www.theclive.co.uk). Open noon-3pm, 6.30-9.30pm Mon-Fri; noon-9.30pm Sat, Sun. £££. Modern European.*
There are 15 spacious rooms providing accommodation for wayfarers in this large building, but the dining room is also popular with locals. The venue was redecorated in early 2007 to a crisp modern finish; you could pretty much say the same about the menu. Ingredients are sourced locally where possible: Wenlock Edge Farm ham is a kind of English prosciutto, here suitably served with fig and melon. Often-robust mains might include braised and roasted rabbit (a tad dry on a recent visit), and seafood and fennel casserole (more engaging). Chocolate mousse with green tea ice-cream makes a pleasing end to a meal.

De Grey's
5-6 Broad Street (01584 872764/www.degreys.co.uk). Open 9am-5pm Mon-Fri; 9am-5.30pm Sat; 11am-4pm Sun. ££. Café.
Beamed ceilings, copper pots and aproned waitresses provide a nice retro feel to Ludlow's famous tearoom, which dates back to 1570 and is bustling almost every day. Afternoon tea is De Grey's raison d'être, but it also dishes up breakfasts and is a hugely popular spot for lunch. The menu includes tempting own-made soups, fresh sandwiches, jacket potatoes and more substantial dishes (roasted confit of duck leg, for instance). The medley of cakes, buns and pastries would break the resolve of even the most determined of dieters. A shop at the front offers takeaway treats.

Koo
127 Old Street (01584 878462/www.koo-ook.co.uk). Open Summer 7-10pm Tue Sat. Winter 7-10pm Wed-Sat. ££. Japanese.

This cosy venue strikes an unexpected note in such a quintessentially English town, but it's by no means an inharmonious one. Tucked away at the bottom of Old Street (a five-minute stroll down the hill from the town centre), turquoise-tinted Koo is Ludlow's sole Japanese restaurant. The four-course menu offers a few choices, but usually begins with a selection of sushi. Other courses might include tsukune (glazed chicken and sweet potato cakes) and buta yuan yaki (a marinated pork dish).

Mr Underhill's
Dinham Weir (01584 874431/www.mr-underhills.co.uk). Open 7.30-11.30pm Wed-Sun. ££££. Haute cuisine.
The hotel side of this operation is very good (see p330). The Michelin-starred restaurant, though, is nothing short of exceptional. While Judy Bradley oversees proceedings in the long, thin dining room (a comfortable space, with tables at the end overlooking the river), husband Chris takes charge in the kitchen, compiling a daily changing, seven-course tasting menu with considerable élan. Highlights during our visit included a blissful foie gras custard layered with sweetcorn cream and a sesame glaze; a perfectly balanced medley of slow-roasted fillet of beef, ox cheek pie and roasted vegetables; and, for dessert, a wonderfully playful Highland parfait. The wine list is strong enough to keep pace with the food at what is arguably the best restaurant in this most food-oriented of towns.

Shop

The great beauty of Ludlow is that it's far from being a staid museum: it remains a thriving market town with a strong sense of local community. Regular **street markets** are held on Monday, Wednesday, Friday and Saturday in Castle Square, which also hosts an antique and flea market (first and third Sundays of the month), a books and crafts market (second Sunday of the month), a local produce market (Mar-Nov second and fourth Thursdays of the month. Dec-Feb second Thursday of the month) and a handful of other more sporadic events.

Away from the market, Ludlow's twin shopping fortes are **food** and antiques. Despite its small population, the town supports a range of butchers and bakers (although no candlestick makers we could find) that would shame many a city. Apart from those mentioned in the listings below, R Walton (7-8 Market Street, 01584 872088) and Richard C Swift (5 Parkway, off Corve Street, 01584 874767, www.swifts.bakery.co.uk) are excellent establishments for your daily bread. There's an astonishing array of specialist food shops too, selling everything from cheese to chocolate. For more information on local food, see www.localtoludlow.org.

Antiques shops are ten a penny in Ludlow, especially on Corve Street. For old furniture, porcelain and glass, Corve Street Antiques

(141A Corve Street, 01584 879100) is good value; at the other end of the price scale, G&D Ginger (5 Corve Street, 01584 876939, www.gdgingerantiques.com) specialises in high-quality, antique oak and country furniture. Somewhere in the middle lies the Ludlow Period House Shop (141 Corve Street, 01584 877276, www.periodhouseshops.com), which sells an enticing range of curios and accessories (including reproductions). But the most striking shop is Dinham House (Dinham, below the castle, 01584 878100, www.clearviewstoves.com). The largest Georgian house in Ludlow, this was once occupied by Lucien Bonaparte, Napoleon's brother, who lived here for six months in 1811. These days, it's a showroom for wood-burning stoves (by Clearview) and handcrafted furniture, but the premises manage to retain a grand period feel.

Andrew Francis

1 Market Street (01584 872008). Open 7am-5pm Mon-Sat.

It would be a shame to miss the free-range pork and chicken sold by this butcher's, hidden away in Market Street. The pies are own-made and the sausages are among the best around.

Chocolate Gourmet

16 Castle Street (01584 879332/www.chocolate gourmet.co.uk). Open Summer 10.30am-5.30pm Mon-Sat; 11am-5pm Sun. Winter 10.30am 5pm Mon-Sat; 11am-5pm Sun.

The name tells you all you need to know. When she opened her shop in 1999, Janette Rowlatt combined her love of chocolate and Ludlow in the one premises. Since then chocoholics have come here for high-quality truffles, pralines and fudge, and organic and fair trade chocolate.

Deli on the Square

4 Church Street (01584 877353/www.delionthesquare ludlow.co.uk). Open 9.30am-5pm Mon-Thur; 9am-5pm Fri, Sat.

Cheeseheads are well served in Ludlow, with the Deli and Mousetrap Cheese (*see below*) selling a wide range of the excellent local specimens, as well as foreign interlopers. Here, you'll find over 140 types of cheese, as well as charcuterie, mustards, oils and vinegars.

Farmers' Produce Market

1 Mill Street (01584 873532). Open 7am-5.30pm Mon-Sat. No credit cards.

An excellent fruit and veg retailer that has been in business for 45 years. Most of the produce is grown locally and many of Ludlow's restaurants buy their green stuff here.

Fruit Basket

2-3 Church Street (01584 874838). Open 8am-5.30pm Mon-Sat. No credit cards.

Ludlow's other greengrocer (ignoring Tesco at the bottom of the hill) also sells local fruit and vegetables, as well as dairy produce and eggs, and a good range of cut flowers too.

A H Griffiths

11 Bull Ring (01584 872141). Open 8am-5pm Mon-Fri; 7am-4pm Sat.

One of Ludlow's trio of independent butchers, A H Griffiths buys its pork, beef and lamb from local farmers. The meat pies are excellent stomach fillers on a long ramble up nearby Clee Hill – especially the award-winning pork pies.

Mousetrap Cheese

6 Church Street (01584 879556). Open 9am-5pm Mon-Sat. No credit cards.

Mousetrap specialises in unpasteurised British farmhouse cheeses, and we can recommend the delicious little Hereford variety made at its own dairy.

Price & Sons

7 Castle Street (01584 872815/www.pricesthe bakers.co.uk). Open 9am-5pm Mon-Wed, Fri, Sat; 9am-4pm Thur.

A family bakery since 1940, Price & Sons would now more accurately be called Barnett & Daughters. However, Sid Price was the current owner's father, and he ran the business with his sons, so the name has stuck. Just as lasting are the traditional long-fermentation methods used here, so the bread contains just flour, water, yeast and salt, without any flour improvers. The cakes, pies, pasties and sarnies are excellent too. A good place to stock up for a picnic down by the river.

D W Wall & Son

14 High Street (01584 872060/www.walls butchers.co.uk). Open 7.15am-5pm Mon-Wed, Fri; 7.15am-1pm Thur; 7.15am-4pm Sat.

The third of Ludlow's butchers, Wall & Son is the place to go for meat from rare breeds of cattle, pigs and sheep reared in Shropshire and Herefordshire. Wall sells the excellent Ludlow sausage and many other prize-winning bangers.

Stay

In addition to the hotels, B&Bs and inns listed below, take a look at the **Shropshire Hills** chapter for other places to stay (*see p50*). **De Grey's** also has nine distinguished-looking rooms.

Dinham Hall

By the Castle (01584 876464/www.dinhamhall.co.uk). £££.

This elegant Georgian pile dates back to 1792, but it has served as a hotel only since the early 1980s. Beforehand the building spent the better part of two centuries as a private residence and, latterly, a boarding house for boys at the local grammar school. Happily, the rooms have been redecorated since the brats left, in a fashion that's both handsome and highly sympathetic. Each of the 13 rooms, some of which overlook the castle or the river, is furnished in a slightly different style: variations on the same crisp, plush theme. Downstairs, the public rooms are country-house posh; a new atrium holds a dining area that's more casual than the (excellent) main restaurant.

Ludlow Food Festival

This quaint market town might be small, but don't underestimate its appetite for food and drink. Ludlow is now widely acknowledged to be a centre for gastronomy (playing host to two Michelin-starred restaurants is only one aspect), and the annual Food Festival is a huge draw to visitors who are serious about their tucker.

Now in its 15th year, the event is bigger than ever, attracting more than 130 independent food and drink producers from the area, who convene to flog their most excellent wares. Expect the likes of artisanal bakers and cheesemongers, small-scale producers of organic draught ciders and perries, and experts in meat, fish and poultry – and that's just the beginning.

The festival itself was founded with the simple aim of celebrating the sheer diversity and quality of food and drink found in Ludlow and the Marches. Food is at the centre of Ludlow life, so it's hardly surprising that the population puts so much effort into this grand three-day bonanza set against the handsome backdrop of Ludlow Castle. The rules are strict – only producers who are directly based in the counties on either side of the Welsh-English border are allowed to trade in the marquees, so everything on show is well and truly local.

One of the festival's unique features is the prestigious Sausage Trail. Ludlow takes great pride in having a trio of traditional butchers still

trading in the town; every year each one (along with a couple of other invited producers) creates a new sausage recipe for the round of tastings and voting by visitors. Don your sausage connoisseur hat, purchase your voting form and get stuck into tasting a sample of each butcher's competition entry, giving a mark out of ten. For your efforts, you'll get your preferred sausage, piping hot in a bap.

Another highlight is the Slow Food marquee, showcasing a vast range of genuinely impressive comestibles; look out for rare Three Counties perry, Old Gloucester beef, and traditional Worcestershire apples among the culinary delights.

Festival events also include the all-important cookery demonstrations and talks, tastings, workshops and oddities such as the Waiters' Race, as well as various cook-offs and competitions. Though the main three-day bash takes place in mid September every year, in 2009 there was also a food event held in May ('celebrating local beers, bangers and bread – and much more', www.thespringevent.co.uk), in the castle gardens. If successful, it's likely to become a fixture.

But in September gastronomes have no excuses – pull on your most forgiving pair of trousers and experience the food festival of the year for yourself.

Ludlow Food Festival, 3 days in mid Sept, www.foodfestival.co.uk.

De Grey's.

Feathers

The Bull Ring (01584 875261/www.feathers atludlow.co.uk). £££.

Possibly the most famous building in Ludlow, the crooked yet characterful Feathers looms over the Bull Ring from the top of Corve Street. You can almost hear its 500-year-old timber frame creaking on windy days. The hotel looks small from the outside, but contains 40 rooms spreadeagled across a network of corridors that extends over the adjacent shops. The decoration in the rooms is in tune with the building's heritage: rich, heavy and a bit ragged around the edges. A similarly opulent restaurant offers three-course dinners nightly; the adjoining bar, redecorated in eyebrow-raisingly modern style in early 2007, is rather less formal.

Fishmore Hall

Fishmore Road (01584 875148/www.fishmore hall.co.uk). ££££.

Owner Laura Penman took a run-down old reform school set on a hillside overlooking Ludlow and turned it into a model boutique hotel. In this she was helped by the fine Georgian proportions of the building and the expansive views over the Shropshire countryside – Clee Hill, the highest point in the county, looms to the east from the dining room. The difficult feat of fitting modern decor into a traditional building has been achieved impressively, in part because of the attention paid to lighting. The restaurant is exceptional, with chef David Jaram producing a regularly changing market menu dependent on what's in season, a fine à la carte, and a six-course Marches taster menu, featuring salmon, wood pigeon, scallops, rabbit and local cheeses. This is food worth starving yourself for.

Mr Underhill's

Dinham Weir (01584 874431/www.mr-underhills.co.uk). £££.

Tucked away behind the castle, this collection of buildings sits spectacularly on the banks of the swimmer-friendly River Teme, the weir causing the water to rush right around Mr Underhill's justly famed restaurant (*see p327*). To make the most of the space in the main house, hosts Judy and Chris Bradley engaged the services of a designer who usually works with the interiors of motor cruisers.

The results are stylish and cultured, with specially made blond-wood furnishings and crisp white linens offering a handsome backdrop to the river views. The Shed is a capacious addition to the property containing plush suites, as is the two-storey, two-bed suite in the Miller's House across the road. Ten minutes away lies the Old School, a lodging house that will open in summer 2009 for self-catering guests.

> 'The rest of the house, from the oak-panelled breakfast room to the plush library, retains a pleasingly old-world feel.'

Mulberry House

10 Corve Street (01584 876765/www.ten corvestreet.co.uk). ££.

Located in a Georgian building right in the heart of Ludlow, this discreet B&B is marked only by a small sign next to the front door. Inside, owners Anna and Robert Reed have decorated the sturdy property in an elegant style. Rooms are painted in eye-catching Georgian shades (Chinese blue, crimson, orchard green), with beds covered in plain white linen. Antique furniture and toile de Jouy fabrics add to the period feel. The ingredients for breakfast come from the local butcher's and baker's just up the road.

Overton Grange

Old Hereford Road (01584 873500/www.overton grangehotel.com). £££.

Once fusty and traditional, this stately Edwardian house was recently subjected to a long-overdue makeover, eradicating the chintz and china dolls in favour of a plainer, more 21st-century look: white bedding offset by rich plums and silvery greys; tactile suedes, satins and velvets; and occasional retro touches. The rest of the house, from the oak-panelled breakfast room to the plush library, retains a pleasingly old-world feel. The restaurant has a good reputation too.

Factfile

When to go

Ludlow is quiet in winter, and the castle is closed on weekdays. Spring, summer and autumn are the best seasons to visit.

Getting there and around

The train station at Ludlow (01584 877090) has regular services to Swansea, Cardiff and Shrewsbury. On Sundays there's a **coach** service (the 192) between Birmingham and Ludlow.

By car

By car, Ludlow is reached via the A49, which goes north to Shrewsbury and south to Leominster and Hereford. The town itself is perfect for walking around.

Tourist information

The tourist information centre is in the Assembly Rooms on Castle Street (01584 875053/www.shropshiretourism.co.uk). Open 10am 5pm Mon-Sat.

Clockwise from top left:
Tate; Godrevy lighthouse;
Porthminster Café;
Primrose Hotel.

St Ives

A jewel on the north Cornwall coast.

The approach to St Ives by train – a journey holidaymakers have been making since the line was built in the 1870s – is a veritable sight for sore eyes. The single-carriage train chugs along the curve of St Ives Bay, opening up gasp-worthy vistas of golden sands and, nearer the bumpers, treating you to a bird's-eye view of the UK's most perfect seaside town: a pretty old granite harbour scooped out of the Bay, filled with water the colour of lime cordial, with a tangle of cottages and lanes nudging for space behind.

Long a magnet for artists, on account of the extraordinary quality of light in the Bay, St Ives still has a wonderfully exotic feel. The vivid colours rebel against the restrained English palette, and its island-like setting means soft white-sand beaches and emerald sea glimpses at every touch and turn. A scattering of palms – not to mention the more recent arrival of chic white beachside cafés and restaurants – combine to bring a real French resort feel to the Cornish Riviera.

A thriving centre of the fishing industry in the 19th century, pilchard stocks had declined by the time the town began to attract schools of artists instead: the likes of Barbara Hepworth, Ben Nicholson, Naum Gabo and Bernard Leach put St Ives firmly on the creative map. And for art, the small seaside town still has a big reputation, cemented by the construction of the third branch of the Tate in 1993 – right on the beach, naturally.

The advent of more affluent tourists to the area in recent years has yielded frothy cappuccinos, fancy restaurants and fluffy white towels, but the fudge shops, buckets and spades, and fish and chips of yore remain – in short, all the essential ingredients for the modern British seaside holiday.

Explore

ST IVES

One of the great pleasures of a visit to St Ives is taking an aimless stroll through the twisting 'downlong' alleys and lanes (where the fishermen used to live) behind the harbour. These endlessly picturesque streets, forming an 'old town' of sorts, are lined with pretty pint-sized white and granite cottages, decorated with bursting flowerboxes and pastel-coloured paintwork. The town's main shopping drag, handsome pedestrianised **Fore Street** – now as much home to interiors boutiques, delis and cafés as it is to the old-fashioned pasty and sweet shops – is a good place to dive in. In the area, take a stroll through **Trewyn Subtropical Gardens** to see banana trees, palms and bamboo – all of which manage to make themselves at home thanks to the mild Cornish climate.

Up until the decline of the pilchard stocks at the turn of the 20th century, St Ives was a thriving fishing centre. Between the shell shops and alfresco drinkers, it might now be hard to envisage that the lovely old harbour would once have been piled high with fish and – at the height of the lucrative pilchard trade – up to 400 fishing boats would have sheltered here.

At the entrance to Smeaton's Pier you can take a peek in the miniature stone-built **St Leonard's Chapel**, where fishermen prayed before they went to sea. On the opposite side of the harbour stands the **Lifeboat Station** (the original is now the Alba restaurant next door), which opens to visitors in summer. Between the two is the atmospheric **Sloop Inn** (www.sloop-inn.co.uk), one of the oldest pubs in Cornwall – with tables right on the harbour. Stretching out north of the harbour like a big toe is the area known as 'the Island', an outcrop whose grassy footpath takes you on a short walk around the headland to Porthmeor Beach – and the **Tate** – on the other side.

It's hard to imagine a town of such diminutive dimensions with more (or better) beaches: if you count the harbour, which also transforms into a big sandy beach at low tide, St Ives has four beaches, all with clear waters and soft, clean sand: little **Porthgwidden**, hidden away in a nick on the Island, which is great for kids; Atlantic-facing **Porthmeor**, St Ives's surf star and home to the Tate gallery; and Mediterranean-feeling, palm-trimmed **Porthminster**, whose waters and sands are so clean they have been awarded Blue Flag status.

Barbara Hepworth Museum & Sculpture Garden

Barnoon Hill (01736 796226/www.tate.org.uk/stives/hepworth). Open Mar-Oct 10am-5.20pm daily. Nov-Feb 10am-4.20pm Tue-Sun. Admission £4.65; £2.74 reductions. Joint ticket with Tate £8.55; £4.40 reductions.

This small museum, owned and managed by Tate, is an engaging tribute to one of the 20th century's most important artistic figures. Sculptor Barbara Hepworth made this her home and studio from 1949 until her death at the age of 72 in

0 — 50 miles

St Ives

Historic sites
● ● ● ● ●

Art & architecture
● ● ● ● ●

Hotels
● ● ● ● ●

Eating & drinking
● ● ● ● ●

Nightlife
● ● ● ● ●

Shopping
● ● ● ● ●

St Ives
●

St Ives   Penzance →

Top: Hayle; Leach Pottery; middle: Godrevy Beach; bottom: Porthminster Beach.

Fired up

For a town of its size (a resident population of just 10,000) and peripheral location (nearly 300 miles from the capital), St Ives carries extraordinary artistic clout. It became a hotbed of artistic talent in the 1930s, when artists, attracted by the clarity of the light and the inspiring landscapes of the Penwith peninsula – set up studios in the seaside town.

Among the modernist heavyweights of the era (Barbara Hepworth, Ben Nicholson, Naum Gabo) was the pioneering potter Bernard Leach, widely hailed as the 'father of studio pottery'. After long years of neglect, his internationally renowned Leach Pottery (see p337), founded in 1920 with Japanese potter Shoji Hamada, reopened in 2008 after a £1.7 million restoration and redevelopment programme – furnishing St Ives its third major artistic attraction, alongside the Tate and the Barbara Hepworth House.

'In the world of pots, we have been messengers between cultures on opposite sides of the world,' Leach is said to have told Hamada – and his status as a global artist, fusing Far Eastern techniques with traditional English pottery, is key to understanding the significance of his work today. Born in Hong Kong, the son of a colonial judge, Leach spent his formative artistic years mingling with the

artists of the Japanese Shirakaba folk craft movement. They were a major influence on his work, and the Leach Pottery was the first in the Western world to install a Japanese wood-burning kiln. Now a scheduled monument, the multi-chambered kiln stands – just as it was in the 1970s – in the most evocative part of the museum: the old pottery. Here you are free to nose around the clay room, the pottery wheels, the glazing workshop and the fireplace where Leach would hold court with his potters – all left gloriously unpolished.

Though heritage is key, the Leach Pottery isn't merely about the preservation of a relic – crucial to the success of the project is the re-creation of the space as a working pottery. In an Asian-inspired extension to the old building, there is slick new studio space occupied by MA students under the supervision of lead potter Jack Doherty – plus an exhibition space with a sharply curated, Leach-inspired programme.

The Leach Tableware collection, produced on site and sold in the pottery shop (prices from £10 per piece), makes a classy souvenir – the design is beautifully functional and the earthy tones draw on the local land- and seascape. The shop also sells a well-edited selection of cutting-edge ceramics from contemporary local, national and international names.

a fire here in 1975. It now offers fascinating insight into the sculptor's life, with her studio and garden preserved as she left it. Her beautiful, curving sculptures, including *Fallen Images* (completed only a few months before her death), are complemented by background material on the artist (including some captivating quotations), while the garden, which she helped to design, displays many of her larger pieces in a peaceful subtropical setting. Many demonstrate her fascination with Cornwall's ancient menhirs and dolmens.

Leach Pottery

Higher Stennack (01736 799703/www.leach pottery.com). Open Mar-Sept 10am-5pm Mon-Sat; 11am-4pm Sun. Oct-Feb 10am-4pm Tue-Sat. Admission £4.50; £3.50 reductions.
See p336 **Fired up**.

St Ives Museum

Wheal Dream (01736 796005). Open Easter-Oct 10am-5pm Mon-Fri; 10am-4pm Sat. Admission £1.50; 50p reductions. No credit cards.
This museum (closed in winter) is an absorbing exploration of the history of this Cornish port, with displays on pilchards, art, mining, farming, shipwrecks and the railways, supplemented by an eccentric collection of ephemera.

Tate St Ives

Porthmeor Beach (01736 796226/www.tate.org.uk/ stives). Open Mar-Oct 10am-5.20pm daily. Nov-Feb 10am-4.20pm Tue-Sun. Admission £5.65; £3.20 reductions. Joint ticket with Barbara Hepworth Museum £8.55; £4.40 reductions.
The undisputed flagship of the art scene in Cornwall, the UK's smallest Tate, opened in 1993 in a striking, curvy building in an even more striking location: built into the cliff on Porthmeor Beach, looking out to sea. At the heart of the building is an open-air rotunda (representing the gas-holder that once occupied the site at the old gasworks), and the brightly coloured glass display is the work of the late Cornish artist Patrick Heron. The museum's changing exhibitions (there is no permanent collection) showcase the work of 20th-century painters and sculptors, particularly those associated with St Ives, as well as showing contemporary artists as part of its artist-in-residence programme. Look out for St Ives School heavyweights such as the naïve art of the fisherman-turned-artist Alfred Wallis; the simple geometrical paintings of Ben Nicholson (who moved to St Ives with his second wife Barbara Hepworth); and the studio pottery of Bernard Leach (*see p336* **Fired up**). Take a breather in the chic top-floor café (*see p338*), which has the best views of all – over the old town and way out to sea.

OUTSIDE ST IVES

For guaranteed sand castle-building space, make for the eastern reaches of St Ives Bay, and the impressive three-mile stretch of sand from Hayle up to Godrevy Head, including the popular surfing beach of **Gwithian Beach** (the middle part) and **Godrevy Beach** (the eastern end). The **Godrevy Lighthouse**, thought to have been the inspiration

for Virginia Woolf's novel *To the Lighthouse*, stands at the entrance to the bay.

In the opposite direction, the scenic B3306 road heads west towards **St Just**, taking in the heart-stopping coastal scenery and the charming village of **Zennor**. West again is the **Geevor Tin Mine** (Pendeen, 01736 788662, www. geevor.com); the huge clifftop site was a working mine for 300 years before its closure in 1990. In 2008, it gained the new Hard Rock Museum after a multi-million pound development programme to protect its heritage. The underground tour of the 18th-century mining tunnels is as fascinating as it is claustrophobic.

Eat

See also the **Gurnard's Head** (*p339*).

Alba

Old Lifeboat House, Wharf Road (01736 797222/ www.thealbarestaurant.com). Open 11am-2.30pm, 5-9.30pm daily. £££.
Beautifully converted from a skeleton of the old lifeboat station, and with direct views over the harbour, this sleek restaurant serves top-flight Modern European cuisine with an emphasis on locally sourced and organic ingredients (line-caught fish, Newlyn crab, free-range local chicken, Cornish cheeses). The slate grey-and-glass front and the pared-down aesthetic lend an air of sophistication – and make a refreshing change from the obligatory palette of blues of Cornish-chic restaurants. One of St Ives's finest.

Blas Burgerworks

The Warren (01736 797272/www.blasburgerworks. co.uk). Open 6-10pm Tue-Sun. (Easter & school hols open daily, times vary). ££.
St Ives's very own gourmet burger company occupies a pint-spaced space hidden down a pretty, narrow lane (look out for signs from the railway station). Seating is on stools at communal tables – and elbow room is scarce – but once you've sunk your teeth into one of Blas's char-grilled burgers, you'll probably find yourself surprisingly uninterested in comfort and conversation. Our tip: grab a burger and walk a few yards to the seafront (minding the circling seagulls, renowned for barefaced swoop-and-steal operations). Cornish meat is used in all burgers and Blas boasts a green agenda: all organic waste is composted, the furniture is made from reclaimed timber and local produce is king. Try the cornish blue cheeseburger, made with a slice of the celebrated local blue cheese. Alternative garnishes include spicy chilli relish, watercress and wild garlic mayo.

Digey Food Hall

Porthmeor Beach 6 The Digey (01736 799600). Open 10am-5pm Mon-Sat. £.
This cosy deli and café, down a pretty lane leading off the main shopping drag to Porthmeor Beach, specialises in the ever-expanding stable of premium Cornish food produce,

including sandwiches with a local twist – Village Green cornish goat's cheese with cranberry jelly baguette, say, or hot Cornish sausage with chutney – as well as Italian and Spanish deli classics (platters of Parma ham and salami and Serrano ham and manchego cheese with quince jelly). Pair with a glass of St Austell Brewery ale, or Cornish Orchard's Summer Cup.

Porthminster Café
Porthminster Beach (01736 795352/www.porthminster cafe.co.uk). Open Summer noon-4pm, 6-10pm daily. Winter noon-3pm Tue-Thur, Sun; noon-3pm, 6-9pm Fri, Sat. ££££.
The name rather understates its case: far from being your average beachside caff, the Porthminster Café is a serious restaurant in the body of a laid-back beach hut (albeit a very classy one). Ever since opening in a gorgeous old white deco house on the sands of glorious Porthminster Beach, Australian chef Michael Smith's kitchen has been attracting accolades. The sun-kissed menu sets the perfect tone for holiday dining, with the emphasis on Mediterranean flavours, as well as posh fish and chips (with white balsamic vinegar, naturally). Friendly and slick service, fresh decor and dreamy views make this the perfect perch from which to contemplate the light in the Bay dancing off the water with a glass of local bubbly. A hot contender for St Ives's best kitchen, and quickly making inroads into the upper echelons of Cornwall's burgeoning restaurant scene. Open all year round – book ahead even in low season.

Seafood Café
45 Fore Street (01736 794004/www.seafoodcafe. co.uk). Open noon-3pm, 6-9.30pm daily. £££.
This gleaming modern restaurant on the main street combines clean, airy Conranesque decor with concept dining: you go up and choose your catch (chicken and beef also available) from the iced display and pick a sauce to go with it: roasted pepper and mango, fresh hollandaise, ginger and spring onion glaze and so on. Desserts aren't so globe-trotting, taking in much-loved classics like bread and butter pudding, a platter of Cornish cheeses and sticky toffee pudding. Prices are geared more towards visitor Visa, but service and quality both consistently hit the mark and it's invariably packed. Book ahead.

Tate Café
Porthmeor Beach (01736 796226/www.tate. org.uk/stives). Open Mar-Oct 10am-4.50pm daily. Nov-Feb 10am-3.50pm Tue-Sun. ££.
The museum's airy top-floor café – offering uninterrupted Atlantic views – is the ideal spot for a post-Tate tête à tête. The short but classy menu is all about light lunches (soups, gourmet sandwiches, grilled mackerel with potato salad) with the emphasis on local flavours: we loved the cornish yarg and smoked ham sarnie on granary bread and the Newlyn hand-picked white crabmeat. The ingredients are top-notch, service is unfailingly friendly, and the food is prepared with care and precision – but for all its accomplishment, the main story here will always be the glorious views over Porthmeor Beach, out to sea and over the higgledy-piggledy roofs of the old town.

Shop

As well as having three significant art museums, all with classy shops – the Tate, the Barbara Hepworth Museum and the newly refurbished Leach Pottery – St Ives's thriving art scene has spawned dozens of smaller galleries and studios around town, showing the work of local artists, ceramic artists and jewellery makers. They run the gamut from tourist tat – and the inevitable clichéd beach scenes – to serious collector material, and offer hours of browsing.

Seasalt
4 Fore Street (01736 799684/www.seasalt cornwall.co.uk). Open 9.30am-5.30pm Mon-Sat; 10.30am-4pm Sun.
Cornwall mini chain Seasalt is a specialist in organic cotton clothing, producing its own range of colourful, comfortable basics, as well as buying in choice pieces from the likes of Camper and Helly Hansen. The clothes have an outdoorsy feel, so key items are soft-wool stripey scarves, eco fleeces and colourful patterned wellies made from natural rubber.

Halzephron Herb Farm
62 Fore Street (01736 791891/www.halzherb.com). Open 10am-6pm daily (winter times may vary).
This little shop is packed to the rafters with jars and bottles of delectable chutneys, dressings, dips, honeys, marinades, mayos and stir-fry sauces – all made with ingredients from the Halzephron Herb Farm, grown on the well-drained soil of its clifftop setting near Gunwalloe on the Lizard. A fine souvenir alternative to sickly-sweet fudge.

Stay

Blue Hayes Private Hotel
Trelyon Avenue (01736 797129/www.bluehayes.co.uk). ££££.
The 'private' tag is fair: tucked discreetly away above Porthminster Beach (and just ten minutes from the harbour), Blue Hayes has just five luxuriously appointed suites and a guests-only restaurant. Owner Malcolm Herring spent two years overhauling an old 1920s guesthouse, halving the number of rooms, creating a clean, fresh interior design, and adding more than a touch of glamour. The rooms have spacious terraces, glorious sea views and big pampering bathrooms (thick white towels, huge baths, shower body jets, Molton Brown minis), but the icing on the cake is the glamorous balustraded white terrace, where you can take breakfast (or a cocktail at sunset) overlooking the harbour and the Bay, and the palms of the lush hotel garden. All in all, more St Tropez than St Ives.

Boskerris
Boskerris Road, Carbis Bay (01736 795295/ www.boskerrishotel.co.uk). £££.

Over the past five years, this '30s-built hotel has been transformed by the Bassett family into a haven of contemporary coastal chic, furnished with impeccable taste (think metallic Osborne & Little outsized floral print wallpaper, perspex coffee tables and crisp white rugs) and run with extraordinary attention to detail (perfectly placed mirrors to reflect the ocean, satnav references for popular day trips in the in-room info, fresh milk offered for tea). Located on the southern edge of St Ives, in the coastal village of Carbis Bay (just above the big sandy beach of the same name), the hotel has an eye-wateringly beautiful setting: the hotel's panoramic terrace is in pole position to take in the sweep of the whole bay, with St Ives on one side and the white horses crashing into the Godrevy Lighthouse on the other, and nearly all rooms have direct ocean views.

Breakfast is sure to satisfy the fussiest of foodies – a named-local-source menu includes ricotta hot cakes with berry compote and French toast with pan-fried bananas and maple syrup – and the friendly, professional service is in a league of its own. Nothing is too much trouble for the Bassett family, who chalk up suggested walks and activities (in the manner of a restaurant specials board) and have collaged a huge OS map of Cornwall on the wall to help you plan activities. The centre of St Ives is most picturesquely accessed via a 20-minute walk along the coastal path or a three-minute train journey on the charming branch line train. Highly recommended for affordable luxury.

11 Sea View Terrace

11 Sea View Terrace (01736 798440/www.11 stives.co.uk). £££.
Technically it's a B&B, but aesthetically this Edwardian townhouse is breaking well out of its bracket. The three rooms are one hundred per cent chintz-free, with clean white walls and bedspreads, navy blue accents and spotless white bathrooms. In terms of views, the address says it all: located on a terrace at the top of town, it has two rooms with views over the harbour and old town below, and the other has a private south-facing terrace by way of compensation.

Gurnard's Head

nr Zennor, 5 miles W of St Ives *Gurnard's Head (01736 796928/www.gurnardshead.co.uk). ££.*
With the desolate Penwith moorland on one side and the foaming Atlantic on the other, this country inn with restaurant and rooms is ideal for that weekend when you really want to get away from it all. Located a touch west of the pretty village of Zennor, the coastal pub sits a few fields away from the namesake Gurnard's Head, a spectacular rocky outcrop (shaped like a gurnard's head) that takes you out into the Atlantic for great views of the cliffs on either side and the feeling of the wind in your hair (and quite possibly the Cornish drizzle on your anorak).

Rooms are simple and comfortable, and though the upmarket menu and rustic chic decor place Gurnard's squarely in the gastropub category, the food is fuss-free – this is hearty British comfort food of the highest order: the likes of pork belly with mash, cabbage, cider and thyme; rabbit and partridge terrine; and, of course, the mother of all Sunday roasts. The Inkins are firm believers in 'simple things in life done well'. So, now, are we – along with hundreds of other hungry hikers, urban refugees and locals getting together for a big family roast – so booking is recommended.

Primrose Valley Hotel

Porthminster Beach (01736 794939/www.primrose online.co.uk). £££.
One of St Ives's best boutique options, this lovingly run hotel has a quiet but central location, contemporary styling and keen attention to guests' needs. Just yards from the soft sands of Porthminster Beach, white-fronted Primrose Valley has the feel of a seaside villa – ask for a front-facing room with sea views. Despite hip hotel accents (kitschy floral wallpaper, neat retro lamps, polished wood floors, pink and purple hues) this is a thoroughly friendly place. So, expect a superb organic breakfast, personal service, a small bar that goes well beyond the call of duty (a 50-strong wine list), and it is green accredited with the Cornwall Sustainable Tourism Project. It even has a one-room spa on site with a range of treatments, massages and primping and preening services, all using REN's products.

Factfile

When to go

Summer is the classic time for a bucket and spade holiday in St Ives, but to find quieter streets it's better to go slightly off-season. For beach-to-yourself moments – and seriously discounted hotel rooms – go for a winter break, when you'll still find the big attractions like the Tate gallery open, and you'll have a better chance of booking a table at the town's finest restaurants.

Getting there & around

The train station is in the centre of town and the loveliest way to arrive to St Ives is via the branch line train from St Erth, which connects direct to London Paddington (journey time 5-7 hours).

Getting around

St Ives is best tackled on foot – its narrow winding streets are no place for a car and parking is problematic. The distances involved are incredibly short – the town can be walked from end to end in 15 minutes.

Tourist information

The tourist office is located in the centre of town at the Guildhall, Street-an-Pol (01736 796297). Open Winter 9am-5pm Mon-Fri. Summer 9am-5pm Mon-Fri; 10am-4pm Sat; 10am-2pm Sun.

Internet

St Ives Library, Gabriel Street (01872 322005).

Top: River Ouse
& Guildhall
left: National Railway
Museum; right: Minster.

1434

MULBER

York

A small but perfectly formed cathedral city.

From the moment the train pulls in under the majestic curved domes of York railway station, or you drive past the great green swathe of the Knavesmire racecourse, you know you are in one of England's special places. This beautiful medieval city is compact enough to be explored on foot, yet big enough to sustain sophisticated shops, restaurants and bars. It has breathtaking architecture and world-class museums. And, for an escape from city bustle you can walk its superbly intact ancient city walls or along its river, bordered by footpaths and cycleways.

Dominating the skyline is the unmissable York Minster, awesome in its size and grandeur, yet exquisite in its detail of stone, wood and stained glass. It will never be free of scaffolding – work has been going on now for 800 years – but it is one of the world's great churches. There's a mass of detail, too, in the hidden York, with its ginnels and snickets, its quaintly named Whip-Ma-Whop-Ma-Gate and Mad Alice Lane, and the 22 cat statues placed on city buildings by the mog-obsessed York architect Tom Adams.

But this small city is not just about history. It is home to a booming university and an annual Science and Technology Festival. A thriving arts scene bursts on to the streets each summer with contemporary sound and light shows in St Mary's Abbey ruins, along with outdoor film shows, with films projected on to the Minster walls. Paintings from the National Gallery are hung in the streets. And the vibrancy shows no signs of diminishing: currently closed, the Yorkshire Museum is preparing to open with three new galleries charting the story of the city; the restored *Flying Scotsman* will steam out of the National Railway Museum in 2010, and the four-year cycle of mystery plays returns to the city the same year.

Explore

Three miles of city walls (open 8am-dusk daily) – the most complete medieval walls in Britain – all but encircle York's city centre, and walking them is a great way to explore the city. You can pick up a guide from the Visitor Information Centre (01904 550099, www.visityork.org) in Exhibition Square. Children may also enjoy the 'rubbing kit', so they can build up a map of the walls from the steel plaques en route. There's a sensational show of daffodils on the grass ramparts in spring.

Begin at **Bootham Bar**, one of the five gateways to the city. From here you have a good view into the beautiful private gardens behind the Minster. At **Monkgate** the portcullis is still intact and at **Walmgate** there are still doors. In 1501 knockers were added to keep out 'Scots and other vagabonds and rascals'. Micklegate Bar was the monarch's entrance to the city, and also the spot where traitors' heads were displayed on spikes.

The major sights are within the walls, including the ever-dominating presence of the **Minster** *(see p345)*. The only exception is the **National Railway Museum**, and you can pick up the museum's black and gold train from Duncombe Place to take you to its door.

Pedestrianisation also makes shopping a delight. **The Shambles**, with its overhanging buildings, is probably York's best-known thoroughfare. And while the city fills up in high season, it rarely feels overbearing, and if it does the tranquil **Museum Gardens** or a bench on the riverbank will provide some calming respite.

Never lovelier than when the sun reflects the medieval Guildhall or at night when the floodlights shine spookily under the bridges, the **River Ouse** was once the city's lifeline. Now it's a flood risk – in 2000 it rose near-catastrophically to 17 feet above normal levels – and rowers and pleasure boaters are the main water traffic. **York Boat** (01904 628324, www.yorkboat.co.uk) run pleasant one-hour trips from King's Staith from 10.30am through the day, along with evening dinner cruises. Or you can hire self-drive motor boats to go and down the river at your own pace (maximum speed seven mph).

A fun way to learn about the city is to join one of **York Walks** (01904 622303, www.yorkwalk.netfirms.com), which depart twice a day at 10.30am and 2.15pm from Museum Gardens. Walks are themed to include Roman York, an historic toilet tour, secret passages, even a confectionery tour – York was home to former chocolate giants Rowntree and Terry's and the sweet smell of chocolate still occasionally wafts downwind from the Nestlé works. In addition, Voluntary Guides run free, two-hour historical walks from outside York Art Gallery in Exhibition Square (www.btinternet.com/~york.touristguides). Supposedly the most haunted city in Britain, York also has half a dozen guided ghost

York

Historic sites
● ● ● ● ●

Art & architecture
● ● ● ● ●

Hotels
● ● ● ○ ○

Eating & drinking
● ● ● ● ○

Nightlife
● ● ○ ○ ○

Shopping
● ● ● ● ○

0   50 miles

York

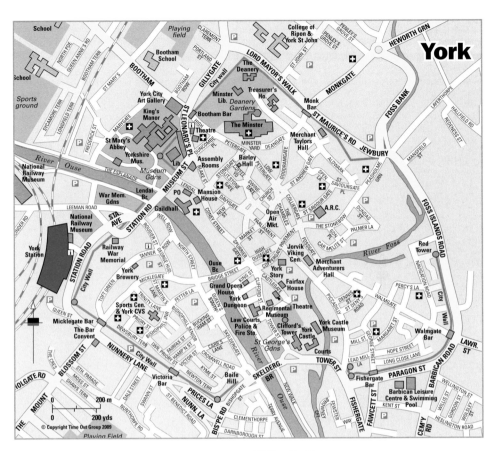

York

walks to prove it. One that doesn't take itself too seriously is the **Ghost Hunt**, (www.ghost hunt.co.uk 01904 608700) led on our tour by a cadaverous man in a top hat and frock coat. Walks start at 7.30pm from the Shambles every night of the week, whatever the weather. Also recommended is the **Original Ghost Walk of York** (www.theoriginalghostwalkofyork.co.uk 01904 764222), starting at the King's Arms, Ouse Bridge at 8pm. No need to book for either, just turn up.

Barley Hall
2 Coffee Yard, off Stonegate (01904 610275/543400/ www.barleyhall.org.uk). Summer 10am-4pm Tue-Sun. Winter 10am-4pm Wed-Sun. Admission £4.50; £3-£3.50 reductions.
In the 1980s, when developers moved in to demolish a mess of decaying buildings in Coffee Yard, they had no idea that 'lost' amid the junk of a plumbers' merchant, was a spectacular medieval townhouse, which has now been impressively restored by York Archaeological Trust as if it were 1483 again.

Clifford's Tower
Tower Street (01904 646940/www.english-heritage. org.uk). Open Mar-Sept 10am-6pm daily. Oct 10am-5pm daily. Nov-Feb 10am-4pm daily. Admission £2.90; £1.50-£2.30 reductions.
Impressive but with a dark history, Clifford's Tower stands ruined and alone on a conical mound by the Castle Museum. A fortress was first built here by William the Conqueror, but the structure burned down twice, most significantly in 1190 when the Jews of York took refuge in the tower during a ghastly pogrom. Besieged by a mob, the rabbi called for the people to take their own lives rather than succumb. Fathers cut the throats of their wives and children before committing suicide themselves. The survivors were tricked and then slaughtered. Some 150 people died in the massacre and no Jewish community has ever re-established itself in York. Walk round the top for an unsettling bird's-eye view of the city.

DIG
St Saviour's Church, St Saviourgate (01904 543403/ 615505/www.yorkarchaeology.co.uk). Open 10am-5pm daily. Admission £5.50; £5 reductions.

Top & centre right: Melton's; left & lower right: Café No8 Bistro.

Budding archaeologists (under the age of 12) can learn how to excavate a Roman, Viking, medieval or Victorian remains. Combine it with a ticket to the Jorvik Viking Centre (*see below*).

Fairfax House

Castlegate (01904 655543/www.fairfaxhouse.co.uk). Open mid Feb-Dec 11am-4.30pm Mon-Thur, Sat; 11am-2pm Fri; 1.30-4.30pm Sun. Admission £6; £5 reductions.
The finest Georgian townhouse in England, according to York Civic Trust. The kitchen, saloon, grand staircase and bedrooms are all impeccably decorated and furnished to Jane Austen perfection. There are different events each month: a tour of the house by candlelight, perhaps, or the 'Keeping of Christmas', when the whole house is made period festive.

Jorvik Viking Centre

Coppergate (01904 543400/www.jorvik-viking-centre.co.uk). Open Summer 10am-5pm daily. Winter 10am-4pm daily. Admission £8.50; £6-£7 reductions.
In 866 a huge armada of Viking ships sailed up the Ouse, seized the city and made it their capital. One thousand years later, while preparing to build a new shopping centre, archaeologists uncovered Viking remains – timber buildings, garden fences and a Viking rubbish tip that contained old socks, shoes and combs complete with head lice. They went on to uncover 40,000 objects from the peaty layers. In 1984 the ever-popular Jorvik Viking Centre opened to the public. Visitors travel by electric pod through the reconstructed streets and homesteads, see how the Vikings lived (and smelled) and see the artefacts. Avoid the queues by booking ahead; tickets are valid for 12 months. Each February a citywide, five-day Viking Festival takes place.

Minster

Minster Yard (01904 557200/www.yorkminster.org). Open 9am-5pm Mon-Sat; noon-3.45pm Sun. Admission (Minster) £6; £5 reductions. (Undercroft, Treasury and Crypt) £4; £3 reductions. (Tower) £4; £3 reductions. (Joint entry) £9.50; £8 reductions.
When the ten-tonne Big Peter tolls each day at noon it makes its presence felt right across the city – as does everything about the Minster. The biggest Gothic cathedral in northern Europe, it's 200ft high, took 250 years to build and is genuinely awesome. Inside, the nave is 500ft long and 100ft wide. Until it was dismantled for restoration in 2008, the Great East Window, the size of a tennis court, was the largest area of medieval stained glass in the world (the Minster as a whole contains two million individual pieces of glass). Now, using 16 miles of scaffolding, it is being restored piece by piece, as part of a decade-long programme. In its place, a photographic replica is amazing enough, the largest single photograph ever printed. In compensation for missing East Window, visitors can marvel at the Five Sisters window in the North Transept, climb the 275 steps up the Central Tower for the definitive view of the city or book a tour of the Glaziers' Studio (01904 557216, 2pm Wed, Fri, departing from the Minster desk). Other highlights include the Chapter House, the Astronomical clock, the Quire Screen with sculptures of all the Kings of England from William the Conqueror to Henry VI, and the Roman remains in the Undercroft.

National Railway Museum

York Station, Leeman Road (01904 621261/www.nrm. org.uk). Open 10am-6pm daily. Admission free.
Indisputably the best railway museum in the world. The show-stopping centrepiece of the National Railway Museum is the vast Great Hall, where 22 giant steam engines compete in size and grandeur. Among them is the record-breaking *Mallard*, capable of 126mph under steam and still looking futuristic, and a scale replica of Stephenson's *Rocket*. The biggest is a 93ft monster built for the Chinese National Railway in 1935. Elsewhere, you can clamber aboard a Japanese bullet train, check the restoration of the *Flying Scotsman*, take a rock 'n' roll journey from London to Brighton on the simulator, and take the kids for a ride on the miniature railway. True railway buffs, meanwhile, can scour 750,000 items of railway memorabilia in the warehouse. Revive with tea in the Brief Encounter café right on a platform. Train enthusiasts may also enjoy York Model Railway, next to the railway station. It's a bit fusty by comparison, but control freaks of all ages will enjoy pushing buttons to make the trains run on time in its miniature world.

York Castle Museum

Eye of York (01904 687687/www.yorkcastlemuseum. org.uk). Open 9.30am-5pm daily. Admission £7.50; £4-£6.50 reductions.
One of York's gold-star attractions, this museum of everyday life, with its period rooms, sweet shops, prison cells and its famous re-creation of Kirkgate, a Victorian street, has something for everyone, from exhibitions of Victorian childbirth and gynaecological instruments, to the vintage Ewbanks, Hoovers and Dysons in the 'Spotless' exhibition. The costume collection is one of the best in the country, so is the military section. Among the toys, an early Cindy, a box of Meccano or a Super Mario computer game will have you crying 'Ooh I had one of those.' Book early for a Dickensian Christmas with 'Carols in Kirkgate'.

Yorkshire Museum/Museum Gardens

Museum Street (01904 687687/www.yorkshiremuseum. org.uk). Open 7.30am-5.30pm daily. Admission free.
Set among the evocative ruins of St Mary's Abbey, the Museum Gardens are the much-loved green heart of the city. On sunny weekends and summer lunchtimes the young spread out on its lawns with tourists and office workers. Otherwise it is a peaceful oasis for tame squirrels and pigeon feeders. History is unavoidable, too. Apart from being strewn with the Abbey's stones, it contains the Roman multangular fort and the timbered medieval Hospitium. A delightful old Observatory holds star-spotting parties on Saturday evenings in winter.

Here, too, is the Yorkshire Museum. Closed at the time of writing, it is set to reopen in August 2010, with three new galleries charting the history of York. The city's Roman heritage will be a central theme.

Shop

Shopping in York is great – it's compact and virtually traffic free. Explore Micklegate, Gillygate and the Quarter for the best independents. Take a look, too, at the tourist board's themed shopping trails (www.visit york.org/shopandthecity).

Ken Spelman Rare Books
70 Micklegate (01904 624414 www.kenspelman.com). Open 9am-5.30pm Mon-Sat.
This shop is a real treasure, a second-hand bookshop where you can lose yourself for hours among the well-ordered shelves of rare and not-so-rare books. There's even a little fireplace at the back with a real fire burning in the grate.

Mulberry Hall
Stonegate (01904 620736/www.mulberryhall.co.uk). Open 9am-5.30pm Mon-Sat; 11am-5pm Sun.
A beautiful half-timbered shop in Stonegate that is crammed from floor to beamed ceiling with crystal, china and everything for the table. Don't miss the cool and contemporary Dining Warehouse at the back nor, in season, the winter wonderland of Christmas decorations.

Selkie
45 Low Petergate (01904 626242/www.selkieclothing. co.uk). Open 10am-5.30pm Mon-Fri; 10am-6pm Sat; 11am-5pm Sun.
A pretty, independent boutique run with quiet charm by Lucy Weller, who cleverly mixes one-off pieces by northern designers with casual wear, glamorous evening wear, gorgeous jewellery, bags and scarves.

Snowhome
42 Gillygate (01904 671155 www.snow-home.co.uk). Open 10am-5pm Mon-Fri; 10am-5.30pm Sat.
This shop is sheer indulgence for designer homeware that's both functional and fun, contemporary and international. It ranges from Italian lighting to a terrorist teapot with balaclava cosy and lots of stylish knick-knacks to take home.

Eat

Betty's Tearooms
6-8 St Helen's Square (01904 622865/www.bettys. co.uk). Open 9am-9pm daily. ££. Tearoom/café.
Locals, visitors – everyone loves Betty's, so hang the expense and join the queue. You could dine modestly on an egg mayo sandwich or the classic Fat Rascal (a large scone made with citrus peel, almonds and cherries), less modestly on the sublime Swiss rosti – fried grated potato mixed with cream, bacon and raclette cheese – but Betty's full afternoon tea is the works, presented on a tiered cake stand, heavy with sandwiches, scones, jam, clotted cream and little cakes, served with a pot of Yorkshire tea. As essential to York as the Minster.

Blake Head Café
104 Micklegate (01904 623767/www.theblakehead. co.uk). Open noon-3.30pm. £. Café.
A vegetarian café hidden away within a bookshop. The pleasing conservatory extension has newspapers on sticks and a democratic clientele of single shoppers, families, visitors and locals. The self-service counter does big bowls of salads, a daily quiche and a hot dish that might be stuffed peppers or a savoury crumble. Good cakes and a fine selection of juices.

Café Concerto
21 High Petergate (01904 610478/www.cafe concerto.biz). Open 10am-10pm daily. £££. Café.
'Music for the mouth' is how the owners describe this much-loved York institution, within earshot of the Minster bells. Yellowing sheet music covers the walls and scrubbed tables and old school chairs complete the relaxed, lived-in look. It's open all day for soup, sandwiches or quiche. There's also a selection of fabulous home-made cakes. The owners also let a two-roomed holiday apartment upstairs.

Café no8 Bistro
8 Gillygate (01904 653074/www.cafeno8.co.uk). Open 11am-11pm Mon-Fri; 10am-11pm Sat; 10am-5pm Sun. £££. Modern European.
The tiniest and cosiest restaurant in York, Number 8 has just half a dozen tables in one long narrow room, but it packs a lot in, with breakfast, brunch, lunch and dinner and a sweet little garden that extends to the city walls for sunny days. Main dishes might include spiced meatballs and couscous or slow-braised lamb shoulder with bubble and squeak; puddings are comforting classics such as banoffi pie and cheesecake.

City Screen Café Bar
13-17 Coney Street (0871 704 2054/www.picture houses.co.uk). Open 11am-9pm daily. ££. Café.
There's no better location on a summer evening than the terrace of the old *Yorkshire Herald* building, now the city's independent three-screen cinema. Movie-going or not, it's worth dropping in for drinks and simple scoff of sandwiches, burgers, meze plates, pizzas and salads. The service is friendly, the atmosphere informal, the sort of place you can happily eat alone, in or bring your boss or your baby. Bag a table outside for watching the gulls, the geese or the fit young things from York Rowing Club on the Ouse below.

DCH at Dean Court Hotel
Duncombe Place (01904 625082/www.deancourt-york.co.uk) Open 12.30-2pm, 7-9.30pm daily. ££££. Modern European.
Don't expect gloomy hotel dining here. After a total restyle of the lounge and dining room a few years ago, DCH is a smart venue with a menu of modish dishes to match – the likes of wood pigeon and puy lentil ragout or pumpkin and sage risotto, which diners enjoy with views overlooking the Minster. The Court bistro serves light meals, sandwiches and afternoon tea, and hosts 'First Tuesday' jazz suppers every month. *See also p349.*

Hotel du Vin.

de'Clare Deli

5 Lendal (01904 644410//www.declaredeli.co.uk).
Open 8am-5.30pm Mon-Sat. £. Café.
The pristine white interior of Clare Prowse's deli is the backdrop for help-yourself salads, great-value toasted ciabatta sandwiches, olives and antipasti, Spanish and Italian hams and cheeses, lovely cakes, brilliant brownies and some distinctive Yorkshire produce. Though this is principally a deli and a takeaway, three tables provide a welcome coffee stop when everywhere else is heaving. Better still, put together a picnic and find a shady tree in Museum Gardens across the road.

J Baker Bistro Moderne

7 Fossgate (01904 622688/www.jbakers.co.uk). Open noon-2.30pm, 6-10pm Tue-Sat. £££. Modern European.
When Jeff Baker opened his bistro in Fossgate after a star-studded career in Leeds, he said he wanted to move away from the stuffiness that comes with a Michelin star, and while Bistro Moderne is not especially informal, the food is terrific and full of fun. 'Fun' could mean a seven-course dinner that includes pot noodle, guinea hen served with its own feed, and fish and chips with chip shop curry sauce. But this is not junk food. Take pudding: a 'fruit shoot' Baker-style is sarsparilla and rhubarb with Pontefract liquorice ice-cream and ginger parkin. In less lavish mode, the lunchtime 'grazing menu' offers small plates for between £4 and £6. And upstairs a room is dedicated to chocolate in various incarnations. Who's resisting?

Le Langhe

The Old Coach House, Peaseholme Green (01904 622584/www.lelanghe.co.uk). Open 10am-5.30pm Mon-Sat. ££. Italian.
This pure Italian deli has a restaurant at the back that serves brilliantly simple dishes, done really well. Wooden boards of cured meats or Italian cheeses from the shop served with good bread are always pretty irresistible – as is the soup of the day, with tomatoes, cannelini beans, Italian sausage and a slug of olive oil, perhaps. And there could be a special of pasta, stew or polenta with mushrooms. Owner Otto Bocca makes it look dead simple. Distinctive Italian wines too.

Little Betty's

Stonegate (01904 622865/www.bettys.co.uk). Open 10am-5.30pm Mon-Fri, Sun; 9am-5.30pm Sat. ££. Tearoom/café.
Just what it says, a little Betty's in the cutest of old-fashioned shops in historic Stonegate. Downstairs, girls in white pinnies will sell you some de luxe patisserie or a bag of single estate Darjeeling. Up the rickety staircase, they sit you down for all the delights of Betty's menu (*see p346*).

Melton's

7 Scarcroft Road (01904 634341/www.meltons restaurant.co.uk). Open 5.30-9.30pm Mon; noon-2pm, 5.30-9.30pm Tue-Sat. ££££. Modern European.
A trusty favourite ever since Michael and Lucy Hjort opened it nearly 20 years ago: consistent and assured cooking full of seasonal Yorkshire flavours has ensured it has remained one of York's best restaurants. Dinner might begin with carpaccio of Yorkshire-reared Galloway beef served with devilled muffins; local venison comes with mulled pears, red cabbage and polenta. Desserts charm, with combinations like pannacotta, rhubarb and vodka. Melton's hosts Champagne brunches on race days and a four-course 'First Saturday' lunch every month, themed around a seasonal ingredient which might be mutton, lobster, fish or offal, repeated the following Monday.

Melton's Too

Walmgate (01904 629222/www.meltonstoo.co.uk). Open 10.30am-midnight Mon-Sat; 10.30am-11pm Sun. £££. Bistro/British.
From the Melton's stable, the lovely old 'Mtoo' is an informal café/bar/bistro housed in a rambling former 17th-century saddlery. Open every day from breakfast until midnight and with all sorts of menu options, you can go for lunchtime tapas of black pudding and apple, deep-fried squid or meatballs in tomato sauce; a good-value early-doors dinner, or a full-blown evening à la carte. Owner Michael Hjort is director of September's York Festival of Food and Drink (www.yorkfoodfestival.com), so he knows all there is to know about local produce. Look out for his Yorkshire game pie or rare breed Yorkshire pork shoulder with cider and apples from Ampleforth Abbey. Yorkshire-produce dinners run throughout the year, there are music gigs in the loft, and monthly dinner and wine tastings.

Nineteen Restaurant

19 Grape Lane (0845 873 0931/www.nineteenyork.com). Open 11.30am-3pm, 6-10pm Mon-Thur; 11.30am-10.30pm Fri, Sat; 11.30am-3pm, 6-9.30pm Sun. £££. Modern British.
Wonky walls and low ceilings remind you that this is one of the oldest buildings in York. The food, on the other hand, is pleasantly contemporary, with a three-course menu that may bring you escabeche of red mullet, followed by slow-cooked lamb shank, and end with banoffi Eton mess. There are also simpler snacks and lunchtime dishes.

Pig & Pastry

5 Bishopthorpe Road (01904 675115). Open 9am-3pm Mon-Sat. ££. Café.
Just south of the city walls, this newish café has quickly become a neighbourhood favourite. Easygoing, warm and welcoming staff serve simple savoury dishes, sandwiches, scones, muffins, cakes and brownies and delicious, giant meringues spiked with flaked almonds.

Treasurer's House

Minster Yard (01904 624247/www.nationaltrust. org.uk). Open Mar-Nov 11am-4.30pm Mon-Thur, Sat, Sun. ££.
If the queues for Betty's are too daunting, try the National Trust tearooms in the beautiful 17th-century Treasurer's House behind the Minster. The house is well worth a visit in its own right, but entry is free for the basement café, which serves the expected good-quality National Trust selection of light meals, scones and cakes.

Stay

Alexander House
*94 Bishopthorpe Road (01904 625016/
www.alexanderhouseyork.co.uk). £.*
A charming B&B on the south bank with pleasant rooms, good breakfasts and free parking, and the city centre just a five-minute walk away.

Bootham Gardens
*47 Bootham Crescent (01904 625911/
www.bootham-gardens-guesthouse.co.uk). £.*
This handy six-bedroom B&B close to the city centre majors on breakfast. And with home-made bread, jams, teas, and tisanes; smoked salmon and scrambled eggs; ham and Yorkshire cheese; Whitby kippers, or a full English, no guest need go hungry. Rooms are comfortable and contemporary.

Dean Court
Duncombe Place (01904 625082/www.deancourt-york.co.uk). ££££.
It may not be as glamorous as Middlethorpe Hall (*see below*) or as sumptuous as the Grange (*see below*), but Dean Court has pole position for location, sitting in the shadow of York Minster. You can almost pick the nose of a gargoyle from your four-poster. There are 37 smartly decorated, well-equipped rooms, ranging from family rooms to de luxe suites. With good food and bars, and welcome valet parking, this place has plenty going for it. *See also p346.*

Grange Hotel
Clifton *1 Clifton (01904 644744/www.grange hotel.co.uk). ££££.*
An impressive Georgian mansion decorated country-house style, this place is stuffed with antiques, oils of venerable old gents, thick drapes, crackling fires and well-stuffed sofas. Rooms also major in traditional comfort. It's all rather lush – with prices to match. There are two restaurants, an informal Cellar Bar and the posher Ivy Brasserie upstairs.

Hotel du Vin
89 the Mount (01904 557350/www.hotelduvin.com). ££££.
In a recently remodelled grade II listed house, this branch of the boutique hotel chain is as elegant as you'd expect. There are 44 rooms, all with snow-white linen, soft towels, thick bathrobes and own-brand toiletries. The public rooms are small and intimate, choc full of buttoned-back leather chairs, feather-filled sofas and plumped-up cushions. The bistro is done out rather self-consciously with racing paraphernalia and the menu is a modish if safe collection typified by duck confit, salmon and cod fishcakes, and wild mushroom ravioli. Wines are reliably excellent.

Middlethorpe Hall
*Bishopthorpe Road (01904 641241/
www.middlethorpe.com). ££££.*
Just the place for pushing the boat out after a big win at the adjoining racecourse – or better still if you owned the racehorse. This handsome 17th-century Queen Anne pile, converted to a classic country house hotel in the 1980s, was recently bequeathed to the National Trust. Traditionally and comfortably furnished rooms are in the main house and a coach house, with three suites tucked away in a nearby cottage. Whether you're being preened and pampered in the spa or floating around the drawing rooms among the antique furniture, flipping through *Tatler* and *Country Life*, it's easy to come over all lord and lady of the manor here.

Factfile

When to go
The city is a very popular tourist destination, and summer sees the biggest influx of visitors, although it doesn't usually feel uncomfortably packed. In the run-up to Christmas, York hosts the St Nicholas Fair and the Festival of Angels.

Getting there
York is a railway hub, with a high-speed link to London (journey time 2 hours 10 mins). Leeds/Bradford airport is 40 minutes' drive away.

Getting around
Driving is difficult: traffic in the city centre is notoriously congested and parking expensive. Many shopping streets are pedestrianised during working hours. Park and Ride schemes work well, with free parking on the edge of town and buses every ten minutes into the city centre. Walking is generally the best way to get around.

York aspires to be a cycling city and there is a network of cycle lanes on roads outside the city walls. Like cars, cycles are prohibited in the city centre during working hours, when much of the area is pedestrianised.

Tourist information
Visit York De Grey Rooms Visitor Information Centre, Exhibition Square (opposite York Art Gallery).
Visit York York Railway Station Information Centre.
Both (01904 550099, www.visityork.org). Open Summer 9am-6pm Mon-Sat; 10am-5pm Sun. Winter 9am-5pm Mon-Sat; 10am-4pm Sun.
A one-day York Pass (www.yorkpass.com) costs £28 for adults and £18 for children and gives free entry to some of the main attractions. The more visits you make, the better the value. Two- and three-day passes also available by post or from the tourist office.

Mountains

Top: Glencoe;
Bottom: Steall Falls (left)
Glencoe.

Glencoe, Ben Nevis & Ardnamurchan

Extreme scenery in the Scottish Highlands.

Nothing can quite prepare you for the majesty of Glencoe. With its towering peaks, fast-flowing burns and deep glens set beneath an often-brooding sky, it is Great Britain at its rawest and most dramatic. This extreme landscape has seen its fair share of human drama over the centuries, too – Hagrid, Rob Roy and Richard Hannay have all played out scenes beneath the dark, pyramidal mass of the glen's most famous mountain, Buachaille Etive Mor.

At Glencoe's western end, the mountains peter out as the road dips down towards the village of Ballachulish and the edge of Loch Linnhe. Here the maritime climate has produced a more gentle, but no less stunning, landscape, with wild flowers and woodland able to thrive along the shores. The narrow loch cuts off the road to the Ardnamurchan peninsula; a ferry provides a gateway to the peninsula – one of mainland Britain's last great wildernesses and home to its most westerly point. If you're looking to get away from it all, you've come to the right spot – less than 2,000 people are scattered across this 50-square-mile expanse.

Back on the tourist trail, a few miles further along the A82 sits the self-styled 'UK outdoor capital', Fort William. The town itself may not be much to get excited about, but it's what lies on its doorstep that will get the heart of any outdoors explorer beating a little faster. Looming over the town is the mighty bulk of Britain's highest peak, Ben Nevis, and just beyond, the mountain gondola up to Aonach Mor, the country's ninth highest peak and home to some of the country's best skiing and its most challenging mountain biking.

Explore

GLENCOE

The valley of Glencoe is renowned for being home to some of the most famous climbing and walking routes in the British Isles, with the ridges of **Stob Coire nan Lochan** and **Aonach Eagach** towering above the A82, which cuts through the valley. But it is perhaps even better known for an incident that took place more than 300 years ago, one of the most notorious clan massacres in Scottish history – that of the Macdonalds by the Campbells. In August 1691 King William III offered a pardon to all Highland clans who had fought against him or attacked their neighbours, as long as they took the oath of allegiance before a magistrate by 1 January 1692. The Macdonald clan chief agreed to take the oath, but mistakenly went to Inverlochy in Fort William instead of Inveraray near Oban. He finally reached Inveraray on 6 January, five days after the royal deadline. The Macdonald chief believed that, despite this delay in taking the oath, he and his clan would now be safe. But unknown to him, a force had already been given orders to massacre the whole clan. The force left for Glencoe on 1 February, led by Captain Robert Campbell of Glen Lyon. On the night of 12 February 1692, Campbell received orders to kill all Macdonalds under 70 years old at 5am the next morning. Although only 40 were killed, many more died of hunger and exposure as they ran for the hills.

Standing like a sentinel at the head of Glencoe is the famous old **Kings House Hotel**, which was built in the 18th century to house troops. Dorothy Wordsworth visited with her brother, William, in 1803 and was unimpressed, writing in her journal: 'Never did I see such a miserable, such a wretched place – long rooms with ranges of beds, no other furniture except benches, or perhaps one or two crazy chairs, the floors far dirtier than an ordinary house could be if it were never washed.' Standards at the Kings House have improved considerably since Wordsworth's visit (it's still a hotel, *see p361*), but outside, the hostile natural surroundings have remained virtually unchanged in the intervening centuries.

From here, **Rannoch Moor**, a National Heritage site, stretches eastwards at an altitude of a little over 1,000 feet for some 50 square miles of boggy emptiness, pretty much desolate except for the single train track that takes the London to Fort William sleeper back and forth six nights a week. The track, begun in 1889, took some 5,000 navvies and nearly five years to build, a task made nearly impossible by the dual problems of peat and water. The peat had to be overlaid with brushwood, tree roots and thousands of tons of ash so that the line wouldn't sink into the bog. Progress was so slow that the company ran out of money, and the whole project was on the brink of collapse until one of the directors of the West Highland Railway gave part of his private fortune to bring the project

Glencoe, Ben Nevis & Ardnamurchan

Historic sites
● ● ● ● ◦

Art & architecture
● ● ● ● ●

Hotels
● ● ● ◦ ◦

Eating & drinking
● ● ● ◦ ◦

Nightlife
● ● ◦ ◦ ◦

Shopping
● ● ● ◦ ◦

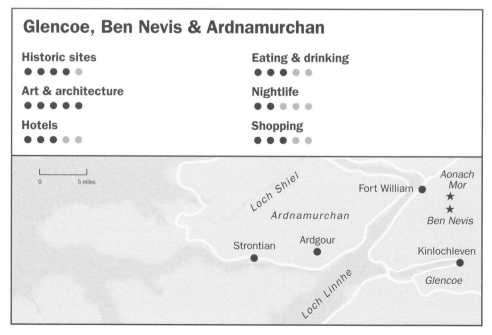

0 — 5 miles

Loch Shiel
Ardnamurchan
Strontian
Ardgour
Loch Linnhe
Fort William
Aonach Mor ★
Ben Nevis ★
Kinlochleven
Glencoe

Glencoe.

Crannog.

ror & coriander
ym Smoked mackere
nnog fishcakes wit
b crusted cod F
red Seabass fillet
t coast langousti

to completion and create an iron road from London to Fort William. The walk across the moor from Kings House to Rannoch station, a journey of some 14 miles, is a wonderful wilderness trek. Take care, though – this is one of the most inhospitable corners of the British Isles, and help is a long way away.

Just across the road from the Kings House Hotel is the **Glencoe ski area**. Hemmed in by the desolate expanse of Rannoch Moor on one side and the craggy peak of Buchaille Etive Mor on the other, this is skiing on the wild side. Originally known as White Corries, Glencoe was the UK's first commercial ski area, with the construction of a ski lift on Meall A'Bhuiridh in 1956. Since then expansion has been slow, with just seven lifts and 19 runs today. For several years things have been very tough, with mild winters, decreasing snowlines and visitor numbers. But when the resort does open (and the snow falls), the area is a magical place to ski, with Scotland's biggest vertical, its steepest on-piste black run and some of its longest queues – being just 75 miles from Glasgow, white weekends see the resort rammed with skiers and snowboarders, although numbers are limited to 1,500 skiers a day on the mountain. From the base area a chairlift and tow take skiers up to the main bowl, and then on to the area's highest point at Meall A' Bhuiridh. From here, one side leads to a series of blues back down towards the Plateau café, while the other side leads to a couple of reds and Scotland's steepest black – the Flypaper – which shoots down through craggy terrain with stunning views of the surrounding hills before joining up with a green run to the Plateau café. The piste map optimistically marks three pistes (blue, red and black) all the way back down to the car park at 1,000 feet – a near-alpine vertical of some 2,500 feet – but this is a rare treat indeed.

Glencoe Visitor Centre
1 mile E of Glencoe Village *off A82 (0844 493 2222/www.nts.org.uk). Open Mar-Oct 9am-6pm daily. Nov-Feb 10am-4pm Thur-Sun. Admission (exhibition) £5.50; £4.50 reductions.*
The new National Trust for Scotland visitor centre, which replaced the old, obtrusive 1970s building when it was demolished in 2002, is a much more harmonious affair. Located nearer to Glencoe Village, it was built at a cost of some £3 million, and contains a shop and café, plus a permanent exhibition, Living on the Edge, which covers everything you need to know about the area before you hit the hills.

The Ice Factor
Kinlochleven *Leven Road (01855 831100/www.ice-factor.co.uk). Open 9am-7pm Mon; 9am-10pm Tue-Thur; 9am-7pm Fri-Sun. Admission (ice wall courses) from £45/person.*
Despite its handsome natural setting, the town of Kinlochleven, six miles from Glencoe and a stopping point

on the West Highland Way, was always a rather dreary place – home to an aluminium smelting plant and not much else. But now the plant has closed and the building has been transformed into the Ice Factor, home to the largest indoor ice wall in the world, plus over 6,400 square feet of climbing wall, a high-level rope route and access to mountaincraft courses and guided climbs in the nearby hills. The centre also has a shop and café, and next door is the home of award-winning boutique brewer Atlas (www.atlas brewery.com), which runs guided tours from Easter until September (5.30pm Mon-Sat).

FORT WILLIAM
Leaving behind the brooding valley of Glencoe and passing Glencoe Village, its only major settlement, at the western end, you soon reach the shores of Loch Linnhe and a change of scenery, with forest aplenty contrasting strongly with Glencoe's bare slopes. The road skirts along the loch edge and finally arrives at Fort William, a fairly unprepossessing town which totes itself as the UK's outdoor capital, and is prefaced by a good mile of B&B signs as every last local attempts to cash in on some of the most awesome scenery in the country. The centre of the town is pedestrianised and lined with a mixture of pubs, restaurants, outdoors shops and tartan tat gift shops. The buildings themselves, many in thick, solid stone, are often more attractive than what lies beneath. Fort William is no Highland beauty in its own right, but the company it keeps makes it the perfect place to hole up. Whether it be a walk up Ben Nevis, a snowboarding lesson on Aonach Mor (see p358), a long-distance trek along the West Highland Way to Glasgow, a boat trip down Loch Linnhe to Seal Island, a trip on the 'Harry Potter' Jacobite steam railway to Mallaig or a berth on the overnight sleeper service to London, the range of experiences available make the tartan tat just about bearable.

Jacobite Steam Railway
Leaves from Fort William station (01524 737751/ www.westcoastrailways.co.uk). Phone or check website for timetable. £30 day return; £17 reductions.
During the summer the Jacobite steam train, run by West Coast Railways, takes steam enthusiasts and Harry Potter fans on the stunning 84-mile round trip from Fort William to Mallaig and back. The route takes you through wonderful Highland scenery, including the 21-arch Glenfinnan viaduct made famous by the flying car sequence in Harry Potter and the Chamber of Secrets, before halting in the charming fishing port of Mallaig for a few hours at lunchtime. If you're not fussed about Harry's exploits, you can lose the steam and save yourself a few quid by using Scotrail instead, which runs a couple of standard trains a day on the same route.

West Highland Museum
Cameron Square (01397 702169/www.west highlandmuseum.org.uk). Open Summer 10am-5pm

Mon-Sat; 2-5pm Sun. Winter 10am-4pm Mon-Sat. Admission £3; reductions 50p-£2. No credit cards. The West Highland Museum, founded in 1922 and housed in a handsome former bank building just off the high street, provides a decent overview of the often harsh life in the area, with rooms devoted to natural history, crofting and Jacobite relics, including Bonnie Prince Charlie's death mask and bagpipes dating back nearly 700 years to the battle of Bannockburn.

BEN NEVIS

Fort William's USP, the brooding mass of 4,406-foot Ben Nevis, sits a few miles outside the town to the north, although the chances of actually seeing the top are fairly remote – the summit is only clear every few days on average and receives twice as much annual rainfall as Fort William. The main route up the mountain, the pony track, which starts from the **Visitor Centre** a couple of miles up Glen Nevis, was built in 1883 to service the Ben Nevis summit observatory. The observatory housed meteorologists who made hourly observations on the peak for 21 years from 1883 to 1904, when it finally closed. Its crumbling walls now provide limited shelter from the wind for those who reach the top. The ascent generally takes between four and five hours, with another three back down, and with some 100,000 people heading to the summit every year, numbers can feel a bit overwhelming in high season. But unfortunately there aren't many alternative options, unless you fancy scaling the infamous 2,000-foot cliffs on the north-east face, regarded as some of the toughest climbing in the country, with classic cliffhangers like Zero Gully, Point Five and Orion Direct to contend with. Once on top, weather permitting, the views are astounding. And if you can't see beyond your hand, you can at least console yourself that it's only 4,000 feet of downhill from here to the Ben Nevis Inn (see p361) and a well-deserved pint. If you fancy a real challenge, the first Saturday in September is the traditional date for the Ben Nevis race, from Fort William to the summit and back. The race began in 1899; the women's record stands at one hour 43 minutes, and the men's at one hour 25 minutes.

If you don't fancy charging up the ben or the weather's poor, then drive on past the Visitor Centre and instead head up the breathtakingly beautiful and sheltered **Glen Nevis** to the start of one of the most stunning walks in the area, up to the **Steall Falls**. From the Upper Falls car park, an amazing natural water slide can be seen cascading down the western slopes of Ben Nevis, and a danger sign at the start of the walk warns that people have fallen to their deaths on the path. The walk winds up the gorge and, although a little exposed in places, it's not quite as forbidding as the sign implies – although you need to take care, especially when it's wet underfoot. You can hear the river flowing beneath and occasionally catch glimpses of deep pools and little waterfalls through the trees. Then, after 30 minutes or so, the path emerges out of the top of the gorge and on to a wide, grassy plateau, with, at the far end, the dramatic Steall Falls. They are the third highest falls in Scotland, cascading some 344 feet down the mountainside. After gazing in awe, you can return the way you came or, if you have the legs, plough on to **Corrour** some 14 miles to the east, where the Fort William sleeper still stops (request only) on its nightly journey south to London.

If your stroll up to the Steall Falls has given you the walking bug, Fort William is also the finishing line for one of the most dramatic long-distance treks in Britain, the **West Highland Way**. The path starts in the Glasgow suburb of Milngavie and then winds its way for some 95 miles through the gentle Trossach hills, and up along the wild side of Loch Lomond, and then heads across the high mountain scenery of Glencoe before emerging after a week or so's walking at Fort William. Recommended reading is The West Highland Way by Anthony Burton, a comprehensive guide to the route.

AONACH MOR

Just north of Ben Nevis sits the peak of Aonach Mor, Britain's ninth highest mountain and home to the Nevis Range (www.nevisrange.co.uk) resort. This is Scotland's highest skiing area, with a fairly respectable top height and a better recent snow record than some of its competitors, although the strong winds that whip across the slopes can quickly blow off any fresh snowfall and turn the pistes into an icy nightmare. Access from the valley is by the UK's only mountain gondola (ski lift accommodating six people in each cabin). The beginners' area is right next to the gondola top station, which also contains a passable café, loos and a ski shop. Although this makes life easy for novices, it also means that the nursery slopes can often be shut due to a lack of snow, although there is a dry slope when things get desperate. From the base area, lifts lead up to a top height of 4,000 feet and things get progressively steeper as you head further up the slopes of Aonach Mor, with a decent selection of blue and red pistes from the top down the main snowgoose bowl. Where Nevis Range trumps its rivals is with the back corries, with evocative descents like Yellow Belly, Chancer and Lemming Ridge. Opened up a few years ago with the construction of the Braveheart chairlift, they have expanded the skiable area considerably. When the snow's fresh, they provide intermediate and experienced skiers with an off-piste expanse unrivalled in Scotland. In summer, the gondola also gives access to one of the UK's most challenging mountain bike courses, which drops 2,000 feet over its 17 mile length, with huge drop-offs, rock steps and jumps.

Clachaig Inn.

ARDNAMURCHAN

After all that adrenaline-filled action, the perfect spot for a bit of R'n'R lies just across the loch from Fort William. The Ardnamurchan peninsula is one of the country's last real wildernesses. To access it, it's a seven-mile drive from Fort William back towards Glencoe to the Corran Ferry. Then it's a short chug across the loch to **Ardgour** (there is a road route from Fort William but it's at least 35 miles). The ferry leaves every 20 minutes or so from 6.30am to 9.30pm for the five-minute crossing and then it's a 50-mile drive along mostly single-track road from Ardgour to the end of the peninsula, mainland Britain's most westerly point, with not much except sheep, streams and stunning mountain scenery in between. A few settlements line the road west, including the village of **Strontian**. Its name comes from Gaelic and means 'point of the fairies'. In the 1790s, French prisoners of war working in the lead mines to provide shot for the British war effort against France found the first signs of a new element, which was named Strontium (atomic number 38, if you're curious) after the village.

There are some beautiful walks in the area, especially through the ancient Ariundle oak forests a few minutes inland from the village. These rare maritime oakwoods are rich with ferns and mosses, providing shelter for pine martens, wildcats and red squirrels.

It's a long, tortuous drive west from Strontian to the **Ardnamurchan lighthouse**, but the visual rewards are majestic, especially as you round Ben Hiant and head down towards the tip of the peninsula. The lighthouse sits on a windblown promontory, and from April to October you can climb the 152 steps (and two ladders) to the top for a stunning view of the Inner Hebrides, and the local white sand beaches. Back down the road a couple of miles, pull into a grass layby (ask the lighthouse keeper to point it out from his eyrie), where you can park and then follow a path for about ten minutes down to one of the most beautiful beaches in the area. Ignore the tired-looking campsite along the way and instead head down to this wonderfully isolated stretch of white sand and crystal-clear water. As you take in the amazing panorama before you, just think – you're about as far away from everyone else as you can be without getting your feet wet.

Ardnamurchan Lighthouse

Signposted from Kilchoan (01972 510210/ www.ardnamurchanlighthouse.com). Open Apr-Oct 11am-4.30pm daily. Admission £5; £3 reductions.
The lighthouse stands 118ft tall, and was built in 1849 using granite from Mull. It was designed by Alan Stevenson, uncle of Robert Louis. The lighthouse became fully automated in 1988. The former head keeper's house has been converted into an exhibition centre, where you can visit the restored engine room and workshop to learn how the original fog horn operated and how keepers kept the lighthouse in working order. If you fancy tasting life as a lighthouse keeper, one of the old keeper's cottages is available for rent during the summer.

Eat

Crannog

Fort William *Town Pier (01397 705589/ www.crannog.net). Open noon-2.30pm, 6.30-11pm daily. £££. Modern European.*
The word 'Crannog', which refers to an ancient loch dwelling, was chosen by local fisherman Finlay Finlayson to showcase his concept of catching, curing and cooking the finest West Coast seafood. The restaurant is located in his old bait shed at the end of Fort William's town pier, with large picture windows to enjoy the views across Loch Linnhe. Starters might include breaded haddock with a bean broth, followed by mains of pan-seared king scallops with belly of pork served with apple purée and pancetta or Crannog bouillabaisse. Crannog also offers cruises on the loch (see website for details).

Kilcamb Lodge

Strontian *(01967 402257/www.kilcamblodge.co.uk). Open noon-1.30pm, 7.30-9.30pm daily. ££££. Modern European.*
The setting of this small, luxury country house hotel, right down on the shores of Loch Sunart, would be reason enough to make a diversion, but the views are matched by the food and handsome dining room. Dinner is £48 per head, but for that the award-winning kitchen turns out outstanding dishes such as roast breast of wood pigeon on celeriac and spiced pear or pan-fried filleted Mallaig skate wing with baby capers and lime burnt butter, with poached winter fruits glazed with dark rum sabayon and black cherry ice-cream to finish.

Lime Tree Gallery

Fort William *Achintore Road (01397 701806/ www.limetreefortwilliam.co.uk). Open noon-2pm, 6.30-9.30pm daily. £££. Modern European.*
The award-winning, boutique-style Lime Tree combines hotel, restaurant and art gallery under one handsome 19th-century roof. The restaurant is the star, though, hitting just the right note with starters such as cheese and chive soufflé with poached onion and sweet chilli tomato salsa, followed by mains such as Lochaber lamb slow cooked with orange and bay leaf and served with creamy parmesan risotto. There are nine en-suite rooms if you fancy sticking around for breakfast.

White House Restaurant

Lochaline, Morvern, Ardnamurchan *(01967 421777/www.thewhitehouserestaurant.co.uk). Open 12.30-2.30pm, 6.30-9.30pm Tue-Sun. Closed winter. £££. Modern European.*
Everything at this remote restaurant (apart from the wine, of course) is sourced locally, down to the salads, herbs and vegetables grown in the garden next door. The award-

winning kitchen specialises in local produce – prawns from Lochaline; venison, beef and lamb from local estates; and Isle of Mull mussels. Starters might include Sound of Mull scallops and nutmeg butter, followed by Ulva sirloin, celeriac purée and savoy cabbage or Lochaline langoustines with aioli and bitter leaves. The dining room may be rather functional, but the food is a rare treat indeed.

Stay

Ben Nevis Inn
Achintree, 1 mile NE of Fort William *(01397 701227/www.ben-nevis-inn.co.uk). £.*
If you're not averse to cosying up with a few strangers (bunkhouse accommodation is in three dormitories), then there couldn't be a much more convenient spot to lay your head before an ascent of the big mountain – the main path up Ben Nevis starts right outside the door. Sleeping conditions are a little cramped, to say the least, but to help you drop off in such confined surroundings there's a lively bar with reasonably priced simple meals and a decent selection of malts on offer.

Clachaig Inn
Glencoe *(01855 811252/www.clachaig.com). £.*
Situated right in the heart of Glencoe, a couple of miles south-east of Glencoe village, this 300-year-old inn is a classic climbers' and walkers' staging post. There are 23 en-suite bedrooms. Food is a Highland theme menu, with haggis, venison casserole and clootie dumpling all making an appearance. The boots bar, with a cracking open fire, has loads of live music and malts galore, perfect for elaborating on that overhang you climbed earlier in the day.

Inn at Ardgour
Ardgour *(01855 841225/www.ardgour.biz). ££.*
Handsomely situated on the Ardnamurchan side of the Corran ferry, a few miles south of Fort William, this whitewashed, family-run inn has 12 basic but comfortable en-suite bedrooms, all with wonderful views down Loch Linnhe. The oldest part of the inn began life as cottages for the Corran ferrymen, and now houses the cosy bar. Food-wise, expect standard pub fare – the setting is the star here.

Inverlochy Castle
Torlundy, 2 miles NE of Fort William *(01397 702177/www.inverlochycastlehotel.com). ££££.*
Inverlochy Castle has a stunning position beneath Ben Nevis and just a couple of miles outside Fort William, and an equally majestic interior. Built in 1863, it was converted into a hotel in 1969 and has 17 luxurious rooms, with the Queen's Suite coming in at about £600 a night. This is no highland hostel, with 500 acres of wooded grounds leading up to the foot of Ben Nevis, a one-Michelin star restaurant and a handsome wood-panelled snooker room. If you're after a five-star treat and don't mind sharing it with an international moneyed crowd, then it's just about worth the steep prices.

Kings House Hotel
Glencoe *(01855 851259/www.kingy.com). £.*
Built in the 18th century, the Kings House Hotel sits in splendid isolation, just off the A82 opposite Glencoe's most famous peak, Buchaille Etive Mor. The 22 bedrooms could do with some updating, but after a day on the hills, most guests are generally after a comfy bed, a hearty meal and a large dram, and the Kings House wins through on all three counts. The climbers' bar at the back of the hotel is a lively place to numb the pain after a day on the hills.

Factfile

When to go
Fort William is a lively town throughout the year, with mountain biking, walking, climbing and skiing all bringing in the crowds. Similarly, Glencoe is an all-season destination, with skiing in the winter, and walking and climbing throughout the year. Ardnamurchan is best visited during spring to autumn, as many attractions close up during winter. Snow permitting, the ski season in the Highlands usually lasts from January to April, although, sadly, Scottish winter sports are increasingly a case of 'if' rather than 'when'.

Getting there
Glasgow and Inverness are the nearest airports. There are four buses (www.citylink.co.uk) and four trains (www.scotrail.co.uk) a day from Glasgow to Fort William (the bus stops en route at Glencoe), and there are several buses a day from Inverness to Fort William. From the south,

the overnight Caledonian sleeper train from London Euston (Mon-Fri, Sun) is the most civilised way to hit the Highlands, arriving at Fort William at around 9am, and departing at around 7.30pm.

Getting around
There are buses from Fort William to Nevis Range, Glencoe and Ardnamurchan, but a car is fairly essential to enjoy the area to the full, especially if you plan to explore the Ardnamurchan peninsula thoroughly.

Tourist information
Fort William's tourist information centre is on Cameron Square (0845 225 5121/ www.visitscotland.com). For planning your trip, the website www.visithighlands.com is packed full of information, ideas and accommodation suggestions.

Brecon Beacons.

Brecon Beacons

Mountains, moorland and deep, dark forests.

The Brecon Beacons National Park packs in an amazing diversity of scenery. Between the Black Mountain in the west and the Black Mountains in the east, via the Fforest Fawr and Brecon Beacons ranges in between, you'll find everything from waterfalls and sandstone escarpments to sculpted cliffs and fertile valleys, dense forests, glacial lakes, springy moorland and miles of caves. And with more than half of the area 1,000 feet or more above sea level, it's very easy to get up high and enjoy the wildlife, adventure activities and, of course, walking – there are more than 620 miles of public footpath criss-crossing the 519 square miles that make up the park, and pretty much every inch of them is worth covering.

To experience the vastly differing landscapes and atmospheres it's best to think of the park as three distinct areas: in the east, Abergavenny across the Gospel Pass up to bibliophiles' mecca Hay-on-Wye and back to the lovely valley town of Crickhowell; in the centre, the range of the Brecon Beacons studded with towering peaks like Corn Du and Pen-y-Fan in the north and shimmering reservoirs to the south; and finally the western quarter, boasting the rugged and remote terrain of the Black Mountain and Fforest Fawr, where limestone ravines and caves close in around you as you descend to sea level from mountainous heights.

Explore

THE BLACK MOUNTAINS

The Black Mountains are a very special introduction to the Brecon Beacons National Park, an ethereal rural landscape that's bleakly beautiful, its rugged hills, flat-topped mountains and deep valleys stretching between Hay-on-Wye in the north and **Abergavenny** in the south, to the River Usk in the west and the Vale of Ewyas on the Welsh/English border in the east, where a section of the Offa's Dyke Path runs south from Hay Bluff. Here are myriad opportunities for walking, horseriding, climbing, canoeing, white-water rafting and sailing, and if you're into none of those but just seek solitude and beauty in which to think deep thoughts, Hay and its surrounding countryside is perfect.

At the border village of **Skenfrith**, home to a beautiful stone bridge over the gurgling River Monnow, you'll find the impressive remains of a 13th-century castle, an unusual medieval church (pop in for a bag of Cath's daily-made Welsh cakes, all proceeds going to the restoration fund) and six exhilarating circular walks across the sheep-dotted hills – maps are available at the excellent Bell at Skenfrith inn (see p368, p372).

Neighbouring **Abergavenny**, a one-time centre of the weaving trade, is no great shakes in terms of looks, but its position, accommodation and

eating options make it a good base – convenient for climbs up the 1,955-foot **Sugar Loaf** or Skirrid Fawr, or excursions further afield to the magical 12th-century **Llanthony Priory**, where atmospheric ruins cling to a lovely little pub and a walk up to the ridge offers stunning views back across the valley. This glorious scenery is worth exploring in detail; head north through the Gospel Pass on the super-curvy road that reaches its highest point at **Hay Bluff**, within striking distance of fabulous walks along the dramatic **Offa's Dyke Path National Trail**, before descending towards bookish **Hay-on-Wye**, home of the literary Hay Festival.

This pretty border town is a delight to potter about in, exploring the crumbling castle, trying a sheep's milk ice-cream at Edwardian-style ice-cream parlour Shepherds (9 High Town, 01497 821898, www.shepherdsicecream. co.uk), and browsing the numerous book and crafts shops. On the western side of the range, little **Crickhowell** is equally worth exploring, with its curious 17th-century bridge (with 13 arches visible from one side and only 12 from the other), castle ruins, pretty high street and impressive medieval church of St Edmund. From here, it's a fairly gentle five-mile hike to the top of **Table Mountain**, whose brown cone provides such a spectacular backdrop to the little town. The 1,480-foot summit, complete with Iron Age fort, has magnificent views over the Usk Valley.

Brecon Beacons

Historic sites
● ● ● ● ○

Art & architecture
● ● ● ● ○

Hotels
● ● ● ● ○

Eating & drinking
● ● ● ● ○

Scenery
● ● ● ● ●

Outdoor activities
● ● ● ● ●

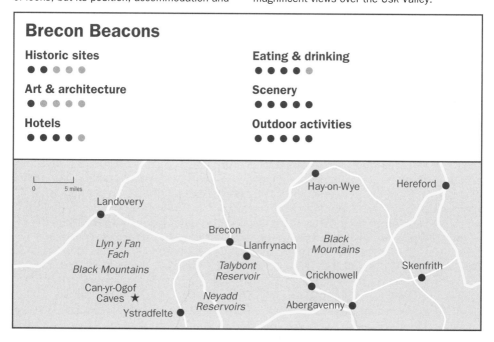

Left: Ystradfellte;
right: Brecon Beacons;
bottom: Pen-y-fan.

THE CENTRAL BRECON BEACONS & FFOREST FAWR BORDERS

Hugely – and deservedly – popular with walkers and pony trekkers, the central Brecon Beacons are characterised by their mountainous terrain and stunning reservoirs hemmed in by densely conifered slopes – not that you'd guess at such splendours from the town of **Brecon**. While initially exuding all the hustle and bustle of a thriving market town, its slightly down-at-heel feel makes its appeal limited, but it does offer a convenient base if you're planning to explore both the central Brecon Beacons and the Black Mountains in the same trip. The best day to visit is the second Saturday of the month, when the Brecknockshire Farmers' Market is held in the covered Market Hall (High Street, 01874 636169, 10am-2pm, www.brecknockfarmersmarkets.org.uk).

"Sgwd yr Eira has a six-foot overhang that allows intrepid explorers to walk behind the roaring 20-foot curtain of water."

However, for most visitors, this area is about the outdoors, beginning with the most popular hike in the central Brecon Beacons, the five-mile ascent of **Pen-y-Fan** (South Wales's highest mountain at 2,907 feet), and its near neighbour **Corn Du**, half a mile west of it. Enthusiastic walkers can opt for the 10.5-mile alternative from **Llanfrynach** village, which approaches the summit of Pen-y-Fan via the lower peak of Fan-y-Big – a name Dylan Thomas would have surely approved of.

Heading south from Llanfrynach, the terrain begins to close in as you wend your way towards the serene, secluded reservoirs that supply the water for most of South Wales and the Midlands; the most remote are the **Neuadd reservoirs** just beyond **Talybont**, where you can circumnavigate the upper and lower bodies of water without seeing another soul, or strike off up into the hills for spectacular views back over the water and the valleys. Below these, the more popular **Pentwyn** and **Pontsticill reservoirs** are equally enchanting, as is the tiny **Brecon Mountain Railway** which chuffs waterside for two miles before arriving at the hamlet of **Pant**. A few miles west will bring water fans even more excitement as they arrive at **Pontneddfechan**, jumping-off point for Fforest Fawr's fabulous eastern border waterfalls – there are falls a mile north of the little hamlet and, more famously, at **Ystradfellte**. Here the River Mellte

rushes pell-mell into the mouth of the Porth-yr-Ogof cave before it emerges into daylight a few hundred yards on to merge with the River Hepste and tumble through three miles of limestone ravines as a fast-moving river and a series of stunning waterfalls, the last of which, the **Sgwd yr Eira**, has a six-foot overhang that allows intrepid explorers to walk behind the roaring 20-foot curtain of water.

FFOREST FAWR & THE BLACK MOUNTAIN

Heading west, the terrain changes again as the upland forest becomes still more dense and the landscape darker and wilder. It's a perfect setting for the wonderfully atmospheric **Dan-yr-Ogof showcaves** (www.showcaves.co.uk, 01639 730801; open Apr-Oct 10am-3pm daily; admission £11.50, £7 reductions), three separate sites featuring a meandering and mesmerising series of caverns, a cathedral cavern and a bone cavern, all of them wonderfully spooky despite being relentlessly tacky and touristy. North of the caves, the terrain becomes increasingly mountainous and barren as the land climbs towards the **Black Mountain** range, characterised by flowing, towering smooth-humped peaks and ridges like **Fan Brycheiniog** (at 2,631 feet, the highest peak in the western Black Mountain region) and criss-crossed by streams and glacial lakes that shimmer like liquid silver. The most bleakly, serenely beautiful of these is **Llyn y Fan Fach**, which, set against the impressive backdrop of the 2,458-foot **Bannau Sir Gaer**, is the lake associated with the Welsh legend of the Lady of the Lake. It's easy to imagine a young shepherd staring awestruck as a beautiful maiden emerged from the water – particularly if you do the exhilarating four-mile circular walk that brings you out on the westernmost of the high peaks of the Black Mountain. From here, the views back down to the lake and out across the ridge and mountain range are magical enough to make you believe anything of this country. In **Llandovery**, an appealing market town at the very northern tip of the park, the **Heritage Centre** (Kings Road, 01550 721228) tells the story of the Lady of the Lake (and her sons, the Physicians of Myddfai), via a series of startling talking statues.

Eat

Aber Organic Farm Shop & Tea Room
Trecastle, 10 miles W of Brecon *(01874 636108/ www.aberorganic.co.uk). Open 11am-6pm Wed-Fri; 11am-4.30pm Sat, Sun. £. Café/tearoom.*
It's only open during the day, but the Aber is definitely worth a lunch or teatime stop. The food at this pretty stone-built café and tearoom is mostly sourced from the family-run organic Aberhyddnant Farm in the Crai Valley, and made into dishes

Bell at Skenfrith.

like dense, full-flavoured casseroles of pork, beef or lamb and fresh local vegetables, served with chunks of local bread and Welsh butter, all for £4.50. Or try a Drover's Lunch, a selection of welsh organic cheeses served with chunks of granary bread, salad and Pen Cae Mawr chutney. Afternoon tea is top notch, and you'll be spoiled for choice with a Welsh tea (Welsh cakes and Bara Brith with a pot of tea of your choice), traditional tea (home-made scone, Pen Cae Mawr jam and organic double cream with a pot of tea of your choice), or selection of cakes.

"There's a selection of 'simple things done well', like braised pork cheeks with pearl barley risotto and garden peas.."

Bell at Skenfrith
Skenfrith (01600 750235/www.skenfrith.co.uk). Open noon-2.30pm, 7-9.30pm daily. £££. Modern European.
In the light and airy Bell at Skenfrith, a blackboard lists the restaurant's food suppliers – from the free-range eggs to the meat, fish and vegetables. It's an impressive list and a testament to the consciousness with which the owners source their ingredients. Menus cover everything from fancy sandwiches to an à la carte featuring mains such as grilled Talgarth rib-eye with hand-cut chips and béarnaise sauce or fillet of sea bass with couscous and fennel. Melt in the mouth pan-fried calf's liver was deliciously pink, while starters of celery and apple soup and a ham hock salad, both light and refined, set up the mains perfectly. Alongside the expected desserts like hot chocolate brownie and a local cheeseboard was an adventurous – and surprisingly successful – lemongrass crème brûlée with Thai green curry ice-cream. The Bell also has comfortable rooms upstairs. See also p370.

Bridge Café
Brecon 7 Bridge Street (01874 622024/www.bridge cafe.co.uk). Open Mar-Oct 10am-5pm Wed-Fri; 10am-6pm Sat (Sun during bank hol weekends). £. Café.
Whitewashed walls, wooden tables and floors and a couple of comfy leather sofas by the wood-burning stove make up the simple interior of the Bridge Café. Food is similarly unpretentious and honest, with robust stews and soups in winter, along with snacks and salads, and home-made organic cakes. Drinks include local Penderyn whisky.

1861
Cross Ash, 7.5 miles NW of Abergavenny (0845 388 1861/www.18-61.co.uk). Open noon-2pm, 7-9pm Tue-Sat; noon-2pm Sun. £££. Modern European.
The 1861 is less than two years old but is already garnering praise, thanks largely to the skills of chef Simon King, who trained with the Roux brothers at the two Michelin-starred

Waterside Inn at Bray and then worked for Martin Blunos at Lettonie. In this picturesque former pub, decorated in simple but warm contemporary tones and textures, King uses local seasonal produce – including fresh vegetables from his father-in-law's nursery in nearby Nantyderry – to create unfussy menus that might include glazed onion and cider soup or salad of perl las cheese and poached pear as starters, with roast rump of lamb or honey-glazed pork belly for mains. Desserts are stunners, little bright jewels of apple and calvados parfait with bramble sorbet or strawberry crème brûlée with polenta biscuits.

Felin Fach Griffin Inn
Felin Fach, 3 miles NE of Brecon (01874 620111/www.eatdrinksleep.ltd.uk). Open 7-9.30pm Mon; 12.30-2.30pm, 7-9.30pm Tue-Sun. £££. Modern European.
Laden with impressive awards and enthusiastic reviews from the likes of A A Gill, Charles Inkin's Griffin Inn is regarded as one of the best places to eat in west Wales, no mean feat when the Walnut Tree (see p373) and Bell at Skenfrith (see above) are in the picture too. For lunch, there's a carte, a set menu and a selection of 'simple things done well', like braised pork cheeks with pearl barley risotto and garden peas. In the evening, à la carte starters include foie gras terrine or dressed Portland crab with ginger mayonnaise, with the likes of wild halibut with summer vegetables and venison with butternut squash as mains. There are some lovely rooms here too.

Gliffaes Country House Hotel
Crickhowell (01874 730371/www.gliffaes.com). Open noon-2.30pm, 7.30-9.15pm daily. ££££. Modern European.
The elegantly appointed drawing rooms at this relaxed country house hotel are perfect for sipping a good sherry while choosing from the daily-changing and very reasonable menu: three courses for £34 or two courses for £27.50, with service, buys you a feast. A modern slant on the classics is reflected in perfectly executed starters like scallops on black pudding with a beetroot purée. Mains can be hearty – a big-flavoured seafood and chorizo paella topped by a succulent fillet of pan-fried John Dory, perhaps, or a pork medley (fillet, confit of belly, and leek and basil sausage). Desserts such as a beautifully executed vanilla parfait with spun sugar and glazed figs tasted as wonderful as it looked. See also p372.

Nantyffin Cider Mill Inn
Crickhowell Brecon Road (01873 810775/www.cider mill.co.uk). Open noon-2.30pm, 6-9.30pm Tue-Sat; noon-2.30pm Sun. £££. Pub.
With its bright pink exterior and bold roadside position, this sprawling 16th-century drovers' inn is unmissable. The menu has an equally confident character. In the two dining rooms – the two-storey Mill Room restaurant and the more informal bar and lounge – you'll find starters such as seared pigeon supreme with braised puy lentils, or a baked Welsh goat's cheese tartlet, followed by hearty, substantial mains using local produce, like grilled rack of Old Gloucester pork or confit of home-reared local mountain lamb with creamed herb mash and rosemary and garlic sauce. If you've room for pudding, the rum and raisin bread and butter pudding or sticky toffee and date pudding are as good as they sound.

Number 18

Crickhowell *18 High Street (01883 812429).*
Open 9am-5.30pm Mon-Sat; 10am-4.30pm Sun. £.
No credit cards. Café.
Samantha Devos opened this lovely little café two years ago, keen to offer Crickhowell a simple place that offered good food, with maximum use of local and organic produce. And it has been a real hit. Whether you choose to eat in – the cellar is surprisingly inviting, thanks to skylights and comfy sofas – or out, you'll appreciate Samantha's efforts. Takeaway choices feature the likes of Caroline's organic ciabatta rolls, baps or wraps filled with Welsh mature cheddar and Avril's home-made chutney, or Mr Richard's Welsh-baked ham, or Black Mountains Smokery chicken breast or beef. Indoors, choose from the daily-changing specials board and salads such as Pantysgawn goat's cheese salad. A great selection of cakes, teas and coffees makes this place a great pit-stop for walkers and cyclists in need of an energy boost too.

Peterstone Court

Llanhamlach, 4 miles E of Brecon *(01874 665387/www.peterstone-court.com). Open 7.30-9.30am, noon-2.30pm, 7-9.30pm Mon-Fri; 8-10am, noon-2.30pm, 7-9.30pm Sat, Sun. £££. Modern British.*
Just seven miles from Peterstone Court is the Llangynidr farm that provides 90% of the meat served in the hotel restaurant. Its quality shows: pressing of ham hock and split pea is dense and intensely meaty; roast lamb is pink, succulent and juicy. Local produce is also evident in other dishes, such as a delicate leek and potato soup served with perfectly tart and creamy Bower's Farm crème fraîche. In keeping with the rest of the hotel, the restaurant is positively fairy-tale like, its cream walls flickering with candlelight, firelight and twinkling chandeliers. Philippe Starck Ghost chairs and delicate muslin curtains add to the ethereal feel. Desserts are as pretty as the setting – a rhubarb trio (of rhubarb crumble jelly, rhubarb and custard ice-cream and ginger rhubarb mousse) quivered perfectly on the plate. *See also p372.*

Swan Hotel

Hay-on-Wye *Church Street (01497 821188/www.the swanathay.co.uk). Open noon-2pm, 7-9pm daily. £££. Bistro.*
A bright and spacious dining room and a cosy, warm bistro make this Grade II-listed Georgian coaching inn a welcoming eating option; alfresco dining with views of the gorgeous gardens are a bonus. Chef Harry Mackintosh trained in France, which obviously influenced his menu, which might include a white bean and lentil soup or chicken liver parfait, followed by confit pork belly or scallop and crab risotto. Puds might be a chocolate fondant or apple and berry crumble.

Walnut Tree

LLandewi Skirrid, 3 miles NE of Abergavenny *(01873 852797/www.thewalnuttreeinn.com). Open noon-2.30pm, 7-10pm Tue-Sun. ££££. Modern British.*
Shaun Hill bought the Walnut Tree in 2008 as 'somewhere I could start winding down as I headed towards retirement'. The Michelin star he brought with him from the Merchant House in Ludlow put paid to his plan, and the Walnut Tree is packed most nights – and deservedly so. There's plenty of

offal on the menu, such as calves' brains and ox tongue, but this is matched by the likes of salmon tartare, or puntarella salad with anchovy, chilli and endives. Mains are delicate, delicious fish dishes – monkfish, sea bass, lemon sole or turbot – or hearty red meat and juicy fowl: rib-eye of beef, saddle of venison, roast wood pigeon, perhaps. Vegetarian options are equally good; a little tower of milk-white parsley root pudding was exquisite. Desserts are delicious too, like a wobbly buttercream milk pudding teamed with sticky roast figs. Add to that an impressive selection of wines (many by the glass or carafe) and it's easy to see why you need to book well ahead to eat here at weekends.

White Swan

Llanfrynach *(01874 665276/www.the-white swan.com). Open noon-2pm, 7-9pm Mon-Sat; noon-2.30pm, 7-9pm Sun. ££££. Pub.*
With a pretty, airy bar, a formal dining room filled with big old flagstones and wooden beams, and a lovely terrace covered by a wisteria-clad pergola, the first decision at the White Swan comes in choosing where to eat. There's a lot of choice with the food too: dishes range from homely favourites such as shepherd's pie and whole lemon sole in parsley butter to adventurous, orientally inspired dishes like curried lamb's kidneys with stir fry vegetables, pak choi and egg noodles. Meat is local and accompaniments are hearty, delicious and occasionally unexpected – celeriac mash and parsnip purée on the one hand, deep-fried beetroot risotto balls on the other.

Stay

There's no shortage of friendly, family-run B&Bs in the Brecon Beacons, but when it comes to hotels, especially those with a dash of style, choices are more limited. Plan well ahead for the Hay Festival (late May to early June), and the Brecon Jazz Festival (August), as accommodation gets snapped up months in advance.

Good accommodation is also available in some inns listed in our Eat section: the **Bell at Skenfrith** (*see p368*), **Felin Fach Griffin Inn** (*see p368*) and the **Swan Hotel** (*see above*).

Angel Hotel

Abergavenny *15 Cross Street (01873 857121/ www.angelhotelabergavenny.com). ££.*
The 36 rooms at this former Georgian coaching inn have been undergoing a stylish refurb, hoping to capitalise on Abergavenny's excellent location as a gateway to the Black Mountains. Some of the newly renovated rooms are in an annexe, which offers seclusion but can be a little noisy, others are in the main hotel. All share wonderfully comfortable beds and ultra modern bathrooms featuring smart, efficient showers, with nice touches like White Linen toiletries and DAB radios. The standard rooms are perfectly presentable too, and both categories are good value for money. Breakfast – Dorset cereals and a superb full English for the devil-may-care, bran flakes or Special K and perfectly poached eggs on toast for the abstemious, say – is first class.

Walnut Tree.

Bell at Skenfrith

Skenfrith *(01600 750235/www.skenfrith.co.uk). £££.*
Settings don't come much better than that of the Bell at Skenfrith, and as if rising to the challenge of the magnificent scenery, owner Janet Hutchings has turned her one-time coaching inn into one of the most stylish hotels in mid Wales. The 11 rooms are all gorgeous, with unique home-made oak beds, art and antiques dotted around and pretty Welsh blankets on the beds. The Heckham Peckham is a stunner – a double-height space with oak beams and a sumptuous galleried bathroom. However, they all have something special about them, as well as ground coffee, a dinky thermos of fresh milk and a jar of handmade biscuits. As you might expect, dinner in the restaurant is excellent *(see p368)*.

"It's filled with roaring log fires in winter, huge flagstone hearths, lots of wood and heaps of cosy nooks and crannies."

Cantre Selyf

Brecon *5 Lion Street (01874 622904/ www.cantreselyf.co.uk). ££.*
Dating from the 17th century, with mainly 18th-century interiors, this beautiful townhouse boasts heaps of original features, including moulded ceilings, elegant fireplaces and oak beams. The three double rooms are all simply furnished in country-house style, and there's a very comfy sitting room and gorgeous walled garden too. Owner Helen Roberts is famed for her breakfasts and serves up a choice of full English, smoked salmon and scrambled eggs, vegetarian cheese-and-leek sausages, omelette of your choice or french toast, yoghurt and fruit.

Coach House

Brecon *Orchard Street (0844 357 1301/ www.coachhousebrecon.com). ££.*
The National Trust paint job on this elegant boutique hotel's exterior offers a good indication of what's inside – cool neutral colours and crisp white linens, with lots of careful attention to detail combining to create a very comfortable base for a few days of exploration in the central Brecon Beacons. Breakfasts come highly recommended, and a range of holistic therapies, including a one-hour Swedish massage, is available too. Or guests can simply chill out in the peaceful decked garden behind the converted townhouse.

Gliffaes Country House Hotel

Crickhowell *(01874 730371/www.gliffaes.com). ££££.*
The effortlessly posh and laid-back Gliffaes is a huge favourite with anglers, thanks to its stunning location in sight – and sound – of the River Usk. But even if you don't know one end of a rod from the other, Gliffaes is still heavenly, whether you choose to sit on the terrace with just the sound of the river, sheep and hens in the background; to explore the extensive grounds; or curl up with a book in front of a roaring fire. That's assuming you can drag yourself out of your lovely room, all 23 of which are luxuriously comfortable and individual. Owners James and Susie Suter are a keen cyclist and walker respectively, and are happy to offer tips and advice on where best to do both – a great idea after filling up on the top-class breakfast, featuring home-made marmalade, local organic apple juice and locally smoked salmon.

Llandovery Castle Hotel

Llandovery *Kings Road (01550 720343/ www.llandoverycastle.co.uk). ££.*
With its picturesque castleside setting and pretty beer garden, oak beams, genial staff and welcoming leather chesterfields gathered round ancient open-fired hearths, Llandovery Castle makes a very respectable alternative to the nearby New White inn *(see below)*. The 20 rooms are all individually decorated and very comfortable. A key attraction for some is the welcome for dogs; book a dog-friendly room and for £5 per night your best friend will get a doggie towel, a Burns pet food doggy bag and access to the bar and adjacent dining area, where he or she can stretch out in front of the open fire while you enjoy a well-earned beer after tramping the glorious countryside together.

Manor Hotel

Crickhowell *Brecon Road (01873 810212/ www.manorhotel.co.uk). ££.*
This sister hotel to the Peterstone *(see p373)* occupies a pretty spot, set back from the A40 just north of Crickhowell, and takes the same serious approach to the business of looking after visitors and feeding them well, though with a slightly less sybaritic ambience. Decor is more boutique hotel than country house, with muted palettes and bright accents. A leisure centre includes an indoor pool and gym. So if you're a get up and go rather than a lay back and stay kind of person, this is the one to go for. And you get to use the spa at the nearby Peterstone too.

New White Lion

Llandovery *43 Stone Street (01550 720685/ www.newwhitelion.co.uk). £££.*
Gerald and Sylvia Pritchard's hugely impressive little hotel offers all the intimacy and warmth you'd expect from somewhere with just six rooms, but with the luxury, style and great food you'd expect from a larger hotel. With the help of their designer daughter Jeanette, the warmly welcoming Pritchards renovated this former pub (owned by Gerald's mother) into rooms drawing on Welsh folklore and history to create highly individual looks. The silvers and shimmering blues in the Lady of the Lake room make it a must for the romantically inclined, while rugby fans might prefer the more manly hues of 'Bread of Heaven' composer's William Williams' room. Whichever you choose, be sure to spend some time in the fascinating sitting room, stuffed with found objects like the ingenious, Tardis-like Indonesian honesty bar. And don't miss eating in the cosy dining room; veg is grown by Gerald at his allotment, Welsh cakes are made by Sylvia, breakfast features terrific home-made jams and marmalade and the dinner is first-rate.

Peterstone Court

Llanhamlach, 4 miles E of Brecon *(01874 665387/ www.peterstone-court.com). ££££.*

Wales has a good share of country house hotels that offer luxury combined with great food, but the Peterstone has something else too; a stylish contemporary twist on the more usual decor that makes it romantic and chic. The wood-panelled library features lovely armchairs clad in plush, funky-patterned velvets, and the same effort is applied to the 12 bedrooms (four in an adjacent converted stables, and dog-friendly), all of which are individually decorated with unexpected patterns and rich textures. Bathrooms are unfussy, beautifully appointed and filled with Circaroma Soil Association-certified organic toiletries, soft robes and slippers. A spa in the atmospheric cellars features a Moroccan chillout room, sauna and double treatment room, and an impressively equipped gym, lovely outdoor terrace, deck and outdoor pool make leaving the Peterstone very hard once you've checked in. *See also p370.*

Seven Stars Hotel

Hay-on-Wye *11 Broad Street (01497 820886/ www.theseven-stars.co.uk). ££.*

This quirky 16th-century building looks unprepossessing from the outside, but inside it's a little cracker, particularly for the price. Packed with character, the eight bedrooms are all simply furnished with pine, good beds and cosy duvets, the bathrooms are sparkling clean and, best of all, if you bag the pool room, French doors allow you to step through into a lovely indoor heated pool. Both this and a sauna are open year-round for hotel guests and, combined with the lovely original features of thick stone walls, huge oak beams and gently sloping floors, make the Seven Stars one of the nicest places to stay in Hay. And that's before you sample the terrific breakfasts, which should set you up perfectly for a day of walking and book browsing.

Three Cocks Coaching Inn

Three Cocks, 4 miles SW of Hay-on-Wye *(01497 847215/www.threecockshotel.com). ££.*

From the outside, the rambling 500-year-old Three Cocks looks like it would be warm: it's filled with roaring log fires in winter, huge flagstone hearths, lots of wood and heaps of cosy nooks and crannies. Seven spacious bedrooms are comfortably kitted out in crisp white linens and sparkling modern fittings that contrast nicely with the criss-crossing olde-worlde feature beams. The public spaces are equally appealing; celebrate the fact that your room doesn't have a TV by spending time instead in the gorgeous first-floor limed oak-panelled residents' sitting room, the perfect place to read, gaze out over the lovely garden or enjoy a large brandy from the equally comfy little bar downstairs.

Factfile

When to go

Spring and summer are obviously the busiest times, but coming out of season has its advantages: in late autumn the emerald fronds of bracken turn russet-gold, setting the mountain escarpments on fire; in late winter/early spring the springy moss on the Gospel Pass and tiny lambs leaping across it offer a wondrous sense of nature's ebulliance. Late May heralds the prestigious Hay Literary Festival (www.hay festival.com), when the world's literati revel in ten days of full-on bibliophilia.

Getting there

Abergavenny is served by direct train connections with Newport in South Wales or Manchester in northern England, while Llandovery can be reached easily from Swansea in South Wales. London trains to Newport and Swansea depart from Paddington station, with journey times of two hours and two hours 55 minutes respectively. The Beacons Bus (www.breconbeacons.org/visit-us/transport/beacons-bus-1) runs throughout the summer, connecting all the major towns in South Wales with Brecon; it can carry bikes.

Getting around

Roads and spectacular routes around the entire National Park arc easily navigable by car or bike.

Bus services are infrequent and connections complicated, with some areas barely serviced at all. Visit www.countrygoer.org/brecon.htm for timetables and details.

Tourist information

Abergavenny Monmouth Road (01873 853254/ www.abergavenny.co.uk). Open Summer 9.30am-5.30pm daily. Winter 10am-4pm daily.
Brecon Cattle Market Car Park (01874 622485/ www.visitbreconbeacons.com). Open Summer 9.30am-5.30pm Mon-Fri; 9.30am-5pm Sat; 9.30am-4pm Sun. Winter 9.30am-5pm Mon-Sat; 10am-4pm Sun.
Crickhowell Beaufort Chambers, Beaufort Street (01873 812105).Open Summer 10am-5pm daily. Winter 10am-4pm Mon-Sat; 10am-1pm Sun.
Hay-on-Wye Craft Centre, Oxford Road (01497 820144/www.hay-on-wye.co.uk/craft centre). Open Summer 10am-5pm daily. Winter 11am-4pm daily.

Internet

Brecon Cyber Café 10 Lion Street (01874 624942/ www.breconcybercafe.co.uk).
Crickhowell Library Silver Lane (01873 810856).
Hay Tourist Information Bureau Oxford Road (01497 820144/www.hay on wyc.co.uk/tourism).

Top left: Ashness Bridge;
right: Bowderstone;
bottom left: Lodore Falls;
right: Derwent Water.

Lake District: Around Keswick

The sheer beauty of water and fell.

It sometimes feels as though every shade and shadow that influenced the Lake District poets can be found within a ten-mile radius of Keswick: from picturesque waterscapes and sublime ranges of rolling fells to bleak scrub-covered crags. Depending on the foliage of the season in which it is dressed, the landscape can vary from quaintly pastoral to awesomely majestic, but it is seldom short of awe-inspiring, its many mysteries – ancient stone circles of unknown provenance, boulders balancing precariously on their edges – adding to the sense that this is a place apart, touched by a rough magic.

Whether looking out over Bassenthwaite Lake, walking along the Cumbria Way, clawing a path towards the peak of Blencathra or soaking up the views of Derwent Water from Cat Bells, it's not hard to imagine you can still hear the whispered voices of Wordsworth, Coleridge and Southey, whose obsession with the place makes more sense with each passing moment.

Explore

KESWICK & DERWENT WATER

Its medieval incarnation as a market town still echoes in Keswick's main square (Saturday remains market day), dominated by the 19th-century **Moot Hall**, with its unusual one-handed clock; the building is now home to Keswick's tourist information centre (*see p385*), although its ominous appearance betrays its former role as town hall and prison. Historic local landmarks are otherwise limited, although the soft pink sandstone of 19th-century **St John's Church** (Ambleside Road, 017687 72130) houses the grave of novelist Sir Hugh Walpole, who lived and worked in nearby Brackenburn.

Keswick's main draw is its quaint jumble of old coaching inns, cluttered antique shops, traditional tearooms and unusual museums. Of the latter, **Keswick Museum & Art Gallery** (Station Road, 017687 73263), should be first on any to-do list, housing a fascinating collection of Lakeland ephemera preserved in vintage glass cabinets – from geological oddities and stuffed animals to letters penned by the area's literary giants (Wordsworth, Southey and Walpole are present and correct). However, the 'musical stones' remain its most famous exhibit, a series of slate hornfels set in a wooden frame and played like a xylophone. Other cultural collections worth perusing can be found at

the **Cumberland Pencil Museum** (Southey Works, 017687 73626, www.pencilmuseum.co.uk), which charts the discovery of graphite in the Borrowdale hills and Keswick's erstwhile monopoly on pencil-making, and the bizarre **Cars of the Stars** (Standish Street, 017687 73757, www.carsofthestars.com; open 10am-5pm daily; admission £5, £3 reductions), at which Keswick artist and car collector Peter Nelson exhibits famous automobiles from film and television – including three Batmobiles and a staggering number of vehicles driven by James Bond.

For most people, however, a trip to the lakes is an excuse to escape car culture, something that's easily done with a short walk down Lake Road – passing the excellent **Theatre by the Lake** (017687 74411, www.theatrebythe lake.com), particularly buzzing during Keswick's jazz (February), film (May) and literary Words by the Water (March) festivals. This in turn leads to the shimmering expanse of **Derwent Water**, barely three miles long and never more than a mile wide, but one of the Lake District's most astonishing lakes, thanks to its majestic frame of shadowy fells.

The **Keswick Launch** (017687 72263, www.keswick-launch.co.uk) runs trips to six points around the lake, although surroundings can be just as pleasantly soaked up on a leisurely walk. Most people choose to follow the shore south, passing by **Derwent Island** – still home to a grand house built by the eccentric banker Joseph Pocklington

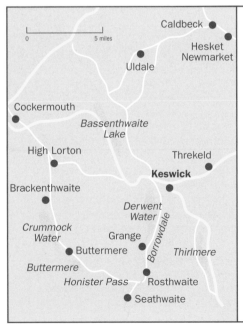

Lake District: Around Keswick

Historic sites
● ● ● ○ ○

Art & architecture
● ● ○ ○ ○

Hotels
● ● ● ○ ○

Eating & drinking
● ● ● ○ ○

Scenery
● ● ● ● ●

Outdoor activities
● ● ● ● ●

– and stopping at **Friar's Crag**, from which pilgrims once embarked by boat to nearby St Herbert's Island in search of blessings from the hermitic saint reputed to live there. Friar's Crag was also a favourite childhood spot of John Ruskin, remembered in a bronze memorial.

Other waterside sights (all served by the Keswick Launch) include Ashness Bridge, from which a minor road accesses picturesque Watendlath farmstead and tearoom (which rents boats and rods for trout fishing on the tarn); **Lodore Falls**, site of the intermittent waterfall (spectacular after heavy rain) described in Southey's *The Cataract Of Lodore*; and **Cat Bells** (1,481 feet), one of the Lakes' most visually dramatic easy climbs. The latter is best accessed from the Hawes End launch pier with a return via the Swinside Inn (017687 78253, www.theswinsideinn.com) for a much-needed pint, or by a leisurely meander through Brandlehow Woods and Manesty Park (where Hugh Walpole once lived in the house he called Brackenburn).

Those hoping to take to the water themselves can rent rowing boats at northernmost **Nichol End** (017687 73082, www.nicholendmarine.co.uk), which also has a lakeside café.

BORROWDALE

The Borrowdale Valley is a mysterious place, lent an aspect of the Tolkienesque by the tangled trees that shroud its paths in shadow and the verdant mosses that matt its rocky summits. The potential for hikers is limitless, although there's also a useful bus service – the Borrowdale Rambler (*see p385*) – running regularly along the B5289, which conveniently links the valley's several villages.

Grange-in-Borrowdale, the most northerly, is a quaint clutter of slate houses on the far side of a picturesque packhorse bridge that crosses the flood-prone River Derwent. Its cafés make it a convenient stop for walkers on the Cumbrian Way; most favour the expansive garden of the traditional Grange Bridge Cottage Tearoom (017687 77201).

South of Grange the valley becomes increasingly otherworldly, its jagged peaks rearing overhead with a menace befitting their nickname: the 'jaws of Borrowdale'. A woodland track off the main road leads to the famous **Bowder Stone**, a single large rock (roughly 1,900 tons) balancing precariously on one edge; interested parties may argue over whether it was deposited by a glacier or fell from a nearby mountain, although most people simply prefer to climb the wooden ladder to its summit, worn smooth by generations of feet.

Further south is **Rosthwaite**, another small slate village most famous for its prized Herdwick sheep – many of which end up in the sausages and 'herdi burgers' so beloved by hikers refuelling at the Flock-In (*see p381*). Rosthwaite is also

home the Scafell Hotel (017687 77208, www.scafell.co.uk), starting point for the annual 18-mile Borrowdale Fell Race, which takes place on the first Saturday in August.

Immediately south of Rosthwaite is the Glaramara Outdoor Centre (017687 77222, www.glaramara.co.uk), organiser of countless land- and water-based adventure activities in the surrounding hills. After that the valley funnels into three tiny villages: **Stonethwaite** is home to the excellent Langstrath Inn (*see p381*); **Seatoller** is the site of both enigmatic Seatoller House (*see p385*) and the traditional Yew Tree café (017687 77635), as well as a path into neighbouring Johnny Wood; while **Seathwaite** is a popular departure point for hikers attempting to scale neighbouring **Scafell Pike**, England's highest mountain, and also boasts the Borrowdale Trout Farm (017687 77293), which offers a café, picnic area and the potential for fishing with hired boats and rods. Alternatively, a sharp westward turn on the B5289 at Seatoller leads to **Honister Pass** and the still-working **Honister Slate Mine** (Honister Pass, 017687 77230, www.honister-slate-mine.co.uk; open 9am-5pm daily; admission £9.75, £4.75 reductions), where fascinating guided tours offer an insight into this most dangerous of local industries from Elizabethan times to the present day.

BASSENTHWAITE LAKE & AROUND

It's perhaps best known as the only true lake in the Lake District (the others are all referred to as 'waters', 'meres' or 'tarns'), but there's more to long, narrow Bassenthwaite than geographical terms. A National Nature Reserve, Bassenthwaite is home to countless species of wildlife: below the surface mingle roach, salmon and the super-rare vendace; above it circle herons, cormorants and, since 2001, osprey.

The best place to witness the animal kingdom up close is **Dodd Wood**, on the lake's eastern shore; there's parking near the Old Sawmill Tearooms (017687 74317, www.theoldsawmill.co.uk), from where a quarter-mile uphill slog leads to an open-air viewing platform with telescopes provided. Closer to the shoreline is neighbouring **Mirehouse** (*see p379*). Also worth a visit is the nearby **Church of St Bega**, a restored Norman chapel that some might recognise from the opening lines of Tennyson's *Morte d'Arthur*, which the poet was inspired to write while staying at Mirehouse.

Also on the Bassenthwaite shoreline is **Trotters World of Animals** (Coalbeck Farm, 017687 76239, www.trottersworld.com), a renowned conservation centre mixing familiar farmyard animals with formidable beasts such as Canadian lynxes (the only ones in Britain), capybara (the largest rodents in the world) and a European eagle owl of the same family as Malfoy's

award-winning sculpture set in stunning woodlands

bring this advert for two-for-one admission to the sculpture estate

cass sculpture
foundation
at goodwood

registered charity number 1015088

open april – october every year
10:30 to 5pm, last entry 4:30pm
directions at **www.sculpture.org.uk**

owl in the Harry Potter movies. Signs throughout highlight the plight of endangered species the world over, plus there's an adventure playground, a decent café and a picnic area.

It's also worth traversing the lake's western edge, beneath the towering crags of Barf (notable for a white pillar marking the spot where the Bishop of Derry is reputed to have died falling from his horse after drunkenly betting companions he could ride all the way up), through the village of **Thornthwaite** with its charming gallery of Lakeland arts (017687 78248, www.thornthwaitegalleries. co.uk), to the Whinlatter Forest Park. This is England's only true mountain forest, and offers biking and hiking trails, an excellent education centre, the superb Siskin's Café and an adrenalin-fuelled treetop canopy run incorporating bridges, wires and slides.

Mirehouse

Underskiddaw, 1 mile E of Keswick *(017687 72287/www.mirehouse.com). Open (Grounds) Apr-Oct 10am-5.30pm daily. (House) Apr-Oct 2-5pm Wed, Sun. Aug 2-5pm Wed, Fri, Sun. Admission £6; £3 reductions.* This secluded 17th-century manor-turned-museum is filled with everything from antique toys and paintings by Constable to letters from the writer and historian Thomas Carlyle, a close friend of former resident James Spedding.

THRELKELD TO THIRLMERE

Avid ramblers should make time to follow the disused railway line running east of Keswick, being sure to turn off half a mile in and follow signs to the **Castlerigg Stone Circle**, heavily weathered lumps of Borrowdale stone arranged with brooding symbolism and dating back to roughly 3200 BC. Competing theories peg them as everything from an astrological timepiece to a forum for trading axes; less historically minded hikers can simply relish the astonishing views of the surrounding fells.

A ramble further east along the railway path leads to the village of **Threlkeld**, home to two charming pubs – the Horse and Farrier (017687 79688, www.horseandfarrier.com) and the Salutation (017687 79614, www.thesalutation. co.uk) – most appealing at the end of a gruelling slog up and down **Blencathra** (2,848 feet), for which Threlkeld makes an ideal starting point. Otherwise, the village's main attraction is the **Threlkeld Quarry & Mining Museum** (*see below*). South of Threlkeld, a footpath passes through the splendid isolation of **St John's in the Vale** – notable both for its squat Victorian chapel and for the charming tea garden and craft workshops of Low Bridge End Farm (017687 79242, www. campingbarn.com) – before reaching **Thirlmere**, an awe-inspiring five-mile reservoir created from two smaller lakes to satisfy Manchester's industrial water demands in the late 19th century. Flooding as it did the hamlet of Armboth and

numerous nearby farms, the action enraged early environmentalists, among them local vicar Hardwicke Drummond Rawnsley, whose failure to stop the project inspired him to co-found the National Trust in 1893. These days Thirlmere is surrounded by lush forestry, the best of which is sampled at **Launchy Gill** on the reservoir's south-western shore.

Threlkeld Quarry & Mining Museum

Threlkeld *(017687 79747/www.threlkeldmining museum.co.uk). Open Mar-Oct 10am-5pm daily. Admission (Guided tour of the mine) £5; £3 reductions. (Museum) £3; £1.50 reductions.* The area's past as a centre of granite quarrying and mining for lead and other metals is brought to life with artefacts, photographic records and a range of heavy machinery. There are also 45-minute tours through a re-created lead mine.

BACK O' SKIDDAW

There's not much in the way of conventional sights in the rugged hinterland known as Back o' Skiddaw – lying on the dark side of the famous Skiddaw fell – but that is music to the ears of those travelling here to escape the more self-consciously touristy elements of Lakeland towns and villages.

A right turn at the Castle Inn junction of the A591 will take you on a roughly eight-mile meander over vividly rolling hills, with plenty of scenic spots where you can pull over and soak up the surroundings. **Uldale**, a farming hamlet en route, served as a setting for more than one of Walpole's novels and boasts a decent pub, the Snooty Fox (016973 71479, www.snootyfox-uldale.co.uk). Most, however, carry on to **Caldbeck**, named after the fast-flowing river (the 'cold beck') that once powered its many mills; one such building, the Priest's Mill, has been restored to house the Watermill Café (016974 78267, www.watermillcafe.co.uk). In terms of sights, Caldbeck is most notable for its **Church of St Kentigan**, resting place of both John Peel, the famous British huntsman and subject of the Scottish folk song 'D'ye Ken John Peel', and Lakeland beauty Mary Robinson, the 'Maid of Buttermere', whose life story was mentioned in Wordsworth's *The Prelude*.

It's also worth driving the extra mile or so south to **Hesket Newmarket**, home of the co-operatively owned Old Crown (016974 78288, www.theoldcrownpub.co.uk), noted for its local ales and excellent food. Suitably refreshed, a return journey along the eastern borders of the fells can be broken up with climbs of such spectacular peaks as **Carrock Fell** (2,174 feet), best accessed from Stone's End Farm, and **Bowscale Fell** (2,360 feet), from where it's possible to descend into **Mungrisdale**, site of the celebrated Mill Inn (017687 79632, www.the-millinn.co.uk).

Derwent Water.

Eat

Flock-in

Borrowdale *Rosthwaite (017687 77675/www. borrowdaleherdwick.co.uk). Open Feb-Oct 10am-5pm Mon, Tue, Thur-Sun. Nov 10am-5pm Mon, Tue, Fri-Sun. ££. No credit cards. Café.*

In a small slate building at the working Yew Tree farm in Rosthwaite, this delightful café makes a convenient pit stop for hikers doing the Cumbria Way, Coast to Coast or Allerdale walks. Tea is served in pint or half-pint china mugs alongside snacks ranging from steaming bowls of soups to the famous 'herdi burger', a meaty mouthful of own-reared Herdwick lamb, which can be enjoyed either indoors or in the expansive café garden with stunning fell views. The florally decorated rooms in the affiliated inn have hosted Prince Charles.

George

Keswick *St John's Street (017687 72076/www.george hotelkeswick.co.uk). Open 5.30-9pm daily. £££. Pub.*

This 16th-century coaching inn is warmer and more welcoming than most, its timber-beamed interior and open fire popular with locals and their dogs, its walls replete with framed Lakeland ephemera. The lunch menu offers simple pub fare along the lines of scampi and chips or Cumberland sausages and mash, although the main draw is a gargantuan 'cow pie' that would intimidate even Desperate Dan. There's an adjoining dining room in which to sample the more formal evening menu – featuring the likes of locally reared steaks, slow-braised belly pork and Jack Daniels-marinated barbecue chicken – and 13 simple rooms.

Ivy House

Braithwaite, 4 miles W of Keswick *(017687 78338). Open 5.30-8.30pm Mon-Sat. £££. Modern European.*

The imposing Ivy House Hotel is a members' affair open only to holiday property bond-holders. Its restaurant, however, welcomes the public, but you'll need to book in advance – with a chef with experience at both London's Le Gavroche and the Berkeley, tables are in great demand. Food is robust, the likes of Lakeland beef casserole topped with honey roasted parsnips, with desserts like Jamaican gingerbread and white chocolate parfait. Prices are surprisingly low (£22.95 for three courses) and the interior decidedly low-key, with little more than a few candles, framed mirrors and a crockery-filled antique cabinet to constitute decoration.

Langstrath

Borrowdale *Stonethwaite (017687 77239/www.the langstrath.com). Open Apr-Oct noon-2.15pm, 6-9pm Tue-Sat; noon-2.15pm, 6-8.30pm Sun. Nov-Mar noon-2.15pm, 6-9pm Tue-Sat. £££. Modern European.*

At the end of an impossibly long farm track in the diminutive rural hamlet of Stonethwaite, the Langstrath is one of the Lake District's best-loved inns: both the traditional wood-panelled pub warmed by an open fire and serving a reliable range of casked beers, and the sparingly decorated dining room decked out with modern wood furnishings. The latter serves an excellent menu of locally inspired cuisine, with starters such as Cumbrian cheese soufflé and Morecambe Bay potted shrimps alongside mains like slow-cooked Rosthwaite Herdwick lamb, or rich beef bourguignon made with local Keskadale Farm steak. Eight comfortable bedrooms cater to overnight visitors, and full Cumbrian breakfasts are provided.

Morrels

Keswick *34 Lake Road (017687 72666/www.morrels. co.uk). Open 5.30-9pm Mon-Thur; 5.30-9.30pm Fri, Sat. £££. Modern European.*

Located in a grand house near lakeside Hope Park, this well-loved restaurant's luxurious interior features cream and chocolate upholstered chairs, chunky dark wood tables divided by branded glass partitions and a handful of verdant potted palms, all presided over by cult movie stars gazing back from a few modern prints – Steve McQueen as Bullit, Pacino as Scarface. Food is first-rate: expect starters along the lines of smoked haddock with grain mustard rarebit on buttered baby spinach, and mains such as chicken breast stuffed with salami in a brandy and black pepper sauce. There are two smart self-catering apartments upstairs.

Pheasant

Cockermouth, 7 miles W of Bassenthwaite Lake *(017687 76234/www.the-pheasant.co.uk). Open noon-1.15pm, 7-8.30pm daily. £££. Pub.*

It's perhaps best known as one of the region's most characterful coaching inns – its 15 rooms mixing traditional English aesthetics with modern amenities like flat-screen televisions – but the Pheasant also serves great food. Light lunches can be enjoyed at one of the leather banquettes in its delightful bolt-hole of a bar, a mix of tan walls decorated with ageing paintings and a few bronze pots of dried flowers, or the brighter and better-aired guests' lounge. Typical dishes include hearty chicken caesar salads, ploughman's lunches or open sandwiches with the likes of roast chicken and crisp Cumbrian bacon. The smart timbered dining room is reserved for more formal dinners.

Square Orange Café

Keswick *20 St John's Street (017687 73888/ www.thesquareorange.co.uk). Open 10am-11pm Mon-Thur; 10am-9pm Fri; noon-3pm, 6-9pm Sat; noon-3pm Sun. ££. Café/bar.*

This colourful hideaway neatly straddles the line separating 'happening bar' from hip, continental-style café, satisfying cravings both culinary (there's a decent range of tapas and popular stone-baked pizzas) and cultural (live bands and musicians perform every Tuesday night on the makeshift stage). The limited space makes for a bit of a squeeze that only adds to the friendly informality, and the vintage wooden bar is a lovely place to sip one of the excellent hand-pulled beers – from local offerings courtesy of the Keswick Brewing Company to the likes of Erdinger and Birra Porretti. Staff are amiable and upbeat, and the coffee is counted among Keswick's finest.

Sweeny's

Keswick *18-20 Lake Road (017687 72990). Open Easter-Oct noon-9pm daily. £££. Modern European.*

Simultaneously cosy and cosmopolitan, Sweeny's provides upmarket eating without feeling pretentious or pricey, in a setting of chunky blond wood furnishings, artful light fittings and large silver-framed mirrors that contrast pleasantly with the timber-beamed ceiling and old-fashioned wood-burning stove. The smart, black-shirted waiters are friendly and efficient, and prices are notably low: there's a £5 three-course set lunch, and a £15 set dinner (smoked salmon and cream cheese parcels followed by sirloin steak and horseradish mash, say), alongside an a la carte. There's also a decent tapas menu and a popular weekly steak night.

Unique
Keswick *23 St John's Street (01 7687 73400/ www.uniquedining.co.uk). Open 6.30-9.30pm Mon, Tue, Thur-Sun. £££. International.*
When it opened in late 2007, Unique couldn't have looked more incongruous amid its sleepy Keswick surroundings, its black and gold exterior more akin to a nightclub than a restaurant, and its glamorous interior mixing hardwood floors and black leather chairs with striking red walls, crisp cream linen and elaborate floral displays. Luckily, the staff have had the culinary verve to back up their aesthetic bravado, with starters such as smoked duck breast in a port and orange sauce with a toasted sesame seed and spring onion salad. Mains could be Lakeland sirloin in a brandy and peppercorn sauce, perhaps, or baked Borrowdale trout with lemon and hollandaise dressing.

Stay

Armathwaite Hall
Bassenthwaite Lake *on B5291 (01 7687 76551/ www.armathwaite-hall.com). £££.*
No other hotel complements the local landscape with such grand majesty as Armathwaite Hall, a 17th-century stately home surrounded by 400 acres of woodland and with breathtaking views across neighbouring Bassenthwaite Lake. Despite extensive renovation from the 1970s onwards – including the 2009 opening of a £5 million spa complex featuring an enchanting outdoor hot tub – the house retains the 'perfect and irresistible atmosphere' described by a smitten Hugh Walpole. Explorers will find luxurious wood-panelled lounges complete with roaring fires, elaborately framed paintings and wall-mounted gaming trophies; a billiards room decorated with vintage Punch comics; a stone terrace perfect for afternoon tea; and a vaulted dining room offering an elaborate six-course dinner (formal dress, non-guests welcome). Rooms are smart, spacious and traditionally decorated, and offer views across either the lake or the surrounding grounds, which incorporate Trotters World Of Animals (*see p377*), free to guests.

Borrowdale Hotel
Borrowdale, 3 miles S of Keswick *on B5289 (01 7687 77224/www.lakedistricthotels.net). £££.*
Its squat slate frame may pale in the shadow of the neighbouring Lodore Falls Hotel (*see p382*), but the

Borrowdale is perfect for those seeking traditional Lakeland accommodation with a few frills but none of the fuss. Supremely friendly staff help generate a homely atmosphere that extends from the roaring fireside lounges to the wood-panelled bar – heaving during the evening with guests and locals – through hallways decorated with local curiosities to the smart dining room, where guests linger over dinners served without the self-conscious stuffiness of some similar establishments. Rooms are pleasantly if plainly decorated (disabled access rooms are available alongside four-poster and family suites), and guests are able to make full use of the spa and sports facilities at Lodore Falls.

Coledale Inn
Braithwaite, 4 miles W of Keswick *(01 7687 78272/www.coledale-inn.co.uk). ££.*
A functional, unfussy affair set in the comfortable frame of a former Lakeland mill, with a hilltop location and stunning views across the valley to Skiddaw, the lemon yellow Coledale Inn remains a firm favourite with families. Facilities are limited to a suitably cavernous Victorian bar, a bright and airy restaurant (serving cheap and cheerful pub-style grub) and a small residents' lounge furnished with a few battered sofas, a handful of antique lamps and a well-worn Persian rug. The 24 rooms are simply furnished, but all are clean and cosy and many have superb valley views.

Lodore Falls Hotel
Borrowdale, 3 miles S of Keswick *on B5289 (01 7687 77285/www.lakedistricthotels.net). ££££.*
It's hard to miss the looming Lodore Falls Hotel, sandwiched between Derwent Water and the rolling Castlerigg Fell, and snuggling up to the enigmatic Lodore Falls waterfall after which the hotel is named. The upmarket interior welcomes guests with a grand bar, the aptly named Lake View restaurant and various lounges decorated in red and gold, their wood-panelled walls replete with photographs and paintings of local landmarks. Facilities include tennis and squash courts and the Lodore Leisure Suite, complete with swimming pool, sauna and gym; guests can also play a complimentary 18 holes at nearby Keswick Golf Course.

Lyzzick Hall
Underskiddaw, 1 mile E of Keswick *(01 7687 72277/www.lyzzickhall.co.uk). ££££.*
Lyzzick Hall manages to combine the visual splendour of a traditional country house hotel with a fun, informal air – the latter in no small part due to its affable owners Alfredo and Dorothy Fernandez, and their team of partly local, partly Spanish staff. Smartly upholstered furniture, regal green carpeting and an ornately tiled open fireplace characterise the lounge, while a small, slightly retro bar opens on to a pale blue dining room, where a daily-changing menu mixes Spanish and English influences to superb effect. There's also an indoor swimming pool, sauna and jacuzzi, plus a delightful terrace overlooking the gardens. Rooms range from simple to strikingly modern, but all are clean and effortlessly cosy.

Langstrath.

Armathwaite Hall.

Mary Mount Hotel

Borrowdale, 2.5 miles S of Keswick *on the B5289 (017687 77223/www.marymounthotel.co.uk). £££.*

The Mary Mount's proximity to the shimmering expanse of Derwent Water means that many guests leave their cars at the hotel and instead cross into town on the Keswick Launch (*see p376*). The hotel has a homely atmosphere, with regular return guests treated by manager Mike Mawdsley as old friends, and while the decor of the adjoining bar and restaurant feels a little dated (the former teeming with board games and well-thumbed books, the latter offering sweeping waterside views), both are as clean and comfortable as the 20 affordable and well-appointed bedrooms. The menu is also a cut above the average, and dinner is open to non-guests.

Seatoller House

Seatoller *(017687 77218/www.seatollerhouse.co.uk). £££.*

This 17th-century cottage was once home to historian GM Trevelyan, whose inaugural trip to Seatoller as a Cambridge undergraduate in 1898 inspired him to found the infamous Lake Hunt, a local sport in which both hares and hounds are played by men. The hunt continues every year to this day, and the staircase of this enigmatic dwelling is lined with portraits of hunt masters through the ages. The ten rooms are quaint and cosy, furnished with antiques and offering views of the large garden. There's a charming guest lounge complete with an honesty box bar, and a small dining room for indulging in sumptuous six-course Cumbrian dinners.

Skiddaw Hotel

Keswick *Main Street (017687 72071/ www.lakedistricthotels.net). £££.*

For many, a trip to the Lake District is about isolation and escape, but those seeking a more central base of operations would do well to consider this large, modern hotel in Keswick's central square. The Skiddaw feels very much like a function hotel – and does a suitably roaring trade in weddings, Christmas parties and conferences – but it is also a warm and welcoming establishment, with red-carpeted halls, walls replete with sepia-tinted photographs of old Keswick and a decent restaurant, 31 The Square. The 44 bedrooms range from functional singles to family suites and glamorous four-poster bedrooms; there's also free Wi-Fi in communal areas.

Underscar Manor

Applethwaite, 2 miles N of Keswick *(017687 75000/www.underscarmanor.co.uk). ££££.*

Amid a host of typically British country house hotels, the Italianate exterior of Underscar Manor comes as something of a surprise when it appears at the end of its long, conifer-lined driveway (the hotel is set in 40 acres of grounds) – arched windows, campanile tower and all. Inside, the decoration is more traditional English, the rooms grand and glamorous but leaning towards the floral end of the spectrum. Underscar's conservatory restaurant is justly revered for its food, and there's a delightful terrace with views over Derwent Water and the slopes of Skiddaw looming behind the hotel. Guests also have use of Oxley's health/beauty spa. The hotel also has some self-catering apartments available.

Factfile

When to go

Spring and summer are the most popular seasons to visit the Lake District but crowds can infringe on the sense of rural isolation and prices tend to be sky-high. Autumn is cheaper and arguably more beautiful, the landscape a russet collage of rich browns and oranges, and snowy winters provide the most stunning views of all – provided you come prepared with appropriate clothing.

Getting there

Penrith is the closest major train station, with services to and from London, Manchester and Birmingham. For drivers, the M6 makes for a mostly direct route from London to the Lakes, turning off at Penrith and following the A66 to Keswick.

Getting around

A comprehensive network of local buses runs from Keswick into the surrounding countryside. Bus 73/73A (Caldbeck Rambler) runs via the Castlerigg Stone Circle, Threlkeld, up the Back o' Skiddaw to Caldbeck and thence to Mirehouse. Bus 77/77A (Honister Rambler) accesses Honister Pass via Grange, Seatoller and Whinlatter Pass. Bus 79 (Borrowdale Rambler) runs a straight service to Lodore, Grange, Rosthwaite, Seatoller and back. Bus X4/X5 takes in Threlkeld, Braithwaite and Bassenthwaite Lake, among other destinations.

Tourist Information

Keswick Moot Hall (017687 72645/www.lake-district.gov.uk). Open Apr-Oct 9am-5.30pm daily. Nov-Mar 9am-4.30pm daily.

Internet

Java & Chocolate 23 Main Street, Keswick (017687 72568). Open 10am-5pm Mon-Sat; 10am-4.30pm Sun.
Keswick Library Heads Lane (017687 72656). Open 10am-7pm Mon, Wed; 10am-5pm Tue, Fri; 10am-12.30pm Thur, Sat.

Need to know

ACCOMMODATION

CAMPING & CARAVANNING

Camping and Caravanning Club 0845 130 7631/www.campingandcaravanningclub.co.uk
Camping and Caravanning UK www.camping.uk-directory.com. UK and European camp- and caravan site directory.
UK Parks www.ukparks.com. Another directory site that also lists cottages, lodges and caravans to buy or hire.

SELF-CATERING

English Country Cottages 0845 268 0788/www.english-country-cottages.co.uk. Directory of self-catering rural accommodation for large and small groups.
Helpful Holidays 01647 433 593/www.helpful holidays.com. Specialises in holiday cottages in the West Country.
Landmark Trust 01628 825 925/www.landmarktrust.org.uk. Self-catering accommodation in historic buildings owned by the Landmark Trust charity.
National Trust 0844 800 1895/www.national trust.org.uk. The National Trust offers some holiday cottage accommodation as well as camp- and caravan sites on NT land and B&Bs run by NT tenants.
Visit Britain www.visitbritain.co.uk. Another website offering details of many different types of accommodation: hostels, campsites, hotels, self-catering etc.
YHA 01629 592 700/www.yha.org.uk and www.escape-to.co.uk. The Youth Hostel Association offers many different types of accommodation including self-catering, cottages, mansions as well as youth hostels.

ELECTRICITY

The UK uses the standard European 220-240V, 50-cycle AC voltage, along with three-pin plugs.

EMBASSIES & CONSULATES

American Embassy 24 Grosvenor Square, London, W1A 1AE (020 7499 9000/www.london.usembassy.gov). Bond Street or Marble Arch tube. Open 8.30am-5.30pm Mon-Fri.
Australian High Commission Australia House, Strand, London, WC2B 4LA (020 7379 4334/www.uk.embassy.gov.au). Holborn or Temple tube. Open 9.30am-3.30pm Mon-Fri.
Canadian High Commission 38 Grosvenor Street, London, W1K 4AA (020 7528 6600/www.canada.org.uk). Bond Street or Oxford Circus tube. Open 8-11am Mon-Fri.
Embassy of Ireland 17 Grosvenor Place, London, SW1X 7HR (020 7235 2171/passports & visas 7225 7700). Hyde Park Corner tube. Open 9.30am-1pm, 2.30-5pm Mon-Fri.
New Zealand High Commission New Zealand House, 80 Haymarket, London, SW1Y 4TQ (020 7930 8422/www.nzembassy.com). Piccadilly Circus tube. Open 9am-5pm Mon-Fri.
South African High Commission South Africa House, Trafalgar Square, London, WC2N 5DP (020 7451 7299/www.southafricahouse.com). Charing Cross tube/rail. Open 9.45am-12.45pm (by appointment only), 3-4pm (collections) Mon-Fri.

EMERGENCIES

Ambulance, Fire Brigade, Police 999.

LOST CREDIT CARDS

American Express 01273 696933; **Diners Club** 01252 513500; **Mastercard/Eurocard** 0800 964767; **Switch** 0870 600 0459; **Visa/Connect** 0800 895082.

PUBLIC HOLIDAYS

On public holidays (bank holidays), many shops remain open, but public transport services run to a Sunday timetable. On Christmas Day, almost everything, including public transport, closes down. There are eight bank holidays: **Good Friday**, **Easter Monday**, **May Day Holiday** (first Monday in May), **Spring Bank Holiday** (last Monday in May), **Summer Bank Holiday** (last Monday in August), **Christmas Day** (25 Dec), **Boxing Day** Sat (26 Dec), **New Year's Day** (1 Jan).

SMOKING

Smoking is now banned in all enclosed public spaces, including pubs, bars, clubs, restaurants, hotel foyers, shops and public transport. Many bars and clubs have smoking gardens or terraces.

TELEPHONES

If you're calling from outside the UK, dial your international access code, then the UK code

(44), then the full UK number, omitting the first 0 from the code. To call abroad from within the UK dial the international access code (00) followed by the relevant country code: Australia 61; Canada 1; New Zealand 64; Republic of Ireland 353; South Africa 27; USA 1. The London area dialling code is 020.

US cellphone users will need a tri-band or quad-band handset.

Public payphones take coins and/or credit cards. International calling cards, offering bargain minutes via a freephone number, are widely available.

TIME

The UK operates on Greenwich Mean Time (GMT) and British Summer Time (BST). GMT is five hours ahead of US Eastern Standard time. In Spring (on the last weekend in March) the clocks switch forward one hour to BST, returning back to GMT in autumn on the last weekend in October.

TIPPING

Tip in taxis, minicabs, restaurants (some waiting staff rely heavily on tips), hotels, hairdressers and some bars (but not pubs). Ten per cent is normal, with some restaurants adding as much as 15% for service. Always check whether service has been included in your bill: some restaurants include a service charge, but also leave space for a tip on your credit card slip.

TOURS & ACTIVITIES

ACTIVITY HOLIDAYS

Acorn Adventure 0800 074 979/www.acornfamily holidays.co.uk. Family adventure/activity holidays.

British Activity Holiday Association 01244 301 342/www.baha.org.uk. Trade association that lists companies that offer activity holidays around the UK.

Sherpa Expeditions 020 8577 2717/www. sherpa-walking-holidays.co.uk. Walking holidays in the UK.

Skedaddle 0191 265 1110/www.skedaddle. co.uk. Biking holidays in the UK.

CULINARY TOURS

Cooking Holidays www.cookingholidays.co.uk. Website listing cooking holidays across the UK as well as the rest of the world.

On The Menu 08708 998 844/www.holiday onthemenu.com. Tour operator running cooking holidays in the UK and abroad.

CULTURAL TOURS

Inscape 020 7839 3988/www.inscpacetours. co.uk. This company specialises in fine art and architecture tours.

Martin Randall Travel 020 8742 335/www. martinrandall.com. High-brow cultural tours with themes of art, architecture, music and history.

Tailored Travel 0845 230 9966/www.tailored-travel.co.uk. Offers tailor made art and culture tours to UK and other countries.

TOURIST INFORMATION

British Tourist Board www.visitbritain.co.uk.

English Tourist Board www.enjoyengland.com.

London Tourist Board www.visitlondon.com.

Northern Ireland Tourist Board www.discovernorthernireland.com.

Scottish Tourist Board www.visitscotland.co.uk.

Welsh Tourist Board www.visitwales.co.uk.

TRAVEL

AIRPORTS

Edinburgh Airport (EDI) (0870 040 0007/ www.edinburghairport.com.

Gatwick Airport (LGW) 0870 000 2468/ www.gatwickairport.com.

Heathrow Airport (LHR) 0870 000 0123/ www.heathrowairport.com.

Luton Airport (LTN) 01582 405100/ www.london-luton.co.uk.

Manchester Airport (MAN) 08712 710 711/ www.manchesterairport.co.uk.

Stansted Airport (STN) 0870 000 0303/ www.stanstedairport.com.

CAR HIRE

Avis 0844 581 0147/www.avis.co.uk.

Enterprise 0870 350 3000/www.enterprise.co.uk.

Europcar www.europcar.co.uk.

Hertz 08708 415 161/www.hertz.com.

Thrifty 01494 751 500/www.thrifty.co.uk.

TRAINS

National Rail Enquiries 08457 484 950/ www.nationalrail.co.uk.

Network Rail 08457 114 141/ www.networkrail.co.uk.

VISAS & IMMIGRATION

EU citizens do not require a visa to visit the UK; citizens of the USA, Canada, Australia and New Zealand can also enter with only a passport for tourist visits of up to six months as long as they can show they are able to support themselves during their visit and plan to return home afterwards. Use www.ukvisas.gov.uk to check your visa status well before you travel, or contact the British embassy, consulate or high commission in your own country. You can arrange visas online at www.fco.gov.uk.

Festivals & Events

JANUARY

Edinburgh
Burns Night
Robert 'Rabbie' Burns was born on 25 January 1759 and Scots gather on the anniversary of his birth to eat haggis, sup whisky and listen to readings of his works in events all over the city.
www.rabbie-burns.com

London
London International Mime Festival
Innovative and visually stunning theatre from across the globe.
www.mimefest.co.uk

New Year's Day Parade
The capital's New Year effort features more than 10,000 performers from 20 different countries all strutting their stuff around central London.
www.londonparade.co.uk

FEBRUARY

Bath
Bath Literature Festival
Fairly new but fast-growing bookfest with over 100 literary events and talks from leading authors spread over nine days.
www.bathlitfest.org.uk

London
Chinese New Year Celebrations
A bright spectacle of dances, martial arts, music and costume takes place in Leicester Square and Trafalgar Square.
www.chinatownchinese.co.uk

Great Spitalfields Pancake Day Races
Shrove Tuesday brings out charity pancake racers across the capital. Don a silly costume and join in the fun at the Great Spitalfields Pancake Race (you'll need to register in advance) or watch City livery companies race in full regalia at the event organised by the Worshipful Company of Poulters.
www.alternativearts.co.uk

York
Jorvik Viking Festival
Hundreds of Vikings descend upon the city in order to demonstrate their battle drills; other less bloodthirsty events include lectures, arts and crafts fairs, encampments, river events and saga telling.
www.jorvik-viking-centre.co.uk

MARCH

Cornwall
St Piran's Day
On 5 March all over Cornwall celebrations are staged, including a play at Perran Sands, to celebrate St Piran's Day (he being Cornwall's patron saint).
www.an-daras.com

Cumbria
Pasche Egg Play
Local Morris Men put on Pasche egg plays over Easter – 'pasche' comes from the Hebrew word for passover – in the Furness area villages of Baycliff, Broughton, Cartmel, Coniston, Elterwater, Hawkshead, Near Sawrey and Ulverston.
www.thecumbriadirectory.com

London
Kew Spring Festival
Kew Gardens is at its most beautiful in spring when five million flowers carpet the grounds.
www.rbgkew.org.uk

Oxford & Cambridge Boat Race
Watched by tens of millions worldwide, Oxford and Cambridge students race each other along the Thames from Putney to Mortlake in a pair of rowing eights.
www.theboatrace.org

APRIL

Edinburgh
Beltane Fire Festival
This druidic tradition, marking the transition from winter to spring, is a mass of fire, drumming and exhibitionists, watched by roughly 10,000 people.
www.beltane.org

Edinburgh International Science Festival
The UK's largest science festival, with around 200 events, from free talks to hands-on workshops.
www.sciencefestival.co.uk

Kirkaldy, Fife
Links Market
Kirkcaldy's Promenade transforms under the weight of the largest funfair in Europe. A mile long, it hosts every conceivable fairground attraction, as well as food stalls for those who can stomach it.
www.linksmarket.org.uk

London

Chelsea Art Fair
Chelsea Old Town Hall becomes home to one of the best collections of contemporary and 20th-century art in Europe. Roughly 40 galleries show off paintings, ceramics, drawings and prints.
www.penman-fairs.com

Flora London Marathon
From Greenwich Park to St James's Park via the Tower of London – this spectacular event attracts about 35,000 starters.
www.london-marathon.co.uk

Spill
A festival of international contemporary performance, live art and experimental theatre with world premières and commissioned works.
www.spillfestival.com

Morpeth, Northumberland

Morpeth Northumbrian Gathering
The Gathering celebrates ancient local traditions over three days each spring. There are concerts, singarounds, a barn dance, storytelling, street theatre and the Border Cavalcade re-enactment.
www.northumbriana.org.uk/gathering

MAY

Bath

Bath International Music Festival
This highly regarded event features orchestral, chamber and contemporary classical music as well as world and electronic sounds. The programme includes some free outdoor events.
www.bathmusicfest.org.uk

Bath Fringe Festival
Bath Fringe is a jamboree of arts and ents across the city, one of the largest in the country.
www.bathfringe.co.uk

Cornwall

Daphne du Maurier Festival
The novelist's festival takes place in and around her home town of Fowey and attracts an array of writers, performers and celebrities.
www.dumaurierfestival.co.uk

'Obby 'Oss Day
This world-famous, 900-year-old May Day festival in Padstow features two 'osses, monstrous effigies made out of hoop-work, tarpaulin and horse hair, which are paraded through the streets with wild singing, drumming and accordion music.
www.padstow.com

Derbyshire

Well Dressing
From May to September, Peak District village wells are traditionally dressed with elaborate mosaic-like pictures made from flower petals, seeds, grasses, leaves, tree bark, berries and moss.
www.welldressing.com

Gloucestershire

Cooper's Hill Cheese Rolling
If you want to see people risking life and limb chasing cheese, head for Cooper's Hill in Brockworth, where competitors battle it out in pursuit of an eight-pound Double Gloucester.
www.cheese-rolling.co.uk

Tetbury Woolsack Races
Each Spring Bank Holiday local teams relay a 60lb woolsack (35lb for ladies) up and down Gumstool Hill between the Crown and Royal Oak pubs.
www.tetburywoolsack.co.uk

Hay-on-Wye, Powys

Hay Festival
The apex of literary festivals, with celeb authors, critics, fine wines, storytelling and comedy.
www.hayfestival.com

Isle of Bute, Argyll

Isle of Bute Jazz Festival
Jazz sessions from morning till night over the first weekend in May. On the Saturday there are also marching bands, a street parade and jazz cruises.
www.butejazz.com

Kendal, Cumbria

Spring Bank Holiday
Kendal was granted its market charter in 1189, and relives those days each year on Spring Bank Holiday with a medieval market, as well as pageantry, music and other entertainment, including jesters and jugglers.
www.southlakeland.gov.uk

London

Chelsea Flower Show
Held on the 11-acre grounds of the Royal Hospital in Chelsea, this is the mother of all flower shows.
www.rhs.org.uk

Speyside

Speyside Whisky Festival
The festival brings out a quarter of a million drams of malt and single-malt whisky, plus a merry selection of entertainment.
www.spiritofspeyside.com

JUNE

Cambridge

Cambridge Midsummer Fair
Held on Midsummer Common since the early 13th century, this is East Anglia's largest funfair.
www.cambridge.gov.uk/public/summerinthecity/

Strawberry Fair
Held on Midsummer Common on 6 June and now into its third decade, Strawberry Fair is a popular music, arts, theatre and crafts event – and it's free too.
www.strawberry-fair.org.uk

Edinburgh
Royal Highland Show
Scotland's annual Royal Highland Show, running since 1822, embraces every pastime and pursuit related to farming, the countryside and rural living.
www.royalhighlandshow.org

Glastonbury, Somerset
Glastonbury Festival
The UK's most famous music festival. Pre-registration (essential to even be in with a chance of buying a ticket) starts in with a in February.
www.glastonburyfestivals.co.uk

Isle of Wight
Isle of Wight's Round the Island Yacht Race
This yacht race is one of the world's biggest. Almost 2,000 yachts and 12,000 sailors set sail on a 50-nautical-mile chase west from Cowes.
www.roundtheisland.org.uk

Old Gaffers Classic Boat Festival
The island is a boaties' paradise in the summer and Old Gaffers is a unique chance to inspect and delight in more than 100 gaff-rigged boats.
www.yarmoutholdgaffersfestival.co.uk

London
Coin Street Festival
Celebrating London's cultural diversity, this free summer-long Thameside festival features a series music-focused events.
www.coinstreet.org

Open Garden Squares Weekend
Visit roof gardens, prison gardens, children-only gardens and those in private squares that are temporarily thrown open to the public.
www.opensquares.org

Wimbledon Tennis
The grandest slam of them all, if the rain stays off. Join the public ticket ballot or join the queue.
www.wimbledon.org

Ludlow, Shropshire
Ludlow Festival
Open-air Shakespeare in the grounds of the castle, plus opera, dance, poetry, music and a fireworks display.
www.ludlowfestival.co.uk

Penzance, Cornwall
Golowan Festival
A celebration of ancient Celtic traditions and the midsummer Feast of St John (Gol Jowan) including traditional dance, street theatre and music.
www.golowan.org

West Sussex
Chichester Festivities
The festival, based around Chichester's Norman cathedral, features talks, walks, candlelit concerts, sculpture, classical music, jazz, comedy, street art, fireworks and more.
www.chifest.org.uk

Corpus Christi Carpet of Flowers
A 100-year-old celebration: on Corpus Christi eve a magnificent 90-foot carpet of flowers is placed down the central aisle of Arundel Cathedral.
www.arundelcathedral.org/corpuschristi.htm

Goodwood Festival of Speed
Arguably the world's biggest and most diverse celebration of the history of motor sport and car culture, with everything from 19th century steam carriages to current Formula One.
www.goodwood.co.uk

JULY

Cambridge
Cambridge Folk Festival
Long-running, eclectic and popular festival with traditional British and Irish folk artists, American country, blues and roots artists, contemporary acts, plus gospel, cajun, jazz, world and a ceilidh. *See p308.*
www.cambridgefolkfestival.co.uk

Gloucestershire
Cotswold Show & Country Fair
Cotswolds' homespun charm is put on jolly (and large-scale) display in Cirencester each summer. Livestock, arts and crafts and gastronomic delights attract over 35,000 people.
www.cotswoldshow.co.uk

Westonbirt Arboretum Concert & Fireworks
This famous arboretum hosts various events and festivals throughout the year. This is one of the finest.
www.forestry.gov.uk

Harrogate, North Yorkshire
Great Yorkshire Show
A 150-year-old countryside showcase featuring show-jumping, pole-climbing, marching bands and cattle parades.
www.greatyorkshireshow.com

Harrogate International Festival
A celebration of classical, jazz and world music performed by contemporary stars.
www.harrogate-festival.org.uk

Henley, Oxfordshire
Henley Royal Regatta
The first week of July sees the River Thames and the town of Henley-on-Thames become one large sporting and social arena where the world's best rowers compete.
www.hrr.co.uk

London
BBC Proms
Summer sees some of the most important music festivals of the year – namely, the BBC Sir Henry Wood Promenade Concerts, or the Proms, running from July to September.
www.bbc.co.uk/proms

London Literature Festival
The South Bank two-week-long programme combines superstar writers with stars from other fields.
www.londonlitfest.com

Music Village, Hyde Park
Europe's longest-running – and free – festival of world cultures is always inspirationally themed and magical, bringing global musicians together and showcasing London's own diaspora performers.
www.culturalco-operation.org

Manchester
Manchester International Festival
Biennial international arts festival launched in 2007.
www.mif.co.uk

Sandringham, Norfolk
Sandringham Flower Show
The Queen's Norfolk retreat is even more splendid than normal when it's ablaze with flowers.
www.sandringhamestate.co.uk

AUGUST

Arundel, West Sussex
Arundel Festival
Held at Arundel Castle, the festival attracts visitors from all over the world for a feast of concerts, Shakespeare and opera both indoors and out.
www.arundelfestival.co.uk

Eastnor Castle, Herefordshire
Big Chill
Held at Eastnor Castle in the Malvern Hills, the Big Chill is a rather grown-up festival featuring music, art, dance and film.
www.bigchill.net

Edinburgh
Edinburgh International Festival, Edinburgh Festival Fringe, Edinburgh Film Festival
Edinburgh becomes the envy of the world every August with its famous International Festival, of which one of its offshoots, the Fringe Festival, is the shining glory. Every type of theatre is on, with some 1,500 different shows.
www.edinburghfestivals.co.uk

Grasmere, Cumbria
Grasmere Sports & Show
This historic and energetic Sports Day involves Cumberland wrestling, hound trails, the Fell Race, gundog and sheepdog displays, junior races, mountain bike dashes and a tug of war.
www.grasmeresportsandshow.co.uk

Isle of Skye
Isle of Skye Highland Games
Dating from 1877, the event takes place in the Lump, a natural amphitheatre. The Gathering Hall hosts the piping competition, while the island itself is circumnavigated in a sailing competition.
www.skye-highland-games.co.uk

Isle of Wight
Cowes Week
August on the Isle of Wight is heralded by the longest-running, most prestigious and largest sailing regatta in the world.
www.cowesweek.co.uk

London
London Mela
Dubbed the Asian Glastonbury, this exuberant celebration of Asian culture attracts thousands to Ealing's Gunnersbury Park each year for urban, classical and experimental music, circus, dance, visual arts, comedy, children's events – and yummy grub.
www.londonmela.org

Notting Hill Carnival
A vibrant highlight of the London summer over the Bank Holiday weekend but be prepared for serious crowds.
www.rbkc.gov.uk/NottingHill

Manchester
Manchester Gay Pride
One of Europe's most splendid Prides – you'd be hard-pressed not to get caught up in the ten-day spate of parties and parades.
www.manchesterpride.com

SEPTEMBER

Abergavenny, Monmouthshire
Abergavenny Food Festival
Foodie fun set against the mountains of Skirrid, Sugar Loaf and Blorenge on the edge of the Brecon Beacons.
www.abergavennyfoodfestival.com

Bristol
International Festival of Kites & Air Creations
Up to 50,000 enthusiasts convene to see trad, Chinese and funny-shaped kites let loose on the skies over the 850-acre Ashton Court Estate.
www.kite-festival.org.uk

Kendal, Cumbria
Kendal Torchlight Carnival
Around 100 floats and 2,000 people parade through the pretty market town in a spectacle featuring classic cars, folk dancers, street entertainers, marching bands and carthorses.
www.kendaltorchlightcarnival.co.uk

London
Open House London
Snoop round palaces, private homes, corporate skyscrapers, pumping stations and bomb-proof bunkers normally closed to the public.
www.openhouse.org.uk

River Race

The alternative Boat Race (*see p388*) – and much more fun, with an exotic array of around 300 traditional rowing boats from around the globe racing the 22 miles from Richmond to Greenwich. *www.greatriverrace.co.uk*

Thames Festival

A giant party along the Thames. A spectacular, family-friendly mix of street arts, pyrotechnics, art installations, carnival, river events and live music alongside craft and food stalls. Don't miss the last-night lantern procession and firework finale. *www.thamesfestival.org*

Ludlow, Shropshire

Ludlow Food & Drink Festival
Food-centric Ludlow's festival is not to be missed. There will be rare and speciality breed meat available, as well as local cheese, game, cider, perry, ale and much more. *See p328*. *www.foodfestival.co.uk*

St Ives, Cornwall

St Ives September Festival
Annual arts festival brimming with music, theatre, poetry, literature and visual arts. *www.stivesseptemberfestival.co.uk*

OCTOBER

Argyll

Cowalfest
A ten-day event based around over 80 walks in the Cowal Peninsula. Art installations and exhibitions are dotted about the area too. *www.cowalfest.org*

Chichester, West Sussex

Autumn Countryside Show
The Weald & Downland Museum hosts this tribute to the harvest, with steam engines, threshing boxes, plough horses, vintage tractors, and local craftspeople displaying their skills. *www.wealddown.co.uk*

London

Diwali
A brilliant celebration of the Festival of Light by London's Hindu, Jain and Sikh communities. Expect fireworks, food, music and dancing. *www.london.gov.uk*

Pearly Kings & Queens Harvest Festival
London's Pearlies gather at St Martin-in-the-Fields for their annual thanksgiving service dressed in spangly pearl button Smother Suits. *www.pearlysociety.co.uk*

Manchester

Manchester Literature Festival
What was once the Manchester Poetry Festival has expanded and now also welcomes prose writers from all over the world as well. *www.manchesterliteraturefestival.co.uk*

Norwich

Bidwells Norwich & Norfolk Food Festival
Celebrating Norfolk produce and healthy eating, this week-long binge encompasses food tasting, demonstrations and recipe swapping. *www.norwichfoodfestival.co.uk*

NOVEMBER

London

Bonfire Night
Celebrations of Guy Fawkes's failure to blow up the Houses of Parliament in 1605 take place all over London: Battersea Park, Alexandra Palace or Victoria Park, or pre-book a late ride on the London Eye.

Lord Mayor's Show
London's new Lord Mayor heads to the Royal Courts of Justice amid a procession of floats, bands and thousands of people. At 5pm fireworks are set off from a Thames barge. *www.lordmayorsshow.org*

State Opening of Parliament
Pomp and ceremony attend the Queen's official reopening of Parliament after its summer recess. *www.parliament.uk*

Ludlow, Shropshire

Ludlow Medieval Christmas Fayre
Vendors in medieval garb set up shop outside Ludlow Castle. The event aims to reconstruct a traditional Shropshire Christmas. *www.ludlowmedievalchristmas.co.uk*

Windermere, Cumbria

Powerboat Record Attempts
The world's fastest powerboat racers break the silence on lovely Lake Windermere. *www.conistonpowerboatrecords.co.uk*

DECEMBER

Edinburgh

Edinburgh Hogmanay
A four-day extravaganza with non-stop concerts, processions and a massive street party that end with a concert and spectacular fireworks display. *www.edinburghshogmanay.org*

London

New Year's Eve Celebrations
Full-on fireworks display launched from the London Eye and nearby rafts on the Thames. *www.london.gov.uk*

Tetbury, Gloucestershire

Westonbirt Arboretum's Enchanted Christmas
Take a walk through the famous Enchanted Wood and see the arboretum lit up at night. Meet Father Christmas and enjoy carols from local choirs and bands, roast chestnuts and mulled wine. *www.forestry.gov*

Advertisers' Index

Please refer to relevant sections for contact details

Index

Page references in italics indicate illustrations.